Crossed Swords

Pakistan, its Army, and the
Wars Within

SHUJA NAWAZ

OXFORD
UNIVERSITY PRESS

OXFORD
UNIVERSITY PRESS

Great Clarendon Street, Oxford OX2 6DP

Oxford University Press is a department of the University of Oxford.
It furthers the University's objective of excellence in research, scholarship,
and education by publishing worldwide in

Oxford New York

Auckland Cape Town Dar es Salaam Hong Kong Karachi
Kuala Lumpur Madrid Melbourne Mexico City Nairobi
New Delhi Shanghai Taipei Toronto

with offices in

Argentina Austria Brazil Chile Czech Republic France Greece
Guatemala Hungary Italy Japan Poland Portugal Singapore
South Korea Switzerland Turkey Ukraine Vietnam

Oxford is a registered trade mark of Oxford University Press
in the UK and in certain other countries

ISBN 978-0-19-547660-6

Second Impression 2008

Typeset in Minion Pro
Printed in Pakistan by
Kagzi Printers, Karachi.
Published by
Ameena Saiyid, Oxford University Press
No. 38, Sector 15, Korangi Industrial Area, PO Box 8214
Karachi-74900, Pakistan.

Crossed Swords

Also by the author:
Journeys (1998)

PAKISTAN TODAY

N

CHINA

AFGHANISTAN

Kabul
● Jalalabad
NWFP*
Peshawar ■
Rawalpindi ·
☆ Islamabad

JAMMU
AND
KASHMIR

Gujranwala ·
Faisalabad ·
Lahore ■

PUNJAB

Multan ·

■ Quetta
· Sibi

● New Delhi

BALOCHISTAN

Larkana ·

IRAN

INDIA

SINDH

Gwadar
Hyderabad
■ Karachi

ARABIAN
SEA

NORTH WEST FRONTIER PROVINCE*

Dedication

This book is dedicated to the memory of a very special group of persons who did not live long enough to read it:

my father, Raja Abdul Ghafoor Khan and my mother, Khawar;

my uncle, Brigadier Mohammad Zaman Khan, and his wife, Surraiya (*nee* Sarwar)—my surrogate parents, with whom I spent my early life;

my father-in-law, Lt. Col. J.D. Malik;

and my brother, General Asif Nawaz,
Chief of Army Staff of Pakistan, 1991–3, a Soldiers' Soldier.

It is offered with love and thanks to my constant sources of inspiration and joy

my wife
SEEMA

and our daughters
ZAYNAB, AMNA, and ZAHRA

CONTENTS

List of Photographs

Army Chiefs of Pakistan

1. General Sir Frank Messervy
2. General Sir Douglas Gracey
3. Field Marshal Mohammad Ayub Khan
4. General Mohammad Musa
5. General Agha Mohammad Yahya Khan
6. Lt. Gen. Gul Hassan Khan
7. General Tikka Khan
8. General Mohammad Ziaul Haq
9. General Mirza Aslam Beg
10. General Asif Nawaz
11. General Abdul Waheed
12. General Jehangir Karamat
13. General Pervez Musharraf
14. General Ashfaq Parvez Kayani

LIST OF ACRONYMS

ACR	Annual Confidential Report
ADB	Asian Development Bank
ADC	Aide-de-Camp
AFRC	Armed Forces Reconstitution Committee
AIG	Afghan Interim Government
ASF	Airport Security Force
AZO	Al Zulfikar Organization
BCCI	Bank for Commerce and Credit International
BD	Basic Democrats
BJP	Bharatiya Janata Party
BNR&R	Bureau of National Research and Reconstruction
BSF	Border Security Officer
Centcom	Central Command
CEO	Chief Executive Officer
CGS	Chief of General Staff
CIA	Central Intelligence Agency
CID	Criminal Investigation Department
C-in-C	Commander-in-Chief
CJCS	Chairman Joint Chiefs of Staff
CMLA	Chief Martial Law Administrator
CTBT	Comprehensive Nuclear Test-Ban Treaty
CTBTO	Comprehensive Nuclear Test-Ban Treaty Organization
CO	Commanding Officer
COAS	Chief of Army Staff
COS	Chief of Staff
CPC	Chemical Plant Complex
CRO	Commonwealth Relations Office
CRS	Congressional Research Service
CSP	Civil Service of Pakistan
CSS	Central Superior Services
DCC	Defence Committee of the Cabinet
DCM	Deputy Chief of Mission
DG ISI	Director General Inter Services Intelligence Directorate
DG ISPR	Director General Inter Services Public Relations

DGMO	Director General Military Operations
DHA	Defence Housing Authority
DIB	Director Intelligence Bureau
DMO	Director Military Operations
DPD	Defence Production Division
EBDO	Elective Bodies Disqualification Ordinance
FATA	Federally Administered Tribal Areas
FC	Frontier Corps
FCNA	Force Commander Northern Areas
FCR	Frontier Crime Regulation
FDI	Foreign Direct Investment
FDO	Fysscish Dynamisch Onderzoek
FIA	Federal Investigating Agency
FSF	Federal Security Force
GDP	Gross Domestic Product
GHQ	General Headquarters
GOC	General Officer Commanding
GSO	General Staff Officer
IAEA	International Atomic Energy Agency
IAF	Indian Air Force
IB	Intelligence Bureau
ICS	Indian Civil Service
IG	Inspector General
IISS	International Institute for Strategic Studies
IJI/IDA	Islami Jamhoori Ittehad/Islamic Democratic Alliance
IJT	Islami Jamiat-e-Talaba
IMA	Indian Military Academy
IMF	International Monetary Fund
INA	Indian National Army
ISI	Inter Services Intelligence Directorate
ISPR	Inter Services Public Relations
JCS	Joint Chiefs of Staff
JCO	Junior Commissioned Officer
JCSC	Joint Chiefs of Staff Committee

JUI	Jamiat-ul-Ulema-i-Islam
JUP	Jamiat-ul-Ulema-i-Pakistan
KANUPP	Karachi Nuclear Power Plant
KC	King's Commission
KCO	King's Commission Officer
KESC	Karachi Electric Supply Corporation
KRL	Khan Research Laboratories
LFO	Legal Framework Order
LOC	Line of Control
MAAG	Military Assistance Advisory Group
MGO	Master General Ordnance
MI	Military Intelligence
MLA	Martial Law Administrator
MMA/UAF	Muttahida Majlis-e-Amal /United Action Front
MO	Military Operations Directorate
MQM/RFG	Muhajir Qaumi Mahaz; Muttahida Qaumi Movement/ Refugee National Front
MRD	Movement for the Restoration of Democracy
NAB	National Accountability Bureau
NAP	National Awami Party
NCO	Non-Commissioned Officer
NDC	National Defence College
NEFA	North East Frontier Agency
NLC	National Logistics Cell
NLI	Northern Light Infantry
NPT	Nuclear Proliferation Treaty
NSC	National Security Council
NWFP	North West Frontier Province
OIC	Organization of the Islamic Conference
OSS	Office of Strategic Services
PAEC	Pakistan Atomic Energy Commission
PAF	Pakistan Air Force
PCO	Provisional Constitution Order
PDA	Pakistan Democratic Alliance

PDP	Pakistan Democratic Party
PEMRA	Pakistan Electronic Media Regulatory Authority
PIA	Pakistan International Airlines
PINSTECH	Pakistan Institute of Nuclear Sciences and Technology
PM	Prime Minister
PMA	Pakistan Military Academy
PML	Pakistan Muslim League
PNA	Pakistan National Alliance
PNE	Peaceful Nuclear Explosion
PNG	Pakistan National Guard
POW	Prisoner of War
PPP	Pakistan Peoples' Party
PRODA	Public and Representative Offices (Disqualification) Act
PTV	Pakistan Television
QMG	Quartermaster General
RAW	Research and Analysis Wing
RPAF	Royal Pakistan Air Force
RSS	Rashtriya Swayamsevak Sangh
SAC	Strategic Air Command
SEATO	The South-East Asia Treaty Organization
SSG	Special Services Group
UAE	United Arab Emirates
UNCIP	United Nations Commission for India and Pakistan
US MAAG	United States Military Assistance Advisory Group
USUN	US Mission to the UN
VCGS	Vice Chief of General Staff
VCO	Viceroy's Commissioned Officer
VCOAS	Vice Chief of Army Staff
WAPDA	Water and Power Development Authority
WASAG	Washington Special Actions Group

PREFACE AND ACKNOWLEDGMENTS

This is a book that I have lived with most of my life. Born into a military family with a long tradition of soldiering, in an area that has produced warriors and still does, I could not help but learn the ways of the soldiers and follow their activities with a knowing eye. This book is an attempt to understand and explain Pakistan's soldiers and its army within the context of the country's search for nationhood and a place in the global order of things. For the story of Pakistan in many ways is the story of the Pakistan Army. And in order to understand Pakistan's position in the emerging regional and global order, in a world beset with terror and the threat of regional nuclear wars, it is important to understand the nature and role of the Pakistan Army and its leadership.

In taking on this venture, I realize that the Pakistan Army today is different from the institution that I grew up in, which was then a newly instituted post-colonial force with a young but dedicated officer class that had not been fully trained to take on the task of running a national army. In its early days it was also removed from civil society. I have seen it grow into a large force, and observed it at close quarters in peace and in war. It is now more of a national army than at its birth with a much better trained officer corps and soldiers. However, it has also suffered defeat in war and has become deeply embroiled in the politics of Pakistan. Its influence pervades civil society in ways that are pernicious, and in tasks for which it has not been trained. The army is now involved as a major protagonist in the wars raging within Pakistan today, and as I write these words, large swathes of public opinion seem to be challenging its hold on state power.

I have chosen to tell the story of Pakistan and its army not as a seamless or definitive history but through reportage and examination of important episodes in order to help understand why things have turned out the way they have. In this endeavour, I have tried to shed light—by presenting new information and re-examining earlier data and analyses—on the nature and operation of the army in Pakistani society and its actions in war.

But this story is incomplete without the role of the United States, which allied itself (for its own interests, of course) with the new Pakistani state which was seeking military aid in order to secure its borders against a large and hostile India. The US proved to be too willing a military partner in the early stages, and even after doubts emerged in the minds of its policy-makers about the nature and efficacy of its relationship with Pakistan, the US continued to engage with the new country for the first couple of decades of its life as an independent state. The relationship had its ups and down through the 1960s. After the end of the war against the Soviet occupation of Afghanistan in 1989, in which Pakistan played a key role as a base and ally for covert US efforts to dislodge the Soviets, the relationship became dormant in the early 1990s. Things then soured between the two countries because of the US's insistence that Pakistan stop and roll back its nuclear programme, something that Pakistan refused to do. However, the US–Pakistan alliance has been revived with gusto in recent years, specifically since 2001 when the US re-entered Afghanistan in force to begin its global 'War on Terror'. However, there is a barely-concealed mistrust on both sides of the alliance—scars of prior experience.

In the first decade of the twenty-first century, as the forces of militant and conservative Islam appear to be on the rise in Pakistan and elsewhere in the Middle East and South Asia, and talk of another 'Clash of Civilizations' crowds the airwaves, this book is a close examination of the Pakistan Army. It looks at the current recruitment patterns of the Pakistan Army and its demographics, and what this portends for the future. From being a colonial army in the 1940s, 50s, and 60s, with a restricted recruitment base, today the ranks of the army—a highly advanced military machine with nuclear weapons—increasingly represent a wider base of the population. Should this inspire fear or confidence within Pakistan and among its allies?

This book also examines the army's relationship to politics and the role of major civil and military personalities at different points in the history of Pakistan and its relationship with the United States, first during the Cold War, then in the period when the United States became the single superpower. And, by tapping the memories of key participants in the country's history in recent decades, this book tries to shine some light on key episodes in the growth and development of Pakistan.

The book is based on over thirty years of reading, discussions with serving and retired army officers (including most of my and my wife's relatives in the army), personal experience as a newsman for Pakistan Television in the coverage of the period before, during, and after the 1971 war with India, and on research in the voluminous US government archives on US–Pakistan relations and the Public Records Office of the United Kingdom, as well as the archives of the General Headquarters (GHQ) of the Pakistan Army at Rawalpindi.

My family has been a source of great strength in this effort. My wife, Seema, and our three daughters, Zaynab, Amna, and Zahra, have provided constant cheer and encouragement. Zaynab stepped in at the last minute to help with transcription of interviews too. Seema's eagle eyes scanned my drafts with unerring aim to point out infelicities of prose, and kept me writing even when the creative juices did not flow!

My elder brother, General Asif Nawaz, deserves the blame for keeping me, the civilian 'black sheep' of the family (as he jocularly called me in front of his military friends), deeply interested in the army. It was he who persuaded me not to join the army in 1964 when I graduated from St. Mary's Academy in Rawalpindi, and encouraged me to pursue further education. And it was he who encouraged me to read all the military strategy and history books that he had to swot himself for his various courses and promotion exams. We did not know when I began work on this book that he would become the Chief of the Army Staff (COAS) in 1991 and leave an indelible mark on the army and the country before he died in office on 8 January 1993—well before this book was completed. He encouraged me to write this book but never asked to vet it at any point. In return, I did not seek nor get access to Pakistan Army archives or materials during his tenure as COAS. Neither of us wanted to make things difficult for the other. After his death, I put the book aside and only recently was encouraged by my wife to complete the task.

Anand Chandavarkar, a former IMF colleague and sagacious friend, kept me fed with information, scholarly references, and good advice. He was also willing to comment on some early drafts. My childhood friend, schoolmate, and then collegemate, Ambassador Arif Ayub, took time off from his very busy life in Cairo to read and comment on chapters in detail and provide valuable suggestions and corrections. My friend and mentor Shahid Javed Burki encouraged me to complete this book and refreshed my memory on some episodes in which he was a figure. He also read the first draft and provided valuable feedback and advice, as did Paula Newberg, Stephen Cohen, and Parvez Hasan.

General Mirza Aslam Beg and his 'Glasnost' policy opened the hitherto shut doors of the GHQ in Rawalpindi and granted me a detailed interview on the record, and then Major General Jehangir Karamat, the Director General Military Operations in 1990 (later Corps Commander under my brother and COAS on 12 January 1996), helped me find my way around GHQ. General Karamat was always a source of guidance and a key check on my ideas. I am grateful to my escort officer in 1990, Major Mussarat, and then Deputy Military Secretary, Brigadier Aziz Khan, for opening up hidden files to me, and many others, notably Brigadier Mahmud Ahmed (later lieutenant general), for helping me understand key episodes in the army's history. At the GHQ, Brigadier Riazullah, then Director General, Inter Services Public Relations (ISPR) Directorate, Brigadier Aziz Khan, then Deputy Military Secretary, Major Shabbir Husain, Lieutenant Colonel Shaukat Mahmood, and Mr Mohammad Anwar (micro-filming officer) were extremely helpful in finding documents for me during my short stay in 1990.

Many years later, President General Pervez Musharraf sat down for a candid interview with me, as did his Vice Chief General Ahsan Saleem Hyat. I am grateful to them for further access to the GHQ archives, where Major Imtiaz Ahmad and I spent many hours in profound conversations, laced with copious amounts of tea. Major General Shaukat Sultan Khan (now General Officer Commanding [GOC] of a division in Lahore) and his colleagues at the ISPR Directorate, particularly Brigadier Shahid Masood and Major Murad

Qayyum Khan, were very helpful in setting up these contacts and also in tracking down materials.

My wife's cousin, Major Saeed Akhtar Malik, provided portions of the unpublished memoirs of his uncle, the late Major General Abdul Ali Malik, and also gave me insight on the Attock Conspiracy and the subsequent trial. Thanks also to Brian Cloughley for his early review of some chapters and his encouragement. My former colleague from *The New York Times*, Barbara Crossette, also helped with her comments. Ayesha Jalal, herself a student of the Pakistani military and a brilliant historian, kept the challenge alive with advice and commentary during the early stages of my research. Ashraf Janjua of the State Bank of Pakistan helped with budget data for the period up to the 1990s. Parvez Hasan provided a useful paper on economic policy and defence spending. Mohammad Sadiq of the Pakistan Foreign Service was extremely helpful in providing some useful background material at short notice. My former classmate at St. Mary's, Rawalpindi, Ali Yahya Khan, provided a rare look inside the workings of his father's mind, by giving me a copy of General Agha Mohammad Yahya Khan's personal file on Pakistan's role in the US opening into China. General Yahya also spoke with me after he was out of power, while under treatment for a stroke in the United States. Ambassador Robert Oakley was the source of much useful information about the late 1980s and early 90s. And the 'Man of Many Secrets', my wife's cousin, Lt. Gen. Javed Ashraf Qazi, provided a lot of valuable inside information on the events of the 1990s. I also wish to acknowledge the many hours of conversation with a brave man, my late father-in-law, retired Lt. Col. J.D. Malik, whose incredible memory provided many a glimpse into the workings of the British Indian Army and the early days of the Pakistan Army. My thanks are due also to my brother-in-law, Nabeel Malik, Saqib Qureshi, and others who read some of the earlier chapters and gave me useful feedback.

I am very grateful to the many persons, military and civilian, in both Pakistan and the United States, who took the time to give me detailed interviews on important events in the life of our country. One of the most gratifying aspects of this work was that almost everyone that I approached agreed to talk on the record. A complete list of Primary Sources carries their names. A number of other serving and retired senior and junior officers provided me insights and sometimes access to their private cache of documents that helped me understand the Pakistan Army better. I wish I could quote their names but cannot, to protect those sources and our friendships.

My thanks also go to Rashid Chaudhry of the Sarah Foundation in Potomac, Maryland which provided financing for some of the logistical work connected with the production of the final manuscript. Accentance of Chantilly, VA provided valuable digitizing services for the interviews and some transcriptions. Virginia Baker helped shape the final document before it went to the publisher. And I am grateful to Farook Ahmed, who took precious time off from his graduate studies at Georgetown's School of Foreign Service to produce transcripts of many interviews that often meandered through both Urdu and English. Thanks also to Massoud Etemadi for the maps that help explain the text.

I must acknowledge also the continuing support of Ameena Saiyid, Managing Director of OUP (Pakistan), Ghousia Ali, and editor Alia Amirali, who helped me through the publishing process with their advice and well-directed questions.

Many other persons, in the United States and Pakistan, provided information and guidance on specific issues. My thanks to all of you. The strengths of this book are yours. Its mistakes are mine alone.

Shuja Nawaz
Alexandria, Virginia
February 2008

DRAMATIS PERSONAE

MOHAMMAD IQBAL, a philosopher and pre-eminent Urdu and Persian poet. Came up with the idea of Pakistan. Died in 1938.

MOHAMMAD ALI JINNAH, also known as *Quaid-i-Azam* or the Great Leader, by the Muslims of British India and independent Pakistan. A London-trained lawyer, he left the Indian National Congress to join the Muslim League which he then headed and fought for a separate homeland for the Muslims of India. A modern and secular thinker, he died on 11 September 1948, just over a year after Pakistan came into being on 14 August 1947.

LIAQUAT ALI KHAN, an aristocratic lawyer, also trained in England. Was the first lieutenant of Jinnah and became the first Prime Minister of Pakistan. Inaugurated the relationship with the United States. Assassinated on 16 October 1951 in Rawalpindi.

ISKANDER MIRZA, Sandhurst-trained officer in the British Indian Army, later joined the civil service. Held many posts (in chronological order): secretary of defence in independent Pakistan, governor of East Pakistan, home minister, governor general (he was the last one to hold this post before it was abolished), and finally the first president of the republic of Pakistan. Overthrown and sent into exile in October 1958 by General M. Ayub Khan. Died in London on 12 November 1969, nearly nine months after Ayub himself was overthrown by General A.M. Yahya Khan.

GENERAL SIR FRANK MESSERVY, first Commander-in-Chief (C-in-C) of the Pakistan Army, took charge of his post at independence on 14 August 1947. Had differences with civilian leadership over the surreptitious conduct of the First Kashmir War with India. Left office in February 1948.

GENERAL SIR DOUGLAS GRACEY, second C-in-C of the Pakistan Army, took over from Messervy with whom he had served as deputy C-in-C. Left office in January 1951.

GENERAL, later FIELD MARSHAL M. AYUB KHAN, first native C-in-C of the Pakistan Army, succeeded General Sir Douglas Gracey on 17 January 1951. Later made defence minister and then chief martial law administrator by Iskander Mirza on 12 October 1958. Overthrew Iskander Mirza on 27 October 1958 and became president. Cemented the relationship with the United States but then broke with his former ally to shift toward China. Instituted a form of controlled democracy called 'Basic Democracy'. Overthrown by his chosen C-in-C, General A.M. Yahya Khan in April 1969. Died 19 April 1974.

GENERAL MOHAMMAD MUSA KHAN, succeeded Ayub as army chief in 1958. Saw action in the British Indian Army in Waziristan and North Africa. Was the first chief to rise from the ranks, having joined the army as a soldier. Failed to influence planning for the Kashmir war in 1965 and was generally overshadowed by Ayub Khan. Retired in 1966 and then served in various civilian positions, as governor of West Pakistan and later as governor of his native Balochistan. Died in 1991.

GENERAL AGHA MOHAMMAD YAHYA KHAN, a decorated officer in the British Indian Army in the Second World War. An energetic and hard working young officer, he rose rapidly in independent Pakistan as a member of the team that helped Ayub Khan overthrow Iskander Mirza in October 1958. Was made C-in-C of the Pakistan Army after General Musa Khan by Ayub Khan in 1966, and ended up removing Ayub from power in 1969 and taking over as President. Held elections (generally accepted as free and fair) in 1970 that allowed the Awami League of Sheikh Mujibur Rahman in East Pakistan, and Zulfikar Ali Bhutto's Pakistan Peoples' Party in West Pakistan, to come to the fore. A simple and well-meaning man, he found himself out of his depth in politics and as a result of bad advice and poor decisions led Pakistan into a military debacle against India that resulted in the birth of independent Bangladesh and a stalemate in West Pakistan. He played a key role in the United States' connection with the People's Republic of China by arranging Secretary of State Henry Kissinger's secret visit to Beijing and was rewarded by President Richard Nixon's undying gratitude. He died on 4 August 1980, following complications resulting from a stroke.

LT. GEN. GUL HASSAN KHAN, Chief of General Staff (CGS) during 1971 war with India, became Chief of Army Staff (COAS) on 20 December 1971 after Bhutto took over as President and changed the title of C-in-C to COAS. Bhutto removed him suddenly on 3 March 1972 after accusing him of 'Bonapartist tendencies.' Became ambassador to Austria but resigned in protest against Bhutto's refusal to call fresh elections in 1977. Died in Rawalpindi on 10 October 1999.

ZULFIKAR ALI BHUTTO, a young lawyer from Larkana in Sindh province, educated at the University of California at Berkeley and at Christ Church, University of Oxford, was inducted into Ayub Khan's martial law government in October 1958 as minister for fuel, power, and natural resources. Later made foreign minister. Broke with Ayub after end of 1965 war with India that he had helped provoke with the support of guerrilla operations in Kashmir, and set up the Pakistan Peoples' Party. Took over as president on 20 December 1971 after war with India and Pakistan's loss of East Pakistan (which became independent Bangladesh). Introduced new parliamentary constitution in 1973 and became prime minister. Was overthrown in a coup d'etat by his chosen COAS General M. Ziaul Haq on 5 July 1977. Imprisoned by Zia on a charge of murdering a political opponent's father, he was convicted and later executed on 4 April 1979 in Rawalpindi.

GENERAL ZIAUL HAQ, successor of General Tikka Khan as COAS from 1976 until his death in an air crash on 17 August 1988. Overthrew Prime Minister Zulfikar Ali Bhutto on 5 July 1977 and became president and COAS concurrently. Instrumental in helping the United States launch a covert *jihad* (holy war) against the Soviet invasion of Afghanistan and building up the Inter Services Intelligence (ISI) Directorate as the executing agency for that war. Introduced Islamist reforms and economic and social systems in Pakistan and Islamized the Pakistan Army.

GENERAL AKHTAR ABDUR RAHMAN, Director General of the ISI under President Ziaul Haq and the key figure in the execution of the Afghan *jihad* against the Soviet Union. Promoted to General and made Chairman of the Joint Chiefs of Staff (CJCS), a largely ceremonial position, in 1987. Killed in the same air crash that claimed the life of General Ziaul Haq in August 1988.

GENERAL TIKKA KHAN, COAS from March 1972 to March 1976. Succeeded Lt. Gen. Gul Hassan Khan. Gained notoriety in army actions in Balochistan and later in East Pakistan in 1971, as an officer who followed orders without question. Later joined Bhutto's PPP and served as defence advisor to both the father and his daughter, Benazir Bhutto.

GENERAL MIRZA ASLAM BEG, VCOAS under General Ziaul Haq, took over as COAS after Zia's death in August 1988 and facilitated the constitutional handover of power to the then chairman of the Senate, Ghulam Ishaq Khan. Retained his hand in Pakistani politics however, and was instrumental in the dismissal of Benazir Bhutto's government in August 1990. Publicly opposed Prime Minister Nawaz Sharif's decision to send troops to aid the coalition forces that helped evict Iraq from Kuwait in 1990. Wished to be elevated to a re-defined and more powerful position of CJCS when his three-year tenure was coming to an end, but President Ishaq Khan did not accede to that plan and instead named the newly-appointed CGS, Lt. Gen. Asif Nawaz, as Beg's successor. On retirement, Beg created his own think-tank and set up a political party that failed to gain much popular support. Continues to write commentaries on national and international topics for the press.

GENERAL ASIF NAWAZ, the tenth army chief, became COAS on 16 August 1991 and died in office after a heart attack on 8 January 1993. Served as commander of V Corps in Karachi, responsible for Sindh, and then briefly as CGS before being selected by President Ishaq Khan to succeed General Aslam Beg as COAS. Last of the Sandhurst-trained army chiefs. Worked hard to rebuild fractured relations with the West. Developed differences with Prime Minister Sharif over the government's one-sided policies against terrorists and violence in Sindh and over the prime minister's attempts to intrude into military promotions and other matters.

GENERAL ABDUL WAHEED, commander of XII Corps in Quetta when General Asif Nawaz died in office on 8 January 1993. Named COAS by President Ishaq Khan on 12 January 1993 and completed his three-year tenure in 1996, refusing to accept an extension that was offered to him by the then Prime Minister Benazir Bhutto. Instrumental in ousting both President Ishaq Khan and Prime Minister Sharif in 1993. Key supporter of Pakistan's quest for a nuclear weapon and did his best to keep the covert programme going. Led a private, reclusive life in Rawalpindi after retirement.

GENERAL JEHANGIR KARAMAT, named COAS by President Farooq Leghari in 1996 when General Waheed retired. Resigned in 1998 after a difference of opinion with Prime Minister Nawaz Sharif over Karamat's proposal of a National Security Council to formalize the army's role in governing the country. Earlier he had refused to enter the battle between President Leghari and Prime Minister Sharif over the removal of the chief justice. Succeeded by General Pervez Musharraf who later appointed him as ambassador to the United States. After retirement, he remained active as a lecturer on politico-military matters at home and in think-tanks abroad.

GENERAL PERVEZ MUSHARRAF, succeeded General Karamat as COAS in 1998. Key supporter of the Pakistani action in Kashmir near Kargil that produced a short and fierce battle over several months in 1998 and that was brought to an end after the intervention of President Bill Clinton of the United States in July 1999. Had strong differences with Prime Minister Sharif after that event and following further quarrels, including about the appointment of senior officers in the army close to Sharif, the prime minister removed him from office and replaced him with Lt. Gen. Ziauddin Khawaja on 12 October 1999, while Musharraf was in an aircraft returning from Sri Lanka. Musharraf's colleagues launched a coup d'etat and removed Sharif from power. Musharraf became chief executive and then president of Pakistan, while retaining his position of army chief till late in 2007. He broke with the Taliban after the Al Qaeda attacks on the United States of 9/11 and became a key US ally in the 'War on Terror,' becoming the target of various assassination attempts in the process.

BENAZIR BHUTTO, daughter of Zulfikar Ali Bhutto, became prime minister of Pakistan twice (1988–90 and 1993–6). Educated at Radcliffe College, Harvard, and at Lady Margaret Hall, Oxford, she took up the banner of the Pakistan Peoples' Party after her father's ouster and execution by General Ziaul Haq. Both times her government was ousted on charges of corruption and mismanagement, the second time by the president she herself had appointed—also a former party member—Farooq Leghari. She went into exile and divided her time between Dubai and London, before returning to Pakistan to challenge President Musharraf's regime in October 2007. She survived an attack on her first procession on arrival in Karachi on 19 October but died following another attack on her outside Liaquat Bagh in Rawalpindi on 27 December 2007.

MIAN MOHAMMAD NAWAZ SHARIF, twice prime minister of Pakistan (1990–3 and 1997–9). Earlier, finance minister of Punjab during the Ziaul Haq regime, having been recommended to Haq by the former DG ISI and then governor of Punjab, Lt. Gen. Ghulam Jilani Khan. Chief Minister of Punjab during the first Benazir Bhutto government (1988–90) and a key member of the Islami Jamhoori Ittehad (IJI) coalition of Islamist parties formed by the ISI to oppose her government. His first term as prime minister ended after a battle with President Ishaq Khan, when the army chief persuaded both the prime minister and the president to resign and called for fresh elections. Overthrown the second time around by the Pakistan Army acting on behalf of General Musharraf in October 1999 and sent into exile first to Saudi Arabia and then London (United Kingdom).

LIEUTENANT GENERAL HAMID GUL, then major general was appointed DG ISI after the promotion of then Lt. Gen. Akhtar Abdur Rahman to CJCS. Active in the Afghan war during its final stages and takes the credit for setting up the IJI, a coalition of Islamist opposition parties that fought against the Pakistan Peoples' Party in the 1988 elections. Later promoted to lieutenant general, he was removed from the ISI on Prime Minister Benazir Bhutto's request in 1989 and made corps commander in Multan. Moved by COAS General Asif Nawaz in early 1992 to the Heavy Industries Complex in Taxila but refused to go and was retired from the army. Continued to remain active in politics, taking a staunch Islamist stance on national and international issues.

GHULAM ISHAQ KHAN, bureaucrat-turned-politician, rose from the provincial civil service to become secretary general of the government under President Yahya Khan. Later served as finance minister under General Ziaul Haq and was elected to the Senate and became its chairman. Became president after Zia's death in August 1988 until he resigned at the instigation of army chief General Waheed in 1993. Keen supporter and guardian of Pakistan's nuclear programme. Led a private life after retirement and died in October 2006 in Peshawar.

Army Chiefs of Pakistan

General Sir Frank Messervy

General Sir Douglas Gracey

Field Marshal Mohammad Ayub Khan

General Mohammad Musa

General Agha Mohammad Yahya Khan

Lt. Gen. Gul Hassan Khan

General Tikka Khan

General Mohammad Ziaul Haq

General Mirza Aslam Beg

General Asif Nawaz

General Abdul Waheed

General Jehangir Karamat

General Pervez Musharraf

General Ashfaq Parvez Kayani

Pakistan was created as a separate state on 14 August 1947, in the name of the Muslims of British India. Today, more than sixty years after independence, the country is struggling to become a nation. Its political reins have been effectively in the hands of the Pakistan Army for more than thirty-eight years, while it continued to exercise control even when civilians were titular rulers of the land. It has fought three major wars and a number of smaller wars with its powerful neighbour, India. The country is now wracked by internal divisions between provinces and between modernist forces and the forces of militant and radical Islam, whose continuing wars in the federally administered area of the North West Frontier Province (NWFP), Swat, and in the hinterland's cities have created political uncertainty and chaos that has allowed the military to step in and dominate the stage yet again.

Though Pakistan came into being in 1947 as one country comprised mainly of contiguous Muslim-majority areas, the country consisted of two wings West and East Pakistan, separated by 1000 miles. Separating the two wings, of Pakistan was a hostile India. The events leading up to the creation of Pakistan also made the path to statehood very difficult: more than a decade of civil unrest as Indians of all races and creeds sought independence from Great Britain was followed by a massive migration involving some fourteen million refugees who crossed what became the Pakistan–India border. Nearly one million persons—Hindus, Sikhs, and Muslims—died during this bloody upheaval.

Although the Muslim way of life was a motive behind the call for Pakistan, its early political leadership did not provide an Islamic blueprint for its political development or goals. In fact, the movement for Pakistan was not an Islamic movement as much as it was a movement by Indian Muslims to seek greater social and economic opportunity for themselves. Indeed, according to one view, it was the movement of the salaried classes and hence was not supported either by the Islamist parties or by the rural masses in the Muslim majority provinces.[1]

The Pakistan Army, the largely Muslim rump of the British Indian Army, too was saddled at birth with this paradoxical identity: the symbols of Islam but the substance of a colonial force, quite distant from the body politic of the fledgling state. As a result, Pakistan's history is one of conflict between an underdeveloped political system and a well organized army that grew in numbers and political strength as a counter weight to a hostile India next door and in relation to the domestic political system. 'Whenever there is a breakdown in...stability, as has happened frequently in Pakistan, the military translates its potential into the will to dominate, and we have military intervention followed by military rule,' states former army chief General Jehangir Karamat. 'But,' he states, 'As far as the track record of the military as rulers in the past is concerned, I am afraid it is not much better than the civilians.'[2]

While the army gained the respect of Pakistan's population for its spirited defence of the country's borders against India, for example, and continued to attract large number of youth to its ranks, its dominance of the polity of Pakistan eventually produced public questioning of its role. Over time, through coups and largely unfettered access to state resources, the army used its significant coercive powers with the underlying threat of its military might to challenge the authority of the state and capture power time and again, leaving the instruments of state weakened and unable to function whenever the military returned to its barracks.

POWER BROKERS

The paradox that hobbled Pakistan's political development was that as the army grew in strength and size, it stunted the growth of the political system whose leaders either made no attempt to redress the power imbalance between the institutions of the state and that of the army, making the latter effectively the centre of power; or worse, they invited the army to settle political differences amongst themselves. In one view, the country's power is diffused among three broad centres, creating political instability:

> In moral and spiritual matters, the 'ulama' and the 'mashaikh' [religious scholars and leaders] still command the undivided loyalty of the bulk of the people. In temporal matters, the coercive authority is seen to reside clearly with the military and civil bureaucracy. Political leadership, therefore motivated mainly by the power of patronage, is burdened with a constant struggle for legitimacy; unlike European countries, in the popular perception [among Pakistanis] no moral legitimacy is conferred by elections, with the result that politicians seldom have been able to control the bureaucracy.[3]

Successive political leaders suborned and eviscerated the vaunted bureaucracy that had been seen as the steel framework of the system of governance in British India and also managed to weaken the educational system, thus depriving the country of alternative governance mechanisms and an informed electorate. This reduced the bureaucracy and civil society's role relative to the army. The army meanwhile learned over time to establish patron–client relationships with the bureaucracy and with Islamist parties whom it used in its efforts to fight populist leaders in both East and West Pakistan and fuel the Kashmiri insurgency against Indian rule. The result: a persistent praetorian state with military or quasi-military rule for most of its life after independence from the British.

In an analysis steeped in irony, former army chief General Mirza Aslam Beg, known for his penchant for manipulating the political system when he was in power, identified three 'power brokers' that emerged after Pakistan's first martial law government of 1958, namely 'the Military, the Judiciary, and the United States...[which] have since manipulated power in Pakistan to their advantage. The military has acted as the catalyst; the judiciary as the facilitator under the cover of the Law of Necessity, and the United States as the manipulator, using the political parties and the vested interest groups to bring military dictators to power to accomplish the agenda of "regime change".[4]

The Law or Doctrine of Necessity that Beg referred to was described by one legal expert as 'a talisman' evolved by the superior courts of Pakistan to legitimize the illegitimate. Coup d'etats (sic) in the history of Pakistan have been validated by the superior courts by the misinterpretation of three maxims of Roman Law: '*Id quod alias non est, licitum, necessitas licitum facit*' (that which otherwise is not lawful, necessity makes lawful), '*Salus populi est suprema lex*' (the public welfare is the highest law), and '*Salus republicae est suprema lex*' (Safety of the State is the supreme law).[5] Pakistan's judiciary continued to apply these rationalizations to their judgments on various military coups, except in one case: the refusal of six out of the eleven judges of the Supreme Court plus five other judges to take an oath under the Provisional Constitutional Order (PCO) of General A.M. Yahya Khan. It was left to a later court to declare Yahya a 'usurper,' but only after he had been overthrown. Another Supreme Court in 2000 declared that General Pervez Musharraf's extra-constitutional coup d'etat of 12 October 1999 was 'validated on the basis of the doctrine of State necessity and the principle of "*salus populi [est] suprema lex*"', and deemed his coup to be 'in the interest of the State and for the welfare of the people.' The court went even further to state that he had 'validly assumed power by means of an extra-constitutional step.'[6] Even when the Doctrine of Necessity was not directly cited as the basis of decisions, the Supreme Court found ways of validating extra-constitutional actions of the executive;[7] most recently by accepting the move by General Pervez Musharraf in his capacity as chief of army staff to declare a state of emergency on 3 November 2007. He dismissed the chief justice and other members of the court, put the constitution in 'abeyance' and promulgated a new PCO to run the affairs of the state. A number of compliant justices signed on with the new order and assumed office. Others were removed summarily. Leading broadcast media were shut down and politicians taken into custody. Within weeks the new Supreme Court, once again using the crutch of the Doctrine of Necessity signed off on Musharraf's eligibility to run and be elected as president of Pakistan. Meanwhile, with the National Assembly having retired after its five-year term, the president resorted to ruling by presidential ordinances, a return to rule by fiat.

Pakistan's existence has been marked by attempts to build a nation but without first building the institutional foundations that are needed to allow a stable federal entity to evolve in a democratic and pluralistic setting. Ethnic and regional strife, sectarian violence, and the persistent intrusion of foreign powers into the region in the pursuit of their global agenda, all have created the setting for uneven political and economic development. Its rulers, both civil and military, have fallen into the category of Mancur Olson's 'roving bandits' more than the 'stationary bandits' that might foster the broadening of the economic base for the longer term.[8] Pakistan has suffered three national martial law regimes in 1958, 1969, and 1977 and the military has had a hand on the tiller in civilian regimes since 1988. The 1999 coup that brought General Pervez Musharraf to power resorted to legal legerdemain to avoid being classified as a martial law regime but effectively operated under a temporary legal dispensation that allowed it to operate beyond the ambit of the constitution of the country.

A widely held view is reflected in the analysis by two scholars:

> For the most part, thus military rulers have been the final arbiters of Pakistan's destiny. Dominated by Punjabis and representing the landed and industrial interests, the military regards its dominance of Pakistani politics not only as a right but as a duty based on the need to safeguard the territorial integrity of the country in the face of lingering ethnic, linguistic, and religious fissures.[9]

While the extent to which it represents interests other than its own is debatable, the army has gradually expanded its domain to include protection of the national ideology, as defined by itself. Over time, that ideology has changed from a loose definition of a Muslim state at birth to an Islamic polity under Ziaul Haq and now back again to a newly defined 'enlightened moderation' of General Pervez Musharraf, even as the large and growing urban population appears to be heading toward the conservative end of the social and political spectrum.

IN THE BEGINNING...

786: these three numbers represent the numerological equivalent of the opening sentence of the Quran, *Bismillah ir-Rahman ir-Rahim* (In the name of Allah, the Merciful and Beneficent), the words that all Muslims intone before the start of anything worthwhile in their lives. 786 became the identification number for the GHQ of the new Pakistan Army when it took over the operations and offices of the British north command in India in Rawalpindi after independence. This numerical code was emblazoned on all gate posts and vehicles, as a reminder that this was the army of a Muslim country. But the Islamic identity was only in name at that stage. The senior echelons were still British officers who had opted to stay on, and they were in turn succeeded by their native clones, men who saw the army as a unique institution, separate and apart from the rest of civil society and authority. This was the dominant cultural ethos of the army at the time. And as the country grew in age, this initial schism between the cantonment (military reservation) and the city pervaded the army's thought processes and seemed to guide as well as bedevil the military's relationship with the civilian sector in Pakistan. The army initially retained its largely moderate and secular nature. As Pakistan moved from being a newly post-colonial state (in the latter days of President Mohammad Ayub Khan's rule) which represented a hybrid of the British Raj and Pakistan but in which Pakistan was an ally of the United States, to being a true post-colonial state (under President Ziaul Haq) which saw an attempt at forging a new national identity through forced Islamization of the army and state. It is still searching for its identity as a nation. Zia, for better or worse, tried to give it an autonomous identity based on his idea of Islam, and minus the US for a while. The US came back into the picture but not as part of a formal pact. The key factors at play in the country's history eventually became three, sometimes conflicting, entities: the Army, America, and more recently Allah.

Contrary to the more recent view of an ancient nexus between the army and Islamist groups that has become fashionable especially in the West and among scholars pandering to the worst fears of the West about Pakistan, the Pakistan Army has not had a close relationship with Islamic parties in the past, except in certain instances when the army tried to use these groups to undermine populist opposition parties in what was once East Pakistan and in certain areas of West Pakistan. Indeed, under the first military ruler, General (later Field Marshal) M. Ayub Khan, there was rank antipathy toward the nullahs. As Ayub Khan noted in his diary in 1967:

> The fight with the mullah is political. It started from the time of Sir Syed [Ahmad Khan, a leading Muslim reformer in the late nineteenth century]. The mullah regards the educated Muslims as his deadliest enemy and the rival for power. That is why several of them opposed Pakistan and sided with the Congress. They felt that with the help of the Hindus they will be able to keep educated Muslims out of power. So we have got to take on all those who are political mischief-makers. This battle, though unpleasant, is unavoidable. It has to be waged sometime or the other in the interest of a strong progressive Pakistan.[10]

It was only during the regime of General Ziaul Haq that the military–mullah nexus was formed, first for the Afghan *jihad* against the Soviet Union and then to help the Kashmiris against the Indian Army. Ironically, the United

States fostered the military–mullah alliance since the alliance was directed against its arch-rival, the Soviet Union. The military–mullah alliance continued in one form or another till an electoral alliance under General Pervez Musharraf, the current military ruler, allowed the mullahs to support Musharraf in his bid to remain COAS and president concurrently. This deal allowed the mullahs to gain political traction on the national scene for the first time ever.

TODAY'S HEADLINE: 'WAR ON TERROR'

Today, Pakistan is at another crossroad: as a partner of the West in the global 'War on Terror.' Its army is operating in a changed and highly charged domestic political environment where a controlled form of democracy exists. After decades of conflicts with India, including one that led to the break up of united Pakistan and the birth of Bangladesh in 1971, today, for the first time, Pakistan's army is waging a largely futile war against an unseen enemy— 'Islamist terrorists'—within its own borders. The eastern front against India is relatively calmer and there is promise of some progress on the Kashmir dispute, though that may be illusionary, given the mood swings of rulers on both sides. But the western front bordering Afghanistan is awash in insurgent activity spilling over from Afghanistan and also home-grown radicalism, involving the Islamist Taliban who are intent on fighting the United States in Afghanistan and putting their stamp on the tribal areas of the Federally Administered Tribal Areas (FATA) of Pakistan. Even the settled areas of the NWFP, including Swat, and the urban heart of Pakistan and its capital, Islamabad, have become havens for the radicalized Islamists who wish to impose Islamic law or *Sharia* on their fellow citizens and who have challenged the military with some success.

The army effectively rules the country through a de facto presidential system of government, the constitution having been transmogrified at the hands of a compliant judiciary and a parliament that operated under the PCO following Musharraf's first coup of 1999. As 2007 rolled to a chaotic and noisy end, the country was once more under a state of emergency and a fresh PCO. Fresh elections were called but confusion reigned about the ability of the political parties to wage effective campaigns under the state of emergency and while the private broadcast media remained silenced. One man, General Musharraf, was both the president and the army chief. Modernist though Musharraf was in intent and speech, his new form of autocracy had all the internal weaknesses of any monopoly. Having come into power through his extra-constitutional Guardian-style coup d'etat in October 1999, his avowed aim was to bring about true democracy in place of what he called 'sham democracy'. Here he was referring to the largely personality-driven, dynastic and familial ruling groups that dominated most of the mainstream parties such as the Muslim League or the Pakistan Peoples' Party. Most of these parties do not practice internal democracy while talking of it on the national scene. Appointments to senior party posts are more often than not based on selection rather than election, and rarely do they present an elaborate agenda for change. It is only the Islamists and the urban-based parties such as the largely Karachi-based Muttahida Qaumi Movement (MQM) of Altaf Hussain, who have presented a real political agenda. But even the MQM deteriorated over time into a cultish and personality-driven machine and became known for its strong-arm tactics on its own membership as well as its opponents. Musharraf's avowed aim of restoring true democracy could not be realized and the army continued to loom large over the political landscape, stunting political development with its wide shadow.

For the first time since the army's ill-considered action against the civilian population of East Pakistan in 1971 under General A.M. Yahya Khan and against the tribes of Balochistan in 1973 under Zulfikar Ali Bhutto, and more recently against the Bugti tribe and other groups seeking a greater share of the province's resources for the locals, today the Pakistan Army is operating in force inside its own borders again. The 'enemy' this time is a growing Islamist militant movement known as 'Talibanization', after the radical right wing and fundamentalist former regime of Afghanistan. The enemy also comprises 'foreign' elements aligned with Al Qaeda, the amorphous network of well trained terrorists begun by Osama Bin Laden and operating in the FATA that form the no-man's land between Pakistan's NWFP and Afghanistan's eastern border, the Durand Line. A mis-directed military approach by the Musharraf regime, which bypassed the local population and civil administration and isolated the local tribal leadership, has given the insurgents and Islamists the upper hand. Plus, the army itself has been beset with a breakdown in its discipline, as some members of the Frontier Constabulary and the Frontier Corps are reported to have balked at conducting operations against their fellow tribesmen in this area. Also, the army was neither equipped or trained for counter-insurgency warfare, and is now searching for other ways to resolve the issue.

Pakistan's strategic location at the cusp of the Middle East, the Persian Gulf, and South Asia, and as the door to Central Asia and China, gives it added significance and makes it a key player on the regional and global scene. It is an ally of both the United States and China, the only country in the world to boast of such a relationship. And it is seen as a champion of the Islamic world, with close relations with Saudi Arabia and the Gulf states, and a teetering relationship with Iran. Its proximity to a largely hostile and dominating neighbour, India, that has not been shy in asserting its military and economic strength to dominate or effect events in smaller neighbours in South Asia, shapes Pakistan's foreign and defence policies on the one hand and informs its domestic debates on the other.

The presence of nuclear weapons and missile delivery systems in both Indian and Pakistani hands makes this an even more volatile region than in the past. Although the army has now taken control of the nuclear command and control system through the Strategic Plans Division of the army headquarters and oversight by the National Security Council (NSC), the fear persists that radical elements in the country or within the military may one day decide to use Pakistan's arsenal of nuclear weapons regionally or resort to proliferation, especially to other Muslim nations. The nuclear command and control system appears to have met the approval of strict Western referees[11] but the fear remains that nuclear assets might fall into the hands of radical Islamists in the military or fissile materials might fall into the hands of militants inside Pakistan or abroad. The fuse for a constantly brewing conflict with neighbouring India remains the Muslim-majority state of Kashmir, representing the unfinished part of the 1947 partition of British India that has been the cause of at least three wars between the two countries.

Pakistan came into being as the most populous Muslim nation on the planet, giving up that title to Indonesia after losing its eastern half with the birth of Bangladesh in 1971. But the debate over its national identity has not been conducted democratically nor concluded. Is it an Islamic nation along the lines of other religious states such as Israel, Iran, or Saudi Arabia? Or is it a state with a majority Muslim population that supports the rights of its Muslims to live their lives according to Islamic precepts and allows other Pakistanis to participate in the life of the country without any constraints?

It has also yet to craft a stable political system that establishes the supremacy of the civil over the military, as envisioned by its founder Mohammad Ali Jinnah. Its political parties too have yet to root their thinking and actions in well-crafted mandates and manifestos. Without a powerful base of support in the country as a whole, they have not been able to provide the counter-point to the Pakistan Army that is all too well equipped and ready to step in to fill the power vacuum.

THE CORPORATE ARMY

Increasingly, the Pakistan Army is seen by many as a corporate entity that functions as the most effective political party in the country, protecting its interests, sometimes even at the expense of national interests. A recent study of 'Milbus', or military business interests, focuses on Pakistan to characterize the role of the military as 'predatory'. While this study does not ascribe acquisition of assets through legalized means solely to the military (recognizing the prevalence of these actions among the civil sector too), it assigns personal aggrandisement as the motive force behind the actions of senior serving and retired military officers.[12] In a country where a Culture of Entitlement has taken hold since the late 1970s, this criticism is valid against all actors on the political stage. The army's prominence on this stage and reluctance to submit its management and operations to parliamentary and public scrutiny makes it an easy target.

Unlike other single-party autocratic polities, the dominant ruling party in Pakistan is the military. Its senior leadership is criticized for being more interested in wealth creation than protecting the country's frontier or imposing the writ of law throughout the country. A small group of some 150 officers of general rank (two to four star[13]), perhaps an even smaller group of some twenty corps commanders and principal staff officers at GHQ effectively helped the president, who was also the COAS, control the political destiny of Pakistan. Both supporters and critics of the army agree on one thing: it is the most powerful and well-organized institution in the country today, and therefore deserves to be properly understood.

The questions that arise are many and complex:

- What are the roots and the nature of the Pakistan Army?
- How has it changed over the life of the country?
- What separates and distinguishes it from the civil sector?
- How has it fared in war and peace?
- Can Pakistan revert to the ideal state that its founder, M.A. Jinnah, envisioned in which a civilian government had sway over its military in a country that allowed Muslims to practice their faith and allowed all other religions equal opportunity to practice theirs?
- Can the country avoid repeated coups d'etats? If so, how? (See final chapter for my suggestion to reorient the Higher Command structure).
- If not, what is the future of Pakistan in today's rapidly democratizing world?

NATURE OF THE ARMY

Pakistanis proudly point to the fact that theirs is a volunteer army with a long historical tradition. In many ways, it is often talked about in the same terms as the army of its political ally and brother country, Turkey. In the words of an experienced observer of Turkey, Stephen Kinzer: 'Turks…feel deep gratitude and a genuine connection to their army. They believe it exists and works for them. But at the dawn of the twenty-first century, the Turkish army, like the Kemalist tradition it so fervently defends, risks losing the admiration of the Turkish people and hence its leading position in Turkish society.... Turks want to escape from its political power, which has become intrusive and suffocating. They have learned the lessons of democracy and now want to live by them.'[14] While many may debate whether Pakistan has learned the lessons of democracy, the sentiments in Pakistan today are similar to those in Turkey—whose army is often cited as a model for the army of Pakistan.

Yet there are those who see a closer resemblance between the Pakistan Army and the army of Indonesia under Presidents Sukarno and Suharto, in which the *dwi fungsi,* or 'dual functions', of the army became entrenched. Army officers saw themselves as 'saviours of the country'[15] and also developed a role in ruling the country via a revolving door policy under which military officers were given civilian jobs and then moved out to make room for new officers. Like Pakistan's troika of the president, the prime minister, and the army chief, Indonesia had its own version of a tripod that involved the *Angkatan Bersenjata Republik Indonesia* (ABRI), with the Indonesian armed forces as the central pillar. The other two were 'the elite of the civil executive headed by the President, and the elites within the general population. These elites include the key elements of the predominant religion Islam, and the entrepreneurial Chinese.' Like any tripod, if any one of the legs became weak or disappeared, the structure became unstable and vulnerable to collapse.

The 'Guided Democracy' system of Sukarno relied on many of the attributes of previous colonial and tribal rulers: a seemingly permanent position at the helm of affairs, an ability to distribute largesse, and a largely monarchical style of operation. Under his successor, Suharto, 'military officers...used their public position to further their private interests. Military involvement in the economy had become well established...at the same time, many army officers became involved in private business activities. Under the New Order, army-sponsored businesses continued to flourish as the military kept supplementing its allocations from the government budget by means of independently raised funds.'[16]

Some recent literature assigns many of these characteristics to the Pakistan Army and its relationship to the polity of Pakistan. In her recent book, *Military Inc.*[17] Ayesha Siddiqa attempts to quantify the extent of the military's business interests in Pakistan and comes up with a figure of $10 billion. She challenges the rationale for military business ventures and the creation of a system of easy access to state resources that, according to her, allow individual senior officers to profit at the expense of the state and the private sector. While some of her calculations may be open to dispute, the gist of her arguments raises relevant questions: to what extent is the military's access to state resources crowding out the private sector and preventing expenditure on other more productive sectors, such as health and education? More important, is this model sustainable?

As Indonesia expert Harold Crouch asserts, a patrimonial system can only survive if the ruling elite—in this case the military elite—is ideologically homogenous. Further, the masses need to remain passive and isolated from the political process. Which model, the Turkish or Indonesian, will the Pakistan military choose to follow? That is the challenge facing Pakistan's army today—a challenge that has confronted the army since the creation of Pakistan.

THE WIDE FOOTPRINT OF THE ARMY

Both the size and nature of the Pakistan Army have a huge impact on the country's economy and society. Rising from a relatively small force at independence, Pakistan today has an army of around 800,000 plus, including over 550,000 regular army and the rest as reserves. It is larger than the regular army of the United States. It increased its force size even after losing half the country in 1971 with the independence of Bangladesh (formerly East Pakistan). In the process, Pakistan's security threat from India grew, forcing it to meet India's rapid growth of military might on the one hand, and on the other the appearance of the Soviet armed forces in Afghanistan to its west in the 1980s further propelled its expansion.

As Parvez Hasan stated in a recent analysis of the growth of the military and defence spending during the period of Ayub Khan's rule:

> The biggest impact of 1965 war was to change the priorities of public spending.... It is significant that Ayub Khan, a former commander-in-chief of the army, kept the size of the army under strict control, even though India's defense expenditure was rising rapidly after its confrontation with China in 1962. But following the war with India in 1965, defense expenditures were given high priority and phasing out of US military assistance after 1965 put additional burden on domestic resources. Real defense expenditure almost doubled between 1960–65 and 1965–70. This took its toll on development.[18]

As the accompanying table shows, a serious conflict became evident after 1965 between development and defence. The Third Five-Year Development Plan (1965–70) aimed for a sharp expansion in public development spending while reducing defence spending as a proportion of GDP. In fact, development spending remained stagnant as a percentage of GDP while defence expenditures nearly doubled from 2.8 per cent of GDP in 1960–5 to 4 per cent in 1965–70.

Table 1
Defence vs. Development (in billions of rupees)

	1960–5 Actual	1965–70 Planned	1965–70 Actual
Development spending	13.95	30.0	21.75
	(7.1)	(9.8)	(7.1)
Defence spending	5.50	6.89	12.38
	(2.8)	(2.2)	(4.0)

Note: The figures in parenthesis are in per cent of GDP.
Source: Fourth Five-Year Plan, pp. 45–47, cited in 'State and Pakistan Economy: Where have we come from? Where do we go?' by Dr Parvez Hasan.

During Ziaul Haq's period, there was a tremendous increase in public spending, which raised the share of government expenditure in GDP. 'Equally serious, there was a major shift in the public expenditure priorities from development to defence. Real defence spending increased on average by 9 per cent per annum during 1977–88 while development spending rose 3 per cent per annum; by 1987–8 defence spending had overtaken development spending.'[19]

Indeed, defence spending appears to follow overall spending, as another study by Mahmood-ul-Hasan Khan confirms. After the Soviet withdrawal from Afghanistan, in the 1990s and despite tensions with India defence spending dropped from 26.8 per cent in the 1980s to an average of 18.7 per cent for FY2001–03.[20] Yet, according to World Bank data, defence spending as a percentage of GDP in Pakistan was around 3.4 per cent in 2005 compared with India's 2.34 per cent,[21] among the highest burdens of military spending in the world. As Pakistan develops and its economy grows, the opportunity cost (that is the foregone benefits in the development sector) of its defence spending will rise dramatically. This is a huge challenge for the regime, as it ponders its political future on the one hand and the nature of the army that Pakistan needs to ensure its security on the other.

The issue facing Pakistan and its military today is one that faces many other developing countries. Apart from crowding out other more useful investments, the relatively large size of the defence sector and its gradual expansion into other economic activities, as has been the case in Pakistan, Turkey, and Indonesia, for example, spawns a host of ills associated with such parastatal (government and semi-government owned) enterprises: feather-bedding or over-employment, heavy and often hidden subsidies, privileged access to scarce resources, and the creation of a powerful and new vested interest group in economic activities: the serving military and ex-servicemen. Further, these activities lead to other spin-offs in the economic field, including non-military industries, hospitals, real estate, banking, insurance, airlines, and even consumer goods such a cereals and clothing, often in the guise of benevolent schemes for ex-servicemen. As stated earlier, there is little financial scrutiny or supervision of these enterprises or, more importantly, overall defence spending. This distorts the allocation of scarce domestic resources and retards economic development. A study at the University of London established that higher rates of defence spending was associated with lower savings rates in fifty developing countries and the proportion of GDP devoted to investment was negatively associated with the ratio of defence spending to GDP.[22]

Accompanying this economic domination of the political landscape, the army has also strengthened its political status within the rubric of the state's system of assigning seniority to different representatives of government.

ARMY VS. CIVIL HIERARCHY

Successive civilian heads of government have allowed this imbalance between the civil and the military to grow. When I asked former Prime Minister Nawaz Sharif if he was familiar with the Warrant of Precedence, he shook his head and asked what it was. I reminded him of the list that Pakistan inherited from the British and that established the relative ranking of civil and military officials for protocol purposes.[23] Beyond simple protocol, this list symbolizes the relative roles of officials from the civil and the military in the nation's polity and provided a map of their relationships. The Warrant of Precedence issued by the Ministry of Interior from Karachi in February 1950 ranked the top officials of the then dominion of Pakistan, with the governor general at the head, followed by the prime minister, the governors of the provinces (within their own areas of responsibility, i.e. provinces), foreign ambassadors, the chief justice of the Supreme Court, the president of the parliament, ministers of the dominion, then governors (outside their immediate domain), then premiers of the provinces, and so on. Notably, the commander-in-chief of the Pakistan Army came in at number 15, below, among others, the judges of the federal court, the chief justices of the high courts of the provinces, and deputy ministers of the dominion. The chief of staff of the Pakistan Army came in at number 20 while lieutenant generals came in at number 21, followed by general officers commanding divisions at number 22, both below federal secretaries and the governor of the State Bank of Pakistan.[24] I reminded Prime Minister Sharif that Bangladesh had reverted to this early Warrant of Precedence. He then recalled that when he landed at Dhaka on the invitation of Prime Minister Khaleda Zia, he was 'looking for the army chief in the reception line and then [I] saw him, far down the line, after the other officials!'[25] Recent events in Bangladesh appear to suggest that the civilian ascendancy was short-lived, as the army re-asserted its guiding role in the country's polity.

Pakistan changed this warrant de facto when General Ayub Khan, the C-in-C of the army, was made defence minister, and again when he took over as CMLA and then also became president. By 1960, other changes had been introduced, with rulers of some princely states that had joined Pakistan being elevated to higher status. But the commander-in-chief was still maintained at number 15. Corps commanders were elevated to number 20, in the company of the attorney general and the army's chief of staff and the commanders-in-chief of the navy and air force (who were considered lower than the army chief).[26] By 1970, the warrant had been amended a number of times to accommodate the changing priorities of different offices. The attorney general was moved up to number 5 (if he held the rank of a federal minister), while the chiefs of army, navy, and air staff were bumped up to number 6, along with the chairman of the joint chiefs of staff committee, but who would be considered to rank above the chiefs of staff of the three armed services. Officers of the rank of lieutenant general (including corps commanders) were promoted further to number 16 and were now at par with federal secretaries.[27]

Today, the attorney general retains the same rank (number 5) but is joined by the rector of the International Islamic University at that level (a sign of the Islamic times!). The chairman JCSC, and chiefs of army, air, and naval staff are now ranked at number 6, while lieutenant generals remain at par with federal secretaries at number 16.[28] That is the theory, but given that the president and COAS are the same person, by virtue of the warrant, the COAS becomes number 1. And corps commander can assert their rank in their domains and move up to the head of the receiving line whenever the president or other guests come to visit. While not important in itself, the Warrant of Precedence is both an instrument of protocol and a means of ensuring that relative rankings of the civil and military are maintained. None of the civilian prime ministers in recent decades has attempted to change this order. Indeed, all of them have elevated military officers to levels beyond those envisaged by the founders of Pakistan and then complained publicly about the military asserting itself in the polity of Pakistan. Will Pakistan follow Bangladesh's example? That is a question that confronts the prime minister now and will do so in the future as well.

PROTECTING ITS OWN

A frequent complaint about the army in today's Pakistan stems from its overwhelming power and ubiquity in all spheres of civil endeavour, and its ability to operate outside the bounds of normal legal systems. As a result, when its members choose to ignore the law or take it into their own hands, the first instinct of the higher command is to keep the matter out of the public's eye. Concomitant with this tendency has been the growing power and involvement of the ISI agency and the Military Intelligence (MI) in domestic political and civil issues as policy advisors and implementers rather than providing policy-neutral intelligence for military purposes or conducting counter intelligence against the external enemies of Pakistan. The ISI, a highly effective counter intelligence entity, has often been called a 'rogue' agency or a 'state within a state'. But it operates at the behest of the government, civil and military, and because its role has been confused by its masters, who want it not only to serve an intelligence function but also to implemente policy, it takes the heat for some of its actions on their behalf. The civilian Intelligence Bureau (IB), which used to be tasked with internal security matters is now an appendage of the military agencies. Under the Musharraf regime, it was headed by a retired brigadier, a friend of the COAS and president. Under the previous civilian regime of Prime Minister Sharif, the IB was used for political purposes and even then it was headed by a former military officer. To make these agencies effective and to remove from them the opprobrium associated with their extra-legal actions, they need to be subjected to public scrutiny and controls, not only within the army's structure but also before the parliament.

The army and the armed forces in general remain a key element in Pakistan's polity. They are well entrenched and powerful and have moved to fill whatever power vacuum or gap that they see. While, unlike the Turkish army, they do not have any constitutional role in the country's polity, they have crafted a role for themselves and equipped themselves to tackle whatever problems they face, without an invitation from the government. This has created an inherently unstable system.

An examination of the historical record of the Pakistan Army in this book yields a number of major themes over time:

- The Pakistan Army today reflects Pakistani society more than at any time in its history. Increasingly it is going to be based on urban recruitment, especially of its officer corps, and the pool of recruits will come from bigger towns and cities in areas other than its traditional recruitment ground in the Potohar plateau of northern Punjab.
- Internally weak political parties, tied to individual personalities or brought together by temporary and short-sighted common interests, have turned to involve the army in political affairs, only to later lament its active role and taking over of the reins of power.

- The army has gradually acquired a corporate structure and identity that appears to trump broader national interests. It tends to act autonomously in foreign dealings, particularly with the Middle East and the United States. It has penetrated the civilian sector and now controls large segments of civil administration. And, it has a wide economic footprint that goes well beyond the welfare needs of its ex-servicemen and women. Increasingly, the central decision making on political issues involves the corps commanders and the army chief. The newly instituted National Security Council gives the army and the other armed services a formal role in national policy-making.

- The increasingly important role of the army has been given a boost by the US relationship. The United States has at various times given its strategic and often short-term foreign policy interests precedence over sustaining democracy in Pakistan, by aligning with the army as a centre of power. It has been ready to deal with autocrats and dictators at the expense of fostering democracy. The powerful nexus between the US Department of Defense and the Pakistan Army has been a key element of this approach. Yet, whenever the crunch comes, the Pakistan Army acts in its own or national interest rather than bending to the dictates of its US partners.

- The army has generally performed well in its primary task of defending the country against external threats but it has failed to gauge the political will of its own people, leading to the loss of half the country in 1971 and to ill-thought out and autonomously executed military adventures beyond its borders in 1948, 1965, 1971, and 1999. Its junior officers and soldiers rank among the best in the world, but its senior leadership has let down the lower echelons in each of its wars.

- The Pakistan Army's history also shows how it protects its corporate image and structure even against its own leadership when the leadership appears to be threatening the respect and operation of the army as an autonomous entity. It up-ended the Ayub Khan and Yahya Khan dictatorships, when public discontent arose against the army. It also failed to follow up on the investigation of the death of General Ziaul Haq and was reluctant to investigate the suspicious death of General Asif Nawaz. Interestingly, when a civilian prime minister removed General Jehangir Karamat, the army took the change in its stride and rallied behind its new leader.

- Related to the preceding theme is the selection and composition of the senior leadership of the Pakistan Army. It is a highly personalized system of selection in which the army chief plays a dominant role, and the longer a chief remains in power the more likely he is to promote compliant clones. This deprives the senior military leadership of the useful capacity of argument and debate in making decisions.

- Finally, Pakistan remains a key and strategically important country in a troubled region of the world, sitting as it does on the cusp of South Asia, Central Asia, and the Gulf. It also has nuclear arms, whose control and safeguarding is the key to the future stability of the region. For now the army has maintained effective control over the nuclear weapons. But that has not allayed concerns.

These are the broad themes that emerge from a historical analysis of the Pakistan Army at key junctures in the nation's history, and they lay the ground for a re-examination of the army's role in Pakistan's polity and suggestions for change. The army remains a key player on the political scene and will not easily relinquish its hold on power. Whatever new structure emerges over time will have to take the army's nature and role into consideration and bring it into the equation, while increasing the role of the civil sector. The army's leadership needs to be a willing participant in this effort to effect a smooth transition. Without such a shift, Pakistan's search for nationhood and a stable political system may remain an elusive quest.

NOTES

1. Hamza Alvi, 'Pakistan and Islam: Ethnicity and Ideology', *State and Ideology in the Middle East and Pakistan*, Fred Halliday and Hamza Alavi, eds., London and New York: Monthly Review Press, 1988.
2. General Jehnagir Karamat, 'The role of the military and the future civil–military relations in Pakistan.' Talk at Brookings Institution, Washington DC, 19 June 2000.
3. Arshad Zaman, former chief economist, planning commission, 'National Security and Development Strategy in Pakistan.' Paper presented at the National Defence College, 26 September 1998.
4. General (retd.) Mirza Aslam Beg, 'The Powerbrokers of Democracy', *The Nation*, Lahore, 6 April 2007.
5. Kamal Azfar, 'Doctrine of Necessity', *The Nation*, 2 April 2006.
6. Kamal Azfar, 'The Swing of the Pendulum', *The Nation*, 10 September 2006.
7. In an interview with the BBC on Saturday, 17 November 2007 he declared 'Have I done anything constitutionally illegal? Yes, I did it on November 3', he said, referring to imposition of emergency rule. 'But did I do it before? Not once.' *The News*, Islamabad, 18 November 2007.
8. Mancur Olson, 'Dictatorship, Democracy and Development', *American Political Science Review*, Vol. 87, No. 3, September 1993, pp. 567–576 and Mancur Olson, *The Logic of Collective Action* (Cambridge: Harvard University Press, 1965).
9. Mahmood Monshipouri and Amjad Samuel, 'Development and Democracy in Pakistan: Tenuous or Plausible Nexus?' *Asian Survey*, Vol. XXXV, No. 11, November 1995.
10. Craig Baxter, ed., *Diaries of Field Marshal Mohammad Ayub Khan 1966–1972* (Karachi: Oxford University Press, 2007). Entry for Sunday, 15 January 1967, p. 49.

11. The International Institute of Strategic Studies, *Nuclear Black Markets: Pakistan, A.Q. Khan and the Rise of Proliferation Networks—A Net Asessment* (London: IISS, 2007), pp. 109–113.

12. Ayesha Siddiqa, *Military Inc.: Inside Pakistan's Military Economy* (London: Pluto Press, 2007).

13. The Pakistan Army has a legion of brigadiers also who represent the one-star generals, but who are not referred to as generals, unlike, say, in the old British Indian army or the United States army.

14. Stephen Kinzer, *Crescent and Star: Turkey Between Two Worlds* (New York: Straus, and Giroux, 2001), pp. 164–65.

15. Interview with Ambassador John Monjo, former envoy to both Pakistan and Indonesia. See also Harold Crouch, 'Patrimonialism and Military Rule in Indonesia,' *World Politics*, Princeton University Press, 1979, pp. 571–587.

16. Crouch, 'Patrimonialism'.

17. Siddiqa, *Military Inc.*

18. Dr Parvez Hasan, 'State and Pakistan Economy: Where have we come from? Where do we go?'

19. Ibid.

20. Mahmood-ul-Hasan Khan, 'Defence Expenditure and Macroeconomic Stabilization: Causality Evidence from Pakistan,' State Bank of Pakistan, Working Papers, No. 6, December 2004.

21. World Bank *World Development Indicators 2006*.

22. Saadat Deger and Ron Smith, 'Military expenditure and Growth in Less-Developed Countries,' *The Journal of Conflict Resolution*, 27 June 1983.

23. Interview (conducted by author) with Prime Minister Nawaz Sharif.

24. Provisional warrant of precedence. Notification. Ministry of the Interior (Home Division), Karachi, 22 February 1950.

25. Sharif interview.

26. Warrant of precedence for Pakistan published in Ministry of Home and Kashmir affairs (Home Affairs Division). Notification no. 21/2//61-Public, 7 March 1963 as amended from time to time. Corrected up to 26 June 1968.

27. Notification. Government of Pakistan, Ministry of Interior, Islamabad, 6 July 1970. Signed by AMS Ahmad.

28. Revised Warrant of Precedence. Government of Pakistan, Cabinet Secretariat, Cabinet Division. No. 7-2-2003-Min. I. Islamabad, 31 October 2006.

1 | IN HISTORY BOUND

The Pakistan Army of today is rooted in the ancient history of the region that now constitutes Pakistan, and is bound as much by the geography of the region as by the forces that contributed to the culture and civilization of the Indian subcontinent. The peoples of Pakistan represent the ebbs and flows of tribal migrations into ancient India in the midst of countless invasions, mainly from the north-west. Cradled in the security of the Himalayas in the north and north-east, and separated from other lands by the Bay of Bengal and the Arabian Sea on the south-east and the south-west respectively, India offered only its western frontier to intruders. And many came, leaving behind a culture and a congeries of tribes that, despite the passage of centuries, still retain the memories of ancient warring tribes of Central Asia, the Middle East, and even Central Europe.

The western marches of Pakistan are guarded by a range of mountains that spin off from the Pamir Knot and head westward toward the Hindu Kush range into the area now called Afghanistan and southward into the Sulaiman range into Balochistan. Though seemingly impregnable, this wall of mountains is broken by over a dozen major passes, some at high altitudes, others through deep chasms in the body of dried rocks that characterize much of this western frontier. Some geographers estimate as many as 23 passes. Yet, two entrances have gained prominence in history and folklore: the Khyber and Bolan passes, one feeding from the road that follows the Kabul River gorge eastward to Jalalabad and then veers south-east into the valley of Peshawar, and the other from the desert-like wastes of Kandahar into the plateau that now contains the city of Quetta. Further to the south and west is the almost perfect defence of the Makran desert adjoining the Iranian deserts of Balochistan and Dasht-i-Lut.

The northern wall of mountains is backed up by a series of parallel valleys with high and steep mountains which have made invasion for wayward intruders a death-trap. Even Alexander of Macedon, who stumbled into what was perhaps the worst invasion route into India, through the mountains of what is now Bajaur, nearly lost his life fighting entrenched mountain tribes of this region. It is not surprising, therefore, that invaders who had some knowledge of the topography of the area used the Khyber Pass to enter India. For most, the base camp was the area of Kabul, where the mountains of the northern area of what is now Afghanistan debouched onto a plateau with rivers and orchards that offered promises of the sweeter waters of the Punjab and the riches of the Gangetic plains of India. The easterly flow of the Kabul River had carved a gorge in the mountain shield that protected the Indian frontier; this gorge became the path most frequently taken by invaders.

According to previously accepted histories and local folklore, the earliest documented invaders of India came from Western and Central Asia. More recent historians have challenged this interpretation of Indian history, blaming the Aryan theory on Western prejudices, favouring instead the possibility that all inhabitants of India came from elsewhere.[1] These were the fair-skinned 'Aryans', who routed and pushed into the South of the subcontinent the darker-skinned aborigines whom they called 'dasyus' or enemies and 'Dasas' or slaves. Since the Aryans took pride in their fairer colour, the Sanskrit words for colour *varna* came to mean 'race' or 'caste' and Aryan poets who composed the Veda some 3000–4000 years ago celebrated their gods who slayed the 'Dasyus and protected the Aryan colour.' They heaped scorn on the 'noseless' or flat-nosed natives while praising their own 'beautiful-nosed' gods.[2] These Indo-Germanic people, the Aryans, were said to be the ancestors of the latter day Brahmin, Rajputs, and even the Englishmen who much later ruled India.[3]

The Aryans flooded the plains of India, setting up kingdoms and fortresses, and over time becoming absorbed into the culture of India. They came to constitute the caste of 'Brahmin', the priestly class of rulers and the Rajputs or 'sons of rulers'—in other words the warriors—while relegating others to more menial occupations. Their southward spread was celebrated in the epic poems of the *Mahabharata* and the *Ramayana*. War was elevated by them to a noble, almost religious experience.[4]

ALEXANDER'S INVASION

Alexander the Great, himself of Aryan stock, contemplated Asia after subduing the Greek tribes. With some 32,000 infantry and 5,100 cavalry, he set foot on Asian soil in 325 BC. He augmented his force with about 10,000 Greek soldiers already in Asia and turned to do battle with the Persian emperor, Darius.[5] The Persian Army is said to have included mercenaries from as far east as the Punjab, as the Greek Aryans met their Rajput counterparts for the first time. The defeat and retreat of the Persians, followed by the death of Darius, allowed the youthful Greek emperor to enrich his force with local garrisons and head east. He stumbled into the Hindu Kush and took among the worst routes into the subcontinent, through the steep mountain valleys of the Hindu Kush. He fought his way through numerous mountain fortresses across the Indus River to Taxila, where the local chief, Abisares (known as Ambhi in Indian literature), submitted to him and sought his help in defeating a major local rival, Porus, the king of the Pauravas in the land between the Hydaspes and Acesines rivers (modern day Jhelum and Chenab).

Camping in the area of what is now Haranpur (close to my village Chakri Rajgan) and perhaps crossing at the site of modern Jalalpur in Jhelum district, Alexander took on his formidable local opponent in a highly mobile battle that lasted most of the day, as Indian elephants and Greek cavalry sparred for advantage, until the moment when Porus's elephant was struck in the eye and fled, giving his forces what they perceived as the signal for retreat.[6] Alexander took advantage of this and routed the fleeing army of Porus. When the Indian raja was brought before him, Alexander asked, 'What do you wish that I should do with you?' 'Treat me as a King ought,' replied Porus. Having become used to the bargaining and self-seeking behaviour of defeated Persian and other rulers of Asia, Alexander asked, 'But is there not something that you would wish for yourself? Ask it.' 'Everything,' said Porus, 'is contained in this one request.' Overwhelmed by this dignity in a fellow warrior, Alexander restored Porus's lands to him and sought safe passage to the East. Even today, the region carries memories of that epic battle. Many locals still name their sons Sikandar (the local variant of Alexander). I too recall my father's uncle sending us Greek coins and even a shield and a short sword once (which we donated to the Taxila museum). These had been found in his fields during ploughing, leading me to believe that our village area had once been the burial ground for Alexander's army after the battle with Porus. The fact that this story of Porus's exchange with Alexander is still repeated in Pakistan today is testimony to the strength of tradition that grows deep in the area and its people.

The tribes that inhabit today's Pakistan and people its army are the remnants of numerous movements across the north Indian landmass. Except for the Pathans, who largely remained in the north-western reaches of the land and the Baluch, who came from their Syrian and Persian homes to settle in the Kirthar and Sulaiman ranges, most of the warrior tribes of the Punjab and Sindh emerged from battles among the leading army chieftains of ancient India, battles that led to the creation of diasporas, often westward from their homes, in north and central India.

THE MARTIAL TRIBES

Pakistan's army continues to rely on certain areas for its soldiers, a tradition that goes back to pre-British India and became enshrined in the near-mythic formula of the 'martial races.' Punjabi Mussalmans (PMs) dominated recruitment during the British period, and were mainly from these 'martial races' that inhabited the Potohar plateau and the Punjab plains. Pathan recruitment began at a late stage under British rule, while Sindhi and Baluch tribals were mostly outside the principal recruiting networks, and remain so today.

On the Potohar plateau, the Gakkhar tribe—descended from Gakkhar Shah, a general of Mohammed Ghori (although many Gakkhars seek other, more glamorous origins in Arabia)—dominated the area. The other major tribal group, although in much smaller numbers, is the Rajput tribe, the Janjuas, an offshoot of the Rathors and Chauhans of Rajputana. This tribe travelled back from the hinterland, fought unsuccessfully against Mahmud of Ghazni, and embraced Islam. In his *Baburnama*, Babur refers to them as ruling several other tribes of the Salt Range and specifically mentions the Janjuas, (my tribe), which has its headquarters, fort of Malot, in the Salt Range.[7] Later, the Janjuas sided with Sher Shah Suri against the Gakkhars. Other Rajput tribes of the area also contributed to the armies of the Mughals and the British Raj.

Also in the Salt Range, the Awans have contributed profusely to the ranks of the army. While they claim descent from the Prophet Muhammad's (PBUH) son-in-law, Ali, through Kutb Shah, a general of Mahmud of Ghazni, there appears to be some evidence in favour of a Hindu origin of the tribe. Pandit Harikrishan Kaul in his report of the 1911 census refers to the Sanskrit term 'Awan' as meaning defender or protector.[8] There appears to be some evidence that the tribe was converted to Islam by Kutb Shah, hence the practice of calling themselves Kutb Shahis.

On the Punjab plains, the Jats, a pastoral people, have been the mainstay of the armies of successive rulers of the area. While they are now seen as a separate tribe, there appears to be some evidence that they share a common root with the Rajputs. In fact, some Jat tribes do claim Rajput origins. Both Muslim and Sikh Jats have been known as brave soldiers. Mahmud of Ghazni fought them near the Chenab, and overcame them after great difficulty. The Mughal emperor Babur mentions the Jats of the Salt Range in his memoirs as having been subdued by the Awans, Janjuas, and other Rajput tribes of the area.

Another major military group are the Gujars, again linked to the same roots as the Rajputs and Jats, but differentiated now mainly because of their occupations. Wikele speaks about the Scythian tribe of Yuch-Chi that had been established in Kabul, Kashmir, and northern Punjab at the time that the Jatii or Getae (modern day Jats) moved into India. Around the third century some of them moved southward and became separated from their northern cousins by the inroads of the Getae from the Bolan.[9] Later, the Gujars ruled a major Indian empire from Kanauj. Today, the settlements of these Gujars are still marked by names such as Gujrat, Gujar Khan (near Rawalpindi), and Gujranwala.[10]

Among the many other warrior tribes that populate the army of Pakistan today are those that came back from the hinterland either during the reign of Alauddin Khilji or most recently in the aftermath of the Partition of India in 1947. The Kharrals, Tiwanas, Ghebas, and Chaddars are among the many tribes of Rajputs that emigrated from Hindustan to the Punjab. The Manj, Punwar, and Chauhan Rajputs figure prominently in this reverse migration.

A smaller number of Pathans who had settled in the *bastis* (settlements) of Jullundur also turned westward when East Punjab became part of Hindu India in 1947 and settled mainly in Pakistani Punjab. These included the Burkis, formerly of Afghanistan's Logar valley, and Kanikurram in Waziristan.

Many Pathan tribes from both the Punjab and the current NWFP also became prominent in the military during various regimes. Among them, the Niazis, Jaduns, Chagarzais, Akkazais, Tanaolis, Tareens, and Utmanzais are notable. In the Pakistan Army and in the latter days of the British Indian army, the Mahsuds and Khattaks also became well-known recruits. Meanwhile, in Sindh and Balochistan, despite the more recent efforts at recruitment, the fierce tribes retain their independent ways and still avoid military service in any but their own tribal forces.

This tribal background provides a powerful glue of tradition for the recruitment of manpower into the Pakistan Army. A volunteer force, the Pakistan Army uses these tribes' historical links to the military to ensure a regular stream of recruits and to assure discipline among those that it brings into its ranks. There is no room among the tradition-bound tribes for anyone who fails to make the grade once he has enlisted, while the demonstration effect of relatives and fellow tribals often is enough to turn many a recalcitrant recruit into a pliable soldier.

PRISONERS OF THE PAST

But it was much more than sheer tribal spirit that brought the warrior tribes of the area that is now Pakistan into a seemingly permanent marriage with the army. Economics too played a part. The region that they inhabit is largely hostile and unproductive. Rain-fed agriculture and subsistence pastoral pursuits ensured that these tribes had to rely on forays into more productive regions or loot from passing caravans heading from the west towards mainland India. The Koh-i-Jud (named after Jodh, one of the two sons of the Rajput leader Raja Mal, the first chieftain of my own Janjua tribe), now known as the Salt Range, provided a safe haven for these brigands. The Potohar plateau and the Salt Range produced little of value, except manpower.

By the time of the Mughals, the area that now comprises the western reaches of the districts of Rawalpindi and Attock (called Campbellpur in the latter part of British Indian history), up to the Indus River, was known primarily as a breeding ground for cavalry horses.[11] The only other economic pursuit was the production of salt from mines near Khewra (Khoora in earlier times), Makhiala, and Khurd. Between the Jhelum and Chenab rivers (i.e. the Chaj Doab, or land between the two rivers), the principal products were swords, daggers, and embroidered muslin. As one proceeded eastward and the land became irrigated, agricultural products and related activities began to appear.

The Mughals built upon the inherent qualities of these peoples and set up a sophisticated recruiting and payment system to ensure a regular supply of troops from recognized warrior tribes. They refined a system of honours, using imperial '*mansabs*' or royal edicts for recruiting by rank, according to the number of soldiers to be provided by a local chieftain. *Mansabs* were not necessarily confined to the military, and were in use in the case of civil appointments too. The *mansab* entitled the holder of the edict to petition the state for funds or honours. This system came from Central Asia. The highest rank held by anyone other than a member of the royal court was commander of 7,000 men, though there have been instances of persons with higher numbers under their command.[12] In brief, the Mughals set up a system for honouring local chieftains and for ensuring a steady supply of soldiers for their regional campaigns. This helped firm up a relationship between local rulers and the central authority, a relationship which became critical for the maintenance of a vast empire in India, first under the Mughals and then under their successors, the British. Moreover, it strengthened the creation of mercenaries from among the warrior tribes, who were available for service in distant areas.[13] The nucleus of the future 'volunteer' army of Pakistan was being formed in these early days.

ENTER THE BRITISH

The next major rulers of India, the British, built on the Mughal traditions and systems. 'As long as we rule India, we are the greatest power in the world. If we lose it, we shall drop straight away to a third-rate power.' With these words, Viceroy Lord Curzon in 1901 outlined the relationship beween India and Great Britain. The decline of the Mughal empire had led to the formation of numerous regional nodes of power, leading to conflicts between competing local interests. The rise of autonomous rule in distant fiefdoms produced a highly dynamic economic and political situation. Freed of central control, these kingdoms embarked on vigorous economic and political expansion. The arrival of European traders and their accompanying forces added a potent new ingredient to this cauldron. The Europeans brought with them their own feuds. The war of Austrian succession, for example, drew the French and English East India companies into conflict for control of trading privileges in the coastal areas of southern India. In this process, they drew in local surrogates and partners. According to noted British historian, C.A. Bayly, 'The British had been drawn into the politics of coastal India by lust for profit' and their representatives benefited also from revenues from markets as well as rich political perquisites.

The British began by acquiring the prized possession of Bengal, their military commander, Robert Clive having successfully installed Mir Jafar as his puppet ruler in August 1757, with its £4 million worth of revenues and booty. This gave the British a powerful foothold on the Indian subcontinent in both political and economic terms, allowing them to penetrate further inland and to destabilize petty potentates who attempted to withstand their inroads. The East India Company controlled the valuable saltpetre, salt, indigo, and betel nut monopolies.[14] This not only allowed the company to profit immensely but also made its officers extremely wealthy and willing to use military force to penetrate and eventually control the ailing Mughal empire. This was exemplified by the views of the brothers Richard and Arthur Wellesley in favour of the British right to conquer India.[15] They favoured the extension of British 'protection' over native states while maintaining a semblance of civility with the Mughal emperor. At the same time, the company began a process of military recruitment and alliances that would eventually give it the wherewithal to take on all independent native rulers.

It began recruiting from 1765 in eastern Awadh and the area around Benares, home of the famed *poorbias* or 'easterners' who had staffed the armies of the Muslim rulers since the fifteenth century.[16] These Bumihar and Rajput soldiers found it increasingly difficult to get meaningful employment in the armies of the fading Mughal empire, becoming good targets for British recruiters. By 1857, this area provided some 80 per cent of the troops of Bengal, providing links between the British rulers and rural society. This army also became the backbone of operations against native rulers of southern India and in operations in Ceylon, Java, and the Red Sea area. These soldiers were paid well (Rs 80 per annum), and regularly. Supported also by a strong navy and armed with modern muskets, the British Army gained an advantage over their native rivals. An exasperated Haider Ali of Mysore is reported to have said of the British: 'I can defeat them on land, but I cannot swallow the sea.'[17]

The fluid movement of men and materials around Indian shores, coupled with efficient siege methods and a well-trained cavalry, gave the British additional advantages over increasingly divided opponents. Local chieftains drew the British into their regional quarrels, allowing the East India Company to negotiate important economic and sometimes military benefits in return. This subsequently led the company into direct conflict with other local rivals for land revenue and commerce. Gradually, the fiscal and the military aspects of the company's operations became inextricably intertwined. Out of this emerged a system of local alliances and the creation of a network of surrogates upon whom the company built its superstructure of power.

The ultimate aim of the British was the economic conquest of India. This was slowly but surely accomplished, often with the use of local soldiery. Revenues from India were used to cover the company's deficits in London and to continue to provide dividends to shareholders there and, of course, funded the large and expensive army that helped further British aims in western India and even overseas in the Middle East.

The role of the army within the hierarchy of government grew immensely during this period. Indeed it became the virtual engine of growth of British rule in India. The commander-in-chief in India ranked second only to the governor general to whom he reported, unlike his other military counterparts at home who came under the commander-in-chief of the British Army in London. His pay, at Rs 100,000, made the Indian commander-in-chief the highest paid soldier in the British empire.[18] His titular control extended over the armies of Madras and Bengal, though direct control was confined more or less to the Bengal Army. The later addition of the Punjab Irregular Field Force (the legendary 'Piffers') came under the lieutenant governor of the Punjab. The commander-in-chief did not control the armies of the princely states either.

By 1828, British rule held most of India under its sway, except the Punjab and the North West Frontier region. British machinations following the two wars against the Sikhs and the death of Ranjit Singh gave them control over a well-disciplined force of Muslims and Sikhs, mainly from the Jullundur area and the Rechna Doab (the tract between the Ravi and Chenab rivers). After the end of the Second Sikh War in 1848–9, the western frontier was extended to the mountainous borderlands at the edge of Afghanistan, further widening the potential recruitment area.

Meanwhile festering grievances within the lower ranks of the army and dissatisfaction with the British monopoly over the politics and economy of India bred a violent reaction.

THE MUTINY

The causes of the great Indian mutiny of 1857, as it came to be called by British historians, were many. The final spark came from within the soldiery at Meerut, when the eighty-five *sowars*, or horse-soldiers, of the 3rd Light Cavalry refused to use a new cartridge that was alleged to have been greased with the fat of cattle and pigs. The new cartridge was designed for the Lee-Enfield rifles that replaced the smooth-bored muskets used by the army till then. Being smaller and tighter than the rounds used in the earlier muskets, the new cartridge had to be greased to allow it to be plunged easily into the barrel. Colonel Carmichael Smyth of the 3rd Light Infantry tried to explain to his troops that they did not need to bite the covering off the cartridge. Instead they could tear it with their fingers. He showed this method to his havildar major (a non-commissioned officer) and an orderly. That night the havildar major's tent was burned down and the orderly is said to have fired his carbine twice to protest being used for this demonstration. When the cartridges were issued, only four men accepted them whereas eighty-five did not. Smyth sought direction from General Hewitt at army headquarters in Meerut. A court martial was ordered. All eighty-five pleaded 'not guilty' and then interrupted the testimony of the acting Adjutant Melville Clark with shouts of, 'It's a lie!'[19] The proceedings ended quickly with the passing of a guilty verdict that was confirmed by the British army commander, General Anson, in Simla by cable.

Indian soldiers by that time had also accumulated various other complaints against their British superiors. The case of sepoy Mangal Pandey had caused much concern earlier in 1857. Pandey had rushed out onto the parade ground of the 34th Regiment on 29 March, shouting for his colleagues to rise against the British for the sake of their religion—the cause, greased cartridges. He shot and wounded the British sergeant major, then fired at the adjutant's horse. Later in the day, a charge by Brigadier General Hearsey led Pandey to fire his weapon at himself. Pandey failed in his suicide bid and was captured, tried, and hung. Thereafter, all native soldiers who rose against authority were known as 'Pandies.' Officers were seen as overbearing and distant. Some officers even tried to convert their native soldiers to Christianity; (the colonel of the 34th Bengal Native Infantry freely admitted to this).[20] Many soldiers felt that the company had broken its promises to them. Instead of being sent home on pensions, many were retained to work in the military cantonments. Moreover, special pay or 'batta' for service outside British territory was stopped once those areas were brought under British control.

British prejudice against the native was seen as excessive by the soldiery. The Meerut mutineers were paraded publicly before a hollow square of English and Indian troops on Saturday, 9 May 1857. The British troops—the 6th Dragoon Guards and the Queen's 60th Rifles—faced each other across the square bearing loaded weapons. The third side of the hollow square contained the Indian troops of the 3rd Light Cavalry without their horses, and the 11th and 20th Native Infantry, all carrying weapons without ammunition. The Bengal Artillery had two batteries at the ready under the command of Brigadier Archdale Wilson, just in case things got out of hand. The sentences were read out: older soldiers were sentenced to life or sent to 'Kala Pani,' the dreaded 'Black Water' prison of the Andaman Islands. Younger men received 10–20 years jail sentences. The men were fettered on the spot. 'Remember us!' they shouted to General Hewitt as he turned away. They also cursed Colonel Smyth profusely. Discontent simmered in the barracks that night and the next day. Even the bazaar prostitutes are said to have taunted their Indian clients with news that the British soldiers would attack them. On Sunday, while the British rested after church services, the soldiers attacked them with a view to freeing their jailed comrades.[21]

The fire of the mutiny spread far and fast, mainly because of the 4,044 miles of telegraph cable that had been strung up in India. In the Punjab, the chief commissioner, Sir John Lawrence, based in Lahore, was away in Rawalpindi. His deputy Robert Montgomery asked the local brigadier commanding the four native regiments near Lahore to disarm them. This was done under the shadow of twelve cannons in British hands that were pointed at the Indian troops and ordered to be loaded for firing. The Punjab was thus 'saved.' Some soldiers, the Sikhs and the Gurkhas among the most prominent, remained loyal. Indeed, the Punjab provided most of the troops that helped break the siege of Delhi and with it the back of the uprising against British rule. In the process, the British learned to turn their attention to the west to solidify the recruitment of the bulk of their soldiery.

THE ARMY OF THE RAJ

The 1857 uprising led the British to rethink their approach to the army of the Raj and to the recruitment of soldiers, shifting away from the south and eastern provinces towards the Punjab and the north-west. Increasingly, the Punjab became the 'sword arm of the Empire,' with the *barani* (rain-fed agricultural) districts of Campbellpur (Attock), Rawalpindi, and Jhelum taking on importance as being the most prolific providers of soldiers for the army of the Raj. Apart from the Muslim soldiery of the Punjab, Sikhs, who had been a major component of the forces that helped quell the Great Mutiny (as the British called the uprising of 1857), acquired prominence in the British Indian forces of the time.

The first efforts in this direction involved setting up regimental recruiting centres in the Punjab. But by 1892, a new recruitment process emerged, based on a class system, with most regiments recruiting soldiers of the same ethnic class or religious caste. Some regiments also divided the component companies on the basis of class or ethnic background, leading to the creation of recruitment categories such as Punjabi Mussalmans (or Muslims), Pathans, and Sikhs.[22] The British officers relied heavily on self-governance by these caste or ethnic-based regiments and companies, using the viceroy's commissioned officers (VCOs) to act as intermediaries as well as potential recruiters of soldiers from their own groups or regions.

The emphasis on the Punjab is reflected in the rapid growth of Punjabi regiments in the Indian Army, rising from 28 in 1892 to some 57 in 1914, at the outset of the Great War. At the same time, recruitment efforts in other regions and from other groups (except the Gurkhas), began to slow down, with the Bombay and Madras presidencies going down from 30 to 18 regiments and 40 to 11 respectively in the same period.[23] Meanwhile within the orbit of the new recruitment pattern, a discernible shift occurred toward favouring certain tribes or classes that were perceived to be intrinsically warlike.

THE 'MARTIAL RACES'

The biggest proponent of the idea of the 'martial races' was the celebrated Lord Roberts of Kandahar, eventually the commander-in-chief of the British Indian Army (1885–93), who spent some forty years in the military service of the Raj.[24] By 1885 he had come to the conclusion that, 'The time had arrived for us to prove to the people of India that we had faith in their loyalty and in their recognition of the fact that their concern in the defence of the empire was at least as great as ours, and that we looked to them to take their part in strengthening our rule and in keeping out all intruders.'[25] He went on to say that, 'From the time I became Commander-in-Chief in Madras until I left India the question of how to render the army in that country as perfect a fighting machine as it was possible to make it, was the one that caused me the most anxious thought, and to its solution….the first step to be taken towards this end was, it seemed to me, to substitute men of the more warlike and hardy races for the Hindustani sepoys of Bengal, the Tamils and Telegus of Madras, and the so-called Mahrattas of Bombay.' Roberts found no comparison between the 'Gurkhas of Nepal or the warlike races of Northern India' and the 'effeminate peoples of the south.'[26]

   Roberts was not alone in his thinking along these lines. Indeed, the current recruitment patterns of the Pakistan Army reflect many of these ideas, although the reason for the continuation of the recruitment patterns is not solely based on the 'martial races' theory. Geography and economy play a key role in supporting recruitment patterns. The tribes of the North West Frontier and the Punjab sat astride the major invasion routes into India. As such, these tribes traditionally relied heavily on their military prowess to eke out a living in a largely arid and rough terrain. Moreover, as the British Raj solidified its hold on India, there was a distinct lack of industrialization and economic development in these regions from where the majority of the soldiery was recruited. Indeed, the first industrial plant in the Jhelum district was not set up until after partition, when the Prime Glass Factory and then the Fauji (i.e., Military) Textile Mill, after much debate on their negative effects on military recruitment, were set up to provide employment for retired soldiers. The

British feared that local employment opportunities would draw potential recruits away from the army of the Raj. The recruitment areas of northern India were also likely to have a low literacy rate, making their population unfit for pursuits other than the military. In 1902, for example, according to the 1901 census of India, the literacy rate for the Punjab (including the NWFP) was only 64 per 1,000 persons less than one-half that of Madras.[27]

Even in the Punjab, the recruitment centred on the rural areas and away from the less hardy townsfolk. Retired General Imranullah Khan[28] of the Pakistan Army recalls that his father spoke of how the British recruiters would come to his area (in the NWFP) and ask all potential recruits to hold out their hands. The recruiting officer would then pass his palms over the extended palms of these men and reject anyone whose hands were soft, indicating an absence of manual labour. Extensive writings in the district gazetteers and specialized handbooks such as Colonel Wikele's *Punjabi Mussalmans* defined the characteristics of the tribes and clans of the Punjab, even stereotyping them into particular types of soldiers. My own Rajput tribesmen, the Janjuas, were seen by Wikele as being 'Fine soldiers, most suitable for cavalry, as they are of light build.'[29]

The recruitment process involved not only the roving recruitment parties from the various regimental centres that were established in the target districts, but also involved serving soldiers who were encouraged to bring their relatives into the fold. A list of *umeedvars*, or contenders/applicants, was kept for each regiment and was added to by serving or retired soldiers so that recruiting officers would know how many were in the pipeline and would then give preference to relatives of the soldiers or ex-servicemen who had placed the applicants on the list of potential recruits. A common Punjabi prayer for women was 'May you have seven sons' since the Raj provided special stipends to families with a large number of male children. Every now and then, senior British officers would tour the catchment area of potential recruits, visiting villages that had substantial numbers of ex-servicemen and honouring them publicly. Often, as was the case of Field Marshal Sir Claude Auchinleck, the visiting officer would be briefed about the names and relatives of the ex-servicemen whom he might meet in a village. He would then address them by name in Hindustani (or Urdu) and ask about the health of a senior retired relative. This created the impression that the British officer knew the names by heart and was highly regarded by the locals. The British avoided recruitment from the cities and towns and also categorized tribes so tightly that recruitment officers were trained to ask trick questions to catch young men who tried to pass themselves off as belonging to the more favoured war-like tribes.[30]

At the same time, the members of many tribes that were classified as martial continued to enlist in the British Indian Army, even when economic conditions were favourable to them. The Tiwanas of Shahpur district, though owners of large tracts of irrigated land, had over half of their 1,500 strong male population enlisted in the army.[31] Cognizant of the need to provide good benefits to the fresh recruits, the army paid them well and provided services to both serving and retired soldiers, making them more prosperous than their non-military peers. Remittances from soldiers provided substantial benefits to their home regions. Soldiers and pensioners from the three major recruiting districts in the Punjab, Jhelum, Attock, and Rawalpindi received some fourteen million rupees from the government of India in 1939. War-time services brought extra pay and bonuses, as the reality of war, especially the distant and costly conflict in Europe in 1914, caused recruitment to lag.

SOME DISENCHANTMENT

There were other reasons for the lag in recruitment as well. While many in the rural areas appreciated the developments that the British had brought to their regions in the form of roads and railways, the deployment of Punjabi soldiers to distant parts of India or even to other continents 'across seven seas' brought its own form of protest. This was reflected, among others, in local songs. The shift in tune from praise for the 'firangi' (foreigner), as present in the following verse:

Putt jeen ve firangiya tere
Pind vich rail aa gayee
(O Englishman! May your progeny live long!
Now that rail has come to my village)

Or

Sohna raj Angrezi
Pind pind dakiya firey
(The English rule is good
Every village now has a postman)

to a lament against enlistment and overseas service that took men and specially married men far, far away:

Rana wale jang jit de
Kitthe likhiya firangiya, das ve
(The soldiers with wives win wars?
Where is it written, O Firangi, tell me!)

And, even that earlier welcome train bore the brunt of the local complaints:

> You separated my husband and I
> *May you break down!*[32]

The naiveté and resentment of the folk songs captures the reality that the British introduced mass transit, and the railroad especially, as a means of building and expanding their forces, whether in the arid wastes of the North West Frontier or in Sindh. Yet, mobility and the introduction of education raised expectations and led to increased ambitiousness among the rural gentry which occupied a high social status but a relatively low economic status in its home regions. Young men aspired to reach the higher ranks of the military, studying by lamplight and walking miles to go to high schools that prepared them to enter the world of the British.

LAND GRANTS

British colonial policies were clearly tilted toward the military, providing service awards, pensions, and land grants to soldiers from the Punjab. In doing this, the British built on the age-old policies of the Sikhs and the Mughals. With the gradual introduction of canals into the Punjab, lands which were once arid and fallow came under the plough and were distributed to servicemen starting in 1865. Sizeable portions of land in the newly colonized areas of the Jech or Chaj *doab*, (the tract between the Jhelum and Chenab rivers,) and the land between the Sutlej and Beas rivers to the south and east, were allocated to soldiers from the *barani* areas of Punjab.

As a result of this policy, agricultural land in these once barren areas rose from some 3 million to 14 million acres. This not only allowed the state to exercise greater control over what were hitherto 'wastelands', but also gave it the power to provide largesse to favoured segments of the population, furthering these peoples' dependence on the state.[33] The Jhelum colonies were heavily tilted toward the military by virtue of a new policy that favoured allocation of lands to military personnel who would breed horses and mules for the army. Despite opposition from civil officials, who contended that soldiers from the Potohar already raised horses, the army proceeded with the scheme. This scheme survived all the way into the twentieth century, well after the army had no more need for horses or for mules! The minimum size of these land grants of 2 squares (55.5 acres) gave the soldier class a foot up the socio-economic ladder, making it more beholden to the state. Land or *jagir* grants often accompanied civil or military awards to local officers. In the 1880s, they were of the order of 500 acres each. After 1890, the size of the grants in the canal colonies was reduced. The selection of the grantees was done by the military not civil authorities and was aimed at soldiers and officers from the Punjab who served the British Indian army. Even natives who chose to serve in distant parts of the empire, such as Hong Kong, were excluded.[34] The aim was to provide incentives to the tribes that provided the most recruits for the army in India.

INDIANIZATION

Between 1914 and 1918, the size of the British Indian Army nearly quadrupled to over half a million men, more than 136,000 of whom were Punjabi Mussalmans. The demand was fuelled by the fighting in Europe and Mesopotamia. Immediately after the war, the size of the army was drastically reduced. A new trend of thought was emerging as the British realized that they could not hope to run such a large force with the relatively small number of officers they had brought over from England. A lively debate had been brewing for decades about the need to 'Indianize' the army of the Raj. As early as 1836, Colonel John Biggs of the Madras Army suggested that Indians be given higher command in the British Indian Army and soon afterwards Henry Lawrence had suggested the introduction of a native officer class.[35]

Yet, there was an entrenched opposition to these ideas among the British. Their general reaction centred on the education and ability of the Indians compared with the British officers. Among the leading critics of 'Indianization' was General Wilcocks, who commanded the Indian forces in Europe during the First World War. He considered the Indian innately inferior to the British, with the latter being able to command and the former only able to follow.[36] There were views also along the lines of one English general's comments, in which he maintained that native officers' wives would speak only Hindustani and that this would bring the native language into the guarded confines of the officers' mess![37]

The general view against giving the Indians greater responsibility was reflected in the comment by Lord Curzon, the viceroy, that only 6,500 European and 22,000 Indian civil servants held sway over 230 million Indian subjects. Despite this economic divide between himself and the local rajas, Curzon remained what leading British historian Niall Ferguson terms a 'tory-entalist,'[38] someone who broke with the previous generation of British Orientalists to re-create the imperial grandeur of the British. He only consorted with the local rajas and aristocratic landowners whom he regarded as best suited to be surrogates of the British rulers.

WORLDS APART

The British Indian cantonment or military camps were self-contained units with everything that the army needed: shops, housing, barracks, and even brothels.[39] Ancillary bazaars sprung up in these areas, such as the celebrated Lalkurti (or Red Shirt, the colour of the British Tommies' uniforms) of Rawalpindi where the northern command headquarters was located, or the R.A. (Royal Artillery) Bazaar and *Athaaees* (28th) Bazaar of Lahore. The gap between the cantonment and the city, where the civilians lived, was huge and almost insurmountable. This divide continued well into the first couple of decades of independent Pakistan, leading not only to separate economic and social systems for these entities, but also to a different worldview and indeed to a different view on national issues. Even today, the cantonment functions as an autonomous economy within the cities and towns of modern Pakistan.

In 1917, the British decided that the following year, Indian officer cadets would be inducted into the Royal Military Academy at Sandhurst in England, starting a trend which, with some breaks, continued well into the first few decades of both independent India and Pakistan.[40] Ten places were to be set aside for Indians who would be eligible for the king's commission (KC), with recruitment confined to members of the martial races and families that had provided valuable services to the British during the First World War. Further, some non-commissioned officers and graduates of cadet colleges would be granted KCs directly. Notable among the early Sandhurst-trained KCOs was Iskander Mirza, the first president of Pakistan.

As expected, the early appointments of this kind did not yield perfect results, further strengthening the views of opponents of Indianization. But the trend could not be reversed, fuelled also by the growing Indian dissent with British rule in general and the desire that the British should quit India. The presence of a British 'caste' system did not make things easier. British officers rarely socialized with their native counterparts and natives were not allowed membership in many local clubs that admitted only British officers.[41] Despite these constraints, Indians competed actively for the select positions that were being made available to them in the British Indian Army in search of a higher station in life, or in some cases in search of a return to the favoured status of old military families. To better prepare them for service in the army, the Prince of Wales Royal Indian Military College was set up in Dehra Dun in March 1922 to act as a feeder school for Sandhurst and a career in the military. Ten years later, the Indian Military Academy (IMA) was set up in Dehra Dun to prepare some sixty officers for the Indian Army.

Native officers, who gradually replaced the VCOs, were deputed to serve for the first year with a British regiment with a view to teaching the natives the skills of troop management as well as social etiquette. Some of them acquired the pronounced *Koi Hai* accents and mannerisms of their British colleagues and superiors, which persisted well into the years after independence![42] Others found it hard to adjust but hunkered down and managed to survive this 'ordeal'. By then, military commissions had become much sought after because of the prestige associated with them and places had to be reserved for sons of military families. A new breed of officer had begun to appear: the urban middle and upper class officer. Yet, the total number of Indian officers remained rather small, growing from nine holding the KC in 1919 to a total of only 400 KCOs and Indian commissioned officers at the start of the Second World War, few of whom attained field rank in an officer corps of some 3,000.[43]

What made matters difficult in the relationship between the rulers and the ruled was the fact that there was almost no private social intercourse between the British and the Indian officers whom they commanded, except in very formal contexts. Indeed, the British Army officer rarely consorted even with British civil officers, except the favoured members of the Indian Civil Service (ICS). No VCO or even Indian KCO or his family was ever expected to be invited to a British officer's home. As Byron Falwell notes in his magisterial *Armies of the Raj*: 'It has been said, with some truth, that the British in India knew only servants and maharajahs.'[44] In the numerous autobiographical books by British officers in India, there is rarely a mention of native counterparts or friends. Even as late as the period of the Second World War, an American observer, Edmond Taylor, who served with the OSS (Office of Strategic Services, the CIA's precursor), noted that '…the British in India did not have any significant native contacts. Most Britishers had none, except bearers. They worked with Indians as colleagues—usually very humble colleagues—in their offices and their regiments, but such contacts are not emotionally fruitful contacts, except some of the military ones....Mask meets mask instead of man meeting man.'[45]

THE SECOND WORLD WAR

The Second World War prompted the return of the VCOs[46] and the setting up of officer training schools that allowed a larger number of young men to enlist in the officer corps as emergency commissioned officers. By 1945, the number of Indian officers had grown to 8,300, while the number of British officers had risen from the 1939 base of 3,000 to 34,500.[47] The IMA course was shortened to push through the number of officers available for war duty. Despite the rising political opposition to British rule in India, the British Indian Army of some 2.5 million volunteers continued to play an important role in the war effort, accounting for some 80 per cent of the forces in the South East Asian theatre of operations. Some 24,338 Indians were killed, 64,354 wounded, 11,754 missing, and 79,489 were taken prisoner[48] during the war, with most of the casualties occurring in South East Asia where a large Indian contingent was among the force that surrendered to the Japanese in Singapore and Malaya.

Politics was a taboo subject within the confines of the army mess, the other taboos being women and shop talk. Yet, the rising freedom movement in India, with its powerful proponents in both the Hindu and the Muslim camps (such as Gandhi, Nehru, and Jinnah, among others), had some effect on the more politically aware Indian officers.

The surrender of British forces at Singapore led to the formation of the first Indian National Army (INA) under Japanese aegis. Led by Mohan Singh, this was succeeded by the INA of Subhas Chandra Bose, a charismatic Bengali intellectual, who rallied a coalition of Muslim, Sikh, and Hindu officers from among the surrendered forces in Singapore into a force that fought against the British army in Burma. A large number of the leaders of the INA came from the 1st Battalion of the 14th Punjab Regiment (later 5 Punjab Battalion of the Punjab Regiment in Pakistan), home of Mohammad Ayub Khan, later president of Pakistan. (He was not serving with the regiment when it was captured.) Among them were Captain Shahnawaz Khan and Mohammed Zaman Kiani, both from the Potohar area of the Punjab.[49] Kiani describes how he had resisted joining the INA initially. He recalls in an unpublished manuscript of his book on the INA that when they first saw the INA of Mohan Singh at Ferrer's Park they were wearing arm bands with F written on them, 'which we took to meaning Fifth Columnist....The curious part was that they seemed proud flaunting these arm bands. It was only later that we learnt that it was an abbreviation of "Fujiwara Kikan" the organization headed by Fujiwara.'[50] (Fujiwara was the Japanese officer who was deputed by their captors to recruit the Indian prisoners for the INA.) The British officers were separated from the Indians and they took with them all the tinned food and petty cash from the messes, leaving the Indians at the mercy of the Japanese. The Indians were further outraged when the POWs were assembled at Ferrer's Park and a Lt. Col. Hunt addressed them, telling them that they were being handed over to the Japanese whom they ought to obey in the future, as they had earlier obeyed the British.[51]

Much has been written about the motivation of the Indian officers that joined the INA. Major General Syed Shahid Hamid, a highly patriotic Muslim officer from Lucknow in northern India who opted for Pakistan in 1947, in his memoir of partition *Disastrous Twilight*,[52] calls the INA soldiers 'traitors,' a sentiment echoed by many others. However, and understandably, the INA soldiers and officers thought of themselves as patriots, attempting to rid their homeland of foreign rule and not beholden to their Japanese sponsors. The British put three of the INA officers on trial, including the Muslim General Shahnawaz, a Janjua Rajput from Rawalpindi district. This created a huge stir among the politicos, and specially the Indian National Congress that deputed its leading lights to form a committee of lawyers to defend these 'heroes.' Among the lawyers was Jawaharlal Nehru.

Eventually, these officers were pardoned by the government of India and General Shanawaz Khan opted for India, becoming a junior minister in the Nehru government.[53] General Kiani, who was Chief of Staff (COS) of the INA and had opted to return to his native Pakistan, thought that the reasons why former INA officers were not re-inducted into the Pakistan Army were many.[54] For one, some of these ex-INA officers would have superseded the serving officers, being senior to them in rank and often with greater military command and battle experience. Professional jealousies also played a part. As a result, most of the former INA officers were sidelined into civilian jobs. Kiani and Habib-ur-Rehman[55] both served as political agents in remote Gilgit in the Northern Areas. Kiani, despite having been promised by Ayub that he might be re-inducted into service, was never called back into uniform, a fact that he lamented in his memoirs. The INA officers suffered a similar fate in India.

Overall, the Muslim officers who attained senior ranks in the fledgling army of independent Pakistan, played little or no part in the political thinking of the freedom movement. They had little contact with or inclination towards politics, and they stayed away from the Muslim League. A few officers who tried to raise political issues with the leader of the Muslim League, Mohammad Ali Jinnah, found themselves rebuffed by him with the direction that they concentrate on their profession. Despite this, a group of Muslim Indian Army officers prepared a detailed brief for Mr Jinnah on the division of the Indian Army.[56] Meanwhile, some of the educated young Muslim men of northern India who would have a political role as military leaders in independent Pakistan decades later (such as Mirza Aslam Beg, later COAS 1988–91, of Azamgarh in the United Provinces), were growing up politically aware and involved in the student freedom movement. The military men who would later take the helm of political affairs in Pakistan, including Ayub Khan and Yahya Khan, apparently had little love for politics and even less love for politicians, factors that coloured their actions later in life.

PARTITION

The abrupt partition of British India into two entities took place under the aegis of the last viceroy of India, Lord Mountbatten. Bharat or India (as its constitution proclaims) took the old name for the subcontinent, while Pakistan, divided into two wings more than a thousand miles apart, took as its name both an acronym and a *Farsi* word meaning Land of the Pure.[57] Partition brought along with it not only the need for demarcation of boundaries, but also for the transfer of assets, including military formations and material.

The run-up to partition included heated debates within the corridors of power in New Delhi. Field Marshal Sir Claude Auchinleck, the commander-in-chief of the British Indian Army who had a deep association with his institution, initially favoured a joint army command for the two dominions though he recognized the impracticality of this idea and ended up suggesting a division of the army into two parts. He had early in his career served as the commanding officer of the 1st Battalion of the 1st Punjab Regiment ('First First') and developed a deep emotional attachment to the British Indian Army.[58] After his wife left him for the British air force chief in India, many felt that he was wedded to the Indian Army. In a paper that he presented to the viceroy, he outlined the reasons for the division and its formula, with Pakistan's entitlement to be 'either on the present Muslim and non-Muslim ratio in the armed forces (30–70 per cent)—or in proportion to the total population of Pakistan areas as compared to Hindustan. The latter alternative is probably fairer.'[59] His strategic analysis of the defence needs and issues facing Pakistan recognized the need for a huge force in the western marches, but, as his deputy chief of general staff was to note on a separate paper on the military implications of Pakistan: 'The main enemy of Pakistan will be Hindustan [India], but we think that a concerted attack on Pakistan, sponsored by a Hindustan government is unlikely.'[60]

Against this backdrop of debate within the higher command of the British Indian Army, Mountbatten proceeded apace with the plans for partition of British India and its army. By July 1947, the defence department was divided into Indian and Pakistani sections and further subdivided under three categories: personnel, moveable stores and equipment, and installations. As mentioned earlier, Muslims accounted for some 30 per cent of the army, with Hindus and Sikhs comprising most of the remaining force. After the war and demobilization of the 2.5 million strong British Indian Army, the total number of active soldiers numbered only 400,000, of which some 140,000 were earmarked for Pakistan. The infantry had nearly 7 Muslim regiments out of 23 (excluding the Gurkhas).[61] Under the rules agreed to by the Joint Defence Council for the partition of the army 'a Muslim soldier domiciled in Pakistan and a non-Muslim domiciled in the rest of India had no option but to serve his respective dominion, or be discharged. But a Muslim from India or a non-Muslim from Pakistan could elect which dominion he would serve' after filling out a questionnaire, 'with a subsequent entitlement to reoption.'[62]

Sir Rob Lockhart was named the first commander-in chief of the army of the dominion of India, with General Sir Frank Messervy as the first commander-in-chief of the Pakistan Army. Messervy had earlier commanded the 7th Division (Golden Arrow) in battle. Auchinleck remained as the supreme commander with the remit to prepare for the gradual withdrawal of British forces in the six months after independence.

THE ARMY SPLITS IN TWO

The division of the army took place amidst much emotional outburst, with regiments being split and trading components. Hindu or Sikh squadrons of cavalry regiments, for example, were sent to new regiments in India while Muslim counterparts were moved to Pakistani regiments. The first native commander-in-chief to-be of the Indian Army, General Cariappa, had had serious misgivings about the British departure and its aftermath and about dividing the Indian Army. He was quoted by Lord Ismay in a letter to Mountbatten as having put forward 'the amazing suggestion that the Indian Army, with either Nehru or Jinnah as commander-in-chief, should take over power when we left in June 1948. I [Ismay] at once said that the proposal was not only wholly impractical, but highly dangerous, and that throughout history the rule of the army had always proved tyrannical and incompetent, and that the army must always be servants and not masters.'[63]

Farley recounts the scene at partition poignantly: 'Men exchanged presents, sang "Auld Lang Syne", and swore to remain friends.' In Delhi, the Hindu and Sikh officers gave a 'farewell comrades' party for their Muslim counterparts. According to General Shahid Hamid, the senior Indian officer, General Cariappa, presented a silver trophy to his Pakistani counterpart and then gave a toast, predicting that: 'We shall meet each other frequently as the best of friends and in the same spirit of good comradeship that we have had the good fortune to enjoy all these years.' The senior Pakistani officer, A.M. Raza, replied in kind and they all linked arms and sang 'For they are all jolly good fellows.' 'Three days later, four Muslim officers who had sung that night were among the 150 Pakistani officers and officials, with their families, who were hacked to death by Sikh *Jathas* (armed lawless gangs) who attacked the train carrying them to Pakistan.'[64] Indian General Menezes quotes then Major Agha Mohammad Yahya Khan at the 'break up' party at the Staff College in Quetta as saying to Colonel S.D. Varma, the chief instructor: 'Sir! What are we celebrating? This should be a day of mourning. As a united country, we could have been a strong and powerful nation. Now we will be fighting one another.'[65] Prophetic words indeed, from a man who later presided over the break-up of an independent Pakistan in December 1971 after a defeat by India.

A 'Tattered Dawn'[66] or a 'Disastrous Twilight'[67] ushered in independent Pakistan on 14 August 1947. A day later, on a date selected by numerologists and Hindu holy men to be a good augur, India came into being as an independent dominion. Mountbatten became the governor general of India. Mohammad Ali Jinnah, the leader of the Muslim League, took over as the first governor general of Pakistan. Shortly thereafter, the same officers who swore eternal friendship would be taking up arms to do battle, while the remaining British officers (some 2,800 of them out of a total of 13,500 British officers in post-war India) would grapple with their sentimental ties to either their Muslim or predominantly Hindu or Sikh units on the one hand and their Crown on the other. Unbeknownst to the political leaders of India and Pakistan, Auchinleck had issued a secret order to all British officers who opted to serve India or Pakistan to stand down in case the two countries went to war.[68]

The seeds of this conflict were laid in the final map of partition that ceded territory to India in the Punjab which gave it a land bridge to Kashmir, and in the spontaneous and horrific breakdown of civil order that led to attacks on Muslim, Hindu and Sikh caravans and trainloads of refugees moving from their homes to the safety of their respective new country. By the time order was restored in both countries, Pakistan had gained eight million refugees from India and India had to absorb some six million Hindus and Sikhs from the areas that came under Pakistan.[69] A 30,000 strong Punjab Boundary Force, set up under command of Major General Thomas W. (Pete) Rees, a veteran commander of Indian troops in Iraq, North Africa, and Burma, proved less than effective at controlling the violence in an area of some 37,500 square miles populated by warring factions of Sikhs, Muslims, and Hindus. His headquarters were in Lahore, and under him were Indian officers and troops of different ethnic backgrounds, all trying to put into effect Operation Rail Cross for the refugees seeking a land route into India or Pakistan. This was later augmented by Operation Sea Cross for refugees taking the sea route from Bombay to Karachi.

Under General Rees was Colonel M. Ayub Khan, a Sandhurst commissioned officer, who had recently been 'sent back' from a difficult assignment with the Assam Regiment in Burma.[70] Reports soon emerged that a train load of Muslim refugees had been slaughtered under his watch in eastern Punjab. Whether true or not, this created an emotional reaction in the NWFP. His close friend and fellow Sherdil (then 1st Battalion 14th Punjab Regiment and later 5 Punjab Regiment) officer, Colonel M. Zaman Khan (my uncle) heard reports that a group of tribals was preparing one night to attack Ayub Khan's home in Rawalpindi, where his wife and children were staying. My uncle rushed over in the evening and brought Ayub's family over to his own home. In the end, there was no attack. But, clearly the emotional storm was brewing, and as news of attacks on Muslim caravans trickled to the north-west, attacks began first on Hindu and Sikh caravans and then, as the accession of Kashmir to Pakistan became uncertain, the tribesmen provided manpower and arms to the battle for Kashmir.

It was in this uncertain climate that Pakistan came into being.

NOTES

1. See, for example, John Keay, *India: A History* (HarperCollins, 2000): '...there are now grounds to suppose that the *dasa* were in fact survivors of an earlier wave of the Indo-European diaspora and were not therefore indigenous. It has also been suggested that *arya–dasa* contact may have taken place in Afghanistan before the *arya* reached India,' p. 24. A recent study done by Dr Qasim Ayub for the 'World Genome Project', at least for NWFP and Balochistan, shows a minimal Aryan gene, with Central Asian and Middle East genes predominant. (Source: Arif Ayub).

2. Sir William Wilson Hunter, *A Brief History of the Indian Peoples* (23rd Edition, Oxford, Clarendon Press, United Kingdom, 1903), pp. 40–41.

3. Ibid.

4. Published in the Smithsonian Institution War Background Studies, Number Eighteen (29 April 1944).

5. Arrian gives figures for Alexander's forces that are confirmed by Diodoros. See *The Campaigns of Alexander by Arrian* (Flavius Arrianus Xenophon), trans. Aubrey de Selincourt (United Kingdom: Penguin Classics, 1981).

6. Arrian, op. cit. See also Johnny Torrens-Spence, *Historical Battlefields of Pakistan*, pp. 8–14. (Karachi: Oxford University Press, 2006).

7. 'Seven *kos* [about a mile and a quarter] to the north of Bhera is a mountain called Koh-i-Jud in the *Zafarnama* and her other books. I had not known why it is was so named but later found out that there are two clans on this mountain descended from a single ancestor, and one is called Jud and the other Janjua [the author's tribe].... As soon as we stopped in Janjua [territory], Langar Khan [nephew of Malik Hast, the Janjua chieftain] was sent to Malik Hast. He hastened there, convinced him of our good intentions and favour and brought him back that night. He presented a mail-clad horse and paid homage.' Thus writes the Emperor Babur in *Baburnama: Memoirs of Babur, Prince and Emperor*, about his encounter with my ancestors. Translated, edited, and annotated by Wheeler M. Thackston, Freer Gallery of Art and Arthur M. Sackler Gallery, Smithsonian Institution, Washington DC and Oxford University Press, New York and Oxford (UK), 1996.

8. J.M. Wikele in his *Punjabi Mussalmans*, reprinted by Book House, Lahore, dwells at some length on the arguments surrounding the origins of the Awans.

9. Ibid., p. 9.

10. Although curiously, a small isolated segment of the Janjua Rajputs has survived in Gujranwala in modern times. Pakistan's well known civil servant, poet, and journalist, Altaf Hussain 'Gauhar' (this being his poetic name) belonged to this Janjua family.

11. Irfan Habib, *An Atlas of the Mughal Empire* (New Delhi: Oxford University Press, 1982). Habib notes that the *Ain i Akbari* mentions that Punjabi cavalry horses were seen to be equal to Iraqi horses.

12. William Irvine, *The Army of the Indian Moghuls* (reprint, New Delhi: Eurasia Publishing House, 1962).

13. D.A. Washbrook, 'Progress and Problems: South Asian Economic and Social History c. 1720–1860,' *Modern Asian Studies*, 22, 1, 1988 refers to the work of B. Stein in documenting the emergence of this 'military fiscalism' during the Mughal period that laid the grounds for the relationships forged by the East India Company and later British imperial rulers.

14. Ibid.

15. Ibid.

16. Ibid., p. 84.

17. Bayly, ibid.

18. Byron Farwell, *Armies of the Raj* (New York: W.W. Norton and Company, 1989), p. 27.

19. James Leasor, *The Red Fort* (New York: Collier, 1956).

20. Farwell, *Armies*, p. 27.

21. Ibid.

22. Stephen P. Cohen, *The Indian Army* (University of California Press, 1971) offers a succinct view of the background to the emergence of the army of the Raj.

23. *Indian Army, Recruiting in India Before and During the War of 1914–18,* cited in Cohen.

24. Field Marshal Lord Roberts of Kandahar, *Forty-One Years in India: From Subaltern to Commander-in-Chief*, 2 vols. (New York: Longmans, Green and Company, 1987, and London: Richard Bentley and Son), was a highly successful book, that came out in 25 editions in the first year of its publication, including a Braille edition.

25. Ibid., p. 41.

26. Roberts, *Forty-One*, Volume 2, p. 442.

27. Cohen, ibid.

28. Conversation with author.

29. J.M. Wikele, *Punjabi Mussalmans* (reprint Lahore, Pakistan: The Book House), p. 98. Our family provided horses and cavalry soldiers to, among others, the 19th Lancers and Probyn's Horse.

30. See the excellent study of recruitment patterns and techniques in David Omissi, *The Sepoy and the Raj: The Indian Army, 1860–1940* (London: Macmillan, 1994).

31. Ibid., p. 52.

32. Kumkum Srivastava and Vinay Kumar Srivastava, 'National Consciousness in Punjabi Folksongs,' *Guru Nanak Journal of Sociology*, Volume 10, Nos. 1 and 2, April and October 1989.

33. This discussion owes much to the excellent volume by Imran Ali, *Punjab Under Imperialism, 1885–1947* (Princeton University Press, 1988).

34. Ibid., p. 115.

35. Omissi, *Sepoy*, p. 155.

36. Ibid., p. 161.

37. Cohen, *Indian Army*, p. 117.

38. Niall Ferguson, *Empire* (New York: Basic Books, 2002), pp. 204–206.

39. General Sir Ian Hamilton, who was posted in 1873 to the 92nd Gordon Highlanders in India and served until 1898, describes in some detail in his memoirs, *Listening For the Drums* (London: Faber and Faber, Mcmxliv) the red light district in Bombay where he was taken soon after his arrival and from which he escaped after being importuned by an Armenian amazon! British commanding officers or their deputies were often sent on 'recruiting' missions to the hill country to select women for the officially sanctioned and regulated red light districts attached to regiments. See also Niall Ferguson's *Empire* (Basic Books, 2002), p. 181 for a description of cantonments.

40. My uncle Muhammad Afzal Janjua was the senior Indian cadet at Sandhurst when Mohammed Mohammad Ayub Khan, later commander-in-chief and president of Pakistan, arrived there. One of my uncle's memorable stories was running a 100 meters race against Harold Abrams (who later won the Olympic gold medal in Paris—celebrated in the movie *Chariots of Fire*) at White City and being allotted the heavily rutted inside track. This

handicap allowed Abrams to pip him at the tape, he recounted! My elder brother, Asif Nawaz was at Sandhurst in the mid-1950s (at the same time as Gohar Ayub Khan, Asif Afridi, and Aftab Sher Khan), later on becoming the last Sandhurst-commissioned officer to head the Pakistan Army.

41. Farwell, *Armies*, p. 295. There were instances of British officers who fought these segregationist policies. Indeed, the last club that agreed to admit native officers was the Peshawar club that changed its policy of not admitting natives when the commanding officer of a local cavalry regiment threatened that he would not allow any of his officers to join the club if native officers were not admitted and further he would withdraw the provision of his regimental horses from the Peshawar Vale Hunt!

42. *Koi Hai! Or Qui Hee!* (Anyone there?!) Was the preferred shout from British officers on entering the mess or their own quarters that brought a mini-army of servants to tend to their immediate needs. Some Indian officers found the British officers' habits difficult to understand. My father-in-law, Lt. Col. J.D. Malik recalled how he would get up early in the morning and wash and shave in the warm water that his batman (orderly) brought in a washbasin. He was astounded when his fellow British tent mate asked: 'J.D., would you mind if I use the water now?'

43. Farwell, *Armies*, p. 301.

44. Ibid., p. 97.

45. Edmond Taylor, *Richer by Asia* (New York: Time-Life Books, 1947), p. 100.

46. My father Raja Abdul Ghafoor Khan also joined as a VCO during this period but left soon after, as the youngest son, to look after the family's interests in our village Chakri Rajgan in Jhelum district.

47. Roger Beaumont, *Sword of the Raj: The British Army in India, 1747–1947* (Indianapolis and New York: The Bobbs-Merrill Company, Inc., 1977), p. 174.

48. Among the celebrated POWs in North Africa were A.M. Yahya Khan (later commander-in-chief of the Pakistan Army and president of Pakistan 1969–71) and his fellow Baluchi Abdul Hameed Khan (known as Burmee because of his appearance), and Sahibzada Yaqub Khan. Yahya Khan recalled in a conversation with the author that he proposed escaping but Yaqub demurred. 'He wanted to complete learning Italian!' joked Yahya. So, at one point when their Italian captors became lax, Yahya and Hameed escaped and rejoined their regiment. Yahya was decorated for his effort. Yaqub Khan who made a reputation as a linguist and diplomat in later life was foreign minister in the governments of General Ziaul Haq, Prime Minister Benazir Bhutto, and Prime Minister Nawaz Sharif.

49. Shahnawaz was 30 years old and the father of a one-year old son when he left for the war. He belonged to a military Janjua family of the Potohar plateau and had some sixty relatives in the armed forces. (See Abdullah Malik's Urdu work *Hindu Muslim Sikh Fasadaat aur Pakistani Fauj ki Nafsiat: Volume 2* of *Fauj aur Pakistan (The Army and Pakistan)*, Lahore: Kausar Publishers, 1988). Kiani, also from the same area, specifically Shakarparian, near modern Islamabad, was a brilliant officer cadet at the Indian Military Academy in Dehra Dun where he won both the sword of honour, awarded to the best all round cadet, and the gold medal for the academically top cadet.

50. M.Z. Kiani, was made a major general in the Indian National Army, his colleagues, Colonel Habib-ur-Rehman and Lt. Col. A.I.S. Dara all were friends of my uncle Brigadier M. Zaman Khan. Habib was the sole survivor of the plane crash in which Subhas Chandra Bose died in Formosa. Dara became legendary as the father of Pakistan field hockey. General Kiani served later as a political agent in Gilgit. Our families stayed in close contact and he gave me a draft of his unpublished manuscript with a view to getting it published in the USA.

51. Kiani, ibid.

52. Major General S. Shahid Hamid, *Disastrous Twilight* (London: Leo Cooper with Martin Secker and Warburg, 1986).

53. Shahnawaz, however, chose to send his son Mahmood, to Pakistan and married his daughters to Pakistanis but could not visit his ancestral village of Maira Matore, home of a number of Pakistani army generals, including Tikka Khan and the brothers, Ahmed Jamal and Ahmed Kamal. Mahmood was commissioned in his father's regiment, 5 Punjab, also known as the Sherdils, and served under my elder brother Asif, also a Sherdil. He fought in the 1965 war, an action that led many Congressites in India to question the patriotism of Shahnawaz Khan. But Nehru stuck with his loyal soldier and retained him as minister.

54. Kiani, ibid.

55. Habib-ur-Rehman, who was given the rank of brigadier in the INA, was the sole survivor of the plane crash in Formosa in which Subhas Chandra Bose died. As a family friend, we used to visit his home in Rawalpindi in the 1950s and 60s. He was burnt over parts of his body, specially his hands and carried the scars of that event till his death in the 1970s.

56. Major General S. Shahid Hamid, *Disastrous Twilight* (London: Leo Cooper with Martin Secker and Warburg, 1986), Appendix VI, p. 324.

57. PAKISTAN was said to be an acronym of Punjab, Afghania, Sindh, Kashmir, and Balochistan, a name coined by a group of Indian Muslim students at Cambridge University, including Chaudhry Rehmat Ali, who has been popularly given authorship of the name. Ironically, he became disillusioned with the idea of Pakistan as it emerged and died and was buried in England. Efforts in late 2005 to exhume and re-inter his remains in Pakistan did not reach fruition.

58. I recall clearly the time he visited my school St. Mary's in Rawalpindi after he had retired from service and how fondly he spoke with me (a young schoolboy) about my uncle Afzal, who was the first native commanding officer of the Auk's 1st Punjab Regiment.

59. Hamid, *Disastrous*, Appendix VI, p. 326.

60. Ibid., p. 339.

61. Farwell, *Armies*, p. 359.

62. Lt. Gen. S.F. Menezes, *Fidelity and Honour: The Indian Army from the Seventeenth to the Twenty-first Century* (New Delhi: Viking Penguin Books, 1993), p. 428.

63. Menezes, *Fidelity*, quoting The Transfer of Power documents, p. 423.

64. Farwell, *Armies*, p. 358.

65. Menezes, *Fidelity*, p. 435.

66. The Pakistani poet Faiz Ahmed Faiz's take on independence day.

67. Maj. Gen. S. Shahid Hamid's view of partition.

68. 28 October 1947 letter to UK chiefs of staff from Auchinleck. C. Dasgupta, *War and Diplomacy in Kashmir 1947–48* (New Delhi: Sage Publications 2002), p. 19.

69. Shahid Javed Burki, *Pakistan: A Nation in the Making* (Boulder and London: Westview Press, and Karachi: Oxford University Press), p. 41.

70. Sher Ali Khan Pataudi, *The Story of Soldiering and Politics in India and Pakistan* (Lahore: al Kitab, 1983), p. 114. A report by Sir Gilbert Laithwaite, the UK high commissioner to Pakistan in 1958 also states 'I would not put him [Ayub] in the highest intellectual class by any means. He was, according to our records, a failure as a commanding officer (lieutenant colonel) on active service and had to be relieved. But in senior post in Pakistan, since that country obtained its independence, he has built himself up a very considerable position, both within the army and in the country. He is a vigorous personality with a reputation for getting things done.' DO 35/8944 dated 28 October 1958, UK Public Records Office, cited in Roedad Khan's *The British Papers* (Karachi: Oxford University Press, 2002), p. 47.

This tattered dawn is not what we longed for

– Faiz Ahmed Faiz[1]

As the witches' brew of communal conflict was bubbling in the Punjab, fuelled, among others, by the Sikh leader, Master Tara Singh, who vowed to settle issues with his '*kirpan*' or dagger, the Pakistan Army was being created in a hurry. Mountbatten had rushed through the plans for partition, even sooner than the original plan of June 1948, to 14 August 1947. He announced on 3 June 1947 that the subcontinent would be divided into two dominions by August. Pakistan was to come into being on 14 August with India a day later. This left a gigantic logistical task for the civil and military officials entrusted with the division of forces of the British Indian Army. Accompanying the division of manpower was the division of fixed assets that is the training schools, military production facilities, workshops and documentation of the British Indian Army. Since most of these fixed assets resided in what was to become India, Pakistan was at a severe disadvantage. It had to start almost from scratch: setting up a new capital in Karachi and a new military headquarter in Rawalpindi, at the site of what was till then the headquarter of the British Indian Army's northern command from where operations in the tribal areas were directed. An interesting counterpoint to this situation on the Indian side is provided by Lt. Gen. L.P. 'Bogey' Sen's view that the 'Army Headquarter, India, was in a very unhappy state. While Pakistan had established itself in the well-equipped Northern Command Headquarters in Rawalpindi and was able to commence functioning without impediment, its analogue in New Delhi found itself engaged in an accommodation-cum-location battle with Supreme Headquarters.' Additionally, Sen believed that the Muslim director of the civilian Intelligence Bureau had spirited away all valuable files to Pakistan.[2]

The road to independence for the Pakistan Army was fraught with great difficulty. It lacked officers, especially those with command experience, and was faced with the huge task of transport of personnel and assets from India. At the time of independence, the British Indian Army was still proceeding with its planned demobilization of forces after the Second World War, with the aim of reducing its strength of emergency commissioned officers from some 8,000 to around 450. A series of selection boards was constituted to assess the individual officers who had been commissioned during the Second World War to decide on who ought to be given regular commissions. Among the officers selected to head these boards was Colonel Ayub Khan.

Meanwhile discussions had begun at the highest levels of the British Indian government and the UK government about the division of the British Indian Army. In May 1947, the issue was brought directly to Prime Minister Attlee's notice during the deliberations of the India–Burma Committee when the committee discussed a paper from Field Marshal Auchinleck on the division of forces in the subcontinent.[3] By 12 June, the Partition Committee in India had considered the terms of reference of an Armed Forces Reconstitution Committee (AFRC) which was then approved by the Indian cabinet on 16 June. The AFRC was charged, among other things, with the task of producing proposals 'to ensure that the disposition of troops on the 15th of August, or as soon thereafter as possible, shall be such as to contain the maximum number of units of the State to which they are eventually going to belong, i.e. by endeavouring as far as possible to have the majority of Muslims in Pakistan and the majority of non-Muslims in the rest of India.'[4]

The pace picked up in June, with meetings between Mountbatten and Mr Jinnah and meetings of the Indian cabinet on the reconstitution of the armed forces, leading to approval by the cabinet of the viceroy's proposals. These included the setting up of a Joint Defence Council that would include the 'Governor General or Governors General'[5] of India and Pakistan, the defence minister of the two dominions and the commander-in chief of India (Auchinleck later changed this title to Supreme Commander as of 15 August). Both India and Pakistan were to have their own commanders-in-chief, with operational command of their national forces.

DIVISION OF FORCES

The issue of the division of the armed forces was key to the future of both countries since it would determine their ability to patrol and defend their respective frontiers. Pakistan had a hot western border, with an independent Afghanistan that harboured claims to the western marches of Pakistan as part of a greater Pushtunistan (or Land of the Pathans). Indeed, Afghanistan voted against the newly independent Pakistan's entry to the United Nations on that basis. Given the tinder box of communal feelings in pre-partition India, Pakistan also had to contend with a potentially hostile India on the eastern border and looming over it was the northern menace of the Soviet Union. It needed an independent and sufficiently well-equipped and trained military to sustain itself. The British however were like jealous parents, reluctant to let go of the reins of power. Not content with the situation where the heads of the armies (and air force and navy) of the two new dominions would be British officers, Mountbatten wanted to retain control through the supreme commander and possibly his own position as a potential joint governor general of the two dominions. Even Lord Ismay, Mountbatten's right hand man, did his best to persuade Jinnah to accept a joint military command and control structure, calling the division of the army 'the biggest crime and the biggest headache.'[6]

Opposition to the splitting of the army came from another unexpected source. Chaudhry Muhammad Ali recalls that he was approached by the then Brigadier K.M. Cariappa and a Muslim officer during that period. Cariappa was at that time the senior-most Indian officer in the British Indian Army. He argued before Ali against the division of the army and called for a jointly controlled army. According to Ali, Cariappa thought that 'it was better for the army to take charge of both Dominions than be divided.'[7] Earlier, the plan for the division of the armed forces drawn up by Liaquat Ali Khan, the Muslim League's representative and the person responsible for the Finance Ministry had been opposed by Baldev Singh, the Congress representative as defence minister, as well as by Auchinleck, though for different reasons.

Soon after independence and while the division of military assets was still underway, Auchinleck summed up the situation for the British cabinet and chiefs of staff in a note on 28 September 1947 in which he blamed the distance of the Pakistan government from the action in New Delhi as a major factor hindering Pakistan's ability to assert its rights given the 'open enmity between the two Dominions,' adding that 'in the opinion of many they are on the verge of open conflict.'[8] After much debate, the AFRC had agreed to division of assets in the proportion of 64 per cent to India and 36 per cent to Pakistan, but Auchinleck felt the Indian government was 'determined to contest it to the last ditch.' To allow Pakistan an even chance, he suggested that the meetings of the committee take place alternatively in New Delhi and Karachi, thus further strengthening the view in Indian circles of him as being pro-Pakistan.

'I have no hesitation whatever in affirming that the present Indian cabinet are implacably determined to do all in their power to prevent the establishment of the dominion of Pakistan on a firm basis,' he stated in the second, political part of his assessment. 'Since 15th August...the situation has steadily deteriorated and the Indian leaders, cabinet minister, civil officials and others have persistently tried to obstruct the work of partition of the armed forces.' According to Auchinleck, the Indians were trying to persuade Mountbatten to dissolve the supreme headquarters 'so that the one impartial body remaining in this country shall be removed.' He believed that Pakistan's approach had been 'reasonable and cooperative.' 'This is natural in the circumstances,' he observed, 'as Pakistan has practically nothing of her own and must obtain most of what she wants from the reserves of stores, etc. now lying in India.' Meanwhile the situation in the Punjab was going from bad to worse, with retaliatory killings by both Muslims and Sikhs. Auchinleck reported that in his view, 'the Sikhs led the massacre, to effect which systematic reconnaissance had been carried out for weeks beforehand. The result is that, today, in my opinion, few think that the Indian government is now able to control the Sikhs.' He blamed the rulers of the Sikh states of the

Eastern Punjab for being 'behind the campaign of extermination.' On the Pakistan side, he thought that there were 'equally horrible occurrences, though the general impression is that these are more spontaneous and less organized than those in east Punjab.'

Near the end of this report, Auchinleck reminded his bosses in the United Kingdom that he had issued his officers the order to stand down in the event of war between the two countries, under which the British commanders and officers would not participate in any hostilities between the two dominions. With time, pressures mounted against Auchinleck and his frustration with the slow pace of action in the division of assets grew. Barely a week after his report of 28 September, he sent up a note to the Joint Defence Council that the supreme headquarters be disbanded on 30 November. The Indian members of the council supported this proposal at a meeting in Lahore on 16 October. Liaquat Ali Khan opposed it. The Indians pledged to deliver Pakistan's share of the combined military resources. The council reached a deadlock, and the matter was referred to the two governments of India and Pakistan. The governments' failure to resolve the issue affirmed the British government's decision to withdraw the supreme headquarters in November. Soon thereafter the flow of divided resources from India to Pakistan slowed down, and then, in the words of Chaudhry Muhammad Ali, 'even the trickle stopped.'

BIRTH OF THE PAKISTAN ARMY

On 14 August 1947, Pakistan not only came into being as a 'moth-eaten' political entity, but it also came with a 'moth-eaten' military which was under the firm command and control of the British officers who chose to remain ostensibly under Pakistan control, (notwithstanding the secret 'stand down' order of the supreme commander). Out of the 46 training establishments that existed in pre-partition India, only 7 were in Pakistan. These included the Staff College in Quetta, the School of Military Intelligence and the Anti-aircraft Artillery School, both in Karachi, the Royal Indian Army Service Corps (RIASC) School in Kakul, the No. 1 RIASC Training Centre (Supplies) in Lahore, the Armament Artificer Wing of the Indian Electrical and Mechanical Engineering Corps in Chaklala (near Rawalpindi), and the Military Farms Department Training Centre in Lahore. Certainly not an adequate framework for the creation and sustenance of a fledgling army!

The Pakistan Defence Council at its second meeting on 2 and 3 October 1947 agreed to set up the Pakistan Military Academy at Kakul, which was to start operations in January 1948. The first commandant of PMA was Colonel F.H.B. Ingall of the 6th Lancers. His main deputies were Lieutenant Colonel

M.A. Latif as battalion commander and Lieutenant Colonel Atiqur Rehman as chief instructor. The first trainees were from the group of Muslim officer cadets from the Indian Military Academy in Dehra Dun who were flown to Lahore in October 1947. In this group were members of the second and third post-war IMA courses. Members of the second course were immediately given commission in the Pakistan Army. The members of the third course were temporarily parked with units and then joined the PMA when it began functioning out of the former Army Service Corps School premises. By 26 February 1948, when the PMA actually began its operations, it included some 66 IMA/PMA cadets, 63 university graduates who were members of the First Special Course and 78 cadets of the First PMA Long Course.[9]

A key training establishment that came into Pakistan's share at partition was the celebrated Staff College at Quetta. It was closed down in September 1947 when the non-Muslim staff members left, but it was re-opened on 2 February 1948 under the British Brigadier J.C.A. Lauder.[10] Of the pre-partition instructors of the Staff College, Lt. Col. A.M. Yahya Khan remained. Others who joined him when the college re-opened were Lt. Col. Akhtar Hussain Malik and Lt. Col. Gul Mawaz Khan,[11] the latter a highly decorated officer during the Second World War when he gained the Military Cross, and the former destined for military fame and high decorations in the 1965 Indo–Pak War.

The logistical foundations of the Pakistan Army were severely short-changed by the division of assets at partition. The three key command workshops of the British Indian army that helped maintain armoured fighting vehicles, radar repairs, and crystal cutting, were all left in India, at Secunderabad, Kirkee, and Agra. Of the 40 ordnance depots, only 5 small retail depots were located in Pakistan. The major depots were situated on the main supply routes which were providing support to the army during the war in South East Asia, with major stocks of material kept in the major ports such as Bombay, Madras or Calcutta or in ancillary depots inland in southern India. The depots in Pakistan had a minimal stock. Similarly, there were twelve engineer stores depots in British India, of which only three small depots came to Pakistan. Even the munitions industry that was expanded during the Second World War came to reside primarily in India, with only 3 of the 17 ordnance factories located in Pakistan.[12] In short, even with the greatest willpower and determination of its fighting forces, Pakistan began life with a weak logistical infrastructure and serious dependence on Indian goodwill to transfer assets to it.

As mentioned above, the Indian members of the Joint Defence Council worked hard to make life difficult for the fledgling dominion of Pakistan. Once trouble began in the border regions and in Kashmir, they were given ample grounds for refusing to transfer those assets, without which Pakistan could not fight. Lt. Gen. S.P.P. Thorat, commissioned in the Sherdils, and a fellow officer of General Ayub Khan and my uncle, Brigadier M. Zaman Khan, recalls that when hostility had begun in Kashmir, '...we were sending train loads [of arms and ammunition]...to Pakistan, each one of us was painfully conscious that we were indirectly helping Pakistan to kill our own men.' General Bucher, the Indian commander-in-chief, insisted that the transfer take place as agreed. Thorat states that he urged Bucher to stop or at least slow down this movement, but was rebuffed. He then went to Sardar Patel, the deputy prime minister, who told him: 'Don't be too prompt in doing your duty.' Thorat notes in his autobiography: 'From then onwards, there was a sharp decline in the quantities of arms and ammunition sent to Pakistan but a corresponding increase in innocuous items to make up the tonnage.'[13]

Even the human resources of the new Pakistan Army were severely constrained. Following the agreed formula for division of shared assets, Pakistan received 6 out of the 14 armoured regiments, 8 of the 40 artillery regiments, and 8 of the 15 infantry regiments (although India also had additional Gurkha regiments that were not subject to division). Yet of the infantry regiments, comprising individual battalions, Pakistan got only 33 versus India's 88, and those too at reduced strength, with the departure of many Sikh or Hindu companies that were not fully compensated for by the transfer of Muslim counterparts from India. Its paper army of roughly 150,000 officers and *jawans* (literally 'young men' or soldiers), comprised some 508 units of various sizes, according to Fazal Muqeem Khan, but on Independence Day, 40 per cent of this force included units that were still in India! And further depleting its officer corps, some thirty Muslim officers were posted to supreme headquarters in the first week of August 1947.[14]

Even the command levels were firmly in British control. The commander-in-chief of the Pakistan Army was General Sir Frank Messervy, who was the GOC northern command in Rawalpindi at the time of independence, but he did not last very long. He was succeeded by the COS General Sir Douglas Gracey, on 10 February 1948. The chief of general staff, the master general ordnance, and the quartermaster general were all British, as were the heads of key directorates (signals, artillery, and military training, to name just a few) of the GHQ and even field formations. Senior-level Pakistani officers were few and far between, most of them not even having attained field rank in pre-partition India. Some of these were quickly promoted, unfortunately some beyond their experience or capacity. Brigadier Sher Khan, who headed the military operations directorate, and Colonel M. Akbar Khan, who headed the weapons and equipment directorate, were among the early senior appointees in GHQ.[15]

The senior-most Pakistani officer at the time was Major General Mohammad Akbar Khan, who was designated Pakistan Army number 1 (PA1 for short), followed by Brigadier Faiz Muhammad Khan. Akbar Khan, who was involved with the remount depots was generally known as Akbar 'Khachar (Mule)-wallah' (due to his association with transport services involving mules), to distinguish him from the other Akbar Khan who gained notoriety in Kashmir and later in the Rawalpindi Conspiracy Case. Ayub Khan was PA10, being outranked, among others, by Fazal ur Rehman Kallue (PA5), my uncle Muhammad Afzal Janjua (PA6), and Nawabzada Agha Mohammad Raza. Two senior medical officers who were KCOs also were given special numbers: S.M.A. Faruki was PA100001, while Wajid Ali Khan Burki, who had been approved for major general before partition, was designated PA100002.

With this motley crew, Messervy set up the Pakistan Army GHQ with the same structure as the GHQ in New Delhi. The Rawalpindi GHQ headed six static area commands: Lahore, Rawalpindi, Peshawar, Waziristan, Sindh, and East Pakistan. The GHQ operated with a skeleton staff till October 1947, when most of its staff arrived from New Delhi, *sans* their personal belonging and families in many cases but, more importantly, often without key documents. Indian officials had put an end to the dispatch of documents other than those that were with the publications department!

The government of Pakistan decided almost immediately to re-orient its military posture and launched Operation Curzon between 6 and 27 December 1947. Named ironically after the British viceroy who had propagated the Forward Policy of pushing forces towards the Oxus River in Central Asia, this operation in fact reversed that approach by withdrawing the army from the border regions of north and south Waziristan. Pakistan had decided to leave it to the tribes to control their own affairs, with policing provided by the Frontier Scouts. This freed the troops for other critical areas and set the stage for the reorganization of the army from its previous static formations to an operational basis. The 7th Division was set up in Rawalpindi, 8th Division in Karachi/Quetta region, 9th Division for the NWFP, 10th Division for the Lahore area, and 14th Division for East Pakistan, with the 3rd Armoured Brigade in Risalpur.[16]

SETTING A ROLE FOR THE ARMY

Among the first order of business for the Pakistan government was to establish the role of the Pakistan Army. At its inaugural meeting on 5 and 6 September 1947, the Pakistan Defence Council,[17] headed by the prime minister and minister of defence, Liaquat Ali Khan, outlined both the internal and external functions of the army. These functions were: to support the civil government and police in maintaining law and order, and to support the political authorities in the tribal region while ensuring that there were no tribal incursions into the hinterland. Despite the relatively small resource base of the army, the external role was defined in the anachronistic British imperial defence terms, 'to prevent aggression by a minor power,'[18] while preparing to defend against a major power. The task facing the army was huge. Pakistan's geography made its borders difficult to defend. It shared 3,250 miles with India (1,250 in West Pakistan and the rest in East Pakistan, the latter of which was surrounded on three sides by India), and some 1,350 miles with Afghanistan. The Iranian border apparently did not figure in the calculus of defence at that time. And then there were the 450 hottest miles of contested boundary in Kashmir!

In the hurly burly of those early days, a scheme was concocted to set up a defence system based on a first line of the regular army, supported by a second line of the volunteer Pakistan National Guard (PNG), which would also include women. On paper, the PNG appeared to be a major operation, but on the ground, as its second commander, Brigadier M. Musa, was to discover, it was an amateurish affair with no real military capabilities. He essentially told the women to go home! It took another two years before this PNG Directorate was morphed into the Infantry Directorate under Brigadier Latif.

On the whole, the GHQ of the Pakistan Army in the immediate post-independence period was a chaotic place, with new officers coming in almost daily from India. There was a shortage of offices and even of normal office supplies that are the life-blood of any establishment. The chain of command, though well defined on paper, was also hazy at best, as the civilian leaders, who had run a campaign for independence under the flag of the Muslim League, attempted to consolidate their positions in the new state. Moreover, the distance between Karachi, the new capital of Pakistan, and Rawalpindi, the military headquarters, intruded on the ability of the political leadership to interact frequently and directly with the army. Just a decade later, this distance helped precipitate a military coup. The prime minister had to rely for political advice on the border areas on local governors, who were British, or on local politicians, many of whom until recently had not fully subscribed to the idea of Pakistan as an independent state.

The prime minister concurrently held the defence portfolio, but had to rely extensively on his secretary, Iskander Mirza, a Sandhurst-trained ex-army man. He had very few other senior-level military confidants or advisers. The British commanders were competent soldiers but certainly not imbued with the nationalistic spirit that the new state demanded. Their military thinking too was coloured by their experience in the Great War and their training (and that of their Pakistani subordinates), which leaned towards long and drawn-out campaigns rather than the swift wars that were to characterize relationships between emerging Third World adversaries such as Pakistan and India.

Indeed, the thrust of much British thinking at that time was still geared towards a defence against the threat of communism and the Soviet Union.

Within a matter of months, the new country and its army were embroiled in a crisis that was forced upon them by the dynamics of partition and the complications regarding the accession of princely states to either India or Pakistan. India's rapid military move into the small state of Junagadh (which had a Muslim ruler but a predominantly Hindu population) caught the Pakistani military unawares. Not that it could have done anything to counter that move. Pakistan also was incapable of doing much about the subsequent Indian invasion and absorption of the Muslim state of Hyderabad in southern India. Both Junagadh and Hyderabad were not contiguous to Pakistan. But the State of Jammu and Kashmir, better known simply as Kashmir, was a different issue altogether.

THE KASHMIR ISSUE

Kashmir was the stuff of legend and dreams. The favourite holiday spot of the great Mughal emperors and their British successors in India, it captured the imagination of poets and travellers alike. The Frenchman, Francois Bernier, visited Kashmir in the entourage of the Mughal emperor Aurangzeb and gave a detailed account of the place for western readers. As the British writer John Keay noted: 'Explorers talked of making Kashmir "a little England in the heart of Asia", and of "opening up Central Asia" and "bagging the Pamirs".'[19] Not that much came of these plans. The natural beauty of Kashmir and its surrounds was made untouchable by its geography, with waves of steep mountain ranges converging at the Pamir Knot. With little knowledge of the place, many British explorers took to carrying with them the fictional extended poem *Lalla Rookh* by Thomas Moore,[20] as a guide!

If geography is destiny, Kashmir inherited an important role in the history of the subcontinent, situated as it was between Afghanistan and the Soviet Union to the north,[21] China to the north-east, Nepal to the south-east, India to the south, and Pakistan to the west. The great Himalayan Range meets the Hindu Kush, the Karakorams, and Central Asia in Kashmir. Almost literally the Top of the World, its high mountains and narrow valleys made it a military nightmare for invaders, many of whom (Greek and Central Asian alike) either got lost in its mountainous maze or decided to stay, carving out their own Shangri-Las in its distant redoubts. At the time of partition, Kashmir as a whole had an area of 84,471 square miles, roughly the size of Great Britain and the climate of Switzerland. Wrapping around this territory are the arms of two mighty rivers of the Punjab: the Indus and the Ravi, with the Jhelum and the Chenab cutting their own deep swathes through the middle of the region before debouching onto the plains of the Punjab.

Islam came into this region as early as the late eleventh century, when King Harsha of Kashmir (1080–1101) employed Muslim soldiers and officers. Over the next two centuries, Islam spread in the region largely due to the influence of Muslim holy men, i.e. saints, one of whom, Bulbul Shah, is said to have converted one of Harsha's successors, King Rinchana Bhotta, a Tibetan, to Islam in 1339. When the decline of, first the Mughals, and then the kings of Kabul, began, the rising new power in the region became Ranjit Singh, the celebrated ruler of the Punjab who conquered the valley of Kashmir in 1819. He gave the local authority for Jammu and Kashmir to Gulab Singh.

As the East India Company extended its reach farther into northern India, it came up against the border of the Punjab. During the British war of 1845 against the Sikhs, Gulab Singh initially remained aloof, though he emerged as an adviser of the British after their victory at Sobraon. As a result, the British made the vanquished Sikhs sell the entire state of Jammu and Kashmir to Gulab Singh for one million pounds through the Treaty of Amritsar of 16 March 1846. However, Gulab Singh found it difficult to control the Muslim rulers of various territories in the region. One of these rulers, Gauhar Rehman of Hunza, defeated the Sikhs and established the Indus as the western boundary of Kashmir in 1852 till the British, apprehensive of Russian moves in Central Asia, took control of Hunza and appointed a political agent. It was not until the twentieth century that the British attached that territory, i.e. Hunza to the state of Jammu and Kashmir, a state which had a predominantly Muslim majority but a Sikh ruler.

Over time, the successors of Gulab Singh were seen by their Muslim subjects as dictators of the worst kind. This growing unrest led to the formation of the All-Jammu and Kashmir Muslim Conference by a charismatic Kashmiri Muslim named Sheikh Muhammad Abdullah and his partner, Chaudhry Ghulam Abbas, and other leaders of the Reading Room Party. They broke up their partnership but both ended up being jailed for their efforts in favour of greater representation for the Muslims of Kashmir. When fresh elections were held, in the absence of these two leaders, Abbas's Muslim Conference claimed victory. Until this point, the Muslim League of India had kept its distance from Kashmiri politics under Jinnah's dictum that the princely states needed to make up their own minds about accession to either dominion. So, while other princes acceded or prepared to accede to one of the two successor states to British India, Hari Singh, the maharaja of Kashmir went into what appears to be a state of denial. Even his son, Karan Singh, recalls him as being 'alone and friendless.'[22]

ACCESSION

Once India and Pakistan came into being on 14 August 1947, the pressure mounted on Hari Singh to make up his mind. Pakistan's expectation had always been that Muslim majority provinces that were contiguous to Pakistan would accede to it. India, which also had a small area that abutted Kashmir, had similar hopes, with Nehru, himself a Kashmiri Pandit (Brahmin) seeing the state as an integral part of the Indian Union. According to the Indian census report of 1941, out of a total population of 4,021,616, Kashmir had a Muslim population of 3,101,247, which is about 77 per cent. Muslims were in the clear majority in all three areas of the state: Jammu province, Kashmir province, and the Frontier districts. The only districts where non-Muslims were in a slight majority were Jammu and Udhampur.

The two major routes connecting Kashmir to British India passed through what was to become Pakistan: the Rawalpindi-Murree-Baramula-Srinagar road that followed the Jhelum River for part of the way, and the Sialkot-Jammu-Srinagar road that crossed the 9,000 foot high Banihal Pass in the Pir Panjal Range. An ancillary dirt road connected Pathankot to Srinagar. In the north, the Indus River valley provided a connection for Gilgit to the area that would become Pakistan. As Mahnaz Ispahani explains, routes determine the security of nations and also their potential, providing the opportunities for trade and commerce.[23] The criticality of these links between Kashmir, India and Pakistan was to be borne out as the drama of partition unfolded.

A key element of the partition plan of the British government was the setting up of two boundary commissions, one for Punjab and the other for Bengal. A lawyer named Sir Cyril Radcliffe, who had never set foot in India before, arrived on 8 July in New Delhi and was made head of a small team of British and Indian officers to assist him in his deliberations. He alone was to make the final award. His remit from the government was the demarcation of 'the boundaries of the two parts of Punjab on the basis of ascertaining the contiguous majority areas of Muslims and non-Muslims.'[24] Both the Indian National Congress and the Muslim League were part of his 'team'. A first draft of the award was ready by 8 August, and the final draft was delivered to the viceroy's staff on 12 August but remained unannounced by Mountbatten till after partition.

The final boundary, known as the Radcliffe award, allotted some 62 per cent of the area of undivided Punjab to India, with 55 per cent of the population. The boundary ran from the border of Kashmir State south along the Ujh River, leaving one *tehsil* of Gurdaspur district to Pakistan and allotting the remainder to India. Where the Ujh met the Ravi River, the boundary followed the Ravi south-west, until it met the existing administrative line dividing Amritsar district from Lahore district. Radcliffe was careful to specify that the relevant administrative boundaries, not the course of the Ujh or the Ravi, constituted the new international boundary. The boundary then ran through Lahore district, along *tehsil* and village boundaries, leaving the district's easternmost corner in India. When the Radcliffe boundary met the Ferozepore district line, it turned to follow the river Sutlej along the administrative boundary between Ferozepore and Montgomery districts. The Radcliffe line ended where it met the border of Bahawalpur, a princely state whose ruler, like the maharaja of Kashmir, had the choice of acceding to Pakistan or India.[25]

Radcliffe gave India most of the Muslim majority district of Gurdaspur which was located at the northern peak of East Punjab, allowing India land access to Kashmir as well as control over some of the headwaters of rivers flowing from Kashmir into Pakistani Punjab, thus not only spawning a controversy over whether Mountbatten influenced him to change his draft Award, but also providing fuel for a number of wars between India and Pakistan. Radcliffe is said to have destroyed his notes and working documents after leaving India, but Beaumont, Radcliffe's secretary, believes that Mountbatten influenced Radcliffe at a lunch (from which Beaumont was excluded) to change the Award. Mountbatten denied doing any such thing till his death.

Chaudhry Muhammad Ali also describes his own meeting with Lord Ismay, Mountbatten's chief of staff, whom he had gone to see before the Award was made public to highlight Mr Jinnah's concerns that Muslim area of Gurdaspur might be going to India. Ismay professed ignorance of the topic. To illustrate his point, he writes about walking over to a map hanging on a wall of Ismay's office. 'There was a pencil line drawn across the Punjab. The line followed the boundary that had been reported to the Quaid-i-Azam [Mr Jinnah]. I said that it was unnecessary for me to explain further since the line, already drawn on the map, indicated the boundary I had been talking about. Ismay turned pale and asked in confusion who had been fooling with his map.'[26] Ali recalls that the difference between the draft and the final award was only that in the draft, the Ferozepur and Zira *tehsils* were seen to be on the Pakistan side.

Lionel Carter, who edited Mountbatten's *Report on The Last Viceroyalty*, a collection of Mountbatten's contemporary records of the period dated 22 March to 15 August 1947, states that although Mountbatten denied any meddling in the Radcliffe Award, 'there is evidence that he did so'[27] in the case of the Ferozepore, Zira, and Fazilka *tehsils* (or subdistricts). Among other things, he cites Justice Mohammad Munir, a member of the Radcliffe Commission allegedly being assured 'by Radcliffe, in "the most unequivocal terms" that the three *tehsils* were going to Pakistan.' He also cites the Transfer of Power documents to indicate a 'secraphone message from the Viceroy's

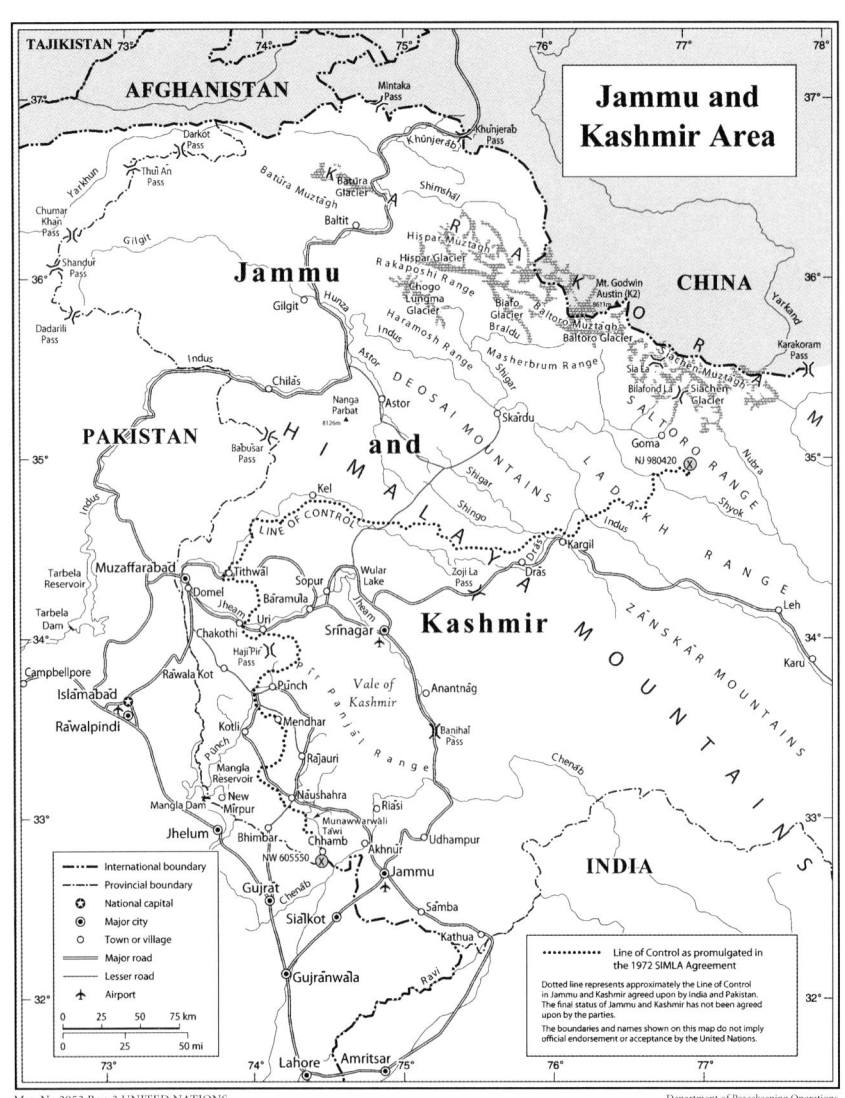

Author's Note: River Jhelum is spelled "Jheam" in this map.

House' to the Punjab authorities around 10–11 August, containing the order: 'Eliminate Salient.' This meant that the three *tehsils* were to be given to India and presumably the earlier maps indicating them in Pakistani territory that had been sent to the governor of the Punjab should be updated. This change in the original recommendations of the Radcliffe Commission is also alluded to by a leading Indian jurist, H.M. Seervai.[28]

Regardless of the reasons behind the Radcliffe Award, it connected India to Kashmir by a land route, thus allowing India direct access to the state and the freedom to transport troops and materials to the area over time. Many in Pakistan believe this was all Mountbatten's plot to give India the advantage in attaining and securing the accession of Kashmir. Naturally, the Indian view is different and relies on the need for equitable distribution of irrigation water from the rivers that flowed from Kashmir into India and then Pakistan. The seeds of conflict had been sown. (See the United Nations map of Jammu and Kashmir)

Mountbatten's personal reports, (written and edited with a view to history) indicate his desire to keep a neutral position between the two new dominions even though he was designated the governor general of India. The Pakistani view was less kind, and attributed to him and his close friendship with the Indian Prime Minister Jawaharlal Nehru the desire to deprive Pakistan of its assets and its strategic territory of Kashmir so that it would collapse under the weight of its independence and revert to some kind of a confederate or subservient status within a United India or *Akhand Bharat*. Interestingly, the Indian view of Mountbatten has been less than enthusiastic. Even while Nehru was using his friendship to plant ideas in the viceroy's mind at critical junctures in the run-up to independence, he was frequently in argument with the viceroy. More recent Indian historians have been downright critical of Mountbatten. C. Dasgupta, a senior Indian Foreign Service official in his *War and Diplomacy in Kashmir, 1947–48*,[29] discerns a British tilt toward Pakistan in the post-partition era, and paints Mountbatten as serving British interests above those of the dominion of which he was governor general.

The Punjab, meanwhile, was ablaze. Sikh arson and mass murder in East Punjab resulted in the deaths of thousands of Muslim men, women and children. There were often retaliatory killings of Hindus and Sikhs by Muslims in western Punjab and even in the NWFP, where tribesmen were enraged at the news of Muslims being massacred. A bigger conflagration was in the works.

Under the terms of the partition of British India, the contiguous Muslim and Hindu areas of the subcontinent were to form the twin dominions of Pakistan and India, with the 565 rulers of the princely states with whom the British had separate bilateral arrangements opting for either one or the other dominion, based on the religious make-up of their populations and contiguity.

The largest such state was Hyderabad in the southern area of the Deccan, ruled by a Muslim but with a Hindu majority in his 16 million subjects. Kashmir, contiguous to both India and Pakistan, was among the handful of such states that did not accede to either union by the time of partition, (Hyderabad and Junagadh, in the west, being the others). Thus was laid the ground for an eventual conflict that would reverberate in history.

NOTES

1. 'Freedom's Dawn', August 1947, a poem by Faiz Ahmed Faiz from *Dast e Saba*, 1952.
2. Lt. Gen. L.P. Sen, *Slender was the Thread* (Orient Longman, 1969), pp. 26–28.
3. I am indebted for much of the background to this discussion to the compilation of materials by Major General Shaukat Riza in his *The Pakistan Army 1947–1949* (Pakistan: Services Book Club, 1989).
4. Riza, ibid.
5. Mountbatten was harbouring the ambition to remain the joint governor general of India and Pakistan, a dream that was shattered by Mr Jinnah, who insisted that two countries could not function under one representative of the Crown and kept the governor generalship of Pakistan for himself. This act created further antipathy in Mountbatten's heart against Jinnah, which became evident in his contemporary secret reports and later public ruminations, including those with the authors of *Freedom at Midnight* Larry Collins and Dominique Lappiere.
6. Lord Ismay, *Memoirs* (London: Heinemann, 1960), quoted in Chaudhri Muhammad Ali, *The Emergence of Pakistan* (New York and London: Columbia University, 1967), p. 186.
7. Chaudhri Muhammad Ali, *The Emergence of Pakistan* (New York and London: Columbia University, 1967), p. 187.
8. This section benefits from Major General S. Shahid Hamid, *Disastrous Twilight*, pp. 269–61.
9. Riza, *Pakistan*, pp. 228–29.
10. Ibid., pp. 225–26.
11. His father and my grandfather served together and were great friends in the British Indian army, when both were first VCOs and then honorary officers. My grandfather Mohammed Nawaz Khan retired as honorary captain, then the highest rank available to native officers.
12. Major General Fazal Muqeem Khan, *The Story of the Pakistan Army* (Karachi: Oxford University Press, 1963), pp. 26–27.
13. Lt. Gen. S.P.P. Thorat, *From Reveille to Retreat* (India: Allied Publishers, 1985), pp. 100–101.
14. Fazal Muqeem Khan, *The Story of the Pakistan Army* (Karachi: Oxford University Press, 1963).
15. Akbar was replaced by Col. M.H. Hussain in February 1948 and then onwards devoted his efforts to the Kashmir front.
16. Khan, *The Story*, p. 47.
17. In addition to the prime minister, the council meeting was attended by the three chiefs: Messervy, Rear Admiral J.W. Jefford (commander-in-chief, Royal Pakistan Navy), and Air Vice Marshal Perry Keene (Royal Pakistan Air Force), Ch. Muhammad Ali (secretary general), Lt. Gen. Sir Douglas Gracey (chief of staff, army), Lt. Col. (retired) Iskander Mirza (secretary, ministry of defence), Ghulam Abbas (financial adviser, ministry of defence), Group Captain Elworthy (station commander Drigh Road, Karachi), and S.I. Haque (deputy secretary, defence).

18. Riza, *Pakistan*, p. 150.
19. John Keay, *When Men and Mountains Meet: The Explorers of the Western Himalayas 1820–75* (John Murray Publishers, 1977).
20. *Lalla Rookh* by Thomas Moore (Longmans, 1861).
21. The narrow Wakhan corridor, in fact, separated Kashmir from the Soviet Union.
22. Schofield, *Kashmir*, p. 117, quoting Karan Singh's memoir entitled *Heir Apparent*, Oxford, 1982.
23. Mahnaz Z. Ipashani, *Roads and Rivals: the Political Uses of Access in the Borderlands of Asia* (Ithaca and London: Cornell University Press, 1989).
24. Alastair Lamb, *Kashmir: A Disputed Legacy 1846-1990* (Karachi: Oxford University Press, 1991).
25. 'The 1947 Partition: Drawing the Indo–Pakistan boundary' by Lucy Chester. http://www.unc.edu/depts/diplomat/archives_roll/2002_01-03/chester_partition/chester_partition.html accessed 17 May 2007.
26. Muhammad Ali, *The Emergence*, p. 219.
27. Lionel Carter, ed. (and a new introduction), *Mountbatten's Report on the Last Viceroyalty, 22 March–15 August 1947* (New Delhi: Manohar, 2003).
28. H.M. Seervai, *Partition of India: Legend and Realilty* (Bombay: Universal Book Traders 1989, 90, and 94). pp. 146–147.
29. C. Dasgupta, *War and Diplomacy in Kashmir, 1947–48* (New Delhi: Thousand Oaks and London: Sage Publications, 2002), based on research in the papers of the Commonwealth Relations Office and other sources in Britain.

3 | THE FIRST KASHMIR WAR

In 1947, with the issue of Kashmir's accession still under contention, feverish activity proceeded in the corridors of power in New Delhi to effect a smooth transfer of power from the British to the successor dominions. No one wanted a war but almost everything that was done made war inevitable. The viceroy, Lord Mountbatten, is said to have tried to persuade the maharaja not to take action but to ascertain the wishes of his populace before committing. With a view to keeping options open and under the Muslim League leader, Mohammad Ali Jinnah's careful approach so as not to upset the delicate balance of accession of a number of key states that were still weighing their options (Kashmir and Hyderabad, being major illustrations of this case), Pakistan signed a standstill agreement with the maharaja of Kashmir. India held off from doing so. The viceroy's special aide V.P. Menon was deputed to discuss matters with the maharaja. The concern among Indian political leaders was that the longer Kashmir held out, the greater the possibility that the maharaja might either take an autonomous position or, much worse, opt for Pakistan or allow Pakistan to enter Kashmir.

The Indian National Congress leader and India's first Prime Minister, Jawaharlal Nehru, sat down and wrote an assessment to fellow Congressite and deputy prime minister, Sardar Vallabhbhai Patel, on 27 September 1947, which summed up the situation succinctly from the Indian point of view:

> It is obvious to me that the situation there [Kashmir] is a dangerous and deteriorating one. The Muslim League in the Punjab and the NWFP are making preparations to enter Kashmir in considerable numbers. The approach of winter is going to cut off Kashmir from the rest of India. The only normal route then is via the Jhelum valley. The Jammu can hardly be used during winter and air traffic is also suspended....
>
> I understand that the Pakistan strategy is to infiltrate into Kashmir now and to take some big action as soon as Kashmir is more or less isolated.

He then proposed the release of the Kashmiri politician Sheikh Abdullah and the National Conference leaders followed by a declaration of 'adhesion to Indian Union', for once this was done '...it will become very difficult for Pakistan to invade it officially or unofficially without coming into conflict with the Indian Union.'[1]

Patel joined hands with Nehru in continuously pressing the maharaja to accede to India. V.P. Menon meanwhile acted as the viceroy's emissary and a flurry of visits to Kashmir ensued.

Meanwhile, the maharaja was making matters worse by reacting badly to the efforts of the people of Poonch (in western Jammu) to assert their political rights. Poonch is a strategically important location as it is surrounded by the Jhelum and Chenab rivers, and the Pir Panjal range on the border with Kashmir. The southern spurs of the Pir Panjal range gradually descend into hilly areas which merge into the plains of the Gujrat district in Pakistan. While possessing pine forests in the higher reaches of the mountains, most of the rest of the area is arid and has little agriculture potential. The main towns are Bagh, Poonch, Mendhar, Kotli, Naoshera, Bhimbar, Rajauri, and Akhnoor, with the major communications links running along the rivers toward Pakistan. Before independence, a road that ran from Jammu to Bagh, crossing over the Chenab at Akhnoor and from there on to Beri Pattan, Noashera, Mendhar, and then Poonch, was improved. With Indian help, the Dogra government tried also to establish an alternate route from Bagh across the Jhelum River valley to the Srinagar valley to provide year round access. The track from Poonch to Uri over the Hajipir Pass was also improved but remained unusable due to snow for much of the year.[2] (Many of the key battles of the First Kashmir War centred on these roads and this region and the names of even small towns such as Akhnoor entered military lore in both India and Pakistan.)

TROUBLES IN POONCH

This critical location gave the region great importance in a strategic context. Its population, largely Muslim, also had close ties to the contiguous regions in Pakistan in the districts of Jhelum, Rawalpindi, and Gujrat. The people shared a strong martial tradition with their relatives across the border. The martial tribes in Poonch included Sudhans, Abbasis, Chibs, Rajputs, Dainyals, Mardyals, and Gakhars, mainly from the Poonch and Mirpur districts. Poonchis had traditionally been active soldiers, in contrast to Kashmiris from the valley. Some 60,000 of them had served in the Second World War and they had strong links, because of geographical, economic, and religious reasons, with the contiguous areas of what was now Pakistan. On return from the war, the soldiers found that they had become the subjects not of the benign maharaja of Poonch but of the maharaja of Kashmir and were liable for all of the latter's onerous taxes. Dogra troops were billeted in the region to help collect the taxes. The Poonchis also responded badly to news of the slaughter of Muslims in East Punjab. A public meeting was held in August 1947 at Nila Bat, a village near Dhirkot, to support the demand for accession of Kashmir to Pakistan. The maharaja sent his Hindu Dogra forces to quell the unrest with a heavy hand. The troops opened fire on the gathering. On 27 August, Sardar Abdul Qayyum Khan, a local *zamindar* or landowner (and later president of the Azad Kashmir government), led an attack on a police-cum-military post in Dhirkot and captured it, leading the maharaja to unleash the full force of his Dogra troops on the population. This effectively drew the lines in Poonch between the Hindu ruler and the Muslim population, all of whom were now seen as enemies. Muslim villages were attacked and burned.[3]

The Poonchis reacted sharply to these events. Many ex-servicemen from Poonch exfiltrated across the (as yet undefined) border to Pakistan in order to leave their families with relatives, and then began to prepare themselves for an armed rebellion. Among the leaders of this rebellion was the young Sardar Mohammed Ibrahim Khan, a lawyer and member of the state assembly, who fled across the border to Pakistan and attracted around him a core group of supporters, including retired military officers and former members of the INA. He was introduced to Colonel Akbar Khan of the Pakistan Army at one point and he asked for Akbar's help.[4] According to Akbar, Ibrahim 'thought that the time for peaceful negotiations was gone because every protest was being met with repressions and, therefore, in certain areas the people were virtually in a state of revolt...if they were to protect themselves and to prevent the maharajah from handing them over to India, they needed weapons.' The number of weapons requested was only 500 rifles. Akbar states that a few days later Mian Iftikharuddin, a leading member of the ruling Muslim League (and later publisher of repute), arrived in Murree and said that he was being asked to go to Kashmir to see if he could facilitate accession to Pakistan. If that did not work out, he said, there ought to be a plan to help Kashmiri Muslims take action against any likely accession to India. Iftikharuddin asked Akbar to prepare such a plan but warned that 'any action by us was to be of an unofficial nature, and no Pakistani troops or officers were to take an active part in it.'

Akbar discussed this issue with Ibrahim and others and then returned to Rawalpindi to prepare the action plan. As director of weapons and equipment at GHQ in Rawalpindi, he had a good idea of the weapons situation in Pakistan—a situation which was not very good. Moreover, the secrecy enjoined on him meant that he could not take the army chief into confidence and have orders issued to support the Kashmiris. He found that 4,000 rifles had been sanctioned for the Punjab police that could somehow be diverted for this new cause (his military mind had already assessed the need for a force larger than the 500 sought by Ibrahim), and he also arranged to find some condemned ammunition that was to be 'thrown into the sea.' His friend Colonel Azam Khanzada agreed to allow this shipment of condemned ammunition to be diverted 'secretly for use in Kashmir.'

Once the basic weapons had been acquired, Akbar concentrated on organizing support for the Kashmiris. A critical need was trained military manpower. In the absence of serving Pakistani officers, he assumed the use of ex-INA officers who had not been re-inducted into the army after their release at the end of the Second World War. His plan entitled 'Armed Revolt inside Kashmir' concentrated on 'strengthening the Kashmiris themselves internally and at the same time taking steps to prevent the arrival of armed civilians or military assistance from India into Kashmir.' The plan assumed that roughly 200 Muslim troops of the State army would not fight against their co-religionists, leaving a force of 7,000 to contend with, most of whom were scattered across the territory.

AKBAR'S ACTION PLAN

The action plan thus focused on severing two major routes that linked Kashmir to India: first, the Kathua–Jammu route, an unmetalled road that passed through 'broken territory' where guerrilla action could hold up any traffic till the rains and winter snows made it impassable. Second, the aim was to make Srinagar airport, the terminus for the likely air supply route from India, unavailable to Indian planes.

Akbar gave this plan to Iftikharuddin on the latter's return from Kashmir. Soon thereafter, Akbar was summoned to a meeting in Lahore with Prime Minister Liaquat Ali Khan and Sardar Shaukat Hayat Khan, a minister in the Punjab government. Shaukat Hayat had another plan in hand, which included the use of INA officers such as M. Zaman Kiani and Khurshid Anwar, a commander of the Muslim League national guards, to mount cross border operations under the overall command of Shaukat Hayat. According to Akbar, there was a meeting later that evening, attended by the finance minister, Ghulam Mohammad (later governor general), Mian Iftikharuddin, Zaman Kiani, Khurshid Anwar, Shaukat Hayat, and Akbar himself. As his precise military mind, understood it 'again the enthusiasm was there but there was no serious discussion of the problems involved...the allotment of funds received much attention [but]....operational details and their pros and cons were not discussed.' At the end of the meeting, Khurshid Anwar told Akbar privately that he was not going to take orders from Shaukat Hayat. Soon thereafter, Shaukat Hayat in turn told Akbar that he had no confidence in Anwar. And thus the master plan for Kashmir was off to a less than auspicious start, with amateur enthusiasm leavened by some military fervour and a good deal of bickering among the principals.

Upon his return to Rawalpindi, Akbar took then Colonel M. Sher Khan, deputy director of Military Intelligence (and future director of MI), into confidence so that he may get military information for planning purposes.[5] He also arranged with Colonel 'Tommy' Masud of the cavalry to collect and store the condemned ammunition. Air Commodore Janjua and others from the air force also offered to help with logistics, as did Khwaja Abdul Rahim, the civilian commissioner of Rawalpindi division.

By early October, it had become obvious to the Pakistan Army that the situation in Kashmir was becoming critical, with the maharaja's apparent reluctance to declare accession to either dominion and a popular uprising in Poonch that was increasingly being abetted by relatives and other forms of support from across the Jhelum River in Pakistan. An exchange of telegrams took place between the Pakistan and Kashmiri governments in early October, with Pakistan protesting the use of 'armed bands, which include troops' against Muslim villages in Kashmir. 'These stories are confirmed by the large number of villages that can be seen burning from Murree hills.' The Kashmiris responded on 15 October with a telegram saying that they had proof of Pakistani infiltration into Kashmir but were open to a neutral inquiry. However, the words to note in the Pakistani message were: 'The situation is fraught with danger'; a message that was probably not lost on the new chief minister of Kashmir, Mehr Chand Mahajan, who had worked on the Radcliffe Commission and had recently given up his home in Lahore where he had been a judge.[6]

SHER KHAN'S ASSESSMENT

Either before or soon after Akbar approached him,[7] Colonel Sher Khan wrote a secret two-and-a-half page appreciation of the situation in Kashmir in typically clinical military style.[8] Copied to the secretary defence, the personal secretary to the commander-in-chief, the chief of staff, the Intelligence Bureau in Karachi, the deputy chief of general staff, the director Military Operations and Intelligence and his colleagues at the GHQ, the main objective of the letter was 'to assess the likelihood of an uprising in Kashmir and, if it is likely, when it might occur.'

Proceeding from the assumption that 'the general desire of the Muslims of Kashmir and those others is that the State should opt for Pakistan,' Sher Khan noted that the 'Maharaja is definitely nervous of a general uprising, and is wavering about an open declaration of the State's option for India. Under pressure, however, from the maharani, Mr Batru ICS [Indian Civil Service], and some Indian leaders, it is reported that a secret agreement has been reached in which the maharaja has agreed to opt for India, and India has promised military assistance if necessary.' He then analysed the attitudes of the non-Muslim groups in Kashmir. Of the three main groups, he wrote that the Kashmiri Pandits, though small in number, were very influential but they were 'afraid of losing their privileged (sic) position if the State opts for India, and are therefore against it.' Hindus and Sikhs, other than the Pandits, were expected to favour the India option. They were the bulk of the State's forces. Also, refugees from NWFP and Western Punjab had been 'armed by the State authorities ostensibly for self defence.' They too were seen as being in favour of opting for India.

Sher Khan's analysis of the local inhabitants found the dwellers of the valley of Kashmir to be 'not very martial.' But the inhabitants of the hills to the west and the south, who constituted a majority of the population, were deemed to be martial. Many of them were ex-soldiers or serving soldiers. They were reported to have clashed with the State forces 'over Pakistan celebrations' on 14 August and 'are continuing to resist now.' Sher Khan felt that Sheikh Abdullah had been 'bought over but the indications are that he is not likely to command any substantial following over [the] Pakistan–India issue.'

The arrival of large bodies of armed Sikhs and Hindus in Jammu, especially the import of INA and Rashtriya Swayamsevak Sangh (RSS) (a right wing Hindu fanatical group), was what Sher Khan termed 'the outside influences' at work in Kashmir. (Ironically, Mohan Singh of the INA was organizing his forces against his erstwhile Muslim INA colleagues in Eastern Punjab.) He also identified Pakistan and the NWFP tribes as 'clamouring for Kashmir to opt for Pakistan.' But he noted that 'so far no reports have been received of any move by armed reinforcements from the Punjab to Kashmir. On the contrary, people along the border are vacating their homes and moving inland. But there is no doubt that there are some hundreds of religious fanatics and adventurers who are prepared to, and will, cross the border.' Himself a Pathan, Sher Khan well understood the mood of the Frontier province. 'The Frontier tribes.' he stated, 'are a totally different problem. Their tempers are dangerously high as a result of the East Punjab atrocities stories.' Concluding that while it had been difficult for the tribesmen to cross the NWFP and Punjab governments to go to East Punjab, he wrote that 'it will be quite easy for them to go to Kashmir should oppression against the Muslims continue there.' In brief, in his view, all the factors 'which ordinarily make for trouble exist or may be created in Kashmir'. The timing depended on various factors.

He identified the factors as follows: First, the maharaja's declaration of opting to accede to India. This depended on Indian pressure and her assurances of effective military support. This support, including equipment and supplies, 'cannot be effectively given until the road Pathankot–Kathua is fit for MT [Motorized Transport] traffic.' In his view, 'the earliest this is to be expected to be through is the end of October. The declaration, therefore, might be expected then.' The second factor was the oppression of the Muslim population by the non-Muslim troops of the State of Kashmir and other armed bodies. He mentioned that in Poonch, several villages had been burned and refugees had started arriving in Pakistan. He warned that this might 'inflame the already incensed tribesmen from as far as…Afghanistan' to cross the border to the assistance of the Muslims. 'The report of their casualties etc. will keep a regular stream…going into Kashmir. This might start any day.'

The third factor he identified as the Indian attitude over the Junagadh option. He thought a referendum might be held and the results 'cooked.' The final and 'important' factor was the weather. Large parts of Kashmir will be under snow in 'six weeks time,' wrote Sher Khan, and the local population 'with their limited food and severe winter condition will not be in a position to stage any serious trouble. It will also be very difficult for the tribesmen to go to their assistance in large numbers.' His assessment was that the Maharaja was well aware of this situation and thus might delay his announcement until the weather started changing.

On the basis of this assessment, Sher Khan concluded that 'trouble in Kashmir is likely…The NWFP incl[uding] Afghan tribesmen are likely to be involved.…[and] The trouble is likely to start any time from now.' He was not far off the mark. Yet, GHQ did not appear to get into high gear at that point, operating as it was at that time with a skeleton staff and that too, far away from the political decision makers in Karachi. There does not appear to be any evidence of a master plan for the invasion of Kashmir with which the Pakistan Army was formally associated. Moreover, the prime minister had already decided not to involve the British commanders of the Pakistan Army in his planning for the Kashmir war, relying instead on a collection of semi-trained officers and civilians with pretensions of military knowledge. Given the nature of the prime minister's relationship with Mr Jinnah, it seems unlikely that all this planning was being done without Mr Jinnah's tacit approval although there has been some debate among Pakistanis about this issue. Regardless, a plan was approved by the prime minister and action initiated. Reflecting the highly romanticized view of his own role in this venture, Akbar Khan took on the *nom de guerre* General Tariq, after Tariq bin Ziad, the legendary Berber Muslim invader of Spain after whom Gibraltar is named (Jebel el Tariq) and who ordered his boats burned at the beachhead so there was no retreat once his force landed on the mainland. Indian sources maintain to this day the formation of a formal Operation Gulmarg, giving this hodgepodge of plans and activities a shade more formality and substance than they probably had in fact.

THE INVASION BEGINS

It was against this background that Khurshid Anwar managed to cobble together a force of some 2,000 tribesmen from the NWFP, aided by the Kashmiri-born Chief Minister Khan Abdul Qayyum Khan and the commissioner of Rawalpindi division Khwaja Rahim. Early on Thursday, 23

October 1947, they crossed over into Kashmir through the Jhelum valley and hit the road to Muzaffarabad, Domel, and Baramula *en route* to Srinagar. This invading force was a congeries of tribes, reflecting the tribal map of the frontier province. The main elements were the Mahsuds and Waziris. The other tribes that had responded to the call for help in Kashmir included the Mohmands, Orakzais, Turies, Mangals, Zadrans, Maqbuls, Gurbaz, Khattaks, Bittanis, Ghilzais, Rajouries, Yousafzais, and the Bangash. Hazara tribes from faraway Balochistan, and Zadrans, Sulemankhels, Ahmadzais, and Ghilzais from astride the Durand Line that separated Afghanistan and Pakistan also participated. Meanwhile, from within Pakistan, Diris, Swatis, and Chitralis also joined the fray.[9]

On Friday night, Nehru informed Mountbatten at a dinner for the Siamese foreign minister that tribesmen were being transported in 'military transport up the Rawalpindi road' toward Kashmir.[10] The following day, at the defence committee, attended by Mountbatten, General Rob Lockhart, the Indian Army chief, read out a telegram from the GHQ[11] in Pakistan that 'some five thousand tribesmen had attacked and captured Muzzafarabad and Domel and that considerable tribal reinforcements could be expected.' Other reports indicated that the invaders were only 35 miles from Srinagar. The defence committee began discussing ways of providing military assistance to Kashmir but Mountbatten insisted on the need for accession by the maharaja before any aid could be sent. Moreover, Mountbatten felt that 'accession should only be temporary, prior to a plebiscite.' No decision was taken but V.P. Menon was dispatched to Kashmir to speak with the maharaja.

ACCESSION AND INDIA'S ENTRY IN FORCE

It was during this trip that Menon managed to persuade the maharaja to escape with his family to Jammu. It was claimed—and this became a major bone of contention for times to come—that the maharaja signed the letter of accession to India on 26 October in Jammu, where Menon had followed him. Menon then brought the letter back to Delhi. On the basis of that letter, Mountbatten agreed to authorize Indian troop deployment in Kashmir. However, plans for such an airlift had begun much earlier. Indeed, Patel had written to the defence minister, Baldev Singh, on 7 October to be prepared to send arms and ammunition to Kashmir by air. 'I think the question of military assistance in time of emergency must claim the attention of our Defence Council (sic) as soon as possible. There is no time to lose...' he stated.[12] Commandeered civil and military aircraft were part of the airlift, with some 330 troops departing from Palam airport in a Dakota that first night and arriving and securing Srinagar airport almost immediately.[13] Future flights took place from Willingdon (Safdarjang) airfield. By 11 November, 'over 600 aircraft sorties carrying over 5000 men and several thousand pounds of stores' had been dispatched to Srinagar.[14]

India was lacking in good intelligence at the time. Even the commanding officer of the 1st Sikh Regiment, Lt. Col. Dewan Ranjit Rai, who was tasked with the first flight into Srinagar, was not given very specific information. According to Sinha, who took the minutes of the meeting where operational orders were drafted for the Kashmir operation, India did not even know whether Srinagar airport was available for landing at the time. So Rai was told to divert to Jammu in case landing was impossible at Srinagar and to immediately head up the road to Srinagar as far as he could.

The arrival of Indian forces in Srinagar was not a smooth operation, given the poor communications and the abject condition of the state forces whose commander had been killed early on in the fight against the raiders. The commander of the 161 Brigade, L.P. Sen, wrote that he was short of manpower for the defence of Srinagar and only discovered by chance that 1,850 state troops had been holed up in their Badami Bagh barracks ever since hostilities began. Most of them were veterans of earlier wars. It was only at the end of the first week of December when a request for rations for 2,000 men was received by 161 Brigade HQ at Uri. Assuming there was a misprint and an extra zero had been added, a query was sent back with the authorization for the issuance of the rations. That is when Sen discovered that there were indeed 1,850 fully armed state forces available to him who had chosen to sit out the action![15]

Inside Kashmiri territory, the tribesmen from the NWFP linked up with the forces of the Azad (or Free) Kashmir Army. Indian reports indicate that they were well armed with a 'complete range of infantry weapons including machine-guns and heavy mortars.'[16] But Akbar Khan described a rag-tag force equipped with outdated rifles or home-made weapons in the gun factories of the Frontier province. Indeed, the 1,000 men that were supposed to be ready to cut the Jammu–Kathua road were not there 'because their country-made rifles having broken down, they had returned to Pakistan—and the 200 rifles meant for the Srinagar landing ground had not been given by Khurshid Anwar to the people concerned.' Reinforcements were produced in the form of a hundred ex-servicemen volunteers from Rawalpindi. But, as Akbar admits 'it was too late then...as the Indian troops had already taken up defence of the landing ground.' Till this day, however, the story that has taken root in Pakistani minds is that the raiders had taken the hills surrounding Srinagar and could see the lights of the city.

The same evening that Indian forces landed in Srinagar, the Pakistani prime minister had called an 'unofficial conference' in Lahore that included Iskander Mirza (Defence Secretary), Chaudhry Muhammad Ali (then

Secretary General), Abdul Qayyum Khan (Chief Minister of the NWFP), Nawab Mamdot (Chief Minister of the Punjab), and Colonels Sher Khan and Akbar Khan, to evaluate the situation. Akbar states that he proposed cutting the Jammu road with three tribal *lashkars* of 1,000 persons each and offered to go with them. Everyone, except the chief ministers of NWFP and Punjab, opposed this idea since they feared this might provoke a full-scale Indo–Pakistan war. Akbar, of course, felt these fears were groundless since India knew the tribesmen had gone through Pakistan to get to Kashmir and had it so desired, India would have launched a cross border attack on the fledgling Pakistan earlier but it did not. In Akbar's view, this was because India 'was not militarily strong enough to take such a risk.' He was also of the view, though mistaken in his calculation, that the Indian army was only twice the size of Pakistan's. Perhaps he was looking at the troops in Kashmir alone. Regardless, Akbar's idea was shelved and, in his view, an opportunity was lost to attain an advantage in the battle for Kashmir. He regretted the lack of daring on the part of Pakistani leaders at that time.

He was not aware at that time that the same evening, Mr Jinnah had ordered General Gracey, the acting commander-in-chief (while Messervy was on leave), to send the Pakistan Army into Kashmir in response to India's military intervention. Gracey is said to have demurred, citing the need to get the supreme commander's permission and most probably referring to the stand down instructions of Auchinleck that would have meant the loss of Pakistan's entire crop of senior British military commanders. Further, the Pakistan Army was in no position to launch and sustain a military operation against India at that time. Auchinleck flew to Lahore to meet Jinnah and explain the reality behind the stand down order.

The Lahore meeting on Kashmir under Prime Minister Liaquat Ali Khan concluded at 2 a.m. the next morning with the approval of Akbar Khan's idea for the formation of a Liberation Committee to coordinate actions in Kashmir. Next morning, Akbar was asked to meet the prime minister and was informed that he was now a member of this committee and would leave his post at GHQ to become military adviser to the prime minister. He was to stay on in Rawalpindi for this work which was to be kept secret from the British officers and the GHQ. Included in the Liberation Committee were Sardar Ibrahim, Ghulam Mohammed, and Major Yousaf, who was to deal with the tribals. Akbar sought a clarification of the military aim of the effort. According to him, the prime minister 'wanted...to keep the fight going for three months which would be enough time to achieve our political object by negotiations and other means.' Weighed down by the fears that his forces were operating on short supplies, and that they were especially short on ammunition, Akbar rushed back to Rawalpindi on the afternoon of the 28 October 1947 to ensure that the tribesmen received their ammunition on time.

It is interesting to note that Messervy had a view that was somewhat congruent with that of Akbar Khan's for the solution of the Kashmir problem. In a conversation with Nawabzada Sher Ali Khan Pataudi, who was visiting him in early 1948 at his home in Rawalpindi, Messervy stated that 'he had given Iskander Mirza a piece of his mind [on the way the Kashmir situation was being surreptitiously handled and planned in those early days].' In Messervy's view, 'all it required was a battalion in plain clothes, who would have been there within 12 hours—a battalion less two companies at the air field in Srinagar and two companies at Banihal Pass and that would have been the end of the story.'[17] But no one approached Messervy for his views or plans. Somewhat presciently, this soldier's soldier commented that 'politicians using soldiers and soldiers allowing themselves to be used, without the proper approval of their superiors, were setting a bad example for the future.'[18] Messervy had by then told the prime minister that he was planning to leave but did not brief him on the political activities of officers at the GHQ, 'as the PM had not asked for his advice.'

Akbar Khan left on 29 October for Kashmir, accompanied by a reporter named Ali Akhtar Mirza. They drove along the Jhelum River beyond Kohala and reached Muzaffarabad, which was the hub of the tribal forces. More and more buses loaded with tribal warriors were arriving, armed with an assortment of colourful weapons of British, German, French and local manufacture, including pistols and hunting guns, and many had come with just their daggers! Another 50 miles down the road at Uri, where State forces gave battle to the tribesmen and blew up the bridge across the river, Akbar noted that locals had helped cut a new road through the hillside to enable the tribal warriors to proceed to Baramula. The tribal force had hit Baramula on the 26th and fought a battle against the retreating State forces which blew up buildings and a key bridge over the Jhelum River to hinder the movement of the attackers. The tribals had also rampaged through the town. Finally, the Indian Air Force attacked them in the city, adding further to the devastation. Indian newspaper accounts and reports, including those from L.P. Sen whose forces took Baramula back during the campaign, accused the tribesmen of rape and pillage, with victims including members of a convent.[19] The attack stopped at Baramula for two days—two days which may have been critical in the battle for Srinagar and Kashmir.

According to Akbar, his talks with the locals led him to believe that Khurshid Anwar had waited for Kashmiri leaders with whom he wished to confer about the future government of Kashmir. Yet another view was that the leaders of the force, including Khurshid, squabbled about who would lead the victory march into Srinagar. The Indian view is quite different. They saw the tribals as having been distracted by the prospect of loot, and, having won time, Indian forces were able to move out of Srinagar and give battle on the road between Baramula and Srinagar. Akbar Khan's own reconnaissance of Srinagar indicated that much of its boundary was waterlogged, and the best way was by road but that this would need armoured cars that only the Pakistan Army could provide. He found his way back to Pakistan and discovered that his friend 'Tommy' Masud was willing to take 'a whole squadron of his unit's armoured cars.' Masud said his men 'would go in plain clothes without official permission and at their own risk.' But this proposal was shot down at a meeting with Sher Khan, Lt. Col. Arbab, and Raja Ghazanfar Ali Khan, a central government minister from Jhelum, since this action might precipitate war between India and Pakistan. No action was taken and the tribal attack appeared to have ground to a halt some 35 miles from Srinagar.

PAKISTAN ARMY HELPS OUT

Despite the halt in the attack, Akbar and his cohort were being kept busy by the arrival of Indian forces in large numbers. Battles between the two sides spread across the map of Kashmir towards the north and the south-west of the state. By December, the army chief had been brought into the picture, though in a peculiar fashion. A meeting was held on 4 December with the prime minister, but Messervy was kept in a separate room and communicated with Akbar via chits. After that meeting, Messervy told Akbar that 'you will not have to do it with sticks alone any longer. I am going to help.' He ended up allotting a million rounds of ammunition for the war and the release of twelve officer volunteers from the Pakistan Army for three weeks. By the end of December, India had taken the issue to the United Nations. But the fighting continued, both on the field and off. The Azad Kashmir Forces had set up a GHQ that was trying to acquire all the trappings of a major military enterprise. Akbar was amused at the attempts by the 'defence minister' to set up separate branches of command for the GHQ, all according to the British field service manual that this individual carried with him at all times. Rivalries persisted between field commanders in Poonch who kept promoting themselves to field ranks, rising from captain to major to colonel and brigadier, until both field commanders became field marshals. At this point, the 'defence minister' himself, seeing no other title available, 'came to adopt the German rank of captain general'! While this Gilbert and Sullivanesque opera was underway, sporadic fighting continued as Indian forces attempted to regain control in some areas. A major operation was occurring in Poonch, where a temporary ceasefire was sought and granted by the local Azad commander to allow Indians to evacuate the wounded. But then winter set in, and with it came a slump in the action and time to regroup and plan for the spring, when melting snows would allow for freer movement of troops.

Akbar Khan, reverting to his alter ego General Tariq, drafted a note on 8 February 1948 on the organization of Azad Forces HQ and future plan of action[20] for the battles ahead. His overall assessment was that the administrative organization was 'in danger of collapse' because of a lack of coordination between existing organizations and the influx of thousands of 'out of control tribesmen.' He saw the need for an organization that would integrate the different headquarters into one and also saw the need to 'send the tribesmen back to Afghanistan' from concentrations in Sialkot and Gujrat districts to avoid lawlessness in Pakistan, and 'replace them with Pakistani tribesmen in controllable *lashkars* under our leaders.' Meanwhile, he wanted the 1,000 Darband *lashkar* and Azad Forces to keep Indian troops in Jammu involved and to provide cover for raids in Sialkot district.

At that point, Akbar Khan estimated a total of three Indian divisions: two divisional reconnaissance regiments (with armoured cars and light tanks), one armoured regiment, plus two field and one mountain regiment deployed as follows: Force HQ at Jammu, with 50 Para and 70 Brigade in Naushera and Beripattan; 80 Brigade to maintain line of communication (L of C) between Akhnoor (sic) and Beripattan; 77 and 268 Brigade in Jammu and on the Kathua–Jammu LOC; 161 Brigade in Srinagar–Uri sector; Poonch Brigade in Poonch; 36 Brigade in Jammu or on the way; and ten State forces in Jammu and Srinagar, including one battalion from the eastern state of Patiala.

Akbar Khan expected India to build up quickly for an offensive against Bhimber from Akhnoor (using armour), and then the Naushera (also Noashera) force would break out west to Jhangar. Once successful, this force would try to link to Poonch via Kotal or attempt to link up from Uri and try to capture Muzaffarabad. Just a few days earlier, Indian forces had fought a pitched battle against the raiders at Noashera, who gave the Indians an opportunity to use their heavy weapons (including one squadron of armoured cars and one battery each of field and mountain guns) and thereby inflict heavy casualties. The raiders had attacked from three directions but were met by well-entrenched Indian troops. The Indian author, Lt. Gen. S.K. Sinha estimated that there were some 2,000 dead out of a tribal force of 15,000 (both numbers are hard to verify). He admits to a total of 963 bodies that were left on the battlefield. Thirty-three Indians were killed and 102 wounded.[21] This battle gave the Indians a chance to regroup and then prepare for an advance on Jhangar under the newly named local JAK (Jammu and Kashmir) Force Commander Kalwant Singh.

To counter these Indian forces and their likely plans, Akbar Khan proposed:

- Preparations for an anti-tank defence around Bhimber, with demolitions, road blocks, mines etc. on the road between Akhnoor and Noashera and setting up of ambushes between Noashera, Jhangar, and Kotli 'to restrict the enemy in Noashera.'
- Raids on bridges/culverts on the Jammu–Srinagar road in the area of Ramban from a base in Rajauri, accompanied by raids on the Srinagar—Uri road in the Baramula district by the Titwal battalion to force the Indians to disperse their forces towards Handwar and thus prevent any concentrated move on Muzaffarabad.
- Use of the Uri force to prepare bridges/culverts on the road between Uri and Domel for demolition, establish roadblocks between Uri and Chinari and strengthen its own positions south of that road.
- Block the Uri–Poonch road in the hills, and
- 'Liquidate Poonch, before its relief by Indian (sic).'

According to this assessment by Akbar Khan, the battle for Kashmir was being run by an Azad Force HQ under a commander-in-chief and comprised mainly of ex-soldiers under arms in Azad Kashmir, plus a Tariq Force HQ comprising three Pakistan Army officers, a political officer, a Pakistan audit and accounts officer, and a civil supply organization under an officer appointed by the Punjab government. The Azad Forces HQ was to deal with strategic and tactical advice and the routine logistical and supply issues. However, he felt that the administration and training of the Azad Forces needed to be better organized on 'sound lines by [the] Pakistan Army accepting tr[ainin]g and adm[inistration] responsibility to these forces as allies, non-regulars or PNG [Pakistan National Guard].' He established priority on the organization of training centres and record offices, training of officer cadets and technical personnel, reorganization of battalions, brigade headquarters and Lines of Communication facilities. Finally, and most important, he suggested 'closing down of the ad hoc Tariq HQ as soon as GHQ Pakistan take(s) over commitments.' Akbar Khan then asked the prime minister to be relieved of his duties on Kashmir. By mid-February, Sher Khan was to take on the mantle of General Tariq. The ground was being laid for the formal involvement of the Pakistan Army in the Kashmir war.

OVERHAULING THE SHOW

Less than two weeks later, on 19 February, Brigadier Sher Khan, now responsible for managing the effort in Kashmir, reported to the prime minister in Karachi in his usual succinct and cut-to-the-chase style on the latest situation in the execution of the war in Kashmir.[22] 'The show was thoroughly disorganized and completely out of control,' he started. 'My first action, therefore, was to reorganize and overhaul the show and set-up.'

Clearly picking up on Akbar Khan's earlier 'General Tariq' memorandum of 8 February, Sher Khan stated that he had integrated the three headquarters into one and cleared out the thousands of Pathans sitting in camps in the Sialkot and Gujrat districts. 'These Pathans were a serious menace to law and order and [the] cause of a very serious drain on our resources of food, transport and ammunition and caused a lot of dishonest dealings, e.g. the camp staff were drawing thousands of *maunds* [local measure of weight equal to about 82 pounds] of food grains, ammunition and petrol and selling them.' He said he was preparing to send tribesmen in controlled groups directly into Kashmir and was closing down all fixed camps in Pakistan, using only transit facilities. He shut down the headquarter in Gujrat.

At the operational level, Sher Khan saw the Poonchis 'who have been our hard core' showing signs of disintegration. Having fought hard for three months, they 'are now melting away from the front', he wrote, giving the Indian garrison a chance to hit out successfully. He proposed rushing 1,000 persons to reinforce the Poonchis right away with another 1,000 in a week or ten days. There was no fresh development on the Uri front. In Noashera, Sher Khan reported that the tribals had suffered immensely in their last daylight attack on 6 February 'resulting in complete disorganization and melting away of the *lashkars* with their dead and wounded.' He also reported that the Indians were well prepared for an offensive in this sector and prayed that if he was given another ten days' respite he would 'ensure that their advance will not be a walk over.'

In Bhimber, India now had two regiments of light tanks and armoured cars. 'Their intention appears to be to capture BHIMBER with their armour. The country is tankable right upto BHIMBER and it will be a desperate struggle to save it.' He wrote of having made preparations in conjunction with the army and that nothing more could be done at that time 'short of sending in our tanks.' Sher Khan's aim was to 'liquidate' Poonch, 'with some heavy supporting arms. God willing, we should be able to do it.'

Then, he introduced a final note of despondency over the efforts in Kashmir. 'I do not wish to depress you,' he stated, 'but I shall be failing in my duty if I do not give you the absolute facts. I am quite sure you realize that our effort has spent its force. I was hoping and continuing to strive, that with the assistance of the people who have been (sic) such good work we will continue the struggle. But I regret to say a large number of these are throwing in the sponge and backing [out] with one excuse or another.' He cited Zaman Kiani and other INA officers as 'deserting a sinking ship.' Kiani was reported by Sher Khan to have stated that he had hoped his services will be recognized by Pakistan, 'but instead they [the INA] are being debarred from all service.

So, he has asked to be relieved.' (Here again the animosity between the INA and those who had stayed true to the British oath intruded into relationships and actions in Kashmir.) Promising to keep 'the show going as best as is possible,' Sher Khan signed off with: 'I just wanted you to be in the real picture.'

Within the next two weeks, the British high commissioner in New Delhi, Sir T. Shone was writing to the Commonwealth Relations Office (CRO) in the UK on the military situation with the news that 'I understand General Tariq, Commander of the Azad Forces, has resigned.'[23] But he did not identify Akbar Khan by name nor who the new General Tariq was to be. The high commissioner was also keen to draw attention to the news, reported extensively by *The Hindustan Times* on 26 February, that 'Brigadier' Haight, whom he identified as 'USA ex-paratrooper Private, who served with the Azad Forces' had given an interview in America in which Haight was reported to have confirmed the help given by Pakistan to the tribesmen.

The next six weeks or so saw a lot of thrust and parrying on the part of the Indian and the Azad Kashmir and Tariq forces, as winter snow and rains made movement difficult. This gave time for reflection on the original and emerging strategies in the Kashmir war. By 5 April, the new General Tariq (aka Sher Khan) was evaluating the overall picture from a higher perspective.

THE FINAL PHASE

The Kashmir operation, Sher Khan wrote, had begun with the Poonch uprising and the tribal invasion. The initial aim was to try to 'create a situation in which the maharaja would be forced to accept a plebiscite in the State.'[24] The accession of Kashmir to India and the arrival of Indian troops had changed that situation. The objective changed then to make operations difficult and expensive for India so she would 'come to agree to a free and unfettered plebiscite.' The original expectation had been that if the struggle continued till December then this objective would have been achieved. Later this date was extended to the end of March 1948. Although the 'Azad Forces can be said to have carried out this task very successfully', Sher Khan (General Tariq) correctly surmised that the political object had not been achieved. Operations had been carried out 'on an extremely improvised basis and under heavy administrative difficulties.' He considered that it would not be possible to a carry on in this fashion and on the same scale beyond the end of April, presumably when the snow would have started melting.

He then proposed for this 'final phase' of operations that the scope and objective of the Azad Forces needed to be redefined 'to hold the territory now under their control <u>at any cost</u> [original underline] and prevent India from securing a military decision.' This he felt would not be possible without the Pakistan Army openly joining the conflict. However, the introduction of the Pakistan Army 'is not desirable nor in the best interest of Pakistan,' he stated. So, he asked for finance, food, clothing and equipment for the Azad Forces 'on a high national emergency priority.'

Sher Khan's appreciation of the military situation included four main factors. First, India was seen to have introduced into Kashmir two complete divisions and corps troops numbering some 10,000 men. He estimated that the daily supply requirement of this force from Pathankot to Jammu was of the order of 300 tons, plus additional supplies for the civilian population. All this traffic was going through the unmetalled Pathankot-Kathua-Jammu road which was 'likely to be unusable during inclement weather, as was the case during the rains in the second week of March.' Therefore, the Indian Army's ability to undertake large scale operations would depend on the ability of its administrative machinery to meet these demands.

The second factor that Sher Khan identified was the efficient operation of communications and maintaining of mobility and momentum. Of the three forms of communications; road, rail, and air, only the last two were available in Kashmir and both were vulnerable to the elements and to hostile actions. Therefore, he deduced that India 'will make every possible effort to achieve an early decision, military and political.'

He then evaluated the relative strengths of the Indian and Azad Forces, with the Indian Army having 'an overwhelming superiority' in weapons, equipment, organization and resources. Faced with such odds, the Azad Forces 'will not be able to and must not be expected to hold ground.' In his view, 'they should...avoid staged battles.'

The fourth factor was the weather, which had been bad. Snow had hindered the build up of Indian forces in Kashmir but also constrained the ability of Azad Forces to infiltrate around Indian flanks and interfere with their line of communications as well as extend operations to other parts of the valley. 'The approach of summer will enable both sides to intensify operations,' he wrote. In Jammu, however, even in winter the snow had not been a major factor and he expected the Indian Army to launch a bigger effort than the one they had launched against Noashera in March. Yet, he felt that 'the Pathans who have been the biting teeth of the Azad Forces cannot stand upto the heat and are likely to disappear gradually from this front.' His conclusion was that the Azad Forces needed to expand operations into other parts of Kashmir to prevent India from concentrating on any one sector. Meanwhile, more locals needed to take over the role of the Pathans and 'contain the Indian forces' in the south by interfering with their lines of communication and preventing a link up with the Poonch garrison.

Discussing the time factor, Sher Khan thought that the best period for operations in Kashmir from the administrative point of view was from April through June, or until the monsoons broke. He did not expect the Indian Army to be able to build up for another offensive for at least another fortnight. If the Azad Forces were to open other fronts, they could dissipate Indian efforts. If they could keep operations going till August, 'without [the] Indian[s] having achieved a military decision, I believe that they will lose the KASHMIR war for economic and administrative reasons.' He relied on the vulnerability of the Indian line of communication in the south that ran parallel to the front for some 60 miles through hilly and broken terrain, leaving open the possibility of harassment by Azad Forces. In sum, Sher Khan struck a positive cord by deducing that normally time would have favoured India but given the 'special economic circumstances of KASHMIR, geographical conditions and inadequate communications, it would appear... [that time] would be in favour of Azad Forces, provided they can successfully prevent [the] Indian Army from achieving a military decision during the next three months, which it is possible to do.'

Finally, he focussed on Poonch, which had been isolated by the Azad Forces since December 1947. It had a garrison of one brigade strength and approximately 20,000 non-Muslim inhabitants who had been kept supplied by Indian Dakota aircraft. However, since 27 March, the landing ground had been under gun fire and no aircraft had been able to land. The options open to India in Poonch were (as identified by Sher Khan):

- Air drops and supply by planes that could land in Poonch, but letting the garrison fend for itself. Though tactically sound, Sher Khan thought this was not likely to be the course of action since, 'apart from the morale and prestige point of view, it's a running sore for them.' Little did he know that he was almost reading his enemy commander's mind.[25]
- Accept safe conduct that had been offered to them. In his view, the Indian army would be 'only too pleased to do so', but it appeared that the Indian government did not agree to this.
- Try to link the town up with ground forces. This was seen as the most likely course of action.

Sher Khan then proceeded to further penetrate the enemy's brains by exploring possibilities for action open to them. The nearest troops were in Uri but he believed the garrison there was not strong enough for such an operation. The Noashera sector had the required troops but the sector was about 50 miles away and any movement would create a long line of communication through broken territory, subject to attacks. Another option would involve sending a strong column over the difficult Pir Panjal Pass at the same time as the move from Noashera.

India had a number of other options open to it as well, according to Sher Khan's analysis. It could mount an attack from Uri against Domel, a desirable target, but it did not have enough troops for this venture. It could relieve Poonch by a combined offensive from Noashera and the valley over the Pir Panjal: the most likely course. It could also launch an attack from Akhnoor to capture Bhimber, thus securing its line of communications. And finally, it could launch an offensive from Noashera to capture Mirpur but this was not likely since they would need troops for the relief of Poonch. In retaliation, the Azad Forces would need to intensify attacks against the lines of communication and extend operations to divert attention away from Poonch to other parts of the state.

To forestall Indian moves, Sher Khan concluded, the Azad Forces should open other fronts in the state, forcing India to spread thin its troops and thus prevent a build up for an offensive in Poonch. His plan then was to extend and intensify operations in the valley from Muzaffarabad and Gilgit and to attack the lines of communications and destroy transport from Akhnoor to Noashera, Jammu to Srinagar, and from Uri to Srinagar. Their motto, he noted, should continue to be 'a lorry a day keeps the Hindu away.' In all of this, the Azad forces were to avoid staged battles. At least one thousand additional rifles were to be issued to the forces in the Rajauri–Riasi sector 'to enable them to contain the Indian Army in the event of possible disappearance (sic) of Pathans from this front.' Overall, the upbeat theme of Sher Khan's earlier reports continued in this assessment, even as he waited for the Indians' next moves.

INDIAN MOVES

India, meanwhile, had changed its military command for the region, bringing in Lieutenant General K.M. Cariappa[26] in January 1948 to take charge of Kashmir operations. The British commander of the Delhi and East Punjab command, Lieutenant General Sir Dudley Russell, was prohibited from entering the state because of the stand down order. One of Cariappa's moves was to change the name of his command to Western Command, despite the ribbing that its initials might provoke: WC!

Soon after taking over, Cariappa moved his operational headquarters from Delhi to Jammu to be closer to the action, a fact that was dutifully conveyed by the British high commissioner in New Delhi to the CRO in London after receiving the information directly from the army headquarters in India.[27] Soon after ensconcing his headquarters in the residency at Jammu, he began planning for offensive actions to build up on the success at Noashera. The main operations that he reviewed were:

- The recapture of Jhangar
- Advance from Noashera to Rajuari
- Advance to Bhimber, to secure his southern flank, and
- Advance from Uri to Domel.[28]

Given their similar training and knowledge of the terrain, it is not surprising that both the Indian and Pakistani commanders were exhibiting a good understanding of each other's capabilities and plans, almost like two sparring former partners entering the ring for a title fight.

But the weather turned bad and kept the Indian forces stuck at Noashera. The Pathankot–Jammu road was out of commission and even the Jammu airport could not be used. Cariappa decided to head out towards Srinagar through the Banihal Pass, hoping that the snow would soon melt, but he got stuck half way at Batot and had to return to Jammu. The only way out was a road that went from Jammu to Sialkot and then to India. Here occurred one of those bizarre incidents that have often surfaced in wars between Pakistan and India. Officially, India and Pakistan were still at peace. Cariappa asked his staff officer, Sinha, to telephone the general staff officer-1 (GSO-1) of his friend Major General Iftikhar Khan, who commanded the 8 Division in Lahore, to obtain permission to travel back to India via Sialkot and Lahore. Only a month earlier, Iftikhar had invited Cariappa to attend cavalry week in Lahore. The British GSO-1 was taken aback by Cariappa's request and promised to get back to him. Eventually the polite response came that Iftikhar was out of town and Begum Iftikhar 'was indisposed', so 'it would be awkward for them to receive General Cariappa at that time.' The weather held Cariappa prisoner in Jammu for some more weeks until mid-March when it cleared up enough for the Indian attack to be prepared against Jhangar.

The Indian plans to retake Jhangar called for the 19 Infantry Brigade under Brigadier Yadunath Singh to establish a bridgehead at Noashera and then for 50 Para Brigade under the Muslim Brigadier Usman to breakout for Jhangar. This brigade had been selected to avenge its 'defeat of December last.' Usman's Order of the Day concentrated on this aspect of the coming battle: 'I have complete confidence in you all to do your best to recapture the ground we lost on 24th December and to retrieve the honour of our arms.' Then citing from the epic poem 'Horatius' by Thomas Babington Lord Macaulay, (a poem which most missionary-school educated children in India and later in Pakistan had to memorize and still remember as 'Horatius at the Bridge') he wrote:

To every man upon this Earth,
Death cometh soon or late;
And how many can die better
Than facing fearful odds
For the ashes of his father (sic)
And the Temples of his Gods

So forward friends, fearless we go to Jhangar. India expects everyone to do his
duty.
Jai hind![29]

The attack on Jhangar was successful, commencing on 15 March with a
coordinated ground and air attack, and ending the next day.[30] The weather
turned for the better by the end of the month, ending the isolation of Srinagar.
Meanwhile, Kalwant Singh was preparing for the attack on Rajauri. As the 50
Para Brigade carried out a deception towards Kotli in the north, the 19
Infantry Brigade headed towards Rajauri, which was captured after a fierce
fight. Sinha describes evidence of what he called 'a general massacre of the
local non-Muslim population' by the defenders, evidence of which he says
was later shown to Dr Wenger of the International Red Cross.

Preparations then began for the summer offensive. First, the large Kashmir
force was split up into two divisions. The Srinagar Division or Sri Div (later
19 Division) was placed under Major General K.S. Thimayya,[31] a decorated
veteran of the Burma front (where he won the Distinguished Service Order),
while Major General Atma Singh was given command of the Ja (Jammu)
Division (later 26 Division) in the south.

The Pakistan Army was by then fully involved with the Kashmir war and
keeping close tabs on developments. Despite the ban on British officers taking
active part in hostilities between the two dominions, the new army chief,
General Gracey, prepared an appreciation of the Kashmir situation[32] for
delivery at Rawalpindi on 20 April 1948. He summed up the general military
situation in terms of the rapid build-up of the Indian forces in Kashmir. By
his count, India now had eight brigade groups, with supporting artillery,
armour, engineers, bombers, fighters, and transport aircraft in Jammu and
Kashmir.

GRACEY'S ANALYSIS

On 15 March, the Indian defence minister had told his country's constituent
assembly that the Indian Army would clear the raiders from Kashmir within
the next two or three months. The offensive had begun already with Rajauri
having been captured. 'This was followed by a reign of terror which included

burning villages, massacre of civilian population and other atrocities. Four thousand men are reported to have been victimized in this manner, and great panic and confusion prevails in the area,' wrote Gracey.[33] He expected the major offensive to begin shortly with Bhimber and Mirpur as its objectives, with a view to coming 'right upto the Pakistan border.'

Gracey feared that any such Indian moves and, given the recent ill effects on the civilian population in areas that India had recaptured, Pakistan may be faced with a 'big refugee problem...as the move into the RAJAURI area has already done.' In his view, Mangla headworks across the Jhelum River would be impossible to defend and if the Indians took Bhimber and Mirpur, they would 'have crossed the Ravi and Chenab rivers, and will be within striking distance of the JHELUM bridge, thus constituting a direct military threat to PAKISTAN.' He saw a similar refugee situation developing in the Poonch area to the south, with the Azad Forces unable to stop the massive Indian Army presence between Rajauri and Poonch. The result would be 'a drain on PAKISTAN's food and other resources.'

In the Kashmir valley itself, India was seen to be preparing for an offensive along the Srinagar-Baramula-Muzaffarabad road with a view to capture Muzaffarabad and Kohala. Again, Gracey saw the modern equipment and overwhelming superiority of Indian forces as well as their complete supremacy in the air as giving them 'a distinct advantage over the Azad Forces who are unlikely to be able to stand up to a heavy onslaught.' The military implications of such a move would be very bad for Pakistan, since capture of either Muzaffarabad or Kohala would mean that the Indians would have crossed the Jhelum River and 'will be knocking at the back door of Pakistan', posing 'a serious and a direct threat to Abbottabad, Rawalpindi, and ultimately Peshawar from the rear.' The refugee problem would be as bad as the expected one in Poonch.

On the political front, Gracey saw India making overtures to Khan Abdul Ghaffar Khan, the Pathan leader who was known as the Frontier Gandhi and was close to the Indian leadership. They had also started 'making overtures to the Fakir of Ipi, through Afghan authorities, and are known to be supplying him with funds to stir up widespread trouble in Waziristan.' Ghaffar Khan was reported to be sending messages to the Fakir of Ipi and both were seen as 'working in concert to overthrow the govt.' Afghanistan was also seen as getting encouragement and financial assistance from India to stir up trouble in the NWFP.

In sum, Gracey produced a set of far reaching recommendations that would only lead to one conclusion, the entry of the Pakistan Army into a state of war with the Indian Army in Kashmir:

If PAKISTAN is NOT to face another serious refugee problem of about 2¾ million people uprooted from their homes; if INDIA is NOT to be allowed to sit on the Doorsteps of PAKISTAN to the rear and on the flank at liberty to enter at her will and pleasure; if the civilian and military morale is NOT to be effected (sic) to a dangerous extent; and if subversive political forces are NOT to be encouraged and let loose within Pakistan itself, it is imperative that the Indian army is not allowed to advance beyond the general line URI-POONCH-NAUSHAHRA. If necessary, regular units of PAK ARMY must be employed to hold this line at all costs [author's emphasis added]. Technically, this might constitute a breach of international conventions but in the vital interest of the security of the country the risk should be accepted and it should be possible to justify this step before any impartial world tribunal.

In putting forward this blunt and very nationalistic assessment, Gracey was venting his own frustration with the half-hearted official support for the Kashmir effort and reflecting the views of some of his senior commanders, including the commander of 7 Division, Lt. Gen. Loftus Tottenham. The army was also not happy with the manner in which elements within the military high command were being used by the politicians to run this private war in Kashmir, knowing that in the end the defence of Pakistan would rest with the armed forces. As a contemporary lecture on higher planning[34] delivered at GHQ spelled out, there existed a number of mechanisms for formulation of national defence policy. These included the defence committee of the cabinet, the defence council, the joint services commanders committee and the joint services liaison committee. Yet, 'no government orders were issued' to the Pakistan Army to support the Kashmir war.

Indeed, the first policy indication the commander-in-chief received was towards the end of December 1947, two months after the operations had been in progress, and by which time India had already referred the matter to the UN Security Council. Even at that time, the army chief was told 'that he should help Azad Forces with material without unduly weakening the Pak[istan] Army. The government maintained that this action was permissible and quoted the example of America helping Great Britain with material when she was not a belligerent.' The second official policy directive from the government to the Pakistan Army on Kashmir came around the time that the Indians were preparing their offensive and the Security Council discussions were dragging on. 'The Primary task of the Pakistan Army,' it stated, 'is to be prepared to meet the aggression from India.'[35]

This was a tall order, since the Pakistan Army at that time had effectively only the 10 Division (with three fully committed brigades), 8 Division (with one brigade in Malir, far from the Kashmir front), 7 Division (with two brigades, one in Abbottabad and one in Rawalpindi), and the 9 (F) Division (a static division deployed in the Frontier region with three brigades). Loftus

Tottenham's 7 Division and the armoured brigade were the GHQ reserve. After much debate in the GHQ, the 7 Division was given the task of defending Pakistan. In reality, all it could do was adopt a policy of 'plugging the hole' wherever India broke through the Azad Forces. The senior brass at GHQ knew that this meant surrendering the initiative to the enemy, which no commander or troops like doing. It was only later in the summer when the Indians gained some momentum that the commander-in-chief 'had to gamble on completely turning his back on the N.W. Frontier and commit the whole of 9 (F) Div in Kashmir.'[36]

'GENERAL TARIQ'S' NEW ASSESSMENT

Unaware of the battles of ideas going on in the Pakistani GHQ and in the corridors of power, 'General Tariq' continued making his assessment and plans for the summer ahead.[37] He was fully aware of the Indian reinforcements that had streamed into Kashmir and also of the changes in command and the structure of forces in Kashmir. He expected 'a general offensive in the South and probably also in the valley in the next ten days', that is by the last week of May 1948. But his own assessment of the troops in Kashmir was less than ideal. 'On the whole, morale is reasonably good but [the troops] are tired, feeding has been difficult, [they] have tattered clothes [and they] are worried about the safety of their families [in Kashmir].' He suggested that political leaders and workers should 'get busy immediately to prepare them [soldiers and the general population in Azad Kashmir] for further sacrifices and strengthen their resistance.'

From the general build-up of the Indian forces, Tariq tried to gauge Indian intentions. He thought they would:

- Try to link up with Poonch 'at the earliest date', attacking from Uri, Jhangar (through Kotli), and also from the east, with the Uri thrust being the main effort.
- Attack against Bhimber from Akhnoor, with a supporting action from the direction of Noashera.

The Indian aim, according to General Tariq, would be 'to draw our forces away from the L of C [Line of Communication] of their forces operating towards Poonch.' If they succeeded in capturing Bhimber, the Azad Forces L of C to Noashera would be cut off. Once these two operations had succeeded, Tariq expected India to launch an attack against Muzaffarabad and Mirpur.

In the face of these expected actions, he saw Azad Forces as gaining ground or being in attacking formations in the north from Gilgit towards the valley, and also at Uri where the front was narrow, allowing the forces to hold out against Indian attacks. He was less sanguine about the ability to hold out in Poonch, where the local soldiers might leave with their families for the safety of Pakistan across the border. The country in the south was open and India was expected to use its tanks and field guns to good effect there, making a defence by the Azad Forces harder to sustain. Moreover, 'the Pathans who have fought extremely well and have been a great encouragement to the Azad Forces and a terror to the enemy are finding the heat too much. The heat is reducing their numbers and also their fighting efficiency.'

Summing up the situation, Tariq saw India building up for a military decision 'during the next six weeks' that is by the end of June 1948. Militarily, he thought the Azad Forces could prevent India from achieving this overall aim but warned that 'there may be some loss of territory.' At the political level, he asked for help from the leadership and workers in Kashmir to prepare for 'a last-ditch stand.'

The Indian offensive began in May, as expected, and before the onset of rains that would have made movement difficult. A strong Indian column, Brigadier Harbaksh's 163 Infantry Brigade, advanced from Handwara and captured Tithwal on 24 May. Another column, the 161 Brigade under Brigadier L.P. Sen, advanced from Uri along the main road to Muzaffarabad and reached Chakoti on 25 May, by which time it had come upon the first strong resistance in the shape of a Pakistan Army brigade comprising the 4/15 Punjab Machine Gun Regiment, 4/16 Punjab, 1/13 Frontier Force Rifles, and the 4/13 Frontier Force Rifles. Little did Sen know that the brigade commander facing him at Chakoti was none other than General Tariq, now back to his normal identity of Akbar Khan, whose brigade had been moved from Kohat to Kashmir for this defensive operation. The Indian advance came to a halt at Chakoti. Thimayya now decided to revise his approach and attempted to outflank Chakoti, giving Brigadier Nair's 77 Para Brigade the task of advancing in a right hook along the northern bank of the Jhelum River to the area behind Chakoti. The aim was to reach the objective Point 6065 by 31 May. Harbaksh was tasked to send a battalion from Tithwal towards Muzaffarabad. The aim was to pressure the Pakistani and Azad forces at Chakoti, allowing Sen to advance. The right hook failed because of logistical difficulties due to the bad terrain and lack of air supplies (Srinagar airport was shut down due to rains). The surprise element was lost and the operation was 'reluctantly' called off by Thimayya.[38]

Meanwhile, taking advantage of the remoteness of the northern reaches of the state, Azad Forces, using their established base in the Northern Areas, captured Kargil, Dras and a substantial portion of the Leh valley, isolating Leh in the process. However, these thrusts by the Azad Forces could not be sustained and the fear was that the entire territory that had been wrested from the maharaja's control could be overrun, creating a huge refugee problem. This would have had a serious affect on the economic life of Pakistan and placed Indian forces just across the major rivers and within easy striking distance of Pakistan's lifeline of roads and railways.

THE PAKISTAN ARMY JOINS THE BATTLE

To prevent the collapse of the Azad Forces in the face of the concentrated Indian attacks, Pakistan Army troops were sent into battle with General Gracey's instructions which stated that 'the Indian army is not [to be] allowed beyond the general line Uri-Poonch-Naushera.' They were to avoid, as far as possible, direct clashes with the Indian Army, and they were also to buttress the Azad Forces while preventing 'any sudden breakthrough to the Pakistan border by the Indians.'[39] At the same time, the Pakistan Army took over formal control of the war in Kashmir.

By mid-June, Indian forces advanced from Rajauri and finally managed to link up with Poonch on 23 June. But their attempt to link with the Uri–Poonch force was successfully halted by the Pakistan Army and Azad Forces. The following month, India managed to capture Gurais in the north. In the south, Azad troops drove out Indian forces from the Mendhar area and Poonch was again isolated. August rains brought about a lull in major operations. The Indian summer offensive had failed to achieve a major breakthrough.

General Gracey complained to his Indian counterpart and fellow Briton, General Bucher, 'that atrocities committed by Indian troops in Kashmir are causing large number of Kashmiri Muslims to take refuge in West Punjab.'[40] The British high commissioner in New Delhi reported to the CRO in London on 12 July, that 'General Bucher promised to inquire personally into this and, as a result of his visit to Jammu on 7 July, has sacked commander 268 Brigade, Brigadier Bikram Singh, and one brigade commander.'[41]

The United Nations had in the meantime agreed to send a special team to the subcontinent to investigate the situation in Kashmir and to try to prevent further hostilities. The UN Commission for India and Pakistan (UNCIP) under General Delvoie arrived soon after the Indian summer offensive had ended.[42] Pakistan, meanwhile, took the opportunity to straighten out its defensive lines. In the remote Northern Areas, Azad Forces finally wrested Skardu from the Indians after having laid siege to it since February 1948.

Meanwhile, India was not sitting idle. The western command began examining plans for a number of operations in the autumn. These included Operation 'DUCK' to recapture Kargil and thus link up with Leh, 'EASY' to link up with Poonch via Rajauri, 'CAMEL' to capture Hajipir Pass, 'SNOOK' to capture Bhimber, 'STEEL' to capture Kotli, 'CRAB' to capture Muzaffarabad, and 'BLOOD' to capture Mirpur. To effect these plans, Major General Shringaesh was promoted to lieutenant general and made corps commander of V Corps, which took over the tactical headquarters of the western command at Jammu in September 1948. Cariappa wanted to move to the offensive but did not wish to bring the army high command into the picture, particularly on Operation 'EASY'.[43] He concentrated his forces on the objective of linking up with Poonch, and managed to achieve that on 20 November 1948 after a hard fight, leading to the exodus of some 60,000 Muslim refugees from the region into Pakistan. In the north, India managed to regain control of Kargil by 22 November. By then, winter was upon the region and there was not much further Indian activity in the north. In the south, Pakistani forces had held up an Indian advance on the Kotli road.

LAST MOVES

The UN discussions were moving into high gear in the autumn and the Pakistan government was keen to wind up hostilities. But the military commanders were aching to take the Pakistan Army on the offensive rather than playing the largely defensive role they had so far assumed in Kashmir. Gracey came up with Operation 'Venus', designed to get control of the Beri Pattan road and of the Indian dumps in the region through which most of their supplies passed to Noashera, Poonch and Jhangar. A subsidiary plan, 'Little Venus', to capture the hills overlooking this area was vetoed by the cabinet in Karachi on the grounds that it would create political complications. Iskander Mirza approved the idea of Venus and gave it to the prime minister, arguing that it would not only allow Pakistan to capture Akhnoor but also allow them to destroy, or at least incapacitate, five Indian divisions.[44]

The prime minister sat on the plan for a week and then decided to go with the UN resolution instead. The Pakistan Army and the 7 Division decided to press ahead with Venus anyway. According to his then GSO Habibullah Khan Khattak (later lieutenant general), the commander of 7 Division, Loftus Tottenham, wanted to 'strengthen our position territorially before the order [for ceasefire] were received by the army.'[45] Habibullah was asked to proceed to the front. Loftus Tottenham told him: 'Habib, pressure is building on me to do nothing on our front.' The plan was that when Habibullah was told on the phone to abort Venus he was to pretend not to have heard what was said and proceed regardless. At the tactical headquarters near Qazi Baqar, Habibullah got a call from his division commander but the message was that the prime minister needed to speak to him. Having served as liaison officer to the prime minister, Habibullah knew him and so took the call. 'I distinctly remember the prime minister telling me: "Habibullah, we are getting Kashmir on a plate and if one Pakistani soldier is killed I would call it murder by you."' Habibullah retorted with: 'Sir, in human history how many territories have been given on a plate?' Nevertheless, Habibullah was asked to call off the attack.

Habibullah recalls calling 10 Brigade and 14 Para Brigade (under Sher Ali) to stand down. But 'some gunner officer told me that the guns were charged and could not be unloaded without firing. I telephoned the GOC and he said, 'Let the bastard have it!' Each gun fired the round in its breach and some medium guns fired extra rounds also.' The result was the blowing up of the India dump near the Beri Pattan bridge and damage to the bridge itself. The expected infantry attack that would have followed the artillery attack never materialized because of the government of Pakistan's instructions. Interestingly, Sinha, who as then a junior officer on the Indian side, notes in his later book on the Kashmir operation that this was a typical Pakistan Army action: artillery fire without infantry attacks!

Sher Ali has choice words for being asked to hold off on the overall plan that called for a surprise attack towards Jammu with his force and beyond to Pathankot and Gurdaspur. Such a move he felt would have put him in a position to threaten the flanks of any force that might have attacked Lahore. 'The surprise, of the concentration of so much force, was so complete that it caused panic in the Indian divisional headquarters and they abandoned their positions and the troops started for Jammu in haste. This caused panic in Jammu and the jail was broken and prisoners escaped,' writes Sher Ali.[46] He bemoans the political decision to accept the ceasefire at 23:59 hours on 1 January 1949 which, he believes, deprived Pakistan of the one chance of achieving a military breakthrough in Kashmir. Iskander Mirza too opposed the ceasefire and sought a time limit of three months for the ceasefire to prove its effectiveness in resolving the Kashmir problem. He was overruled by the prime minister.[47]

Two weeks after the ceasefire, on 15 January 1949, General Gracey and the new Indian army chief Cariappa met in New Delhi to give the ceasefire line a more formal status. The truce sub-committee at its later meeting on 12 March, agreed on the ceasefire line 'from Munawar in the south to the Jhelum in the north with the exception of certain disputed pockets like Aniwas, Pirkanthi and Ledigali. No agreement could be reached on a line beyond the Jhelum to Keran in the north and thence east to Ladakh valley.'[48] From that point, the Kashmir conflict slipped into a series of surreptitious advance patrols to gain local advantage, and the UN became part of the local scenery until the next major war of 1965.

However, the thinking in the GHQ at Rawalpindi had not paralleled the changes in the political field. Gracey, while adhering to the ceasefire instructions of his political masters, toyed with the idea of retrieving Kashmir militarily. He scribbled a note on his little scratch pad adorned with the simple words commander-in-chief on 1 October 1949 to that effect, ending with the words: Surprise in all its aspects and at all stages is vital. On 1 November he put on the same scratch pad a plan 'To infiltrate' but then scratched that out and put in its place the following:

> To capture and hold the Vale of Srinagar up to and incl. the BANIHAL Pass.
> Tps. [troops] Available
> Two Divisions
> Two Lt. Amd Recce Regts [regiments]
> One Mtn Regt.
> Two F. Regts.
> AK [Azad Kashmir] Forces and forces in Gilgit, Astore, Chitral, Baltistan.
> Tribesmen.
> RPAF [Royal Pakistan Air Force] until danger threatens Pakistan elsewhere, then spasmodic and uncertain.

Clearly, the Pakistan Army still felt it had not been allowed to complete the job. There was much rethinking of the campaign that had just ended. And this would continue for decades. Habibullah recalls that on 21 July 1947, soon after he had returned from Srinagar, he spoke to his next door neighbour Sher Khan in Rawalpindi, 'requesting him to smuggle one company of infantry strength into Srinagar to make the Srinagar airfield unusable by cutting the orchard trees surrounding the airfield. He [Sher Khan] laughed at my suggestions and assured me that GHQ had far better ideas than my unsophisticated plan.'[49]

WHY THE WAR FAILED

In retrospect, Pakistan's higher planning and leadership failed to clearly see the advantage of intervening in Kashmir and to gauge the Indian reactions in a manner that they could counter effectively. A guerrilla operation was launched without trained manpower to direct and control the tribals, and certainly without laying the ground for local support in the valley of Kashmir. It is not enough to dismiss the inhabitants as 'non-martial,' as Sher Khan did in his assessment. Later events in Kashmir in the 1990s were to prove that assumption wrong. Further, the military support from the Pakistan Army was severely constrained, with the political leadership unable to come to terms with the fact that they were in fact fighting a war. The leadership pretended that this was a minor operation and that the ultimate aim was to internationalize the Kashmir issue so that a ceasefire could come about and a plebiscite arranged. What is hard to understand in retrospect is why they continued with this point of view even after Indian troops were on the ground in Kashmir.

There was also a lack of bold and unorthodox thinking. Habibullah's idea or even Messervy's own idea of infiltrating trained soldiers into Srinagar to render the airfield useless, coupled with a concentrated attack by the Pakistan Army with adequate artillery and air support to cut the Jammu road, may have brought a checkmate to the Indian moves in Kashmir. Operation Venus, the final attempt to retrieve the situation, was too late and moreover, it was aborted on the orders of the prime minister.

The Kashmir war produced many after-effects. It further strengthened the view (among a coterie of officers) that Pakistan needed stronger central leadership. Akbar Khan and his friends who aided the informal Kashmir effort were to sow the seeds of discontent that later showed itself in the Rawalpindi Conspiracy Case. Despite Akbar Khan's disavowal of the action plan for this first attempted *coup d'etat* in Pakistan, it clearly marked the beginnings of Bonapartism in Pakistan's polity. The intellectual distance between the army and the politicians was heightened by the physical separation of the two: the political leadership in Karachi and the army in Rawalpindi, that too at a time when communication was more complicated and uncertain. This led to a greater autonomy of thought and action in the army leadership. A curious sidelight to the Kashmir war is that the eventual military leaders of the country that dominated its politics for the following two decades did not figure much in the military action. Ayub Khan's memoirs, *Friends not Masters*, skips the war entirely. He was involved in Operation Curzon and then sent off to East Pakistan in 1948. Musa was not among the front line commanders. Yahya was at Staff College in Quetta and then at the GHQ.

At the military level—as the assessment by General Loftus Tottenham of the Kashmir war indicated—there was no central command set up to manage the Kashmir war.[50] 'The Kashmir war was queer in that it was fought under certain restrictions—the attitude was and had to be—you can hit them so hard but NOT too hard, otherwise there will be all kinds of repercussions.' It also had its strange moments. The Indians, for example, who were using the same radios as the Pakistanis to transmit operational orders to their troops in the field, began sending out messages that were meant to mislead the Pakistani forces which were tapping into the Indian networks. According to Tottenham, given the few choices of actions available to both sides, once the Pakistani forces knew what the Indians were not going to do, they could deduce what their real intentions were and often were ready for whatever moves the Indians made! It was an almost amateur affair run largely by relatively inexperienced officers with a boy scout enthusiasm, many of whom may have been too deep over their heads. As General Musa recalls in his own memoirs, senior military officers were not kept informed of developments.

Brigadiers Nazir and Iftikhar for example, who were among the senior most Pakistani officers and major generals soon after partition, were kept in the dark and asked Musa what was happening.[51]

In contrast, at the local and tactical level, the Kashmir war was marked by numerous instances of unorthodox thinking and bravery on the part of junior officers and men on both sides of the conflict. On the Pakistani side, the capture of Pandu and Chunj, for example, were two remarkable actions where individual soldiers and officers took it upon themselves to attack strongly held positions and managed to carry heavy artillery pieces, bit by bit, near the top to assemble them in higher altitudes and thus surprise defenders. Among the newly promoted officers to command positions, Brigadier Hayauddin, who had earlier won himself a Military Cross and then been given the honour of Member of the British Empire (MBE) during the Second World War, led his artillery in daring actions that prevented the Indian attack on Poonch from breaking through in February 1948. His commanding general, Loftus Tottenham, recommended him for the Hilal-e-Juraat, the Pakistani equivalent of the Distinguished Service Order.[52] But at the national level, the army felt betrayed by an indifferent and weak political leadership. It was not surprising that many junior officers felt a sense of betrayal by the higher command when the conflict ended in a stalemate.

In the absence of higher-level planning and of the involvement of the senior commanders of the army in the early stages of the Kashmir war, there was no coordination of the political and military actions. For example, while the prime minister and the very able foreign minister, Sir M. Zafrulla Khan, were trying to make a case for plebiscite in Kashmir, the only troops in action on the ground were locals in the Poonch area with light weapons, supplemented by tribal forces of indeterminate and inconsistent quality, also armed with poor weapons. Putting in the regular army into action, as India did on its side, might have righted the balance and allowed Pakistan to take advantage of its road access from Rawalpindi in the west into the heart of Kashmir.

The Pakistan Air Force played almost no role in the action, giving the Indian Air Force supremacy in the region. The Azad Kashmiri and Pakistani efforts were further hampered by the serious constraints imposed on the military when they were deployed. The army units were ordered to take a defensive posture to the extent possible, with the aim of buying time for the politicians to get a solution on the negotiating table at the United Nations.

Military planners were further hamstrung by the politicians' fears that there might be a full-scale war between India and Pakistan if Pakistan were to press its advantage in the area of Jammu and Kashmir bordering on Sialkot in the south. The situation on the ground did not support this eventuality. The Indian Army was as unprepared for a full scale war as Pakistan. Further, the boundary force, with British, Indian, and Pakistani officers and troops, was still situated in the Punjab. If anything, the threat of an all-out war might have provoked direct and immediate international attention and action. Pakistan had the advantage of surprise in the first few days of the war and might have achieved some success in cutting off Srinagar airport had it relied on its regular troops rather than the rag tag bunch of tribals. Similarly, it could have effectively routed the State forces that were in poor fighting readiness in the south and cut off communications between India and the valley, something that was left to be tried till late into the war. Pulling the plug on Operation Venus—the one daring move by the Pakistani forces—near the end of the war epitomized the thinking on the part of the prime minister and his advisers. If anything, given that Pakistan had limited reserves of arms and ammunitions, it could have tried to put them to maximum effect with a plan for a short, sharp conflict rather than going for a slowly progressing conflict on the ground while trying to seek a diplomatic victory in the United Nations.

The end result was an unfinished war that contributed to the political instability of Pakistan. The unhappiness with the ponderous and meandering decision-making of the politicians led to tensions—some overt, others hidden—between the military and the politicians. This internal conflict fuelled the eventual expansion of military influence in Pakistan and created a serious imbalance between military and political decision-making in the fledgling nation. Kashmir became both a reason for not allowing a democratic polity to emerge and a massive financial haemorrhage for the new nation state. It was to become the cornerstone of Pakistan's foreign policy and domestic politics for decades, as civilian and military leaders struggled to keep the issue alive enough to further their own careers. In the process, the Kashmiri people were soon a forgotten part of the trilateral equation and were not able to play a role until the 1990s.

NOTES

1. C. Dasgupta, *War and Diplomacy in Kashmir, 1947–48* (New Delhi: Sage Publications, 2002), p. 37.
2. Pakistan Army GHQ (Restricted), *The Kashmir Campaign 1947*, Pakistan Army GHQ.
3. See also Alastair Lamb, *Kashmir: A Disputed Legacy 1846–1990* (Roxford Books, UK 1991 and Oxford University Press, Pakistan 1992), pp. 124–125.
4. Akbar Khan, *Raiders in Kashmir: Story of the Kashmir War, 1947–48* (Pak Publishers, 1970), pp. 11–18.
5. In his book, Akbar refers to Sher Khan as 'Brigadier and Director of Military Intelligence', a rank and title that Sher Khan did not posses at the time of these activities.
6. Lars Blinkenberg, *India and Pakistan: The History of Unsolved Conflicts* (Copenhagen and Arhus, Denmark: Dansk Undensrigkppolitik Institut, 1972), pp. 82–83.
7. Akbar Khan does not give any specific dates for his meetings with the prime minister and others.

8. Pakistan GHQ archives Number 1497/60/CI (ii) Appreciation of the Present Situation and Possible Development (sic) in Kashmir, 10 October 1947 by Colonel M. Sher Khan, DDMI.

9. Pakistan Army GHQ (Restricted), *The Kashmir Campaign 1947*, Pakistan Army GHQ.

10. Ian Campbell-Johnson, *Mission with Mountbatten* (New York: Atheneum, 1985), p. 224.

11. Dasgupta, (*War*, p. 43) relying on the Mountbatten Papers refers to this telegram as emanating from the commander-in-chief of the Pakistan Army, Lt. Gen. Sir Douglas Gracey. At that time, however, Gracey was the chief of general staff and acting in Messervy's absence. Messervy was the army chief. Campbell-Johnson does not identify the author of the telegram.

12. Ibid., p. 42.

13. *The Official History of the Operations in Jammu and Kashmir*, published by the Ministry of Defence of India in 1987 gives details of the first flights on 27 October that total 464 soldiers and officers transported to Srinagar, p. 28.

14. Lt. Gen. S.K. Sinha, *Operation Rescue* (New Delhi: Vision Books, 1977), p. 22.

15. Lt. Gen. L.P. Sen, *Slender was the Thread: Kashmir Confrontation 1947–48.* (Orient Longman 1969), p. 84.

16. Sinha, *Operation*, p. 17.

17. Sher Ali Khan (aka Sher Ali Pataudi), *The Story of Soldiering and Politics in India and Pakistan* (Lahore: al Kitab, 1983).

18. Ibid., pp. 116–117.

19. Sen, *Slender*, pp. 103–104. 'Bogey' Sen was the acting brigade commander of 161 Brigade of the Indian Army that defended Srinagar and fought its way to Baramula.

20. Hand corrected typewritten draft in Pakistan Army GHQ archives.

21. Sinha *Operation*, p. 57.

22. Brigadier M. Sher Khan, secret and personal note of 19 February 1948, to the prime minister, carried by hand by Sardar Shaukat Hayat Khan to Karachi. Pakistan GHQ archives.

23. 494 MilSit, UK High Commissioner to CRO, 28 February 1948. Public Records Office, Surrey, UK.

24. An analysis of the Kashmir situation by Sher Khan under the *nom de guerre* 'General Tariq', 5 April 1948. Pakistan Army GHQ, Rawalpindi archives. All quotations in this section are based on this source.

25. Writing about the 'Punch' [Poonch] operations, Lt. Gen. Russell stated that: 'It is really in the tribesmen's best interest to use their normal tribal that is, dispersal tactics. In the Kashmir Valley, they tried to fight like regular troops. They gave us a good target, a solid objective and were completely thwarted. In future, they will eschew open country.' He thought that the tribesman was 'far more difficult to deal with, when he is playing his own guerrilla game in the hills and this is the game I see him playing in Punch, in strength and continuously. Should he do this, we would be landed with a permanent frontier commitment, which I might describe as **a running sore** (emphasis added), requiring us to lock up a large and increasing number of troops, from which we will get very few tangible results.' Cited in Sinha, op. cit., pp. 42–43.

26. Later general and then field marshal and chief of army staff of India.

27. In addition to regular oral briefings or conversations that the Indian chief of general staff and other senior officers had with the UK high commissioner, the CGS routinely forwarded cyclostyled copies of the latest reports on the Kashmir War from the AHQ (I) Military Intelligence Directorate, signed by Brigadier Chand Das, whose own removal eventually and replacement by Brigadier Dubey also made the news reports to the CRO. Originals of these reports with the compliments slip from the CGS, India are in the PRO, Surrey, UK.

28. Sinha, *Operation*, pp. 57–58.

29. Sinha, *Operation*, pp. 61–62. This poem is better known to all who memorized it in school as Macaulay's 'Horatius at the Bridge'. Usman or Sinha clearly took some liberty with the

words and the line structure of the fourth stanza of this epic poem which runs as follows in the original version: 'Then out spoke brave Horatius, the Captain of the Gate: "To every man upon this earth Death cometh soon or late./And how can man die better than facing fearful odds,/For the ashes of his fathers, and the temples of his Gods". Brigadier Usman was killed by an artillery shell near Jhangar later on in the war and was given a state funeral in New Delhi.

30. A timeline produced by GHQ Pakistan Army shows Jhangar being captured 18 March after 'fourteen days fighting.'

31. Thimayya, known to all officers as Timmy (though the JCOs and soldiers called him Timmy Sahib) was later to become general and chief of army staff.

32. Document No: 2014/58/DMO, Pakistan Army GHQ, Rawalpindi archives.

33. Ibid.

34. Document in Pakistan Army GHQ archives. No additional indexing information available. This section is based on material from this document.

35. Ibid.

36. Ibid.

37. Situation report on the Kashmir situation, 17 May 1948, Pakistan Army GHQ, Rawalpindi, archives.

38. Sen, *Slender*, pp. 72–75.

39. Akbar Khan, *Raiders*, p. 101.

40. Document in Public Records Office, Surrey, UK.

41. Ibid.

42. For details of the history of the war and the UN role in the conflict see *Danger in Kashmir* by Josef Korbel (the father of former US Secretary of State Madeleine Albright), (Princeton University Press 1954 and 1966) and Lars Blingenberg, *India and Pakistan: The History of Unsolved Conflicts* (Copenhagen and Arhus, Denmark: Dansk Undensrigkppolitik Institut, 1972).

43. As indicated above, my research into the archives at the Public Records Office in Surrey, UK indicated that routinely all operational reports were being copied and sent by courier from Indian Army headquarters to the British high commission. A complimentary slip was attached to each report.

44. Humayun Mirza, *From Plassey to Pakistan: The Family History of Iskander Mirza, the First President of Pakistan* (Lanham, New York, and Oxford: University Press of America Inc., 1999), p. 163.

45. Lt. Gen. (retd) Habibullah Khan Khattak, 'The First Kashmir War: The Untold Story,' *The News*, Lahore, Friday, 12 July 1991.

46. Sher Ali, *The Story*, p. 119.

47. Mirza, *From Plassey*, p. 163.

48. Sinha, *Operation*, p. 134.

49. Khan, *The News*, 12 July 1991.

50. Lessons of Kashmir campaign by Comd 7 Div, File No K/18/Hist Sec, GHQ Pakistan Army archives

51. General M. Musa, *Jawan to General: Recollections of a Pakistani Soldier* (New Delhi, 1985), quoted in *Operations in Jammu and Kashmir*, published by the Ministry of Defence of India in 1987.

52. Information confirmed by his son, Asad Hayauddin. Hayauddin, known to all his friends as 'Gunga' (after the movie *Gunga Din*), a Sandhurst-commissioned officer was PA 18, that is the 18th senior-most Pakistani at partition and later commanded Pakistani troops in the orderly withdrawal from the NWFP's border areas under Operation Curzon.

THE LEGACY OF CONFLICT:
CHAOS AND AMBITIONS

I have no spur
To prick the sides of my intent, but only
Vaulting ambition, which o'erleaps itself
And falls on th'other

– William Shakespeare, *Macbeth* Act 1, Scene 7, 25–28

As the Kashmir war continued to be fought in the corridors of the United Nations, Pakistan lost its first soldier: Mohammad Ali Jinnah, passed away on 11 September 1948 from medical complications on his way back to Karachi from Ziarat, Balochistan. (Jinnah had been suffering from tuberculosis for some time.) He left behind a house divided and rudderless. Jinnah had so dominated the political scene in India and Pakistan that he had few equals to carry forward his mission. His first Prime Minister Liaquat Ali Khan, a portly and gentlemanly lawyer with a soft demeanour and the look of a schoolboy with his round wire-rimmed spectacles, was not quite ready for the cut and thrust of emerging politics in the country and specially the machinations of the provincial chieftains who saw little of the national picture and were blinded by their own ambitions and parochial concerns. Jinnah had not allowed him to acquire the strength of his position during the short period that the two worked together after independence. After Jinnah's death, Liaquat engineered the choice of an East Pakistani, Khwaja Nazimuddin, as the governor general, another kindly but largely ineffective soul. But he retained for himself the presidency of the Muslim League while supporting another East Pakistani, Maulvi Tamizuddin, as the president of the constituent assembly that was charged with providing a constitution for the new state.

Liaquat tried his best to pull the nation together, to ensure that the international negotiations on Kashmir did not roll back whatever gains Pakistan had made towards making it a part of the new state. In this quest, he relied heavily on the erstwhile rulers, the British, on the one hand and the emerging superpower, the United States on the other. At the United Nations, the United Kingdom was being seen as supporting the Pakistani point of view, because—according to one Indian scholar—of the efforts of Noel Baker.[1] Meanwhile, behind the scenes the United States, which had pressured the United Kingdom to accelerate the divestiture of its imperial holdings (especially India), pushed for UN resolutions seeking a plebiscite. Liaquat also looked to the other side of the post-war divide, to the Soviet Union, for support. But when push came to shove, he opted for the Western alliance over the Soviets, giving the Americans the impression that he was cancelling a trip to Moscow in favour of one to the United States.[2]

To continue the military struggle, Liaquat sought economic aid and arms from both Britain and the United States, while stressing the message of democracy that Jinnah had espoused. He attempted to draw parallels between the United States and Pakistan during his first visit to the country, while trying to rely on Britain to make up for the lost materiel that Pakistan should have acquired after partition from India but did not.

At home, Liaquat faced the continuing scourge of provincialism that Jinnah had tried to fight even as he struggled to stay alive himself. Speaking to an East Pakistani audience in Dacca (now Dhaka) on 21 March 1948, Jinnah had stated that:

> You belong to a nation now; you have now carved out a territory, vast territory, it is all yours; it does not belong to a Punjabi or a Sindhi, or a Pathan, or a Bengali; it is yours. You have your central government where several units are represented. Therefore, if you want to build yourself into a nation, for God's sake give up this provincialism.[3]

POLITICAL ROT SETS IN

But Jinnah's words fell on closed ears and minds, as provincialism took hold and factional politics rather than transnational political leadership held sway. The Punjab—which had always been the hotbed of internecine political warfare, enough to exasperate Jinnah during his campaign for Pakistan—in the days after partition,[4] it fell into trench warfare of the worst kind with a clash of ambitions that pitted Mumtaz Daultana against the chief minister, the Khan of Mamdot. Sardar Shaukat Hayat Khan, a latecomer to the Pakistan Movement, had joined the Muslim League government in the Punjab as the revenue minister. But the League was starting to fracture as it struggled to make the difficult transition from a movement for freedom to a ruling party. Soon Hayat and Daultana quit the Punjab government. Mamdot tried to cobble together a new coalition but fresh squabbling prevented the government from functioning and it was soon dismissed. Citing 'the failure of the members of the legislative assembly elected in different circumstances to rise to the greater responsibility which Independence brings', the governor general imposed governor's rule on the province. The political rot had begun.

Similar fissures emerged in the other provinces. The NWFP, where the Muslim League had established a strong position at the time of partition, (in large part due to the strength of Chief Minister Khan Abdul Qayyum Khan and the commissioner in Peshawar, Iskander Mirza,) witnessed clashes between the ruling party and the losing Red Shirts of the separatist leader Khan Abdul Ghaffar Khan. Apart from this political conflict, the autocratic style of Qayyum and his use and condoning of 'jobbery, bribery, and nepotism' that had drawn even the attention of an angry Jinnah,[5] led to a ceaseless battle for control of the province.

Political warfare in Sindh had earlier led to the dismissal of the powerful chief minister, Ayub Khuhro, in April 1948 after frequent clashes between him and Governor Ghulam Hussain Hidayatullah. The motive force behind this action was Jinnah. A judicial inquiry found Khuhro guilty of a number of charges relating to poor administration and misconduct. But the wily Khuhro got himself elected president of the Sindh Muslim League even while he was still being tried. This prompted the enactment of the Public and Representative Offices (Disqualification) Act, or PRODA, which disqualified a person from politics if they had been found guilty of misconduct. This was the first of many such acts that subsequent governments used to eliminate troublesome opponents. But Khuhro's departure did not mean the end of troubles in Sindh, as his successor Ilahi Bux was also removed shortly after assuming office and succeeded by Yusuf Haroon. The political sniping continued, enough to provoke governor's rule in Sindh as well. Balochistan continued to be ruled from the centre, thus papering over whatever dissension lingered there.

The only province that had any semblance of normal political activity was East Pakistan, though even there the rumblings of discord were being heard. Khwaja Nazimuddin had been succeeded by Nurul Amin in the province as chief minister, who was able to maintain things on an even keel though a number of major figures (Maulana Bhashani, among them) jumped into the opposition. And Huseyn Shaheed Suhrawardy returned from exile in Calcutta to join the ranks of the opposition not only in East Pakistan but also as part of a broader coalition that drew Mamdot and others in West Pakistan.

In brief, the Muslim League was unravelling. As Muhammad Ali commented on its membership:

> The pillars of society, the landlords, the well-to-do lawyers, the rich businessmen, and the titled gentry, were its main support. With some exceptions, they were not men noted for their total commitment to any cause. Their willingness to sacrifice their personal interests or comfort for the sake of the nation was often in doubt, and not unjustly.[6]

Jinnah had managed to draw into the fold the masses and the middle class in the struggle for freedom but once Pakistan was achieved, the ruling cliques of the League fell back into its old ways, and factionalism ruled the day. Provincial leaders paid little heed to the needs of the nation as a whole, becoming warlords who negotiated with the central command to gain benefits for themselves and their cohorts.

LIAQUAT BUILDS UP ARMY

Against this background, Liaquat attempted to build up the armed forces of his new nation. The Pakistan Army had tasted war in its first few months of independence, seen the civilian decision-making up close, and found it wanting. The army though was still an amalgam of British and Pakistani officers with the latter slowly taking over responsible positions. Many of the promotions were engineered by the senior British officers. Messervy, the first commander-in-chief, and after him Gracey, had a say in most of the postings and promotions and applied rigorous standards that were often not to the liking of the individuals affected by them. They had little patience for the officers who exhibited strong political leanings. Akbar Khan was one such officer who was indeed initially passed over for promotion to major general but then restored. He was promoted to CGS in 1950. Akbar and others who were promoted in those early days were often accelerated to higher levels, often well before they had the experience or the *gravitas* for command. In retrospect, Ayub Khan saw the birth of Bonapartist tendencies in the officer corps in the early years of Pakistan with young men wearing high ranks and thinking that they had the wherewithal to run the country.

Ayub Khan himself was also superseded and sent as a brigadier to East Pakistan where he took over command of the provincial troops with the local rank of major general.[7] According to Sher Ali Khan, Ayub approached him to speak with his friend Messervy, who assured Sher Ali that he would decide all such cases entirely on merit.[8] 'He then said that correct selection and promotion at this time would mean the correct man for the top job when the British had all gone,' recalls Sher Ali. Ayub felt that Messervy and his deputy, Gracey, did not like him.

FIRST PAKISTANI CHIEF

As Gracey prepared to bow out, preparations were under way to prepare a successor from among the ranks of the Pakistani senior officers. Major General Iftikhar Khan, who was previously junior to Ayub, having been commissioned as an officer a year later than Ayub, and who commanded troops in Lahore as a major general was seen as the most likely to be the first Pakistani army chief. To equip him for this task, Iftikhar was asked to proceed to the Imperial Defence Course in the UK. Accompanying him was the other rising star, Sher Khan, who had commanded the Kashmir operations as 'General Tariq' after Akbar Khan. But fate intervened, as it has so many times in Pakistani history. Iftikhar, his wife and son, and Sher Khan were among the passengers of a Pak Air aircraft that crashed at Jungshahi near Karachi. There were no survivors.

Suddenly the nomination of the first native Pakistani army chief was thrown wide open. Liaquat, who did not know all the senior commanders personally, invited the senior-most officers to a conference in Rawalpindi so he could better assess them and their thinking. He is reported also to have had some interviews with the more senior among them and asked some of them to speak on the current issues facing Pakistan. According to General Burki,[9] Ayub Khan made a fine presentation in the meeting at Circuit House. Ayub was a tall and very impressive looking man and exhibited great confidence. He was also a quick study and able to grasp rapidly the critical details of an emerging situation. Liaquat was sold on him as the first Pakistani commander-in-chief, apparently without bringing into account any regional or other considerations. The ever-dutiful Gracey then proceeded to write his final annual confidential report on Ayub Khan on 15 January 1951, clearing him for promotion to the rank of commander-in chief of the Pakistan Army two days later.[10]

Earlier, Gracey had sorted out another issue: Ayub's relative seniority within the ranks of the senior officers of the army. Given that Ayub had been sent to East Pakistan as a local major general, he was effectively superseded by others. Gracey cleared up that situation with a handwritten note on his commander-in-chief letterhead that was sent to Ayub Khan 'c/o Khwaja Mohd Khan, Bus Stand, Haripur, Hazara'—we assume it was meant for onward delivery to Ayub Khan at his village of Rehana, near Haripur. A footnote by Gracey to the MS (military secretary, responsible for postings and promotions etc) states: 'Gen. Ayub Khan to see this and initial as seen.' The note reads as follows:

> In case of any misunderstanding Brigadier (local Major General) Ayub Khan, when promoted to Major General, will be antedated to the date of his local Major General i.e. to the end of January [A superscript inserted '8 January' here], and NEXT below Maj. General IFTIKHAR KHAN, and next above Major General Nasir Ali Khan.

This establishes the fact that Iftikhar Khan was seen as senior in order of rank to Ayub Khan. The latter, in his official memoir *Friends not Masters*, however, challenges the fact that Iftikhar had been designated army chief before his death. He refers to the divisional commanders conference in Rawalpindi and a meeting with Liaquat Ali Khan at Circuit House where Liaquat raised the issue of the next army chief stating that it might not necessarily be the senior-most officer. He asked for views. Ayub recalls stating: 'Our drill is simple and clear, as army officers we serve to the best of our ability and leave the judgement (sic) to our superiors. Whatever the decision they take, whether we like it or not, we must accept it. And if somebody is not prepared to accept that decision, he should get the hell out of the army.'[11] While the general sentiments of this statement appear to be in line with his thinking, it is doubtful that Ayub would have taken such a firm stand and used the language of his last sentence at that stage in his career and in front of an iconic leader like Liaquat.

He further writes that: 'There was a great deal of talk about General Iftikhar, a good officer; there was a general impression that the British were backing him.' But then he adds a churlish comment, that 'Iftikhar was a difficult man to get along with, and he was short-tempered. I do not know how he would have done as commander-in-chief but I am certain he would have met with considerable difficulty.'[12] Ayub recalls that after he was brought back to GHQ as adjutant general and talk heated up about the next army chief, he proceeded to go on leave into the hills at Changlagali, an hour's drive from Rawalpindi. There he was called by someone from the Ministry of Defence on a September night in 1950 and was told that he was to be the next chief and appointed as deputy chief to Gracey, who 'took the announcement in very good part,' according to Ayub. Yet, on his part, Ayub held a grudge against Gracey for many years, even discouraging the retired Gracey from visiting Pakistan as a director of the Attock Oil Company.[13]

Sher Ali Khan, who was later superseded for promotion to COS by Ayub Khan, makes an argument that Ayub is not telling the whole truth by skirting over his own knowledge of the appointment of Iftikhar as the C-in-C designate. Sher Ali states that the day the prime minister informed Iftikhar about his selection, Sher Ali was with him in Lahore. 'He [Iftikhar] told me about it. Ayub Khan was also in Lahore and as usual staying in my father-in-law's house.... He came up to me and asked for me to arrange to meet Ifti. He said he was to be our commander-in chief, and he had never really met him, which he would like to, before he went.' Sher Ali failed to set up this meeting. So, Ayub must have known about this appointment and did not know Iftikhar Khan well.

Sher Ali's assessment of Iftikhar is one of a 'very shy person, which gave the impression of his being a conceited person, which he wasn't. He was well read, and a highly intelligent and wise man. After his interview with the PM…he was quite worried. He discussed the danger of the politicians using the army for their own ends and in the name of the country. In fact he once said to me that it would be better if we both got out before our hands were stained and garments polluted.'[14] This was the man who could have led the Pakistan Army as the first native chief.

An interesting footnote on the choice of Ayub Khan is provided by General Burki. He had gone to stay in Swat as a guest of the Wali (the ruler of the state). Burki states: 'The Wali of Swat mentioned that Sikander Mirza (sic), who was Secretary of Defence at the time, told him that it was a question of choosing a one-eyed man out of a number of blind men (*annan cho kana* [in Punjabi]). Sikandar Mirza was jealous.'[15]

ENTER AYUB KHAN, FACING A CONSPIRACY

Given the situation and the circumstances facing the Pakistan Army, Ayub seems to have been the right choice. He was not an extrovert but a man with a presence who affected others around him with his willingness to work very hard and to think equally hard when faced with issues. Ayub never forgot his humble roots and often returned to his village of Rehana, especially to see his mother. Many around him believed that his mother's prayers saw him through many difficulties. He assiduously cultivated the habit of reading. And he wrote his diary regularly, an old British Indian Army habit. But he was not the caricature of the British officer that many others in the Indian Army and the Pakistan Army had become. Generally quiet and unassuming, he did not exhibit great airs. He was a good listener and managed to make and retain a wide range of friends, who remained loyal to him. He liked to have his drinks, by himself or with chosen friends. And he loved to hunt, especially duck. He gathered around him colleagues whom he felt comfortable with and also who did not challenge him. But he was also astute and gradually exhibited all the qualities of a political soldier that he had to be under the circumstances, unwittingly providing a role model for many others that followed him.

Ayub Khan thus entered the national scene on 17 January 1951 as a deserving though accidental army chief at a critical time in the nation's history and was instrumental in charting the country's course indirectly or directly for the next eighteen years. Little did he know at that point of the turbulent times ahead. During the handing over of command from Gracey to Ayub, Gracey had remarked on the possibility of some Young Turks in the army that Ayub should keep an eye on. He mentioned Akbar Khan specifically but, according to Ayub, did not go into more detail.

Yet, Ayub Khan in his reshuffling of responsibilities after taking over as the new army chief, agreed with Gracey to the promotion of Akbar to major general and gave him the key slot of CGS, the effective coordinator in GHQ of all the field formations and the voice of the commander-in-chief in all operational matters. Ayub justifies this move with hindsight thus: 'I knew of his ambition, of his family background, and also of his political leanings....I decided to post him to General Headquarters as Chief of General Staff, I did this to ensure that he remained under my eye and also not in direct command of troops.' A surprising statement, given that there were many other jobs at

GHQ where Akbar might have been kept under surveillance and yet made ineffective.[16]

Within a matter of months, Ayub was to learn from Prime Minister Liaquat Ali Khan that a conspiracy had been uncovered by the NWFP government under which a group of army officers and others were planning to overthrow the government and install a military-style nationalistic government. Liaquat called Ayub to the Sargodha railway station during the middle of an electioneering campaign to break this news to Ayub and Iskander Mirza. Ayub then launched his own inquiry. On 9 March 1951, Liaquat informed the country from Lahore of the plot that was henceforth to be known as the Rawalpindi Conspiracy. He announced the arrests of Akbar Khan, Brigadier Muhammad Abdul Latif Khan, and Faiz Ahmed Faiz, the editor of *The Pakistan Times* (Lahore), and Mrs Nasim Akbar Khan. Other military officers who were implicated included the senior-most Pakistani air force officer Air Commodore M.K. Janjua, Maj. Gen. Nazir Ahmed, Brigadier Sadiq Khan, Lt. Col. Ziauddin, Lt. Col. Niaz Mohammed Arbab, Captain Khizar Hayat, Major Hassan Khan, Major Ishaq Muhammad, and Captain Zafarullah Poshni. In addition, the accused included Muhammad Husain Ata, the secretary of the provincial communist party of the NWFP and Syed Sajjad Zaheer, an Indian Muslim who was operating underground in Pakistan to help set up the communist party of Pakistan. Two others who were involved with the conspiracy became approvers or turned state witnesses: Lt. Col. M.M. Siddique Raja (who had served with Ayub Khan in his regiment 1/14 Punjab) and Major Khwaja M. Eusoph Sethi.[17]

A significant linking factor of the co-conspirators was their involvement with the Kashmir conflict. Akbar had used a number of them as his contacts during that conflict and tried to induct others into the plot. Among those that he failed to win over were the two friends, Habibullah and Gul Mawaz Khan (his name is spelt Mowaz in the documents). Indeed, Habibullah was asked by Ayub to provide a detailed account of what the latter had learned. This statement that was delivered to Ayub on 4 March carried the rather droll and misleading title of *Duffer's Drift*, a celebrated slim volume that all army officers were encouraged to read.[18] Habibullah used this opportunity to paint himself as a patriotic individual who was trying to control Akbar Khan's machinations even while meeting him during the conspiracy phase.

As the case unfolded it became clear that the roots of the unhappiness that fuelled the conspiracy lay in the abortive attempt to win over Kashmir through military means. Akbar felt that the civilians had let the country down and that the presence of British officers in senior slots in the Pakistan Army was a hindrance to a nationalistic view of things. Others, including Major Ishaq, Ziauddin, and Sadiq Khan, felt that the ceasefire in Kashmir had prevented Pakistan from liberating Kashmir. A view from London indicated that the US Assistant Secretary of State for the region, George C. McGhee, found the cause of the conspiracy to be based 'largely in the personality of Gen. Akbar Khan, whose ego had been played upon.'[19]

In the process of gathering evidence and presenting it at the trial, it became clear that Akbar had approached the communist party membership for support even though he appeared to regard the Soviet Union as a potential threat to the new country. But some communist party members, such as Eric Cyprian, a professor of English at the Government College, Lahore, testified that the party was reluctant to be involved in such an adventure. The circumstantial evidence also indicated that Habibullah Khan may have also harboured ambitions of taking over government and had played along with Akbar Khan, although his later reports to Ayub and testimony painted him in a different light. It was clear that there was rising resentment within the newly promoted senior Pakistanis in the army against the British commanders and suspicions that these commanders had British interest more at heart than those of Pakistan, especially in the matter of the conduct of the Kashmir war. A number of them—Latif, Habibullah, and Gul Mawaz,—also regarded themselves as better soldiers than Ayub and potentially more suited to command than Ayub. The fact that Habibullah and Gul Mawaz were good friends also created further tensions between them and Ayub.

The conspiracy trial ended with convictions and substantial jail sentences for most of the accused but had exposed the fault lines within the military establishment on the one hand and between elements in the army and the civilian government on the other. (Yet, in 1955, all the accused were released after their sentences were commuted. Akbar returned as a minister of state for defence in the first Bhutto government.) Liaquat Ali Khan, meanwhile, was trying his best to resolve the splits within the Muslim League in the provinces and attempting to control their governments from a weakened centre. It appears that this prevented him from concentrating efforts on producing a constitution for Pakistan that might have helped him in the quest for provincial stability. In this process, he appears to have ceded the work on the constitution to the bureaucrats who gained an ascendant position in the hierarchy, allowing them to prepare to enter the political arena over the next few years. Political systems abhor vacuums much like the laws of physics. A weak and dithering central authority gave both the bureaucrats and the Pakistan Army a chance to assert their role in shaping policy nationwide.

CONFLICTS WITHIN

Contributing to the precariousness of Liaquat's position was the opposition that was emerging in the armed forces on the one hand and the recrudescence of the Punjabi landlords and political caretakers on the other. A number of Punjabi politicians saw Liaquat as weak, ineffective, and lacking a strong political base in Pakistan. To some extent this was true. Liaquat owed his position to Jinnah and his own role in pre-partition India as a representative of the upper crust of the Muslims of India. However, he was an outsider in Pakistan where a battle was brewing between the provincial 'insiders'—those who belonged to the four provinces that formed Pakistan—and the *muhajir* 'outsiders', who had migrated from India to the new state.[20]

Adding to these tensions were economic factors, as the refugees were allocated property to replace lands and houses that they had abandoned in India to make their trek to Pakistan. While the elite had indeed left large properties and great wealth behind, most of the refugees belonged to the middle or lower middle class. In the chaos of the migration and the quest to acquire property, it became fair game for individuals who had access to the bureaucracy to suddenly acquire substantial urban assets. This was not restricted to the civil sector. Even army officers managed to get property allotted, often multiples of their family holdings in India, with one parental home in East Punjab or Delhi being counted against allotments to every member of a clan that had migrated from India. A celebrated case of an allotment that was challenged even within the military was the acquisition by Sher Ali Khan of *Bachan Niwas*, one of the palatial homes of the brothers Mohan Singh and Sohan Singh on the Mall Road in Rawalpindi. Although Sher Ali had left a regal home in India, his allotment of this property raised eyebrows in Rawalpindi and was the cause of great unhappiness and tension between him and Ayub Khan.

Against this backdrop of tension on different fronts, Liaquat Ali Khan made his way from Karachi to Rawalpindi on 16 October 1951 on the governor general's Viking aircraft to address a gathering at the Company Bagh on the north side of the Leh Nullah (or stream) that divided the city from the cantonment. A crowd of some 30–40,000 had gathered to hear him speak. Liaquat had been taking a bellicose stance against India in recent weeks. At a speech in Lahore he had raised his clenched fist and promised to fight any aggression with force, a moment captured for history by a photographer in a pose that remained etched in the collective memory of Pakistanis henceforth. He reached the site of the public meeting around 3:45 p.m., inspected a guard of honour, and took his place on the dais. A prominent local politician, Sheikh Masud Sadiq welcomed the prime minister, and then as Liaquat stood up to begin his speech with the words 'Muslim brethren', two shots rang out and he fell, wounded mortally.

Syed Nur Ahmad (aka Mir Nur Ahmed) describes the scene vividly:

His political secretary, Nawab Siddiq Ali and some others tried to support him. Liaqat (sic) first recited the Holy Kalima [La Illah illilah ho Muhammad ur Rasul Allah: there is no God but Allah and Muhammad is his prophet] and then said 'Goli lag gayi hai' (the bullet has hit me), then recited the Kalima again and said 'God protect Pakistan.'[21]

He then faded into unconsciousness and was rushed to the hospital but lost his life. The police immediately pounced on the assailant, identified later as Said Akbar, who had travelled from Peshawar to Rawalpindi, and shot him dead. An inquiry commission was set up by the government. Subsequent efforts to inquire into the cause of the assassination, even with help from Scotland Yard, proved futile. As usual, a cloak of secrecy covered the investigation and the full report never saw the light of day, setting a standard for many such events in Pakistani history. Adding to the mystery was the fact that the inspector general of the special branch of the police, Nawab Aitzazuddin, who had been entrusted with the investigation, was killed in an aircraft accident a few days after the publication of the public version of the commission's report while he was on his way to report to the new prime minister, Khwaja Nazimuddin. All the documents related to the case were reportedly burnt in the air crash.

THE POST-LIAQUAT MESS

Political plots continued to thicken around the country. Nazimuddin took on the role of president of the Muslim League a month after ascending to the prime ministership and elevated finance secretary, Ghulam Mohammad, to the rank of governor general, bringing the first of the bureaucrats to a position of political power, a move that reverberated in Pakistani history in years to come. Turmoil in the provinces continued to dominate the news: Bengali agitation in East Pakistan, corruption charges against yet another Khuhro government in Sindh, a battle over allocation of Muslim League seats in the upcoming elections between chief minister (also provincial president of the League) Qayyum Khan, and Yusuf Khattak, the secretary of the national Muslim League, and a brewing battle over the emerging constitution of Pakistan that saw the Punjab trying to ensure that it did not lose its powerful position on the national front. Adding fuel to the fire was a movement first launched by a group called the Ahrars in the Punjab against the Ahmadiyya sect which professed that its founder Mirza Ghulam Ahmad of Qadian (in India) was the returned prophet, a claim that ran counter to the orthodox Islamic view that the Prophet Muhammad (PBUH) was the last prophet. Rioting ensued and the civil authorities could not quell it.

An embattled Nazimuddin, who was facing a challenge to his election as Muslim League president, suddenly found himself facing serious social and political unrest in the Punjab. He turned to the army for help and imposed martial law on 8 March 1953. Enter the army. Major General Muhammad Azam Khan, who had earlier endeared himself to the population of Lahore by using the army to fight the ravages of floods and protect Mughal emperor Jehangir's mausoleum from the encroachment of the swollen Ravi River, was a Pathan who did not believe in half measures. Imposing a curfew that he enforced ruthlessly and showing himself all over the city, he quickly quelled the unrest and gave the government a breather, enough for it to set up a commission headed by Justice Mohammad Munir to investigate the cause of the riots. This commission's activities resulted in an amusing spectacle of leading Muslim scholars from all branches of the faith failing to agree on the simple definition of who was a *momin* or true believer. It thus buried the conflict over the Ahmadis till later in the country's history when Prime Minister Zulfikar Ali Bhutto in 1977 sought to buy the support of the *ulema* in the face of growing political opposition by declaring this sect to be non-Muslims.

Azam Khan's swift actions and the army's presence had also established the presence of the army as a new major force on the national political scene. Azam Khan personally, and the army in general, was regarded by the local population of Lahore as saviours of law and order. Slogans of 'Jarnail Azam Khan *Zindabad*' (Long Live General Azam Khan) and 'Pakistan Army *Zindabad*' (Long Live the Pakistan Army) were often heard at public events. Azam Khan also took the chance of running affairs in the provincial capital to sort out what he considered to be a sorry state of administration in all sectors, education included. He denigrated the religious leaders by ordering his PR people to refer to them as *mullah* not *maulana*. In this he was reflecting a view held also by Ayub that religious leaders were often not well-read and willing to mislead illiterate people with their misguided views. A clear divide was created between the civil and the military with the military taking the view that the civilians had botched affairs. To some extent this was correct. Syed Nur Ahmed, the local director of public relations (and later author of the Urdu book *Martial Law Se Martial Law Tak* or *From Martial Law to Martial law*), had been instrumental in producing inflammatory press releases, apparently at the behest of Chief Minister Mumtaz Daultana, highlighting the campaign against the Ahmadis. The army put a stop to all that.[22]

While the army gained prestige, Nazimuddin and the political leaders lost prestige. Nazimuddin was sacked by the governor general on 17 April. Despite pleading with the British high commissioner to get the Queen of England to intercede on his behalf, he was replaced by a political non-entity.[23] The new prime minister was Muhammed Ali Bogra, another East Pakistani, who was brought back from his position as ambassador to the United States. Other moves also presaged later events. Among them, Iskander Mirza was appointed governor of East Pakistan in 1954 and later inducted into the central cabinet, positioning him to become governor general in 1955 and then the first president of the republic of Pakistan in February 1956.

Yet, it was not solely the first martial law that got the army thinking about how well it could do the job of running the country. After the Kashmir war, there was a dormant wave of scepticism about the ability of the politicians to run Pakistan. Even as early as 1948, Jinnah detected misunderstanding in the minds of senior Pakistani army officers about their role. In his customary crisp and clear manner he addressed the officers of the Staff College in Quetta on 14 June 1948. While praising the high morale of officers and soldiers, he introduced a note of warning:

> ...during my talks with one or two very high-ranking officers I discovered that they did not know the implications of the oath taken by the troops of Pakistan. Of course, an oath is only a matter of form; what is more important is the true spirit and the heart.
>
> But it is an important form and I would like to take this opportunity of refreshing your memory by reading the prescribed oath to you.
>
> 'I solemnly affirm, in the presence of Almighty God, that I owe allegiance to the constitution in the Dominion of Pakistan (mark the words Constitution and the Government of the Dominion of Pakistan) and that I will as in duty bound honestly and faithfully serve in the Dominion of Pakistan Forces and go within the terms of my enrolment wherever I may be ordered by air—land, or sea and that I will observe and obey all commands of any officer set over me....'
>
> As I have said just now, the spirit is what really matters. I should like you to study the Constitution which is in force in Pakistan at present and understand its true constitutional and legal implications when you say that you will be faithful to the Constitution of the Dominion....the executive authority flows from the Head of the Government of Pakistan, who is the Governor-General and, therefore, any command or orders that may come to you cannot come without the sanction of the Executive Head.[24]

We know that Yahya Khan (then an instructor) was among the audience at Staff College on that day. It is not clear how widely this speech was distributed among the Pakistan Army and how many officers took Jinnah's homily to heart. As later events were to prove, the army reserved the right to act as it saw fit in the interest of Pakistan and in its own interest.

AYUB KHAN AND POLITICS

When Ayub Khan took over as the first Pakistan army chief in January 1951, he issued an Order of the Day that urged the army to 'Keep out of politics.... you must avoid taking any active part in party politics and propagation of any such views....we are the servants of Pakistan and as such servants of any party that the people put in power.'[25] Yet, only three years later, Ayub Khan, while on an official trip to the United Kingdom, sat down in the Dorchester Hotel and penned a fateful document that presaged his view of the future political system in Pakistan, one with a single unit in West Pakistan and another in East Pakistan and the creation of a supreme commander's position to head the joint staff. 'In addition to other duties, he should be made the defence member and *ex officio* member of the cabinet. This will not only knit the services together and lead to economy in pooling things common to all services, but would put a stop to any attempt by politicians to interfere in the internal affairs of the services to promote their personal interests.'[26]

Ayub was thinking at that time not only of the domestic situation but also about the foreign policy of Pakistan. As the domestic political edifice crumbled and headed for a fall, the army was already working towards a future in which it would control the direction of the country, at first from the sidelines and later directly. Helping them unwittingly in this quest were the political leaders of Pakistan, making and breaking short-term alliances for individual advantage, while ignoring the need of the country for a home grown constitution that would last. This continuing internecine warfare among the politicos strengthened the role of the bureaucrats and the army. Ayub found himself being invited to take over the country by Governor General Ghulam Mohammad and declined the offer, according to his memoir. Meanwhile the country stumbled its way out of a series of government changes to the dissolution of the constituent assembly and the production of a new constitution under the guidance of another bureaucrat, Chaudhry Muhammad Ali, who was elevated to prime minister. In 1956, former army man and then civil servant, once colonel but by then major general, Iskander Mirza was brought back from East Pakistan and inserted into the cabinet and then promoted to the rank of president of Pakistan. But by then Ayub and the army, clearly seeing a need to take charge of their own destiny and with it the destiny of the country, had set a new course for Pakistan's foreign policy that had serious implications for its domestic policies and political structure. Seeking 'friends not masters', Ayub engineered the opening to Washington to build a relationship that he hoped would stand Pakistan and the army in good stead.

NOTES

1. C. Dasgupta, *War and Diplomacy in Kashmir 1947–48* (Sage, 2002). This view is contradicted by S.A.D. Qureshi and S.M. Burke in their *The British Raj in India* (Karachi: Oxford University Press, 1995), p. 562, appendix F.
2. The impression given at that time was that Liaquat had received an invitation from the Soviet Union to visit Moscow. In fact, no record of such an invitation exists in the Foreign Office of Pakistan. I am indebted to my friend Ambassador Arif Ayub for this important clarification.
3. Jinnah, *Speeches* (Karachi: Pakistan Publications, 1963), p. 84.
4. Ch. Muhammad Ali, *The Emergence of Pakistan* (New York: Columbia University Press, 1967), p. 367.
5. Speaking to a gathering in Peshawar on 20 April 1948, Jinnah declared: 'We are watching your government, your province, your ministry, and your civil services. It is under our searchlight and there is no doubt we shall soon be able to X-ray it and throw out the poison from our body politic.' *Dawn*, Karachi, 21 April 1948, quoted in Ali, p. 368.
6. Ali, *The Emergence*, p. 371.
7. A local rank as opposed to a substantive rank denoted a temporary situation and the individual was supposed to revert to his previous substantive rank, in this case brigadier, when returning to a normal posting.
8. 'Sher—am just off to East Pakistan. Have been superseded. Could you do something?... Grateful. Thanks Ayub' was the brief scribbled note on a torn sheet from a note book that Ayub sent Sher Ali. Sher Ali Khan (aka Sher Ali Pataudi), *The Story of Soldiering and Politics in India and Pakistan* (Lahore: Bakhtyar Printers, 1983), p. 116.
9. Lt. Gen. Wajid Ali Khan Burki, *Autobiography of An Army Doctor in British India and Pakistan* (self-published limited edition. Rawalpindi: Burki House, 1988), pp. 344–5.
10. I have seen this original ACR in the Pakistan Army GHQ archives and was impressed that Gracey showed great spirit by not resorting to fulsome praise but to evaluating Ayub in a matter of fact yet positive manner and thus cleared him for his promotion, without reservation.
11. Mohammad Ayub Khan, *Friends not Masters: A Political Autobiography* (London: Oxford University Press, 1967), p. 34.
12. M. Ayub Khan, Ibid., p. 35.
13. Letters to this effect are in the Public Records Office, Surrey, UK.
14. Sher Ali, *The Story*, pp. 125–126.
15. Burki, *Autobiography*, p. 345.
16. Ayub Khan, *Friends not Masters*, p. 38.
17. Details of this case have been made available in an excellent book, Hasan Zaheer, *The Times and Trials of the Rawalpindi Conspiracy 1951* (Pakistan: Oxford University Press, 1998), based on the declassified documents of the case that the author saw during his official service. The following discussion profits from this work.
18. E.D. Swinton, *The Defence of Duffer's Drift* appeared in 1907 in the British Royal *United Services Magazine*. It is a wonderfully engaging account of the tactics of a small military operation set in the Anglo-Boer War, under which different scenarios are enacted out for the defence of Duffer's Drift, each with a changed situation. It was a useful training tool for young officers in the British Army, the German Army (they added a few chapters of their own), the US army and now the Pakistan Army. It remains in print even today Army Publishing Group Inc, Wayne, New Jersey, 1986. I first read it in the library of the Pakistan Military Academy at Kakul as a young man and now have my own copy of the reissued book.
19. Top Secret Memorandum of a conversation between US and British officials in London, 3 April 1951, *Foreign Relations of the United States 1951*, p. 1691.

20. Shahid Javed Burki has developed this theme in his many essays and books. The US embassy also focused on it and evaluated many governmental postings and squabbles through this prism.

21. Syed Nur Ahmad, *From Martial Law to Martial Law: Politics in the Punjab 1919 to 1958.* Craig Baxter, ed. Mahmud Ali trans. from Urdu (Lahore: Vanguard, 1985), p. 311.

22. An eyewitness account of this period is contained in *The Military in Pakistan: Image and Reality* by Brigadier A.R. Siddiqi, who was then a junior officer in the ISPR Directorate and later headed that directorate during the 1971 war with India. (Lahore: Vanguard, 1996).

23. Nur Ahmad quoting Raja Ghazanfar Ali Khan's recollection of a talk with the member of the British high commission staff.

24. Quaid-i-Azam Mohammad Ali Jinnah, *Speeches as Governor-General of Pakistan 1947–1948,* Government of Pakistan. It is remarkable how Jinnah managed to keep his speeches short and to the point. His legal training must have prepared him for this. Few of his speeches ran longer than a few pages, a tradition that was never kept up by his successors who thought that to be prolix was to be eloquent.

25. *The Pakistan Times*, 23 and 24 January 1951, quoted in Hasan Askari Rizvi, *The Military and Politics in Pakistan, 1947–86* (Lahore, and Konark, Delhi: Progressive Publishers, 1988), p. 56.

26. Ayub Khan, *Friends not Masters*, pp. 186–191, also reproduced as Appendix A in Rizvi, *The Military*, pp. 265–270.

5 | COURTING UNCLE SAM

O lofty birds, death is better than the gifted food
That hinders your ability to soar

– Muhammad Iqbal

When the poet-philosopher Muhammad Iqbal, who is credited with being one of the visionaries of the Pakistan Movement, wrote the above-quoted verse, he was referring to the self-imposed chains of colonialism. For him, the choice between food and freedom was an easy one. He would rather die than be subservient. Years later, when Pakistani strongman Field Marshal Mohammad Ayub Khan dictated his book *Friends not Masters* to his amanuensis Altaf Hussain Gauhar, the latter, himself an Urdu poet of no mean quality, chose Iqbal's verse for the title of the book in Urdu: *Jis rizq sey aati ho parwaaz mein kotahi* (The food that hinders your ability to soar). The reference in this case was updated to the relationship between the United States and Pakistan not Britain and Pakistan. It took barely a quarter century for Pakistan and specifically Ayub Khan to acquire American friendship and then for this most ardent American friend to want to portray himself as independent of that relationship. Yet, in that quarter century, the US–Pakistan relationship grew and matured to such an extent that it continued to exert a powerful influence not only on Pakistan but also on the whole of West and South Asia.

The roots of US interest in India lay in the emerging US policy toward the British empire during the final years of the Second World War. As influential US thinkers saw the British unable to sustain their control over vast colonial territories with increasingly restive native populations. Rising levels of education, political awareness, and mobility during the war years, especially in the case of the military, had exposed large numbers of Indians to the possibility of self-rule. The idea of self-determination for these colonies had taken root in the American psyche as early as the period of Woodrow Wilson and expanded its foothold in the American imagination during the period between the two world wars. Franklin Delano Roosevelt took the idea of the League of Nations and reshaped it into a world resting on regional security that would follow the independence of former colonies. This idea was picked up by the influential US media. Quoting from *Life* magazine's 'Open Letter to the People of England' which appeared at the time of the Quit India Movement in October 1942: 'one thing we are *not* fighting for is to hold the British empire together.'[1] Much to Winston Churchill's consternation, Roosevelt also tried to persuade the British to accept the idea of self-determination, spelled out in the Atlantic Charter of 1941, for the colonies of the British empire. A key individual furthering this idea was Sumner Wells (Under Secretary of State), while Cordell Hull (Secretary of State) called for opening up the global economic system. As a result, the partition of British India—and the subsequent birth of India and Pakistan—was seen as a major achievement for the Americans.

The United States took up the issue of Kashmiri self-determination at the newly formed United Nations. As early as 6 January 1948, the US Secretary of State was instructing his ambassador to the United Nations that 'in the opinion of the Department...the only solution acceptable to all parties concerned in the Kashmir problem will eventually be a determination, probably by plebiscite, of the wishes of the inhabitants of Jammu and Kashmir, with respect to their long-term affiliation with either India or Pakistan, taking into account the possibility that some form of partition may be proposed.' The secretary also advised his ambassador that the United States would be prepared to take the lead, if the British desired, to introduce resolutions that would facilitate appropriate actions by the United Nations.[2]

Before and during the war, America had relegated itself to a secondary role in the politics of South Asia, allowing the British to call the tune. However, with the rise of anti-communism in the United States, a shift in that stance began to occur at the policy-making level at home. The general public was still unaware of the drama of independence and partition unfolding halfway across the world. Indeed, as Saqib Qureshi cites Chester Bowles: 'As late as 1951, there were more employees at the US embassy in Athens than at the embassies of Delhi and Karachi combined.'[3]

TURNING TO WASHINGTON

On the Pakistani side, the idea of an alliance with the United States did not begin to take firm shape till after partition. Earlier, during a meeting with Lord Ismay, Mr Jinnah had examined the possibility of Pakistan after the British left and determined, according to Ismay, that 'Pakistan could not stand alone.'[4] It would need to be friends with a superpower. 'Russia had no appeal for them. France was weak and divided; there remained only England and America, and of these the former was the natural friend.' According to Ismay, Jinnah 'jokingly' added: 'Apart from anything else, the devil you know is better than the devil you don't.' Jinnah did not know the United States well and dispatched his trusted aide M.A.H. Ispahani to reconnoitre the landscape and try to set up contacts. He was the recipient of numerous unsolicited letters from well-meaning Muslims who had established themselves in the United States and offered to represent the cause of Pakistan, some even suggesting themselves as potential ambassadors, a post that eventually went to Mr Ispahani.

The United States meanwhile was taking a cold and calculated look at the map of the Middle East and South Asia and saw the need for Pakistan's airfields and strategic location as an essential part of its plan to defend the trade routes of the west to the east as well as the northern frontiers of the region against the Soviet Union. The US saw the need to fill the emerging political and economic vacuum, as Britain shed its colonial wealth and indeed became burdened with debt to its erstwhile colonies. It also viewed Egypt, Iran, Syria, and Iraq as being vulnerable to the influence and direct intervention of the Soviet Union.

Immediately after independence, Mr Jinnah asked the US to provide some $2 billion in military and civilian aid to Pakistan, making the US potentially the largest donor for the fledgling economy. Though this request was rejected by the US in the aftermath of the First Kashmir War, Pakistani politicians continued to stress their strategic location and potential role as a US ally against the encroaching Soviet empire. The ground was being set for the new Pakistani prime minister to head to the emerging superpower and make a very favourable impression on his American hosts. Liaquat Ali Khan played an interesting card before taking the trip to the United States. He announced a visit to Moscow, apparently to counter-balance Nehru's much publicized planned visit to the United States but then cancelled that visit to come to the United States instead. At least that is the way he wished to present the situation on the aborted Moscow visit at the time. Later information suggests that the Soviets had become cool to the idea and delayed the visit, enough to push Liaquat to agree to the Truman invitation.[5] Accompanied by his smart wife Raana,[6] an articulate Foreign Secretary Ikramullah, and Ambassador Ispahani, Liaquat Ali Khan played on the US's new worldview, depicting Pakistan as a partner in the battle against communism.

He was helped in this task by the condescending attitude of the Indian leadership to the United States and their own desire to seek closer relations with the Soviet Union. Nehru's trip to the United States in the summer of 1949 had been preceded by great publicity, especially from the media and US politicians, and expectations were raised sky-high as to the future role of India on the global stage and as a potential friend of the United States. But US foreign policy officials, including the ambassador to New Delhi, Loy Henderson, had already started reading very negative meaning into Nehru's frequent public and private fulminations against the United States and Nehru's desire to steer a neutral course on the global political sea. Compounding the difficulty was the lack of chemistry between Truman and Nehru, with the patrician Nehru unable to understand the down-home style of his host. As Robert McMahon asserts: 'Nehru's much ballyhooed tour of the United States must be judged one of the most curious and least successful state visits in recent history.'[7] Truman and Nehru appeared to talk 'past each other.' Following that visit, the US stopped talking about huge aid packages to India, leaving it to fend for itself and to seek help from the World Bank. Subsequently, the US also increased pressure on India at the United Nations to accept demilitarization in Kashmir.

LIAQUAT MAKES NEW FRIENDS

The focus of the US thus shifted from India to Pakistan, as the latter appeared much more willing to act as a bulwark against communism and to provide military assistance to other countries in the Middle East. Liaquat was given red carpet treatment during his visit to the US. President Truman had sent his personal aircraft, the Independence, to ferry the Pakistani prime minister from London to Washington, D.C. and accorded him the highest honour by personally welcoming him at the national airport on 3 May 1950, accompanied by his entire cabinet. A photograph from that time shows Truman, hat in hand, and his wife smiling at the camera, surrounded by his Pakistani guests and their elegant wives in traditional 'gharara' outfits in front of Blair House, the state guest house across the street from the White House.

Liaquat, wearing a Western suit but adding a 'Jinnah' Karakul cap for effect, was effusive in his own thanks to Truman. Replying to Truman's welcome speech, Liaquat Ali Khan said:

> Mr President:...United States of America have done great honour to us and to our country. I bring you and the great American nation the most friendly greetings of eighty million men and women of Pakistan. Although we come from a distant country in the heart of Asia, and this is my first visit to your land, the American people are not strangers to us. We have known them as educators[8] and as men and women engaged on missions of peace. We have known them as soldiers who fought on our plains, our hills and our jungles. And again since the birth of Pakistan we have known them as messengers of your goodwill.

After Nehru's lectures and critical commentaries, such friendliness was music to the ears of the US administration and the media. Liaquat continued to educate the US public about Pakistan and its unequivocal stand alongside the United States against the communist menace. (More than two decades later, the United States recounted Liaquat's words to welcome Prime Minister Mohammad Khan Junejo on his maiden and final voyage to Washington, with President Ronald Reagan invoking Liaquat's anti-communist pledges to indicate that relations between the two countries had remained firm on that front.) At the same time, Liaquat pressed his hosts for military assistance. Pakistan had been less than successful in getting additional Fury aircraft from the United Kingdom and needed a new source to bolster its military. Though the Liaquat visit did not produce any such dividends, it did prepare the ground for an emerging US view that Pakistan was a necessary and willing ally in the Middle East.

Liaquat laid the foundations for a deeper friendship with the Americans also by supporting the US in UN-sponsored actions against North Korea. The Korean War became the political glue for the new relationship, with the United States seeking Pakistani troop commitments and support at the United Nations. Pakistan was unable to oblige with troops, citing its own defence commitments on two fronts at home: against India and against Afghanistan on the western front. It stuck to this position although the United States offered to equip a brigade of Pakistani troops for Korea. However, Pakistani politicians and military leaders rather adroitly played the Korean card to their maximum benefit to paint themselves as partners in the defence of the Middle East and against the communist threat worldwide, in sharp contrast to India's neutral and at times pro-Soviet stance. Economically too the Korean War caused an economic boom in Pakistan, further strengthening its government's resolve to cosy up to the United States.

SEEKING MILITARY AID

Pakistan did not take no for an answer from its new found friends in the United States and pressed for specific military aid. Even in preparing for the Liaquat visit, Iskander Mirza spelt out Pakistan's requirements from the US.[9] These included 'Sherman tanks, transport, motorized transport and tank spare parts, and recoilless guns (sic)'. The 1949 defence mission to the US had been told that in the absence of [the] Enabling Act that was expected to be passed by Congress, the US could not provide direct military supplies from its own military stockpile to Pakistan. However, 'the representative of the State... stated that there was no objection to Pakistan obtaining her requirement through civilian manufacturing firms in USA subject to concurrence of that ministry', and Mirza said the mission was assured that such concurrence would be forthcoming. Pakistan subsequently made some purchases through those channels but wished to get direct military aid. Mirza's impression was that 'America was doubtful of Pakistan's attitude towards communism.'

Three weeks later, Mirza prepared a brief for the prime minister advising him not to 'press for the supply of anything as Dollar position is uncertain. We would like H.P.M. [honourable prime minister in the carryover of the old British parlance] to open up an avenue for future supplies of tanks, recoilless guns and Radar equipment from America. The Americans do not like to even discuss tanks with our representatives,' he stated.[10] The Pakistanis were prepared to seek military aid during the Liaquat visit but would not be sad if not much emerged. Yet, they sometimes read too much into US words. And in the wake of the prime minister's successful US visit, they thought that approval of military aid from the US was imminent.

Pakistani ambassador Ispahani, while helping facilitate the procurement of US arms, showed a greater degree of realism and caution than his Pakistan-based colleagues. Replying in a letter sent by diplomatic bag to Iskander Mirza soon after the Liaquat visit, Ispahani warned Mirza that:

> I am inclined to feel from the tone of your letter [of 17 May] that you are being overly optimistic. We have had in the past promises for the sympathetic consideration of our demands but unfortunately none of them have so far brought fruit. I shall, therefore, be pleasantly surprised if anything materializes on this occasion as well.... As for the 200 latest type tanks, your optimism really startles me. Those are still on the top secret list and have not yet been made available to even the Atlantic Pact countries.[11]

Ispahani then proceeded to check if the M24 light tanks that could be upgraded from their 75mm guns to 76mm guns might be of interest to Pakistan. Mirza responded on 9 June that his optimism had been based on a letter from G. Ahmed (later ambassador to the US) who had accompanied the prime minister during his meeting with Defense Secretary Louis Johnson. Mirza was delighted to accept the proffered M24 light tanks with the upgraded 76mm guns.

But there were strings attached to such aid. The US sought assurances that Pakistan would use any military aid 'to foster International peace and security within the framework of the charter of United Nations through measures which will further the ability of Nations dedicated to principles and purposes of the Charter.' It also understood that Pakistan would require the items provided by the US 'to maintain its internal security, its legitimate Self Defense or built it (sic) to participate in Defense of [the] area of which it is a part; and that it will not undertake any act of aggression against any other State.'[12] Mirza's reply to this was that this was nothing new since the 'undertakings required [of Pakistan] by the Govt. of United States of America are the same they require from other countries to whom they supply arms and equipment. Para 3 might mean that Pakistan will be expected to help with her armed forces in a situation like Korea where the United Nations asked the nations for armed help against North Koreans. But in view of what has happened in the past, Pakistan can limit her help to declarations in favour of the United Nations.' It was clear that this was an emerging relationship between consenting adults! Pakistan was willing to dance along to the US tune but also had its own agenda.

AYUB'S ANTI-COMMUNISM CARD

The new army chief, Ayub Khan, had started playing the anti-communist card. Having been scared by the association of socialists with the conspiracy within the army to overthrow the government and military leadership, he stressed the importance of chasing out the leftists and communists from whatever corner of the country's political and social system they occupied.[13] In addition, he harped on the ability and willingness of the Pakistan Army to send troops to defend the Middle East's oil resources. His eye, however, was on domestic defence needs, especially against India.

Ayub's views were helped to a great extent by the internal analyses in the US government. In a report to the National Security Council on South Asia on 19 August 1952, David Bruce, the acting secretary of state warned of the 'noticeable increase in the activities of the *mullahs* (orthodox religious leaders) in Pakistan.' It cited 'growing doubts' in Pakistani minds about the lack of 'real friends', meaning the United States. 'Were this trend to continue the present government of enlightened western-oriented leaders might well be threatened, and members of a successor government would probably be far less cooperative with the West than the present incumbents.'[14] Bruce also cited the lack of a positive US response to a Pakistani request of July 1952 for $200 million of military supplies, including armour and aircraft. Citing legal constraints, the US failed to meet this request. Pakistan had also asked for economic assistance in the form of a shipment of 200,000 tons of wheat. 'To date Pakistan has seen little tangible evidence of US friendship, and failure to respond to the request for wheat would almost inevitably affect our national interests adversely,' the note concluded.

By October 1952, the US was re-evaluating the role of Pakistan in light of its review of the communist threat. It noted the 'large number of excellent airfields and air base sites (notably in West Pakistan) within medium and heavy bomber range of major industrial and governmental centres in Soviet Central Asia and the interior of communist China and the presence of major ports and other facilities that would support communications between Western Europe and the Far East.'[15]

But the US was also concerned about the stability of the Pakistani regime, as there was a battle being fought between the 'insiders'—the local (largely feudal) landlords and political fixers—and the 'outsiders', the relatively better educated and committed immigrants from northern India and Bombay who had fought hard for independence. The elitist rulers of Pakistan—many of whom came from northern India—were not seen by the 'insiders' as being very representative of the Pakistani population and its wishes. Indeed, most of the provinces that formed West Pakistan had not shown great support for the Muslim League during the freedom struggle, except near the end of the

British programme to partition India. Thus, the veneer of pro-western thinking was indeed thin and presented more for effect. Moreover, the bureaucracy, largely populated by the so-called 'outsiders', began to form an alliance with the army, another institution that was not particularly integrated into the country as a whole, being comprised mainly from three districts in the Punjab (Rawalpindi, Jhelum and Campbellpur—later re-named Attock) and the NWFP.

It was with some satisfaction that the US noted in 1952 that:

> The Government of Pakistan has recently been strengthened as a result of Governor General Ghulam Mohammed's [a former bureaucrat] summary dismissal of Prime Minister Nazimuddin on 17 April. This move, which brought to the premiership Muhammed Ali [aka Muhammed Ali Bogra, after his place of origin in East Pakistan], then Pakistan Ambassador to the US, represented a vigorous effort by a strong element within the Muslim League, spurred on by the permanent Secretary of the Defense Minister [Iskander Mirza, a former military man bureaucrat] and the army Commander in Chief [Ayub Khan], to halt the decline in government effectiveness, strength, and popularity.[16]

While the US continued to eye Pakistan's strategic location and potential for helping defend US interests in the Middle East, it did not see Pakistan possessing the capability at that time to send troops outside its border nor to effect a 'sizable increase of present forces' because of the 'shortage of qualified officers and administrative personnel and the lack of adequate logistic organization.' But, the US also recognized that Pakistani leaders were keen to be included in a Middle East defence organization, 'though there are indications that they have been motivated largely by a desire to strengthen Pakistan's military position vis-à-vis India.' The assessment concluded that 'in entering into defence arrangements with the West, Pakistan would probably seek to drive as hard a bargain as possible.'

PAKISTAN PART OF THE ALLIANCE

By February 1954, a draft policy being proposed for the NSC was reiterating support for the Pakistan government 'so long as it remains friendly to the United States', while making clear to Pakistan that on its Kashmir conflict with India it would not support 'either country against the other'. Pakistan was being seen as part of an alliance which, in the 'case of a general war' against communism, would provide 'manpower, resources and strategic facilities for mutual defense efforts with the West.' In light of these factors, it was proposed that 'special consideration be given to Pakistan in providing grant military assistance.'[17] The signals from the White House were clear to the US bureaucracy. Only a month later, in a special meeting of US ambassadors in South Asia (comprising Iran, India, Afghanistan, Pakistan, Burma, and Ceylon) held at Nuwara Eliya in Ceylon, 'all of those present agreed with the decision to give military aid to Pakistan'. The meeting noted that 'the linking of military aid to Pakistan with the beginning of a regional defense arrangement in the Middle East will probably be politically beneficial to the United States and the free world.'[18] By that time, Pakistan had purchased some $26.5 million of military equipment from the United States under the reimbursable military assistance programme, compared with $36.3 million by India. Pakistani purchases included three hundred and fifty-two medium tanks, seventy-five 90mm M-63 gun carriages and ammunition, up to 90mm. But it needed much more.

This was on the mind of the Pakistani leadership and it was reflected in almost all exchanges between them and their US counterparts. Ambassador Horace Hildreth, reported on a meeting of the new Vice President Richard Nixon held with Governor General Ghulam Mohammad, the then Prime Minister Muhammed (this was the official spelling of his first name) Ali Bogra, and Defence Secretary Iskander Mirza, during which all of them pressed Hildreth to seek US military aid for Pakistan even before any arrangement had been made to join Turkey in a defence pact.[19] The Pakistanis' argument (reported Hildreth) was that Indians would huff and puff but the issue would blow over in a matter of months. At the same time, 'the prime minister said aid not forthcoming now would be like taking a girl down primrose path and deserting her in the limelight of world publicity.'[20] He painted this outcome as a potential victory for Russia and China. He also stated that Pakistan did not wish to become 'tail of dog' of Russia and China, even if piqued. Hildreth's embassy subscribed 'wholeheartedly' to the frank views of the Pakistani officials, except in the matter of the likely Indian reaction. In the view expressed by the embassy, 'the basic question is simple: Are advantages of Pakistan's contribution to Middle East defence as active participating free world partner outweighed [by an] adverse reaction [from] India? We venture to express opinion that former is objective worth risk.' On the matter of adverse effects on the government of Pakistan and on US interests in Pakistan and in the area of saying no to Pakistan's request for military assistance, the embassy was unequivocal: 'We believe this is [a] serious consideration.' Hildreth, whose daughter married Iskander Mirza's son Humayun (later a World Bank official), was laying the ground for a closer and much more formal military alliance between the US and Pakistan.

On their part, the civil–military combine in Pakistan, comprising Iskander Mirza and Ayub Khan, had already felt the pulse of the Americans and found them ready, willing, and able to support Pakistan's military build-up. Ayub chose as his targets not only the like-minded leaders of the defence establishment in the War Department but also the Director of the CIA, Allen Dulles, and through him the Secretary of State John Foster Dulles (Allen Dulles's brother). During a series of visits to the United States, Ayub cultivated relations with his counterparts assiduously in both formal and informal settings. Whether he was marching through the corridors of the Pentagon or playing golf with his hosts, he hammered away at the importance of Pakistan for Middle East defence, while avoiding India as a topic of discussion. Yet, he very carefully crafted the impression of Pakistan as a pragmatic partner, not the 'forlorn girl' who was being courted by the Americans. And, as needed, he resorted to moments of unhappiness and pique that only made the Americans work harder at winning him over.

Helping Ayub in this task was Iskander Mirza, who tried to establish his own relationship with the American leadership but lacked Ayub's natural entrée to the intelligence and defence establishment. Another key player was Ambassador S. Amjad Ali, who filled in for Ayub and Mirza when they were not available to deal with the Americans, as roving ambassador. (At some point, he became the object of Ayub's ire for this very reason.) Between the three of them, they launched a sophisticated information gathering and propaganda campaign to convince the Americans of the importance of Pakistan in the global fight against communism. Ayub also had his own person in the Pakistan embassy, who kept him informed privately of developments on the scene. This person was (then) Brigadier M.G. Jilani, the defence attaché, who maintained close ties with the US establishment and reported privately and at length every fortnight to Ayub.[21]

By the middle of 1953, Jilani was evaluating the tour of the Middle East by Secretary of State Dulles against the backdrop of what he described as a battle for control of the Republican Party between President Eisenhower and the forces of ex-President Hoover, General Douglas MacArthur and Senator Taft. According to Jilani, Eisenhower was favouring an approach to foreign policy that included the European allies while his own party's opposition group demanded that the US take on a unilateral and aggressive stance. Based on his conversations with counterparts in the US administration, Jilani informed Ayub that after Dulles's Middle East tour, which also included Israel and Pakistan, the idea of a 'Mid-East Defence Pact is off for the time being. The unfortunate differences between Britain and Egypt, and the apparent backing of Egypt by almost the whole of Asia, has un-nerved the State Department.'[22] There were also some 'scathing comments' about Winston Churchill's 'doggedness' and 'imperialistic' attitude. Jilani noted that a strong policy group in the US favoured breaking the Arab bloc by entering into bilateral pacts with willing members of the bloc. Potential countries included Iraq, Syria, Jordan, and Saudi Arabia. Only Pakistan and Israel 'openly and unreservedly' requested a defence pact. 'However, owing to the hostility of the Arab world, I do not think the US will do anything about it in the near future,' reported Jilani.

According to Jilani, Secretary Dulles's team found the Indian attitude to be 'passive', but they were impressed with the Indian leadership and with India's ability to control the neutral Asia bloc. This made the US 'fearful of taking steps which may throw India's weight against them.' On the other hand, Dulles's team was 'very much impressed with the goodwill they found in our country for the US. To Mr Dulles, especially, it was an eye-opener. It was especially mentioned that on the whole tour, Pakistan was the only country where the team received a hearty welcome, unadulterated by hostile demonstrations.' The net result was that 'Dulles seems convinced that, given stability in the government, our country has strong potentialities.' Dulles was also convinced about Pakistan's genuine support against the communist threat.

Reporting on the delegation's reactions to the Pakistan Army, Jilani stressed that the visitors had been very impressed, starting with the welcome they received. Col. Mead and Counsellor Douglas MacArthur of the Department of State 'maintain that they have never seen a better guard of honour than the one that met them on arrival at Karachi.' Dulles made a similar comment in his report on the visit. The army, according to Mead, 'was 100 per cent efficient.' In contrast, the civilian side was seen to be doing less, especially in comparison with India. Jilani reported that the US team found that Pakistan had not made good use of aid, as had India. 'They seem to attribute this to the instability in governmental affairs at the top, to too much pre-occupation with party politics, religious and language controversies, and to talking too much and doing comparatively little,' reported Jilani. Jilani was told that one of the first remarks of Dulles on his return was: 'We should go ahead and have defense pact with Pakistan. They are friendly and reliable.' Yet, the pact was put on hold. MacArthur floated the idea of a Friendship Pact with Pakistan that would eventually grow into a defence pact. The US also launched some feelers about a Pakistan military mission to Turkey to try to set up an embryonic Mid-East pact.

A NEW MIDDLE EAST PACT

The mission to Turkey soon followed, with both Ayub and Iskander Mirza going to talk not only with the Turks but also with US representatives then in Turkey. Mirza concentrated on building relations with US civilian counterparts, with Ayub handling most of the military discussions. On his return to Pakistan, Mirza noted how in his conversation over dinner with Messrs, Keyes (Deputy Secretary, War Department), and Marsh (State

Department), he was asked for Pakistan's military needs and the current size of the Pakistan Army.[23] While excusing his inability to give a detailed response 'especially after considerable amount of liquid refreshments' he informed his startled interlocutors that Pakistan had an army of 250,000.[24] They had assumed an army of 80,000, according to Mirza. He spelled out Pakistan's demand for additional artillery, doubling of fighter bombers and interceptors from five to ten squadrons, six minesweepers, and a radar to guard against 'attack from the North' [presumably Soviet Union]. When Marsh responded that these demands were not 'exorbitant,' Mirza pressed on to state that even with the increased forces, Pakistan would not be in a position to send forces outside the country to protect the Middle East oil fields or the Shat al Arab waterway, nor to 'mount a diversionary offensive on the Russian flank in the general direction of Mashed.'

In Mirza's view, if Pakistan needed American aid, the government of Pakistan would have to decide: (a) To cast its lot finally and irrevocably with the anti-communist group. (b) To give an undertaking that the aid obtained will not be used to attack India.

While Mirza was showing off his military expertise, Ayub Khan was showing a deft understanding of the broader political issues that underlay the need for military assistance from the Americans. He used the Turkey visit to strengthen ties to the Americans and the Turks and to learn from the Turkish experience in developing a relationship with the United States that was not unequal and certainly gave the US no scope for overbearing actions. While Mirza had returned home from Turkey, Ayub was preparing to head to the United States. Before leaving, he wrote to Prime Minister Muhammed Ali Bogra on the outcome of his visit.[25] In his view, the Turks had set up a balanced relationship with the United States, one in which the US did not attempt 'to force their views in any manner of interfere or influence the internal affairs of the Turks.' He felt 'confident that should there be such a tie-up between us and the Americans, there is no danger of the Americans interfering with our affairs or in any manner forcing their opinions on us.'

Ayub had tried to press the Turks to influence the Americans on Pakistan's behalf and found them reluctant at first. Turkey did not wish to annoy India, and Ayub noted that previous Pakistan ambassadors in Turkey had created the impression that Pakistan was 'engrossed in our [Pakistan's] problems with India.' After a frank talk with Turkey's General Nuri Yamut, Ayub felt he had removed these doubts and concerns. He also reported that the US Ambassador [Avra M.] Warren was 'spending more time publicizing Pakistan than doing his own job.' Warren, a veteran who had some decades earlier served in the US consulate in Karachi in British India, arranged meetings for Ayub with visiting American civilian leaders and also informed him that Admiral Radford, the new 'Chief of the Armed Forces in America [Chairman of the

Joint Chiefs of Staff] has been pleading our cause most vehemently.' Ayub felt that he would get a good hearing on arrival in the United States.

Ayub also took this opportunity of writing to the prime minister to impress upon him the need to examine the Turkish model of command and control and thus to suggest the possibility of a common or supreme commander for all Pakistani forces, which would allow that individual 'to execute [the] defence plan of Pakistan which must again be his [the supreme commander's] plan.' He felt that this was a vital matter requiring the prime minister's urgent consideration 'based on the defence requirements of the country irrespective of what individual service prejudices may be.' Stressing the need for such a new set-up, Ayub referred again to his upcoming visit to the United States and suggested that if his mission was successful, then the need for 're-organisation of the control and command system becomes absolutely immediate so that we can present a united front to the Americans.' He also suggested the idea of conscripting 'all youngsters passing matriculation examination and found suitable as officer material' for an initial period of two years.

A key factor in Ayub's mind, which would help determine the success of the US mission to get military aid was 'how stable our government is considered by the Americans':

> In the larger interest of the country, therefore, I must plead with you to be as firm as possible with the disruptionists and have no mercy on them. By doing so you will not only win outside support but also the support of the country and the Armed Forces. We shall back you up to the hilt.

Ayub was, clearly, slowly drifting into broader issues than military preparedness. But others on the civil side did not quite see his role in such broader policy matters as yet. One such individual was S. Amjad Ali, the Pakistani ambassador, who wrote a top secret, handwritten letter to the prime minister on 14 October 1953, during Ayub's Washington visit to report on his conversations in New York with Colonel Byroade of the United States.[26] Byroade had pressed for consideration by Pakistan of participation in the peacekeeping mission in Korea. Byroade offered the carrot that Pakistani troops could be equipped for this role and then take the equipment and arms back to Pakistan at the end of their tenure. Both the Foreign Minister Zafrulla and Amjad Ali felt that this was a policy issue that required review by the government at home. When Byroade referred to Ayub Khan's visit, the foreign minister 'told Byroade that General Ayub was here to look around and to try to get assistance in making up deficiencies in our equipment. He would not and could not talk on matters of policy which the Govt. alone was in a position to do.' When Byroade asked if he could convey the gist of this conversation to Ayub, he was told he could but again both Amjad Ali and Zafrulla replied that Ayub was only in the US to discuss equipment and not policy matters. Little did they understand the strength and influence of the Pakistan army chief, not only with the government at home but also with his American counterparts. Ayub managed to forge a tight relationship with his US interlocutors, gaining their confidence and support and was quick to claim victory.

Five days later, Secretary Defence Iskander Mirza, who outranked Ayub by virtue of his position as defence secretary but was attempting to forge his own relationship with Ayub Khan as the army chief, noted the gist of a telephone conversation he held with Ayub Khan in Washington.[27] A handwritten note from Mirza to the prime minister states that the 'US defense set-up have agreed to give military aid. States (sic) Department want political agreement before actually giving of aid.' He suggested a case be prepared for the cabinet and once the government agreed in principle, a brief could be sent to the ambassador in Washington who could start talks. But Mirza suggested that 'the commander-in-chief should be asked to be present at the talks as before final agreement is reached we must evaluate the nature of the military task allotted to us and if the aid given to us will enable us (a) to fulfil (sic) the task (b) to defend our country.' He closed with a note that 'Direct rapprochement (sic) with Americans is better than through Turkey or any other country.'

Two days earlier, Ayub had sent Mirza a handwritten report from the embassy in Washington, apologizing for sending it by bag rather than cable 'for security reasons.' This report was the first solid sign that the United States was getting ready to provide military assistance to Pakistan. It also underlined the key role of Ayub Khan in the process of convincing the US to do so, elevating him within the Pakistan hierarchy and in effect allowing the Pakistan Army to begin making foreign policy decisions on behalf of the government of Pakistan. Ayub had met, among others, General Bedell-Smith and Colonel Byroade. He characterized their attitude as 'promising' but 'guarded.' Secretary Wilson, Keyes, Nash, and Ridgway at the Pentagon gave him a better sense of their acceptance of the Pakistan case for military aid. They indicated their readiness 'to give all help.' They wished to send a military team to Pakistan at the 'soonest' provided that 'our Govt. first of all confirms acceptance of political and military obligations connected with such aid.' Ayub told the Pentagon that they needed to spell out these obligations and to approach his government 'through normal channels' while taking into account Pakistan's 'delicate strategic and political situation in the Middle East and South East Asia.' He also advised them to be 'realistic.' Ayub was then invited to a meeting with the Americans to sort out these issues. He suggested including Ambassador Amjad Ali in the meeting and told Mirza that he had apprised the foreign minister too about his exchanges in the United States.

Ayub reported shooting down the idea of sending troops to Korea and agreed with the foreign minister that Pakistan ought to restrict itself to the Middle East sphere. Ayub was requested by the Americans to stop in Korea *en route* to Pakistan. He did not wish to do so but sought guidance from the government of Pakistan. Measuring the significance of the agreements that appeared to have been reached in his discussions in Washington, Ayub wrote:

> Finally, in my view this juncture [is] a turning point in our History. We must aim to get Strong. So let us take the right decision boldly and trust the rest to God. Creating difficulties at this stage will make us loose (sic) this final opportunity.

Mirza immediately sent the handwritten missive from Ayub to the prime minister with a note asking if Ayub should stop in Korea. More importantly, Mirza sought a clear policy from the prime minister on the emergence of a close political relationship with the United States. 'This is only possible if we are ready to form a modern progressive state and are ready to trump fanatics and [...] to take control.'

Thus, Ayub's work in Washington had managed to invigorate discussions on aid to Pakistan and the possible emergence of a Middle East pact. Ayub had met Secretary of State John Foster Dulles and pressed him to push for aid to Pakistan. He already had allies in the US government at the highest level, including Vice-President Nixon, who was beginning to nurture a distrust of the Indians and a trust of the Pakistanis that was to endure. The US raised the issue of aid to Pakistan with their British allies and began preparing for a review of Pakistan's needs.[28] Pakistan in the meantime increased pressure on the US, with official visits by the governor general and the prime minister and repeated reminders from the foreign minister. A calculated series of well-placed newspapers articles about the impending decision was their attempt to force the American hand. Understandably, India reacted badly but neither their protestations nor the repeated pleas of US Ambassador Chester Bowles were enough to dissuade the White House.

EISENHOWER APPROVES AID

On 5 January 1954, at a meeting attended by Secretary Wilson, Governor Stassen, and Secretary of State Dulles and presided over by President Eisenhower, 'the president agreed in principle to proceeding with military aid to Pakistan.'[29] In order to allay Indian concerns, this aid would be presented in the context of 'a regional security project being initiated by Turkey and Pakistan with other countries in the area', and the US would inform India that it would be prepared to provide India with aid under the same type of agreement. The die was cast, even though the US bureaucracy now set into motion a series of studies of the issues related to provision of such aid and the consequences of the US not providing such aid to Pakistan. The sum of these reviews was that Pakistan was likely to be a dependable ally and that despite anything the US did to mollify India, Prime Minister Nehru would not accept the US actions with understanding. On the other hand, if the US were to pull out from a deal to give aid to Pakistan, 'the effect of the decision would be to weaken the position of the pro-Western moderate elements now in control' and 'strengthen the reactionary religious elements.'[30] A negative decision would also send the wrong signals to Middle Eastern allies and encourage elements that opposed ties to the West.

There already were some budding concerns, even among those that the US took for granted as dependent allies in the region. Later that year, when Pakistan's Governor General Ghulam Mohammad shared with Saudi Arabia's King Saud Ibne Abdul Aziz Pakistan's plans to participate in a US-led Middle East defence initiative and reviewed the proposals given to the Saudis by the US ambassador, he received a very frank appraisal of the Americans by King Saud, while supporting Pakistan's role as defender of the Muslim countries of the region. 'It may look to one who had studied the behaviour of United States with Saudi Arabia that this proposed treaty is based on good faith for the help of the Saudi Arabian government. But the past experience is disheartening to the officials of the Saudi government,' Saud wrote in a secret memorandum attached to his cover letter to Ghulam Mohammad.[31] In return for the Saudis' assistance during the war through facilities and other aid, and in the wake of bilateral treaties between the two countries after the war, the king noted that the US gave Saudi Arabia 'some useless armoured cars at very high prices and some other vehicles which were ordered to be replaced with some other good vehicles when Mr Stans visited this country with Mr Dulles.' The Saudis wanted arms but the US promised to study their needs first. Nearly ten years later, 'the result of this promise, discussion enquiry etc. is that we are still without armaments and ammunition. We have not taken arms from other countries because we are depending on God and after that on the promises of American government.' The king stressed that he would be happy if Pakistan were to become stronger. 'No doubt Pakistan's strength is our strength and if the Jews attacked on the Holy Land then Pakistan will be in the front of the defender of the Haramain [Islam's Holy Places] as it has promised.'

Pakistan certainly learned a lot from the Saudi experience. And though it knew that its defence pacts would be geared to protect the Middle East against the communists and not the 'Jews,' it proceeded apace in its negotiations with the United States. This included the sharing by Ghulam Mohammad with the

US ambassador in Karachi of the exchanges between the Saudis and the Pakistanis!

PAKISTAN WAR GAMES THE AID PLAN

While the Americans continued their internal reviews and debates, the Pakistanis lost little time in preparing for the arrival of a US military aid review team. Shortly after arriving back in Pakistan from the US and Turkey, Ayub and Iskander Mirza began planning for their discussions with the Americans. A highly secret meeting was convened on 24 February 1954 at the GHQ premises with General Ayub in the chair. (Iskander Mirza, though a civilian for many years, had been promoted over the course of the previous four years from colonel—his last rank in the army—to major general). Those attending this meeting included the other two service chiefs: Rear Admiral H.M.S. Choudri[32] of the Royal Pakistan Navy and Air Vice Marshal L.W. Cannon of the Royal Pakistan Air Force. Major General Mohammed Musa was the secretary of this exclusive group.[33]

Mirza, as the ranking official representing the government, laid out the main objectives of their exercise, stressing that the 'Government reposed great confidence in the Committee and considered its functions highly important, as it was realized that the entire success of the military aid depended, to a very large extent, on the manner in which our requirements were presented to the American survey team when it arrived in Pakistan to conduct negotiations.' The American team under Brigadier General Harry Meyers was due to arrive within a month. Preparing to war game the exchange with the Americans, Mirza and Ayub had orchestrated a keenly honed strategy. Mirza spelled out the remit of the group:

(a) The committee must at all times keep in view the object of the aid, which is to enable us to repel aggression against Pakistan by communist forces and provide an expeditionary force for the defence of the Middle East under certain circumstances, if required. Any digression from this object was likely to create the impression that we were mainly interested in building our forces for some other purposes. [Note that the name of India was never to be used, even in internal discourse!] This would be fatal and would ruin the prospects of getting any assistance from the USA.

(b) To convince the survey team of the reasonableness of our requirements, the committee had to be very realistic in its appreciation of the forces Pakistan should have to achieve the aim stated in (a) above, and prepare its plans with great care. The Americans would minutely scrutinise (sic) our demands, in the same manner as they had done in Turkey, and we must not appear to be haphazard in our approach to the task.

(c) The success of the committee mission would be seriously prejudiced by any disagreements and the inability of its members to speak with one voice. Differences in their views, if there were any, must be amicably resolved before negotiations with the American started.

(d) The committee's deliberations and decisions must be treated as state secret.

Mirza's aim was to ensure that nothing from these meetings was leaked and, based on the absence of any reference to these meeting in the records of the US and UK governments for this period, the Pakistanis managed to keep their planning close to their chests. But, as Mirza and Ayub anticipated, there were grumblings from the other service chiefs, who wished that the prime minister as defence minister (a portfolio that the prime minister held concurrently), or even President Mirza, should be the one presiding over the committee rather than the army chief whom they considered equal to, if not below, the naval chief in terms of the seniority of service he commanded. Mirza responded by firmly stating that Ayub had dealt directly with the Americans, that he knew how the Turks had dealt with the Americans, and was thus in a better position to 'give guidance to the committee during its discussions'. Mirza stated that his own function was to be a resource for the group, helping resolve any issues that arose. He would also keep the prime minister informed of progress. Ayub was thus positioned at the top amongst the 'equals', with Mirza's blessing.

In a remarkably deft analysis of the situation, Mirza urged the group to bear in mind that 'the USA might not undertake large commitments due to the recent trends in that country to reduce their defence budget, particularly if its military experts were not convinced that our requirements were realistic.' He stressed the need for 'a cast iron case, which was based on a balanced appreciation and represented the unanimous views of all the Services.' He warned that any attempt at 'deceiving' the Americans 'would be fatal'

With these marching orders, the committee began work on its plans before the arrival of the US team. To ensure secrecy, only eight numbered copies of the minutes were distributed. The group met two more times before convening at the GHQ in Rawalpindi on 26 March for its first session with the US survey team.

FIRST DISCUSSIONS WITH THE US TEAM

The 26 March meeting was a larger affair. In addition to the original committee (minus Iskander Mirza), there was a supporting local cast of key officers from all Services, with the Pakistan Army having the largest contingent.[34] Even a cursory look a this list indicates not only the important role of the Pakistan Army in the negotiations but also the emergence of a cohort that Ayub was gathering around him in the Pakistan Army that would in one way or the other be responsible for running the affairs of Pakistan for the next couple of decades.[35]

Arrayed against this stellar group was Brigadier General Harry F. Meyers, assisted by Colonel R.C. Angster, five lieutenant colonels, a commander, one major, and one captain. Colonel Robert L. Ashworth, the army attaché at the US embassy in Karachi joined the US team during its discussions. It is not clear if they were quite prepared for the show that the Pakistanis had arranged for them. Ayub and his team were going to try to build their image with the US hierarchy, not only from the top-down of the hierarchy but also from the bottom-up. For if they were to succeed in transforming the US view of Pakistan and the region, they needed to convince all parties on the US side of the importance of Pakistan as a key ally in the Middle East.

Ayub began the discussions with the US team with a welcoming speech and overview of the military and political situation in Pakistan and the Middle East. He underlined the rough or 'field service conditions' under which the armed forces were operating, also pointing specifically to the ramshackle buildings in which their GHQ was housed. 'Pakistan was a firm believer in peace and would work for peace. She realized that the only way to secure peace would be to get militarily strong,' said Ayub, pointing to the country's strategic location because of which 'neutrality was not...her attitude of life.'[36] Pakistan, he said, was willing to fill the 'power vacuum in the Middle East', now that the pre-partition Indian Army was no longer available for that purpose. He also recognized the 'covetous eye' of the Russians and the US dependence on Middle Eastern oil to meet its growing needs.

Ayub had benefited from his exchanges with Iskander Mirza, who was in London while the US team was in Pakistan. Mirza had told him that he had spoken with the Meyer team and they had told Mirza that the 'American general staff directive to Meyers is, according to him [Meyers], to make a start with 4 divisions and an armoured brigade.' Mirza also conveyed to Ayub that he had 'made it clear that here can be no question of an Expeditionary Force in [the] general area of Persian Gulf unless the present Army is fully balanced and an additional force created for that purpose.'[37]

Very nicely, Ayub then turned to why he found it extremely difficult to put these concepts over to the Americans. He may have been aware of various unsuccessful attempts by the British to influence the US against choosing an alliance with Pakistan over India. If not, he exhibited a good grasp of the situation between the two Atlantic partners. As McMahon has traced in the exchanges between rivals in the US policy hierarchy and between the US and British leadership, as recently as 7 December, British Foreign Minister

Anthony Eden 'had warned of the danger of a military alliance between the United States and Pakistan during a conversation with Dulles in Bermuda.'[38]

But to no avail. Vice-President Richard Nixon had warned on 16 December that if the US backed down from the deal with Pakistan because of Indian objections, it risked 'losing most of the Asian-Arab countries to the neutralist bloc.' Nixon had evidently made up his mind in favour of Pakistan: 'A country I would do anything for. The people have less complexes than the Indians. The Pakistanis are completely frank, even when it hurts. It will be disastrous if the Pakistan aid does not go through.'[39]

Turning back to the events of the meeting, Ayub said he thought the US was constrained in thinking of the Middle East as being in the British sphere of influence and was wary of interfering in the affairs of the countries in this region. Further, 'the fear of India, the lack of knowledge of the Hindu mind and of Pakistan, imposed caution on the United States policy-makers.' He made a parting shot at the previous Truman administration, stating that it had 'socialist tendencies' and that the US thought 'Nehru fair-minded and refrained from hurting his feelings.' Finally, he expressed that the general instability of the Middle East discouraged political and military alliances.

In the face of these odds, a handful of 'determined persons' like the Governor General Ghulam Mohammad and Prime Minister Muhammed Ali Bogra of Pakistan and Ambassador Warren of the US pushed for Pakistan's point of view. Ayub acknowledged that he himself had 'something to do [with] it in a small way' and briefed the US team of the behind-the-scene activities that preceded their visit. Dulles's visit to Pakistan in 1953 had been a 'turning point.' When the government of Pakistan had asked him to go to Turkey and the United States, Ayub told the US team, he had been reluctant to go at first, in the absence of 'a political understanding' between Pakistan and the USA, but then agreed to go ahead with the visit. Ayub then proceeded to praise the attitude of the US officers and other personnel in Turkey and recounted his discussions with the Turkish leadership about the need for Pakistan to protect the Middle East if Russia were to choose to go around the eastern flank of Turkey through Azerbaijan, Iran and Northern Iraq.

In the US, Ayub told the team, he had found it difficult to convince policy-makers to accept Pakistan's viewpoint but he persevered and by the end of his visit, military aid had been agreed in principle. He attributed this to the 'magnificent American leaders' who 'appreciated the truth and acted upon it.' The 'truth', as Ayub put it, was that Pakistan 'did not want preponderance over India'—rather, all it wanted to do was to protect itself against the communists and to assist in defending the Middle East, but it did not have the forces for these tasks. If the US did not act in a timely fashion, Ayub said, 'it would be very costly...to suppress it once it had started.' He said he had assured the US leaders that Pakistan would be 'a trust[ed] associates (sic) of America.'

However, he warned, that 'the aid would raise high hopes in the minds of the general public and they would get utterly disappointed if the USA backed out.' Faced with these arguments, Ayub said, the US leadership had agreed to provide aid to Pakistan and they even showed him a draft before he left the US for Pakistan. And the Americans had stayed the course, Ayub pointed out, even after protestations from India and even the British.

Ayub then spelled out the salient points that he felt ought to guide the discussions:

- 'Pakistan must not be taken for granted.' Anything less than (a sufficient amount of) aid which would enable it to defend itself would be 'futile and a waste of time.' Moreover, it would expose Pakistan to communist and Indian pressure and 'accentuate its internal difficulties.'
- The 'burden of sacrifice' would have to be 'proportionately distributed' between the USA and Pakistan. 'A one-sided deal would not work.'
- Neither side should 'play politics' and 'all concerned must place their cards on the table.'
- Pakistan was buckling under a 'crushing financial burden.' About 75 per cent of the country's budget was being devoted to defence, adversely affecting the economy and its growth, and even then its defence capability was inadequate.
- A long term view of Pakistan's aid requirements needed to be worked and agreed and assistance phased over the years.
- If the US agreed with Pakistan's assessments and committed itself to a long-term plan, the US needed to provide all that was needed to achieve Pakistan's long-term objectives. No tinkering, once the objectives were set.
- And, finally, the visitors needed to apprise the US leadership of the views of the Pakistani civil and military leadership, (something that did not appear to be in the scope of the team's remit.)

This opening salvo was followed by a series of presentations by the army's senior leadership on different aspects of the Pakistan Army. Major General Hayauddin gave an overview of the history, traditions, and socio-economics factors related to Pakistan's defence and the issues that these raised for the fledgling economy. Brigadier Yahya, Captain Ahsan, and Group Captain Asghar Khan presented their respective services' appreciations, plans and requirements to defend Pakistan against the Soviets and to send troops to defend the Middle East, 'provided her forces were not heavily engaged locally.' Admiral Choudri outlined the poor state of the Pakistan Navy and the enormous task it had of protecting the coastline and providing for Middle East defence. Air Vice Marshal Cannon explained how small the Pakistan Air Force was at that time. 'A force of five squadrons was not even a boy in a man's job,' he said.

The MGO, Major General Shahid Hamid, explained how Pakistan had only inherited 20,000 tons of ordnance out of the total 160,000 tons of ordnance stores and 40,000 tons of ammunition in pre-partition India. Most of these stores that Pakistan received were 'spare parts for tanks Pakistan did not possess, oversize boots and shoes used by East African troops in the last war, old vehicles and other unwanted materials.' Pakistan did not have a single ordnance factory in its territory, and it had no funds between 1948 and 1950 to purchase stores from abroad to fill its empty ordnance depots. When funds were available, Pakistani teams found that suppliers could not meet their needs before a period of 2 to 3 years. In sum, the Pakistanis painted a grim picture of their needs and capability to provide a bulwark against the Soviets or to project a Pakistan force beyond Pakistan's borders to defend Middle East oil.

The first question from the US team was about the tie-up between the Pakistan effort in the Middle East and any conflict in Europe. Ayub replied that the major battle ground was likely to be Europe but that the Soviets would wish to come into the south, particularly against Turkey, to 'deny space' to the allies and to increase its bargaining power against the West. The second question was closer to home and focused on the issue of the expeditionary force for the Middle East. Would it be an independent force or part of the field army of Pakistan? Ayub was ready for that too; he did not envisage a separate force on stand by for the Middle East, but rather, he saw an enlarged Pakistan Army capable of 'repelling Russian aggression, provided Pakistan forces were not heavily engaged locally.'

The next day, General Meyers gave an overview of the military assistance programme and the mission of his team. In essence, he stated that his team was restricted in its scope to meeting Pakistan's shortfalls in equipment and training. They were not going to deal with economic assistance or defence support at a broader level. Nor was his team authorized to discuss the programme in terms of its monetary value.

This was not what the Pakistanis expected to hear. Little did they know that indeed this was not what the US State Department had conceived the purpose of the Meyers mission to be.

Nevertheless, Ayub Khan put on as happy a face as he could when he reported to Prime Minister Bogra and key cabinet members on 2 April,[40] prior to the meeting of the prime minister with the US visitors. This meeting included Zafrulla Khan (Foreign Minister), Chaudhry Muhammad Ali (Finance Minister), Sardar Amir Azam (Minister of State for Defence), the three services chiefs, Major General Musa, Aziz Ahmed (Cabinet Secretary), J.A. Rahim (Foreign Secretary), and M. Hamid Ali (Joint Secretary of the Ministry of Defence). Ayub told the gathering that the visitors were 'highly impressed with the presentation made to them and appreciated that the Services were well acquainted with their job, had prepared their plans very thoroughly and had all the information readily available.'[41] But, he explained, the US team had a limited charter and its focus on deficiencies, its inability to discuss the monetary value of needed aid, or to make any commitments about expansion of the present armed forces of Pakistan or broader infrastructural support, was a big drawback. He suggested that Pakistan begin 'agitating for defence support and economic aid straightaway, and keep the Turks informed.' He concluded that the military assistance that the United States envisaged for Pakistan, going by what was conveyed by the Meyers team, 'would be totally ineffective.' He also suggested the setting up of a planning board in Pakistan with a 'powerful chairman' and representatives from key ministries, including defence, industries, communications, and finance to negotiate with the US and to make effective use of any aid that would be forthcoming. Clearly, he saw an opportunity for a broader role for himself.

The finance minister asked many pointed questions about the needs of the services and then opined that the planning for aid would be for nought unless the US was ready in principle to provide aid with a clear and long term objective which he described as 'the Big Concept, for which we sought military assistance from the America.' He termed the survey team's mission as 'the smaller concept', i.e. making good deficiencies in combat items in existing forces.' He suggested that the US ambassador and the visiting team be told clearly that Pakistan had a heavy defence burden that had seriously upset its economy and drained its resources. By approaching the US, Pakistan had antagonized the Russians and India. Pakistan had done all this even when most Asian countries were reluctant to take sides in the global struggle for fear of annoying the Soviets, and Pakistan had taken this step to 'get strong so as to be able to defend herself adequately against communist aggression and make an effective contribution to the cause of peace and stability in the Middle East.' In his view, Pakistan did not seek aid merely to fill the gaps in its current forces. Zafrulla Khan agreed with the finance minister's views. The prime minister said he agreed with the views of his minister and asked that the US ambassador and the team be told that 'by asking America for military help, Pakistan had practically burned her boats, exposed herself to great risks and was now faced with the active hostility of India and disruptive Indian and communist propaganda activities to disintegrate her from within the country.' The meeting also sought a higher level US team to discuss longer-term objectives of military aid.

The next day the visiting team met the prime minister in the company of the army chiefs and senior ministers of the cabinet. The prime minister thanked the Americans for their 'understanding and sympathy' for the Pakistani point of view but also stressed that 'Pakistan's decision to accept military aid was in the interest of both the US and Pakistan. In fact, it would not be wrong to say that USA stood more to gain from this agreement than Pakistan.'[42] In his view, the US had gained considerably in terms of prestige by having Pakistan 'boldly come out into the open and ally herself decisively with the Western democracies' at a time when most countries in Asia were sitting on the fence and '[clinging] to the doctrine of "neutrality"'. Ambassador Hildreth responded that he 'fully realized the importance of what the prime minister had said and that he was sure that it would be given due consideration by his government.' however, he distanced himself from the military team's views whose recommendations he said were theirs alone.

Meyers too recognized the 'importance of the remarks made by the prime minister' but stated that the mission had been given a specific technical job and that the political and other aspects were outside the scope of his team's work. He read out a prepared statement that restated the Mission's objectives, which were: 'to survey the existing military position with respect to your military plans as compared with your present status of military readiness.'[43] They had limited their detailed analysis to Phase-1 of Pakistan's ten-year plan which only covered the first three years. This, he said, was in accord with the rules of the military aid programme and focused solely on deficiencies that fit in with the US's aid programme and would eliminate items that could be produced or procured from local sources. The mission would then accord priorities to these needs and to the delivery schedules. He warned that many items may not be available for 'several years.' Then he proceeded to hedge on the provision of information to Pakistan of what might be available and by when, citing the need for reviews in the US and the need for Pakistan to sign a bilateral agreement with the US. That, he said, would allow the setting up of a military assistance advisory group for Pakistan that would in turn be able to get approval for aid and to 'make changes…found necessary due to changing situations.'

He then proceeded to sweeten his message by praising the Pakistan Army's production plans and state of readiness. 'Unfortunately, the rest of my team have not had the opportunity to see your soldiers under combat conditions. I have seen them and can assure you they can handle their end of the fighting in any land,' he asserted. He concluded with a preview of his recommendations: '(a) That Pakistan be given aid to the maximum extent possible in the initial programme. (b) That necessary actions be taken to insure that funds be made available for future military defense assistance program for Pakistan.'

Given the expectations of the Pakistanis, Meyer's cold-hearted statement elicited a sharp response, with the finance minister pointing out that the Phase-1 plans of the programme being proposed by the mission were 'very modest and limited in scope and of the same order as the plan drawn up by a committee in Pakistan in 1951 with a view to fixing targets for strengthening the country's defence.' Pakistan had been unable to carry out these plans due to the slump in commodity prices and the decline in foreign exchange earnings of US$400 million, 'a very considerable sum in comparison to

Pakistan's total earnings.' The Phase-1 plan had nothing to do with the communist threat or any Middle East venture. Pakistan had never sought US aid merely to meet its own current defence needs or to fill existing deficiencies but to align itself with the US and other democratic countries in fighting the communist threat, said the finance minister. The team's recommended plan was deemed 'exceedingly limited.'

The finance minister went on to say that Pakistan had suffered from increased hostility from India as a result of its alignment with the US and was relying on military aid to reduce the burden on its own resources to protect itself and to play a part in fighting the communists. Even the common man in Pakistan had these expectations. Therefore, not only was Pakistan's army to be strengthened but also her economy, especially the infrastructure.

Meyer responded that the US could only look at Pakistan's current needs and strengths. 'After all…what good would there be if American gave Pakistan military equipment enough for 15 divisions, if Pakistan did not have those 15 divisions?' He reiterated that the issues raised by the finance minister were outside the scope of his team's remit to which the finance minister retorted that unless the objective was agreed upon and Pakistan could start planning accordingly, 'it would never be able to absorb equipment for 15 divisions, not now or in the future.' The meeting effectively ended on that note of disagreement, with Hildreth facing the task of informing his superiors at State Department of the apparent impasse.

US DEBATE ON HOW MUCH AID TO GIVE PAKISTAN

Little did the Pakistanis know that by taking this firm position in these discussions, they were entering the contretemps between different elements in the US government that had debated the scope and nature of the military aid package for Pakistan for a long time, and even now were squabbling over it. The firm Pakistani view forced the US to focus on the nub of the issue: would they build up a stronger Pakistan military or not?

Even before Meyers had left for Pakistan, the Department of State was of the view that the terms of reference drawn up by Meyers were very narrow and sought to have them expanded. They discovered later that Meyers had not changed the terms of reference despite being asked to do so. Not only that, but the State Department officers who met Meyers the day before he left for Pakistan found that 'General Meyers had become so infected with the philosophy of caution and doubt the terms of reference seemed to reflect, that he was taking an extremely alarming line which he planned to take with the Pakistanis.'[44] Byroade therefore arranged a meeting with Admiral Davis (Director, Office of Foreign Military Affairs in Defense) and General Stewart

(Director, Office of Military Assistance), and others, including Meyers. Davis emphatically told Meyers that 'the Pakistan program was not to be regarded as a "one-shot operation" and that if the terms of reference did not reflect that, Davis would change them forthwith.' Meyers was stated to have said that he understood this and would proceed accordingly to take a longer-term view of Pakistan's needs and that the terms of reference did not need to be altered.

Now, faced with reports from Hildreth of how the meetings had gone in Pakistan, Jernegan said that the actions and statements of Meyers 'were at complete variance with the explicit understanding reached at our meeting.' Despite this, the State Department attempted to rectify the situation by speaking of longer-term needs of Pakistan and 'although a clear cut statement may not emerge rapidly, the "glacier is moving"', wrote Jernegan to Hildreth. 'I have no doubts personally that we will be able to follow through on the Pakistan program in a manner which will convince even the doubters that the United States supports its friends.' The pro-Pakistan lobby at State Department and in the White House clearly saw Pakistan as a worthwhile longer term ally and invested in that relationship by making strong efforts to blunt the initial commentary of Meyers on Pakistan's military needs. These efforts paid off. A draft treaty was soon sent to Pakistan for review.

No one in Pakistan was prepared to stop negotiations with the Americans at that point, but there was enough debate and discussion to indicate that Pakistani officials did not want to leave anything to chance or misinterpretation, while leaving enough generalities in the treaty to allow subjective interpretations by the signatory states. A flavour of these reviews is captured in a meeting of the Committee of Secretaries held with the Deputy COAS, Musa to review the draft treaty.

While recognizing that the treaty was a standard one that the US used elsewhere, nevertheless the participants in the meeting felt that mutual obligations needed to be understood and, where necessary, ought to be supported by separate exchanges of notes.[45] Article V, dealing with Pakistan's international role and the effective use of US aid garnered a lot of attention and debate, with fears expressed by some participants that it might allow the US to establish bases in Pakistan. The Foreign Ministry representatives clarified that bases could only be agreed upon by a separate agreement, as was the case in Spain. They stuck to the standard line that Pakistan would only commit to external projection of its forces in light of its own defence requirements at that time and suggested that this needed 'to be separately agreed upon in light of the quantum and character of the aid actually received.' With some minor quibbles and suggestions, the draft was recommended for approval by the government of Pakistan, without any provision for ratification.

In effect, a signature from the executive was all that was needed to put into effect this key document in Pakistan's history.

On 19 May 1954, the United States Charge d'Affaires in Pakistan, John K. Emmerson and the Pakistani Foreign Minister Zafrulla Khan signed the Mutual Defense Agreement between the government of the United States of America and the government of Pakistan in Karachi. Uncle Sam was now officially on Pakistan's side and vice versa. Mirza and Ayub had managed to make foreign policy while strengthening their hands in domestic politics. Unwittingly, India, had contributed to this outcome by taking a bellicose stance and even forcing Pakistan to the edge of another war in 1951, allowing the civil–military combine to assert its position even while the politicians bickered on parochial matters. Ayub and Mirza were able to use India's hostility to build support for a stronger, larger military. The American connection gave them further legitimacy, setting off a trend that later rulers in Pakistan found easy to use to their advantage.

NOTES

1. William Roger Louis, 'American anti-colonialism and the dissolution of the British Empire,' *International Affairs*, 1985, traces the jockeying for advantage by the US in the post Second World War period.
2. 501.BC/1-648: Telegram: The Secretary of State to the United States Representative at the United Nations (Austin), Secret, US Urgent, Washington, 6 January 1948, 1 p.m. *Foreign Relations of the United States 1948, Part 1* (Washington, D.C.: United States Government Printing Office, 1975).
3. 'US Foreign Policy to Pakistan, 1947–1960: Re-Constructing Strategy' unpublished dissertation by Saqib Qureshi for a PhD at the London School of Economics, 2001. This reference is based on Chester Bowles' *Ambassador's Report* (New York: Harper & Row, 1954), p. 14.
4. Record of interview between Ismay and M.A. Jinnah, IOR, Mountbatten Papers, MSS Eur F.200/191, Top Secret, 9 April 1947, p. 646, *Jinnah Papers, First Series Volume 1, Part II*, Z.H. Zaidi (editor-in-chief), National Archives of Pakistan, 1993.
5. See Dennis Kux's comprehensive: *The United States and Pakistan 1947–2000* (Washington, D.C.: Woodrow Wilson Center Press, and Baltimore and London: The Johns Hopkins University, 2001), p. 32.
6. *Nee* Irene Pant.
7. Robert J. McMahon, *The Cold War on the Periphery: the United States, India, and Pakistan* (Columbia University Press, 1994), pp. 55–56.
8. Despite the preponderance of elite British missionary schools, most of them Roman Catholic, in pre-partition India and later in both India and Pakistan, US Presbyterian missionaries had established a stronghold in the area of higher education. Gordon College, the first co-educational college in the country, was set up by American missionaries in Rawalpindi in 1856 as a primary school and in 1893 as a college, and produced many leaders of Pakistani society. Prime Minister Shaukat Aziz graduated with a BSc in 1967, a year before the author. The Forman Christian College (FCC), another similar American missionary college, was set up in Lahore in 1864. It has also contributed to the ranks of Pakistani

leaders. Pakistan's president and chief of army staff, Pervez Musharraf, was educated at FCC, as this college is better known.

9. Secret note for the defence minister, dated 8 April 1950, Pakistan Army GHQ archives.

10. Most Immediate P.M. Secretariat U.O No. S-3339-PMS/50 dated 25-4-50 [note date follows European style, day, month and then year.] from Mirza to Prime Minister's Secretariat. Pakistan Army GHQ archives.

11. Top Secret letter P.O. 75/50/13 dated Boston, Mass., 29 May 1950 from Ambassador M.A.H. Ispahani to Col. Iskander Mirza, Ministry of Defence, Karachi, Pakistan Army GHQ archives. Such handwritten dispatches were the vogue during this and later periods (in the 1971 negotiations of the Kissinger visit to China also) since they provided maximum security in communications. Not even the official typists could see these messages. Pakistan's Defence Attaché then Brigadier M.G. 'Jilly' Jilani employed the same technique during his tenure in Washington from 1952 to 1955 in communicating with his chief, Ayub Khan.

12. Letter from Department of State to the Pakistan Ambassador, 6 December 1950 and sent by telegram to the Foreign Ministry in Karachi. Secret 7040. Pakistan Army GHQ archives.

13. A purge of communists began, both in the civil and military sectors, going to comical lengths at time. Taufiq Rafat of Sialkot recounts the story of a zealous police officer who threw a bunch of people from the city in jail allegedly for their communist connections. When other locals went to the policy officer to explain that these people were in fact 'anti-communists,' he retorted: I don't care what kind of communists they are! So long as they are communists, I'll keep them in jail!'

14. Top Secret Memorandum of the Acting-Secretary of State to the Executive Secretary of the National Security Council (Lay), S/S-NSC files lot 63 D 351, 'MSC 98-Memoranda', 19 August 1952.

15. Secret Special estimate: Consequences of Communist Control Over South Asia, INS-NIE files, Washington, 2 October 1952, in *Foreign Relations of the United States 1952–54, Volume XI Part 2*.

16. Consequences of Communist Control, p. 1079.

17. S/S–NSC files, lot 62 D 351, 'NSC Memoranda' Secret NSC 5409 United States Policy toward South Asia, 19 February 1954 in *US Foreign Relations*, op. cit.

18. 790.5/3-154, Memorandum by the Assistant Secretary of State for Near Eastern, South Asian, and African Affairs (Byroade) to the Acting Secretary of State, Top Secret, Washington, 1 March 1954. *US Foreign Relations*, op. cit., pp. 1118–1119.

19. 033.1100NI/12-853: Telegram Top Secret. The Ambassador in Pakistan (Hildreth) to the Department of State. Karachi, 8 December 1953, 5 p.m. *Foreign Relations of the United States*, op. cit.

20. In a separate message Hildreth noted that the Governor General had earlier chosen the same type of reference when talking about the US–Pakistan budding relationship: 'It would be like taking a poor girl for a walk and then walking out on her, leaving her only with a bad name'.

21. Later a major general and reputedly one of the inner circle of planners of the 1958 coup d'etat, he was not promoted to lieutenant general and retired. He later joined the National Awami Party of the NWFP as a member of the opposition. He moved to the United States in his old age and died in Fairfax, Virginia in 2005.

22. Top Secret handwritten letter from Brigadier M.G. Jilani, defence attaché, Pakistan embassy, Washington DC to General M. Ayub Khan, 28 June 1953. Pakistan Army GHQ archives. This section is based on his letter.

23. Top Secret Aide Memoire by Iskander Mirza, defence secretary, 8 October 1953, Pakistan GHQ archives.

24. Both Ayub and Iskander Mirza seemed to be using this high figure, which appears to be much higher than the regular army at that time and probably includes reservists.

25. Secret Letter from Ayub Khan to Prime Minister Muhammed Ali, from 'Camp Istanbul', 24 September 1953, Pakistan Army GHQ archives.
26. Top Secret handwritten letter from Syed Amjad Ali to Prime Minister Muhammed Ali (no relation) of 14 October 1953, Pakistan Army GHQ Archives.
27. Top Secret DO [Demi-Official] no. 9053/19 on Government of Pakistan, ministry of defence letterhead, Karachi. Iskander Mirza to the prime minister. Pakistan Army GHQ archives.
28. McMahon, *The Cold War*.
29. 790D.5/1-554, Top Secret EYES ONLY *Memorandum of Conversation, by the Secretary of State*, dated Washington DC, 5 January 1954, *Foreign Relations of the United States, 1952-1954*.
30. Top Secret SE–55 Washington, 15 January 1954. *Special Estimate: The Probable Repercussions of a US Decision to Grant or Deny Military Aid to Pakistan. Foreign Relations*, op. cit., p. 1839.
31. Translation of Secret Letter from King Saud to the Governor General of Pakistan, dated 2nd Shawwal 1373 (Muslim Calendar) that is 2 June 1954, plus copy of letter from US ambassador in Karachi to the governor general, declassified 14 January 2003 by Paul Wolf from the National Archives of the United States. See www.icdc.com/~paulwolf/Pakistan/saudaziz2june1954.htm
32. This aptly named chief of the navy caused confusion with his initials. A story goes that before his visit to the British Navy in Portsmouth, a message arrived 'HMS Choudri arriving' and giving the time and date. Back came the reply: 'Please send tonnage'!
33. An interesting sidelight to this gathering, as captured in the meticulous and finely tuned minutes that Musa produced, is the fact that all the participants, except Ayub had garnered fairly distinguished British military decorations for their services. Choudri had an MBE, Cannon had a CB and a CBE, Iskander Mirza had a CIE and an OBE. Even Musa had an MBE. Only Ayub had no such recognition. Within the next decade or so, he had a chest full of medals, including two of Pakistan's highest civil and gallantry awards, the Hilal-i-Pakistan and Hilal-i-Juraat to be followed shortly by his elevation to field marshal.
34. The additional army contingent included: Lt. Gen. Nasir Ali Khan (Chief of Staff), Maj. Gen. M. Hayauddin (Chief of General Staff [CGS]), Maj. Gen. Sher Ali Khan (Adjutant General), Maj. Gen. S.M. Afzal (Quartermaster General [QMG]), Maj. Gen. S. Shahid Hamid (Master General Ordnance [MGO]), Brigadier A.M. Yahya Khan (Deputy CGS), Brigadier Malik Sher Bahadur (Deputy QMG), Brigadier N.A. Qureshi (Deputy MGO), Brigadier Abdul Hamid Khan (Military Secretary; responsible for military establishment and postings etc.), Brig. Choudhry Rahimullah Khan (Director of Organisation), and Lt. Col. M. Barlas (acting Director of Staff Duties; in charge of procedural issues). The navy had Captain S.M. Ahsan (Deputy Chief of Staff), and Commander S.B. Salimi. The air force had Air Commodore L.E. Jarman (Chief of Staff), Group Captain Nur Khan (Assistant Chief of Air Staff and Deputy Chief of Staff Air), Group Captain M. Asghar Khan (Group Commander No. 1 RPAF Group), and Wing Commander A. Qadir (Director of Operations, Air Headquarters). Many of these names figured prominently in Pakistani history.
35. Yahya of course took over from Ayub in 1969 as chief martial law administrator and president. His principal partner in that venture was Hamid Khan. General Hayauddin, who at one time may have been a contender for the army chief position, unfortunately passed away in an air crash of a PIA plane near Cairo. Major General Shahid Hamid, a close confidant of Ayub became the object of US complaints about procurement practices related to US aid and retired early. He later served as information minister in the Yahya administration. When asked about that episode by the author he explained that he may have annoyed the Americans with his tough approach. Asghar Khan and Nur Khan later were both chiefs of the air force and entered politics in due course, with Asghar taking a firm position against military dictatorships. Ahsan became an admiral and governor of East Pakistan during the debacle that led to the birth of Bangladesh. He tried his best to forestall

the military action there that precipitated the civil war and then the Indian invasion and eventual breakaway of East Pakistan into an independent country.

36. Top Secret, Minutes of the 4th Meeting (held at Rawalpindi on 25 and 27 March 1954) of the Committee set up by HPM to conduct negotiations with the American Survey Team, prepared by Major General Musa. Pakistan Army GHQ archives.

37. Cypher Telegram Grade (I), 20 March 1954 from PAHIC [Pakistan High Commission] London to Foreign, Karachi, from Iskander Mirza for General Ayub care of ministry of defence repeated to prime minister (no distribution.) Pakistan Army GHQ archives.

38. McMahon, *The Cold War*, p. 170.

39. Memoranda of discussions at the NSC, 16 and 23 December 1953 and *RN: Memoirs of Richard Nixon,* (New York: Grossett and Dunlap, 1978). Cited in McMahon, p. 171.

40. This incidentally was also the date that Pakistan finally agreed and signed an Agreement for Friendly Cooperation with Turkey that was to be the precursor of the eventual Baghdad Pact and much later the Regional Cooperation for Development (RCD) between Iran, Turkey, and Pakistan. So the Pakistanis felt that they had committed themselves to the path that had been agreed upon with the Americans.

41. Top Secret Minutes of the 5th Meeting (held at Karachi on 2 April 1954) of the committee appointed by HPM to conduct negotiations with the American survey team. Pakistan Army GHQ archives.

42. Top Secret Minutes of the meeting with the US Military Team held on 3 April 1954 at 10 a.m. Pakistan Army GHQ archives. Attendees included the prime minister, the foreign minister, finance minister, minister of state for defence, the three service chiefs, the cabinet secretary, foreign secretary, the defence secretary, the deputy chief of staff of the army, and the joint secretary to the cabinet. The US ambassador also attended with the visiting military team.

43. Meyer's statement was attached to the minutes of the 3 April 1954 meeting.

44. 790D.5 MSP4-954 the Deputy Assistant Secretary of State for Near Eastern, South Asian, and African Affairs (Jernegan) to the Ambassador in Pakistan (Hildreth) Top Secret Official Informal. *Foreign Relations of the United States 1952-54, Volume IX, Part 1,* pp. 500–502.

45. Top Secret Record of the discussion and conclusion reached at the meeting of the Committee of Secretaries held on Wednesday the 5 May 1954 at 8 a.m. to examine the draft Mutual Defense Assistance Agreement between the Government of the United States of America and the Government of Pakistan. Pakistan Army GHQ archives.

No sooner had the ink dried on the US–Pakistan military pact of 1954 than differences seemed to bubble up on both sides, regarding not only the extent of military assistance to Pakistan but also the nature and intent of that aid and its pace. Compounding the difficulties between the countries was the chaotic situation emerging within Pakistan itself, as the political system imploded under the weight of provincial interests and the ambitions of politicians who could not see beyond their regions and bureaucrats who could not see beyond their personal interests. Pakistan still did not have a constitution and was nowhere close to achieving one. A weak Governor General, Khwaja Nazimuddin had been replaced by a wily bureaucrat, Ghulam Mohammad. A former ambassador to Washington, Muhammed Ali Bogra, was prime minister. Other bureaucrats vied for more powerful political positions, and, in the case of Finance Minister Chaudhry Muhammad Ali, got them. Iskander Mirza commanded authority as secretary of defence and had aligned himself with Ayub Khan as the architect of the relationship with the United States. Even Ghulam Mohammad had attempted to build his own relations with the United States by seeking a visit in November 1953, ostensibly for medical treatment, and using it to meet with President Eisenhower, Secretary of Defense Charles Wilson, and Secretary of State John Foster Dulles. Other key bureaucrats aligned themselves with Ayub Khan. Among them was Aziz Ahmed of the Ministry of Foreign Affairs, who was to play a key role in later years as a member of the civil–military combine. This allowed the bureaucracy to assert itself and to attempt a coalition with the military, specifically the powerful army chief, Ayub Khan. The ground was being prepared for a sea change in Pakistan's polity, with the US–Pakistan relationship playing a key supporting role.

On the domestic front, the Pakistani bureaucracy had always seen itself as the inheritor of the mantle of government from the British. As veteran civil servant Altaf Gauhar observed, this group was 'and remains, a self-generating and self-perpetuating class.' Members of the elite ICS 'donned European dress and aped British manners, cheerfully accepting all forms of discrimination.... After Independence, members of the ICS agreed, not without persuasion, to suffix the letters "ICS (Pakistan)" after their names and took pride in their sterling pensions and 'home leave' in England.'[1] They managed to sustain and pass on many of their customs and attitudes to their successors in the Civil Service of Pakistan, the vaunted CSP class that always managed to find itself on the side of the powerful segments of Pakistani society, more often than not the men on horseback who were to rule the country for most of its history as an independent nation. Although comprising some of the best and brightest talents in the country, the civil service group threw up a number of individuals who found it easy to attach themselves as junior partners with politicians or military men, basking in the reflected glory and being allowed to participate in national decision-making and political engineering at the highest levels. Remarkably, when their efforts exploded, few of them were ready to accept their share of the blame. Rather, the pattern was often one of apologia, often through endless columns in the all-too-willing press. The published memoirs of this group of civil servants had become a cliché: a frequent scene would describe high-level meetings in which all other participants favoured the wrong decision (based on 20/20 hindsight of the memoir writer). The only one who favoured the right decision (again with the benefit of hindsight) was the writer himself! Rarely did a senior civil servant exit honourably through resignation. Often, the chosen path was to seek an extension or to move to a parastatal or another lucrative slot until those became difficult to obtain in the face of competition from retired military men.

Arrayed against the elite civil servants was the rum lot of politicians, many of them from rural backgrounds and relying on their inheritances for political power. They had struggled for nearly six years in the constituent assembly to formulate a constitution for the country, tripping over issues such as the nature of an Islamic state and polity in the modern world and the distribution of powers between the centre and the provinces. They also smarted under the emerging control of the bureaucrats, specially the autocratic and idiosyncratic Ghulam Mohammad, who was wont to pull the rug from under any government that did not heed his advice.

BOGRA VS. GHULAM MOHAMMAD

Against this background, Prime Minister Bogra announced in September 1954 that the assembly was ready to go forward with a draft constitution, one that, among other things, would spell out a new relationship between the prime minister and the governor general. According to this draft, the governor general would be obliged to act on the advice of the prime minister, who would be seen to represent the voice of parliament. In short, executive power was to shift from the governor general to the parliament and the prime minister. Bogra did not fully understand the power of the incumbent. Ghulam Mohammad, who had become used to summary dismissal of governments, was not one to shirk from drastic measures. Despite the popularity of the new constitution in the constituent assembly and its support by the powerful religious party, the Jamaat-i-Islami, Ghulam Mohammad dismissed the central government on 24 October 1954 and called for fresh elections so that the 'people' could decide on 'constitutional issues'.[2] To add to the confusion, Ghulam Mohammad summoned Prime Minister Bogra back from a visit in Washington with a view to asking him to form a new government.

Bogra, who understandably was scared of his encounter with the testy and foul-mouthed governor general, asked Ayub Khan to provide him protection. Ayub who too had been recalled from a visit to the United Kingdom recalls in his memoirs that he told Iskander Mirza not to allow Bogra to meet the governor general by himself since it would lead to an 'ugly situation.' Ayub describes the scene when finally he got to Karachi and accompanied by Iskander Mirza, and Chaudhry Muhammad Ali went to see the ailing governor general before he met with Bogra. Ghulam Mohammad was lying in bed, suffering from severe back ache and high blood pressure, and

> ...bursting with rage, emitting volleys of abuse, which luckily no one understood. Chaudhri Mohammed (sic) Ali ventured to say something and received a volley; then Iskander Mirza said something and got another. We were pleading with him to give another chance to Mohammed Ali [Bogra]. His only reply was an angry growl, 'Go, off you go.'

As Ayub was the last to leave, he felt the nurse tugging at his coat. 'I turned and found myself facing a different man. There he was, the sick old governor general, who a moment ago was insane with anger, now beaming with delight and bubbling with laughter. I said in my heart, 'You wicked old man!' He beckoned me with a peculiar glee in his eye. 'Sit down on the bed'. He then pulled out two documents from under his pillow.'[3]

Ayub recalls that one document handed over authority to Ayub Khan and asked him to produce a constitution in three months. The other was a draft of Ayub's acceptance of that task. Ayub states that he argued against this and met with a volley of abuse. But he did not relent. Eventually, Bogra and Ghulam Mohammad made up and Ayub felt that he had done the right thing. 'Had I succumbed to the temptation the course of history might well have been different. We would certainly not have had an army worth the name and the one stabilizing element in the whole situation would have been neutralized,' he wrote in his memoirs.

Yet by virtue of his position as army chief, Ayub now was playing the role of king maker and the next step was a natural one for him: he was asked and agreed to become defence minister in the new Bogra government, the first (but certainly not the last) time that a military man had assumed such a political role in Pakistan. Iskander Mirza became the home minister, responsible for internal security. Ayub asserts that he agreed to enter the cabinet to better serve the army and to protect it from the selfish interests of the politicians. However, it was also around this time that he wrote his own blueprint, while on a trip to London, for the political future of Pakistan. He was also cadging for an extension of his term which he achieved in 1955. At the relatively young age of 48, Ayub Khan was well set on becoming the shaper of Pakistan's political destiny in the decade ahead.

Iskander Mirza's son, Humayun, in his memoir of his father, *From Plassey to Pakistan,* presents a different angle on this episode. According to Humayun Mirza, when Ayub and Iskander Mirza met in London *en route* back to Pakistan, Ayub confided in Iskander Mirza that before going to the US he had been promised by the governor general that he would be taking over the country. Iskander Mirza was shocked and admonished Ayub, 'That would be a very stupid thing to do.' Humayun Mirza also reproduces a message from John K. Emmerson in Karachi to Secretary of State Dulles dated 6 October 1954 giving the gist of a conversation that Ayub held with General Sexton. Ayub expressed great unhappiness with the current political situation in Pakistan and relayed to Emmerson that the 'Prime Minister...[would] ask [the] Pakistan Army to maintain law and order', and if some action was necessary, he 'hope[s] you [the US] will understand.' Discoursing on unpreparedness of a country like Pakistan for democracy, Ayub said 'Hand of God' might be in present situation. Ayub also expressed his concern about the possibility that 'Bengalis [would] dictate government for all of Pakistan,' leading Emmerson to conclude: 'No mistaking he meant [that the] military would take over if necessary. Ayub asked his conversation not [to be] mentioned to any other Pakistani or British [person].'[4]

US WEIGHS ITS CONTENDERS

The United States had a keen interest in these developments and was noting the shifting balance of power in Pakistan. The CJCS, Admiral Arthur W. Radford, who had concluded a visit to Pakistan to review the aid programme reported back in Washington that he had seen little of Ghulam Mohammad during his visit. He was, the admiral said, a very sick man, and might drop off at any time. If he does go, there was certain to be a struggle for power within the country. General (sic) Mirza, the admiral understood, was the No. 2 strong man, but in the admiral's opinion the best man was General Ayub. According to the State Department's John D. Jernegan, Mirza was 'more competent than Ayub.' But Admiral Radford observed 'that very well might be, but as far as honesty and directness is concerned, Mirza was no match for Ayub.' Radford understood that Ayub had been the key in persuading Ghulam Mohammad not to hand over power to Ayub but to keep Muhammed Ali as prime minister. Despite these political shifts in Pakistan, Radford concluded that 'Pakistan was a potential ally of great importance, and...from a military point of view, they have a trained armed force which no other friendly power can match, not even the Turks.'[5]

But despite this distant but powerful vote of confidence in favour of the Pakistan Army, the political system continued to get less than passing grades, and put the United States in a quandary. On the one hand, it favoured constitutional government and rules. On the other, it sought a stable local ally with the military power to provide assistance in the US's battle against global communism.

As expected, Ghulam Mohammad's summary dismissal of the constituent assembly provoked an appeal by the president of the assembly, Maulvi Tamizuddin of East Pakistan to the Sindh High Court. It sought the court's support for the view that the governor general's assent was not needed for the assembly's actions, and his refusal to assent did not invalidate the actions. Finally, this appeal challenged the right of the governor general to dissolve the assembly.[6] The provincial high court came down on the side of the supremacy of the legislature in the area of constitution-making even though the assembly's performance in that area had left much to be desired. But it left open the issue of whether the assembly's actions were those of a truly representative body or not. This allowed the governor general to challenge the Sindh court's decision in the Federal Court.

Even before that decision was pronounced, Ambassador Hildreth was informing the Department of State that 'the present government would take whatever action was necessary in order to confirm its hold on power.' Elaborating further, Hildreth stated:

> In sum, Embassy convinced of following points: 1) Present regime has will and strength to stay in power, regardless of outcomes of Federal Court decisions; 2) promulgation of new constitution desirable, in any event, and will probably occur regardless of court decision; 3) precarious state Governor General's health makes early action to clarify succession imperative; 4) desirable for Pakistan and United States stake in Pakistan that regime maintain itself by methods which have **at least appearance of legitimacy** [emphasis added], and that new constitution be adopted by method which does not set Pakistan off too sharply from community of democratic nations; 5) this last condition can be most effectively met if government secures favourable decision from court....[7]

The Federal Court heard the case against the backdrop of the wheeling and dealing that characterized Pakistan's fractious politics of that time. Even the court itself was riven by differences of opinion, with Chief Justice Munir wishing that the parties would seek a political solution to what was a political issue and Justice A.R. Cornelius (the only Christian on the court at that time and later chief justice of the Supreme Court) making a powerful argument for the sovereignty of the legislature and hence for constitutional norms. The Federal Court dismissed the earlier judgment of the provincial court in favour of Tamizuddin by determining that the governor general's assent was required to legalize the actions of the constituent assembly. Chief Justice Munir then proceeded to pronounce that 'an irremovable legislature...is not only a negation of democracy but is the worst calamity that can befall a nation because it tends to perpetuate an oligarchic rule.' But, as Newberg observes, the constituent assembly **had** completed the task of formulating a constitution. So, the 'Governor General objected to the Assembly's product, not its membership.' In effect, the Federal Court, in dismissing the Tamizuddin case, laid the cornerstone of executive power as the ultimate arbiter of the nation's destiny, superseding the will of the people as reflected in their elected representatives, a decision that was to influence constitutional affairs in Pakistan for decades.

Heartened by the court's decision, the governor general proceeded to rule by edict and proclamations, which were again challenged in the Federal Court, leading to a better definition and some curtailment of his powers. Ghulam Mohammad though was not to be stopped in his quest to create a political One Unit in West Pakistan as a counterweight to the huge majority of East Pakistan in any National Assembly. In this, he was supported by Iskander Mirza and Ayub Khan, both of whom, for their own separate reasons, favoured such an administrative set-up as being more efficient and manageable from the centre. A single West Pakistan would also allow the predominantly West Pakistani army and bureaucracy to exert its influence on the country's politics with more effect. A council comprising the heads of government or senior representatives of the Western Pakistani provinces was set up to put into effect the One Unit scheme. Its report was ready by January 1955 and, as Ayesha Jalal states: 'Based on the twin principles of greater administrative centralization and increased concentration of power in bureaucratic hands, the proposals warmed the hearts of many senior civil servants, especially in the CSP.'[8] Ayub and Iskander also appeared to agree on the need for 'some form of controlled democracy' for the country.

But creating One Unit would not do away with provincialism. And the problems of inter-provincial rivalries persisted. And even in their death throes the provincial assemblies showed signs of deep discord, weakening the Pakistan Muslim League and leading to the emergence of new parliamentary groups. Eventually, to create the semblance of a transnational leadership, Dr Khan Sahib of the NWFP was nominated to be the first chief minister of West Pakistan. Yet, even he was unable to find a safe seat in his native province and had to be slipped into the assembly through an urban seat that was found for him in Balochistan. In East Pakistan, Prime Minister Bogra had a hard time staking a claim to power, faced with rising provincialism and a strong challenge from the United Front of Fazlul Huq and the emerging Awami League.

PRO-WEST ELEMENTS WIN

When elections were finally held to the constituent assembly in 1955, the Muslim League found itself unable to form a majority government, having lost all but one seat in East Pakistan and eking out a bare victory in West Pakistan with 20 seats out of a total of 32. It had to contend with a coalition with the United Front, to carry East Pakistan. In the process, a number of political casualties occurred. Ghulam Mohammad was replaced by Iskander Mirza as governor general, and Bogra disappeared back to his post as ambassador in Washington, with the former finance minister and bureaucrat Chaudhry Muhammad Ali becoming prime minister on 11 August 1955.

The US noted with some satisfaction that the 'pro-United States group which aligned Pakistan with the free world' and that had been 'most directly involved in the Washington conversations of last October' on the military aid programme was in a strong position in the new government. Reporting on the likely new cabinet, Hildreth wrote to Washington that 'Chaudhry Muhammad Ali has become Prime Minister. Amjad Ali will probably be appointed Finance Minister. General Ayub, though relinquishing his Cabinet post [as Defence Minister], continues as Commander-in-Chief of the Army, and **final arbiter of the destiny of cabinets** [emphasis added].'[9]

With the civil–military combine backing the outcome, the new constituent assembly proceeded apace to ratify the emergence of One Unit in West Pakistan and then, under the implicit threat of being turfed out again, it railroaded a new constitution for Pakistan. The result of these efforts was to be more a federal than a unitary form of government, ostensibly grafted onto a parliamentary rather than a presidential system. The biggest optical change was in the name of the country. Harkening back to the Objectives Resolution of 1949 that defined the goal of constitution-making in Pakistan, the country was henceforth to be known as the Islamic Republic of Pakistan. The draft of the new constitution was presented on 8 January 1956. After a heated debate, more often than not led by the East Pakistani members of the assembly, on 29 February the assembly approved the constitution. Two days later, Iskander Mirza signed it into law. The republic came into being on 23 March 1956, a day chosen because of the significance of the Lahore Resolution of 16 years earlier on the same date that first pronounced clearly the call for Pakistan as a separate state. (Ironically, only 15 years later, on roughly the same day, the state with two wings began to unravel, with military action in East Pakistan.)

As Jalal explains, the result of this exercise was a skilful exhibition of legerdemain, with the parliament ostensibly in command but the president in fact being vested with much greater authority than ever resided in the governor general. He could decide on who would be prime minister, by determining an individual who might command majority support. He could dismiss parliament at will. No budget could be presented nor approved without his consent. He also was supreme commander of the armed forces and could appoint the commanders-in-chief of the three services. The president also was the ultimate reporting authority for the civil service and the appointing authority for all provincial governors, who in turn exercised similar powers to his at the provincial level. In brief, a centrally managed political system was introduced.

With so much centralized power, the system was bound to expose the inherent weaknesses of its constituent parts. The bureaucracy, in the shape of the Central Superior Services, led by the Civil Service of Pakistan, continued to assert itself and further concentrated power in the hands of West Pakistanis, often at the expense of East Pakistanis, with the emergence of an elite of Punjabi and North Indian 'muhajir' or refugee officials calling the shots (though often these two groups clashed with each other). The army too began to show signs of similar rifts, as Ayub Khan's extension to a second term provoked criticisms from within the army and led to the retirement of two senior officers, General Yousuf and General Adam Khan (misidentified in a US dispatch as Adnan Khan).[10] Ayub's departure would have allowed them to be considered for promotion to his position. The same dispatch noted that 'the army may not be the sound element for stability [that] our policy assumes it is. This point strengthened by the vigour with which some army men still advocate settling Kashmir issue by force, using United States military aid, of course.'

BACKING AYUB KHAN

Despite these concerns, the US consul general in Lahore suggested 'we should strengthen Ayub's position in Pakistan because he is apparently the only imposing figure who the Army ranks [i.e. ordinary soldiers] will trust and also [the] general public. My populous district rates him alone with Choudhri Mohdzrli [obviously a typo: Muhammad Ali or even Mohd. Ali for short] as statesman with integrity.' Ayub was still on the US favourites list even though he had shown some signs of unhappiness with the meagre and slow military aid. Iskander Mirza was notable by his absence from the analysis of the US consul general.

Chaudhry Muhammad Ali, however, had a short tenure. Pushed into accepting the job of the prime minister, reportedly at the behest of Ayub Khan, he was not made for the cut and thrust of national politics and appeared to be out of his element. Iskander Mirza began trying to consolidate his own position soon after becoming president under the new constitution.

He also found fault with Muhammad Ali's politics, accusing him in conversations with the Americans of having prevented Prime Minister Liaquat Ali Khan from sending troops to Korea at the US's behest and for furthering ties with the mainland Chinese.[11] As the first of many presidents who tried their hands at political engineering, he is said to have spawned a new political group, the Republican Party with support from a Punjabi politician Mushtaq Gurmani and later Dr Khan Sahib, as the front man, that split the Pakistan Muslim League. Prime Minister Ali was seen by the Americans to have 'lacked the decisiveness to cope with the new situation' and was forced to resign on 8 September 1956.[12] He had a severe nervous breakdown after leaving office and proceeded to the United Kingdom for treatment.

The next day, Iskander Mirza 'reluctantly' asked Huseyn Shaheed Suhrawardy, the pre-partition Muslim League chief minister of united Bengal and founder of the opposition Awami League Party, to become prime minister. At that point he was seen by the US as 'virtually the only political leader of national stature.' The independent-minded Suhrawardy had led political demonstrations against the government in East Pakistan when Ayub was commanding the army's only division there and had once been confronted by Ayub who asked him if he was 'looking for a bullet.' But Ayub and he made up before Suhrawardy took the post of prime minister. According to US diplomat and historian of the US–Pakistan relationship, Dennis Kux, Suhrawardy also is believed to have agreed in principle to the setting up of a US listening post at the Badaber air base near Peshawar from where Gary Powers was to take off on his ill-fated U-2 flight over the Soviet Union. At home, heading a coalition with the Republican Party proved beyond Suhrawardy's ability, especially with the Republicans being the senior partners in this endeavour. The government was riven also by competition amongst the West Pakistanis on the one hand and between the West Pakistanis and East Pakistanis on the other. Suhrawardy challenged Iskander Mirza by attacking the Republican Party in public and calling for the National Assembly to convene to determine whether the prime minister had its support or not. Using the extraordinary powers now vested in him, President Mirza dismissed Suhrawardy on 17 October 1957 and brought in a technocrat I.I. Chundrigar to take over as prime minister, heading a West Pakistan dominated coalition that included, in addition to the Republican Party, the Muslim League, the Krishak Sramik (KSP) Party of East Pakistan, and the Nizam-i-Islam Party. Acceding to the biases of the parties that formed his government, Chundrigar promptly re-instituted the system of separate electorates for different religious groups which Suhrawardy had abolished. Paying homage to the US, he also stated continued support for Pakistan's participation in the Baghdad Pact and the South-East Asia Treaty Organization (SEATO). But he too faced a short tenure [two months] and was replaced eventually by a Punjabi feudal chieftain, Malik Firoz Khan Noon, who was a friend of Mirza but also had the singular honour of being the last elected prime minister of Pakistan, before Mirza unceremoniously displaced him and declared martial law in October 1958. In its short life since independence in 1947, Pakistan had had eight prime ministers before the system of government collapsed and was replaced with military rule.

RISING US CONCERN

The continued political instability in Pakistan was a source of concern in Washington even after the signing of the arms agreement in 1954. Compounding that situation was the unhappiness of Ayub Khan with the first aid package proposed by the US. He was quick to convey his feelings to the Americans and used his connections in Washington to effect some changes, leading to an increase of the announced package. Pakistan's army was looking to a major shift in its orientation, equipment and training, away from reliance on primarily British sources to a more worldwide supply network, with the US being the largest of some dozen or more potential military suppliers and partners. Its main opponent continued to be India, which had not relented in its campaign to put pressure on the fledgling neighbour and which was also the object of American advances, though with little reciprocity on the Indian side.

By 1955, the US had, for instance, provided seventeen C-119G aircraft to India under a programme of some $33 million of military aid, and also 'approved' the sale by the British of 'Green Satin' confidential radar equipment. The US hoped that these moves would help 'forestall India's purchase of 60 Soviet light bombers.'[13] It also completed the purchase of thorium nitrate from India. But the US was still not clear on the nature and magnitude of military and economic aid to Pakistan and also was holding up its planned request for base rights in Pakistan, pending a review by the NSC.

The CJCS, Admiral Radford came away from a visit to the region with the view that there was confusion among US agencies on how the US military assistance programme was to be put into effect. Yet he placed great value on the Pakistan Army as an ally 'which no other friendly power can match.'[14] Despite this vote of confidence in Pakistan's ability, the US still did not have a clear idea of how Pakistan was to play a role in a strategic plan to fight communist attacks in the region. There was no discussion of an allied command structure or lines of reporting and communication in case of such a conflict, nor specifically of the Pakistan Army's role in such an eventuality.

Indeed, when Assistant Secretary of State Struve Hensel completed his tour of several Asian and Middle Eastern countries to assess their defence needs, over 5 February–10 March 1955, he found the clear need for Pakistan to receive 'direct forces support.' Hensel saw, or was shown, 'military encampments where the men are living in tattered and torn tents which compare very unfavourably with some of the ramshackle huts, built particularly in the Middle East, by the various Arab and Pakistani refugees.' He was told that 'practically the entire Pakistan Army is under canvas of that type.'[15] While the needs were enormous, General Sexton observed that the flow of equipment into Pakistan was at a pace that allowed the Pakistan Army to absorb it. But he felt that Pakistan's army officers and other ranks needed better emoluments, housing, and subsistence. This created tension in Washington between the relative share of economic and defence aid flows, since some of the economic aid would need to be redirected to meeting the army's needs for better pay and benefits. A further issue that Pakistan had also pointed out in different exchanges at the ministerial and ambassadorial level was the lack of counterpart funds to meet the local share of costs for effective absorption of US military aid.

Hensel noted that Radford favoured increased military strength in Pakistan 'but no one seemed to know precisely why except that Pakistanis obviously make reliable fighting soldiers.' He perceived correctly that almost the entire Pakistan Army was arrayed against India and that 'Pakistan regards the Indian threat as much more serious to Pakistan than the Russian or Communist China threats.' It was also becoming clear to the US that Pakistan did not have the force projection capability that would allow it to send troops to the Middle East and certainly not to South East Asia. In short, the US was seeing itself caught in a bind: having made a pact with Pakistan, based on a potential war against communist advances in the region, it had no idea how Pakistan would play a part in that conflict. It also recognized that Pakistan's focus was entirely against India. Hensel regretted the situation in which the US had shared with Pakistan its plans for military aid of $171 million over three years, the first time probably that information on programmed aid had been shared with a recipient country.

Caught between the twin objectives of military and economic aid to Pakistan, Ambassador Hildreth attempted to clarify for the Pakistani Prime Minister Muhammad Ali the need for Pakistan (and the US) to agree on the relative share of each type of aid, so that Pakistan was not faced with the issue of diverting economic aid for military purposes.[16] When he sensed some support from the prime minister on this issue, Hildreth pressed his advantage to raise an issue that was rearing for the first time: the probable misuse of military aid. Quoting Generals Brown and Sexton, he questioned the need for Pakistan to acquire uniforms from abroad when these could be purchased locally, citing suspicions that this was being done because of the 'chance of a rake-off.' He honed in on the MGO, whom he thought to be 'very poorly equipped to deal with the job.' As mentioned earlier, this attack on Major General Shahid Hamid may have been prompted in part by his tough stance in negotiations with the US. The US, while pushing for the removal of the Pakistani MGO, was careful not to provide any direct evidence of wrongdoing though, a habit that persisted well into the 1980s when leakage from US military aid was ignored in the broader interest of achieving the strategic goals of the relationship.[17] Clearly, things were not going as well as planned.

STAY BEHIND FORCES

On one level though, the US–Pakistan relationship seemed to be working out in 1956. This was in the creation of a force of guerrillas within Pakistan that would be employed to fight the Soviets should they break through and occupy the country. The moving force behind this was not just the Department of Defense but also the CIA, as can be seen from the officers that the United States deployed to Pakistan to begin the training programme. Many appeared to have an intelligence background.

The first commander of the Special Services Group (SSG), as the Pakistani commandos were called, was Lt. Col. A.O. Mitha. The 17 Baluch Regiment, then based at Nowshera, was converted to the SSG and he was named to head it. The operational and training base for the SSG was Cherat, not far from Nowshera. Mitha retained just one company of the 17 Baluch for administrative support and released the rest, since he wanted to have the SSG filled with volunteers from the rest of the Pakistan Army. Mitha himself was sent for training in the United States in March 1956 and from the manner in which his trip was handled by an American officer named Don Bunte and his aide, a man named Russell Miller, Mitha deduced that they were both from the CIA. He was not taken to the Pentagon but to other sites in the Washington DC area and then trained at Fort Bragg and a naval base near Los Angeles (to observe frogman training).[18]

Mitha set up the SSG as a fully operational unit within eighteen months and began selecting officers and soldiers for stay-behind activities. Among those who went through this training was a future COAS, Mirza Aslam Beg. However, progress on this activity was not as fast as expected. At the end of Mitha's tenure of six years as head of the SSG, only some 25 per cent of Pakistan was covered by the planned stay-behind plans. Gradually, differences also arose with the Americans over the training methods as well as the perceptions of the Americans about themselves and their Pakistani counterparts. Soon after the 1958 coup d'etat, the US contingent left Cherat.

FIGHTING FOR MORE AID

In 1955, Ayub was attempting his best to get the US to increase the quantum of aid above the $171 million initially agreed to help Pakistan raise an additional 5½ divisions over the next three years. One tactic that he employed was to separate the force levels from the money needed to support them. For example, he resorted to increasing the numerical strength of each Pakistan Army division. But his major concern was the extremely slow pace of US flows. Ayub also complained bitterly about the arrival of outdated equipment and the Second World War surplus being diverted toward Pakistan and how this placed him in a difficult situation at home.

In a conversation with the US Consul General Fisk in Lahore, Ayub let loose a volley of criticism, stating that the 'US let [us] down on military aid to Pakistan likely to be exposed in Consembly [Constituent Assembly of Pakistan] with result various Mid-East countries will take "I told you so" attitude or argument "You can't trust Americans".'[19] He spoke of how the King of Saudi Arabia had told him in Rawalpindi in 1954 that 'Americans can't be trusted' and felt that the Shah of Iran 'felt the same way.' More tellingly, Ayub stressed his potential difficulties with his army colleagues, stating that he stood to 'lose [his] trousers' and was 'in no position [to] answer [the] growing feeling in Army circles that at least US engaging in "political opportunism" with Pakistan'.

Ayub was not far off the mark. Of the $34.2 million in military aid allotted to Pakistan for US fiscal year 1954, only $7.9 million had actually been delivered as of 31 March 1955 and the US military expected only to complete the delivery of the full amount by December 1956.[20] The JCS had accorded Pakistan third priority! But the Americans understood that Pakistan was having difficulty raising the additional forces 'to properly use all this equipment' and that 'acceleration of deliveries would add to these difficulties and would establish a requirement for increased economic aid.'

But all this put Ayub in a difficult situation, forcing him to use all his contacts to break the log jam. He complained to visiting Congressman Clement Zablocki and then wrote a letter to Admiral Radford, while leaking the letter to James Callahan of *The New York Times* for background use without attribution of source.[21] He found an ally in Hildreth, who carried Ayub's arguments that the force levels, not the US dollar amount of 171 million, should be used to measure the quantum of aid. By these calculations, Pakistan needed more than $300 million rather than the $171 million originally agreed. Using a report from the head of the US Military Assistance and Advisory Group (USMAAG) in Pakistan, Hildreth pressed home the point that the chief of MAAG estimated that rather than achieving the completion of aid within the stated goal of three and half years, 'at the currently indicated pace the program will be extended to six or even eight years."[22] An effort began to convince Ayub that the US could be trusted. The Department of State was coming around to the view that Ayub was propagating.

In a priority, top secret, eyes only message from Hoover to Secretary of State Dulles at New Delhi in March 1956, he presented the nub of the issue:

> It is becoming increasingly apparent that our difficulties in many parts of the world are the result of our not fulfilling military commitments to foreign governments, both large and small, which they had entered with us in good faith. The Pakistan case is typical. A three year commitment for end items and direct forces support, now estimated to cost $350 million, was entered into in September 1954. With the period almost half gone, in early 1956, we have delivered only $21 million of hardware and little if any direct support.[23]

In all the detailed exchanges about the level of military aid, the original differences between the US and Pakistani interpretations of the 1954 military pact appeared to have been purposely brushed under the carpet. The US fully understood that Pakistan needed arms to defend itself against India and was not capable of fighting outside its borders against any future Soviet threat to the Middle East. Pakistan continued to believe that US aid could be used against India and so long as it paid lip service to the fight against communism, it would meet all the criteria for continued aid. The Pakistanis were unaware that President Eisenhower himself was raising doubts about the military relationship. Chairing a meeting of the NSC in January 1957:

> The President observed that we [the United States] had decided some time ago that we wanted Pakistan as a military ally. Obviously it had been proved costly to achieve this objective. In point of fact, we were doing practically nothing for Pakistan except in the form of military aid. The President said that **this was perhaps the worst kind of a plan and decision** [emphasis added] we could have made. It was a terrible error, but we now seem hopelessly involved in it.[24]

His Vice-President Richard Nixon, already an avowed friend of Pakistan, was not at that meeting, otherwise he would have weighed in no doubt with his own views on the Pakistani needs. Just six months earlier, in a visit with President Iskander Mirza in Karachi, Nixon had heard from the Pakistanis of their broader economic and military needs.[25] Mirza had stressed the need for an increase in force levels by one infantry division so there would be an additional five infantry divisions and one and half armoured divisions. He also asked for light bombers to act as a deterrent to India. Former finance minister and then acting Prime Minister Chundrigar also broached, in the context of economic needs, the question of acquiring an atomic reactor so

Pakistan could meet its growing energy needs. He cited India's acquisition of a $14 million reactor from Canada, with Canada providing half of the costs for the foreign exchange components and the US providing $250,000 for heavy water. In contrast, the US had offered Pakistan half the cost of a reactor or $350,000, which he deemed 'of no particular use to Pakistan.' Pakistan, said Chundrigar, needed help in a big way. Nixon said he understood the situation, especially since India was following a neutralist path and Pakistan had aligned itself with the Free World.

But the pendulum was already swinging away from blind friendship toward a more pragmatic relationship on the part of the United States. This was captured succinctly in the new US Ambassador James Langley's letter to William Rountree, the Assistant Secretary of State for Near Eastern, South Asian, and African Affairs near the end of 1957.[26] Characterizing the situation in Pakistan as one in which 'we have an unruly horse by the tail and are confronted by the dilemma of trying to tame it before we can let it go safely,' he wondered if Pakistan had not 'grown wilder of late.' He sought a reappraisal of the situation, particularly in light of the deteriorating political and economic situation in Pakistan and the 'continuation at a constant or increasing level of unproductive expenses (military and government operating costs) and a decline in the productive part of the budget.' Noting that Pakistan's military expenditures absorbed 65 per cent of the government's revenues, he favoured a cut in the military establishment. Then, reverting to the military pact, he stated: 'I fear that it would not be too difficult to make a rather convincing case that the present military programme is based on a hoax, the hoax being that it is related to the Soviet threat.' He then proposed engaging Iskander Mirza and Ayub in a re-evaluation of the Pakistani military programme, 'to set the outer limits' in both military and financial terms. Langley had discerned the 'disturbing' view in higher level Pakistani circles that the US 'must keep up and increase its aid to Pakistan, and conversely, that Pakistan is doing the US a favour in accepting aid.' He questioned the pro-western Pakistani postures in SEATO, the Baghdad Pact, and felt that the United Nations was being in part 'dictated by Pakistan's hatred for India.' The carefully crafted friendship was beginning to fray somewhat, just as the political fabric within Pakistan was showing signs of stress.

As things started falling apart on the domestic political scene, the US had already started gauging the role of the military in any change that might occur. As early as February 1956, Hildreth had asked Iskander Mirza about his relationship with Ayub Khan. 'Pressed on loyalty of Ayub to him, he indicated absolute certainty on this point'.[27] Neither Iskander Mirza nor Hildreth, the much vaunted 'pro-consul' of the United States and confidant of Mirza, knew what Ayub was thinking at the time.

NOTES

1. Altaf Gauhar, *Ayub Khan: Pakistan's First Military Ruler*, Lahore: Sang-e-Meel Publications, 1993, p. 85.
2. *Dawn*, 25 October 1954, in Gauhar, op. cit.
3. Ayub Khan, *Friends not Masters*, p. 52.
4. Humayun Mirza, *Plassey to Pakistan*, pp. 176–177.
5. Memorandum on the Substance of Discussions at a Department of State–Joint Chiefs of Staff Meeting, Washington DC, 14 January 1955, 11:30 a.m. *Foreign Relations 1955–1957*.
6. See an excellent discussion of these constitutional issues in *Judging the State: Courts and Constitutional Politics in Pakistan* by Paula R. Newberg, Cambridge University Press, 1995, pp. 42–51.
7. Telegram 1132, 25 February 1955 from Hildreth to State, referred in Telegram from Department of State to the Embassy in Pakistan, Washington, 5 March 1955, 5 p.m. *Foreign Relations 1955–1957*.
8. Ayesha Jalal, *The State of Martial Rule*, p. 201.
9. Secret Despatch from the Embassy in Pakistan to the Department of State, No 150. Karachi, 26 August 1955. *Foreign Relations 1955–1957*, pp. 435–6.
10. See Secret message from US consul general in Lahore to Department of State, 4 October 1955, 11 p.m. US National Archives.
11. Quoting Iskander Mirza, a top Secret Telegram from the Embassy in Pakistan to the Department of State (Central Files, 611.90D/2-1756) gives details of Mirza's complaints to the US ambassador about Chaudhry Muhammad Ali: 'Fundamentally Prime Minister is timid, weak, and perhaps cowardly and he [Mirza] thinks I should advise Secretary [Dulles] in effect to say very bluntly to the Prime Minister "what's going on here? We don't understand your apparent reversal of thinking. We have started to help you in good faith and intend to continue to do so but we do not understand your flirtation with the communists".' *Foreign Relations 1955–1957*, p. 457.
12. Despatch from US embassy in Karachi to Department of State, no. 339, 1957. US National Archives.
13. Progress Report on US Policy Toward South Asia (NSC 409), dated 30 March 1954. *Foreign Relations 1955–1957*, p. 5.
14. Dennis Kux, *The United States and Pakistan 1947-2000: Disenchanted Allies*, Washington DC, Woodrow Wilson Center Press and Baltimore and London, Johns Hopkins University Press, 2001, p. 79.
15. Secret Memorandum by the Assistant Secretary of Defense for International Security Affairs (Hensel), Karachi, 17 February 1955 on a Conference in Karachi with General Sexton and Ambassador Hildreth. Department of State, Central Files 790D.5-mSP/2-1755, *Foreign Relations 1955–1957*, pp. 418–19.
16. Secret Memorandum of a Conversation, Karachi, 30 March 1955 on military aid. Participants included Ambassador Hildreth, Pakistani Prime Minister Mohammed Ali and Foreign Secretary J.A. Rahim. Department of State, Central Files. 790D.5-MSD/3-155, *Foreign Relations 1955–1957*, pp. 427–9.
17. Major General Shahid Hamid eventually retired from service.
18. Major Gen. A.O. Mitha, *Unlikely Beginnings* (Karachi: Oxford University Press, 2003), pp. 180–226.
19. Secret Telegram from Consulate General at Lahore to the Department of State, 4 October 1955, 11 a.m., from Department of State, Central Files, 790D.5-MSP/10-455, *Foreign Relations 1955–1957*, pp. 444–5.
20. Response to a memorandum from Colonel Robert W. Duke, Military Assistant to Hensel to Brigadier General James K. Wilson Jr., Director of the Office of Military Assistance Policy.

25 June, Department of Defense, OASD/ISA files. NESA Records, Pakistan. *Foreign Relations 1955–1957*, pp. 429–30.

21. Kux, op. cit., p. 80.

22. Secret Despatch from the Embassy in Pakistan to the Department of State, No. 150, Karachi, 26 August 1955, *Foreign Relations 1955–1957*, pp. 435–6.

23. Department of State. Conference Files. Lot 62 D 181, CF 679. *Foreign Relations 1955–1957*, pp. 459–460.

24. Top Secret. Eisenhower Library, Whitman file. NSC Records. Memorandum of Discussion at the 30th Meeting of the National Security Council, Washington, 3 January 1957 *Foreign Relations 1955–1957*, pp. 25–26.

25. Top Secret Memorandum of a Conversation, Karachi, 9 July 1956, 10 a.m.–noon. Participants included President Iskander Mirza, Vice President Nixon, Charge D'Affaires A.Z. Gardiner, Colonel Leroy Watson (OSD/ISA), William Henry and Acting-Prime Minister I.I. Chundrigar, Acting Foreign Minister Firoz Khan Noon, Finance Minister Amjad Ali. *Foreign Relations 1955–1957*. pp. 463–469.

26. Secret Letter from Langley to Rountree, Karachi, 27 December 1957. Department of State, Karachi Embassy files. Lot 63 F 84, 320 Pakistan. *Foreign Relations 1955–1957*, pp. 487–490.

27. Top Secret. Telegram from the Embassy in Pakistan to the Department of State. Department of State, Central Files, 611.90D/2/2-1756. *Foreign Relations 1955–1957*, pp. 456–459.

7 | THE FIRST COUP

The causes which produce military intervention in politics...lie not in the nature of the group but in the structure of society. In particular, they lie in the absence or weakness of effective political institutions in the society.

– Samuel Huntington (1968)[1]

There were forty-seven coups in the post-war world up to 1959.[2] Of these, in 1958 alone, there were at least six coups d'etat in the developing world and one in the developed world (in France).[3] Much like the global revolution of students and youth that spread like a flash fire ten years later in 1968, it seems that the global political order was being infected with a rash of coups. While it may be tempting to blame the post-colonial teething pains of newly independent countries as the main reason for these events, the presence of some thirty coups in South and Central America would counteract that theory. Huntington's view that the political systems of a society best account for military intervention appears to hold water. But that may not present the full picture. Many countries stumble on their way to nationhood and stable polities without fully developed political systems. So, it may well be the interaction of military and political leaders and their respective ambitions and inclinations that account for some of these interventions.

As the decade of the 1950s headed into its final years, both President Iskander Mirza and the army chief, General Mohammad Ayub Khan believed that Pakistan appeared ripe for a drastic change. This secret was not a well-kept one either, as both had shared their ideas with their US friends. In many ways, the personalities and ambitions of these two men who had been thrust into greatness shaped the course of the country's politics in that fateful period.

As the political system imploded and central governments went through a merry-go-round of change, both Mirza and Ayub Khan watched with more than a disinterested eye, with Iskander Mirza playing an active role in contriving a political system that would remain under his control and was headed by politicians who would be beholden to him. Mirza made use of his presidential powers under Section 193 to remove governments that lost his trust and imposed presidential rule for the first time on 21 March 1957 in West Pakistan, when the Muslim League attempted to join forces with the National Awami Party, ostensibly to break up the One Unit (of all provinces in West Pakistan) but in effect to oust the Republican Party led by Mirza's protégé Dr Khan Sahib. The US observers felt that the 'primary reason for Mirza's decision...was his determination to prevent any threat to the maintenance of one unit.'[4] He was seen by the Americans to be acting on his 'fear...that the continuance on power of what might be called the ruling group in West Pakistan would be seriously undermined if the previous system of states in West Pakistan were to be re-established.' The US saw this development as 'unfortunate' given the ongoing discussions with India on Kashmir and on Afghanistan.

Mirza's second chance to impose presidential rule came in 1958 when East Pakistan was wracked by political crises. It all started with the dismissal of the cabinet of Ataur Rehman Khan by the then Governor Fazlul Haq on 31 March 1958. Within hours, the governor himself was suspended by Mirza and replaced by Abu Hussain Sarkar—who had a tenure of just twelve hours! The result was the reinstatement of the Ataur Rehman cabinet that had begun this game of musical chairs in the first place.

The political mess continued to bubble in both wings, with East Pakistan witnessing a series of governments in quick succession. Indeed, on 19 June 1958, the Awami League had the political rug pulled from under it by its erstwhile partner, the National Awami Party (NAP), with the United Front taking over power in Dacca (now Dhaka). But the fallout only lasted some hours, with the NAP returning to support the Awami League and thus bringing down the United Front ministry. This led Mirza to impose president's rule on East Pakistan on 24 June 1958 and allow the reinstatement of Ataur Rehman as chief minister on 25 August. But the political cauldron continued to boil, with a battle royal going on in the provincial assembly. Less than a month later, on 20 September, with Deputy Speaker Shahed Ali in the chair, the provincial assembly carried a motion that declared the absent speaker of 'unsound mind,' provoking a brawl on the assembly floor. Abuse and chairs were hurled across the aisles, with the poor deputy speaker who had made the pronouncement of the assembly's verdict becoming a special target of the assault. He suffered serious injuries and died a few days later. In effect, the 'democratic' political system in East Pakistan died with him. As Jalal observes, 'If developments in West Pakistan gave Mirza good reason to want to banish the spectre of elections…the downfall of four ministries in East Pakistan within six months came as a welcome bonus.'[5] The shenanigans of the politicians in both wings of the country were well reported by the press and created an atmosphere of distrust among the general populace. The poor state of the economy added to people's growing lack of confidence in the politicians.

SERIOUS CRISIS

As Ayub observed in his memoirs, 'By the middle of 1958 the whole country was in the grip of a serious economic crisis. Reckless spending seemed to be order of the day.' Indeed, Pakistan was faced with a serious drain of its foreign exchange reserves and the government in the centre had to resort to new taxes to finance the deficit, thus creating further unhappiness among the businessmen and labour unions. Adding to this was the effect of cut-backs in imports, leading to severe under-utilization of industrial capacity. Inflation was soaring, as price controls were lifted by Finance Minister Amjad Ali. A groundswell of unrest began across the country, fuelled by the economic difficulties and magnified by the bankruptcy of the political system of the time. Student and labour unions took to the streets, demanding change through fresh elections. Elections had been set originally for November 1957 and then delayed into the following year. In retrospect, it appears as if the political engineering at the presidential level had helped create this perfect storm of discontent with the status quo. In Ayub's view, Mirza 'had thoroughly exploited the weaknesses in the constitution and had got everyone connected with political life of the country utterly exposed and discredited. I do not think that he ever seriously wanted to hold general elections: he was looking for a suitable opportunity to abrogate the constitution. Indeed, he was setting the stage for it.'[6] But Ayub's ghost-writer, Altaf Gauhar, who later wrote his biography, suggests that Ayub had a bad feeling about the upcoming elections and warned the Americans in 1958 that 'the politicians were conspiring to hold the election in February 1959 and a large number of persons with dubious antecedents and socialist leanings would get themselves elected by exploiting the electoral procedures and rigging the polls.'[7]

In this season of political turmoil and discontent, a fresh threat to the structure of the newly independent state emerged in the shape of a rebellion in the marcher region of Balochistan. The venerable Mir Ahmad Yar Khan, the Khan of Kalat, chose to lower the Pakistan flag, announce secession from Pakistan, and began talking of a link with Iran. This prompted an immediate action by the Pakistan Army which entered the defenceless state and removed the Khan on 6 October 1958. Ayub felt that Mirza had instigated the secessionist move by the Khan of Kalat to prepare for his own impending coup. Ayub Baksh Awan, who was later Director of the Intelligence Bureau and home secretary under Ayub Khan, states that the Khan of Kalat had been sent for by Mirza and put up at the President's House in Karachi. The Khan was exploring the possibility of regaining control of his state by being allowed to revert to its pre-independence status. After a fortnight in Karachi, he returned to Kalat and 'redoubled his activities. He told his sardars [local chieftains] that the President had given him an assurance that his state would be returned to him.'[8] The Khan in his own book (cited by Awan) provides a much more detailed and colourful account of this episode, even alluding to the seeking of a bribe of Rs 500,000 by Mirza from the Khan and additional amounts from other rulers of the former states of Bahawalpur and Khairpur to allow them also to secede from One Unit. Awan discounts the Khan's suggestions. Regardless, both Iskander Mirza and Ayub had been bemoaning the state of affairs in Pakistan and nurturing the imposition of military rule for some time.

At the end of December 1957, Mirza had addressed the nation:

> I deeply regret the frequent changes of government, and am definitely of the view that they are doing immense disservice to the country....I agree that we must try to get out of this transitional stage and have general elections as early as possible. But I must warn you that unless you all exert yourselves and ensure that only patriots and men with character, ability, and honour are returned, the country will be in a worse condition than ever before.[9]

And in a letter to his son, Humayun, who was then in graduate school at Harvard, he wrote of his deep unhappiness with the politicians of Pakistan:

> The country, to put it bluntly, is being ruined by the politicians....The general state of the country is bad. Many think everything will be all right after general elections. I have my doubts, as people who will come to power will not come from the planets but from Pakistan.[10]

That said, Mirza expressed doubts about his own chances for re-election as the president and warned his son against his own 'innumerable enemies.' Clearly, he saw himself as facing a challenge should elections take place and increasingly sought grounds to support a takeover of the government, something that he had alluded to much earlier in his exchanges with the Americans.

AYUB MULLS TAKEOVER

Within a year or so of taking over as army chief, Ayub too had seized on the idea of a coup, when he first discussed the issue with his division commanders, following talk among some of the younger officers about the military governments in Egypt, Syria, and Lebanon. According to a note from the US consul general in Lahore at that time, 'he [Ayub] told the Divisional commanders that "talk of the Pakistan Army taking over the Government" was to be stopped, and [...] the army was to protect the country. He pointed out that the Pakistan Army did not have trained men in governmental affairs, and such talk was a danger to the country.' At the same time, Ayub told Consul General Raleigh A. Gibson, that 'he had been talking to the leading politicians of Pakistan, and had told them that they must make up their minds to go whole-heartedly with the West....He stated that the Pakistan Army will not allow the politicians to get out of hand, and the same is true regarding the people of Pakistan.' Ayub's view was that it was 'the army's duty to protect the country' and that 'the Pakistan Army was friendly to the United States.'[11] The message could not be more clear cut.

Less than three months later, Ayub was reinforcing it in another conversation with Gibson. While assuring Gibson that there was no danger of either the politicians or the general public overthrowing the then government, he stated that 'in case there was such an attempt the Pakistan Army would immediately declare martial law and take charge of the situation.' At the same time, Ayub was confident that there would be no repeat of the Rawalpindi Conspiracy and that the 'intelligence service of the army GHQ was very good and no plans could be developed without the knowledge of GHQ.'[12] By the end of February, he had engaged the US First Secretary Charles Withers in a half-hour private chat in the presence of General Mohammad Yousuf on the day that the Ahrar agitation had begun in Lahore and repeated the assurance that the army 'would not let the situation get out of hand'. While he said he did not think the army wanted to get into politics, Ayub saw it as 'a stabilizing force in Pakistan and that he would not take any nonsense from the politicians.' Ayub had apparently made up his mind about the politicians even at that stage.

Charles Withers was impressed by Ayub's self confidence and his certainty that he knew his men and that 'army will do what I tell it to do.' In short, 'I got the distinct impression from Ayub and from subsequent conversations with his senior officers who were in Lahore at the same time, that the Pakistan Army is definitely ready to take control should Civil Government break down, although they would be reluctant to do so.'[13] And even while Ayub was busy courting the US for arms, he was undercutting his Prime Minister Muhammed Ali Bogra's visit to Washington in October 1954, disagreeing with the prime minister's views, as conveyed to Ambassador Hildreth over cocktails. According to Hildreth, Ayub began repeating his current mantra that he was 'terribly confident of the ability of the armed services to step in any time as, (sic) if and when necessary.'[14]

Ayub had spent some time thinking about the political situation in Pakistan and produced his Dorchester Hotel blueprint that he shared with the cabinet. Some of his ideas, including the One Unit scheme for West Pakistan had been accepted because that suited the plans of Iskander Mirza and the strong Punjabi clique which did not wish to be overshadowed by its East Pakistani brethren in the National Assembly. After continuing to ponder on the country's political development and the role of the army, Ayub came to the conclusion that the army could not be 'unaffected by the conditions around it; nor was it conceivable that officers and men would react to all the political chicanery, intrigue, corruption, and inefficiency manifest in every sphere of life.'[15] He felt that people were blaming the army for inaction 'while the country is going to the dogs', and expressed the hope that 'someone might rise to the occasion' to save the army from acting as 'a corrective force and restore normalcy.' He wrote that he looked to Iskander Mirza as the person who 'might be able to evolve some pattern out of the chaos which he had created' but found him 'desperate and cornered.' He began suggesting to Mirza 'to give a constructive lead if the country was to be saved.'[16]

INSIDERS VS. OUTSIDERS

While the politicians incurred the displeasure of both Ayub and Mirza, other parts of the establishment were also exhibiting some of the worse traits of cliquishness and intrigue. Among these, the civil service was also beset with rivalries that extended beyond normal professional competition to sectarian rifts and regional divisions. Lines were being drawn between the insiders, the largely Punjabi 'sons of the soil,' and the outsiders, mostly migrants from northern India and other parts of India (Bengalis and other provincial representatives were a small part of the superstructure of the civil service). These divisions were apparent to the keen observers representing Uncle Sam, who spent a lot of effort in gathering information on who was doing what to whom with what effect in the government of Pakistan.

A telling note from the Counsellor for Political Affairs in the US embassy, Geoffrey W. Lewis, discussed at length in early 1958 the transfer from Karachi of Altaf Gauhar, who had been appointed district magistrate in Karachi by H.S. Suhrawardy to 'Dera Ghazi Khan district—the Siberia of Pakistan civil servants.'[17] Within two days after the Firoz Khan Noon government was sworn in, this transfer was cancelled and Gauhar was made deputy private secretary to the prime minister. Lewis thought that these actions illustrated 'the extent to which many civil servants have become identified with provincial and sectarian pressure groups.' He identified Gauhar as a Punjabi, who was a protégé of N.M. Khan, the chief commissioner of Karachi and close to Suhrawardy from their days in pre-partition Bengal.[18] Arrayed against Gauhar was the 'UP group [UP is United Provinces of India—the 'UP group' became the most commonly used term for the immigrants] in the civil service, led by the arch-Shia and striking arm of President Mirza [himself a Shia], Secretary of Interior A.T. Naqvi' and the 'Muslim League organization with its still loyal base in Karachi of refugees from the United Provinces.' Lewis also saw the Sindhi republicans under Mir Ghulam Ali Talpur aligning themselves under a Mirza-sponsored coalition of Prime Minister Chundrigar against Gauhar, the Punjabi, who was replaced in Karachi by a Sindhi, Muzaffar Hussain.

The US embassy continued to examine governmental transfers through the prism of sectarian and regional rivalries, while charting the ups and downs of the leaders. Among these, they identified Aziz Ahmed who had aligned himself with fellow East Punjabi, B.A. Kureshi, while A.G. Riza and I.A. Khan were seen as part of the UP refugees, whose position had been 'eclipsed' during the last several ministries prior to martial law.[19]

A similar conflict appeared to be developing within the Pakistan Army, as Ayub consolidated his position. Having received his first extension as army chief, he was angling for another one. He was also building up his base among the rank and file, largely through the rapid expansion of the army, with American help. This provided opportunities for quick promotions and the building of a stronger base of support for the chief himself. Ayub had never felt comfortable with the upper class, well-educated and more worldly colleagues who came from the leading Muslim families of northern India. He was more at ease with colleagues from the Punjab and Frontier provinces. Although ethnically a Tareen Pathan, Ayub spoke a sweet Hindko version of Punjabi at home rather than Pushto. He had a few very private friendships, some based on regimental ties, and trusted only those who posed no threat to him. Around him the lines were being drawn between the military outsiders and insiders, much like their civilian counterparts.

Conflicts grew as Ayub promoted and placed his favourites (such as Musa and later Yahya) in key slots, often bypassing other more senior officers in the process. Among his more vocal opponents was Sher Ali Khan Pataudi who recalls Ayub telling the army: 'Let me handle politics and you all keep out of it.'[20] According to Sher Ali, Ayub 'wanted to use the army as his power base for a dictatorial position in the political field (administration) while still in uniform; a very dangerous thing in my view for the army, in the future.' Sher Ali warned Ayub against getting involved in politics but was told that the country needed 'shaking up'. He also bemoaned the selling of cantonment land to officers, which he felt had got them 'more interested in building houses and real estate than their work in the army.' When Ayub passed over Sher Ali in promoting Musa to the COS position in October 1956, Sher Ali sent a strongly worded statement of objection to the prime minister in the latter's position as the defence minister, citing favouritism as the basis of army promotions. His objection was not entertained. Later he found out that the prime minister had never even seen the statement. Ayub had dealt with it summarily himself, sending Sher Ali home from the army. Not only that, Sher Ali states that he later found out that a signal had been sent out from Ayub Khan's secretariat 'saying that my services had been terminated because of doubts about my loyalty, which had been known to the authorities for some time.'[21]

It is interesting that Sher Ali was replaced as CGS by Habibullah Khan Khattak, (like Ayub, a Pathan) who had been involved in some of the earlier happenings surrounding the Rawalpindi Conspiracy but had convinced Ayub Khan that he was innocent of participation and indeed helped provide evidence against the conspirators. Habibullah was a highly professional and upright soldier with some ambition and posed a potential threat to Ayub Khan.[22] He and Musa were also among the first IMA graduates to attain high ranks in the army, rather than officers commissioned from Sandhurst Royal Military Academy who had previously held higher commands. Ayub later married his son Gohar Ayub Khan, then a captain in the Sherdils (Ayub's own 5 Punjab Regiment), to Habibullah's daughter, a move some saw as a political marriage to neutralize Habibullah. But then, soon after having sent Habibullah off to the UK for the Imperial Defence Course that would normally have prepared him for higher office, Ayub retired Habibullah suddenly along with a number of his friends, including Brigadier Gul Mawaz. Habibullah later became a very successful entrepreneur and industrialist.

The Americans took note of Sher Ali's departure with some interest. The political officer at the US consulate in Lahore noted a report from a 'sometimes reliable journalist' discussing Sher Ali's allegation that 'Musa was hand-picked by President Mirza over the objection of the C-in-C General Mohammed Ayub Khan who preferred Lt. General Mohammad Azam Khan' for the post of chief of staff.[23] 'The reason for the selection…is that he, like the President, is a Shia' and was 'facilitated by the fact that the influential Secretary of the Ministry of Defence, Akhter Hussain, is also a Shia.' The Americans thought that 'the alleged sectarian motivation for this unusual appointment is plausible.' But, given Ayub's strength within the hierarchy, it is doubtful that he would have accepted Mirza's appointment. By all indications, Musa was Ayub's own choice, largely because he was loyal and a true soldier and would not create any waves, allowing Ayub to concentrate on the political aspects of the job.

FISSURES IN THE ARMY

Other fissures appeared to be weakening the solidity that the army presented to the civilian world, as the army's behaviour began to closely resemble that of Pakistan's civil society. Favouritism based on tribal or kinship ties was creeping into the Pakistan Army or least so the US observers reported. As a detailed contemporary US analysis by Ridgway Knight of the US embassy noted: 'Lines of favouritism are drawn in Pakistan along tribal divisions for Pathans and on the basis of districts for Punjabis, and within districts on the basis of kinship groups, village ties, and caste brotherhood.'[24] Among the factors affecting this behaviour was the changing social composition of the officer group and their involvement in the local politics and disputes of their home districts or villages. 'In the higher ranks, factors other than ability seem to determine promotion in a number of cases,' wrote Ridgway. He noted the potential danger posed by creeping corruption, both political and economic, 'which is recognized to exist in Pakistani civil life all the way to the top', and expressed the view that 'it has not done so to any appreciable extent [in the army which] is a tribute to the corps, linked as it must be with a society in which nearly everyone believes "corruption rules from top to bottom"'. Ayub was seen as a brake on 'President Mirza's inclination to assume a dictatorial role' and at the same time as a reminder to the more radical political leaders that 'the Army stands solidly for law and order and the preservation of Pakistan's ties with the West.' Yet, he noted, 'rumour, unproven in the Embassy's view that Ayub had profited personally from certain military transactions.'[25]

There were two areas where the army mimicked civilian ills. First, there was bitter competition between the outsiders or 'refugees' from northern India and the Punjabis, alluded to earlier. After the initial 'tremendous exhilaration and pace' of the immediate post-partition period had waned, according to Major General Mohammed Latif in his conversations with US officials, there was a decline in the morale of the army. In 1952, Latif reported to his US interlocutors, the COS wrote a secret letter against the refugee officers in which their sizeable numbers were noted. This letter warned that 'they [the UP officers] should not be permitted to rise to top commands since this would allow India to obtain intelligence information by exerting pressure on members of their families who remained in India.'[26] According to the US report, Latif was convinced that the letter was written with Ayub's approval and 'was known only to the Secretary of Defence, himself [Latif?], and Prime Minister Nazimuddin, who ordered the letter destroyed after it was shown to him.'

The sectarian divide within Pakistani society was the second area where the army appeared to suffer the same ill as the civil sector. The US observers noted that Punjabi officers were concerned about Ayub's personnel policies, especially after the removal of Generals Sher Ali and Nasir Ali (misspelled as Nazir Ali in the US document), who feared that Ayub and the president were favouring the 'Pathan clique.' (Sher Ali, of course, was not a Punjabi, a fact missed out by the Americans.) But, as a US officer at the Staff College in Quetta noted: 'Punjabi officers feel that the Pathans have a "closed circuit wired in to Ayub."' The appointment of General Musa as Chief of Staff and General Yahya Khan as Chief of the General Staff fit into this pattern of favouritism towards Pathans.' (Again, this analysis missed the point that Yahya replaced another Pathan, Habibullah Khan.) Adding to this mess was the clash between Shias and Sunnis. While noting that this was a 'growing problem in the army', Latif told the Americans that although both Musa and Yahya were Shia, this was not a factor in their promotion. On the other hand, Nasir Ali, Musa's predecessor, according to Latif, as quoted by Knight, 'was himself a notorious Shia bigot who used his influence to push ahead Shia officers.' Surprisingly, the US embassy did not take into account that Ayub himself was not a particularly fanatical Sunni. Indeed, he took pains to distance himself from the mullahs.

This US analysis concluded also that the same measures that were being used against the UP group of refugee officers were also being applied against Ahmadiyya officers, who 'hold important positions in the armed forces as a natural consequence of their superior education and Punjabi background.' It named members that fell into this group, such as the MGO, Major General Altaf Qadir, as non-practicing members of the Ahmadiyya sect, and included Brigadier Ahktar Hussain Malik and his younger brother Colonel Abdul Ali Malik,[27] as well as the retired Major General Nazir Ahmed, who had left after being implicated in the Rawalpindi Conspiracy. Citing Naval Commander Manzoor ul Haq, it noted that a letter was circulated by the ISI which warned that 'the Ahmadiyya personnel should be carefully watched because they were conducting organized drills and meetings in cantonment areas.' The report also revealed that Commander Manzoor believed that this letter was written 'at the instigation of [Mian Mumtaz] Daultana' during the latter's brief term as defence minister in 1957, and he (Manzoor) also confirmed 'some previous information that a Jamaat-i-Islami group was actively working against his community in the Navy.'

General Latif believed that the army could profit from new leadership under Lt. Gen. Khalid M. Sheikh, the commander of 8 Division, but Ayub was critical of Sheikh, whom he considered medically unfit. This was the time when Ayub was seeking his own extension and it was announced in advance that he would be given another two years (instead of the customary four years) as C-in-C, with effect from 1 January 1959. Ayub refers to the telegram he got from Prime Minister Noon on 9 June 1958 saying that he was 'very glad you have agreed to stay on as commander-in-chief of our armies for another two years....I am confident that the defences of the country are safe in your hands as they have been in the past.' Ayub's reply stated that he would have been 'just as happy to retire as I would be in further serving this magnificent army....you can rest assured that I shall continue to give my best to the army and through it to the country.'[28] It was significant that the announcement of Ayub's extension came from the cabinet and the prime minister and not from the appointing authority, the president. The shadow play continued.

REPLACING AYUB?

President Mirza also apparently had the same idea as General Latif and, according to Humayun Mirza, had decided on appointing Khalid Sheikh to replace Ayub before his new term began in 1959. According to Humayun Mirza, his father 'created a new post of Chairman of Joint Chiefs of Staff and appointed Ayub to it. This was confirmed by Ambassador Langley,' who later checked with Mirza if this was designed to keep Ayub on board even after he retired from his post as army chief, to which Mirza responded 'Yes.' Humayun Mirza reproduces a letter from Ayub to Mirza, thanking him for the appointment and trust reposed in Ayub. In that letter, Ayub praises Mirza for the 'tremendous courage and wisdom' shown by the latter in setting up the new post. 'History will be proud of you,' he wrote, adding that, 'I, personally, am indebted to you for choosing me to shoulder this responsibility. Let us hope I come up to your expectations.'[29] Clearly, Ayub was learning the art of flattery from his politician friends. Having allayed Mirza's concerns, if any, Ayub was off to the US, not knowing what US Ambassador Langley had been told and who confirmed to Mirza's son that Mirza had selected Khalid Sheikh to be Ayub's successor. But events were to overtake Mirza before the year was out.

A key event occurred soon after Ayub made his eventful trip to the US in April 1958. On 20 May 1958, Ayub left by train from Karachi for Rawalpindi, but on receipt of some disturbing information about rumours that were circulating in certain army centres, he got off in Jhelum and spoke with his close friend and the local Division Commander General Azam Khan. Azam told him about the rumour that General Umrao Khan and Brigadier Hisham Effendi had been arrested. Ayub was surprised that the COS, General Musa, was not aware of these rumours and had not told him when they spoke on the telephone while Ayub was in Karachi. Later, at home, he found out more from others, including his wife, and discovered that the rumour, apparently started by politicians, had also implicated him in a plot to sell secrets to India and that the purpose of his US trip was really to 'collect his cheque from Nehru's agents.'[30] Ayub was galvanized by this event to speed up his thinking about the future role of the army in Pakistan so that he could put the politicians in their place.[31]

As Ridgway noted, the US was seeing the army as the only institution that was relatively free of provincial or group rivalries. In its view, the army was 'well disciplined' and had a 'high degree of morale and loyalty to their leaders and **constitute the most stable element in Pakistan today** [emphasis added].'

Meanwhile the machinations within the political system continued to swirl and grow, as the military-man-turned-bureaucrat-turned-president, Iskander

Mirza, continued to try his hand at running the show from his office, disregarding the parliamentary system that he had helped introduce and that had elected him as president. There were two separate but related aspects of his campaign and of Ayub's parallel efforts. First, there was a growing fear and mistrust of East Pakistan and regional politicians in West Pakistan. Second, there was the underlying fear and mistrust between Mirza and Ayub which was evident in their dealings and exchanges with the Americans at all levels of government.

By January 1957, three high level military officers were telling the US Consul General Fisk in Lahore that they 'hold the country's politicians in contempt.' Fisk felt that 'this attitude appears presently (sic) to be even more intense than formerly.' The same officers told Fisk that 'they would not employ such "low characters [referring to West Pakistan's ministers] even as clerks in [their] offices", and said further that 'their [the ministers'] days are definitely numbered.'[32] Not long after that, General Umrao Khan, the GOC East Pakistan, 'expressed grave concern [to his US interlocutors about] increasing Communist and Indian influence in the West Pakistan government and weakness of present Ministry.'[33] Mirza was disturbed by reports emanating from East Pakistan and called Umrao to Karachi to report first-hand on the developments taking place there. Umrao added to Mirza's fears by citing a speech by a Hindu minister of the East Pakistan government in which he did not once mention Pakistan and said that 'the destiny of East and West Bengal was united and common.'[34] Umrao also warned Mirza that 200,000 Hindus from India had overstayed their visas and that East Pakistani officials had no intention of stopping food smuggling out of East Pakistan into India while demanding that the central government make up the food deficit of the east wing. Umrao saw Maulana Bhashani as having 'overwhelming strength while the Prime Minister [Suhrawardy] had very little. Mujibur [Mulibur in original telegram text] Rahman playing double game,' according to Hildreth's report.

Mirza told Hildreth that he 'was going to get one unit in West Pakistan probably by bringing Republicans and Muslim League together.' Mirza had also warned Gurmani 'to stop playing personal politics to get his cronies into office.' Importantly, Mirza felt that the 'Awami Leaguers in West Pakistan were rogues, bums and opportunists,' and that a large number of people were 'sick of being blackmailed' by them and wanted the president to 'do something about it.'

Soon after Hildreth left the country in 1957, the US Charge d'Affaires Gardiner warned the Secretary of State about Mirza's plans and inclinations towards a 'dictatorship.' The US was clearly against imposition of presidential rule in East Pakistan because it would hurt the US image and support the East Pakistani view that the US 'supports Punjabi tyranny and victimization [of] their province.' The US objective was clarified for internal audiences in Foggy

Bottom as being the 'promotion [of] orderly transition from government by small bureaucratic clique to effective parliamentary system conducted by political parties supporting foreign and domestic policies in line with US aims.' Gardiner's powerful conclusion was that the imposition of president's rule 'would lead many to conclude that representative regime cannot (repeat, cannot) exist in same system with expanded Pakistan's military strength.... Embassy does not (repeat, not) believe dictatorship would solve any of Pakistan's basic problems.'[35] The US continued to follow the deteriorating situation in both wings of the country and the struggles for power between Mirza and successive prime ministers. The question now was: would the US support dictator-like behaviour in order to retain Pakistan as an ally against communism?

MIRZA PLANS FOR MARTIAL LAW

Near the end of the year, the new US Ambassador James Langley was passing on to his principals in Washington the gist of his conversation with Mirza in which 'he [Mirza] revealed his low opinion of the East Pakistanis.'[36] Mirza also told Langley that he had persuaded Prime Minister Noon not to allude in his first speech to the nation the specific date of the expected November 1958 elections but to refer to it vaguely. Langley deduced correctly that Mirza was laying the ground for putting off the elections, 'to suit his own purposes.'

These messages appeared to have met a receptive audience. Early in the new year—in 1958—the Secretary of State himself was agreeing with the US embassy's concerns about Pakistan's sliding political structures and suggesting that in the interest of a 'stable representative government', Mirza and Suhrawardy ought to be encouraged to cohabitate politically.[37] Langley was instructed to proceed cautiously in his conversations with Mirza, and that the US government 'must as matter of principle avoid any semblance [of] tutelage of Pakistani leadership.' Dulles added that 'another disruptive political crisis at this time would be unfortunate' and suggested that Mirza be encouraged to 'draw inference that USG [the US government] believes its interests in Pakistan are tied to political stability per se rather than to [the] political future [of] any particularly Pakistani leader or leaders.' Importantly, the US was to stay out of domestic issues such as joint versus separate electorates or one unit. The message was loud and clear. But was anyone listening? Both Ayub and Mirza had their own plans afoot and continued on their parallel paths that would converge before veering away from each other before the year was out.

In the process, Mirza and Ayub continued to share their separate views with the US's representatives at every opportunity. Mirza told Langley in Daud Khel, West Pakistan, on 26 February 1958, that he thought West Pakistan 'should go it alone and let East Pakistan have complete autonomy.'[38] He was counting, he said, on the discovery of oil in the western wing to make up for the loss of foreign exchange earning from East Pakistan's jute and was unmoved by Langley's comment that current governmental policies toward oil exploration companies were such that they would slow down the discovery of oil. On the same trip, Ayub made his pitch for more arms and defence support. When Langley stated that Ayub's talk of the Indian threat rather than the communist threat was not helping Pakistan's cause, Ayub readily blamed the politicians and assured Langley that 'Pakistan would not attack India', but it must be prepared for all eventualities.

While there did not appear to be much discord on the attitude toward India among the West Pakistani politicians, there was growing unhappiness with the eastern wing of the country. This was being shared by various newsmen with the US embassy. According to these scribes, 'certain West Pakistani politicians had begun taking an increasingly hard line toward Bengalis.' Chaudhry Muhammad Ali was mentioned in particular, but other influential individuals in West Pakistan were also said to 'believe that continuing East Pakistan food deficits and political discontent were making it unprofitable [to] maintain [the] political and economic set up of Pakistan,' and were reported as being 'quite prepared to see [the] country divided into its two main constituent parts.' A concurrent and somewhat connected movement was also detected, which supported a union between predominantly Sunni Pakistan and Shia Iran, in which the Shah of Iran would be the head of state! Among the main proponents of this idea, as identified by the US embassy, were the Raja of Mahmoodabad (who had left India to settle in Pakistan) and the Secretary of the Interior Ministry A.T. Naqvi, both well known Shias who had worked with the Shia President Mirza to 'promote their mutual interests.' The activities of this group and the appointment of Prince Aly Khan as Pakistan's emissary to the United Nations were all seen as contributing to the growing theme of Shia domination of Pakistan.[39]

US SIGNALS

In the same analysis that Langley sent to Washington tracking the growth of the Shia group and growing tensions with East Pakistan, he gauged correctly that Mirza was facing a tough situation. Mirza was not liked in East Pakistan and his popularity was slipping in West Pakistan. Dulles and the Department of State had been advising Langley over the previous year that they shared the ambassador's concern about Mirza's inclination toward authoritarian rule but did not wish Langley to 'take any action which could be construed as interference in internal political affairs [of] Pakistan.'[40] But as the political situation continued to deteriorate in 1958, Mirza began showing signs of weakness. He shared with Langley the background to Ayub's appointment as CJCS, which, according to Mirza, Ayub had engineered by putting on a show for Defence Minister Khuhro who favoured the re-appointment of Ayub as army chief while Prime Minister Noon did not. Although Mirza held the power to appoint, he felt constrained by the advice of the prime minister and the minister of defence, leading Langley to conclude that 'Mirza was no longer in command of the situation.'[41] Mirza had told Langley that he favoured General Khalid Sheikh as the new army chief when Ayub's term would expire in 1959. But Ayub's appointment as CJCS would ensure that he stayed on even after he relinquished his post as C-in-C of the army. Clearly, Ayub had outplayed Mirza for the time being, forcing the latter to resort to what Langley called 'desperate politics,' including the dumping of Noon in favour of a Muslim League and Republican Party coalition that also included the Krishak Sramik Party, Congress (Hindu), and scheduled caste members of the National Assembly. Yet, Mirza needed Ayub's support to assume dictatorial powers. Ayub had indicated to Langley that 'only dictatorship will work in Pakistan' but favoured a 'benevolent one [that would] operate in interest of country, not of dictator.'[42] Dulles responded by advising Langley to convey to Mirza that the US favoured democratic government over authoritarian government. '**There may be exceptions which can be justified for limited periods** [emphasis added]. That decision must be left entirely for Pakistan's leaders and people to decide....only as a last resort,' wrote Dulles.[43] In effect, the green light for a change was thus given—and not for the last time in US–Pakistan relations.

Around the same time, Ayub was warning his staff officers of the dangers to the country from the politicians. Having recently come back from the United States, he briefed his officers on the results of his visit[44] and the grand strategy for defending Pakistan against India on the one hand and the communists on the other. A key underlying strategy was that the defence of East Pakistan (from India, that is,) lay in West Pakistan, and that Pakistan needed American aid to provide a deterrent against India in a 'short sharp war.'[45] At the same time, his disgust with the politicians grew apace. As his diary notations reveal, he had little patience for the squabbling and debates of the politicians. He had some choice words for Prime Minister Noon: 'Noon is a nice man, means the country well, but he is very impetuous, lacking in ability and has no guts. He has a very bad memory, can't read anything. So, it is very difficult to do any serious business of life with him. But I am used to dealing with a galaxy of morons starting with Khwaja Nazimuddin downwards.'[46]

Ayub called his corps commanders to a meeting on 6 June and briefed them on his visit to the US and the rumour about his own arrest and that of General Umrao. He was talking himself into shifting from his position as an army man, subordinate to the civil authority, to one who might want to run the country either directly or through the president, whom he also mistrusted.

Oceans away, Mohammed Shoaib, who was then the Executive Director representing Pakistan and seven other Middle Eastern countries at the World Bank, was assuring Frederic Bartlett of the Department of State that 'General Ayub had no serious desire to become President of his country.' According to Shoaib, Ayub did not have grassroot support among the major political parties. He told Bartlett that 'although he [Shoaib] knew General Ayub well as a friend and respected him as a patriot, he did not believe that the General was as highly esteemed for his professional competency by his Pakistani military colleagues as by his American diplomatic friends in Karachi and Washington.'[47] Faint praise indeed from the man whom Ayub was later to hand pick for finance minister! Shoaib went on to warn the US to pay attention to middle rank officers in the Pakistan Army as a potential source of trouble, much like the Egyptian coup leaders.

Ayub headed to a meeting of the Baghdad Pact in Istanbul in mid-July which was overshadowed by news of the bloody coup in Baghdad that led to the death of members of the royal family. It was during this meeting that the Shah of Iran pressed on him the idea of a confederation of Iran and Pakistan with a single army and with the Shah as the head of state. Ayub noted in his diary that he 'gave the Shah no definite answer.'[48] He does not appear to have shared this offer with anyone in Pakistan and even omitted it from his autobiography. The Iraqi coup may have given him some food for thought. But planning continued for a military takeover, with Mirza at the helm. For his part, Mirza continued to pepper the US ambassador with frequent references to the failure of democracy in Pakistan and loud thinking about whether he ought to take over or not. By 27 September, he had enhanced security in Karachi by bringing in an additional 3,000 troops into the city, one-third of whom were navy troops. That day he told Langley that he was 'especially worried at [the] deterioration [of] confidence of [the] army in [a] democratic future of Pakistan.'[49] He was not concerned about Ayub, he said, but about 'officers in lower echelons.'

Langley commented to his superiors in Washington that this may be a reflection of Mirza's growing suspicion that the army thought he too belonged to the league of Pakistan's ineffectual politicians. A detailed report on 30 September from the US consulate in Peshawar, based on frequent contacts with military officers, confirmed the general unhappiness of army officers. According to the report, approximately half of them 'freely criticized the present leaders in Karachi and Lahore for corruption and mal-administration.' A lieutenant colonel referred to Mirza as 'all politician; it has been a long time [since] he has been an army man.'[50] The Pakistani officers generally exhibited a pro-American attitude even when criticizing US actions, including its support of 'an unrepresentative government' in Karachi. Importantly though, they were grateful for US military assistance. The US–Pakistan Army nexus was apparently on firm footing. The Mirza–US nexus was on less firm ground although Mirza apparently felt he had US backing as a result of his frequent reminders to them that he would take over the government.

PLANNING FOR TAKE OVER

Ayub launched the planning for martial law in September 1958 and was satisfied that it would proceed on course. He went off to a holiday in Gilgit on the 18th, leaving it to Yahya, Hamid, and others (including a young Major Majeed Malik) to proceed to Karachi and set up shop. This they did in late September. Meanwhile, in a top secret, eyes only telegram on 4 October, Langley informed the Secretary of State that Mirza '...confirmed to me he would take over the Government of Pakistan probably within a week and simultaneously proclaim Martial Law. The constitution will be suspended, a new commission created to write a new constitution and elections now scheduled for February 15 will not be held.'[51]

Mirza also confided that Ayub would be the martial law administrator, with Umrao taking over in East Pakistan. Ayub was expected to arrive on 6 October and the takeover would occur that night. Mirza's rationale was that he was 'taking over to prevent an army seizure of power in Pakistan. The pressures within the army come from officers below Ayub, both generals and brigadiers.' Mirza said he would retain the foreign affairs portfolio, bring Shoaib back from Washington to be finance minister, and make the Nawab of Kalabagh the minister for food and agriculture. As a sop to the Americans, he said he favoured the US constitution over the British one as a model for future government. Mirza gave a similar heads-up to the British high commissioner but with less specificity on the dates.

Ayub reached Karachi on 5 October, met his commanders, and then went to see Mirza.

'Have you made up your mind, Sir?' he asked Mirza on the lawn at the President's House.

'Yes,' answered Mirza.

'Do you think it is absolutely necessary?' asked Ayub.

'It is absolutely necessary,' responded Mirza.[52]

The die was cast. Ayub had succeeded in ensuring that full martial law authority would reside with him. In effect, by declaring martial law, Mirza was undercutting his own legal authority, having ceded power to the army to run the country.

The US saw the army as having the respect of the people but acting Secretary Christian Herter was concerned about any potential change in the external orientation of the planned coup and on the alleged army pressures triggering Mirza's action. He suggested that Shoaib be approached in Delhi to check out his role in the situation.[53] A day later, a similar missive from Herter spelled out the options for the US in case Mirza took over, and urged the need to reiterate the basic democratic principles that the US favoured:

> While in some instances democracies have had to depart temporarily from basic principles upon which their institutions are found (but only as a last resort and then only to protect those institutions in the long run), we do not have evidence to show this stage has been reached in Pakistan.[54]

Ambassador Langley was clearly in touch with Mirza on a daily basis at this stage and gave further details of the impending coup plans to Foggy Bottom, as well as a contingency 'two hour plan' should anything leak. At 10:30 p.m. on 7 October Pakistan became a dictatorship under President Mirza. Ayub was named chief martial law administrator (CMLA). At 11 p.m. corps commander received their orders and the diplomatic corps were summoned at 11:30 p.m. Ayub sat beside Mirza when the latter briefed the ambassadors. Troops moved into key positions in Karachi, Lahore, and Dacca (now Dhaka). The only politician informed in advance, at very short notice, was Prime Minister Noon, a friend of Mirza, whom he sent a sealed envelope with a letter via Colonel Nawazish, the president's military secretary.[55]

The deed was done. Mirza then sent a personal message to President Eisenhower requesting his 'sympathy and cooperation in the difficult period ahead' and assuring him that Pakistan would 'honour all our commitments and will remain loyal to the free world.'[56]

AN OCTOBER REVOLUTION

Mirza characterized his actions as a 'revolution'. He repeatedly stated that his power derived from the revolution that had become necessary to prevent the spread of the political rot in the country's body politic. Even supporters of the democratic experiment in Pakistan, such as the Americans, were fearful of what might have happened in the period between October 1958 and

February 1959 when new elections were scheduled. Demagoguery had swept the country. For their own tactical benefit, politicians were inciting war against India and resistance to governmental authority. Political processions and mob violence were becoming commonplace. The spectacle of the East Pakistan assembly descending into the scene of an unruly gang war and the death of the deputy speaker as one of the results, captured the attention of the president and the army.

But once Mirza had removed the government and installed Ayub to run the country under martial law, a bigger issue arose: What was Mirza's own position? And how would the two leaders, Mirza and Ayub, both manage to maintain their balance on the narrow pinnacle of the political heap? As US Ambassador Langley observed: 'No true duumvirate has lasted in history.' He even hinted the possibility that another leader might emerge. However, he added:

> If one had to pick between Mirza and Ayub as the ultimate top man, latter with his direct control over the army, which is the solid element and undoubtedly the controlling force in Pakistan today, would be the favourite by a narrow margin. However, whenever Mirza might reach this conclusion himself, he could well turn to one of Ayub's subordinates to form new team preserving his political supremacy. Dangers of such Palace revolutions are obvious.[57]

Langley, at the same time, warned of the possibility of the return of the old regime if the new one could not 'demonstrate real achievement in reasonable time.'

In Washington, the intelligence analysts at the Department of State attributed the take over to Ayub's and Mirza's fears of an electoral defeat at the hands of a Noon–Suhrawardy governing coalition and a new government that would be influenced by Bengali interests who would demand greater autonomy and public funds for East Pakistan. 'Mirza was probably also concerned that the elections would be exploited to inflame sectarian jealousies, to which he was vulnerable as a member of the minority but influential Shia sect,' opined the State Department analysts.[58] At the same time, the view from Foggy Bottom was that the problems that had eluded solution at the hands of 'ineffectual parliamentary politicians...are not likely to be mastered by the military dictatorship of Mirza and Ayub.' The general public was seen as not being ready to accept the arbitrary abrogation of constitutional government and the East Pakistanis were expected to resent it.

Meanwhile, the US embassy and consulates shifted into high gear to gather domestic intelligence about the reaction to the takeover. In this effort, they were assisted by many willing and some unwitting agents. In Lahore, for example, a senior officer of the CID was citing 'very favourable' local reaction, although he said it might change to 'unfavourable' in a month or two. He did not expect any disturbance in the interim. As a bonus, he conveyed (albeit indirectly) to the Americans that their telephones were being tapped and tape-recorded![59] Other middle class informants for the US embassy held General Azam Khan in high esteem and therefore welcomed the new development, expecting moves against black marketers and hoarders. Naseer Sheikh, the publisher of the *Civil and Military Gazette*[60] and also a Muslim League member of the provincial parliament said that 'people as a whole expect [the] army [will] materially improve internal situation, though prospect[s] for long-term stability were not at all certain.' News censorship had been imposed in the country, and members of the press informed the US consulate that the 'angriest and most shaken men in town are Republican politicians who thought they had elections all rigged.' The US consulate in Peshawar also reported similar sentiments of relief and approval of the army takeover.

It is notable that most people viewed the change as an 'army takeover', despite President Mirza's hopes that he would be able to ride the tiger of his self-styled revolution. Within days, it was becoming evident to observers in the media and the diplomatic corps that the duumvirate would not last. Elie Abel of *The New York Times* recounted how he detected a palpable change in the atmosphere of the room when Ayub entered the room for a joint interview with Mirza conducted by Abel, Watson Sims of the Associated Press on 9 October. 'It was immediately clear who was in charge,' said Sims.[61] During that interview, Ayub made a statement to the effect that the army would continue to watch over the nation's interest and had the ultimate responsibility. 'If something goes wrong, which heaven forbid, should he [Mirza] do something senseless and join the politicians, I will act and the decision will be mine alone,' said Ayub.[62] At the same time, Ayub termed the martial law administration 'subservient to the President'[63] while reaffirming that had the president not acted on 7 October, the army would have been obliged to do so alone, 'since it is its responsibility to maintain law and order.' A view that was to be repeated in Pakistan's history. According to Langley, Ayub was already emerging from the shadows, shedding his role as the kingmaker, and giving the impression that having tasted 'direct political power and limelight, he like[s] it.'

DIFFERENCES EMERGE

Ayub's growing role under martial law was not lost on Mirza. Within a fortnight of the institution of martial law, Iskander Mirza was speaking of keeping it for 'the shortest duration possible' and promising a national council 'to clean up the country.'[64] Clearly, if this were to happen, Ayub's tenure as CMLA would be over and so would his potential as C-in-C, since he had already been elevated to CJCS. As mentioned earlier, Mirza had already intimated to Langley that he had selected Khalid Sheikh to be the next army chief. But Ayub had also begun clarifying his interpretation of the direction of martial law. One day after Mirza's statement about the short duration of martial law, Ayub was issuing a statement that talked of not retaining it 'a minute longer than necessary', but with a caveat that it 'will not be lifted a minute earlier than the purpose for which it has been imposed has been fulfilled.'[65] The lines were being drawn between the president and the CMLA. Separately, in a meeting with the Chief Justice, the army's Judge Advocate General, Colonel Kazi, stated his interpretation that martial law in effect removed the president from the chain of command and made Ayub Khan the de jure as well as de facto power in the country.

As positions were being firmed up, Ayub took off for a visit to East Pakistan. While he was away, according to a report that was later made available to Ayub on his return and corroborated by a separate confidential dispatch from the American consulate in Peshawar, Mirza was said to have approached Air Commodore Rabb, then COS of the Pakistan Air Force, and asked him about air force strength in Malir, near Karachi. Having determined that there were some 1,200 air force troops available, Mirza informed Rabb that 'certain army generals were getting "too big for their breeches" and that in the interests of national unity they would have to be removed from the scene.' He then ordered Rabb to arrest four generals present in Karachi. These included Brigadiers Yahya and Malik Sher Bahadur. When Rabb pleaded a bad telephone connection, he was sent a written order within half an hour to carry out the arrest immediately. He was also told, according to the US report, that this had Ayub's assent. An apprehensive Rabb called on Yahya with this plan and a trusted courier was sent to East Pakistan to brief Ayub.[66] General W.A.K. Burki, a close friend of Ayub, recalled a slightly different outcome as a result of Mirza's call to Rabb. He states that Rabb called Brigadier Sharif, who then called Burki. Burki also recalls raising the Rabb story with Mirza, who denied it, stating that someone may have imitated his voice.[67] Air Marshal Asghar Khan, the air force chief, who had also been on a trip to East Pakistan at the time, recalls Rabb meeting him at Malir airport on his return and explaining Mirza's call to him. According to this account, Rabb asked to see President Mirza and went to his home, but the president did not speak to him. Rabb then informed Yahya and Malik Sher Bahadur.[68] Ayub offers a slightly different version in which he found out about the plan on his return to Karachi airport.

Upon his return, Ayub confronted Mirza who denied any such plans, whereupon Ayub said that he told Mirza: 'No monkeying and no tricks. Be very careful. You are playing with fire.'[69] If Ayub was prevaricating and indecisive even at this stage, his more ambitious younger officers made sure he was tipped over the edge into action. General Yahya recalled the final stage of the Mirza–Ayub rift differently. According to him, Mirza had ordered General Musa and then Brigadier Yahya to arrest Ayub. Instead, they went to Ayub and asked him to sign a warrant for Mirza's arrest. Ayub at first refused but at their urging reluctantly signed after which they carried out the arrest and deportation.[70] This conflated account of the actions between the Rabb incident and Mirza's final ouster may be closer to reality. Mirza's son Humayun gives credence also to a report credited to Zulfikar Ali Bhutto, the young minister in the martial law cabinet and at that time a '100% Mirza's man',[71] which attributes the final putsch to Mirza's efforts to bring Musa to his side by promising to make him army chief in place of Ayub.

Asghar Khan cites another incident that may have added to the urgency with which Ayub dispatched Mirza. According to him, military intelligence intercepted a telephone exchange between Syed Amjad Ali and Mirza and reported its contents to Yahya Khan. Amjad Ali's son was set to marry Mirza's daughter. Ali asked Mirza to agree to a date, to which Mirza responded that he had his hands full for the immediate future but would do so as soon as the situation was normal. When pressed, Mirza replied that he would 'sort Ayub Khan out in a few days'. Yahya informed Ayub Khan about this on Ayub's return from East Pakistan.[72]

Unaware of the army's keen eye on his every move, Mirza proceeded to form his advisory council or cabinet. Generals Burki, Azam, and Sheikh were invited to come down to Karachi in the third week of October to be sworn in. Azam was against going since he did not wish to leave the army. Burki persuaded him to accept the job since 'we were all in the same boat and must sink or swim together'.[73] On 24 October, an eleven-person cabinet was named, including the three army generals, four West Pakistanis and four East Pakistanis. Among the West Pakistani ministers, Bhutto (Commerce), Shoaib (Finance), and Manzur Qadir (Foreign Affairs) were to achieve prominence later. The army generals and these three held the commanding heights of government. The East Pakistanis were given ancillary ministries. Ayub was the prime minister and continued to be CMLA. In setting up this cabinet, Mirza in effect further weakened his position vis-à-vis Ayub since no one with a major regional or national constituency was included who might end up supporting him against Ayub in a showdown. In fact, it appeared that he had no cards left to play.

Ayub instructed General Burki to meet Mirza twice to warn him against issuing statements that contradicted the CMLA's orders or statements, and 'to discuss with us beforehand any public announcement he intended to make.'[74] The inner cabinet, comprising Ayub, Azam, Sheikh, and Burki (with Brigadier Yahya as the staff officer) met to discuss the modalities of effecting a change. They decided to ask the president to resign, and if he declined, to dismiss him. Ayub did not wish to take on this task himself because of his long relationship and erstwhile friendship with Mirza. He deputed his trusted friend Burki for the task but Yahya suggested that all three lieutenant generals (Azam, Burki, and Sheikh) might be a better group to make the final demand. D-Day was to be 27 October, H-Hour set at 10 p.m. The cabinet (named earlier) was sworn in on the morning of 27 October, with Ayub taking the oath of office as prime minister. On that fateful morning Burki received an invitation from Begum Mirza to speak with her about forthcoming visits to local hospitals. Mirza also wished to discuss some issues with Ayub, so both Burki and Ayub met at the President's House at 5 p.m., where Ayub had held a press conference half an hour earlier.[75] They had tea on the lawn and then Ayub, Aslam Khattak (the ambassador to Kabul), and Mirza broke off to speak about Afghanistan. Burki and Begum Mirza spoke about her planned hospital visits starting 29 October. Burki recalls how he had to keep a straight face during that exchange since he knew that by then she would no longer be First Lady of Pakistan!

THE COUP

Burki returned to 8 Victoria Road, his residence in Karachi, had dinner, put on his uniform, and returned to the presidential palace in the company of Azam and Sheikh, carrying a hastily typed up letter of resignation that had been prepared by Major Majeed Malik. (Asghar Khan recalls being asked by Ayub to accompany the generals for this job but turned it down, since he 'found the whole exercise…distasteful.') Mirza had just come back from a dinner with his friends, the Ispahanis. When the generals arrived at the President's House, they were told that the president had retired to his bedroom for the night, but due to their insistence on seeing him, they were finally asked to come upstairs. Again, the generals insisted that Mirza come down and meet them. Finally, Mirza descended in his dressing gown and saw the three uniformed generals and Brigadier Malik Sher Bahadur standing behind them. As Burki recalls: 'He sized up the situation. And after some persuasion, [he] signed the letter of resignation.'

Pakistan was now firmly under military rule for the first time. But not the last.

The next morning, the eight ministers who had earlier taken the oath under President Mirza took their oaths again, this time as 'ministers of the presidential cabinet' of Ayub Khan, who assumed the office of president.

Manzur Qadir and Habib-ur-Rehman, who had missed the oath ceremony on the 27th· were sworn in on the 29th. Shoaib was not expected back from Washington till the first week of November and would be sworn in later. Ayub not only continued with the same team but also immediately carried forward all the plans and projects announced at the time that Mirza had taken over earlier in the month. Only the lead actor had changed. Ayub retained for himself the portfolios of Defence, Kashmir Affairs, and the Cabinet Secretariat, and made Azam Khan his senior minister.

The US embassy pronounced its verdict on the cabinet, labelling them 'not an impressive lot and in most cases lack[ing] experience and training in the particular fields for which they are now responsible.'[76] Four generals, including Ayub, dominated the cabinet. The civilians were mainly non-political individuals and not well known beyond their immediate circles. Three of the four West Pakistanis were closely associated with the ousted president: F.M. Khan and Bhutto were known as 'Mirza men'. Shoaib was close to Mirza in the early days after partition and a member of the 'bridge playing clique' around Mirza. Manzur Qadir was known to deliberately avoid politics and best known as a powerful constitutional lawyer but was moved to Foreign Affairs. In terms of their regional affiliations, Bhutto was the only Sindhi, Shoaib a refugee from the former United Provinces of India, Burki from the largely Punjabi-speaking Pathan '*bastis*' (settlements) near Jullundur in East Punjab, Sheikh and Qadir were native western Punjabis, and F.M. Khan and Azam were from the NWFP. Ayub, also from the NWFP, was a Punjabi-speaking Pathan from Hazara district. The rest were all from East Pakistan.

The commentary on individuals accompanying the official bio-data on the cabinet that the US embassy sent to Washington is particularly revealing. While the US observers thought the overall cabinet was unexceptional, Burki was seen as 'highly intelligent, well balanced and well informed. He may well be the most able general in the new Cabinet.' They saw Bhutto, at 30, the youngest member of the cabinet, as 'a personal friend of President Mirza, who [referring to Mirza] has been evidently grooming Bhutto during the last two years for a responsible post....He is married to a highly Westernized girl of Iranian background from Bombay and has two children. Despite the sophistication of the young couple, however, when they visit Larkana each winter, Mrs Bhutto observes strict purdah.' His critics were quoted as seeing in him a 'promising young man but far too young and inexperienced...[for] the Commerce Ministry.' Azam was seen as someone who was well known to the public because of the Lahore martial law, 'primarily a good field soldier' and 'essentially a man of action' who was less happy in staff jobs. Sheikh and his wife were better known to the US consulate staff in Lahore since they rented their home to the US consulate. He had been evaluated at the time when he was seen as Ayub's replacement as army chief. He made a 'fine impression' and was a leader who led 'by persuasion and logic rather than bowling over opposition by force of personality.' He was also seen as tactful and patient and an able negotiator who 'puts listeners immediately at ease' and had a good sense of humour. He was seen as favouring a civilian 'front' government controlled by the army in the background. He was also seen as lacking political ambition and not attracted by the perks of politics 'since both he and his wife are from very wealthy families and have no financial worries.'

Manzur Qadir was highly regarded as legal expert and had played a role on the defence team in the Rawalpindi Conspiracy team alongside Suhrawardy. His father, Sir Abdul Qadir. had been a prominent lawyer and a literary figure in Urdu. Manzur Qadir was seen as 'aloof from politics', although the Americans noted that he had leftwing friends, including Faiz Ahmed Faiz and ex-Major Mohammed Ishaq, a communist who was involved in the Rawalpindi Conspiracy case. Shoaib had been a member of the Indian audit and accounts service prior to partition and was one of the senior officers in finance that came to Pakistan but not a member of the 'so-called Punjabi audit and accounts clique which included Ghulam Mohammad, Chaudhry Muhammad Ali, Said Hassan, S.A. Hasni, and Abdul Qadir, among others.' He had been passed over by Abdul Qadir for secretary of finance by Ch. Muhammad Ali and offered his resignation to Liaquat Ali Khan but was dissuaded by Liaquat. During that period he became close to Iskander Mirza and played bridge with him. In 1952 he was sent to the World Bank as a form of 'political exile.' He was 'well thought of by his World Bank colleagues' and considered 'a thoroughly competent man in the fields of finance and administration.'

With Mirza removed, first to Quetta and then sent in the middle of the night to London, Ayub turned to governing Pakistan. His first declaration, which accompanied Mirza's own statement while Mirza was handing over power to him, emphasized that 'this change would in no way affect my policies which I gave out to the nation in my radio broadcast of 8th October and in other statements from time to time.' While he had considered himself to be a friend of Mirza, he did convey through the British to Mirza that if Mirza spoke to the press, Ayub 'would wreak vengeance.'[77] The local press began publishing reports about Mirza's wealth outside the country. The British also referred to the fact that Mirza was known to have some assets abroad, but Mirza's son Humayun states that all Mirza had was his pension and indeed Humayun helped support him whenever he visited from Washington. General Burki states emphatically that 'Iskander Mirza did not possess much in cash or immovable property, and the propaganda of corruption against him was all lies.' Citing Gunnar Myrdal, Burki wrote that 'in developing countries, the public judges rulers according to their own standards. They visualize what they themselves would do if they had the power, and blame the rulers for these failings.'[78]

The public was quick to accept the change in rulers. Since Mirza had not been a popularly elected president, he was as distant from the masses as Ayub was in terms of electoral politics. It mattered little to the general population which individual sat in the presidential palace. Not only the public, but Pakistan's ever-ready judiciary also pronounced, on the very day of Ayub's takeover, that the usurpation of power to set up a new regime was acceptable. In a remarkable application of Hans Kelsen's theory of revolution and law, Justice Munir ruled that 'where revolution is successful, it satisfies the test of efficacy and becomes a basic law-creating fact.'[79] But was this a revolution or even a coup d'etat? Or simply a political power grab?

Edward Luttwak's seminal *Coup d'etat: A Practical Handbook* would appear to define any successful ouster of a ruling state apparatus by any organized force to be a coup d'etat. Others might classify the October actions, first by Mirza, who was already president, and then Ayub, who was effectively running the country as CMLA, as a *coup de main* or a *putsch*, since the authority figures themselves were seizing total control over government by removing obstacles in their path. In the case of Mirza, he wanted to rid himself of the difficult politicians and, in the case of Ayub, he wished to remove Mirza, who was likely to remove Ayub from his powerful position as CMLA and then from his position as army chief. In effect, the survival mechanism kicked in and the army was the key deciding instrument in the clash of two powerful ambitions.

In the absence of well established civilian dominance over the military, transnational political leadership and democratically organized and powerful national political parties that could have counter balanced any Bonapartist tendencies on the part of the army, the field was wide open and would remain so for decades to come. A compliant and equally ambitious clique of bureaucrats helped the army's ventures, while the judiciary, instead of refusing to give the army legal cover (and by doing so, forcing a showdown with the military government), entered the argument to justify *ex post* its extra-legal moves. As in nature, politics too abhors a power vacuum, and when the army saw the political system disintegrating into regional and sectarian clashes and rank corruption, it expanded its definition of purpose to include guardianship of the national frontiers *and* polity. In doing so, it entered the category of Guardian coups, one of the four types of coups defined by Huntington, thus joining other countries, such as Turkey, Thailand, and Indonesia that went through a series of similar changes of government. With the nation as a trust, the army began the job of trying to rebuild the political system and set up new economic structures. This was not an easy task. The political experiment that began with Ayub in October 1958 was to continue through his cohort group till December 1971, losing half the country and as well as a war with arch-rival India in the process.

NOTES

1. Samuel Huntington, *Political Order in Changing Societies* (Yale, 1968), p. 198.
2. Morris Janowitz, *Military Institutions and Coercion in the Developing Nations* (University of Chicago Press, 1977), p. 52.
3. S.E. Finer, *The Man on Horseback* (Peregrine Books, 1976), p. 269.
4. Confidential memo from SOA Jones to SEA Rountree, 23 March 1957, US National Archives, Washington DC.
5. Ayesha Jalal, *The State of Martial Rule* (Cambridge University Press, 1990), p. 266.
6. Mohammad Ayub Khan, *Friends not Masters: A Political Autobiography* (London: Oxford University Press, 1967), p. 56.
7. Altaf Gauhar, *Ayub Khan: Pakistan's First Military Ruler* (Lahore: Sang-e-Meel Publications, 1993), p. 115.
8. A.B. Awan, *Balochistan: Historical and Political Processes* (London: New Century Publishers, 1985), p. 223. This book provides an excellent account of the past and more recent politics of this strategic province of Pakistan.
9. Speech of 27 December 1957, cited in Humayun Mirza, *From Plassey to Pakistan: The Family History of Iskander Mirza, The First President of Pakistan* (Lanham, MD: University Press of America, 1999) p. 212.
10. Mirza, *From Plassey*, p. 212.
11. Secret air pouch despatch no. 105 from Amcongen Lahore to Department of State, Memo of Conversation: General Mohammad Ayub Khan, Commander-in-Chief, Pakistan Army, and Raleigh A. Gibson. Cited by Paul Wolf at www. icdc.com.
12. Top Secret, Security Information, air pouch despatch number 135 from Amcongen Lahore to Department of State, 13 February 1953. Wolf, op. cit.
13. Top Secret Security Information despatch number 851 of Memorandum of Conversation. Wolf, op. cit.
14. Secret, official Informal letter from Ambassador Horace Hildreth to John Emmerson, Department of State. 14 October 1954. Wolf, op. cit.
15. Ayub Khan, *Friends not Masters,* p. 58.
16. Ibid., pp. 58–9.
17. Confidential Air Pouch Foreign Service Despatch from Lewis, Embassy Despatch number 685, 7 February 1958. US National Archives.
18. In fact, Gauhar is a fellow tribesman of the author, belonging to a very small urban branch of the Janjua Rajputs that were settled in Gujranwala City in the Punjab.
19. Foreign Service Despatch from Hubert H. Curry, Deputy Chief, Economic Section, US Embassy in Karachi. Number 1073, 25 May 1959.
20. Sher Ali Khan (aka Sher Ali Pataudi), *The Story of Soldiering and Politics in India and Pakistan* (Lahore: Bakhtyar Printers, 1983), pp. 159–61.
21. Ibid., p. 162.
22. Habibullah also belonged to an influential political family in the NWFP, which made him a double threat to Ayub, who feared that his strong base in the political system as well as within the army may make him unwilling to bend to Ayub's wishes. Some decades later, Habibullah's son, Lt. Gen. Ali Quli Khan was also seen as a threat by Prime Minister Nawaz Sharif because he was a Pathan and likely to align himself with the then Pathan President Ghulam Ishaq Khan. Thus Ali Quli was not considered for the COAS position.

23. Confidential Foreign Service Despatch: From AMCONGEN Lahore To: The Department of State, Washington. Despatch No 126 13 February 1957. Signed by William F. Spengler, Political Officer. US National Archives. This section quotes from this despatch.

24. Confidential Air Pouch despatch no. 11177 from the American Embassy in Karachi, 23 June 1958 to the Department of State by Ridgway B. Knight, Minister, Deputy Chief of Mission. US National Archives. This section relies on this document for quotations about the changes observed by the US diplomats inside the Pakistan Army.

25. One such allegation in the US files by a friend of Mirza was that Ayub had been given a kickback by the Swedish arms firm Bofors in the installation of the ordnance factory at Wah, near Rawalpindi. But the US was unable to substantiate this allegation. To his credit, Ayub was not seen as keen on personal gain by his contemporaries. His only weakness, as mentioned, among others, by his friend and colleague General Burki, was to allow his children to use their connections to profit from ventures in the private sector. Burki recalls Ayub reacting badly to suggestions that he should curb these actions by his sons. Much of these activities took place after Ayub had taken over and as military dictator ruled over a 'Licence Raj' economy that allowed the emergence of a new *rentier* class.

26. Confidential Air Pouch from American Embassy, Karachi to the Department of State No 1177, 23 June 1958. Subject: Potential Effect on Pakistan Armed Forces of Stresses and Strains in Pakistan. Signed by Ridgway B. Knight, Minister, Deputy Chief of Mission. US National Archives. Also quoted below.

27. These brothers, from Pindori village in Rawalpindi district, were cousins of my father-in-law Lt. Col. J.D. Malik and belonged to the Ahmaddiya sect although their other relatives remained staunch Sunnis. Among these, Malik Mohammed Jaffar, who later became a minister in the first Bhutto government, wrote a strong diatribe against the Ahmaddiya sect. Both Akhtar Malik and Abdul Ali Malik were to receive the highest military honours in the 1965 war with India. Akhtar Malik's son, Saeed, was implicated in an abortive coup against President Bhutto in 1973 and separated from the army.

28. Ayub Khan, *Friends not Masters*, pp. 62–3.

29. Mirza *From Plassey*, ibid., p. 217.

30. The so-called payment was reportedly for vacating some territory to India! Since the rumour was privately circulated and not reported in the public media, Gauhar raises the possibility that it may have been instigated by Military Intelligence to spur Ayub into action. Ayub Khan, *Friends not Masters*, pp. 60–61 and Gauhar, *Ayub Khan*, pp. 123–5.

31. I have a worm's eye view of this event from that time. My father, Raja Abdul Ghafoor Khan, who had been involved with the ex-servicemen's board in Jhelum rushed to Rawalpindi and met urgently with General Burki, my late Uncle Brigadier Zaman's closest friend, and informed him that he had heard a rumour that a plot was underway to arrest Ayub on arrival in Rawalpindi. General Burki was a very close family friend and our next door neighbour in Rawalpindi. He had been introduced to Ayub Khan by my late uncle. My recollection is that General Burki then informed Azam Khan in Jhelum and he intercepted Ayub at the railway station and briefed him on the situation.

32. Limited Official Use Air Pouch, 24 January 1957, Despatch number 109 from Ernest H. Fisk, AMCONGEN, Lahore to Department of State. US National Archives, Washington DC.

33. Secret Telegram Control number 12550, 20 March 1957, 6:44 a.m., from Dacca to Secretary of State. US National Archives, Washington DC.

34. Secret Telegram control number 344 from Ambassador Horace Hildreth, 1 May 1957, after his farewell call on 30 April on President Iskander Mirza. US National Archives.

35. Secret Telegram from Gardiner to Secretary of State, Number 5463, 9 May 1957, 10:13 a.m. US National Archives.

36. Confidential Telegram from Langley to Department of State, Despatch number 540, 24 December 1957.

37. Secret Priority Telegram from Secretary of State John Foster Dulles to American Embassy, Karachi, 4 February 1958, 12:55 p.m. US National Archives.
38. Secret Telegram message from Langley, signed by Corry, from Lahore to Secretary of State, number 258, 25 February 1958, 11 a.m. US National Archives.
39. Secret Telegram message from Langley, to Secretary of State, number 2156, 28 February 1958. US National Archives.
40. Secret cable number 3060 from Dulles of 23 May 1957 and 15 November, number 1144, mulled over the options available to Mirza while hoping he would not upend the political process. US National Archives.
41. Confidential telegram from Langley to Secretary of State, number 5340, 8 May 1958.
42. Secret telegram from Langley to Secretary of State number 13266, 20 May 1958, US National Archives.
43. Secret cable from Dulles to Langley number 2952, 21 May 1958. US National Archives.
44. Mirza had sent his friend Syed Amjad Ali with Ayub, perhaps to keep tabs on him, but Ayub managed to cadge private time with Allen Dulles of the CIA, and General Omar Bradley, the chairman of the joint chiefs of staff, and General Nathan Twining, the vice chief of the US Air Force (with whom he played golf at Burning Tree near Washington DC). Apart from strengthening his bonds with his US counterparts, Ayub may have used his meetings to inject his views on the future of democracy in Pakistan and the role of the army.
45. Gauhar, *Ayub Khan*, p. 127.
46. Ibid., p. 128.
47. Confidential, Limited Distribution Memorandum of Conversation by Frederic Bartlett of the South Asia Office, Department of State, 28 July 1958. US National Archives. Shoaib was to continue as a confidant and sounding board for the US, as other archival documents indicate.
48. Gauhar, *Ayub Khan*, p. 142.
49. Secret telegram from Langley to Secretary of State, number 721, 27 September 1958, US National Archives.
50. Secret Air Pouch dispatch number 4 with Confidential enclosures to Department of State, from American Consulate in Peshawar, 30 September 1958.
51. Secret, Eyes Only telegram from Langley to Secretary of State, number 775, 4 October 1958, 6:42 a.m. US National Archives.
52. Ayub Khan, *Friends not Masters*, p. 70.
53. Secret Night Action (meaning wake up the recipient) Telegram from Herter to American Embassy in Karachi, 5 October 1958. US National Archives.
54. Secret Night Action Telegram, number 791, from Herter to American embassy in Karachi, 6 October 1958. US National Archives.
55. From the unpublished manuscript of Noon's memoirs shown to US consul general Andrew V. Corry in Lahore. Detailed report and extracts sent on 24 August 1959 in Confidential Air Pouch Despatch number 53 to Department of State. US National Archives.
56. Secret telegram from Langley in Karachi to Secretary of State, number 814, 7 October 1958. US National Archives.
57. Confidential telegram from US ambassador Karachi to Secretary of State, number 827, 8 October 1958, 5 p.m. US National Archives.
58. Secret Intelligence Note: Coup d'Etat in Pakistan from R. Gordon Anderson, Director Intelligence and Research to the Secretary of State, 9 October 1958. US National Archives.
59. Secret telegram from Andrew Corry, US Consul General, Lahore to Secretary of State, number 79, 8 October 1958, 5 p.m. The cable also divulges the name of a well known police officer who was the source of this information and rose to higher rank later on. (Name withheld by the author.) US National Archives.
60. This newspaper is associated with Rudyard Kipling whose father started it in Lahore on The Mall, the main road leading from the cantonment (military area) to the city. The newspaper

does not exist nor does the beautiful building that was demolished to make room for the Paramount shopping plaza.

61. Conversation with the author. Eli Abel, later with NBC News, was the Dean of the Columbia Journalism School, New York when the author was studying there and remained a good friend till his death in 2004.

62. Confidential Telegram report on joint interview and subsequent statements by Ayub from Langley to Secretary of State, number 868, 11 October 1958. US National Archives.

63. At the same time he cited Justice Muhammad Munir as having assured him that the president's position was not affected by the abrogation of the constitution. See Paula R. Newberg, *Judging the State: Courts and Constitutional Politics in Pakistan* (New Delhi: Cambridge University Press, 1995), p. 72.

64. *Dawn*, 16 October 1958, cited in Mirza, *From Plassey*, p. 225.

65. Mirza, *From Plassey*, p. 226.

66. Confidential Air Priority pouch message from Robert J. Carle, American Consul in Peshawar to Secretary of State, number 32, 1 April 1959 cites Group Captain A.R. Khan, senior air staff officer of number one group of the Pakistan Air Force as the direct source of this information, which Carle deems to be 'accurate' except for some minor details. US National Archives. Humayun Mirza deems this story absurd. Ayub Khan gives more details of his conversation with Iskander Mirza in *Friends not Masters*, pp. 73–4.

67. Lt. Gen. W.A. Burki. Private conversation with author and in his self-published autobiography, *Autobiography of an Army Doctor in British India & Pakistan* (Rawalpindi: Burki House, 1988), pp. 256–8.

68. Mohammad Asghar Khan, *Generals in Politics: Pakistan 1958–1982* (Vikas, 1983), p. 8.

69. Ayub Khan, *Friends not Masters*, p. 74.

70. Confidential Airgram from American Embassy, London to Secretary of State, number G-630, 8 January 1959. US National Archives. The story contained in this message emerged a few months later courtesy of the UK Commonwealth Relations Office that allowed a representative of the US embassy on 7 January 1959 to read a memo written by an anonymous newspaperman describing an evening with Yahya during the newspaper man's stop over in Karachi. 'According to memo, Yahya accompanied by his aide and latter's Irish wife, spent boozy and extremely informal evening with correspondent providing unusual opportunity for assessing Yahya's character.' Aware of rumours that Yahya was likely power behind the scene in Pakistan, the newspaperman described Yahya as 'worldly, "tweedy," highly intelligent and having an aura of intrigue about him, but thought him hardly man of calibre to either aspire to or attract necessary support for running country.' He also wrote that Yahya 'drank heavily and fondled his aide's Irish wife in front of her husband during rather Bohemian evening.' Then in a highly unusual aside and somewhat ironic comment in light of later close relationship between Yahya and the US, he is reported to have been 'highly critical of British and to some extent Americans and assertive that Pakistan would in future be less submissive and more demanding with both US and UK.' Both the US and UK diplomatic missions relied a lot on such background materials and shared the information with each other. In at least one case, the US also used an Italian military attaché with an intelligence background as the source of information garnered from Ayub Khan.

71. Mirza, *From Plassey*, pp. 227–8.

72. Asghar Khan, *Generals*, pp. 8–9.

73. W.A. Burki, *Autobiography*, p. 256. The following account of the final days of Mirza's rule is from General Burki's recollections.

74. Ibid., pp. 257–8.

75. Mirza, *From Plassey*, p. 230.

76. Confidential Air Pouch from W. Mallory Browne, Counsellor for Political Affairs, US Embassy, Karachi to the Department of State, Dispatch number 426, 6 November 1958. US National Archives.

77. Secret telegram from Whitney in US Embassy London to Secretary of State number 2465, 6 November 1958, 4 p.m., quoting summary given by British officers Twist and Stanley of discussions between Sir Gilbert Laithwaite of the Commonwealth Relations Office of the UK and Iskander Mirza. Mirza expressed befuddlement at Ayub's actions since he did not think there were any real differences between them. Mirza did refer to Ayub's desire to arrest Syed Wajid Ali, brother of Amjad Ali, which Mirza had blocked and the make up of the cabinet which included some of Mirza's choices, certain aspects of the land reforms in the Punjab, and finally Mirza's desire that martial law be for 'several weeks' versus Ayub's desire that it extend for 'period of years.'

78. W.A. Burki, *Autobiography*, p. 262.

79. See Newberg, *Judging*, pp. 73–8 for a lucid and succinct explanation of this case.

MARTIAL LAW AND THE SEARCH FOR LEGITIMACY

> The ruler army chooses the new political order as a reaction to the order that it has replaced
>
> – Amos Perlmutter[1]

After ousting Iskander Mirza, General M. Ayub Khan moved quickly on various fronts to establish his control on the one hand and to show the population that he was trying to effect changes in the way the country was governed on the other. Under the shield of martial law, he promulgated a number of commissions to examine different aspects of the economy and society and to come up with new ways of handling issues that had appeared to bedevil the administration of the country under previous civilian regimes. Obviously, he had not come into office unprepared. Martial law was a long practised and much discussed action within his inner circle, and the army had had its first taste of running civil affairs during the martial law in Lahore, when Azam Khan had extended his writ successfully into all facets of civilian life and administration, with notable public support and acclamation. At the same time, Ayub was looking for continued American support for building up the Pakistan Army, ostensibly as a bulwark against the communist threat from the north-west which was directed not only at Pakistan, but also at Iran and Iraq's oil fields. Ayub immediately launched a number of domestic and external initiatives to strengthen his hold at home and gain support abroad for his military regime. In a global season of military coups d'etat, he wished to portray his own usurpation of civil authority as a benevolent and progressive act that would be in sharp contrast to the preceding civilian governments. But he also sought public approval of his actions and initiated a series of projects aimed at politically re-engineering Pakistani society in accord with his vision.

Setting a trend for later coups, Ayub's coup was planned and carried out by the army alone. The other services were barely involved. Air Marshal Asghar Khan, the C-in-C of the Pakistan Air Force at the time, was informed of the coup only at the last minute. He recalls a meeting attended by Chief Justice Mohammad Munir, and Ayub Khan, soon after Iskander Mirza had declared martial law. Ayub Khan asked Justice Munir about the mechanism that could be used to get a new constitution approved by the populace. Asghar Khan recalls that:

> Justice Munir's reply was both original and astonishing. He said that this was a simple matter. In olden times in the Greek states, he said, constitutions were approved by 'public acclaim' and this could be done in Pakistan as well.[2]

Munir suggested that the draft be published in newspapers, to be followed by public meetings which would be addressed by the new Prime Minister Ayub

Khan, where Ayub was to hoist the document and seek the public's approval! The participants laughed at this suggestion, recalls Asghar Khan. No wonder then that Justice Munir was to declare a successful revolution to be a 'basic law-creating fact'! This from a judge who had earlier stated in the case of *Firoz Khan Noon vs. the State* that 'when politics enters the portal of the Palace of Justice, democracy, its cherished inmate, walks out by the back-door.'[3]

Ayub was not going to allow legal niceties to stand in his way. He proceeded apace with the task of administering the country under martial law. One of the first partners in this task was the civil service. The senior-most civil servant, Aziz Ahmed, who had been designated secretary general, was named deputy CMLA and occupied the prized position to Ayub's left at the first meeting of the martial law cabinet on 27 October 1958. (After that day, the commanders-in-chief of the three armed services were also made deputy CMLAs and three days later Aziz Ahmed was removed from his deputy role.) As if to emphasize his separateness and the basis of his power, Ayub, at that first cabinet meeting, wore his army uniform (with sleeves rolled up in summer style and a leather Sam Browne belt), as did the other three generals in his cabinet: Azam, Burki, and K.M. Sheikh. Among the civilians at the meeting was the 30-year old Zulfikar Ali Bhutto. A photo of that meeting shows him with a politely lowered gaze, sitting across from Ayub Khan. Apart from Bhutto, the newly minted lawyer, all the civilians in the cabinet were men of experience, each well versed in his area of responsibility (despite the US embassy's less than stellar ratings for them at that time). Indeed, some of the civilian members of the cabinet that Iskander Mirza had earlier sworn in were concerned about their own future in Ayub's cabinet. Only Bhutto seemed self-assured, stating, with his characteristic sense of humour, that he had been the choice of both Iskander Mirza and Ayub Khan.[4]

THE NEW GAME PLAN

Ayub laid out his ideas before his cabinet in a wide-ranging talk, citing the need for 'stability in the economic life of the country' as the primary aim. He highlighted food shortages as a critical issue that demanded immediate attention. In a country with enough land and manpower to assure self-sufficiency, Ayub felt that what was needed was 'leadership and direction'. Similarly, he listed land reforms, improvement of the educational system, the problems of displaced persons (from the partition of British India), and civil service reform as key objectives. Achieving these, he felt, might even demand 'drastic measures...in the interests of sound administration'. He saw martial law 'not [as] an instrument of tyranny or punishment; it was an arrangement under which government had acquired certain unusual powers to implement a programme of basic reforms.'[5]

With the Supreme Court giving legal cover to the coup, the country continued to run under the rules of the previous constitution which had been abrogated by the leaders of the coup. Assisting them, but clearly at the secondary level, were the civil servants. A rapid move toward reform and reorganization of the country's administrative and socio-political order was launched. Some fifteen commissions and committees were set up over 1958–9 to investigate a wide range of subjects and present proposals for implementing changes. For the Federal Capital Commission, Ayub selected his protégé Yahya Khan, a self-starting individual who had earlier helped Ayub write up a plan for reorganization of the Pakistan Army. Yahya proved true to form and submitted a report suggesting a new capital near Rawalpindi in the Shakarparian area bordering the Margalla Hills, a city that was to be named Islamabad. This was in accord with Ayub's own preferences: he had often cited the huge distance between the government in Karachi and the army headquarters in Rawalpindi as being a hindrance to good communications and coordination. To some extent, this distance allowed the army to think and act autonomously in the years since partition and independence, perhaps contributing to the divide between it and the civil authority.

Three earlier reports (by different commissions) that had been lying in the government's files were re-examined and their proposals implemented. These included the revolutionary Marriage and Family Laws Commission that provided protection and privileges to females, the Sugar Commission, and the Press Commission. The latter, according to General Burki (whose ministry was responsible for labour relations), extended the suggestions made by Burki's Labour Commission to workers in the news media and provided them set working hours and benefits. Eight new commissions were formed later in 1960 and 1961 to continue the process of reform, including the critical Constitution and Finance Commissions.

Ayub saw himself as a revolutionary leader—even more so than Iskander Mirza—and saw the October Revolution as an opportunity to change the socio-political and economic map of the country. Among his more extreme ideas at that time was a plan to follow the Turkish example and to introduce 'Roman script for all of the languages of Pakistan', a move that he felt 'would help increase literacy and could also help in the creation of a common language.' He instructed his cabinet to consider this idea 'dispassionately'.[6] Although this plan never reached fruition, a mélange of the leading two languages of Pakistan, Urdu and Bengali, was attempted during the waning days of Ayub's regime, more as a propaganda ploy than anything else, with Bengali words introduced into official Urdu statements and broadcasts. East Pakistan, for example, was then to be referred to as '*Poorbo Pakistan*' and not

'*Mashriqi Pakistan*,' the correct Urdu wording, in national broadcasts, notwithstanding the confusion that this created among the many provincial listeners and viewers who had enough trouble adjusting to the high falluting Urdu that was the norm of Pakistan Television and Radio Pakistan broadcasts.

EFFECTING SOCIAL CHANGE

The martial law administrators below Ayub also saw themselves as instruments of social change. Military officers, using the threat of military tribunals and summary punishments, moved rapidly in the cities against price gouging and hoarding of goods. Shopkeepers were asked to clean up their premises. Following the old military adage that 'if it doesn't move, paint it,' they made it mandatory for sellers of foodstuffs to have clean and painted shops, with wire gauze to protect food against flies. A large number of politicians were arrested on charges of corruption and disqualified from public service while raids were conducted against individuals suspected of involvement with smuggling of gold or other items. Although not particularly onerous, the military presence was highly visible in the first few weeks after Ayub took over. However, Ayub was reluctant to expose the army to civil life and its perceived concomitant ills, so in mid-November 1958, he withdrew the military from direct martial law duties while proclaiming success in restoring the efficacy of the civil administration.

Although this action removed the visible presence of the military, it did not prevent key military generals and other officers from playing their roles in the new regime. To bolster the government's propaganda, Ayub brought in the eloquent Brigadier F.R. Khan to set up the Bureau of National Research and Reconstruction (BNR&R), a precursor to the information wing of the president's secretariat (which later became the information ministry under Secretary Altaf Gauhar, a man whom many detractors were to characterize as Ayub's Svengali and Goebbels rolled into one).[7] Among the tasks of the BNR&R was the surreptitious hiring of compliant journalists who were well known and willing to lend their names to commentaries that were published in national newspapers in support of government policies. According to one civil service officer[8] who was brought into the bureau that time, a leading newsman was given as much as Rs 1000 to 2000 a month (a princely sum at the time) for allowing his name to be used in this manner.

The military continued to be suspicious of news media that did not toe its line, especially the well-known *The Pakistan Times* and *Imroze* that belonged to the Progressive Papers Limited (PPL) and whose editors were suspected of socialist leanings. In 1959, Ayub moved to take over PPL, converting *The*

Pakistan Times from a voice of dissent to an official mouthpiece. This action was taken by the government under the Pakistan Security Act on 19 April 1959 ostensibly to 'empower the government to change the management of newspapers—instead of outright banning them—which, in the opinion of the government, published or contained matters likely to endanger the defence, external affairs or security of Pakistan.' According to Tariq Ali,[9] (the son of Mazhar Ali Khan, editor of *The Pakistan Times*), and later accounts by Mazhar Ali Khan himself, the brains behind this scheme was Brigadier F.R. Khan, while General Sheikh and Mr Bhutto participated in the takeover. PPL ownership was auctioned off and given first to a Karachi industrialist, Ahmed Dawood, and later to Chaudhary Zahoor Ilahi before being transformed into the National Press Trust in 1964. Ironically, this takeover was hailed by leading editors and newspapers of the country, including Altaf Husain of *Dawn* and Z.A. Suleri, then editor of the *Times of Karachi* and later editor of *The Pakistan Times* and a staunch supporter of Ayub Khan (and later also of Yahya and Bhutto).[10] In 1960, the military government also introduced a draconian Press and Publications Ordinance that was renewed periodically by both military and civilian regimes to exert control over the news media, holding not only editors and publishers but also printers and distributors liable for punishment if they printed anything counter to the government's views. Such controls clearly violated the publicly professed policies of economic and social development and, in fact, hobbled the government's own ability to communicate effectively with the masses and engender support for its policies.[11]

Official policy continued to celebrate Pakistan's alliance with the United States, aligning itself with US propaganda efforts that were designed to influence both military and civilian opinion leaders. The US portrayed itself as a partner in the growth and development of Pakistan's military. The earlier establishment of the USMAAG as an adjunct to the GHQ of the Pakistan Army in Rawalpindi and the setting up of US information service centres in major cities in Pakistan allowed them to trumpet the names of officers receiving training in the United States in the Pakistani media. Meanwhile, lavishly produced colour publications about the United States were mailed routinely to an expanding list of recipients, with a view to conveying an idyllic picture of life in the United States, perhaps as a model for Pakistan's future development.

RE-THINKING THE CONSTITUTION

While using the military to bolster his position, Ayub was careful not to draw the army too deeply into the day-to-day running of the affairs of state. He was keen to put a civilian face on the government and began pondering changes in the constitutional set-up immediately after taking over. The new US Ambassador Langley reported to Foggy Bottom on a meeting with Ayub on 20 March 1959 during which 'with seeming pride of authorship', Ayub had his secretary prepare a multiple-page document presenting his views of what the next constitution for Pakistan should look like.[12] The final page of this document was a chart of the organization of government that had the president at the head, chosen by an electoral college made up of district commissioners. No term was indicated, according to Langley, but he reported that Ayub had in the past 'expressed preference [for] a single seven or eight year term.' Ayub explained that he had shared the document with Justice Munir and hoped to set up a commission by October to write the new constitution, but added that it might be sooner. With reference to the timing issue, Langley noted that Ayub may have said that only 'because he feels Americans naturally prefer constitutional government and would hasten return to it.'

Ayub foresaw an executive department under the president, comprising a cabinet of ministers chosen from outside the legislative branch 'which could be one or two Houses (perhaps maximum of 200).' Cabinet members were expected to sit in the legislature and also vote, but the president would have 'strong powers' over the legislature, even extending to the point of a veto. Langley recounted Ayub stating that the president must be 'a strong man', but refrained from adding 'like me.' The extent to which Ayub had done his homework and anticipated the future structure of government is indicated by the detail that he shared with Langley even at that early stage. Ayub's chart showed a central government running East and West Pakistan through governors with advisors, all appointed by the president. The next layer below the governors would be the district, and within each district there would be local government units of 10,000 persons each (except cities which would have separate local units). Local boards would be elected by each unit and all board members would elect district commissioners. These local boards would 'participate in the election of legislative members.' Ayub told Langley that he favoured 30 years as the right age for people to be able to vote since this was the 'age at which person became mature enough to vote for local board members.' But he contemplated a party-less system and was prepared to impose a constitution on the country, 'noting [that] it would have within it provisions for its amendment.'

Langley's comment on this exchange with Ayub noted that the president's plan was 'probably purposely silent about an Islamic constitution.' It also would basically preserve many features of the existing form of government under Ayub's dictatorship. He also commented that although lawyers may find fault with the plan, some of them, 'Munir and [Manzur] Qadir included', had evidenced the 'ability to bend with the political winds.' In sharing the document with the Americans, Ayub was testing the waters while playing to their weakness for elections and anything that resembled their own form of government. Ayub was also said to have mentioned that he read some of the earlier American constitutional documents in coming up with his plans. Having worked closely with the Americans, he knew which buttons to press and barring a strong reaction from the US government, he would proceed. And so he did.

But the new administrative form of government that Ayub intended to graft upon Pakistani politics, while aimed at removing the weaknesses that he saw in the disorderly parliamentary form, also laid the foundation for his own eventual fall from grace. For the manner in which he arrived at this new governmental machinery and the way he managed it proved unsustainable in the long run. Ayub began with a premise that the country needed a system of controlled democracy that was in accord with the 'genius' of the people. In other words, the largely uneducated populace did not know what was good for it. It needed a strong father figure, who could control operations, much the way a general commands his troops and the army coddles its soldiers. Paternalism was the hallmark of this approach. In his quest, Ayub found ready support among the bureaucrats and a select intelligentsia. According to Ayub's biographer Altaf Gauhar,[13] Manzur Qadir and K.M. Sheikh toured the country to gauge support for a new constitution and the former came to the conclusion that people were in no rush but had questions about who would formulate the new document.

The document that Ayub shared with Ambassador Langley must have been the presidential directive of 15 March 1959 that Ayub presented to his cabinet and the two provincial governors under the heading 'Outlines of Our Future Constitution'. It was a sharp shift from his earlier 1954 framework (written at the Dorchester Hotel, London) that had hewed closely to the supremacy of the legislature and an elected president. Under the new political engineering, he saw the masses electing an electoral college that would then elect the next layer of government and eventually agree on a president. He saw this approach as a 'simple and cheap' way of introducing democracy that would fill the gap between the government and the people, which was very often 'filled by demagogues whose sole purpose seems to be agitation for the sake of it and disruption.'[14] His answer was resolution and courage that would be 'provided by the top leader—ME.' Reverting to his military drafting skills that use capitals to emphasize words and ideas, he asserted that a strong central government was 'an absolute MUST' for the country, with a president who had more powers than even the US president (something that he had not shared with Langley). Further, he made references to the Islamic character of this strong central figure, comparing it with the caliphs in early Islam. There was talk of the 'essence of an Islamic constitution' from a man who had only disdain for the squabble about 'an Islamic constitution' in the first place.

Against this background, Ayub formulated the idea of a constitutional commission that would present its document for review, (presumably to him). A few violations of democratic practice, he felt, would lead in the end to a document that would benefit all, without drawing all into the process. However, Ayub conceded to his cabinet colleagues that, 'if need be', he would 'do a bit of canvassing to guide the people round (sic) to a sensible [i.e. his] point of view.' As a result, his plan was presented to and approved by the governors' conference in Karachi in May, and Basic Democracy, as this new approach was to be called, was approved by the same body in Nathiagali in June 1959. The next step was to create agreement for Ayub's plan for framing the new constitution. This was done at a meeting in Karachi on 4 August 1959 at a meeting attended by selected ministers, Chief Justice Munir, Justice Shahabuddin (later the chairman of the constitution commission), and a handful of senior civil servants and other invited luminaries. A telling absence was that of the Law Minister Muhammed Ibrahim. Gauhar reports that the meeting received a list of points for discussion under Ayub's signature that presented the framework of the Basic Democracies scheme and different ways in which the constitution could be framed. Ayub's marching orders for the group included a warning against any measures that might foster indiscipline: 'Any form of loose or starry-eyed thinking on our part on this subject will lead us to disaster,' he stated. And he paid a ritual obeisance to Islam by suggesting the adoption of an Islamic ideology that was 'tangible' and 'in the context of the fast moving world of today.' (The army was still in its post-colonial mode and not imbued with a strong Islamic bent. Ayub was loath to cede the grounds to the mullahs, whose antediluvian thinking appeared to him to be the cause of much civil unrest.)

Following a brief review, the group decided to authorize Ayub to appoint a constitution commission and to set the date for the presidential elections after the constitution had been finalized and approved. Ayub had already decided to appoint Justice Shahabuddin as the chairman of the commission and assign the drafting task to Manzur Qadir rather than to the law minister. Qadir and Bhutto were assigned the job of building support for the Basic Democracies idea. Foremost in Ayub's mind was the need to gain legitimacy as the head of the country. The elitist cabinet members did not trust the ability of the elected 80,000 Basic Democrats to understand any complex issues relating to the presidency. Manzur Qadir drafted a sentence that would be the basis of the referendum submitted before the electoral college on 15 February 1960: 'Have you confidence in the President Field Marshal Mohammad Ayub Khan, Hilal-i-Pakistan, Hilal-i-Jurat?'[15] Not surprisingly, the electoral college answered in the affirmative to the tune of 95.6 per cent, paving the way for Ayub to be 'elected' President of Pakistan on 17 February 1960.

Immediately after becoming president, Ayub set the constitution commission into motion. A campaign began to get the commission to support Ayub's ideas, even to the extent of sending a group of senior civil servants before that body to support Ayub's plan. Manzur Qadir and Bhutto both had their own ideas to contribute through papers that each had drafted. Bhutto, citing Alexander Hamilton, favoured 'a basic law without harmful compromises that render the structure into a weak and unworkably legal edifice.'[16] While recognizing that this might draw criticisms from the West, he asserted: 'Let us not be too sensitive to the reactions of democratic countries.' He also suggested keeping Islam out of the constitutional process, other than a mention in the preamble. All in all, Bhutto was positioning himself as an enthusiastic supporter of Ayub's ideology, something that was not lost on Ayub or other observers.[17] And he was not alone. There were many other supporters of the Ayubian vision of a central father figure running the affairs of Pakistan. Altaf Gauhar, who copied and kept Ayub's personal papers while preparing the draft of *Friends not Masters,* cites many examples of sycophantic and gratuitous advice. He also notes how so many of Ayub's advisors appeared to agree with him, leading Ayub to ruminate on his own powers of persuasion: 'It is surprising how people who are totally opposed to me, begin to understand my ideas, once I have talked to them.'[18] Later, Pakistani military leaders would develop the same confidence in their own intellectual and persuasive powers.

The report of the constitution commission on 6 May 1961 was met with a barrage of commentary, harkening the split between the two wings of the country. Bengalis, both in and outside government, hinted at the need for equity between the two wings and the law minister even suggesting rotation of the office of the president between East and West Pakistan. Among the leaders of the attack was the former civil servant and once prime minister, Chaudhry Muhammad Ali, who still favoured the parliamentary system, but whose views were suspect in Ayub's mind because Ali had been the author of the 1956 constitution that Ayub had upended. Ayub disagreed with the commission on the basic issue of universal franchise and this, among other things, led him to appoint another cabinet sub-committee[19] to examine the report and present their views. This they did, as expected, in line with Ayub's stated requirements. After getting his version of the report approved by the governors' conference of 24–31 October 1961, Ayub announced the new constitution to the country on 1 March 1962. He called it 'a blending of democracy with discipline—the two pre-requisites to running a free society with stable government and sound administration.'[20]

Among the voices heard against this *ersatz* constitution was that of Habib Jalib, an Urdu poet who spared no Pakistani ruler (even Benazir Bhutto, whom he had fervently supported when she came to power). In a blistering personal refutation of the new constitution in his poem *Aaeen*, Jalib energized opposition to Ayub with his public and mesmerizing verse:

Aisey dastoor ko,
subah-i-benoor ko,
main nahin manta,
main nahin janta...

This constitution,
this lightless morning,
I do not accept,
I do not recognize.[21]

POWER VS. AUTHORITY

In refusing to accept the constitution commission's report *in toto*, Ayub was to lay the ground for the clash between power and authority that was to dog his regime and those of his civil and military successors. The paternalistic style of government that emerged was a dictatorship, benign though it may have tried to be. It shunned party politics and excluded from public political discourse and action all those politicians who it deemed unfit for such service. And it gave the president, clearly on the basis of his explicit military power, the right to overrule the elected representatives of the people. As a Field Marshal, Ayub carried a rank that would not retire, and he continued to outrank his chosen successor as C-in-C of the Pakistan Army, General Muhammad Musa, a quiet and unimaginative soldier who was content to follow instructions. Other than the army, Ayub had no political standing and no tribal or other regional backing, coming as he did from a humble family background and being a member of the minority Tareen tribe in the predominantly feudal bastion of the Hazara district.

By serving up a constitutional draft that harkened back to the 1956 constitution, the constitution commission had tried living up to the independence of the judiciary. On his part, by accepting the minority view rather than the majority view, Ayub laid down the ground rules for his treatment of the judiciary. However, the judges did not go down without a fight. As Newberg traces the rearguard actions of the next Chief Justice, A.R. Cornelius, Ayub came in for a fair amount of criticism. In the case of *Fazlul Quader Chowdhry and others vs. Mr Muhammad Abdul Haque*, the Supreme Court ruled in favour of the supremacy of the court and against the unbridled power of the president under the 1962 constitution. In Newberg's words: 'The decision told the country that executive rule was fettered by the written constitution and that the constitution's guardians were the courts.'[22] When the following year, fundamental rights were included in the new constitution, the ascendancy of the courts over the presidency became more apparent—much to the dismay of Ayub and his cohorts—laying the ground for legal challenges to the power of the military ruler.

US DEMURRALS

Even as Ayub was coming under pressure from the constitutionalists and rumblings of unrest were emanating from the disaffected and disenfranchised politicos, Ayub was also facing serious scrutiny from yet another front: the Americans, his erstwhile supporters and friends. The US had become more tight-fisted in its dealings with Pakistan by 1958, and was demanding greater accountability and efficiency in the use of its military aid as well as balancing expenditures between military and economic needs. The relationship became yet more troubled when doubts and concerns regarding Pakistan's real intentions in expanding its forces began to be voiced openly. Having led the US to commit publicly to building up the Pakistan Army as a bulwark against communism from the north, Ayub pressed hard for an increase in overall military aid from other sources to allow him to add more formations to his army facing the Indian border to the east.

He began branching out in other directions to strengthen the country's defences, on land and sea. Pakistan approached the United Kingdom for a submarine. The British Foreign Office promptly informed the US embassy in London of this request and its own unhappiness with this request.[23] F. Bartlett, the director of the Southeast Asia Office and his reporting officer, F.S. Tomlinson, said that the British had not yet made up their minds on how to respond. Their ostensible reasons were the high cost of submarines in general as well as the ancillary and recurring costs of maintaining and operating them. They wondered if the US was going to finance this purchase for the Pakistanis and were told this was not the case. Also, they weighed the potential protest from India. The US embassy in London weighed in against such a sale:

> It appears...very questionable that such a purchase would represent the best expenditure of Pakistan's limited financial resources....As the United States is giving substantial assistance to Pakistan, it would seem appropriate to register similar objections to the sale to it of a British submarine **in the absence of overriding evidence that such a vessel is essential to Pakistan's defense against Communist aggression.** [Emphasis added][24]

This position was supported by Ambassador Langley in Karachi, who also noted the 'harmful stimulus to [an] arms race between India and Pakistan' and the 'additional financial burden on Pakistan which even now depends on US aid to finance [a] large share of its military effort.'[25] He recommended that the US discourage the British on this sale and noted that the chief of the USMAAG in Pakistan concurred with this approach. Langley also brought into the open an issue that seems to have bothered him considerably: the implicit understanding between the US and Pakistan that their mutual discussions on military aid were confidential and would not be discussed with any third party. Yet, Langley suggested to Foggy Bottom that 'we should talk with [the] UK on top secret basis in some detail about US military aid to Pakistan over and above bombers.' His reasoning was that the close relationship between the US and the UK justified a frank approach on the part of the US, while recognizing that the British were keen 'to elicit some information from us'. After all, the UK was also in the market to sell bombers to South Asia. Langley acknowledged the need for 'absolute discretion.... particularly now when Pakistanis fear [that the] US and UK are hypnotized by India and Nehru, [and any] leak of military information which [the] Pakistanis might hear of could cause [a] truly grave situation.' It is not clear if the US was sharing just its own aid programme or all the detailed assessments of Pakistan's military formations and plans. Clearly the friendship was waning rapidly.

Ayub may have detected a coolness in the Americans' attitude and was ready to push the American operatives in Pakistan to get his way (while turning on his charm with their superiors in Washington). In an unusually blunt and frank report on a conversation with him on 8 January 1958, Major General Louis W. Truman, the head of MAAG laid out the differences that had emerged between the two and that also brought out the divergence in American and Pakistani views about the intent behind building up Pakistani forces.[26] Truman had arrived in Rawalpindi with Roswell Whitman on 7 January for Whitman's lecture to senior officers of the Pakistan Army GHQ the following day on 'The Economic Problems of Pakistan', and had been invited by Ayub to join him for dinner that evening. Truman recalls mentioning to Ayub that General Musa had been most interested in the lecture and had said that he (Musa) had been unaware of 'the precarious financial condition of the country.' Taking his cue from that comment, Truman told Ayub that 'these economic problems had a direct relationship to, and bearing on, the military problems and budgets.' He had therefore asked Colonel Hollingsworth, Chief of Army Element in the USMAAG in Pakistan, 'to make a study of the Pak Army budget in order to determine how the money budgeted for the Army was to be spent, and in accordance with the April Agreement, what overall US assistance might be required.'[27]

This immediately produced a sharp retort from Ayub, who said that 'it was not his problem to determine from where the money required for the military forces was to be produced. That was a problem for the politicians and financial people to solve. It was his job as C-in-C Pak Army, to build an Army for Pakistan. It was up to the United States to assist in this build up. He said that the US was committed to support Pakistan and that the US should "get along" in satisfying its commitment.' Truman responded by explaining that the US remained committed to meeting certain deficiencies in the Pakistan Army but that cutbacks in foreign aid in Washington might be expected. Ayub's answer was unequivocal. He stated that 'he had to build his forces up quickly so as to be able to defend Pakistan against aggression from India. The US had to assist him in this effort.' But Ayub did not like Truman's riposte that 'I knew he was well aware that the US military aid being given to Pakistan was not for use against India, but that it was being given in order to assist Pakistan in the build up of forces that could be used in the collective defense against communism. Further, the US could not furnish military aid if it was to be used against India.' Ayub volunteered that Pakistan had no aggressive intention against India. But when Truman built up on that by suggesting that it was not in Pakistan's best interest to cite the Indian case to US visitors coming through Karachi, because military assistance was only for 'collective defense against Communism. It would not be given…for use against India,' Ayub blew up. He told Truman that 'If [you] did not agree that…[I, Ayub] should plan for defence against India, using any means possible, then "I don't think much of your military ability."' Ayub asked if General Maxwell Taylor, who was due to come to Pakistan on 17 January, felt the same way as Truman, to which Truman responded that he was reasonably certain this was the case. 'Well, if General Taylor feels that [way], then I do not want to see him,' said Ayub.

The contretemps over, Truman went ahead with his visits to Pakistan Army I Corps HQ and the headquarters of 15th and 10th Divisions, where he was met with briefings by senior commanders who talked only about the communist threat. Both he and Colonel Hollingsworth felt that the Pakistan officers had been 'instructed by GHQ to play up this theme.' The dance continued, with Ayub playing hot and cold in masterful fashion. On 18 January, when Truman reported to Ayub in Karachi that Pakistan would be receiving more M-47 tanks, Ayub referred to the earlier exchange and said: 'Let's forget the difference we had the other evening,' and a day later sent him three ducks that he had shot. But Truman's analysis was that Ayub's 'hostile attitude will continue to increase if we do not give him everything he asks for. His attitude will also change and [has] already changed, as we put more and more pressure on PAK army to obtain better maintenance, warehousing, delivery, and proper end-item utilization of the military equipment which has been...supplied.' Truman feared that Ayub would have him declared *persona non grata* and show him the same level of hostility that had led to the departure of two previous USMAAG chiefs.

COOLING OFF

The downward trajectory of US–Pakistan military relations started early in 1958, even though politically the US was encouraging Ayub as a counterweight to Iskander Mirza. American and Pakistani military officials met in Karachi on 28 February 1958 to review Pakistan's specific requests for increased aid at the instigation of the Pakistani Ministry of Defence. The US believed that the documents prepared by the Pakistanis had earlier been given to Prime Minister Suhrawardy for his visit to Washington in the summer of 1957. As a report from the US embassy in Karachi to the Department of State noted:

> The Pakistani requests for more military assistance received negative responses in almost all cases. The Pakistanis were visibly disappointed at the categorical turndown of their request for family housing at two cantonment areas, Kharian and Jhelum, and indicated that perhaps they had asked for too much. The denial of the Air Force request for F-100 type aircraft brought forth some spirited responses from Air Commodore Rabb, Chief of Staff, Pakistan Air Force.[28]

The Pakistani GHQ's presentations dealt with two aspects of military aid: the current scope of US assistance and recommendations and the enlargement of the programme.[29] US aid being given at the time was designed to meet the deficiencies of four infantry divisions and 1.5 armoured divisions only. Pakistan calculated that to attain this objective, it would require US aid to raise another 56,000 troops. When this figure was considered too high, it was brought down to 40,000, so that it could stay within the current availability of funds. As the GHQ document asserted: 'While appreciating the inadequacy of the support, we accepted the limitation in order to get the programme started.' But they noted that the troops required to achieve a balance in the 5.5 divisions were still 16,000 short of target. These were needed for two infantry brigades, engineers units, anti-aircraft cover for the field army, some signals units, and some logistic support units. Pakistan also felt that the provision of M-47 tanks for one battalion under the current approved programme left a balance of six battalions that still needed M-47s or M-48s. There was also no provision for tank transporters or railway flat cars, leaving the Pakistanis to speculate that 'the tanks will wear themselves out as well as the roads in one year of training.' Similarly, they noted a shortage of motorized battalions, reserves, troop accommodation, storage of fuel, and motor transport to replace the present fleet 'of approximately 36,000 vehicles, a majority of which are of the Second World War vintage.'

Looking to the future, the Pakistanis wanted a two-step increase in US military aid. In Phase I, they suggested making up the deficiencies in the current programme. In the second phase they expected the conversion of the Independent Armoured Brigade into a Division, the completion of the existing infantry divisions beyond the 5.5 divisions and raising of one more infantry division, and the reactivation of a para brigade. Their underlying assumption was that increased military aid would need to be accompanied by the 'provision of troop housing, workshops and depot cover, development of indigenous sources of supply, [and] creation of reserves.' A more practical issue that the Pakistan Army recognized was the need for standardization of equipment. US aid had created a situation where formations and units sometimes had both British and US-supplied equipment, creating problems for spare parts, maintenance, and training. Therefore, the Pakistanis asked that US aid fully equip the 5.5 divisions under review to maintain standardization. They made an argument for building up Pakistan's potential for the provision of technical manpower in support of the Baghdad Pact troops, as well as fostering of indigenous production, linked both to the needs of the military and civil sectors. This, they felt, would ease procurement problems. Specifically, they asked for modification of the facilities of the Wah Ordnance Factory near Rawalpindi to produce automatic rifle and gun ammunition, and spare parts for the US equipment being provided under the military assistance programme.

The Pakistan Army stated that it had carried out an internal reorganization over the previous two and half years to modernize itself, hoping to increase its strength in the process from 181,183 troops before US aid to 221,183 after the induction of 40,000 additional troops funded by the US.[30] However, the reorganization had yielded efficiencies, reducing the starting-point strength of the Pakistan Army to a leaner 165,700. As a result, they made the case that even after an increase of 56,000 troops funded by the US, the total strength of the army would be only 221,700, imposing no additional burden on the Pakistan economy. They emphasized reliance on internal resources for logistical support but warned that the war reserves of supplies and ammunition, which had been large because of the long distances involved in defending the borders of Pakistan, had had to be reduced from the pre-aid level of six months to four months, 'but even this is not catered for in the present programme.'

Despite the case presented by Pakistan, the US did not respond positively. This, however, did not dissuade the Pakistanis, who continued to press the Americans in subsequent meetings and at different levels of government to fulfil their requirements. They also proceeded to explore diversification of sources of supply of weapon systems for the army and the navy. There is some suspicion, however, that some of these actions were more for show than reality (perhaps to put pressure on the Americans), given that the much discussed purchase of a submarine from the UK was eventually overruled by Ayub in his role as defence minister.[31]

Pakistan had started pressing for a broad range of weapons systems from the US in 1958, with the then Finance Minister Amjad Ali, accompanied by Ayub and Air Vice Marshal Asghar Khan, seeking 'early delivery of a light bomber squadron.'[32] The Pakistan ambassador sought to make the argument that Pakistan needed these bombers 'as a deterrent to possible aggression by India' which in the ambassador's view would eventually 'put the screws on Pakistan.' This would happen, he felt, in the context of the Indus Waters dispute. India, using its superior military strength would 'browbeat Pakistan.' But William Rountree of the Near East Asia division of the Department of State (and later US ambassador to Pakistan) countered emphatically that US military aid to Pakistan 'was not based on the premise that Pakistan was to be armed against India.' Indeed, he stated that 'such assumptions by the government of Pakistan and public statements by its leaders implying such premises were hurtful to US interests.' Ambassador Ali immediately retorted that 'Our arming is against any aggression; that has been our position all along.' But that argument did not tilt the US in Pakistan's favour and indeed, Rountree informed the ambassador that the aircraft in question would not become available for another two years. The give and take continued.

BADABER BASE

Among the more concrete results of the US–Pakistan relationship of that time was the agreement to set up the Peshawar air station, about four and half miles south of the city of Peshawar. Construction on this enterprise, better known as the Badaber Base, began in June 1958 and it became operational in December that year as the '6937th Communications Group'. Originally referred to as Operation Sandbag, probably because of the surprise effect on the Soviet Union that was to be the target of eavesdropping and aerial spying by the Americans located in Pakistan, this base used radio receiver and transmitting facilities situated some miles away from the base. The Badaber Base supported the local launching of U-2 spy planes that took off from the Pakistan Air Force facilities in Peshawar. The base came under public scrutiny when Francis Gary Powers (call sign 'Puppy 68') was shot down over the Soviet Union on 7 May 1960 and the Soviets established that he had taken off from Peshawar. This led to a warning from Nikita Khrushchev to the Pakistan ambassador in Moscow that he had circled Peshawar in red on his map and

Pakistan would suffer dire consequences if it continued to allow such activities.[33] As agreed with the Pakistanis, the US stated that Pakistan did not know of these flights and Pakistan 'protested' this US action. But the cat was out of the bag and eventually, given the slide in relations during the waning days of Ayub Khan's regime, the US was told in May 1968 that the agreement would not be renewed in June the following year. Thus ended a colourful episode in the US–Pakistan relationship. Throughout its life, this 'secret' facility was well known to locals, many of whom provided services to the facility.[34] The US personnel used to frequent Peshawar's bazaars and hotels and even had special shoulder badges made by local artisans. The unofficial badge of the base was a colourful shield with a Punjabi curved shoe (*khussa*), an oil lamp, a bolt of lightning, and two clasped hands, with the motto *Khair Sagalie* inscribed beneath it, meaning 'goodwill'.[35]

Notwithstanding the intent or profession of goodwill between the two Cold War allies, the actual collaboration between Pakistan and the US defense establishment had started taking a more critical tone and colour, even as Ayub sought to deepen ties between the two. General Truman brought to bear some of his arguments against unbridled access to US military aid in a memorandum from the US embassy in Karachi to the Department of State on 6 June 1958. Citing the US country team's concerns about the 'seeming inability or unwillingness of the GOP [government of Pakistan] to face up realistically to its own economic difficulties,' Truman recommended that the US 'seek to persuade the GOP to distribute its total economic resources between requirements of defense and economic growth so as to provide the greatest progress toward true self-sufficiency.' He recognized that the US would need to continue its military aid for some time beyond the commitments embodied in the 1954 agreement in order to provide ammunition and support or replace equipment, 'otherwise, the combat effectiveness of the Pakistan forces will suffer to the detriment of the military investment already made by the United States.' But he ended on a broad note of despair:

> A US objective in Pakistan is to create a viable nation; but despite the fact that there has been an American aid program in Pakistan for seven years with total aid amounting to almost $700 million, Pakistan offers little or no hope for viability in the foreseeable years.[36]

'Viability' in this context meant Pakistan's ability to generate its own resources for growth. As an accompanying table[37] showed, Pakistan's GNP was expected to rise from $5,078.7 million in calendar year 1956 to $7,485.5 million by calendar year 1961 with per capita GNP growing from $60.8 to $83.2 over the same period. Yet defence expenditures were also expected to rise from $205.2 million to $213.3 million a year, of which the country's own foreign exchange outlays were rising from $59.3 in 1956 to $72.8 in 1961. A substantial proportion of the resources available for defence were for force maintenance ($216 million in 1961), and a relatively smaller proportion (only $26.4 million) was aimed at force improvement. This compared with $276.3 million for the expected defence requirements in 1961, of which some $206.5 million was for the army alone, leaving a fairly substantial amount to be filled from Pakistan's scarce foreign exchange reserves.

Ayub was not unfamiliar with the line of reasoning adopted by General Truman and chose every opportunity to stress the importance of expanding Pakistan's army. In a meeting on 26 January 1959 with Loy Henderson (Deputy Under Secretary of State), John N. Irwin II (Assistant Secretary of Defense), and General Lyman Lemnitzer (Chairman Joint Chiefs of Staff), Ayub got General Lemnitzer to commit to a force structure of 5.5 divisions in support of US strategic goals and immediately laid out plans for modernizing the equipment of these 5.5 divisions.[38] He said that most of the divisions were equipped with 'obsolescent British weapons' that needed to be replaced. Among them, he cited the need to replace the .303 rifles with newer M-14s from the US, if blueprints and proprietary rights could be secured. Then he lapsed into his traditional sales pitch: 'The value of Pakistan's armed forces [was] not only as a force to protect Pakistan but as a force being available to go elsewhere if needed. He said it would be much less expensive and more useful for the United States to use Pakistan forces in this part of the world than to have to send US forces.' When pressed to reduce expenditures, for example by junking old weapons systems rather than passing them on to other formations in the army, Ayub agreed not to do so but expressed the view that it was essential for Pakistan to solve its underlying problems with India. Finance Minister Shoaib and Foreign Minister Manzur Qadir were asked by him to explain the Canal Waters and Kashmir issues to the American visitors.

US REVIEWS MILITARY AID TO PAKISTAN

As 1959 rolled around, the US was in the middle of an internal review of military aid to Pakistan and recognized the criticisms within its own government of military aid as opposed to economic assistance.[39] However, it also weighed military aid to Pakistan in favour of the creation of 'stability' in the broader area of the Middle East that included Pakistan, Iran, Iraq, and Turkey (members of the Baghdad Pact). While recognizing the growing importance of Soviet economic assistance in addition to military aid to other countries in the region, the US called for a realistic assessment of the military aid programme for Pakistan in response to a number of key questions:

- Is US main objective in Pakistan military or strategic?
- Is Pakistan's main value to the US represented by its airfields with their SAC [Strategic Air Command] potential as part of the essential ring of airfields around the USSR?
- For what specific purpose does the US need Pakistan's 5½ MAP-supported divisions?
- Are we [US] assisting in this ground forces program for its own sake or primarily as a price for the related SAC air base potential?
- Have we [US] sufficiently considered that the 5½ divisions now supported by the US would in all probability remain pinned down along the Indian and Kashmir borders in case of hostilities?

The Americans recognized also certain 'stark realities' among which they knew that although they had committed to supporting 5.5 divisions of the Pakistan Army, they were in fact only supporting about three divisions. India–Pakistan hostilities remained high and Pakistan's military planning appeared to be geared to countering India. Also, despite the government's pro-Western stance, general public opinion was 'basically anti-Western' and the Americans recognized that 'once political parties are restored, we should anticipate the emergence of powerful political forces which may seek to make effective capital out of demanding a re-orientation of Pakistan's foreign policy' including the extreme view of 'throw the Americans out.' US embassy analysts also understood well that the 'defense forces in Pakistan constitute a favored elite. Pakistan exists today because of the strong army…. [and it would] have first call on Government of Pakistan resources.…It may be expected, therefore, that very substantial cuts in military expenditures will not be undertaken, even at the risk of serious economic deterioration.' If anything, one could not accuse the US analysts on the ground in Karachi to be out of touch with reality! Having said all that, the Americans came to the conclusion that 'American assistance is necessary and will be required for some time to come if Pakistan is to continue to make bases and other military facilities available to the US.'

Ayub too recognized that the US support was waning and that the key to building Pakistan was its economy, emphasizing the need to go from being a primarily rural and agriculture-based economy to a modern industrial system. In this endeavour, the creation of a group of economic planners and experts from home and abroad was important. He set up a Planning Commission and drew to it the best and brightest officers of the civil service, many of whom had been or were shortly to be sent abroad for training. A Harvard advisory group and the Ford Foundation also contributed mightily to these efforts to set up a Brains Trust for Pakistan's economic managers. He instituted a series of rolling five-year development plans and encouraged private enterprise, within the bounds of a licensing system, that not only allowed business houses to emerge out of the fledgling economy but also created a new class of *rentiers* who profited enormously from preferred access to scarce domestic and foreign exchange resources and permission to set up heavily subsidized industrial operations. This system also strengthened the hold of the bureaucrats over state resources and the import and export system, creating a bottleneck and a hurdle for the kind of development that would have taken Pakistan up the development ladder, beyond the Rostowian 'take-off' stage.

Having secured his position with the expanding army by getting additional weapons from the United States, even as US interest in Pakistan waned, Ayub made sure that he remained at the helm of things. His rank of Field Marshal made him the supreme commander of the military. With an obedient Musa as the head of the army, Ayub felt safe. He turned to politics, agreeing to head the Pakistan Muslim League and acquiring the support of a huge number of Muslim Leaguers who were ready to follow the trail of power in Pakistan. The only opposition to him was in the inner cities of Lahore and Karachi, where the well organized cadres of the Jamaat-i-Islami were able to muster street power and vote banks against him. In the countryside, the effects of the Green Revolution provided greater production power and income to the farming class, while favourable tax treatment allowed major landlords and feudals to siphon off their income tax-free agricultural income into industrial units near the cities.

However, political shifts abroad, in the shape of a new democrat, John F. Kennedy in the White House, as well as changes in the region—the Sino–India conflict in the Himalayas—were to shift the political balance in the subcontinent. Ayub found himself fighting a rearguard action to preserve his special relationship with the United States on the one hand while opening up doors to China on the other. At home, rising expectations of the rapidly expanding population were to test the stability of a system built on shaky political foundations and an economic development strategy that ignored basic needs while allowing a select few to amass seemingly unbridled wealth.

NOTES

1. Amos Perlmutter, *The Military and Politics in Modern Times* (Yale, 1977), p. 109.
2. Mohammad Asghar Khan, *Generals in Politics: Pakistan 1958–1992* (Vikas, 1983), p. 7.
3. Paula R. Newberg, *Judging the State: Courts and Constitutional Politics in Pakistan* (New Delhi: Cambridge University Press, 1995), p. 75.
4. Asghar Khan, *Generals*, p. 10.
5. Mohammad Ayub Khan, *Friends not Masters: A Political Autobiography* (London: Oxford University Press, 1967), p. 82.
6. Ayub Khan, *Friends not Masters*, p. 85.

7. US files carry a detailed note of an encounter with Brigadier F.R. Khan just before martial law, during which he took over the entire conversation that the visiting political officer had arranged with Major General Bakhtiar Rana, the GOC 7 Division in Peshawar. Brig. F.R. Khan who was visiting from the corps headquarters in Jhelum 'for approximately 45 minutes…kept almost exclusive control of the conversation to present his opinion on US policies in Pakistan and the Middle East.' A key point that he made to the US consul and vice consul was that the 'US is following the path of the British in failing to adapt its educational efforts to the peculiar psychology of the people of this area.' Citing the 'pernicious influence of *The Pakistan Times*' that he saw as being a 'propaganda sheet for the communist point of view,' he said he had suggested to the British that they distribute 200 copies of the *London Times* to officers' messes throughout Pakistan to counter the effects of the communist propaganda but his suggestion was not accepted. *Memorandum of Conversation*, 17 September 1958. Dispatch number 4 from Peshawar. US National Archives.

8. Private conversation with CSP official who was later to become secretary of the ministry of interior.

9. Tariq Ali, *Pakistan: Military Rule or People's Power* (London: Jonathan Cape, 1972), p. 101. Tariq Ali was a celebrated student union leader at Government College, Lahore, the first Pakistani president of the Oxford Union, and editor of several prominent socialist publications in England. This book was written after the fall of Ayub Khan following a visit to Pakistan by Tariq Ali during the period of agitation against Ayub.

10. See Zamir Niazi, *The Press in Chains* (Karachi, Pakistan: Karachi Press Club, 1986), a magisterial survey of the travails of the news media in Pakistan.

11. Shuja Nawaz, 'The Mass Media and Development in Pakistan,' *Asian Survey*, Volume XXIII, No. 8. August 1983 has a detailed discussion of the ill effects of these policies.

12. Confidential telegram from Ambassador Langley, Karachi to Secretary of State, number 2162, 21 March 1959. US National Archives. This section is largely based on this message.

13. Altaf Gauhar, *Ayub Khan: Pakistan's First Military Ruler* (Lahore: Sang-e-Meel Publications, 1993), p. 162.

14. This segment benefits from the citation of Ayub Khan's personal papers, in Gauhar, *Ayub Khan*, p. 163.

15. Note the use of Ayub's newly acquired rank, without having commanded his army in war, and the military awards.

16. Zulfikar Ali Bhutto, 'Thoughts on Constitution,' 10 October 1959. Gauhar, *Ayub Khan*, pp. 176–7.

17. General Burki recalled an encounter in the martial law cabinet when both he and Bhutto seemed to be of a mind against a particular issue that Ayub favoured. In a break during the cabinet meeting, Burki recalls speaking with the young Bhutto and agreeing with him that they both needed to dissuade Ayub from the course of action he wished to pursue on that issue. Much to Burki's surprise, during the subsequent cabinet debate Bhutto showed himself as a staunch supporter of Ayub's idea! Burki confronted him outside the cabinet room, stating that he thought Bhutto was intelligent enough and rich enough to be president of Pakistan himself one day. 'Why did you do what you did today' asked Burki. Bhutto replied that men in his family died young and he did not have enough time on his hands to rise to the top. Burki recounted this story to the author in early 1969, when the street unrest against Ayub had begun. He predicted that Bhutto would become president and deservedly so.

18. Gauhar's personal notes, cited in *Ayub Khan*, p. 179.

19. The cabinet sub-committee that examined the draft constitution included Manzur Qadir (chairman), Bhutto, Shoaib, A.K. Khan, and Muhammad Ibrahim.

20. Ayub Khan, *Friends not Masters*, p. 216.

21. Author's translation.

22. Newberg, *Judging*, p. 95.

23. Message from Edwin W. Martin, First Secretary, American Embassy, London to Secretary of State, Despatch No. 2378, 8 January 1958. US National Archives.

24. Ibid.

25. Confidential telegram from Ambassador Langley, Karachi to Secretary of State, number 1886, 29 January 1958. US National Archives.

26. Telegram from US Embassy, Karachi to Department of State, number 1839, dated 27 January 1958 enclosing a report by Major General Truman to Ambassador Langley of 8 January 1958. US National Archives.

27. Report by General Truman to Ambassador Langley, 27 January 1958. US National Archives. (See footnote above.)

28. Telegram for the Ambassador, American Embassy, Karachi to Department of State, Number 2250, 12 March 1958. US National Archives.

29. 'Brief for the Secretary Ministry of Defence on Military Aid Problem' prepared by Pakistan Army GHQ. Referred to in US Embassy telegram cited above. US National Archives.

30. Second Pakistan Army GHQ paper presented to the US under the heading 'Development of Current Programme Beyond 1959: Current Programme of Aid,' referred to in footnote 26 above.

31. Interestingly, the UK and the US while realizing the sensitivity of the Pakistanis to the issue of keeping their arms aid discussions private between themselves and the US, kept each other fully apprised of all Pakistani moves. The British though kept national interests in the forefront and were prepared to sell Pakistan the submarine (overriding their own concerns about the issue) when it appeared to them that Pakistan might buy one from Sweden. Again, in addition to British sources, including Commodore Beloe, a Royal Navy officer on loan to the Pakistan Navy, Pakistan's Finance Minister Shoaib was cited as a source of this inside information about the cancellation of the Pakistani request for a submarine. See Department of State telegram to American Embassies in London and Karachi, number 1396, 31 December 1958. US National Archives.

32. Memorandum of Conversation, Department of State, 11 April 1958 and again on 22 April, on meeting with Pakistani Ambassador Mohammed Ali. US National Archives.

33. See David Wise and Thomas B. Ross, *The U-2 Affair* (New York: Random House, May 1962 and Bantam Books, November 1962).

34. The author visited this mini-America in the mid-1960s as a representative of an Islamabad-based furniture factory where I was working part-time, to evaluate and bid on the provision of formica-based furniture for the staff club. Lawn sprinklers and Ricky Nelson videos on a closed-circuit television re-created life in suburban America for the denizens of this oasis.

35. A detailed website maintained by the alumni of Peshawar Air Station, under its operational designation as the 6937th Communications Group proudly shares many of the details of this base and its operations, including an updated list of the current whereabouts of former personnel. The existence of this operation was kept so secret, even in the US, that the Military Air Transport Services (MATS) folks who used to process the travel of US staff to this facility sometimes did not know where it was located and in one case sent a staff member to Panama from where he had to return to his US starting point and then connect to a flight to Peshawar! See http://6937th.50megs.com/then%20and%20now.htm

36. Secret dispatch from US Embassy, Karachi to Department of State, number 1109, 6 June 1958. US National Archives.

37. Secret Dispatch, 1109.

38. Dispatch No. 679 from US Embassy, Karachi to Department of State, 29 January 1959. US National Archives.

39. 'Summary of Embassy Karachi's Despatch 762, 26 February 1959. Draper Committee presentation' US National Archives. This section relies on this document for the US views and analysis.

'The art of war is simple enough. Find out where your enemy is. Get at him as soon as you can. Strike him as hard as you can, and keep moving.'

– Ulysses S. Grant (1822–85)

The 1960s saw the rise and fall of Pakistan's strongman, General, later Field Marshal, Mohammad Ayub Khan. The seeds of Ayub's eventual downfall lay in his rapid rise to power and an ill-planned war against India. He seemed to be a man in a hurry to leave his mark on Pakistan. Imbued with a deep-seated desire to correct the perceived wrongs of previous leaders and yet unable to share power with his protégés, he created a system that made rapid progress on many fronts but proved to be unsustainable in the end. He tried to push for land reform, education reform, and a better system for producing power and delivering water supplies to the country's thirsty agricultural system. The specialized agencies that he set up to deal with these issues, giving them autonomous powers and wide discretion, yielded rapid and positive results across the board, except in the area of land reforms where the rhetoric failed to live up to the reality, leaving Pakistan's landed gentry in command of vast resources and retaining its hold on local political systems. The alliance with bright bureaucrats, who flourished in their new-found freedom of action under Ayub's autocratic system, worked very well in the initial period but carried within it the seeds of its own demise, as became evident when systemic continuity and sustainability were needed. Poor leadership of these institutions in later years and the susceptibility of that leadership to political pressures made the same institutions that produced stellar results during Ayub's early rule collapse under their own bureaucratic deadweight.

At the same time, Ayub moved away from his power base—the military—creating alliances with the rag tag remnants of the Muslim League that had spearheaded the move for an independent Pakistan. Emulating his predecessor, Iskander Mirza, who had created his home-grown Republican Party, Ayub tied himself to the Muslim League. The party he chose to become his political base was a mere shadow of the committed entity that drew Muslims from across India to fight against the tide of Hindu domination in British India. Instead, it was a collection of disparate influence groups, more often than not feudal remnants of the Punjabi Unionist Party that saw an opportunity to regain control of the centre, and other camp followers who found it expedient to latch on to Ayub's apparently rising star. Not all Muslim Leaguers joined his party though, leading to the formation of an opposition Muslim League, dubbed 'Council' Muslim League, as opposed to Ayub's Convention Muslim League (later renamed Pakistan Muslim League or PML). Even Ayub's elder brother, Bahadur Khan, joined the opposition Muslim League. Ayub's technocratic cabinet members signed up for the Convention Muslim League, not so much to fulfil the party's mandate as to ensure their own political survival.

The 1960s also saw the emergence of strains in the relationship with the United States, fuelled by much internal debate in Washington on its balance sheet with Pakistan. Also, the US was shifting attention to India as a potentially better partner—being a huge democracy, a counterweight to China, and a nascent market for US goods and services. A series of exchanges with Pakistan about the treaty obligations of the US aimed at providing cover for maintaining the status quo took place while the US forged a new approach to South Asia in general. Ayub, on his part, sought to assuage his critics at home by getting the US to reaffirm its obligations to protect Pakistan. But he was savvy enough to know that in the end he had to protect himself and his country by positioning Pakistan more as a neutral entity rather than a cold warrior on the American side of the fence.

By the early 1960s, the Pakistan Army was finally getting close to the quarter million size that Ayub and his planners had conceived as just right to counter India's large and well established force. US arms and training had prepared the force for a change in its battle tactics and strategy. The largest component of the fighting force, the infantry, was adopting a new approach: shifting to increased firepower and widening its coverage of the battle front per company to close to 1000 yards. (Ayub proudly invited the Shah of Iran to witness a demonstration of company firepower by his own parent regiment, '5 Punjab', in the hills outside Rawalpindi.)[1] Introduction of the American M-1 rifle and the jeep-mounted 103mm recoilless anti-tank rifle (more of a rocket launcher than a rifle) had given the army greater confidence. Although it still relied on the Second World War vintage small tanks, Chaffees, Shermans, and Stuarts, and the 1952 vintage M-47 Pattons, the induction of some newer 200 M-48 Patton tanks had given the armoured regiments greater punch. Air power was still heavily dependent on the old war horse of Korean War fame, the US made F-86 Sabre jet, that provided both ground support and enough agility to take on India's Soviet-supplied MIG-19s, British Gnats, and Hawker Hunters in aerial combat. Twelve F-104 Starfighters were also inducted into the Pakistan Air Force, along with B-57 bombers that matched the Indian Canberra bombers. And Pakistan was negotiating for yet more fighters and bombers—not just to refit its armoury with American weapons, but to provide a counterweight to India's overwhelming military might, while securing its position in the region. Its actions in this regard were jolted by events way outside its borders.

THE SINO–INDIAN CLASH OF 1962

The Sino–Indian conflict of 1962 in the North East Frontier Agency (NEFA) of India suddenly created a new strategic and military imbalance in the subcontinent while shifting the US attention away from their old ally, Pakistan, toward their ideal partner, India. This conflict in the Himalayas had been brewing for a number of years, following the Chinese annexation of Tibet. Talks between India and China had been through their ups and downs, but by 1961, the belligerent Indian defence minister, V.K. Krishna Menon, had taken a hard-line position challenging China to test the Indian resolve with his Forward Policy that would have Indian forces move to the disputed MacMahon Line border with China. He relied on the military skills of his favourite Lt. Gen. B.M. Kaul who was sent to replace the highly respected Lt. Gen. S.P.P. Thorat, who had cautioned against taking an aggressive posture, given the unpreparedness of the Indian Army at that time to fight a war against the Chinese in NEFA. Thorat had written a report on the situation to Menon that Menon never shared with Nehru, according to Thorat's memoirs.[2] Nehru was thus led to believe that India was in a position to oust the Chinese from what it considered disputed territory in that Himalayan border region and accepted Menon's view that the Chinese needed to be challenged strongly in both Ladakh and NEFA.

A battle of words ensued, leading to clashes in NEFA in September 1962 and then again in early October, when the Chinese asked India to pull back from the brink of the precipice.[3] Receiving no Indian response other than more belligerent talk, the Chinese moved forward into the disputed territory in Ladakh and also ousted Indian troops from two posts in NEFA as a precursor to a general offensive that showed how poorly Indian forces were equipped to fight at that altitude in winter conditions. Within three days, the Chinese advanced some 90 miles into NEFA before announcing a ceasefire on 21 November 1962. Immediately afterwards, the Chinese withdrew to their own territory, well behind the line of control between the two countries. But suddenly the geopolitical and military situation in the subcontinent had been changed dramatically by this Chinese foray into India. First, China's swift victory in the Himalayas created, among the Western allies who were still embroiled in a Cold War against communism, the spectre of a communist invasion of India. Second, debate erupted within India about the fighting capability of its army. Kaul was disgraced. Thorat and the like-minded army chief, P.N. Thapar, both of whom had opposed Krishna Menon, were vindicated and Thorat was asked to be part of a commission that Nehru set up to draw lessons from this debacle. Third, Pakistan gained confidence that it could take on a more aggressive military posture against India, given the Indian military's poor show against the Chinese. But Pakistani hopes were soon dashed as its erstwhile Western allies, alarmed by the Chinese incursion, suddenly opened the floodgates of military aid to hitherto non-aligned India.

COOLING US RELATIONSHIP

There was a history to the US's move towards India. Ayub had been carefully crafting a new foreign policy based on a realistic appraisal of Pakistan's strategic location and considerations. As he grew more into his new political role, he grew distant from the Pakistan Army, relying less on his military senior staff to provide him policy advice and tending to lean more on his new cabinet members like Bhutto and foreign office mandarins like Aziz Ahmed. In the process, he favoured settlement of border disputes with China to the north-east of West Pakistan, while treating Afghanistan as a client state that was heavily dependent on Pakistan for its access to the sea. Naturally, the US did not wish to see any cracks emerging in their wall of treaty partners around the communist world's two major countries, the Soviet Union and China. At the same time, they saw India as a potential counterweight to the Chinese giant to the north but felt frustrated by India's loud and often bellicose profession of 'neutrality' and 'non-alignment,' even while India solidified its military and economic ties with the Soviet Union.

By September 1961, the American Deputy Secretary of Defense, Ros Gilpatric, was suggesting to Under Secretary of State Chester Bowles that the US should reopen the question of military sales to India in preparation for the impending visit of Prime Minister Nehru to the United States in November.[4] Recounting the 'slightly degrading effect' of military sales to Pakistan on Indo–US relations and the Indian military's desire to match Pakistan's weapons systems in qualitative terms, Gilpatric spelt out the continued 'predilection for the purchase of Soviet equipment, particularly aircraft' of Indian Defence Minister Menon. He also shared with Bowles inside information from Indian Air Force officers who had told US contacts that they were being forced to make 'other arrangements' while they were mainly interested in US C-130 aircraft, heavy helicopters, Sidewinder missiles, the MK-44 torpedo, radar and engineer bridging equipment. Senior Indian military officials had made approaches to the US Department of Defense representatives 'with specific proposals for circumventing what they consider to be the negative policies of Defence Minister Menon toward the purchase of US equipment.' An Indian general, in the US for medical treatment, had offered to raise the issue of purchase of US material with the Indian ambassador so the latter could bring it to Prime Minister Nehru's notice during his US visit. Meanwhile efforts were underway to use the close relationship of US ambassador John Kenneth Galbraith with both President John F. Kennedy and Prime Minister Nehru to turn India towards acquisition of US military supplies.

Galbraith, who often met Nehru privately in New Delhi, reported on a conversation with the Indian prime minister during which Galbraith raised the issues of arms aid to Pakistan, non-aggression between India and Pakistan, and 'unexpectedly Kashmir.' He told Nehru that the Americans were 'far from satisfied with our present relations with the subcontinent,' using his recent exchanges with President Kennedy and Secretary of State Dean Rusk as the basis for this characterization. He felt that the US could not explain arms aid to Pakistan to the Indian public. One way that would allow it to change its policy would be rapprochement between India and Pakistan through 'a declaration of non-aggression and of their common concern for the defense of the borders of the whole subcontinent,' presumably from China. Nehru's response was 'warm and sympathetic' but he pointed out that as a practical matter, nothing could be done about the Pakistani aspect without bringing in the issue of Kashmir. Nehru said he favoured the ceasefire line in Kashmir as the basis of 'the only possible settlement.' Galbraith countered with the idea of a condominium solution that borrowed from the Swiss experience: the Republic of Geneva joined Switzerland but left a tributary area under French administration. Even if the coveted valley were to remain under Indian administration, Galbraith felt that open access to and trade with the valley by both countries might benefit all sides. Nehru was said to be 'not specifically averse to the idea.' Having trumpeted this minor success, Galbraith then derided his State Department colleague Bill Rountree, whom he saw as not being committed to 'an escape from the military arrangements of which, indeed, he was one of the authors.' As a result, Galbraith felt that the president and secretary of state might want to appoint a person of stature (Lillienthal or Harriman) to tackle Indo–Pakistan issues at a higher level, even offering his own services if the president could expand his charter in the region.[5]

Pakistan was not blind to these shifting sands of US foreign policy and Ayub Khan took the direct approach in a two-paragraph cablegram letter to Kennedy delivered by Ambassador Aziz Ahmed on 4 November 1961:

My dear Mr President,
I understand that Mr Nehru proposes to ask for military aid from the United States during his forthcoming talks with you. You will undoubtedly recall our earlier discussions on this subject. You were good enough to assure me that at no time had your government any intention of giving military aid to India and that if at any time you should come to the conclusion that it had become necessary to do so we would be consulted before a decision was taken in the mater. I do not need at this stage to do more than recall those assurances.

Ayub then proceeded to remind Kennedy of his promise to try to persuade Nehru to proceed towards a settlement of the Kashmir dispute.[6] Kennedy raised the issues of arms aid to Pakistan and the Kashmir dispute during talks with Nehru but his heart was more on the Indian side than in favour of the Pakistanis. 'Many Americans,' he said, 'believe that we would do better to give actual funds to Pakistan and let them decide what they want to spend on military aid and what on economic aid. The difficulty is that it is easier to get funds from Congress for military assistance than for economic assistance.'[7] Galbraith interjected that the US had given India half a billion dollars of economic aid, but when it gave Pakistan twelve planes (referring no doubt to the F-104 Starfighters), there were 'twelve times as many questions in the Indian parliament about the planes as about the aid.' Nehru was not persuaded that democratic India could be equated with the 'military dictatorship' of Pakistan. When Rostow suggested that Nehru had used the same term, 'minor border adjustments', for resolving the Kashmir problem that Ayub Khan had used, Kennedy brushed that aside with the comment that he did not know what Ayub meant when he used that term. But progress was made in discussing the provision of US arms to India, although Rusk was to caution Galbraith and Rountree that the US president had committed to discussing the matter with the government of Pakistan prior to provision of US military aid to India.[8]

The Pakistanis were getting concerned about India's aggressive posture in the region after the Indian invasion of Goa, Daman, and Diu, former Portuguese colonies on India's west coast, and the apparent friendship between the US president and the Indian prime minister. Ayub complained to Kennedy about this posture and cautioned the US against changing its policies towards India. But a shift had started to appear in the US view of the subcontinent. Under the heading, 'A New Look at Pakistani Tie,' Robert W. Komer of the NSC staff wrote to his boss, McGeorge Bundy, President Kennedy's special assistant for National Security Affairs, highlighting the basic differences between the US and Pakistani view of regional issues in the subcontinent.[9] While recognizing Pakistan's insecurity as a smaller country in relation to India, Komer warned against letting Ayub push the US 'into a position which runs contrary to our larger strategic interests in the area,' adding that 'we have failed to get across to him the limitation, as well as the benefits from our support. Instead he seems to have gotten the feeling that we are so attached to him as an ally that he can pursue his aims with renewed vigor, and drag us along with him.' Acknowledging the provision of facilities to the US by Pakistan, Komer wrote 'I'm not sure we've gotten a lot …except paper commitment to SEATO and CENTO.' Strategically, Komer suggested that if the US were to choose between India and Pakistan, its best bet would be to go with the larger India. He suggested, therefore, that the US take a new tack against Pakistan, and not treat Ayub 'with kid gloves,' since Ayub needed the US's help and had few other options of external aid. Finally, he raised the issue of an impending aid consortium meeting in which the US was to commit US$500 million to Pakistan, asking 'whether we are giving too much and not getting enough in return.'

Ayub had other ideas though, and upped the ante by taking the Kashmir issue once more to the UN Security Council, provoking Kennedy to ask Ayub to suspend that action to which Ayub responded firmly but clearly with a reminder that India had massed 85 per cent of its forces, including armoured formations, 'within striking distance of our borders.'[10] The Spring of Discontent of 1962 between the two allies produced many such exchanges, with the US clearly seeking a new way to handle its need to bring India into the fold while retaining Pakistan and its strategic location on the US side. The introspection continued in Foggy Bottom and the White House. A high level meeting in May was convened under Phillips Talbot at the State Department to discuss the 'current unsatisfactory state of US-Pakistan-Indian relations' and noted 'the drift apart of the US and Pakistan.'[11] Noting the importance of Pakistan to SEATO and CENTO and the danger of equal treatment of India and Pakistan as being seen unfavourably by Pakistan, the meeting concluded that 'the US would gain little or nothing by a major shift of our Pakistan policy and a great deal could be lost.' Yet, the participants suggested ways in which the US might have pursued a frank relationship with Pakistan while seeking to enhance ties to India.

It was against this background that the Sino–Indian conflict took place, and the US rushed to take the lead in providing India with armaments, ostensibly to help it fend off an onslaught from the Chinese, down the glaciers of the Himalayas and on to the Gangetic plains. Kennedy, already keen to win Indian friendship, wrote to Ayub to inform him that the US intended 'to give the Indians such help as we can for their immediate needs. We will ensure, of course, that whatever help we give will be used only against the Chinese.' The letter then proceeded to ask if Ayub could send a private message to Nehru to allay any concerns of Nehru that Pakistan might take this opportunity (of India's conflict with China) to create problems on India's frontiers with Pakistan.[12] Ayub confided to US ambassador, McConaughy, that he had no intention of taking advantage of India's preoccupation with China but registered nevertheless his barely concealed anger at the fact that Kennedy had proceeded to aid India without the promised prior consultation with Ayub. In the White House, Komer clearly understood the depth of Pakistan's anger but advised Kennedy that 'there be no give in our position. We have no need to apologize. If we compensate Ayub for our actions vis-à-vis India, we will again be postponing the long needed clarification of our position.'[13]

Ayub's reply, after a considered pause and consultations with his colleagues, was long and argumentative. He expressed surprise at Kennedy's request about giving an assurance to Nehru at that time, given his view that India had moved its formation to battle positions against Pakistan in the west.[14] Ayub's thrust was towards a resolution of the Kashmir dispute as the best way of creating peace between India and Pakistan. Kennedy, for his part, had already done his best to calm Pakistani fears that military aid to India might be turned against Pakistan at some point. His statement of 2 November 1962 emphasized that 'in providing military assistance to India, we are mindful of our alliance with Pakistan. All of our aid is for the purpose to defeat Chinese communist subversion. Our help to India in no way diminishes or qualifies our commitment to Pakistan and we have made it clear to both governments as well.'[15] Ayub Khan quotes this statement and another assurance from the Department of State of 17 November that should the aid to India be 'misused or directed against another in aggression, the United States would undertake immediately, in accordance with constitutional authority, appropriate action both within and without the United Nations to thwart such aggression.' Strengthening this assurance was an aide memoire from Ambassador McConaughy on 6 November 1962 to Ayub that 'the Government of the United States of America reaffirms its previous assurances to the Government of Pakistan that it will come to Pakistan's assistance in the event of aggression from India against Pakistan.'[16] With these assurances in hand, Ayub proceeded to sign a joint statement with Nehru that 'a renewed effort should be made to resolve the outstanding differences between the two countries on Kashmir and other related matters.'[17] This allowed Kennedy to pursue an effort to involve World Bank President, Eugene Black, into a mediation role, based on suggestions from Ambassador Galbraith in India.[18]

US aid to India continued, based on an NSC subcommittee proposal in December 1962, aiming at a target of $120 million to be shared with the UK and the Commonwealth. But despite the 'present strained US–Pak relations', the US came up with a proposed military assistance program (MAP) of $143 million for Pakistan by mid-July 1963, including an additional two squadrons (24 aircraft) of F-104s, despite internal qualms about the lack of leverage that such a long term commitment might create for the US in its relations with Pakistan at a time when the latter was seeking to open ties with China. Komer continued to be the tough voice in the White House, although he noted that the Pakistanis had not 'raised even a finger about Peshawar' and the US base at Badaber.[19] Pakistan welcomed the F-104s since it was ready to phase out the aging F-86s, which in any case were not going to be supported by the US beyond 1968. The US knew all along that the F-104A/B version that it was offering Pakistan, though 'superficially glamorous', was purely a day fighter-interceptor as opposed to the F-104G that India had requested. It also had limited bomb-carrying capacity and could not serve as an interceptor without a controlling aircraft to guide it, something that Pakistan lacked. But Pakistan was not spurning the F-104. It badly needed to upgrade its weapons systems and for now the only game in town was the US.

Ayub went to some lengths to keep the spigot of US aid open. In a long and candid exchange with Under Secretary Ball in Rawalpindi on 3 and 4 September, in the presence of Foreign Minister Bhutto, he assured Ball that 'Pakistan wants to remain friends with the US unless the US drives it away.' But he also warned that: 'Should US policy change, and should we seek to squeeze Pakistan, there would be difficulties...Pakistan,' said Ayub, 'may be poor but it is proud.'[20] Ayub's persistence in this line had an effect on Kennedy's successor Lyndon B. Johnson, who directed Bundy to correct this feeling of insecurity on the part of Ayub 'in a most positive manner' in a meeting in the Oval Office on 30 November 1963. This was followed by a visit to Pakistan by the CJCS, General Maxwell D. Taylor, who reviewed Pakistan's needs and reiterated US support.

But the US–Pakistan relationship was unravelling steadily, as other concerns intruded. The US was becoming embroiled in a draining conflict in South East Asia and was unhappy that Pakistan did not provide troops for the Vietnam war. It also found India to be a better prospect than Pakistan as an economic partner and a potential challenger to China. Pakistan was focusing more on building economic and political ties with China, and Kashmir loomed large as an unfinished business from partition. It was unhappy with the lack of concrete US pressure on India to resolve this conflict. Its leadership was also aware of India's growing military strength, especially after the influx of Western arms in the wake of the Sino–Indian conflict. Pakistan's military had acquired new and improved weapons systems from the US and felt confident that it had a strong deterrent force, should India proceed to exert hegemony in the region. But the increased military force of the Indians created its own dynamic, militarily and politically in Pakistan.

The Pakistan Army was now twice its size at partition and sucking up a larger share of national resources than before. In the words of Sir Morrice James, the UK high commissioner and a long-time expert on Pakistani affairs, 'the Pakistan Army was already the strongest and best organized element in the country.' Moreover, 'the Army was overwhelmingly a local one. Most of its officers and men were recruited from within 100 miles' radius of Rawalpindi.' Re-arming the military on a scale that was occurring with US help 'was to risk creating a situation where it would not be so much a case of Pakistan having an army as of the Army having Pakistan.'[21] The compliant C-in-C of the army, Musa Khan, did not appear to have a voice of his own, given Ayub's towering presence. However, the young Foreign Minister Bhutto was beginning to assert his views with Ayub, particularly in matters dealing with the US and China. Bhutto also had developed close relationships with a number of younger generals, who saw an opening to resolve the Kashmir issue through military means and a window of opportunity that was narrowing with India's growing military strength. While Ayub saw Bhutto as his eventual successor, he confided to the US ambassador and Sir Morrice that he felt his foreign minister needed time to mature. Bhutto also increasingly took on the role of public spokesman for Pakistan's relationships with the US and China, even to the extent of withholding a personal message (that Pakistan would never withdraw from its anti-communist pacts) for President Johnson that Ayub had asked Bhutto to convey, an action that he justified to the US ambassador in Pakistan because of Johnson's reproach on Pakistan's opening to China.[22] Although Ayub did not appear at that point to know it, Bhutto seemed to be staking out an independent position for himself, even sharing commentary on his mentor Ayub with others.[23]

By 1964, Bhutto, along with his like-minded colleagues at the Foreign Ministry and friendly generals, had started concentrating on renewing pressure on India to resolve the Kashmir issue. The Sino–Indian conflict had indicated the relative weakness of the Indian military at that time. However, the inflow of Western military aid was seen in Pakistan as preparing India for mountain warfare and greater mobility to shift its forces around, allowing it to amass its forces against West Pakistan and along the Kashmir border at will. In brief, Pakistan was running out of time if it was to effect a military-induced solution to the Kashmir imbroglio. On his part, Ayub was busy trying to be re-elected president in January 1965 in a bitter campaign that pitted him against the sister of Pakistan's founder, Mohammad Ali Jinnah. Though old and quite inarticulate, his opponent, the much venerated Fatima Jinnah, created a huge political buzz, drawing the disparate opponents of Ayub's regime into a coalition. Her rallies drew large crowds and scared Ayub and his cohort to the extent that Ayub even launched a personal attack against her, referring to the 'unnatural' state of her relationship with Jinnah.[24] (Miss Jinnah was a spinster who lived in her brother's home most of her life.) She gave as good as she got, accusing Ayub of becoming corrupt and attacking the corruption and visible rise to riches of his sons, especially Gohar Ayub Khan, who had left the army as a captain and joined his father-in-law in business. Gohar Ayub had set up Gandhara Industries and became a major importer and assembler of cars and trucks that proved to be a huge success thanks to the license regime of the government that provided windfall profits to the favoured few who got licenses to import goods into Pakistan.

The ruling party got the bureaucrats into action, making it the responsibility of divisional commissioners and district deputy commissioners to persuade local Basic Democrats (BDs), who made up the electoral college, to vote for

Ayub. As a result of these efforts, Ayub eked out a win from his chosen BDs, winning 49,951 to 38,691, but losing critical segments of the population, particularly key districts of East Pakistan and the largest urban centre, Karachi. As a contemporaneous analysis of the results for Ayub by Altaf Gauhar showed, people felt disillusioned and alienated from Ayub and his government. He needed to assert his strength in foreign affairs, especially vis-à-vis India.

Kashmir had already moved to centre stage at the end of 1963, when the guardians of the holy relic of Prophet Muhammad's (PBUH) hair said to be kept at the Muslim shrine of Hazratbal in Kashmir was reported to be missing. This created an uproar in Kashmir and Pakistan with public demonstrations against this alleged 'Indian plot.' Eventually the hair was returned and certified to be true. But by then Kashmiris and Pakistanis alike had been awakened to a fever pitch in terms of their nationalism. Even the Americans had been apprehensive that the incident at Hazratbal 'could provide an excuse for irregular Pakistan infiltrations into Indian-held Kashmir.'[25] Shortly after that, India freed the jailed Muslim leader Sheikh Abdullah and allowed him to travel to Pakistan, where he was given a huge welcome with a spontaneous outpouring of sentiment. But Abdullah's freedom was short lived. In the wake of much public unrest against Indian rule, he was sent back to jail soon after returning to Kashmir.

While Pakistan sought to broaden the international debate on Kashmir, it also undertook an internal review of military options, based on the assumption that India would shortly have an enhanced domestic ordnance capacity with new production facilities and new Western equipment and mountain troops that would give it greater forces to thwart any military moves by Pakistan in the future. Key players in the review of options were Bhutto (Foreign Minister), Aziz Ahmed (Foreign Secretary), Brigadier Riaz Husain (Director ISI), and Major General Akhtar Hussain Malik (GOC of 12 Division and responsible for much of the Kashmir sector). Others who were involved in the thinking about Kashmir were Brigadier Irshad Ahmed Khan (Director Military Intelligence) and Brigadier Gul Hassan Khan (Director Military Operations). But before they were able to come up with detailed plans for the next steps in Kashmir, events in the deep south-eastern tip of Pakistan overtook them.

THE RANN OF KUTCH WAR

The Rann of Kutch was a forbidding, desolate landscape of some 23,000 square kilometres of dried-out salt beds, marshes, and rolling sand dunes that were once thought to have been part of the Arabian Sea. It lay astride the

Indo–Pakistan border that separated the Pakistani province of Sindh from Indian Rajasthan, a boundary that had never been finely delineated. The border region was patrolled by paramilitary forces on both sides, although India had started building roads and supply routes to the border posts in the area. It saw Pakistan as having a potentially stronger military position in the area because of better roads and even an airfield at Badin, close to the frontier. Pakistan maintained that since the area was once a sea and remained underwater during the monsoons. the boundary should run through its middle. India did not accept this and the border was thus left undefined and open to debate. Aggressive patrolling by Indian and Pakistani paramilitary border forces created a number of local conflicts. By February 1965, India had decided to evict Pakistani border troops from Kanjarkot, an old fort that India believed lay some '1370 meters south' of the Indo–Pak border. India began preparations for the eviction of these forces under Operation Kabadi,[26] with operational orders by Major General P.C. Gupta of the Gujarat area command on 21 February to Brigadier S.S.M. Pahalajani of the 31st Infantry Brigade group to 'cross the border' and capture Kanjarkot. These orders appear to contradict the Indian claim that Kanjarkot lay in Indian territory. Pakistan countered the move by having Major General Tikka Khan, commander of the 8 Division, take over the area of operation from the border militia that normally patrolled it and moving the 56 Brigade under Brigadier K.M. Azhar to forward positions. India set up a new defensive line at Sardar Post, in a flat open area that was not defensible. As this military chess game proceeded, Lt. Col. Sundarji, who was officiating as brigade commander in the area, personally reconnoitred the area while dressed in a police uniform and suggested an immediate attack on Kanjarkot, but the government did not approve this plan.[27]

India added to Pakistan's fears of a conflict in the Rann by undertaking Exercise Arrowhead on 27/28 March involving the Indian Navy in the Arabian Sea bordering the Rann of Kutch. Pakistan had earlier countered with Operation Desert Hawk under General Tikka with a view to establishing Pakistani control over the disputed area in the Rann. Tikka, a Second World War veteran who had been captured by the Germans in North Africa and had escaped from a POW camp in Italy, was an artillery man commissioned in 1940. He was known as a man of action and not someone who would get caught up in the cats-paw of politics. His operational instruction of 6 March 1965 to Brigadier Azhar of 51 Brigade was crisp:

> MISSION. You will maintain complete control of territory under our de-facto control in area Kanjarkot and not repeat not allow violation of our territory...Avoid provocation but ensure maintenance of status quo.[28]

Alongside Azhar were 6 Brigade under Eftikhar Janjua, 52 Brigade under Brigadier Sardar Ismail, and Division Artillery under Brigadier S.M. Aslam. Tikka had sent his own appreciation on 16 March to his GHQ in Rawalpindi seeking approval of an attack to control the disputed area 'if attempts for peaceful solution fail.' By early April, talks at the local commander level had not succeeded in clearing the air. The attack to take Sardar Post was readied for the night of 8/9 April. But 51 Brigade was not fully prepared for this action and a confused night of fighting ensued with both Indian and Pakistani forces responding poorly to their first engagement. The immediate result was a stalemate. In the words of the official Indian war historian: 'It would appear that Commander of Pak 51 Bde [Brigade] handled the operation as ineptly as Brig Pahalajani of 31 Inf Bde.'[29] It was left to Brigadier Janjua and his troops to resurrect the situation. They attacked in a series of actions that were to be later known as the Battle of the Bets (after Chad Bet and Biar Bet, two settlements on raised mounds that were the principal objectives of the fighting) to deny India the chance to capture Kanjarkot. In a series of battles marked by great personal bravery on the part of the brigade commander, who insisted on being with his forward troops during the heat of battle, and feats of gallantry by younger officers[30] in his command, Janjua established Pakistan control over the disputed territory, garnering for himself the coveted Hilal-e-Jurat and a reputation for bravado and élan. Meanwhile, in a strange turn of events that often marks Indo–Pak conflicts, Air Marshal Asghar Khan, the Pakistani air chief called his Indian counterpart Air Marshal Arjan Singh on the morning of 14 April to state that no Pakistan Air Force planes were stationed at Badin and none would participate in the action around Kanjarkot. He asked that India do the same to keep the fighting from escalating. Singh agreed. The army chief General Musa states that he was unaware of this exchange with the Indians and that he was mollified by Asghar Khan's aides with the report that the Indian air chief had not acceded to Asghar Khan's request.[31]

After the Battle of the Bets, fighting subsided, an alarmed international community swung into action with British Prime Minister Harold Wilson sending a ceasefire request to President Ayub and Prime Minister Shastri on 28 April 1965. The UN Secretary General U Thant also pressed for a cessation of hostilities. Both Pakistan and India accepted Wilson's proposal for a ceasefire and a return to the status quo as of 1 January, pending the decision of an international tribunal that would examine both countries' demands. Wilson also suggested talks between the two antagonists. Eventually, on 30 June the ceasefire came into effect. The tribunal that was agreed to by both sides eventually gave its verdict on 19 February 1968, recognizing India's claim to the northern border but awarding Pakistan some 802 square kilometres of territory that included Kanjarkot and Chad Bet.

Although much has been said about this action as a precursor to the wider Indo–Pakistan conflict of 1965, even Indian official sources acknowledge that there did not appear to be a Pakistani master plan to engage India at a point of Pakistan's choosing in the Rann of Kutch.[32] Pakistan appeared to have better leadership at the field level and accurate artillery that was effectively deployed. India failed to coordinate its intelligence and also changed its field commander during the conflict. In the words of the official Indian war historian: 'For India, the Kutch Operation was a wrong war with the right enemy, at a (sic) wrong place. For Pakistan, it was a victorious war, out of which it learnt a wrong lesson that it could win a cake-walk victory in Kashmir. This fake sense of victory whetted the Pakistani appetite for Kashmir. This led to the September War ultimately.'[33] Pakistan believed that India had provoked the action in the Rann to try to retrieve its military's reputation after the debacle with the Chinese. Pakistan also claimed that these provocations forced it to move its regular troops into the area, leading to the short conflict. Regardless, Pakistan came out on top in that encounter despite quibbles on the part of many officers, including the Director Military Operations Gul Hassan Khan, that Tikka Khan and Eftikhar Janjua had been prevented from following up on their successes in the Battle of the Bets.

Meanwhile, observers in Washington and elsewhere were fearful of the situation that was developing in the subcontinent. By 20 August, Robert Komer was penning some 'other mood music' for McGeorge Bundy at the White House to help strengthen the US line in tough negotiations with Pakistan on the US intelligence facilities in the country. Komer thought that Phillips Talbot and other 'chickens' at State Department, abetted by Ball, were 'genuinely fearful that we can push the **psychotic Paks** [emphasis added] too far,' adding that, 'the Paks are playing with fire by their continued infiltration in to Kashmir; if the Indians decide to strike back elsewhere or Hindu–Moslem riots occur, we'll have a big mess.'[34] He was right.

OPERATION GIBRALTAR IN KASHMIR

With the Rann of Kutch behind it, Pakistan's government turned its attention again to Kashmir, where civil unrest at the re-imprisonment of Sheikh Abdullah and aggressive Indian military movements had created a sense of urgency. A Kashmir Cell had been established after Sheikh Abdullah's visit to Pakistan in 1964 involving the secretary of the Foreign Ministry, Aziz Ahmed, the secretary of defence, director of the Intelligence Bureau (a civilian body), the CGS, and the DMO of the Pakistan Army. Its remit, was to 'defreeze the Kashmir issue.'[35] Aziz Ahmed took on the role of chairman of this body that was to 'think aloud' about fomenting a popular uprising in Kashmir and providing support for those activities from Pakistan, including the infiltration of irregulars to spark a military uprising against Indian control of the state. As General Gul Hassan recalls, the instructions from Ayub Khan (as conveyed by Aziz Ahmed), were two-fold: First, intensification of the firecracker type of activity that was already current, but the embargo on regular troops crossing the ceasefire line remained. Second: to plan all-out support for any guerrillas who were inducted into Indian-held Kashmir.[36] The commander of 12 Division, Major General Akhtar Hussain Malik, was designated to prepare plans to this effect and to train the personnel to be infiltrated into Indian-held Kashmir. The numbers of this force vary by source. An Irish military historian cites a force of 'about 3,000 Kashmiri "Freedom Fighters".'[37] Indian estimates rise to 30,000.[38]

The overall plan was called Gibraltar, harkening back to the Muslim General Tariq bin Ziad's bold dash from his Berber homeland in North Africa into Spain, when he established a beachhead at the rock that was later to be named Jebel Al Tariq after him (Gibraltar in its anglicized version), burned his boats, and pushed into hostile territory. A second plan named 'Grand Slam' was to follow up on the success of Gibraltar, when Pakistani forces would cross the ceasefire line and head towards Akhnur in the south with a view to cutting off Indian forces in Kashmir from overland contact with India.[39] The two operations had a rough birth with much debate within the Kashmir Cell as well as questioning by Ayub Khan about the basis on which the plans had been conceived by the ISI and the Foreign Office.[40] Another opponent was Colonel S.G. Mehdi, head of the SSG, whose commandos were to be inserted into Kashmir in civilian clothes.[41] But clearly, Bhutto and Aziz Ahmed managed to calm Ayub's fears and proceeded to direct Akhtar Malik to come up with an implementation plan. The army chief, Musa Khan, opposed the plan but did not take a forceful position, although he claimed later that he sent Ayub a note detailing his objections.

Gibraltar was based on the infiltration of trained guerrillas under Pakistan Army officers into Indian-held Kashmir to help foment local dissent and an uprising. The total force was subdivided into subsidiary units named mainly after Muslim military heroes: Tariq (bin Ziad), (Mahmud) Ghaznavi, Salahuddin, (Mohammed bin) Qasim, and Khalid (bin Waleed). One force named Nusrat (incidentally the name of Mrs Bhutto, but also meaning victory) was designated to conduct sabotage behind Indian forces at the ceasefire line.[42] The operation began around 24 July with the forces making their way to, and then across, the ceasefire line over a four-day period. 'The Plan of infiltration was brilliant in conception,' according to the official Indian history of the 1965 war. The guerrillas were supposed to make their way into the crowds attending a Muslim festival at the tomb of Pir Dastgir Sahib on 8 August, and then into Srinagar the next day where they would join a procession announced by the action committee of local Kashmiri politicians to mark the anniversary of the arrest of Sheikh Abdullah. They were then to take over the airfield and radio station and proclaim a revolutionary council, followed by a request for help from Pakistan. This would be the signal for Pakistani forces to cross the ceasefire line to help the Kashmiris.[43]

Pakistan's underlying assumptions were based on the action in Kashmir staying within the boundaries of the disputed state. It had made all efforts not to provoke India to retaliate across the international border. Behind this very subjective reasoning on the part of the Pakistani policy-makers was their contention that there were three types of boundaries that lay between Kashmir and parts of West Pakistan: one, the ceasefire line, the second, a working boundary starting at a place called Abial Dogran (under dispute, because of the original partition of India that lay between parts of Sialkot and Kashmir in the south-western tip of Kashmir), and the third, the international boundary between India and Pakistan which ran south from Abial Dogran (that had a designated Boundary Post number 1) near Sialkot to the Arabian Sea. Bhutto assured Ayub that India was not in a position 'to risk a general war of unlimited duration.'[44] Pakistan did not wish to cross the international boundary but they wrongly assumed that India agreed with their definition of the working boundary not being an international border. It was clear that the army high command would not oppose any plan that Ayub had approved. However, the army did not take it upon itself to ensure that Gibraltar and then Grand Slam would have all the support it needed. As Gul Hassan notes: 'Instead of gearing up all agencies in GHQ to prepare them for the inevitable [war], the problem was conveniently deflected on to HQ 12 Division [under Akhtar Malik]....The Chief [Musa] and the CGS, General Sher Bahadur, had, from its inception viewed Gibraltar as a bastard child, born of the liaison between the Foreign Minister [Bhutto] and General Malik.'[45]

No wonder then that the ground was not prepared adequately for the 'uprising' within Kashmir. An ill-conceived propaganda war against India and its 'puppet government' in Kashmir was launched over the air waves, through Azad Kashmir Radio (that shared offices with Radio Pakistan), and through 'Sadaa-e-Kashmir' the so-called Voice of Kashmir, a pirate radio station ostensibly operating out of Indian-held Kashmir, but in fact located in Race Course Ground, Rawalpindi.[46] In the interest of secrecy, there was no contact with Kashmiri leaders even in the part that was under Pakistan control. They were not alone in their ignorance. Even senior officers at the army headquarters were kept in the dark, as were the formation commanders. No prior ground work had been done with Kashmiri leaders in Indian-held Kashmir. The assumption was that the Kashmiris—leaders and ordinary people—would all rise up spontaneously.

The second part of the plan, Grand Slam, had been given the edge by Ayub Khan who had suggested that Akhnur, a key choke point on the only land route between India and Kashmir, be made the target of the attack by Akhtar Malik's troops. Akhtar Malik, while reluctant to fully tie himself down to that objective, acceded to the request in his meeting with Ayub and others. But, in his operational instructions to his commanders, he kept the option open once he had broken through the Indian defences.[47]

Gibraltar also had some serious internal flaws. Most of the commanders of the infiltrators, if not all, did not speak Kashmiri. Their local contacts had not been established, the assumption being that anyone whom they approached would be anti-India and pro-Pakistan. Even minor details such as the conversion of weights and measures in Indian-held Kashmir to the metric system had escaped them, so they would stand out when they approached anyone to make purchases with the Indian currency they carried for their operations. Many Kashmiri peasants, fearful of Indian reactions, turned in the infiltrators. Other guerrillas found themselves on the run from day one. Major Farooq 'Lalla' Ahmed, son of Brigadier Gulzar Ahmed (a leading military historian), recalled his arduous journey across hostile territory as he hid among animal herds, became infected with fleas and lice, and finally managed to extricate himself to safety.[48] Other officers were captured, and in the words of Brigadier Irshad, the director Military Intelligence, they 'spilt the beans.'[49] Indeed they had. Captain Ghulam Hussain of 8 AK [Azad Kashmir] Battalion and Captain Mohammad Sajjad of 18 AK Battalion were among those captured and reportedly revealed the plans of the infiltrators to the Indians.[50]

Despite these setbacks, the operation succeeded in tying down a large number of Indian forces and inflicted casualties on the Indian Army, as well as destroying some installations. The scale of the operation took the Indians by surprise. Gibraltar had been such a well-kept secret that it took the Indians some days to realize the extent of the infiltration, and that too only after they had interrogated some of the captured officers. Once they became aware of the size of the operation, Indian leaders discussed retaliatory measures and decided upon taking the battle across the Line of Control to plug the gaps through which the infiltrators had come. They attacked quickly and with force, recapturing Pakistani outposts on the Kargil heights that overlooked the road to Leh, and occupying a number of key positions on high ground in the Tithwal area, including the Haji Pir Pass. Among the posts captured by the Indians, one post, Sunjoi, overlooked Mirpur and was close to the Azad Kashmir capital of Muzaffarabad.

The Pakistan Army sought permission to launch Grand Slam but could not get a decision for a number of days. Ayub had meanwhile taken off for Swat from where he sent a signed instruction with Bhutto for both the army chief and the foreign minister (Bhutto), dated 29 August, asking them to 'take such action that will defreeze the Kashmir problem, weaken Indian resolve, and bring her to the conference table without provoking a general war.'[51] However, Ayub did not rule out a war and stated with a false sense of overconfidence that 'as a general rule, the Hindu morale would not stand more than a couple of hard blows at the right time and place.' But the right time had by then been lost. As Gul Hassan recounts, he tried many times (but failed) to get Musa through the CGS to launch Grand Slam. Each time Gul Hassan was rebuffed. Finally, Akhtar Malik was told to attack on the night of 31 August/1 September by which time the Indian corps commander, Lt. Gen. K.S. Katoch had been made aware of the build up of Pakistani forces against Chamb and alerted XV Corps formations to take up their positions accordingly.[52]

The Indians were not all that unprepared, as it turned out. Even as early as the spring, in the wake of the Rann of Kutch clash, Indian Prime Minister Lal Bahadur Shastri had 'given his approval for military action against Pakistan at a time and a place to be chosen by the Army, and General Chaudhuri [the army chief] had indicated that offensive operations could start by 10 May.' Under the name 'Operation Ablaze', preparations began in earnest for the attack against West Pakistan, with the Indian XI Corps getting ready for an attack across the Wagah border to the Ichhogil canal, known in Pakistan as the BRB or Bambanwalla-Ravi-Bedian link canal. The Indian corps commander, Lt. Gen. J.S. Dhillon, moved his troops to their battle stations along the border and made preparations to launch his forces. However, as peace talks over the Rann of Kutch began to bear fruit, the fervour to seek instant revenge subsided. General Chaudhuri arrived on the scene and proclaimed: 'All my experience teaches me never to start an operation with the crossing of an opposed water obstacle; as far as I am concerned, I have ruled out Lahore or a crossing at Dera Baba Nanak.'[53] It appeared that both India and Pakistan had very cautious army chiefs, reluctant to go into battle or to take risks. Gradually, both India and Pakistan moved their troops warily back from the immediate border area...to wait for the next round.

In Kashmir, the Indians had anticipated the Chamb area as a likely point of attack for Pakistan as early as 1956 when General Chaudhuri had been commander of XV Corps. One of his brigadiers, Jogindar Singh, who commanded the 80 Infantry Brigade, had identified gaps in the Indian defences and attempted to get his seniors to do some advance planning for the next war with Pakistan. But he recalls that neither Chaudhuri nor others were interested. 'None of the senior officers wanted to stir a hornet's nest in Delhi, as they had their eye on the next higher rank.'[54] Yet Singh persisted, and he managed to get Chaudhuri to conduct an exercise in April–May 1956 for the 26 Infantry Division that assumed that Pakistan had overrun the 191

(I) Infantry Brigade, captured Akhnur bridge, and, having sent one brigade over, formed a bridgehead. The Indian assumption for this exercise was that the fighting would be confined to the ceasefire line. But, notes Jogindar Singh, the only action that resulted from this exercise was that the commander of 26 Division was sent home on pension! Singh, later in the winter of 1956–7, was to explain to a visiting Intelligence Bureau official that 'if the operations were restricted to J&K [Jammu and Kashmir] only, Pak[istan] would use an armoured brigade from a newly created division, assisted by an infantry division for the rapid capture of Akhnur bridge. These formations would continue to carry out further operations depending on how they developed and most probably would threaten 25 Inf[antry] Div[ision] from the rear, linked with a frontal assault.'[55] He then proceeded to lay out the likely scenario for the deployment of Pakistan's armour into Indian Punjab in the Sutlej–Beas corridor. He maintains that he had developed these ideas during his stint at the Infantry School as the deputy commandant under Brigadier Manekshaw. If true, this was a high order of foresight. It was almost as if he had read Akhtar Malik's mind!

Yet another Indian military exercise conducted in 1958–9 by 19 Infantry Division had looked at likely scenarios for a battle in Kashmir in the Chamb area. It assumed, among other things, that hostilities would be confined to Kashmir and that an increase in ceasefire violations would be followed by infiltration by 'armed tribesmen, intermixed with armed civilians and AK [Azad Kashmir] troops.' As the situation deteriorated, India would induct a fourth brigade from the 26 Infantry Division into the area, allowing a reserve brigade to launch an attack on Haji Pir Pass. India assumed also that 191 Brigade would lose territory to Pakistan, which would reach Akhnur. Another brigade would then be rushed from 26 Division to defend the line of communication to 25 Infantry Division. Limited air force supported was also assumed. The whole clash was supposed to take place over a 25-day period after which XI Corps was to pose a threat to Lahore, drawing UN intervention and leading to the cessation of war. The results of this exercise were sent to the western command, where, according to Jogindar Singh, they were 'filed for good.'[56] The Indian commander of the western command forces in 1965, Lt. Gen. Harbaksh Singh, also narrates a list of lost opportunities. At a meeting in Srinagar on 31 August 1965 between the COAS, the GOC of XV Corps, and the DMO, the COAS identified two possible courses of action available to Pakistan: first, 'to officially associate herself with the infiltration campaign...[and] attack Chammb or in Jhangar-Naushera', and second, to 'take the case to the Security Council, as the Russian veto on its discussion was no longer likely to be operative (sic).' His final analysis was that an offensive by Pakistan 'was unlikely to get very far.' Harbaksh Singh found this assessment to be 'a gross under-estimation of PAK's intentions and

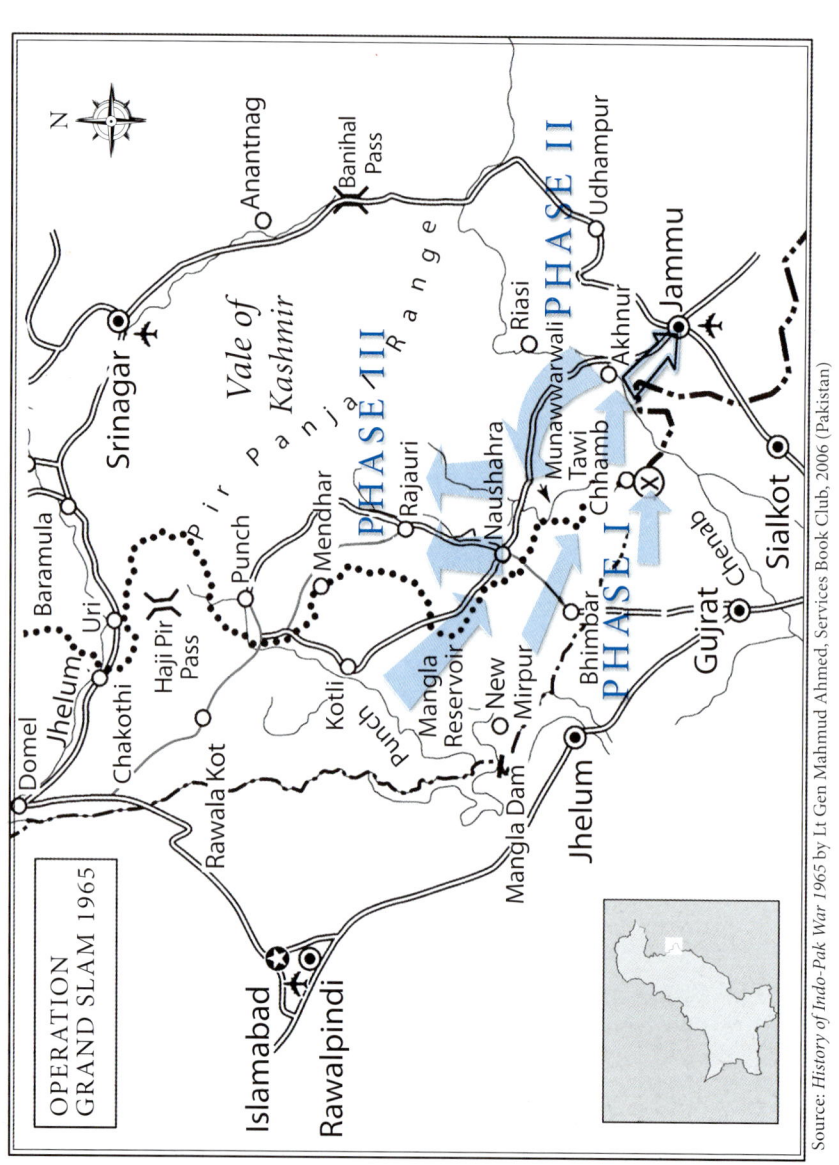

OPERATION GRAND SLAM 1965

PHASE I
PHASE II
PHASE III

N

Anantnag

Banihal Pass

Udhampur

Jammu

Srinagar

Vale of Kashmir

Pir Panjal Range

Riasi

Akhnur

Munawwarwali Tawi

Chhamb

Sialkot

Baramula

Uri

Chakothi

Haji Pir Pass

Punch

Mendhar

Rajauri

Naushahra

Domel

Jhelum

Rawala Kot

Kotli

Mangla Reservoir

New Mirpur

Bhimbar

Gujrat

Chenab

Islamabad

Rawalpindi

Mangla Dam

Jhelum

Source: *History of Indo-Pak War 1965* by Lt Gen Mahmud Ahmed, Services Book Club, 2006 (Pakistan)

capabilities.'[57] Clearly, higher level generalship on both sides left much to be desired in terms of agility in thinking and decision making.

It must be understood that topography dictates military movement and actions. The Chamb sector, with its isosceles triangular appearance (also known as the Chicken Neck), thrusting south to north into Indian-held Kashmir with its peak at Akhnur, limited the use of force.[58] To the left, (as one approached from the Pakistani side,) was a line of hills, and to the right was the Chenab River protecting the Pakistani right flank. Pakistan could employ tanks in the relatively flat land approaching the Tawi, and beyond it to Jaurian, after which the narrow peak of the triangle made movement difficult. The Tawi was not a deep obstacle and eminently fordable, given the right amount of force employed against the expected second line of Indian defence on its eastern bank. As in other conflicts, the daring and momentum of the attacking forces and its generals would determine the end result.

The written orders issued by Akhtar Malik showed his ambitious planning: in Phase 1, he was to destroy the Indian positions in Chamb and up to the Tawi River, (see map of Grand Slam). In Phase 2, he was to swing east to capture Akhnur, and then in Phase 3, he was to send one brigade to capture Rajauri to the north-west of Akhnur. A 'bold and meticulous'[59] artillery plan for the attack was devised by the energetic leader of the corps artillery, Brigadier Amjad Ali Khan Chaudhry and his staff, with medium guns and 8 inch howitzers deployed ahead of the field guns, allowing the Pakistani artillery to dominate the battlefield. As he stated in his official report to GHQ on the Chamb operation, Chaudhary had concentrated his sweeping artillery fire on the forward artillery positions of the Indian Army starting at 07:45 hours on 15 August. The fire was so intense and effective that the Indian commander of the field artillery regiment fled across the Tawi River with the 'debris of his regiment.' According to Chaudhry, a captured Indian artillery officer told the Pakistanis on 2 September that the CO of this Indian artillery regiment was relieved of his command because of this action.[60] General Harbaksh confirms this in his own account of the battle.

The attack was set for 1 September at 05:00 hours, with preceding artillery fire from 03:30 hours. After a brief delay, the Pakistani forces leapt into battle under cover of heavy artillery fire and led by an armoured force that despite heavy attack from entrenched Indian defences, punched its way forward. By 09:00 on the next day, after heavy fighting, Pakistani troops were in Chamb. India brought in air support but the Indian Air Force managed to do more damage to their troops and ammunition dumps than the attacking Pakistani forces, according to the official Indian historian of the war.[61] Pakistan Air Force Sabres, however, provided superb ground support in all phases of the attack.

But confusion reigned over the battlefield, as Akhtar Malik reportedly lost contact with some elements of his force, particularly Brigadier Azmat Hayat's brigade, and the army chief General Musa claimed to have lost contact with Akhtar Malik. Brigadier Amjad Chaudhry also writes about his own inability to rendezvous with Brigadier Hayat during the battle. Musa took off in a helicopter for the battlefield with Brigadier Abid Bilgrami. Not surprisingly, since Akhtar Malik was in the forward area, Musa did not find him at the 12 Division HQ in Kharian. By 11:30, Musa's pilot spotted a convoy of jeeps and landed near them to find General Yahya, the commander of 7 Division. Musa sent out a message for Akhtar Malik to join them at Yahya's 7 Division HQ and then took the most talked-out step of the war: he replaced Akhtar Malik with Yahya, giving 7 Division the remaining tasks of attacking Indian positions in the Chamb sector to the east of the Tawi. With this change of command, the attack virtually came to a halt as Yahya got his commanders together to think through his action plan. With this unexpected pause, the Indian forces regrouped and strengthened the defences around Jaurian and Akhnur. Though Jaurian eventually fell to Pakistan, the attack lost its momentum and fizzled out on the outskirts of Akhnur. Musa had ordered troops away from the Chamb sector by then but deployed 6 Brigade (lately of the Rann of Kutch) to Yahya's command to fill the gap. According to one junior officer attached with Brigadier Eftikhar Janjua of 6 Brigade, Janjua was called to meet Yahya and reported to Yahya that his men were ready to take off for Akhnur. Back came the reply: 'Dig deep, Ifti, my boy! Dig deep! Chaudhuri is no fool! He will counter attack!'[62] That counter attack never came. The Pakistani attack, which India was to term a 'grand plan.... meticulously planned and well executed to some extent,'[63] ground to a halt. Eventually, the safety of the Akhnur bridge, again in the words of the official Indian historian, 'was not the result of Indian generalship, but due to Pak[istani] hamhandedness in crossing Manawar Tawi and changing horses in midstream, i.e. replacing 12 Inf[antry] Div[ision] Commander Major General Akhtar Malik with 7 Inf[antry] Div[ision] Commander, Major General Yahya Khan.'[64]

General Musa was to justify this action later in his book *My Version,* and the officially sponsored history by Shaukat Riza also presents an illogical view that the change of command was pre-planned. In fact, the operational order from GHQ dated 31 August does not mention plans for any change of commanders at any stage of the operation. The original plan had 12 Division handing over the control of the captured territory upto Akhnur to 7 Division leaving Akhtar Malik to proceed further. Riza divides the attack into three phases (see above). A detailed series of studies done at Staff College and supplemented by further research in the GHQ files by Brigadier (later lieutenant general) Mahmud Ahmed fails to bring out any documentation to support the pre-planned change in command. General Yahya, when interviewed by a group of officers from the Staff College, also stated unequivocally: 'I was to come into operations after Akhnur had been captured.'[65]

Akhtar Malik was aware of Ayub's hesitance to cross any international boundary and therefore crafted his written plans to include a move towards Akhnur, followed by a swing to the north-west towards Rajauri. But such a move would not have yielded any strategic benefits, since it would not have cut off the 'jugular' that Ayub had demanded when he suggested Akhnur as a target. Akhtar Malik therefore told his brigade commanders in verbal orders on 29 August: 'Let's get to Akhnur and then we will see whether we go towards Rajauri or turn towards Jammu.' He wanted to keep the attack on Jammu his secret weapon, since that would have effectively cut off all Indian troops in Kashmir from India proper by commanding a choke point that would cut off the road from Pathankot through Jammu via Udhampur and Srinagar. Jammu was not on the official list of targets for that very reason; Pakistan did not want to provoke a wider war. Akhtar Malik did not want to attack along the right bank of the Chenab. His original idea was to attack from the south-east, from an area which is just east of the point where the Tawi River meets the Chenab. By doing so, he would have avoided the Indian entrenched positions along the Tawi and between the Tawi and the Line of Control, saving his forces and his time and coming up on the rear of the Indian forces. But he was not allowed to proceed with this plan by Ayub because it would have meant crossing the border between pre-partition Kashmir and Punjab (extending from Abial Dogran near Shakargarh), considered a working boundary by Pakistan but an international one by India. Akhtar Malik wrote down one plan and wanted to implement another one that would have presented a *fait accompli*.

A telling piece of documentation that Akhtar Malik left behind is a letter he wrote from his post at CENTO headquarters in Ankara to his younger brother Abdul Ali Malik about Gibraltar, the Chamb battle, and the change in command.[66] In that letter, Akhtar Malik takes full credit for keeping the infiltration plan top secret, even from Kashmiris, since that gave his later plans greater strength due to their surprise effect. He also accuses Yahya of subverting his command by getting Brigadier Azmat Hayat to drop communications with him during the battle since Hayat was 'Yahya's brigadier,' a day before the change of command was announced. Malik states that he pleaded with Yahya to be allowed to proceed with the attack, agreeing to work under Yahya's overall command, but Yahya refused and then 'went a step further and even changed the plan. He kept banging his head against Troti (a minor objective east of Chamb), letting the Indian fall back to Akhnur. We lost the initiative on the very first day and never recovered from it.'

This was to be the story of the wider 1965 war with India, as tactical brilliance and gallantry at the lower levels of command were nullified by a lack of vision and courage among the higher levels of leadership of the Pakistan Army. This was a recurring theme of Pakistan's external wars, as senior leaders failed their lower level commanders and ordinary soldiers with poorly conceived military adventures time and again. In the end, what was portrayed as a magnificent victory over India by Ayub Khan's propaganda machine produced only disillusionment and catalysed his eventual fall from grace.

NOTES

1. The author witnessed this impressive firepower demonstration from an observation post, courtesy of my elder brother Asif Nawaz, who was an officer of the 5 Punjab Regiment at that time. Although impressive in peacetime, this approach was not actually employed in the war that ensued.
2. Lt. Gen. S.P.P. Thorat, *From Reveille to Retreat* (India: Allied Publishers, 1985), p. 196.
3. For authoritative accounts of this conflict, in addition to Thorat's autobiography (cited above), please see Neville Maxwell, *India's China War* (New York: Anchor Books, 1972), Brigadier J.P. Dalvi, *Himalayan Blunder* (Bombay: Thacker and Company Ltd., 1969), and Major General D.K. Palit, *War in High Himalaya: The Indian Army in Crisis, 1962* (Lancer International, 1991). Maxwell was the correspondent of *The Times* of London in India at that time, Dalvi was a brigade commander during the conflict, while Palit was DMO at army headquarters in New Delhi.
4. Letter from Deputy Secretary of Defense (Gilpatric) to the Under Secretary of State (Bowles), Washington, 13 September 1961, *US Foreign Relations, 1961–1963, Volume XIX*, US Government Printing Office, Washington 1996, pp. 96–8.
5. Letter from the Ambassador to India (Galbraith) to the Assistant Secretary of State for Near Eastern and South Asian Affairs (Talbot) New Delhi, 21 September 1961. *US Foreign Relations, Volume XIX*, pp. 107–109.
6. Cablegram contained in Letter from Pakistan Ambassador (Ahmed) to President Kennedy, Washington, 4 November 1961, *US Foreign Relations, Volume XIX*, pp. 125–127.
7. Memorandum of Conversation between President Kennedy, Prime Minister Nehru and their aides, Washington, 7 November 1961, *US Foreign Relations, Volume XIV*, pp. 128–34.
8. Telegram from the Department of State to the Embassy in Pakistan, Washington, 8 December 1961, 10:24 p.m. signed by Rusk. *US Foreign Relations, Volume XIX*, pp. 150–151.
9. Memorandum from Robert W. Komer of the NSC staff to the President's Special Assistant for National Security Affairs (Bundy), Washington, 6 January 1962. *USFR*, op. cit., pp. 179–181. This paragraph is based on this memorandum.
10. Letter from Ayub to Kennedy, Karachi, 18 January 1962, delivered via cablegram from US embassy in Pakistan to the Department of State. *US Foreign Relations, Volume XIX*, p. 203.
11. Memorandum of Discussion, Washington, 13 May 1962. *US Foreign Relations, Volume XIX*, pp. 243–5.
12. Letter from Kennedy to Ayub Khan in a Telegram from the Department of State to the Embassy in Pakistan, 28 October 1962, 2:42 p.m. *US Foreign Relations, Volume XIX*, pp. 358–9.
13. *US Foreign Relations, Volume XIX*, p. 375.
14. *US Foreign Relations, Volume XIX*, pp. 377–80.

15. Mohammad Ayub Khan, *Friends not Masters: A Political Autobiography* (London: Oxford University Press, 1967), p. 148.

16. Department of State, 'Report on U.S. Military Obligations to India and Pakistan,' 15 October 1971 (Freedom of Information document obtained and cited by Richard Sisson and Leo Rose in their *War and Secession: India, Pakistan, and the Creation of Bangladesh* (Berkeley and Los Angeles: University of California Press, 1990), p. 51. Also see *Foreign Relations, 1961–1963, South Asia,* released by the Office of the Historian: Document 101–200. The text of the aide-memoire was transmitted to the State Department as enclosure to airgram A-883 from Karachi, 23 February 1963; Washington National Records Centre, RG 84, Karachi Embassy Files: FRC 67 F 74, 320 Pak/US Assurances.

   On 17 November 1962 the Department of State issued a press release that noted the United States had assured Pakistan that if US assistance to India were 'misused and directed against another in aggression, the United States would undertake immediately, in accordance with constitutional authority, appropriate action both within and without the United Nations to thwart such aggression.' (Department of State Bulletin, 3 December 1962, pp. 837–8.) On 19 November, McConaughy wrote to Ayub and enclosed a copy of the 17 November press release. A copy of McConaughy's letter was transmitted to the Department as enclosure 1 to airgram A-613 from Karachi, 5 December (Washington National Records Centre, RG 84, Karachi Embassy Files: FRC 67 F 74, 320 Pak/US Assurances).

17. Ibid., p. 149.

18. John Kenneth Galbraith, *Ambassador's Journal* (Boston: Houghton Mifflin, 1989), p. 299. Galbraith was an ardent supporter of India during his tenure in New Delhi and constantly derided the bureaucrats in Foggy Bottom in personal notes to Kennedy. He opposed military aid to Pakistan tooth and nail, noting regretfully later on that had he known the failure rates of the F-104 Starfighters (that were crashing in large numbers in NATO) he would not have opposed their sale to Pakistan!

19. *US Foreign Relations, Volume XIX*, pp. 622–3.

20. *US Foreign Relations, Volume XIX*, p. 668.

21. Sir Morrice James, *Pakistan Chronicle* (London: Hurst and Company, New York: St. Martin's Press, 1993), pp. 21–2. A variant on this theme was offered some years later by the US historian and political analyst Stephen Cohen to the effect that while some countries have an army, in Pakistan the army has a country.

22. Telegram from the Embassy in Pakistan to the Department of State, Karachi, 1 February 1964, 3 PM. *USFR, 1964-68, Volume XXV, South Asia,* 2000, pp. 24–6.

23. James, *Pakistan Chronicle*, p. 110. Sir Morrice James recounts that a story broke after Ayub's visit to the UK in the summer of 1963 that Ayub had been at a swimming pool party at the home of Lord Astor during which the notorious but comely Christine Keeler (who helped bring down the Secretary of State for War, John Profumo) claimed to the *News of the World* that 'Ayub had ducked [dunked] her as part of the general horseplay.' The Pakistan high commissioner, General Yusuf, denied that Ayub was ever in the pool. Recounts Sir Morrice: 'speaking to me about the incident Bhutto said with mock wistfulness: How incongruous for an interesting thing like this to happen to such a very dull man!'

   Although Sir Morrice got on very well with Bhutto, he had a very dark view of his future that he shared with the CRO in 1965. As he recounts in his memoirs (p. 75): 'Bhutto certainly had the right qualities for reaching the heights—drive, charm, imagination, a quick and penetrating mind, zest for life, eloquence, energy, a strong constitution, a sense of humour, and a thick skin. Such a blend is rare anywhere, and Bhutto deserved his swift rise to power.... But there was—how shall I put it?—a rank odour of hellfire about him. It was a case of *corruptio optima pessima.* He was a Lucifer, a flawed angel. I believe that at heart he lacked a sense of the dignity and value of other people; his own self was what counted. I sensed in him a ruthlessness and capacity for ill-doing which went far beyond what is natural. Except at University abroad, he was mostly surrounded by mediocrities, and all his life, for want of competition, his triumphs came too easily for his own good. Lacking humility he thus came to believe himself infallible, even when yawning gaps in his own experience (e.g. of military matters) laid him—as over the 1965 war—wide open to disastrous error. Despite his gifts I judged that one day Bhutto would destroy himself—when I could not tell. In 1965, I so reported in one of my last despatches from Pakistan as British High Commissioner. I wrote by way of clinching the point that **Bhutto was born to be hanged** [emphasis added]. I did not intend this comment as precise prophecy of what was going to happen to him, but fourteen years later that was what it turned out to be.'

24. Altaf Gauhar, *Ayub Khan: Pakistan's First Military Ruler* (Lahore: Sang-e-Meel Publications, 1993) p. 277.

25. *USFR Volume XIX,* Memorandum from the Department of State Executive Secretary (Read) to the President's Special Assistant for National Security Affairs (Bundy), Washington, 31 December 1963, p. 732.

26. B.C. Chakravorty, *History of the Indo–Pak War, 1965* (India: History Division, Ministry of Defense, 1992), p. 21.

27. Chakravorty, *History*, p. 22. Sundarji was later to become a hawkish Indian COAS and launched the famous Exercise Brasstacks in the same general area in 1986–7 that many in Pakistan believed was a ruse designed to actually invade southern Pakistan. It led to Pakistan moving forces into the Sutlej–Beas gap in the Punjab that threatened India's Punjab heartland and also to send a signal that Pakistan was ready to use all the weapons at its disposal to counter any Indian move.

28. Major General Shaukat Riza, *The Pakistan Army, War 1965* (Pakistan: Services Book Club, 1984), p. 79.

29. Chakravorty, *History*, p. 26.

30. Two actions by Lieutenant Nadir Parvez of 6 Punjab, who came to the battlefield with his left arm in a half cast (as a result of a fight in Quetta, his regiment's home base) led to the capture of Indian arms and troops. He was awarded the Sitara-e-Jurat and was to win a bar (meaning a second medal) for bravery during the later 1965 war with India. Parvez was among the officers who were tried and convicted for an attempt in 1973 to overthrow the government of Zulfikar Ali Bhutto. They were later released and allowed to enter public life. He is now a member of the National Assembly as a follower of former Prime Minister Nawaz Sharif. He is married to the daughter of the author's cousin. His inspiring action prompted my cousin Lt. Farooq Nawaz Janjua of 4 Punjab Regiment to proclaim to me within months of having been commissioned from the Pakistan Military Academy with the Sword of Honour in 1964: 'Lucky Nadir Parvez! He's seen action. I swear if there is a war, you will hear that I have either died or been given the Sitara-e-Jurat!' True to his word, he undertook a daring raid behind Indian lines in the Sulemanki Sector in September 1965 and captured a large number of Gurkha soldiers, gaining his award in the process. He too was allegedly associated with the conspiracy to oust Bhutto in 1973 and was forcibly retired from the army.

31. General Mohammad Musa, *My Version: India–Pakistan War 1965* (Lahore: Wajidalis, 1983), pp. 74–5.

32. Chakravorty, *History*, pp. 36–7.

33. Ibid., p. 39, based on an interview with General P.P. Kumaramangalam, retired COAS, India, 29 September 1986.

34. *USFR, 1964–1968, Volume XXV,* op. cit., memorandum from Robert Komer of the National Security Council Staff to the President's Special Assistant for National Security Affairs (Bundy), Washington, 20 August 1965, pp. 339–40.

35. Lt. Gen. Gul Hassan, *Memoirs* (Karachi: Oxford, 1993), p. 115.

36. Ibid., p. 116.

37. Major Edgar O'Ballance, 'The India–Pakistan Campaign, 1965,' *Defence Journal*, September 1975, p. 27.

38. Chakravorty, *History*, p. 59.
39. This name probably originated with Akhtar Malik, an avid bridge player.
40. Gauhar, *Ayub Khan*, pp. 307–34 has a detailed account of the genesis of these plans, from his rather restricted vantage point as the information secretary who was asked to eventually help with the propaganda aspects of the operations.
41. Seyyed Ghaffar Mehdi, *Politics of Surrender and the Conspiracy of Silence* (Markham, ON, Canada: Crescent International Newspapers, 2001).
42. India identified additional forces named Babar, Murtaza (the name of Bhutto's elder son), Sikandar (the local name for Alexander), and Jacob. India also gives a later timeline for the infiltration of these forces. Chakravorty, op. cit., p. 64.
43. Chakravorty, *History*, p. 65.
44. Gauhar, *Ayub Khan*, p. 322.
45. Hassan, *Memoirs*, p. 223.
46. An interesting footnote to these amateurish efforts was the induction of a 'Psy War' expert in the shape of a young officer named Mujibur Rehman to help run the clandestine radio operation. He was later to parlay this psychological warfare experience into becoming secretary of the ministry of information of General Ziaul Haq.
47. Interview in 1990 with then Brigadier Mahmud Ahmed (later lieutenant general), based on his in-depth study of the 1965 war for the Pakistan Army that included exchanges with many participants. The name of his monumental study of the war is *History of Indo–Pak War 1965* (Pakistan: Services Book Club, 2006). I am grateful to him for helping me capture accurately the details of the plans and operations in the Chamb Sector.
48. I recall visiting him at his father's house behind Ayub Park (Topi Park) in Rawalpindi after his escape and listening to his tale with some awe.
49. Gauhar, *Ayub Khan*, p. 318.
50. Chakravorty, *History*, p. 73.
51. Gauhar, *Ayub Khan*, p. 328.
52. Chakravorty, *History*, p. 104.
53. Ibid., p. 97.
54. Major General Jogindar Singh, *Behind the Scene: An Analysis of India's Military Operations, 1947–71* (New Delhi: Lancer International, 1993), p. 25.
55. Ibid., p. 30.
56. Ibid., pp. 36–7.
57. Lt. Gen. Harbaksh Singh, *War Despatches: Indo–Pak Conflict 1965* (New Delhi: Lancer International, 1991), p. 57.
58. The author served with the Pakistan Army as a war correspondent for Pakistan Television in the 1971 Indo–Pakistan War and observed the area first hand in both the Shakargarh Salient and in the Chamb sector, producing a TV programme on the fight for Chamb in 1971, which turned out to be a near carbon copy of the 1965 clash. General Gul Hassan also gives a useful description of the area of battle in his *Memoirs*, op. cit., p. 184.
59. Shaukat Riza, *The Pakistan Army War 1965* (Lahore: Wajidalis, 1984), p. 116.
60. Secret report on 4 Corps Artillery, Chammb—up to 31 August by Brigadier Amjad Ali Khan Chaudhry, Pakistan Army GHQ archives. See also his book *September '65* (Lahore: Ferozsons, 1977) for a detailed account of Chamb and later battles.
61. Chakravorty, *History*, ibid.
62. Conversation reported by Brigadier Janjua's aide, Captain Khadim Hussain Changezi, to my brother and me soon after the 1965 war.
63. Chakravorty, *History*, p. 112.
64. Ibid., p. 135.
65. Interview with author, 1990. This paragraph relies heavily on Lt. Gen. Mahmud Ahmed's research that led to his monumental *History of Indo–Pak War 1965*. Altaf Gauhar mentions the Staff College study but does not go into details, instead focusing on an attack on Akhtar

Malik. He also writes about an unverifiable incident in which Akhtar Malik wept in his presence: an improbable event, given Akhtar Malik's stoicism and pride.

66. Hassan Abbas, *Pakistan's Drift into Extremism: Allah, the Army, and America's War on Terror* (New York and London: M.E. Sharpe, Armonk, 2005), p. 49.

10 | SEPTEMBER 1965 AND AYUB'S FALL

Ai vatan ke sajeelay jawano
Mere naghme tumhare liye hain
(O splendid soldiers of my Land
My songs are for you!)
— Popular song during 1965 War, sung by Madame Noor Jehan as a paean to
Pakistani soldiers

With the rigour of Newtonian physics, every action in Indo–Pakistan civil and military relations has an equal and opposite reaction. The attacks on Kargil and Tithwal by India in 1965 provoked the Pakistani move into Chamb and Jaurian. The subsequent, though pre-planned, Pakistani threat to Akhnur forced India onto its heels in Kashmir. As India's ambassador to the US, B.K. Nehru, reported to Secretary of State Rusk on 3 September, the government of India 'could not allow Paks to cut [the] road [to] Srinagar. If Paks do, India will have to move across [the] international boundary in [the] Punjab.'[1] A few days earlier, on 1 September 1965, the Indian Prime Minister Lal Bahadur Shastri was pacing in his office, pondering news of the Pakistani attack in Chamb. His aide, C.P. Srivastva recalls Shastri saying '*Ab to kuch karna hi ho ga!*' (*Now we will have to do something!*). He met his cabinet the next day and again on 3 September, and gave the go ahead for an attack against West Pakistan.[2] Thus in retaliation to Operations Gibraltar and Grand Slam, India did what its military planners had rehearsed for almost a decade: it attacked with all its might across the international border at Lahore and other locations on 6 September 1965. But the war was in vain for Pakistan. The failure of the Chamb operation—caused by the delay in the launch of the first attack, the change of commanders and objectives, and then withdrawal of support from the operation itself—sealed the fate of all subsequent efforts on the West Pakistan border with India. Except for a successful initial thrust into Khem Karan in Indian Punjab (followed by a debacle in the subsequent tank attack,) and the blunting of the Indian attack into the Sialkot area, epitomized by the Battle of Chawinda, the war was an exercise in frustration; quite apart from the glorifying media coverage and spontaneous public support through poetry, song, and sacrifice. This war reflected yet again the failure of the high command of the army. Once the dust had settled on this war, Pakistan faced a new political reality: the possibility of a country without Ayub Khan at the helm. Yet, the heavy sacrifices of its military manpower and civilian resources served to keep Kashmir a hot issue in the nation's psyche; a smouldering fire that could turn to flames given the right conditions.

The geography and topography of the Indo–Pakistan border in the Punjab, known to both sides of the conflict, basically limited the options for both. There were, in effect, no surprises. Yet, Pakistan and specifically Ayub Khan, appeared to be surprised by the Indian attack across the international border into West Pakistan. The pre-partition roads connecting Amritsar and Lahore, and Indian Punjab to Pakistan's Punjab, offered a network for logistical support and movement of troops from their peacetime locations not far from the respective borders. Pakistan had had the foresight, thanks to the mighty argument of then Brigadier Eftikhar Janjua, (a local commander in Lahore at the time,) to have constructed the BRB canal (known as the Ichhogil canal in India) east of Lahore, running some 2–10 miles away from and parallel to the international border. According to General Gul Hassan, civilian authorities had asked that the canal be run through Lahore city to provide some natural beauty for the city, but Janjua had persuaded them to move it towards the border. The BRB provided a natural military defence against any attacking force from the east with its 50 foot-wide span and a depth of some 15 feet. Indian General Chaudhuri had commented earlier that he would not attempt to cross this formidable water obstacle. The Grand Trunk (GT) road that linked Peshawar to Calcutta ran across the BRB at a village called Dograi and then swung west and north to provide Pakistan's main line of communications between Lahore, Gujrat, Jhelum, and Rawalpindi. Any Indian attack that reached the GT road would have cut Pakistan in half and forced it to sue for peace.

THE INDIAN PLAN

India planned to 'threaten Lahore' in the first instance, and then 'drive a wedge between the Pak forces deployed around it and those based in Sialkot.' When Indian Prime Minister Shastri met with his defence minister and army and air force chiefs on 3 September, he defined the country's war objectives as follows:

1. To defeat the Pakistani attempts to seize Kashmir by force and to make it abundantly clear that Pakistan would never be allowed to wrest Kashmir from India;
2. To destroy the offensive power of Pakistan's armed forces
3. To occupy only the minimum Pakistani territory necessary to achieve these purposes, which would be vacated after the satisfactory conclusion of the war.[3]

According to the official Indian history of the war (written many years after the war), the idea was not to capture Lahore or Sialkot, but 'to destroy Pakistan's war potential.'[4] But there seems to be some debate about this since it made sense for India to take Lahore: that would have forced Pakistan to withdraw troops from the Kashmir Theatre and from the Khem Karan area, where Pakistan had made some gains initially. The Indian plan was finalized on 9 August—within the first week of Pakistan's infiltration of Kashmir—and the task assigned to the Indian XI Corps by India's western command was to defend against any Pakistan incursion in the Rajasthan area while attacking in the Punjab. The advance was to take place up to the BRB canal from the GT road at Dograi south to its confluence with the Dipalpur canal, with the additional objective of eliminating a Pakistani bridgehead near and capture of the Dera Baba Nanak bridge. Once this was done, XI Corps was to be prepared to 'continue the advance on Lahore'. General Chaudhuri certainly had his eyes on the prize of Lahore, the heart of Pakistani Punjab. H-Hour, the time that attack would start, was initially set at 04:00 hours on 7 September and then changed to 6 September, according to the C-in-C (Indian) western command, Lt. Gen. Harbaksh Singh.[5] The code word for imminent hostilities was 'Bangle'. It was received from army headquarters on 1 September followed by code word 'Banner', the call for the launching of the attack. On 5 September, upon the request of two of the attacking formations (4 Mountain Division and 7 Infantry Division), the H-Hour was changed to 05:00 hours.

General Harbaksh Singh was a busy man in the last days preceding the attack, meeting with his commanders and ensuring that they understood their objectives clearly. He also told them that the attack on Lahore would be undertaken under his direction, after achievement of the earlier objectives. On 5 September, he flew to a civilian lunch in Simla, having arranged for a helicopter to pick him up in nearby Annandale and take him back to the frontlines. He first stopped in Amritsar, briefed the civil officials about the imminent attack, and then ordered a curfew for the city and the creation of a cordon around it, with loudspeakers to broadcast news of the attack. At H-Hour, India moved across the border at four points with a view to capturing Dograi and securing the BRB at a crossing slightly north of the GT road—Jallomor (Jallo crossing). They also moved to capture Bhasin, Dogaich, and Wahgrian, clustered north of Dograi. A fourth thrust from the north skirted Ichhogil Uttar to Bhaini Dhilwal—in short, they went for all locations with bridges across the BRB canal. India was attempting to secure the east bank of the BRB canal and then establish bridgeheads across it to proceed into Pakistan. The speed of these attacks allowed Indian troops to achieve most of their objectives, with a regiment of Major General Niranjan Prasad's 15 Division even managing to cross the canal and advance to Batapur—the site of a shoe factory set up by the multilateral firm Bata—on the outskirts of Lahore. This and the capture of a Lahore omnibus at this location, the image of which was flashed worldwide, may have been the basis of the erroneous BBC broadcast that Indian forces had entered Lahore. Meanwhile, India also captured the bridge at Dera Baba Nanak.

General Prasad had argued strongly with his corps commander, Lt. Gen. J.S. Dhillon, about the plans for the attack. Prasad was seeking air support, which was denied on the grounds that the 'IAF would be in the process of gaining air superiority.' He also sought permission to advance across the international boundary at last light on 5 September instead of on 6 September, allowing his forces to establish themselves on the eastern bank of the BRB canal during the night. All of his requests were denied but he continued to argue with his commanders during the initial stages of the various battles, prompting Dhillon to arrive at his headquarters and to press him to continue with his assigned objectives. The unfortunate Prasad then suffered the ignominy of having his jeep convoy ambushed during the night of 6/7 September, losing his personal jeep and some papers that included his written protest against having been removed from the command of 4 Mountain Division in 1962. Pakistan made hay of this minor victory and broadcast the contents of his papers. The next morning Prasad was replaced by Major General Mohinder Singh.

By taking the war across the international boundary, India forced Pakistan to rethink the battle for Kashmir and concentrate instead on defending the Punjab with its key cities and roads. Yet, general war should not have been as big a surprise as it appeared to be for the Pakistani high command.

PAKISTAN'S PLANS

Apart from knowing that India had the option to fight at a time and a place of its choice, Pakistan had received reports as early as 15 August and as late as 4 September that India was moving troops closer to the international border. Pakistan's 15 Division was asked to set an ambush on the Samba–Kathua road that had seen heavy traffic since the middle of August. At 01:00 hours on the night of 3/4 September, an excited Colonel S.G. Mehdi, colonel staff at division headquarters, called Lt. Col. Sher Zaman of the MI Directorate to report that they had caught an Indian dispatch rider carrying mail for the headquarters squadron of the Indian 1st Armoured Division. This established that the 1st Armoured Division was in the vicinity of Samba, ready for an offensive strike under the code name Operation Nepal.[6] The Lahore, Sialkot, and Kasur sectors all reported heavy Indian activity. A day earlier, Prime Minister Shastri had warned his fellow countrymen in a speech on All India Radio of the 'hard days ahead' when they might have to 'suffer damage from air raids.'[7] Gul Hassan recalls discussing the Indian moves with the CGS Lt. Gen. Sher Bahadur, and suggesting that Pakistan move its forces to defensive positions along the border. Sher Bahadur was reluctant to commit, given the prevailing stricture from the foreign office of 'Do not provoke, Do not escalate.' Musa was visiting Chamb that day and did not get back till late. Gul Hassan asked one of his staff officers to brief the chief who responded that the officer should monitor the All India Radio. Sure enough, All India Radio reported in a flash news item that Prime Minister Shastri had told parliament that Pakistan was moving troops from Sialkot towards Jammu. Clearly something was brewing on the Indian side.

Yet, there was no visible sense of urgency on the Pakistani side. At a higher level, yet again, there appeared to be no attempt to draw the air force or the navy into the strategic planning for the impending war. Indeed, the air force chief, Air Marshal Asghar Khan was replaced by Air Marshal Nur Khan during the summer months when the military action was heating up and plans were being made for the war to come. War was seen as purely a Pakistan Army affair, as Gul Hassan testifies. Yet, the army leadership too seemed unready, as it had since the Rann of Kutch crisis. On the Lahore front, for instance, in April 1965, at the height of the Rann of Kutch crisis, 10 Division had been moved to the border and made ready for action. Defensive positions were taken, mines deployed, barbed wires laid, and bridges over the BRB canal prepared for demolition. However, by July, when the political climate appeared to be cooling, all these preparations were undone and most of the 10 Division was withdrawn from the border. Then, when the action began in Kashmir, the GOC 10 Division, Lt. Gen. Sarfaraz Khan asked the Corps Commander General Bakhtiar Rana at a commander-in-chiefs' conference in Kharian on 31 August: 'Shall we occupy defensive positions?' To which Rana replied: 'Negative!' When Sarfaraz pursued his argument and sought permission to at least 'allow us to lay mines,' Rana responded: 'No. We do not want to provoke the Indians.'[8]

It was in this mindset that Musa gave orders to his troops as late as 4 September to 'take necessary defensive measures' under a flash signal (carrying the highest priority), drafted by the military operations directorate. [9] Shaukat Riza thought the language was not peremptory enough. According to Gul Hassan, the message was quite clear but Lt. Gen. M. Sarfaraz Khan, GOC 10 Division in Lahore, perhaps influenced by his earlier instructions from General Rana, chose to interpret it in a more relaxed manner than the rest, merely asking troops to 'exercise greater vigilance' and warning troops in the rear to guard against air attacks. He also suggested that troops move to defensive positions on the night of 5/6 September. Indeed, on the night of 5 September, he was attending a dinner for visiting foreign aid officials and USAID officials from India in Lahore. Earlier, Pakistan had allowed troops to take leave also, despite the state of war in the Kashmir sector. Complacency seemed to reign in the upper echelons of the army. Indeed, the first news of India's attack reached Pakistan's high command from Pakistan Air Force observers near the border. Ayub Khan then called Musa who said he was trying to confirm the news. At 09:00 on 6 September, the CGS of the Pakistan Army informed the directors at the GHQ that India had attacked Lahore and

Sialkot, concluding with an ominous comment: 'Whatever we have got is in the show window. There are no replacements. Good luck!'[10]

Those sentences seemed to sum up Pakistan's military situation, reliant as it was on US arms and ammunition. It was unprepared for a drawn-out, steady war. The Pakistani high command's decision-making left a lot to be desired, both in the run up to the war and in its execution, as illustrated by the major battles in which lower level officers and troops stood out for their gallant performances, but the higher generalship, particularly in the GHQ, was wanting.

THE BATTLE OF CHAWINDA

The Pakistani GHQ had ordered all formations to move to their defensive positions on 4 September. The 6 Armoured Division, under General Abrar Husain, complied. When news of the Indian attack came, he was told to move his troops to Pasrur on the night of 6/7 September as reserve for the 1 Corps. The move occurred during the night. Then at midnight, the division's staff were told to return to their previous position around Gujranwala by 05:00 hours on 7 September! This was confirmed by the GOC Abrar Husain who said that the DMO Gul Hassan, had given him this order on the telephone. GHQ seemed to be making decisions quite arbitrarily.[11]

But general confusion seemed to reign on the battlefield too. In the Sialkot sector, the 15 Division, apparently on the basis of feeds from the 115 Brigade, reported that the Indians had broken through in the Jassar area, an improbable feat that would have demanded that they cross the Ravi River and then its tributary that was on the Pakistani side of the border. Based on this report, HQ 1 Corps requested GHQ to give it permission to blow up the bridge at Jassar. Meanwhile HQ 1 Corps ordered 15 Division, under Brigadier Sardar Ismail (whom Pakistan military historians were to refer to derisively as 'a Service Corps' officer, not someone who belonged to a fighting arm) to provide assistance to the 115 Brigade. In came two persons who would become part of the Pakistan Army's folklore: Brigadier Abdul Ali Malik[12] (Commander 24 Brigade), and Brigadier A.A.K. Chaudhry (Commander 4 Corps Artillery) who had been moved from Chamb to help protect the Sialkot sector.

Gul Hassan credits Abdul Ali Malik's intuition that prevented him from hurriedly inserting his forces into the confused situation. This allowed Abdul Ali Malik's 24 Brigade and Brigadier Chaudhry's artillery to remain in their defensive positions around Chawinda for what would eventually become a celebrated defence of Chawinda against the Indian 1st Armoured Division.

Abdul Ali Malik recalls getting a call on 7 September from the officiating GOC of 15 Division to say that:

> A critical situation had arisen in Jassar area where the enemy had succeeded in establishing a bridgehead of Pakistan's side of the river....He wanted me to move to Narowal and stabilize (sic) the situation there by counter attack. I pointed out that a large enemy force with armour was concentrated on the other side of the border opposite my brigade, and could attack at any time.[13]

Such a move, Malik said, would be 'quite unsound and dangerous.' In spite of this protest, at 18:00 hours he was ordered to move to Narowal. He chose not to do so with his entire brigade, and instead took only his small operations group. On arrival, Malik learned from Brigadier Muzaffaruddin, commander 115 Brigade, that Jassar bridge had been blown up that morning. The Indian enclave on the Pakistan side of the Ravi River had been cleared by the 115 Brigade. Malik's armour regiment commander, Lt. Col. Nisar Ahmed, warned him that should his regiment be moved to Jassar, 'please do not expect a regiment from me when we get back [to Chawinda].' So Malik told him to bring only one squadron 'in case it was required.' He then asked to speak 'to somebody who had actually seen the Indians on the Pakistan side of the river.' No one came forward.

'The whole picture was one of confusion and uncertainty,' writes Malik. His infantry commander, Lt. Col. Jamshed, whose battalion would have to launch the attack, was of the view that 'due to the uncertainty of the situation abut the enemy, it would be suicidal to commit the battalion in a night attack in an unknown area without any daylight recce of enemy dispositions.' Malik concurred. 'A commander carries a heavy burden of responsibility in war for the safety of his men. I was not fully convinced myself that a large enemy force could have come across the river without a bridge to support it. If the Indians had really intended to make a breakthrough in this area, they could have easily used their large Dharam enclave[14] for initial concentration, where they already had a boat bridge over [the] Ravi. But they had easily abandoned that enclave under slight pressure,' recalled Malik.

While discussions were going on about this with the officiating GOC of 215 Division, Sardar Ismail, an urgent message arrived from Sialkot reporting Indian shelling in Suchetgarh and that an attack appeared imminent. 'That settled it' recalls Malik. 'I took the GOC aside and told him that Jassar was a mere flap and we were both at the wrong place. I pleaded with him to go back to his headquarters, get our orders reversed, and to move us back to our original positions. He agreed and left for Sialkot.' On his own way back during the night, Malik saw a convoy of guns belonging to Brig. Amjad Ali Chaudhry's 4 Corps Artillery heading towards Jassar. He stopped them and told them to return. Lucky for them, they managed to get back before daylight when they could have been sitting ducks for the Indian Air Force.

Even the official Indian history of the war acknowledges that 'the picture of false Indian pressure at DBN [Dera Baba Nanak], as painted [by Brigadier Muzaffaruddin, the Pakistani brigade commander] before his superiors, led to the initial orders for the move of Pak 24 Brigade from the threatened Chawinda Sector. Had the mistake not been rectified, and had the 24 Inf[antry] B[riga]de not re-occupied its original position, the Pakistanis could have lost the crucial Chawinda battle.'[15] Indeed, India expected Pakistan to take advantage of the Dera Baba Nanak bridge and the Pakistan enclave on the Indian side of the Ravi to launch an attack towards Gurdaspur and Pathankot. But having blown up the bridge as a result of Brig. Muzaffaruddin and his division commander's panicky reporting, Pakistan lost that capability of a counter attack.

One of Brigadier Abdul Ali Malik's officers, Farouk Adam, (himself a winner of the Sitara-e-Jurat), recalls how Malik first heard about the Indian forces opposite Chawinda from a 'thoroughly shaken engineer Havildar' who told the CO 2 Punjab, Lt. Col. Jamshed, that 'the Indians had attacked and taken all our positions ahead of Chawinda.' Brig. Malik immediately ordered his staff to cut all communications with higher headquarters 'lest they sow any more confusion in the already confused state of affairs, and ordered the brigade straight to Chawinda.'[16] He was later to confirm this move in a wireless exchange with the new division commander, Major General Tikka Khan. Once at Chawinda, he took the extraordinary decision to order 25 Cavalry with its two squadrons to attack the oncoming Indian armoured division in extended line formation. The audacity of this move was more than matched by the performance of the Pakistani armour in that encounter. Farouk Adam recalls: 'We advanced all day in short bursts, from cover to cover. The Indians were retreating by the afternoon. We reoccupied Phillaurah, then Godgore, then Chobhara. And Major [Mohammad Hussain] Malik [of 2 Punjab that was supporting the 25 Cavalry attack] asked, half in jest, if the Brigadier [Abdul Ali Malik] would have us take Delhi the same day.' By nightfall, the troops were overextended and fell back from Chobhara. Sometimes ignorance is truly bliss. The next day, the puny Pakistani attacking force found a marked map in an abandoned Indian jeep that showed that they had been up against the 1st Indian Armoured Division, 6 Mountain Division, 26 Infantry Division, and the 14 Infantry Division!

The next day, as Brig. Malik assessed the situation with his senior commanders, they came under artillery fire. He knew that his paltry troops could not hold the territory against a concentrated counter attack. So, he chose to go on the offensive once more, reoccupying Chobhara but only to abandon it yet again under a fierce Indian assault. On 11 September, the

Indians broke through the Pakistani defences, and Chawinda was threatened again. But Brig. Malik stood his ground, indeed moving his own headquarters into the forward lines. 'Oh my God,' thought Farouk Adam, 'the Old Man is really determined to stake himself out like the Indian Chiefs!'

The terrain in the Sialkot area is particularly suited for armour operations, being generally flat and rising gently to the north-east, interspersed with small gullies or 'nullahs' that flow north-east to south-southwest. 15 Division had to control a front of some 180,000 yards, aided by seven armoured regiments belonging to the hastily raised 6 Armoured Division. It shared defensive duties with 8 Division that had four infantry brigades and four supporting armoured regiments. IV Corps' artillery brigade was also moved to this sector from Chamb. Opposing it was the Indian I Corps with its 1st Armoured Division and three infantry divisions, with orders to secure the Pathankot–Jammu road by launching a riposte to an anticipated move by Pakistan against Jammu, the private plan of General Akhtar Malik that his superiors had thwarted.[17] The Indian 1st Armoured Division was supposed to establish a bridgehead across the international boundary in Pakistani territory, capture Phillora and then proceed towards Pagowal and Chawinda to the Marala–Ravi link canal. Meanwhile, in a complementary action, 14 Infantry Division was to capture Zafarwal and proceed in a north-westerly direction towards Chawinda. The armour division had a rough start to its operations, running into fierce Pakistani recoilless rifle and armour attacks by the 25 Cavalry Regiment of the Pakistan Army[18] and losing its momentum in the initial phases of the operation. The armour division managed to capture some territory, but then the Indian armour that was to take part in a pincer movement to reduce Chawinda on 14 September ran into a strong anti-tank screen and a fierce battle occurred with a regiment of Pakistani Pattons. In the words of the C-in-C western command, General Harbaksh Singh: 'The progress of battle fell far short of expectations. The armour having failed to create the tactical pre-condition for an infantry assault on Chawinda, the attack …was called off.' Thus ended the first battle of Chawinda. In the words of Brigadier Abdul Ali Malik: 'This battle … enabled Pakistan to seize the initiative from the Indians and blunted the edge of the massive attack of the powerful Indian armoured division, forcing it to retreat.'[19]

The Pakistani high command apparently had not anticipated the Indian moves in this sector despite the capture of the despatch rider on 4/5 September which yielded valuable information about Indian formations and plans. Malik recalls that 'this lucky find was such an important piece of intelligence that I closed the bag immediately and sent it on to HQ 15 Div[ision] for onward despatch to GHQ.…However, I was disappointed to learn later on that GHQ staff did not consider this intelligence to be genuine. People had read too much military history and considered this to be a plant by the enemy.'[20] It was only because of the later capture of an operational order in a knocked-out Indian tank that Pakistan's GHQ was able to find out the disposition of Indian forces in this sector and their intent.

Field Marshal Ayub Khan's son Gohar Ayub Khan has offered a colourful story that Pakistan purchased India's operational plans from a senior Indian officer who needed money for his wife's canning hobby. I recall him telling this story to my brother, his close friend, Asif Nawaz, in the late 1960s, when he named a man who was later a huge Indian military hero and who indeed was under suspicion during that period. An inquiry into this officer's actions was abandoned. As for the veracity of Gohar Ayub's story, if it is indeed true, it reflects poorly on Ayub Khan and his generals who could not take advantage of this information.[21] Gohar Ayub's thinly disguised reference can be traced to one man whose name he took in those days: Field Marshal Sam Manekshaw, who won his Military Cross in Burma on 22 February 1942.[22] It is also eminently possible that this may have been an Indian ruse. Unless more evidence becomes available, it can only be seen as a yarn.

Regardless, it took GHQ 'nearly forty-eight hours to decide upon their next move. Our operational plans had perhaps not taken into considerations (sic) all the options open to aggressor,' wrote Brigadier Chaudhry, the commander of the Pakistani artillery.[23] The Pakistani artillery meanwhile continued to do enormous damage to the Indian armour and infantry attacks, concentrating fire with speed and accuracy on Indian artillery positions with great effect, forcing the latter to keep well behind the front. Pakistan's US-supplied 155mm long-range guns, were especially effective in this regard.

The Indian commanders did not give up their aim to capture Chawinda and thus contain Sialkot and they spent the 15 and 16 September planning afresh. The corps commander reviewed the plans on 16 September along with the commanders of the 1st Armoured Division and 6 Mountain Division, with the 6 Mountain Division being given the job of capturing Chawinda while the 1st Armoured Division and 14 Infantry Division would attempt to get Badiana and Zafarwal. In the run up to the final attack on Chawinda, India got into fierce battles with Pakistani armour and artillery, losing, among others, Lt. Col. A.B. Tarapore of 17 Horse, who was given the highest Indian military honour of the Param Vir Chakra.[24] After that, general confusion took over on the Indian side as misunderstandings arose about the timing of the 35 Infantry Brigade's move. This brigade took off on 16/17 September, earlier than planned and was recalled. The attack, originally planned for 17/18 September was thus postponed by twenty-four hours, by when, due to further confusion, the 1st Armoured Division withdrew some other troops before the 6 Mountain Division could mount its attack. By then, the element of surprise had been lost. Pakistan started shelling the forming-up places (FUPs) while the troops were being marshalled for the attack. The operation was, in consequence, dislocated from the very beginning.[25] Pakistani artillery's pounding unnerved the Indian troops, who ended up firing on each other in the confused fog of battle. The two companies of the 4 J&K Rifles that had managed to reach Chawinda were thrown back by Pakistani infantry and armour fire. About 500 J&K Riflemen 'deserted due to Pak armour threat, and the remnants of Gorkhas were found near Lebbe [close to Phillora, already in Indian hands].'[26]

The failure to capture Chawinda led to the abandonment of plans to capture Zafarwal and Badiana. In a stinging indictment of the Indian operations, the Indian C-in-C western command wrote:

> This battle is a classic study in command failure and poor execution. Lack of control at Corps level paved the way to defeat—an indifferent leadership at lower levels made disaster inevitable. The depressing combination decided the fate of the battle [of Chawinda] and foredoomed the outcome of the entire campaign.[27]

Chawinda was a critical battle of the 1965 war, for had it fallen to the Indian attack, Sialkot's right flank was open and, as Gul Hassan states, India would have forced a fight with Pakistan's 6 Armoured Division in the closed space on the eastern bank of the Marala–Ravi canal, depriving the Pakistani armour freedom of movement. The normally taciturn and modest Abdul Ali Malik writes in his unpublished memoirs that: 'If I had not acted as I did on my own initiative on 8 Sep[tember], to advance and intercept the enemy attack without orders, and perhaps, technically against my orders to stay put at Pasrur, there would have been no battle of Chawinda to talk about. The enemy would have gone beyond Chawinda and Badiana before I Corps or GHQ could intervene in the battle. Thus, there might have been battles of Pasrur, Sialkot or Daska but no battle of Chawinda.'

As it turned out, the Indian attack on a narrow front led to the biggest tank battle since the Second World War. But India's poor generalship came to Pakistan's rescue. India kept attacking Chawinda head-on instead of bypassing it. That, combined with the spirited defence of Chawinda under Major General Abrar Husain, commander 6 Armoured Division, the concentrated use of artillery by Brigadier Chaudhry (according to a fire plan developed by his Brigade Major Aleem Afridi[28]), and the troops of 24 Brigade under Brigadier Abdul Ali Malik, was to save Sialkot from the Indian onslaught. But it was a close call.

The CGS at GHQ in Rawalpindi, General Sher Bahadur, was reported by General Gul Hassan to have wanted to distribute the artillery in pockets throughout the front. That would have dissipated its effectiveness. The director artillery at GHQ, Brigadier Reilly, and Brigadier Amjad Chaudhry persuaded Gul Hassan not to follow this advice. At the field command level, the hesitancy and panicked responses of the acting GOC 15 Division coupled with the reported suggestion of Brigadier Hisham El-Effendi (who had been posted by GHQ as an advisor to General Husain) to withdraw the 6 Armoured Division from Chawinda could have doomed Pakistan's defences.[29] It was evident that Pakistan's senior commanders had been elevated too rapidly to senior levels, without adequate preparation in strategy or even tactics involving large formations. The little training they had dealt with historical campaigns and the Second World War—on a scale that did not fit the canvas of either India or Pakistan. The 1965 war was more of a slug fest between two equally matched amateur boxers.

SAVING LAHORE

Despite the removal of mines and other defensive measures on the Lahore border with India, the fact that Pakistani troops had been deployed there as recently as April 1965 gave them an edge over their Indian counterparts in this sector; they knew the terrain and did not need to rely on maps alone. It was also evident to them that they did not have any defensive depth and that from the northern segment of this sector all the way to the southern end of the BRB canal, there was open land between the advancing Indian forces and key Pakistani towns and cities, including, of course, Lahore, the heart of the Pakistani Punjab. In other words, there was no way for the Pakistani troops to fall back and regroup. Therefore, they had to make a stand at the canal.

The Pakistani troops were given little advance warning from the GHQ. Even on the night of 5/6 September, when 10 Division asked the MO Directorate for permission to move troops to the border, the reply they got from the duty officer was: 'The Foreign Office will not give clearance.'[30] The DMO, Gul Hassan, left it to the discretion of the divisional commander to move his forces. General Gul Hassan's *Memoirs*, while noting the undue influence of the Foreign Office on military planning, does not shed light on the role played by his own MO directorate during those indecisive days. Rather, he blames the CGS and the army chief for their lack of firm decision-making. As a result of this situation at GHQ, when Indian forces crossed the international border on 6 September, none of the bridges over the BRB canal—the first and only line of defence in the Lahore sector—had been prepared for demolition. The engineers had been given orders to start preparing the bridges for demolition on 4/5 September but with twenty bridges to prepare, it was a tall order. They were told this task had to be completed by 8 September. Events overtook them.

Indian troops, using their surprise and momentum of attack, swept through the frontline defences at the border and headed straight for the bridge over the BRB between Dograi and Batapur in the early hours of 6 September. They managed to get troops to the canal and into Batapur. But then, facing intense Pakistani attacks and artillery and tank fire, they withdrew, fearing being cut off. By 11:30 hours, the Pakistani engineers began the job of trying to blow up the bridge, having lost their explosives in a jeep that had been hit by Indian artillery. Major Malik Aftab Ahmad Khan took over the job of improvising with 300 anti-tank mines. By 01:00 on 7 September, they had the bridge set up and then blew it up. Despite intense pressure, India did not manage to establish a bridgehead across the canal and indeed suffered some losses as Pakistani forces counter-attacked. In one encounter, General Mohinder Singh found the CO 15 Dogra battalion running into his headquarters, shoeless, with only one sock on. The CO reported that his troops had been overrun by Pakistani tanks. Mohinder Singh took to the GT road and indeed found the battalion in full retreat toward Amritsar. It turned out that one Pakistani tank had blundered into their position. 'When the tank commander discovered his mistake, he turned his tank away and shouted aloud to the Dogra personnel in the area '*Bhag jao, nahin to tumare upar tank ka bara attack ho jaega!*' (Run away otherwise you will be attacked by a large force of tanks!).'[31] Clearly, the fog of war was having its effect on both sides. India maintained its pressure on this sector, and by the third week of September, she made plans to attack entrenched Pakistani troops at Dograi on the east bank of the BRB canal. In one of the fiercest encounters of the war, they engaged in a bitter street battle and managed to capture the Dograi village, in the process also taking prisoner Lt. Col. G.F. Golwala, the CO of the celebrated 16 Punjab Regiment (formerly 40 Pathans). However, most of Golwala's soldiers made it safely across the BRB canal.[32] India claimed a huge victory at the Battle of Dograi. Pakistan marked it as the Battle for Jallo Mor. However one chooses to phrase it, the Indian move toward Lahore was blunted.

Further south, India ran into fierce resistance at the local level in the Burki area, where well constructed Pakistani pillboxes, resembling the rectangular mud thatched homes that characterize the local landscape, allowed Pakistani defenders to hold on to their positions. Again, at the lower level of command, heavily outnumbered Pakistani troops gave a good display of their valour and training. In perhaps one of the more memorable battles, Major Raja Aziz Bhatti remained with his company under intense Indian attack for days, often standing to get a better view with which to direct fire, before being hit by an artillery shell. He was given the country's highest gallantry award, the Nishan-e-Haider.

This Burki sector was under the purview of the 11 Division of the Pakistan Army under Major General Abdul Hamid and the 1st Armoured Division under Major General Nasir Ahmed (who, like Abrar Husain of 6 Armoured

Division, was an infantry officer). According to Shaukat Riza, Hamid had been designated as 'sort of' corps commander, who was supposed to coordinate the actions of the 1st Armoured Division, but in fact there was little collaboration between the two formations. 11 Division's original mission was to defend Kasur 'as a pivot and destroy en[emy] adv[ance] on Area Ferozepur–Kasur and Khem Karan.'[33] Further, it was to capture the Pakistani side of Hussainiwala bridge and headworks over the Sutlej River, and destroy the Indian forces crossing into the division's area. It was also supposed 'to secure the general line Rajoke 813735-Junc[tion] Rd-Kasur Branch 916740-Bahadur Nagar 939630 with a view to facilitating ops [operations] of Corps SF South.'[34] This was later amended to include the possibility that 1 Armoured Division would launch an offensive operation in conjunction with 11 Division. In that case, the 5 Armoured Brigade of 11 Division would revert to 1st Armoured Division. In effect, 11 Division would provide support for a planned Pakistani right hook into Indian territory in the Sutlej–Beas Corridor which would allow Pakistan a free run in the area behind Amritsar, and as one Indian general put it, a clear road to Delhi. This plan was one that India had anticipated, although Indian defences did not hold in its initial phase.

By 7 September, India had attacked Bedian and was held off during the night. By 08:00 hours, Pakistan had constructed a bridge of the Rohi Nullah [gully] and started its build-up for a move forward in a counter attack led by its tanks, supported by infantry. According to the Pakistani 11 Division official war records, by 11:00 hours, the 'GOC discovered', after meeting the commander of 5 Armoured Brigade and the CO 6 Lancers, that approximately two squadrons of tanks with a motorized battalion had made it across the Rohi Nullah. He then ordered 'an immediate raid on Khem Karan [an Indian railway station]' under the command of the CO 6 Lancers. The raid was successful. Later that day, the operational orders were issued, including three components: a 'breakout' by 5 Armoured Brigade on the Khem-Karan-Bhikkiwind and Khem Karan-Valtoha axes, 21 Brigade with 5 Frontier Force Regiment to move into the bridgehead after last light, and the 1st Armoured Division to build up into the bridgehead and get ready for a 'final breakout.' On the signal from Pakistan Army GHQ, 1st Armoured Division was to break out from the area secured by 11 Division in the direction of Chabal Kalan–Taran Taran and Atari–Amritsar. Pakistan was to try to exploit the lay of the land, following the natural grain of the flat lands that were broken by occasional streams or gullies which ran north to south east, creating lane-like paths between them for movement of troops and armour.

The counter-attack was launched on the morning of 8 September, a little delayed 'on account of administrative preparations.' By 11:00 hours, Khem Karan was captured by the 5 Armoured Brigade with help from the 5 Frontier Force (FF) Regiment. The 24 Cavalry ran up against entrenched Indian positions at Chima, while the 6 Lancers captured Valtoha. But, having moved well ahead of their infantry support, both regiments returned to leaguer (also *Laager*, as in the Boer Afrikaans term for a circle of wagons, used by the army for a safe area to rest and regroup for further action) in Khem Karan. According to the official diary of the 11 Division, the CO of the 24 Cavalry found himself way ahead of his artillery supporting fire and asked the brigade headquarters for infantry support to hold the ground that he had captured. No infantry was available, however, so he returned to square one, giving India a chance to regroup. The next morning, the brigade commander 'was not easily traceable [for] five precious hours, delaying the issuance of orders for that day. The advance re-commenced that afternoon, and by last light had reached a point between Bhura Khana and Asal Uttar, where it leaguered for the night. Pakistani armour went on the attack on 10 September with a view to capturing Chima, using Asal Uttar as a firm base, but 24 Cavalry lost contact with 5 Armoured Brigade until 10:00 hours when they were told that they would have to coordinate their actions themselves with 6 Lancers and 11 FF Regiment. A fierce tank battle ensued in which they claimed nine Indian tanks (no Pakistani losses were recorded in the war diary). India's 4 Mountain Division had meanwhile occupied defensive positions at Asal Uttar and flooded the area south-east of Valtoha from the waters of the local canal, an obstacle that was supplemented by minefields.[35]

Earlier, on 9 September, Pakistani armour made an 'abortive attempt to bypass the defended sector via the Southern flank but most of the tanks got bogged down in the flooded area and were destroyed at leisure,' according to Harbaksh Singh.[36] The main battle that was later to be known as the Battle of Asal Uttar in India commenced at 07:00 hours on 10 September, with Pakistani armour attempting a flanking move this time on the northern flank of the Indian positions. But they fell into an Indian trap where the Indian 3rd Cavalry took advantage of the heavy sugarcane crops to hide, and opened up on the Pakistani armour when they came broadside with devastating results on the attackers. A wider Pakistani flanking move met with similar deadly results, as the heavy Pattons of the Pakistan Army got bogged down and became sitting ducks for Indian tank gunners and artillery.[37] Many tanks were abandoned by their crews with their engines running. The CO of Pakistan's 4th Cavalry Regiment, twelve officers and several other ranks (soldiers) were captured on the morning of 11 September. India claimed to have destroyed some seventy-five Pakistani tanks, while losing only one Centurion and four Sherman tanks in the Battle of Assal Uttar.[38] India was to take seventy of these tanks to erect a battle monument at Bhikkiwind that was to be called Patton Nagar, or the city of Patton tanks. The GOC of the Pakistani 1st Armoured Division attempted to see things for himself at the front and was hit by artillery fire that wounded him and killed the artillery commander, Brigadier

Ahsan Shami, whose body was left on the battlefield and later given a proper burial on the field by Indian forces, with military honours. (His body was later returned to Pakistan after the war and re-interred by his comrades at home.[39])

Thus ended the planned Pakistani counterpunch into the Khem Karan area and beyond it into the heart of the Indian Punjab. Khem Karan was captured but no notable further progress was made. It showed both the strengths and weaknesses of the Pakistan Army in action. Writing about the use of armour by Pakistan, Indian Major General Rajendra Nath stated that 'the way Pakistan used its armour to assault our defended areas came as a great surprise for us, for we had never used our armour in peace time exercises or in war in such a bold and audacious manner.'[40] Light Pakistani tanks would probe Indian defences and then peel off for the flanks to draw Indian tanks and artillery fire, while the main armour attack would commence through the middle. 'The tanks would assault with six to eight abreast....followed by the infantry.' An alternative approach would have the Pakistani tanks coming up in the same formation and then stopping short of and outside the range of Indian anti-tank guns. Having drawn the defenders' attention, other Pakistani tanks would then outflank the Indian positions. But Pakistan persisted with these tactics in both day and night fighting, even though they had the advantage over India in that they possessed infra-red devices that India did not have at that time. And they continued to use the same tactics even when they came up against well defended positions that did not yield. This led to heavy losses, as Pakistani armour kept hitting the same target instead of bypassing it and reaching the Indian rear. In the Battle of Asal Uttar, Pakistan made five night time assaults that came up against a tough Indian defence, manned by 18 Rajputana Rifles, 4 Grenadiers, 1/9 Gorkha Rifles, and 9 J&K Rifles. But in the end the bold plan failed because of poor execution and internal weaknesses that were identified by Pakistani analysts after the event.

General Gul Hassan holds poor leadership of the 1st Armoured Division responsible for the ultimate failure of the attack beyond Khem Karan. According to him, General Nasir stated that he had told General Musa that he was not ready to command an armoured division. Yet he continued in command during the war. He inducted most of the 4th Armoured Brigade into the bridgehead across the Rohi Nullah, creating a congested situation. The first attack beyond Khem Karan could not be sustained as the armour did not have supporting infantry and had to return to base each night. Then, when this brigade was launched on 10 September to bypass Chima, its leading elements ran out of fuel after a few miles![41] This poor planning and leadership was symptomatic of much of the higher command of the army and its responsibility lay with the army chief and his senior commanders, since they had selected and appointed the formation commanders.

Within that first week of the war, both India and Pakistan had made their biggest gains and sustained their major losses. But the results seemed preordained, even to distant eyes. In a telephone conversation between Secretary of Defense McNamara and President Johnson, McNamara acknowledged rather surprisingly that US intelligence was 'really not very good' but 'what little information that I have indicates to me that the Paks are ahead at this point.' McNamara continued: 'And my own impression of the relative military strengths of the two countries is that the Paks could continue to achieve military advantage for a period of, I'd guess off-hand four weeks. And then at the end of that period I would think that the total strength of the Indians in terms of men and equipment, which is roughly four times that of the Paks, would begin to be felt. And then by the end of say 12 weeks, if the conflict continues that long, I would expect the Indians to reverse the trends.'[42] McNamara was generally on target in his assessment but he overestimated the abilities of the local generals to continue the struggle. After the first week, the fighting was localized and without any serious results, and the politicians scrambled for a way out while the international community tried to engineer a ceasefire.

Ayub Khan, the political and military leader of the country was obviously aware of the longer-term effects of the war on his rule. By selecting Musa as his army chief he had found a compliant but professional soldier, not the bold leader that could eventually eclipse Ayub himself. By allowing Bhutto and Akhtar Malik to plan his opening gambit of the war in Chamb, Ayub had abdicated his own responsibility. Yet, when it had a remote chance of succeeding, he withdrew support from that effort to protect the Punjab. Overall, his approach lacked audacity. He played it safe and played Pakistan into a military and political stalemate that could have become a defeat had the war gone on much longer.

A couple of days before the eventual end of the war, Ayub and Bhutto made a secret dash on the night of 19/20 September to Beijing to meet Premier Chou En-lai and Marshal Chen Yi, the Chinese defence minister, and seek their support. They assured him that they would keep the pressure on India but, said Chou, 'You must keep fighting even if you have to withdraw to the hills.'[43] This prolonged war was a foreign concept to Ayub, who had thought India would crumble under a couple of quick blows. He came back tired and depressed, and especially so after he met his army and air chiefs, Musa and Nur Khan respectively, who counselled against prolonging the conflict.[44] His despondency was evident to his own cabinet ministers, one of whom, Shoaib, dutifully reported to the US ambassador during the war on 19 September, that Ayub was 'disenchanted with Bhutto's reckless adventurism, grieved at Pak losses, strongly averse to entering Chicom association and open to a sensible compromise way out.'[45]

On the Indian side, Prime Minister Shastri had asked his army chief, General Chaudhri, 'whether India could win a spectacular victory if the war was prolonged for some days. The general replied that most of India's frontline ammunition had been used up and there had been considerable tank losses also.'[46] In fact, India had barely used 14 per cent of its frontline ammunition by 22 September, and India had twice the number of tanks that Pakistan had![47] Pakistan, meanwhile, had run down its ammunition reserves and lost equipment that it would find hard to replace, given the immediate US embargo on both India and Pakistan at the commencement of hostilities. In the end, the overall defensiveness on the part of both Indian and Pakistani military leaders produced a stalemate that ended with the ceasefire on 23 September 1965.

It was a costly war. Pakistan had spent Rs 7.6 billion (or US$1.6 billion at the prevailing fixed exchange rate of US$1=Rs 4.76) on its defence establishment since the military take over in 1958, averaging close to 53 per cent of total government expenditure in the period 1958–65. Pakistan claimed to have captured territory ranging from 210 square miles (according to Indian sources) to 1,617 square miles (according to Pakistani sources). India's matching claims were 740 square miles (by its own estimate) to 446 square miles (Pakistan's estimate). Pakistan claimed to have lost 1,033 men while Indian claimed 1,333 killed in action.[48] Both sides claimed victory. In fact, both had failed in their military objectives and the immediate effort was to put the best face on a difficult situation.

Ayub's speech to the nation accepting the ceasefire of 22 September produced a new coinage in Urdu for the term ceasefire. Rather than the normal '*Jang bandi*' or cessation of war, a new phrase was invented for him and inserted into the speech by Altaf Gauhar (who credits Zulfiqar Ali Bokhari of Radio Pakistan for this coinage). This was '*Fire bandi*', a pidgin Urdu term made up of the English word Fire and the Urdu word for 'cessation', which was meant to convey that only the firing had stopped but the 'war' continued!

Once the armies had stopped fighting, pressure built up on both India and Pakistan from their allies to work out a longer-term agreement with each other. The US, having failed to step into the fray on Pakistan's side, under the Pakistani interpretation of US commitments to Pakistan, had lost its credibility with Pakistan. Moreover, the embargo on US arms to both India and Pakistan announced by Secretary of State Dean Rusk on 8 September, as always, hurt Pakistan much more than India, given India's larger domestic defence production base and access to Soviet weapons systems, a point eloquently made by Bhutto to the US ambassador in Pakistan on 10 September when he was told of the US embargo. Bhutto stated that 'Pak–US relations would never be the same again.'[49] In fact, as early as 15 July, the US Secretary of Defense had issued instructions to his colleagues: 'Without disclosing the decision to Paks or the Indians, defer until further notice approval of any portion of the FY66 programme of military assistance to those countries.'[50] This had been followed by the refusal of the US to pledge assistance for Pakistan at the aid to Pakistan consortium in July, which prompted the Ayub Khan speech that Pakistan seeks 'friends not masters', (later to be the title of his memoirs). What made matters worse was the fact that US had pledged aid for India, although it tried to rationalize that decision by stating that the aid was a prior commitment to India.[51] The situation between the US and Pakistan further deteriorated with Bhutto making anti-US statements to the press and in the National Assembly. The US, concerned that Pakistan would play tough on further use of US intelligence facilities in Pakistan, started looking for alternative sites in August, with President Johnson's approval.[52] It was also following the internal feuds within Ayub's cabinet, specifically one between Shoaib, the US's inside man, and Bhutto, increasingly at odds with the US position. In a meeting with the US ambassador, Shoaib reported that Bhutto had engineered the call to the United States to fulfil its pledges to Pakistan knowing that it would not be able to respond in a clear and conclusive manner. The war therefore offered the opportunity, in Bhutto's words (as reported by Shoaib), to 'silence once and for all the American party' in Pakistan's government circles.[53]

Iran and Turkey expressed solidarity with Pakistan and sent some arms and ammunition plus Iranian oil. China had an adversarial relationship with India. The only willing and acceptable intermediary left was the Soviet Union under Premier Alexei Kosygin. In the period leading up to the war, Kosygin actively tried to persuade both sides not to get into a conflict. In a letter on 17 September, he proposed that Ayub and Shastri meet in Tashkent in Soviet Central Asia or any other Soviet site, to find a way out of the conflict. Ayub initially demurred. Bhutto was sent to Moscow in late November and emerged from the meetings with an agreement to attend peace talks with India under Soviet sponsorship either at the end of 1965 or in early 1966. The venue would be Tashkent.

Ayub meanwhile readied himself for a visit to New York and then Washington at the tail end of a visit to London in December. His expectation was that Pakistan would be able to approach some kind of a solution of the Kashmir problem at Tashkent, the military option having failed. He did not have high hopes for his visit with President Johnson and Johnson did not disappoint him, making the obligatory references to US interest in preserving Pakistan's territorial integrity but no more. However, Johnson did pass on some unsolicited advice to Ayub about his Foreign Minister Bhutto. As he recounted in a conversation with former President Eisenhower the following year: 'I just said to him—now, Mr President, I know you rely on Bhutto like

I rely on Dean Rusk and like Eisenhower relied on Dulles, but you can't rely on him that way and I am not entering your internal affairs, but this man is damn dangerous as far as you are concerned and you are my friend and I can give you this warning and I know whereof I speak' *[remaining text not declassified].*[54] Ayub got little else that he could make use of during the visit to the United States. Clearly, Uncle Sam was no longer a close friend of Pakistan. He was now counting on the Soviets to pull his chestnuts out of the fire by bringing a face-saving accord with India.

TASHKENT ACCORD

Ayub and Shastri arrived in Tashkent on 3 January 1966 and began a series of meetings bilaterally and separately with their Soviet hosts, Premier Alexei Kosygin and Foreign Minister Andrei Gromyko. Shastri had come prepared to stonewall on Kashmir as a key dispute. On 5 January, however, Shastri conceded to Kosygin his willingness to revert to the status quo in Kashmir as of 5 August 1965. In effect this meant accepting the Ceasefire Line of 1949. Armed with this knowledge, Kosygin met Ayub to see what he would concede in the interest of reaching a settlement with India. But, according to Kosygin's aide Ambassador Zamiatin, Ayub, whom Kosygin found to be 'decent and gentlemanly,' spoke only in generalities, leaving the detailed discussions to Foreign Minister Bhutto. 'Gromyko found Bhutto a really obstructive person. In fact, Bhutto was a destroyer of all ideas.'[55] Bhutto used his knowledge of the English language to good effect, often arguing for small but to him critical changes and sometimes coming back to ask for changes in agreed texts. The bilateral exchanges between Ayub and Shastri were often in chaste Urdu but with a great deal of courtesy. Srivastava, Shastri's aide and later biographer, recalls one exchange at the end of one round of talks, when Ayub said to Shastri *'Kashmir ke mamle men kuchh aisa kar deejiye ki main bhi apne mulk men munh dekhane ke qabil rahoon [On the matter of Kashmir, please do something that would allow me to save face in my country]'* Shastri responded: *'Sadar sahib, main bahut muafi chaheta hoon ki is mamle men apki koi khidmat nehin kar sakta [Mr President, I beg forgiveness that on this issue I cannot be of any service to you].*[56]

By 9 January, after a series of hectic discussions, things seemed to have become bogged down. Shastri was confiding to Srivastava that 'Mr Bhutto does not want an agreement. But I think President Ayub wants peace....Mr Bhutto is driven by passion and anger. He is smarting with rage because of the failure of his grand design on Kashmir. He now wants to retrieve something at this conference and hence he has made Kashmir the pivotal issue. But I have the impression that President Ayub understands the ground realities and very possibly he will opt for peace.'[57] Shastri seemed to have discerned the internal feuds within the Pakistani delegation. Altaf Gauhar too noted the bitter exchanges between Aziz Ahmed and his own foreign minister, especially on the Soviet draft relating to the 'settlement of disputes through peaceful means without the application of force.' Aziz found it acceptable, but Bhutto wanted to remove 'without the application of force.'[58] Three days later, when the Tashkent accord had apparently been finalized by Ayub and Shastri, Bhutto called Gromyko to make some last minute changes to which Gromyko replied: 'No! No! No! Mr Bhutto, you are quite wrong. You had agreed to this and President Ayub himself agreed to this. You cannot go back on it now. It will be very bad, very bad. Please convey this to your president immediately.' A short while later Bhutto called again to withdraw his earlier request.[59] Following long and deep discussions on 9 January, the Tashkent accord was given final shape and was signed at a joint ceremony on 10 January 1966. Bhutto was later to allege that there were secret understandings reached by Ayub at Tashkent. Shastri's aide Srivastava does not hint at any such thing. Altaf Gauhar, who was there, unequivocally asserts: 'There were no secret protocols, appendices, or letters annexed to the Tashkent Declaration.'[60]

Later that night, in a sad epilogue to the exchanges between Shastri and Ayub, Shastri died of a heart attack in his bed. His last exchange with Ayub was marked by customary civility. *Khuda Hafiz (Good Bye* or *May God protect you)* said Ayub. Shastri responded with the same words and then added '*Achcha hi ho gya (It was all to the good)* to which Ayub responded: *Khuda achcha hi karega. (God will do only good).* That was around 9:45 p.m. Three hours later Shastri was dead. The next morning, a visibly saddened Ayub and grim-faced Kosygin helped lift his coffin as it was sent back to India for the last rites. Ayub returned to Pakistan but did not make a statement upon getting home. Bhutto began distancing himself from Ayub. Meanwhile, public agitation began against the Tashkent accord, fuelled by the public's sense of having being let down after having been fed positive news about the war effort. By 5 February, the Ayub–Bhutto split had taken final shape. According to Gauhar, Ayub told Bhutto in Larkana that day that he was going to relieve him of his post as foreign minister. But by then Bhutto had placed himself as a dissenter on Tashkent, and when he accompanied the Chinese President Liu Shao Chi to Lahore on 26 March, he was given a hero's reception. Inadvertently, Ayub had given Bhutto a stage to make his appearance. By that summer Bhutto was gone from the cabinet. Musa was gone from the post of army chief, replaced by Ayub's protégé Yahya Khan. But disillusionment with Ayub had set in throughout the country.

Once the euphoria produced by the official propaganda during the war had died down in Pakistan, people realized that Ayub Khan and the military leadership had failed the nation militarily. Although the lower ranks and younger officers showed remarkable courage, both in Pakistan and India, generalship was not of the highest calibre and the war was marked by indecision and timidity. Pakistan, which had been led to believe it had won the war, was feeling particularly let down and was looking for answers. Ayub himself was disheartened, reportedly stating in a cabinet meeting that 'I want it understood that never again will we risk 100 million Pakistanis for 5 million Kashmiris—never again.'[61] His own political base split. Within the army, the gap between the old guard of ill-equipped generals and the new battle-inoculated officers started to grow. An even more alarming gap appeared between East and West Pakistan, as the East Pakistanis, one thousand miles away felt that the West had forsaken them to a potential Indian attack. (The Indian ambassador to the US had, however, given the US president on 8 September a copy of Defence Minister Chavan's till then secret statement in parliament stating that India would not attack East Pakistan, something that was not shared by the US with its Pakistani allies.[62]) Musa's and Ayub's theory that East Pakistan's defence lay in West Pakistan meant that the army would remain heavily concentrated in the West and dominated by the Punjab and the NWFP. It would be logical for East Pakistanis to feel that they did not belong with Pakistan.

In April 1965, the commander of the garrison in East Pakistan, Major General Fazal Muqeem Khan, had written a top secret memorandum to his CGS, Major General Malik Sher Bahadur, bemoaning the inadequacy of the troops in East Pakistan.[63] He dwelt on the increase in Indian troops in the region and the 'shift' in the 'centre of gravity' to the north of East Pakistan after the 1962 Sino–Indian conflict. 'In terms of number and weapons, we have reached a stage where the present garrison may not be able to secure an effective military operation and may well be destroyed in detail,' warned Fazal Muqeem. He ended his message with a cautionary note about the political situation in East Pakistan:

> Politically, people here are getting more and more vocal about the defence of EAST PAKISTAN. The general trend of feelings is that this wing is not provided with adequate defence. There is an inherent danger in this thinking. My worry is that the people who are rightly or wrongly being taught to think that the defence of EAST PAKISTAN is inadequate, instead of proving a help, might easily, get demoralized and be a problem.[64]

He then went on to cite an editorial in the local newspaper *Pakistan Observer*, that the time for revision of the current Pakistani strategy had arrived.

After the end of the fighting in the West, Fazal Muqeem sent another assessment to the army chief, General Musa, repeating that the 'apprehensions of the people here about the inadequacy of their defence...The feeling is that if WEST PAKISTAN could be attacked without declaration of war, [the] same treachery could be repeated here.'[65]

Musa responded belatedly on 18 October, noting

> ...the difficulty about convincing some of the civilians in EAST PAKISTAN as to the adequacy of the defence of that wing. However, proof of the pudding is in the eating and the recent invasion of WEST PAKISTAN has left no doubt where INDIA wants to really settle the issue. No one can say what line of action INDIA would adopt in similar circumstances in the future and we have, of course, to be prepared for all eventualities.[66]

He then suggested strengthening the force in East Pakistan with paramilitary 'Ansars' (helpers) and 'Mujahids' (Islamic warriors, literally) and told Fazal Muqeem of the posting of ninety-one JCOs from the West for command of the paramilitary forces, plus the dispatch of two batteries (i.e. eight) of 3.7 inch guns with ammunition and personnel, and 10,000 rifles. A reconnaissance and support battalion that Fazal Muqeem had sought had been set up but was being used in the West. Musa also confirmed that the Pakistan Navy would send two patrol craft as soon as they were received from abroad. 'This is all we can do at present, but I assure you that the requirements of EAST PAKISTAN garrison are constantly in our mind,' he stated before signing off.[67] There appeared to be little that West Pakistan could or would do to secure East Pakistan's borders as well as those of the western wing of the country.

Unrest began to bubble in both wings of the country. Bhutto finally broke with Ayub Khan and formed a new party, the Pakistan Peoples' Party (PPP). This new party was initially dominated by committed socialists and other leftist intellectuals but also acquired a strong leavening of traditional feudal politicians, who felt that Ayub was on the decline and wanted to take advantage of the rising star of this new transnational leader. Bhutto came from Sindh but commanded a lot of public adulation in other provinces, especially the Punjab. For the youth attracted to his leftist rhetoric and nationalistic speeches, he symbolized a break from traditional politics. They flocked to his side, as did the urban intelligentsia. In East Pakistan, nationalist feelings were heightened by the announcement in January 1968 of the 'Agartala Conspiracy' that implicated local politicians, including Sheikh Mujibur Rahman of the Awami League, in a plot allegedly hatched with low ranking Bengali officers of the air force and Indian agents across the border in western Bengal at Agartala. The actual trial began in June that year. Mujib quickly displaced the traditional Maulana Bhashani as the voice of the people of Bengal. Suddenly, the Pakistan Muslim League had become redundant. The young satirist Khalid Hasan lamented in a newspaper column: 'PML! O! PML!' as he described his search in vain across the shattered political landscape for the once mighty and ubiquitous governmental party.

Ayub had taken the results of the war with India very hard. He had just become 61 years old but appeared physically older. He was never the same man again. On 29 January 1968, soldiers surrounded the President's House and cut off normal access to Ayub. Altaf Gauhar recounts that even Ayub's secretariat staff were not permitted to enter the President's House. Ayub had fallen ill, with reportedly 'viral pneumonia in the right lung, following a touch of flu.' But it was in fact a serious heart attack caused by a pulmonary embolism. Gauhar states that General Yahya had taken personal control of the situation. 'A coup d'etat had, in fact, taken place.'[68] Ayub managed to recover enough to begin a restricted routine of work. But more trouble lay ahead.

Ayub's advisors helped stoke the fires of resentment by proceeding with plans in 1968 to celebrate a 'Decade of Development' under his rule. A massive publicity campaign orchestrated by the Ministry of Information (that is disavowed by the then secretary of that ministry, Altaf Gauhar, who states that this was Ayub's own idea) was launched, extolling the successes of the Ayub government through the governmentally controlled media: radio, TV, and newspapers. While there was much to celebrate in the way of economic development, the gap between this propaganda and the reality further enflamed the opposition to Ayub. Frustrated youth, perhaps encouraged by the worldwide revolution of students, but definitely seeking redress of very local grievances, took to the streets in 1967 (among other things, to protest US support for Israel in the Arab–Israel War) and 1968. For them, the relatively young Bhutto represented the leader they had been waiting for. His emotional appeal and energy created a new wave of excitement on the traditionally moribund national political scene. His simple slogan of 'Roti, Kapra, aur Makan' (bread, clothing, and housing) appealed to the dispossessed masses, particularly in the western wing of the country. He promised to break the powerful business interest groups whose domination of the economic scene had been in the news.

Ayub's chief economist, a young Mahbub ul Haq, had picked up that theme in a speech in Karachi in 1968 that referred to the 22 leading families of the country controlling most of its industrial and private financial assets, based on research on the Karachi Stock Exchange done by his wife Khadija Haq.[69] Though somewhat flawed because it focused only on the wealthy Pakistanis who were represented on the stock exchange, this analysis captured the public's imagination and 'the 22 families' became a household term. Despite the heavy development expenditure and investment in infrastructure and the advent of the Green Revolution, Pakistan's relatively high economic growth (relative to other developing nations) had not produced any 'trickle down' of its benefits. Meanwhile, the Agartala Conspiracy Case lifted Sheikh Mujib to a new status as a major leader in East Pakistan. The opposition parties united under an umbrella organization and despite Ayub's efforts to meet and discuss with them potential solutions to the problems facing the country, the protests in the streets did not abate.

Perhaps the most telling indictment of Ayub's rule is provided by his own propaganda *meister*, Altaf Gauhar, whom Ayub had decorated with a high civil award on the same day that he recorded his farewell address to the nation:

> There was no recognition that the real cause was the public apprehension of one-man rule, the domination of the centre over the provinces, the inequitable allocation of resources between East and West Pakistan, the extension of bureaucratic control over every walk of life, and the denial of fundamental human rights and freedoms.[70]

By early 1969, protests and strikes spread throughout the country.[71] Yahya, the army chief, had begun to take note of the situation and feared contamination of the armed forces by the issues being raised in the streets. He was under pressure to impose martial law. But Ayub was still titular head of the country and the military. Politicians, sensing the impending change, started switching allegiances and supporting the idea of martial law. Ayub thought that talks with the political parties could resolve the situation. But Yahya had made up his mind. According to Altaf Gauhar, Yahya threatened to 'go to Peshawar [where he had a home] and sit at home while the country burns. I have to do my duty and I am not going to let anyone interfere with that.'[72] History appeared to be repeating itself. And it did. Communications between Ayub and Yahya broke down despite the best efforts of intermediaries, including Ayub's son, Gohar Ayub Khan, who met with Yahya at his home just down the road from the President's House. Yahya was opposed to allowing Ayub to hand over to the speaker of the National Assembly, according to Gohar Ayub.[73] He prevaricated in those days, sending a draft order for imposition of martial law to his corps commanders but then, facing a push back from some (according to one account, from the senior staff of the commander 4 Corps who opined to Gul Hassan that keeping Ayub *in situ* was not a good option), changed his mind and issued fresh orders for martial law that did not include Ayub.[74]

Finally, on 25 March 1969, after pressure from Yahya, who had come up to meet Ayub and receive from him a resignation letter and a set of instructions on how to deal with the situation (that he did not need nor pay attention to, as subsequent events revealed), Ayub decided to call it a day. He handed over the country in an extra-constitutional step to Yahya, the C-in-C of the Pakistan Army, rather than to the constitutional successor, speaker of the National Assembly, Abdul Jabbar Khan of East Pakistan. He recorded his farewell speech before a teary-eyed Yahya, according to Gauhar. Yahya recorded his own speech later in the day, in which he not only imposed martial law but also abrogated the constitution itself. Pakistan was back to square one in its quest for political stability.[75]

Ayub had failed to convert a military dictatorship to a democratic system, largely because he adopted a paternalistic system of governance rather than one that devolved powers and shared them with the provinces. He also learned the hard way, as did other reform-minded leaders that followed him, that any compromise of basic principles leads to the eventual collapse of governments. His land reform agenda, however ambitious, allowed the agricultural fiefdoms to continue. His industrial reforms allowed the creation of monopolies, sustained by privileged access to the Licence Raj that allowed government bureaucrats to exercise undue control over resources. And his policy of playing favourites with his generals allowed the army to be run by senior officers who failed it in war, both during Ayub's reign and later. While he himself was free of the taint of corruption, Ayub did have a soft spot for his children, and as his friend and early colleague General Burki noted, he did not like to hear any complaints about his children's activities. By condoning corruption and favouritism, he allowed the emergence of a new *rentier* class in Pakistan, including his own family members, inviting public criticism, as a result.[76] Yet, despite all his shortcomings, Ayub gave his people a certain sense of dignity and pride, and decades after his death on 20 April 1974, some of them still proudly carry his portraits on the backs of their trucks, while others wistfully refer to Ayub's period as the golden age of Pakistan. Zulfikar Ali Bhutto did not attend Ayub Khan's funeral. However, the Pakistan Army paid him full homage as did a spontaneous crowd that filled the Race Course Ground where his funeral prayers were arranged in Rawalpindi. Along with his bête noire and once protégé Bhutto, Ayub Khan remains a living part of Pakistan's collective memory.

NOTES

1. *USFR, 1964–1968, Volume XXV*, op. cit., telegram from Department of State to the Embassy in India. Washington, 3 September 1965, p. 348.
2. C.P. Srivastava, *Lal Bahadur Shastri: Prime Minister of India 1964–1966, A Life of Truth in Politics* (India: Oxford University Press, 1995), pp. 226–8.
3. Srivastava, *Lal Bahadur*, p. 228.
4. B.C. Chakravorty, *History of the Indo–Pak War, 1965* (India: History Division, Ministry of Defence, 1992), p. 141. This section relies on this volume.
5. Harbaksh Singh, *War Despatches: Indo–Pak Conflict 1965* (New Delhi: Lancer International, 1991), pp. 86–7.
6. Shaukat Riza, *The Pakistan Army War 1965* (Lahore: Wajidalis, 1984), pp. 133–4.
7. *The Hindu*, 4 September 1965, quoted by Altaf Gauhar, op. cit., p. 335.

8. Riza, *The Pakistan*, p. 191.
9. Lt. Gen. Gul Hassan Khan, *Memoirs* (Karachi: Oxford University Press, 1993), p. 189.
10. Riza, *The Pakistan*, p. 136.
11. *Men of Steel: 6 Armoured Division in the 1965 War: War Despatches of Major General Abrar Husain*, Army Education Publishing House, Army Education Directorate, GHQ, Rawalpindi, 2005, p. 205.
12. Younger brother of Akhtar Hussain Malik of 12 Division.
13. 'An account of operations of 24 Infantry Brigade groups in the battles of Phillaura-Gadgor and Chawinda: Indo–Pak War September 1965' by Brigadier Abdul Ali Malik. Unpublished papers from his memoirs. This section relies on this account of the Battle of Chawinda.
14. Dharam enclave was closer to Zafarwal, on the Pakistan side of the Ravi, a location where Malik fought the 1971 war as a division commander. The author served as a war correspondent with him during that period. In 1971 too, the Indian army slipped away from the enclave to their side of the Ravi River, without much resistance.
15. Chakravorty, *History*, p. 182.
16. Farouk Adam SJ, 'Lt. General Abdul Ali Malik—the Ali of Chawinda,' *The News*, Pakistan, 11 February 1992.
17. Harbaksh Singh, *War*, p. 131.
18. Mention must be made here of the tremendous gallantry of Colonel Nisar, the commander of 25 Cavalry, a newly raised regiment, and Major Muhammad Ahmad, originally from the Guides Cavalry, both of whom were to receive the Sitara-e-Juraat for their actions. Major Ahmad was badly burned but managed to knock out four Indian tanks. Interestingly, he returned to the same sector as commander of the 8 Armoured Brigade Group in the 1971 war in the Shakargarh salient, where things did not go too well for the Pakistani armour since he reportedly made some twenty-five plans for counter attacks on Indian forces without coordinating with other formations in the region, and suffered heavy losses of men and materiel. He retired as a brigadier.
19. Adam, 'Lt. General Abdul Ali Malik.'
20. Ibid.
21. Gohar Ayub Khan, *Glimpses into the Corridors of Power* (Karachi: Oxford University Press, 2007) p. 88.
22. 'On 22nd February 1942, occurred the much publicised event when Sam [Manekshaw] was wounded. The retreat through the Burma jungle ended abruptly for him on 22 February 1942, when seven bullets from a Japanese machine gun whipped through his body. The young captain who had just led two companies in the courageous capture of a vital hill was awarded the Military Cross. 'We made an immediate recommendation,' a senior officer explained, 'because you can't award a dead man the Military Cross.' http://www.rediff.com/news/2003/apr/03sam.htm Accessed on 10 August 2007.
23. A.A.K. Chaudhry, *September '65* (Lahore: Ferozsons Ltd., 1977), p. 75.
24. Col. Tarapore's personal tank named 'Fakhr-e-Hind' or Pride of India was captured and used by Pakistan for propaganda purposes.
25. Chakravorty, *History*, p. 217.
26. Ibid., p. 218.
27. Harbaksh Singh, *War*, p. 157. An equally critical examination of the failure of Pakistan's high command by a officer of the Pakistan Army who did not take part in the battle, is available in the *Defence Journal*, March 2001 in 'Battle of Chawinda: Comedy of Higher Command Errors' by Maj. (retd.) Agha Humayun Amin.
28. Information provided by Brig. F.B. Ali.
29. Brigadier Z.A. Khan, 'The Way it Was,' *Defence Journal*, April 1998, cited in Agha Humayun Amin, op. cit., footnote 89.
30. Riza, *The Pakistan*, p. 192.

31. Jogindar Singh, *Behind the Scene: An Analysis of India's Military Operations, 1947–1971* (New Delhi: Lancer International), p. 148.

32. 16 Punjab fought a fierce battle, using whatever arms and ammunition they could get their hands on. My cousin, Captain Nasir Nawaz Janjua, the adjutant of this battalion, left his headquarters and took part in the battle, at one point throwing away his American-made M-1 ('Because it used to get jammed,' he told me) and picking up a much better Indian (Belgian made) FN 7.62mm rifle with its NATO specifications and ammunition, at one point. Although wounded with a shot that grazed his left eyebrow and another that bounced off his elbow, and having received shrapnel in his chest just above the heart, he fought a rear guard action that allowed his soldiers to be evacuated across the canal, swimming across with some of them. (He had been a splendid sportsman at the Pakistan Military Academy, with the rare honour of having received colours in squash, hockey, boxing, and swimming). He was recommended for the Sitara-e-Jurat but received the Imtiazi Sanad (Mentioned in Despatches), mainly because his regiment had already been given too many awards, including one to the Bengali second-in-command who was hit by an artillery shell when he stepped outside his trench. (GHQ had asked that Bengali officers and soldiers be given gallantry awards to show that they were fighting equally hard for Pakistan.) He was evacuated to Rawalpindi's Combined Military Hospital and when we got the news, his mother's first words were: 'Did he get shot in the chest or the back?' When told that he had been wounded in the chest, she proudly proclaimed 'Thank God!'.

33. 'Chronology of Events, 11 Div,' Pakistan Army GHQ Archives.

34. Ibid.

35. Harbaksh Singh, *War*, p. 103.

36. Ibid., p. 107.

37. Among the intrepid Indian defenders was a Muslim Havildar (Sergeant) named Abdul Hamid who used his recoilless rifle to knock out three Pakistani Patton tanks and was honoured posthumously with his country's highest military award, the Param Vir Chakra.

38. Ibid., p. 109.

39. Brigadier Shami was hailed as one of the heroes of the Pakistan Army during the 1965 war and awarded the Hilal-e-Jurat. His son, Sikandar later joined the Pakistan Army, was commissioned from the Royal Military Academy at Sandhurst, and joined the 5 Punjab Regiment. He was the personal secretary (PSC) to my brother General Asif Nawaz, COAS (1991–93) and then to my brother's successor, General Abdul Waheed.

40. 'Indian XI Corps and Battle of Assal Uttar (1965)' by Major General Rajendra Nath, www. orbat.com.

41. Gul Hassan Khan, *Memoirs*, pp. 207–208.

42. Telephone conversation between President Johnson and Secretary of Defense McNamara, 12 September 1965, 9:26 a.m. Tape F65.02, Side B. PNO 1. Cited in *USFR Volume XXV*, pp. 391–392.

43. China had issued an ultimatum to India to remove some structures from the border region in the north-east that India took as an ultimatum of war. A curious sidelight to this incident was the arrival in India of CBS News foreign correspondent Dan Rather from his newly minted slot at the London Bureau to cover the war. Having failed to get his crew close to the action on the frontier with West Pakistan, he was feeling frustrated in New Delhi. Upon receipt of the news of the Chinese threat, against the advice of his local Indian guide, he picked up and left with his crew for the north-east, where he waited in vain for the war to break out. Meanwhile the main action continued on the Indo–Pakistan border. By the time he realized his error and finished exploring the border in search of the Chinese troops, the war was over! See Dan Rather with Mickey Herkowitz, *The Camera Does not Blink*' (New York: William Morrow and Company, 1977), pp. 182–193.

44. Altaf Gauhar, *Ayub Khan: Pakistan's First Military Ruler* (Lahore: Sang-e-Meel Publications, 1993), pp. 351–3.

45. Report of a private meeting between US ambassador to Pakistan and Finance Minister Shoaib 'at home of a mutual Pakistani friend…escaping restrictions on calls at government offices, where in Shoaib's words, 'semi-police state atmosphere now prevails'. In a Telegram from the Embassy Office in Pakistan to Department of State, Rawalpindi, 19 September 1965. *USFR Volume XXV*, p. 411.

46. Hasan-Askari Rizvi, *The Military & Politics in Pakistan 1947–86* (Lahore: Progressive Publishers Ltd., 1987).

47. Chakravorty, *History*, p. 334.

48. Hasan-Askari Rizvi, *The Military*, pp. 124–27.

49. *USFR Volume XXV*, p. 385. Telegram from the embassy office in Pakistan to the Department of State, Rawalpindi, 10 September 1965.

50. Telegram from the Office of the Secretary of Defense to the Commanders-in-Chief, Middle East, South Asia, and Africa South of the Sahara (Adams), Washington, 15 July 1965.

51. Report of a conversation between President Johnson and Secretary of State Rusk. *USFR1964-1968, Volume XXV*, pp. 321–2.

52. Op. cit., National Security Action Memorandum No. 337, Washington, 10 August 1965.

53. National archives and Records administration, RG 59, Central Files 1964–66. POL INDIA-PAK. Cited in *USFR, 1964-1968. Volume XXV*, p. 369.

54. President Johnson discussed Bhutto's resignation with Eisenhower on 4 November 1967. Johnson Library, Recordings and Transcripts, Tape 67.14, Side B, PNO 40. Cited in *USFR Volume XXV*, p. 519.

55. Srivastava, *Lal Bahadur*, p. 365.

56. Ibid., p. 367. Original Urdu transliteration by Srivastava. Translation by author.

57. Ibid., p. 379.

58. Gauhar, *Ayub Khan*, p. 385.

59. Srivastava, *Lal Bahadur*, p. 380.

60. Gauhar, *Ayub Khan*, p. 388.

61. Quoted by Shoaib to Walt Rostow in Washington on 27 April 1966 at 7 p.m. *USFR*, op. cit., p. 627.

62. Memorandum of Record of US President Johnson's meeting with Indian Ambassador B.K. Nehru, 9 September 1965, op. cit., p. 373.

63. Top Secret, note from GOC Major General Fazal Muqeem Khan, HQ 14 Division, Dacca Cantonment, 17 April 1965 to CGS, General Headquarters, Pakistan Army, Rawalpindi. Pakistan Army GHQ Archives.

64. Top Secret note from GOC Major General Fazal Muqeem Khan, 17 April 1965.

65. Top Secret, demi official letter from GOC 14 Division, Major General Fazal Muqeem Khan to C-in-C, Pakistan Army. DO no GOC/Sit/1, 7 October 1965. Pakistan Army GHQ Archives.

66. Top Secret, Demi Official Letter from GOC 14 Division, Major General Fazal Muqeem Khan, 7 October 1965.

67. Top Secret Letter 4037/21/MO2/CinC, 18 October 1965 from General Musa to Major General Fazal Muqeem Khan, GOC 14 Division, Dacca, East Pakistan. Pakistan Army GHQ Archives.

68. Gauhar, *Ayub Khan*, pp. 413–15.

69. An excerpt from a piece written by Mahbub ul Haq, as published in the London *Times* on 22 March 1973 may shed some light on the situation at that time and persisting into later decades: 'While the world was still applauding Pakistan as a model of development—the outside donors always need some "success" stories for their own comfort—we were getting quite concerned that all was not well with the distribution of the benefits of growth.' Haq had been an architect of the Ayubian growth strategy. Indeed his own book *The Economic Strategy for Growth* was seen as a primer for that task. I am grateful to Khadija Haq for this background text.

70. Gauhar, *Ayub Khan*, p. 435.
71. I was at that time a producer for Pakistan TV in a co-production with Czech TV of four documentaries on different aspects of life in Pakistan (including, interestingly a real live wedding of Abida Hussain, daughter of the celebrated Colonel Abid Hussain of Shah Jewana). Our work and travels across the country began in late 1968 in the NWFP and ended in March 1969 in East Pakistan while the National Assembly was meeting under a state of siege in Dacca (now Dhaka). Curfews and protests were evident in nearly every town that we visited.
72. Gauhar, *Ayub Khan*, pp. 473–4.
73. Gohar Ayub Khan, *Glimpses into the Corridors of Power*, p. 112.
74. Background account by the GSO-1 of 4 Corps Brig. Ijaz (Tony) Mahmood, as conveyed to Brig. F.B. Ali.
75. Ayub Khan retired to his own, comfortable but modest (by current Pakistani standards), home that he had built on a promontory overlooking what was once called Embassy Row in Islamabad. His parent regiment, 5 Punjab, gave him an orderly (who incidentally had also been my brother's orderly at one time). He led a simple life but a lonely one as few of his former friends came to see him. Because of old family relations, my brother Asif and I used to visit him regularly and it was always poignant to see this once all powerful, tall and handsome man weighted down with the enormity of his own political downfall. In conversations, he continued to puzzle over what went wrong and why the people whom he so dearly loved failed to trust him. He continued to read regularly and maintained a diary, except for the period of the 1965 war, during which he said he had no time to pen down his thoughts. Today his house is no more. His children sold it to Sadruddin Hashwani, a prominent businessman, who demolished the old structure and replaced it with a re-aligned grand villa. His son, Gohar Ayub Khan, went into politics and became foreign minister and speaker of the National Assembly. Gohar Ayub could not run for office in the 2002 elections because of the graduation requirements imposed by the current government. His son, Omar, became a member of the National Assembly and minister of state for finance.
76. Ayub Khan may have been aware, for example, that the first Aga Khan scholarships for studies abroad that were offered to Pakistan were given to his son Tahir Ayub Khan, Hassan Musa Khan, and Idris Anwar (the son of an army general and a close friend and class mate of Tahir Ayub). Tahir went to Cambridge but returned to Rawalpindi after six months, with an Aston Martin (James Bond's car) that he subsequently smashed into a bullock cart at night on the Murree Road between Islamabad and Rawalpindi! The other two did not complete their studies either under these scholarships.

11 UNTIED PAKISTAN: HOW TO BREAK UP A COUNTRY

Twenty-two years after East and West Pakistan were united under one flag to form one country, the army began the moves that would eventually break that union and divide Pakistan into two separate countries. Within two days of the celebration of Pakistan Day—the day when the Muslims of India first asked for a separate homeland on 23 March 1940, and then in 1956, when Pakistan became a republic—the country came under martial law once again. This time again it was a Guardian Coup, except that the military establishment simply removed its own head, Field Marshal/Supreme Commander Ayub Khan, and replaced him with Yahya, the army chief. Yahya became CMLA on 25 March and assumed the presidency on 31 March 1969. By the time the new martial law regime handed over power to the civilian government (but still under martial law), of Zulfikar Ali Bhutto in 1971, the military had lost a war with India and the East Wing had become independent Bangladesh with the aid of Indian force. Ineptitude in both civil and military operations allowed regional differences to bubble out of control, while wishful military thinking and the faulty judgment of its core leadership group, clouded by blissful ignorance and liberal doses of alcohol, produced a national debacle. The regime ended up believing its own propaganda, creating a vicious circle through which its own disinformation further strengthened its faulty premises for decision-making. The army itself had changed much over the years, becoming top heavy and corrupt at the upper echelons as a result of over-involvement in civilian affairs and martial law duties. This adversely affected its training, thought processes, and actions. The result was military defeat and political dissolution.

In Yahya's first speech to the nation, he, like Iskander Mirza and Ayub, gave his reasons for the coup and outlined its objectives:

> My sole aim in imposing martial law is to protect life, liberty and the property of the people and put the administration back on the rails....I wish to make absolutely clear that I have no ambition other than the creation of conditions conducive to the establishment of a constitutional government....[as] a prerequisite for sane and constructive political life and for the smooth transfer of power to the representatives of the people, elected freely and impartially on the basis of adult franchise.[1]

Within a month, he was telling a gathering of his fellow Baluch Regiment officers at their regimental centre in Abbottabad that 'we must be prepared to rule this unfortunate country for the next 14 years or so. I simply can't throw the country to the wolves.'[2]

Yahya had been present at the launch of the first martial law of Ayub Khan, but as a supporting actor. Now, he was centre stage and brought with him his own cast of generals and other favourites. His right-hand man was his army buddy Lt. Gen. Abdul Hamid Khan, a man who stood by him through thick and thin and did not oppose him on any major action. But the manipulator of political ideas was Lt. Gen. S.G.M.M. Peerzada, whom Yahya named principal staff officer (PSO) to the president and CMLA. Hamid, then the COS of the Pakistan Army (later promoted to full general), and the air chief, Air Marshal Nur Khan and naval chief, Admiral S.M. Ahsan were named deputy MLAs. The latter two were subsequently sent off to be governors of West Pakistan and East Pakistan respectively (reportedly over their objections), leaving Yahya surrounded by his army clique to which he added his own former boss at the GHQ, retired Major General Sher Ali Khan Pataudi. Sher Ali was named minister for information and national affairs, a key post which he used to influence the turn of political events by directing the officially controlled media and other arms of the government to support the Islamic parties. (In fact, Sher Ali coined and popularized the term 'Islam *pasand*—pro-Islam.) Yahya then moved to install junior commanders to the posts of air and naval chiefs, knowing that they would be no threat to him. The activist Nur Khan, as governor West Pakistan, tried to introduce major reforms in education and other social sectors on the basis of advice from his youthful 'whiz kids'. He was to lose his post within the year when One Unit was abolished and West Pakistan reverted to its constituent provinces, a victim of his own overarching ambition and conflict with bureaucracy. As usual, a gaggle of eager constitutional experts gathered around Yahya to provide advice and to facilitate the changing of laws to provide a legal fig leaf for the new administration.

The actual process of imposing martial law was not difficult. Yahya and his colleagues basically copied from the Ayub playbook, dusting off earlier martial law regulations and announcements and issuing them, with minor recasting, before a country that wanted respite from the upheavals of civil unrest. To provide legal cover, a PCO was issued that would allow the country to operate under the 1962 constitution until a new constitution was drafted, but fundamental rights were suspended and martial law was given both supremacy and protection against challenge in any legal forum in the country. With the politicians sidelined again, the military–civil combine took charge of the country. True to form, the martial law government went after troublemakers and allegedly corrupt officials, issuing a list of 303 senior civil servants who were charged with various crimes and misdemeanours, and were asked to come before military courts to clear their names, if they chose to do so. Notable among those was Altaf Gauhar, who had only recently been given a high civil award by Ayub. Although the list was later expanded to 311 persons, the three-naught-three appellation stuck since it was a well-known brand name in Pakistan, being the bore of the celebrated Lee-Enfield rifle of the military for many decades. However, this action had little effect on the condition of ordinary people.

On another front, the new regime moved to control the growing power of the labour unions. The government formulated a new labour policy under the guidance of Nur Khan, the retired air chief and later governor of West Pakistan. Following Ayub's example, the new team dusted off the report of the Services Reorganization Committee and attempted to implement its findings that had been languishing on the shelves. (The civil bureaucracy stymied this effort over time.) As usual, these rapid actions and the appearance of martial law were greeted by the coterie of government-sponsored journalists who inhabited the upper echelons of the media bureaucracy, specifically *The Pakistan Times* and other papers of the National Press Trust. Among them, Z.A. Suleri was among the better known names, a man who managed to find salvation in military rule and served as a vocal supporter of such regimes. As Yahya's chief public relations person, Colonel (later brigadier) A.R. Siddiqi (head of the ISPR Directorate) observed about Suleri: 'Not only did he justify the resort to martial law, but he also lent it a depth and dimension beyond the dreams of the junta.'[3]

Yahya's frankness and his forthright manner were disarming at first. But gradually it reflected his lack of preparedness for the job at hand. Unlike Ayub, he had not come into power after having thought long and hard about the future of the country or its political system. The son of a police officer, whose Qizilbash family had migrated from Afghanistan, Yahya was born in Chakwal, (Jhelum district in the Punjab), and although fluent in Farsi, spoke a sweet Punjabi. After a stellar early military career, with decorated service during the Second World War and a rapid rise in rank after Pakistan came into being, he reached the rank of brigadier at the age of 34. He had commanded three infantry divisions (including one in East Pakistan) as a major general and served in the GHQ as VCGS, CGS, and later deputy C-in-C under Musa, before becoming C-in-C in September 1966. He relied on his inner circle for guidance and took decisions rapidly—or delegated them to Peerzada, who gradually became his *Eminence Grise* and de facto prime minister, or to Major General Ghulam Umar. Rather than drawing senior civil servants into his inner circle, Yahya relied on his trusted military staff to handle matters for him, with two brigadiers, reporting to Peerzada, who decided on issues that senior civil servants brought to their attention. Rarely did the president see these civilians.[4] But the decision making was marked by a paucity of paperwork, analysis, and thought, and, as colleagues observed, the decisions were impulsive and sometimes contradictory. Yahya would often tell his audiences: 'I am a soldier,' as if to absolve himself of responsibility for the wider role that he had assumed or as an excuse for his political missteps. While he may have been ambitious, he did not wish to be seen as such.

The Pakistan Army of 1969 was different from that of 1958. It had started metamorphosing from a colonial, detached, and politically distant force to an immediate post-colonial army that was involved deeply in the running of its country's government, while retaining the social characteristics of the colonial army. It retained many of the trappings and traditions of the earlier force that emerged out of the British Indian Army. Army messes still served alcohol and celebrated dinner nights with bagpipes and dinner jackets. An officer class largely from the Punjab and NWFP commanded troops from the countryside of these two most populous provinces. Most of the officer class still retained some connection with its rural roots but was increasingly settling down in the cities and cantonments. The official business of the army continued to be conducted in English, although officers spoke to soldiers in the basic, imperious, and staccato Urdu of their former British predecessors. A leavening of refugee Muslim officers and some East Pakistanis had started giving the force something of a transnational air. But Ayub's martial law had made the senior commanders more aware of politics and national issues. Further, the Warrant of Precedence that Pakistan (and India) had inherited from the British, designating the order of rank of civil and military officers had been upturned in favour of the military under both the Ayub and Yahya regimes. The 1962 constitution had sanctioned the supremacy of the military by designating that for the next twenty years, the minister of defence would be a military person. At partition, and until Ayub became defence minister, the military chiefs all reported to the secretary of the Ministry of Defence. Indeed, a powerful position was that of the financial adviser, defence at army headquarters, who handled the purse strings for the military. As I.A. Sherwani, one of the last of these powerful civilians explained, the army gradually took over more and more of the decision making, reducing the financial adviser to a rubber stamp role.[5] Now, military officers and service chiefs had a higher rank than their civilian counterparts. In East Pakistan, the division commander ranked next to the governor. Of course, during martial law, the deputy MLA was supreme in each province.

There was also a qualitative difference between the commanders in 1969 and those in 1958. Unlike Ayub's neophyte colleagues, all Yahya's commanders had spent twenty years or more in service and had benefited from training both at home and abroad. They had seen action in 1965 and were better trained and equipped to deal with strategic issues than their earlier counterparts, although vestiges of their formative tactical training under the British left many of them unable to think in broader terms. Promotions to senior ranks, although subject to strict procedures, were sometimes circumvented by the army chief/president to favour regimental, military arm (armour, infantry, artillery etc), ethnic, or tribal ('biradari') ties. But there was generally little overt complaint, given the greater opportunities that emerged for senior military officers to acquire assets and influence national decision making under martial law.

CULTURE OF ENTITLEMENT

Ayub had begun the practice of awarding land in the newly irrigated colonies of Sindh and the border regions of the Punjab to army officers. Military awards also came with land grants. The growth of military cantonments also provided opportunities for military officers to get heavily subsidized plots on easy instalment plans that could, if needed, be sold at a huge mark-up in the open market. Initially, officers could only get one plot or land grant. Later, as regional division and corps commanders acquired the right to autonomously allocate plots in cantonments in their jurisdictions through defence housing societies, the practice of multiple plots was to become common, giving rise to a new 'Culture of Entitlement' that permeated both the military and civil bureaucracies and that would become embedded in Pakistani society. A common practice also emerged, from which the higher ranks of the military were not immune: a heavily subsidized plot would be acquired and a loan generated from a bank or contractor who would then sign an agreement to rent the completed home with an advance payment of rent even before it was complete, thus providing the officer the funds to get the house built. All the paperwork was legal and above board. Sometimes the prospective 'renter' would even supervise the construction of the home. Gradually, the mores of the military changed to make all such 'sweetheart' deals acceptable.[6] According to associates of General Yahya and the Hamoodur Rehman Commission Report,[7] Yahya's own home in the tony Harley Street area of Rawalpindi that he was later to retire to, was built under a similar agreement with a local bank whose executive head was one of his political advisers, making it 'standard' practice.[8] Yahya presents a different picture in his affidavit before the Lahore High Court of 1 June 1978 in which he states that this home at 61 Harley Street was his 'only property' in addition to the two squares of land that the government gave him near the Kasur border when he was awarded the Hilal-i-Jurat. 'The house at Rawalpindi was built by borrowing loans from the banks,' he states.[9]

The military also set up and operated the Fauji Foundation and the Army Welfare Trust, ostensibly to provide for the soldiers and pensioners. But these institutions gradually acquired a life of their own, with forays into virtually all sectors of the economy, competing against the private sector and crowding out other investments as a result of their privileged access to scarce official resources, (often available to them at subsidized rates). No matter that the senior officers who were sent to manage these enterprises had little or no managerial experience, especially in business matters. These and other state-run military enterprises started proliferating in the post-Ayub period, providing sinecures and lucrative post-retirement employment for senior military officers. In effect, the military was acquiring a corporate identity that contrasted with its public statements of a higher purpose and its condemnation of corrupt civilian rulers. To strengthen its hold over the civil society, the army had begun the policy (under Ayub) of inducting young officers into the civil services.[10] Martial law offered even greater opportunities, with around 300 military officers occupying key administrative or judicial positions.[11] Despite the best efforts of successive army chiefs, the emergence of these types of distractions were to have a detrimental effect on the officer class of the Pakistan Army, drawing it away from its main occupation and expertise and fostering a greater tendency to think that it was better equipped to handle civilian and business enterprises than its civilian counterparts.

Once he was firmly in command, Yahya tried to act swiftly on all fronts, while preparing for a new political structure in the country. On 28 November 1969, Yahya announced a detailed plan for the holding of elections to both the national and provincial assemblies in October 1970, and for the tasking of the elected representatives to come up with a draft constitution. He also dissolved One Unit and re-established four provinces in West Pakistan, while creating the idea of parity between East and West Pakistan. Additionally, he promised to re-allow political activities from 1 January 1970. He followed up with a Legal Framework Order (LFO) on 31 March 1970 that made Pakistan the 'Islamic Republic of Pakistan', and allowed, among other things, maximum provincial autonomy while allowing the centre to preserve the independence and territorial integrity of the country. At the same time, Yahya retained for the president the ultimate power to accept, amend, or reject a constitution presented to him by the assembly.

When all was said and done, the mandarins advising Yahya and his army circle of support did not wish to give up their controlling hand in the political process. They attempted to pre-empt the political issues that had forced Ayub to depart in a hurry. But, as in the case of Ayub (and later dictators), their planning was based on self-crafted political frameworks and schemes that had not benefited from public debate or discussion or the input of the major political parties in both wings of the country.

Each party tried to see a silver lining in these plans and began positioning itself for the fray. The martial law regime was unable to address or neutralize the basic issues that bedevilled Pakistani politics, chief among them the issue of disparity in the economic well being and resource allocation of the two wings. This had taken centre stage with the issuance of the fourth five-year development plan under the overall direction of M.M. Ahmad, a much respected civil servant. East Pakistani economists at the Planning Commission and politicians challenged the government's plans, including the prospect of long-term resource allocation being carried out by the temporary martial law regime.

UNDERLYING ISSUES

Yahya's regime had inherited a number of major unresolved issues from Ayub's eleven-year rule. These included the growing economic and political disparity and discord between East and West Pakistan. Despite the 6.5 average annual growth rate of the country as a whole, East Pakistanis felt they had been used as a colony by their West Pakistani rulers who had drained their lands of natural resources (e.g. Jute,) and foreign exchange earned by Jute exports while attracting foreign investment and aid for West Pakistan alone. This average growth rate also hid grave disparities between the haves and have-nots in both wings of the country. Ayub's paternalistic and patrimonial style of rule was not the benevolent dictatorship that he and his friends in the West often portrayed it to be. During his period, the instruments of state control in the shape of the ISI and the civilian IB grew in stature and power. Dissent was curbed, often with a heavy hand. Political opponents were often dispatched to the infamous torture chambers of the Lahore fort. News media were subject to direct and indirect controls which provided a blueprint for subsequent governments. Newsprint was controlled by the government and allocated according to the whims of the Ministry of Information. Government advertising, the primary source of income for many publications, was doled out to friendly or captive media. State controlled television and radio functioned primarily as public relations arms of the government, with no coverage of opposition activities. The first of a series of press and publications ordinances had been introduced by Ayub and his information maestros—first Qudratullah Shahab and then Altaf Gauhar—as an instrument of control which remained in force in one form or another for decades.

The creation of One Unit in West Pakistan had created a false sense of unity in the province. It failed to hide the important differences and needs of the constituent provinces, particularly the important needs of the impoverished parts of Balochistan, Sindh, and the NWFP. The disproportionately large province of Punjab dominated political discourse and use of central government resources. Dissent in the marcher provinces was often countered with either bribery or coercion. The Baluch particularly felt aggrieved and were met with a heavy hand. East Pakistanis were more vocal in their complaints, both within their own province and latterly in the corridors of the central government. Sartaj Aziz, an economist at the Planning Commission, recalls participating in various exercises to assuage Bengali economists at the commission, but without much success.[12] As early as October 1961, Ayub Khan had recognized the grievances of East Pakistani economists by setting up a ten-member commission that delivered its report in January 1962. Even that report was riven with dissent, reflected in not one but three final reports: the chairman's, the West Pakistan representatives', and that of the representatives of East Pakistan! The East Pakistani economists sought to allocate resources not only on the basis of population, knowing East Pakistan's majority, but also weighted by the inverse ratio of per capita income, an indicator in which East Pakistan lagged West Pakistan.[13] In effect they proposed affirmative action to make up for past inequities. Ayub responded by bifurcating major state enterprises such as the Water and Power Development Authority (WAPDA), the Pakistan Industrial Development Corporation (PIDC), and the Pakistan Railway Board, and giving them to each of the two provinces. Public sector expenditures were increased for East Pakistan, leading to parity by 1963–4 but the disparity in per capita income remained.

GROWTH DISPARITY

The 1965 war had cost the country dearly, not only in terms of battlefield losses but also in economic terms. Economic growth stumbled badly as external assistance declined by 25 per cent and defence expenditures soared to make up for the loss of equipment and weapons during the conflict.[14] East Pakistan suffered heavily during this period, with annual average growth declining to 4 per cent during the period 1965–6 to 1969–70. West Pakistan's growth rose to 6.4, well above the planned target under the third five-year plan of the country, with a heavier share of development resources and greater private investment (some 75 per cent) in the West wing. This further exacerbated the differences in the economies of the two wings. Added to the investment in West Pakistan was the heavy expenditure on the Indus Basin Works, following the treaty signed with India to share the waters of the rivers that originated in Indian-held Kashmir but flowed largely through West Pakistan. This expenditure was kept outside the normal plan targets but was evident to the East Pakistani economists working in the Planning Commission. Moreover, the high visibility of these massive infrastructure projects in West Pakistan highlighted the differences in such investments between West and East Pakistan. The result of these trends was a deepening disparity in per capita incomes, with the income gap between the West and East wing widening from 36.4 per cent in 1964–5 to 45.6 per cent in 1969–70.[15] In the military too there were stark differences in representation of East and West Pakistanis, with the latter outnumbering their Eastern counterparts 894 to 14 in the officer ranks of the army in 1955. By 1963, despite efforts to increase the representation of East Pakistanis, the latter had risen to only 5 per cent of total army officers.[16]

The execution of the 1965 war, a recent memory, also showed the real and imagined distance of East Pakistan from West Pakistan, as the military high command relied on war in the West as a means of defending East Pakistan against India. East Pakistanis felt vulnerable and forgotten as a result. Even western commanders of troops in East Pakistan had to struggle to convince their superiors at the GHQ in Rawalpindi of the need to make better preparations for the defence of the Eastern Wing. Attempts to raise East Bengal Regiments were begun but were clearly incapable of making up for the huge gaps between East Pakistani and West Pakistani soldiers or officers. With its substantial Hindu minority and different culture, more akin to West Bengal than West Pakistan, the East Pakistani demand for equal economic opportunity and greater provincial autonomy was painted by the central government of Ayub as a dangerous trend that would lead to the subjugation of East Pakistan by Hindu West Bengal. Supporters of these demands were seen as suspect in terms of patriotism and loyalty to united Pakistan, especially by those in the military (in West Pakistan). This turned out to be a self-fulfilling prophecy.

Politically, the unhappiness and upheavals that led to Ayub's dismissal could not be papered over by martial law. A change of rulers was not enough. East Pakistan was increasingly coalescing under the banner of the Awami League under Mujibur Rahman, who had once been a junior office holder but now had supplanted Maulana Bhashani as the leading political figure of the province. The Pakistan Muslim League, a construct of the Ayub government, was in tatters, an orphan looking for a new master. In the West, the Pakistan Peoples' Party (PPP) of Zulfikar Ali Bhutto, an upstart political party, had caught the imagination of the youth and the opportunistic politicians of the traditional parties (including the Muslim League!), with its broad-based appeal of welfare economics and a nod to religion under the banner of Islamic socialism. The National Awami Party of the NWFP and Balochistan remained a potent provincial force. (Its ties with its East Pakistani namesake under Maulana Bhashani were somewhat tenuous though). The Muslim League was adrift. The Islamic parties, particularly the Jamaat-i-Islami and the Jamiat Ulema-e-Islam, saw their opportunity to grab more attention and power. As mentioned above, they received assistance from Sher Ali Khan Pataudi who found an ally in Major General Ghulam Umar, the newly promoted executive head of the NSC.[17]

Presiding over this simmering discontent, the army under Yahya was not equipped to handle the subtleties of political discourse. Trained to fight external enemies, principally India, the military had a hard time comprehending the complexities of civilian unrest within Pakistan. Its response was often too swift and too harsh, defining opposition to the government as 'treason.' It saw the hidden hand of India in all the troubles in East Pakistan and relied on its military force to quell disturbances, thus fuelling further discord.

A key issue that remained unresolved was the West's response to the articulation of East Pakistani demands that were put forward in the form of the Six Points of Sheikh Mujib as early as 1966. It called, among other things, for a federal constitution that was more of a confederation than a federation, with the centre only responsible for defence and external affairs, separate currencies for East and West Pakistan, autonomy in taxation and the use of tax revenues, the autonomous use of foreign exchange earned by East Pakistan itself, and a separate East Pakistani militia. While these grievances and demands had been made in one form or another as early as the 1950s, Ayub and then Yahya met them with a heavy hand, defining them as treasonous and inspired by India.

EAST PAKISTAN GETS UPPER HAND

Yahya, once in power, began to implement what he conceived to be basic reforms in the political system: doing away with One Unit, and restoring one man-one vote to the electorate. In that process, perhaps unwittingly, he gave East Pakistan a majority in the national electoral rolls. His LFO of 28 November 1969 presented what he considered to be a consensus document that also provided rules for holding elections and subsequently framing a new constitution. On the basis of the populations of the two wings, East Pakistan would have 169 seats in the new National Assembly, compared with 144 for West Pakistan (the latter including FATA along the Afghanistan border). The National Assembly would have 120 days to frame a new constitution. The issue of provincial autonomy was finessed with doublespeak through some guiding principles, with the provinces promised 'maximum autonomy' while the centre would have 'adequate powers' in the administrative and legislative areas. In effect, the definition of 'adequate' was being kept as a prerogative of the centre. Further, the approval of the constitution was left largely in the hands of the president with the National Assembly working under double jeopardy rules: if it failed to come up with a constitution within 120 days it would be dissolved; and if the president did not approve the constitution, the assembly would again be dissolved.

Elections were set for October 1970, and the jockeying among the political parties began. Yahya's cabinet would receive regular briefings on the election campaigns from the head of the IB. But, as his Bengali political adviser G.W. Choudhry recalled, these briefings were often followed by private, more detailed briefings to Yahya's inner cabinet. The ISI had also entered the realm of political analysis, deputing low level officers in each district and division to take the political temperature and report back. Wherever possible, they were encouraged by Sher Ali Khan to help the Islamic parties. But the lack of political knowledge and experience of these operatives continued to hamper their ability to report accurately to headquarters. Jamshed Burki, a civil servant in Sargodha, recalled during that period how the ISI major in his area kept telling him that the PPP had almost no traction in the division. Burki, meanwhile, had come to the conclusion that the PPP would sweep that area. But the GHQ and the President's House somehow never got the message from the grassroots. Wishful thinking continued to dominate political discourse and analysis in Rawalpindi.

With the media taking advantage of the amateurish command and control system of the regime to report on political events and relatively unhindered political rallies of all parties, the parties with the most trenchant messages managed to get their voices heard by the masses. In East Pakistan, Mujib's Awami League and in the West, Bhutto's PPP found resonance in the hearts and minds of the population, especially the dispossessed rural populations, who thronged to their rallies. These parties were helped by the fact that the government did not anticipate their eventual success, otherwise it might have taken steps to change the outcome of the elections. The government had nothing to counter the powerful message of the Six Points in the East and 'Roti, Kapra, aur Makan' (food, clothing, and housing) in the West. Symbolism too played its part. Zulfikar Ali Bhutto chose the sword as his party symbol (with most voters barely literate, pictures on ballots helped them decide on who to vote for). He relied on associating his own given name, Zulfikar, with the name given to the double-headed scimitar of Hazrat Ali, the Prophet's son-in-law and one of the most celebrated warriors of early Islam. Most villagers when asked who they were supporting did not reply 'the People's Party.' Instead they just said, 'Talwar (the sword).'[18] No wonder then that people thronged to Bhutto's rallies in every part of the country. One of his early supporters, Nasrullah Khattak, a Pathan public works contractor with business in Jhelum district, recalled an adulatory crowd clambering over the Bhutto motorcade as it headed over the Jhelum bridge into Serai Alamgir, bringing the emotional Bhutto to tears. Bhutto's magnetism and charisma was getting him the votes that others would have to pay for in hard currency. Arnold Zeitlin, the Associated Press bureau chief, recalled a tribal elder lamenting in the NWFP against universal suffrage: 'If they are all to vote, it will be difficult to pay them all!'[19]

In the East, Mujib was seeing similar reactions to his nationalism for the Bengali cause, provoking his famously repeated statement to various Western media: 'My peoples loves me and I loves my peoples (sic)!' His student wing had trounced the traditional Islamic parties in the university elections in the spring of 1970. With more than half the population of East Pakistan under 40 years of age, the youth had a greater affinity for Bengali nationalism than the Islamic ties that bound them to West Pakistan or the fear of Hindu India that kept their elders exercised. Mujib, however, kept his ties to West Pakistani business interests alive. He had close relations with G.A. Adamjee, the owner of the largest Jute mills in the province and for whose insurance company he had once worked. He also had good relations with the influential Haroon family of Karachi, who were, among other things, owners of *Dawn*, the major English daily newspaper.

PREPARING FOR ELECTIONS

As the jockeying continued for electoral advantage, the military intelligence estimates gave the Awami League no more than 46–70 seats out of 167 seats in East Pakistan, and gave the PPP no more than 20–30 seats out of the 144 allotted to the West. Relying on these estimates, the regime counted on a divided parliament that would be managed by the ruling junta with ease. A secret GHQ assessment of the run-up to the elections characterized the Awami League campaign for Six Points as thus:

> Its modus operandi...stemmed from a callous and deep rooted conspiracy to create regional hatred. The Party's propaganda machinery was geared in that direction only and it must be admitted became a rallying cry....The Six Points envisaged a weak centre and ultimately a weak Pakistan. Therefore, Indian Government seized [t]his chance to exploit the situation to her advantage. The Indian propaganda media began voicing the grievances of the 'oppressed' people of 'Bangla Desh'. Their propaganda organs actively infiltrated (sic) in East Pakistan. The local Hindu community came in the forefront in support of Bangal (sic) language and Six Points....Six Points became a movement, actively guided by foreign governments.[20]

The reference to 'foreign governments' in the plural encompassed the US ambassador, who was reported to have 'met Sheikh [Mujib] on several occasions. He reportedly assured the latter of US economic aid for large scale development of East Pakistan, in the event of secession.'[21]

Even the politicians underestimated the relative strengths of the Awami League and the PPP. Mian Mumtaz Daultana's Convention Muslim League turned down an offer of twenty-nine uncontested seats in East Pakistan from Mujib in exchange for collaboration after the elections. The Bengali expert in the regime, G.W. Choudhry also underestimated the potential of the Awami League, telling the Pakistan Society of London in September 1970: '...there is no question of East Pakistan members forming one single group in confrontation—if that comes, then it means the state comes to an end, and we are quite optimistic that this will never happen.'[22] He was right on one count: the state coming to an end, and wrong on the other: that it would never happen.

There were other forces at work. Rains in East Pakistan in the summer months of 1970 created massive flooding and brought Yahya to East Pakistan, showing the flag and his concern. The flood led Yahya to postpone the October 1970 elections to 7 December. But the worst blow was yet to come. At night, on 13 November, a huge cyclone accompanied by tidal waves swept up the Bay of Bengal and hit the unprotected underbelly of East Pakistan. Over 200,000 people lost their lives and millions were rendered homeless. Mujib feared that Yahya would further postpone the elections. But the Yahya regime was to give Mujib an important electoral weapon.

Yahya dropped into Dacca (now Dhaka) on his way back from China. Apparently flushed with drink from his long flight, he mumbled his way through a statement at the airport, interrupting it at one point to point to a quivering Bengali who was holding a microphone up to his face to say in Urdu: 'Who are you? You are nobody!'[23] A junior civil servant recalled him saying at the end; 'Good speech that! Whoever wrote it!' He flew over the flooded area and left giving Mujib an opportunity to deem the regime callous. Questions arose about another postponement of elections, given the destruction caused by the cyclone. But Yahya stuck to his guns and announced that elections would be held on schedule, confident that he would preside over a hung parliament and fashion a pliable civilian government, while retaining presidential powers.

ELECTION SHOCK

The elections to the National Assembly on 7 December produced an even bigger cyclone in both wings of the country. Millions of hitherto disenfranchised persons, a vast majority of them youth who had never before exercised their right to vote, turned out to cast their ballot and upended the ossified political structures of the past. Party organizers did not even have to provide transport or other inducements, as the people of Pakistan voted freely for the first time in their collective memory. Pakistan Television scheduled non-stop twenty-nine hours of coverage for the National Assembly elections and seventeen hours for the provincial assemblies on 17 December, with anchors sitting in front of a huge electoral scoreboard, reporting the results live, without fear or favour.[24] PTV's own reporters in each district got the latest running totals and sent them to a central desk that then posted them without filters in front of the audiences that were virtually glued to their TV sets. For the first time, Pakistanis were being told exactly what was happening at the ballot boxes around the country, without any governmental control. The results shook the regime.

The Awami League of Sheikh Mujib swept East Pakistan, garnering 161 out of 163 open National Assembly seats in East Pakistan. The Awami League also won seven seats that were reserved for women on the basis of East Pakistan's majority, and got nine more in January when delayed elections were held in the areas devastated by the cyclone. The Awami League won no seats in West Pakistan, where Bhutto's PPP swept an unexpected majority with 81 seats that later grew to 88, with the acquisition of women's seats and independents who joined him—but a majority in the West was not enough to provide an effective deterrent to Sheikh Mujib's absolute majority in the National Assembly. Bhutto's strongholds were Sindh and Punjab. The PPP had not contested any seats in the East. The result was a clear political divide that provided heartburn to the regime and left it scrambling to somehow retrieve the situation. Ayub's much vaunted Muslim League was nowhere in sight, neither were the other older parties. Only the most powerful feudals were able to salvage their seats. The traditional powerhouses of Pakistani politics were swept out of the way by newcomers, fuelled by fierce nationalism in East Pakistan and a mélange of socialism and youthful contrarian politics in the West. Two weeks later, the provincial elections on 17 December produced very similar results. The regime was astounded by the results, having been misled by its own intelligence reports.

At the army headquarters, Gul Hassan took in the results and started looking ahead. 'Let's back Bhutto!' he proclaimed to A.R. Siddiqi, the military's PR chief. Siddiqi felt that this statement was based on Gul Hassan's calculation that Bhutto had got most of his support from the Punjab, the main recruitment ground of the army, and that Bhutto would not do anything to hurt the military, but Mujib may well downsize the forces.[25]

Mujib and the Awami League initially celebrated their success with considerable restraint but then held a massive rally on 3 January at the Paltan Maidan (ironically named Regiment Ground) in Dacca, where the party members took an oath to support the principles on which they had run for election. Bhutto meanwhile positioned himself for two-party rule with two prime ministers. Caught in the middle, Yahya attempted to patch things up, flew to Dacca and even seemed to anoint Mujib by referring to him at the airport as the 'future Prime Minister' of Pakistan. But things seemed to be getting out of the military's control and it began thinking of other means of exercising control over the political process. Among other things, it began strengthening forces in East Pakistan. Yahya went to Larkana to meet Bhutto immediately after visiting Mujib in Dacca, and Bhutto impressed upon him the need to avoid giving control of the National Assembly, and hence the country, to Mujib. Bhutto ended up going to Dacca for an abortive round of talks with Mujib. The regime was facing a serious breakdown of the constitutional process.

Adding to its woes was an unexpected event, the hijacking of an Air India Fokker Friendship aircraft, the Ganga, by two alleged Kashmiri militants who flew it to Lahore and demanded the release of jailed Muslim militants in Indian Kashmir. Taking advantage of this situation, Bhutto went and met the hijackers, calling them heroes. When negotiations failed, the aircraft was set ablaze on 27 January, prompting India to ban the passage of Pakistani aircraft over India to East Pakistan.[26] This ban led to a long detour via Sri Lanka for future Pakistan International Airlines (PIA) and military flights to Dacca. The military was now truly scrambling, with Peerzada and Umar trying their best to resurrect the situation that was increasingly getting out of their control. Umar shuttled around the country trying to get the other parties to stay away from the assembly if the PPP chose not to attend.

Bhutto was not ready to sit in the opposition. On 15 February, Yahya set 3 March as the date for the meeting of the National Assembly in Dacca. Bhutto immediately sought more time. The senior brass of the regime was already thinking of a military solution in case the politicians did not follow their instructions. 'Generals like Hamid, Umar, Gul Hassan, and Peerzada, who seemed to be opposed to any real transfer of power were now planning for a Turkish-type of military–civilian (i.e. concealed) regime,' writes G.W. Choudhry, Yahya's Bengali advisor on constitutional matters.[27] By mid-February, the junta had decided to scrap the cabinet—replacing it with 'advisors'—and prepared to deal with the Awami League. Major General Rao Farman Ali, an advisor at the martial law headquarters in Dacca, came up with a plan to arrest Awami League leaders. This was discussed and approved at the governors' conference on 22 February. Interestingly, no one anticipated a mutiny by the East Pakistani soldiers and officers in the province. Bhutto seemed to be the man whom the generals favoured over Mujib. On 27 February, Bhutto addressed a rally in Mochi Gate, Lahore, demanding either extension of the 120 days needed to formulate a new constitution or postponement of the assembly. He threatened those who attended the assembly session with physical harm.

Mujib, meanwhile, was prepared to stand his ground. The deadlock persisted despite repeated attempts by Yahya to get an agreement on a postponement to gain time for a resolution, or failing that, for military action (which required a proper build up of forces in the East). Finally, on 1 March, hard on the heels of Bhutto's refusal to participate in the National Assembly session on 3 March, Yahya postponed the assembly *sine die,* citing as his reasons the refusal of Bhutto to attend the session, increased tension with India, and the need for more time to resolve the constitutional issues that were still open. In fact, Yahya did not personally make this key announcement.

Instead, I (Shuja Nawaz), then a newscaster for PTV in Rawalpindi-Islamabad, was asked to read his statement that evening in the first person, Yahya supposedly being unavailable to deliver the speech at that time![28] Having failed to broker an understanding between the regime and the Awami League, Admiral Ahsan, the governor of East Pakistan, resigned on the same day. Yahya did make a speech to the nation on 6 March, announcing this time that the assembly would meet in Dacca on the 25th but using it to attack the Awami League. 'I will not allow a handful of people to destroy the homeland of millions of innocent Pakistanis. It is the duty of the Pakistan Armed Forces to ensure the integrity, solidarity and security of Pakistan—a duty in which they have never failed,' Yahya thundered.

Yahya also cancelled a round table conference that had originally been planned for 10 March. Bhutto, meanwhile, hardened his stance. At a public meeting on 14 April 1971 in Nishtar Park, Karachi, he said that it was 'only fair that in East Pakistan, it [prime ministership] should go to the Awami League and in the West to the Pakistan Peoples' Party.' This speech was reported the next day in the Urdu newspaper *Azad* under the headline coined by its editor Abbas Athar: '*Uddhar tum, Iddhar hum*' (You stay there, we stay here), words that have been wrongly ascribed to Bhutto since that day.[29] Clearly, Bhutto's arguments and the hawkish views of his other close advisors had prevailed. Yahya also had a military plan in his back pocket that may have led him to take a firm position against the Awami League. This puts all his actions during the post-election period in a cynical light.

OPERATION BLITZ

Following a discussion between the DMO, Brigadier M.A. Majid, and commander eastern command and MLA of Zone B, Lt. Gen. Sahibzada Yaqub Khan,[30] a plan code named 'Operation Blitz' was evolved well before the December elections. An operation directive was signed and issued by Yaqub Khan on 11 December 1970, within four days of the National Assembly elections. The plan 'authorized the Commander Eastern Command to relieve the Governor of his duties and take control of the entire civil administration of the province. He [the former] was then to implement the plan to restore law and order...[and] was given complete freedom in exercise of his powers[...].'[31]

Brigadier Siddiqi recalls Yaqub stating words to the effect that 'we may have to give him [Mujib and his party men] a whiff of the grapeshot, should they refuse to behave and go berserk.'[32] Strong words indeed from a man who had cultivated an image in the army as a cultured, sensitive, and liberal individual, and who had begun learning Bengali upon taking command of troops in East Pakistan.[33] He had built a name as a thinking officer, and in the 1965 war gained a reputation as perhaps one of the few if not the only senior officer in the entire subcontinent at that time who really understood operational strategy, and went to the battlefield as an armour advisor to the corps commander, Lt. Gen. Bakhtiar Rana. He had come up with a bold and innovative strategy for the defence of the Sialkot front against India, using a 'scheme of manoeuvre' to launch an engulfing armour movement against the attacking Indian forces. He knew his military strategy backwards—at least on paper. (His 1965 plan was not fully followed by General Abrar, the armour division commander, because theory apparently did not stand up to the reality of the battlefield.)[34]

The top secret paper entitled 'Operation Blitz' that Yaqub issued on 11 December was available in only six numbered copies which were distributed to Major General Khadim Hussain Raja (GOC 14 Division), Major General Rao Farman Ali (in charge of civil administration), Brigadier S. Ali El-Edroos (COS Eastern Command), Lt. Gen. S.G.M.M. Peerzada (PSO to the President and CMLA), and Brigadier Majid (DMO). One copy was retained for Yaqub's own office.[35] The operation could only be put into effect on the 'recommendation from MLA Zone B', that is Yaqub Khan, after personal clearance of the CMLA, Yahya Khan, conveyed through the martial law headquarters. Operation Blitz would follow the declaration of an emergency in East Pakistan under the following conditions:

a. Open defiance of martial law and/or declaration of 'Independent Bengal', rejection of the Legal Framework Order ending up in a 'mass movement' similar to the sporadic outbreaks which shook the Province in the period January 69–March 69.
b. An anarchist movement sparked off by extremist Naxalite/Communists [Indian separatist movements] or even NAP [National Awami Party of Maulana Bhashani] and other groups of province-wide dimensions.
c. If frustrated in their designs, the majority party [Mujib's Awami League] may resort to a mass movement for enforcing their (sic) will outside the Assembly, to the jeopardy of the integrity of Pakistan.

The operation was meant to be put into effect only in the most 'grave situation when the normal law and order machinery had broken down, and the situation on a province-wide scale, is beyond the control of the civil administration, police, and EPR [East Pakistan Rifles, a paramilitary force].' Yaqub suggested that the operation be carried out with:

[…]the greatest vigour and determination to create an unmistakable impact and remove any doubts regarding the type of martial law which is being imposed in contra-distinction to the deliberately watered-down martial law to which people have become conditioned. **Shock action would therefore be imperative** [Emphasis added]…There should be no hesitation in using force for effect[…]This will save lives in the long run.

He then laid out the details of the operation, identifying who was to be detained and who would carry out the actions, using as a model the military operations at Dacca University for the arrest of political dissidents Manto and Saleem in July 1970. Interestingly, at that time, the EPR forces were seen to be loyal and a necessary part of the operation. The main operation was expected to be completed within 24 hours and everything would be kept under wraps. 'Complete censorship will be imposed,' stated Yaqub.[36]

But, within a matter of three months, Yaqub was to change his mind about the efficacy of this approach, citing the need for more time and more troops on the one hand, and reportedly stating that a political solution was the only way out on the other. When Ahsan resigned on 1 March, an embattled and isolated Yaqub followed suit four days later via telegram:

Only solution to present crisis is a purely political one. Only the President can take this far-reaching decision by reaching Dacca by March 6 which I have repeatedly recommended. I am convinced there is no military solution which can make sense in present situation. I am consequently unable to accept the responsibility for implementing a mission, namely military solution, which would mean civil war and large scale killings of unarmed civilians and would achieve no sane aim.[37]

An angry Yahya came close to court-martialling Yaqub for failing to obey orders. Despite this, Yahya did return Yaqub back to his substantive rank of major general. Word spread within the army that Yaqub had lost his nerve. This was further strengthened by the choice of Lt. Gen. Tikka Khan as Yaqub's replacement. Tikka, a Janjua Rajput from a village near Kahuta in Rawalpindi district, was seen as a commander who followed orders to the letter. He was a low key officer who was given the sobriquet of 'Butcher of Balochistan' for his vigorous prosecution of military action in 1958 against dissident tribesmen in that province fighting under the flag of Nawab Nowroz or Nowroz Khan (also known by Baluchs as Babu Nowroz), the head of the Zarakzai tribes of Balochistan.[38] Tikka's mind was reportedly unclouded by strategic thinking or complicated vocabulary. He was expected to get the job done in short order.[39] With both Ahsan and Yaqub out of the way, the regime had nobody to provide a counter balance to its chosen path of military action.

TALKS FAIL, OPERATION SEARCHLIGHT LAUNCHED

Both Yahya and Bhutto made more trips to the East to cajole Mujib into working with them. But each time Yahya appeared ready to recognize Mujib as the rightful prime minister, he was dissuaded by his colleagues who suspected that Mujib might use his majority in the assembly to legally secede from Pakistan, or worse, to reduce the army's power and influence. Meanwhile, the army began flying in new troops dressed as civilians on the circuitous PIA flights via Colombo. They came without equipment and weapons, but they were noticed by the locals. The political discourse spiralled downwards as the Awami League showed its muscle. Army officers were attacked or humiliated. Non-Bengali residents of East Pakistan found themselves under attack in sporadic incidents. Reports of such events began circulating, creating panic and fear among the West Pakistanis living in East Pakistan. Surprisingly, the army maintained its discipline in the face of insults and even the suspension of their food supplies by Bengali contractors. They became strangers in their own country. But nerves were wearing thin and anger was building up.

As Pakistan neared the celebration of its national day on 23 March, both Yahya and Bhutto were in Dacca. Discussions with Mujib fell apart. Mujib's forces raised the Bangladesh flag over most of East Pakistan, turning Pakistan Day into Resistance Day. The army had its plan. When talks broke down, they launched an operation under the code name 'Operation Searchlight' on the night of Thursday, 25 March. By 8:00 p.m., Mujib had got word that soldiers of EPR, at their station at Road Number 2 in Dhanmondi, (some two miles from Mujib's own home on Road Number 32,) had been disarmed by their largely West Pakistani commanders. He told Bengali journalists that he expected the army to move that night, citing the possibility of 'selective killing.' He said he would stay but suggested that other leaders of the Awami League take off.[40] By 10:00 p.m., Tajuddin had left, first to stay with friends and then to head for Calcutta (now Kolkata), India, where he was to become the prime minister of the government-in-exile of Bangladesh. Yahya took off that evening for West Pakistan, telling General Tikka Khan to 'sort them out,' and leaving Bhutto behind in his eleventh floor room of the Hotel Intercontinental.

The Pakistan Army had around 45,000 fighting soldiers in East Pakistan, including a brigade in Dacca under Brigadier Jahanzeb 'Bobby' Arbab, who was operating from the modern red brick second capital designed by celebrated US architect, Louis Kahn. Overnight, the army cracked down with full force, a group of Special Services Group (SSG) commandos capturing Mujib but allowing other leaders to slip away. The commandos destroyed the students' dormitories at Dacca University which had been used for housing militants who underwent training with mock weapons.[41] They were especially brutal in their attacks on newspapers offices and printing presses that had produced vitriolic articles against them in the preceding months. From his vantage point, Bhutto saw the military operation for about three hours:

> A number of places were ablaze and we saw the demolition of the office of the newspaper 'The People.' This local English daily had indulged in crude and unrestrained provocation against the Army and West Pakistan. With the horizon ablaze, my thoughts turned to the past and to the future. I wondered what was in store for us. Here, in front of my eyes, I saw the death and destruction of our own people.[42]

The army occupied all the key installations and took over the broadcast centres in Dacca. They failed to do so in Chittagong, the second major city, where the 8 East Bengal Regiment (EBR) rebelled under its second-in-command Major Ziaur Rehman, in the process killing its West Pakistani CO, Lt. Col. Rashid Janjua (my cousin).[43] Zia took over the radio station and broadcast messages over it for four days before a well-directed air attack destroyed the transmitter.[44] Similar uprisings took place all over the province, leading to fire fights and the eventual slipping away of the Bengali officers and soldiers to sanctuary in India. Foreign journalists in Dacca were bundled into trucks and taken to the airport to be sent away immediately, a key mistake that was to haunt the regime. Tikka ordered this action but the man who exercised tight control over the media, Roedad Khan, a civil servant, was a hawk among the information advisors of Yahya, having recently been promoted from his slot as managing director of PTV to secretary of Ministry of Information.[45] Most of these journalists ended up covering the ensuing events from India. Three of them, Michel Laurent, Simon Dring, and Arnold Zeitlin, remained behind in Dacca (whether on purpose or inadvertently; Zeitlin had been at dinner with Roedad Khan the night of the army action), and filed critical and graphic reports on the military action taking place. The propaganda war had been lost already.

Bhutto was evacuated the next day and on arrival in Karachi uttered his memorable words: 'By the Grace of God, Pakistan has been saved.'[46] He feared that if the regime had not acted the next day, the Awami League would have declared the independence of Bangladesh unilaterally. Even as late as September that year, when he published his account of this period, Bhutto supported army action although he differed in the details of the execution of the military's plan:

> The Army will have to act with alacrity but not with brutality. The rebels will have to be ferreted out individually. Mass destruction will not do. It will only aggravate the problem. Innocent people will get exposed to military action, thereby making them enemies and further military action necessary....The final solution must be

of a political nature. Military measures become meaningless unless they are part of an over-all political policy....East Pakistan must be satisfied if it is to be saved.[47]

Bhutto favoured a return to democratic government but he evaded discussing his own role in bringing the inter-wing dispute to a head (by precipitating the political crisis that culminated in military action). He was still hoping that the army would resolve the situation and give him a share of power at the centre.

The most scathing criticism of the army's action comes from an improbable source, the disaffected Lt. Gen. A.A.K. Niazi, who was promoted (over many officers) to lieutenant general by Yahya, and took over as commander East Pakistan from Tikka on 10 April, when the latter became governor and MLA. Niazi had served in the region during the Second World War and had commanded the 5 Punjab Regiment in Dacca in 1958. Writing in his memoirs many years after the event, he states that:

> General Tikka, instead of carrying out the task given to him, i.e., to disarm the Bengali units and persons and to take into custody the Bengali leaders, resorted to a scorched earth policy. His orders to his troops were: 'I want the land and (sic) not the people'....Major General Rao Farman [Ali] had written in his table diary, 'Green land of East Pakistan will be painted red.'[48]

These comments need to be put into the proper context, coming as they did so far after the event. Niazi, who had a reputation for strong arm tactics himself and, according to some officers who served with him, condoned if not encouraged the atrocities committed by the Pakistan Army under his command in East Pakistan, had much to cover up himself.

As is usual with a change in command, Niazi brought in new officers to replace Tikka's principal officers, sending (among others) Major General A.O. Mitha back to West Pakistan. Mitha, a former commando and commandant of the PMA, was a no-nonsense soldier who became part of Yahya's inner circle. He had sought additional troops for East Pakistan but the promised reinforcements had not been supplied by the time the army action began. Among the staff that Niazi collected around him was Brigadier Ghulam Jilani Khan, his COS in place of El-Edroos whom Niazi called a 'drawing room soldier'. (Jilani was later to become DG ISI and the man responsible, when he was governor of the Punjab, for suggesting that General Ziaul Haq induct a young businessman named Nawaz Sharif into his government). Niazi also took action against some officers for events related to the army action, including against Brigadier Arbab who, Niazi states, 'on the recommendation of Major General Rahim GOC 14 Division, was removed from command on charges of looting and theft. He was found guilty in the court of inquiry and sent back to West Pakistan to be court-martialed.'[49] (No action was taken against this officer, despite the Hamoodur Rehman Commission's own recommendation about this issue.)

The preparations that the Awami League had made seem to have paid off. Deserting troops of the EPR and the EBR, all trained and equipped soldiers, took charge of the countryside, offering stiff resistance to the Pakistan Army, which found itself operating in a hostile environment. Niazi writes:

> The Pakistan Army was fighting in and around cantonments and camps and these became their fortresses of power. Their only link with Dhaka [a later spelling of the name] and each other was by air. All other communications were cut, blocked, or out of commission. The rest of the country was under the control of the Mukti Bahini [the name taken by the rebel forces], whose morale was sky high and who had the initiative with them.[50]

Niazi's force of 45,000–34,000 army and the rest paramilitary—was ill-equipped, not being able to bring its heavy supporting equipment or tanks from the West. Only one squadron of aircraft at Dacca was present to provide air cover and support.

Niazi, who was proud of his sobriquet 'Tiger', chose to go on the offensive in a plan that involved troops racing toward the Indian border and taking over the major towns along the perimeter of East Pakistan, and then opening the communications system within the province—all this while trying to eliminate the peoples' army that he was now fighting under his eponymous opponent, Colonel M.A.G. 'Tiger' Osmany, who had taken over as chief of the Mukti Bahini. He states that he wished to take the battle to India in hot pursuit but lacked the troops and equipment.[51] Moreover, he states that General Abdul Hamid Khan forbade him from any such actions.

THE INDIAN PLAN

Had Niazi chosen to 'take the battle to India', India was not yet fully prepared for battle in the region. It had not been able to muster its regular forces around East Pakistan and would have to wait for the end of the monsoon. Indeed, from New Delhi, the army chief, General S.H.F.J. 'Sam' Manekshaw, conveyed to the COS of his eastern command, Lt. Gen. J.F.R. Jacob, the Indian Prime Minister Indira Gandhi's wish that the eastern command move quickly into East Pakistan. Jacob states that he refused because such a suggestion was 'impractical' and told Manekshaw the earliest he could begin operations would be 15 November, after the end of the monsoon.[52] Manekshaw told Mrs Gandhi that 'in East Pakistan when it rains, rivers become like oceans. If you stand on one side you can't see the other. I would be confined to the roads. The air force would not be able to support me, and the Pakistanis would thrash me.' Despite a request from Defence Minister Jagjivan Ram to accede to the prime minister's wishes, (*Sam, Maan bhi jao! [Sam, Do agree!]*), Manekshaw persisted in his view, citing the need to muster his troops into the region and their lack of preparedness.[53] This gave Niazi freedom to fight the 'miscreants,' as the Mukti Bahini were called by the Pakistani military. But India began providing logistical support and surreptitious manpower to the Mukti Bahini, helping set up training camps and penetrating Pakistani border defences for sabotage and subversion.

The 1st, 3rd, and 8th EBR, formerly of the Pakistan Army, now in Indian territory, were moved by Col. Osmany to the Meghalaya border areas, while the 2nd and 4th EBR went to the eastern border. Three more regiments were raised from newly trained Bengalis who had fled to India. All these activities provided propaganda fodder to the Indians, who encouraged the exiled foreign journalists from Dacca to cover the activities of the Mukti Bahini and even helped sneak some of them—including Nichlaos Tomalin of *The Sunday Times* of UK, Sydney Schanberg of *The New York Times*, Tony Clifton of *Newsweek*, and crews from NBC and CBS TV from the US, and Granada TV from Britain—into East Pakistan.[54] Roedad Khan's and the army's folly in sending these journalists out of East Pakistan came back to haunt Pakistan, as stories flooded into the Western press about alleged Pakistan Army atrocities and the successes of the Bengali freedom fighters. Pakistan was caught flat-footed. Its leadership seemed to be stuck in neutral gear—and for good reason: Yahya had been distracted by his heavy personal involvement in a secret venture to bring the US and China together.

THE CHINA CARD

President Richard Nixon first raised the idea of Yahya becoming an intermediary between the US and China during a short stop in Lahore on 1 August 1969 during his worldwide tour, and found Yahya more than willing to be of help. The US was simultaneously using another dictator, Nicolae Ceauşescu of Romania, as a contact with the Chinese, knowing full well that the Romanian link would be in the knowledge of the Soviet Union. Given the history of bad relations between the US and China and the explosive nature of these moves should they become public, the US wanted total secrecy. Yahya and his cohort were perfect for the job. Over the two years that followed, they participated in detailed and secret negotiations with the Chinese and the Americans, relying on handwritten notes and letters to convey messages to and from Beijing for the Nixon government, and setting the ground for what would be a momentous surreptitious visit by Nixon's national security advisor, Henry Kissinger, to Beijing on 9 July 1971.

Eventually, Nixon would make his own journey to Beijing in February 1972, by which time his friend and facilitator Yahya would be gone from the political scene.

The amazing aspect of this venture was not so much that the US and China came together but that Yahya and his closest staff officers and senior officials of the Foreign Office spent so much time tending personally to the details of the arrangements related to the Kissinger visit at a time when critical developments were occurring within Pakistan and between Pakistan and India. Clearly Yahya felt that the investment was worth it in terms of the goodwill from both the US and China, both Pakistani allies. On Friday, 10 October 1969, Sher Ali Khan was conveying to Kissinger at the White House Yahya's willingness to play this role and seeking confirmation of the US line to be taken in discussions with the Chinese 'at the top level.' In Sher Ali's view, Nixon wanted to 'normalize American relations with Peking [contemporary spelling], but it should be obvious to the Chinese that this would take some time as it had to [be] effected gradually since American public opinion had to be prepared carefully for the change.' To ensure secrecy, Kissinger suggested that Yahya deal directly with the Chinese ambassador in Islamabad. 'It was essential to keep both State Dept. and the Pakistan Foreign Office out of this affair,' noted Pakistan's ambassador to the United States, Agha Hilaly.[55] This helped ensure that that there were no leaks. But it required the heavy personal involvement of Yahya and his close aides, and yeoman work by Foreign Secretary Sultan M. Khan in Islamabad and Agha Hilaly in Washington, giving them direct access to the heart of the US presidency.

Almost weekly notes were exchanged, as details of the policy stances of both sides were garnered by the principals in Pakistan and shared with the other negotiators, and later logistical arrangements were discussed at the most detailed level. Yahya, of course, leveraged his access to the Chinese leader, Premier Chou En-lai, and built up his relations with Nixon and Kissinger. Both would stand him in good stead as Pakistan became embroiled in its civil war and the battle with India. Notably, it was this activity alone that could be said to have been critical in persuading the US president to 'tilt' in favour of Pakistan in the ensuing conflict with India, the first time that such behaviour was seen in the White House. What helped matters also was Nixon's pronounced allergy to the Indian leadership and specifically Prime Minister Mrs Indira Gandhi. By the time Yahya and Nixon met in the Oval Office on 25 October 1970, a positive image of Yahya had already emerged in the White House:

> Yahya is tough, direct, and with a good sense of humor. He talks in a very clipped way, is a splendid product of Sandhurst [incorrect, Yahya being a graduate of Dehra Dun in India] and affects a sort of social naivete, but is probably much more complicated than this. [...]

The President began the conversation by saying that we have had difficult times in our relationships with our allies produced by Congressional opposition, but that we will stick by our friends. And we consider Pakistan our friend.[56]

Yahya assured Nixon of Pakistan's friendship, referring jokingly to the incident when US Ambassador Keating in Delhi had overslept and missed seeing off Mrs Gandhi when she was headed to the US. 'It would be unthinkable,' said Yahya to Nixon, 'that in Pakistan people would deliver a broken alarm clock...to an American Ambassador.' Nixon replied: 'Your people are too proud to do a thing like that.' To which Yahya responded: 'We will never put you in an embarrassing position. Your gesture to give us military assistance against all advice is appreciated by our people.' Thus was the relationship cemented, with Yahya taking on the intermediary role in his forthcoming visit to China. Yahya was true to his word. By 9 December, Hilaly was in Kissinger's office dictating a reply from Chou En-lai 'after three days of deliberations' in which Chou confirmed that the response had been discussed with Chairman Mao and Vice Chairman Lin Piao:

We thank the President of Pakistan for conveying to us orally a message from President Nixon. China has always been willing and has always tried to negotiate by peaceful means...In order to discuss this subject of the vacation of Chinese territories called Taiwan, a special envoy of President Nixon's will be most welcome in Peking.

And, Chou En-lai added, in the course of the same conversation with Hilaly:

We have had messages from the United States from different sources in the past but this is the first time that the proposal has come from a Head, through a Head, to a Head. The United States knows that Pakistan is a great friend of China and therefore we attach importance to the message.

President Yahya's comments:

I think it is significant that Chou En-lai did not accept or reject the proposal as soon as it was made and that he consulted Mao and Lin Piao before giving the answer....Further, at no stage during the discussions with the Chinese leaders did they indulge in vehement criticism of the United States.[57]

The game was afoot and picked up pace in the coming months, as Pakistan made logistical arrangements with Kissinger and his team to set up a secret dash from Rawalpindi to Beijing. Yahya and his team took personal notes on these arrangements, down to the minutest details of who would come with Kissinger, (a chosen few staffers plus body doubles from the secret service for both Kissinger and his aide Winston Lord), where they would stay, and who from the Pakistani bureaucracy would play a part in the subterfuge involving Kissinger's trip. General Umar was designated as the 'main coordinator throughout' according to a handwritten note on a scratch pad from the President's House in Rawalpindi. M.M. Ahmad was designated to be the Pakistani official accompanying US Ambassador Farland, (acting as the Kissinger double and who himself by then had been brought in on the secret of Kissinger's trip to China at Pakistani insistence), and Ambassador Hilaly on a road trip to Nathiagali hill station near Rawalpindi, where Kissinger was said to hole up under the pretence of a stomach upset.[58] Farland was to dissuade the embassy doctor from going to Nathiagali. Meanwhile, Kissinger would make for Chaklala airport on the night of 9 July. He was seen off by Sultan M. Khan, the Pakistan foreign secretary, as he boarded a PIA Boeing, accompanied by three Chinese navigators and four senior Chinese officials who had flown to Pakistan to greet Kissinger, and headed across the Karakoram mountains to Beijing. Kissinger's own team included Winston Lord, John Holdrich, Richard Smyser, and two secret service men.

By the time Kissinger got back from Beijing on 11 July, history had been made. In his 27-page report to Nixon on his seventeen hours of talks with Chou En-lai and his associates, Kissinger stated that his two-day visit to Peking:

> [...]resulted in the most searching, sweeping and significant discussions I have ever had in government...Another four hours were spent with Huang [Hua] and Chang [Wen-chin, head of the West European and American Department of the Chinese Foreign Ministry], mostly on drafting the communiqué. These meetings brought about a summit meeting between you and Mao-Tse Tung, covered all major issues between our countries at considerable length and with great candor, and may well have marked a major new departure in international relations.[59]

After reviewing the details of his talks and presenting notes on regional topics, Kissinger covered the gist of his discussion on South Asia. Below are selections of some of the salient features of Kissinger's report to Nixon:

> Chou described the South Asian subcontinent as a prime area of 'turmoil under heaven.' This was because India had long ago under Nehru adopted an expansionist philosophy, not only committing aggression against Pakistan but against China as well...
>
> India was responsible for the present turmoil in East Pakistan. It was supporting Bangla Desh and had allowed Bangla Desh 'headquarters' to be set up on Indian territory....
>
> China would stand by Pakistan in the present crisis....
>
> I told Chou that we were trying very hard to discourage an Indo–Pak war. I assured Chou that we were bringing all the influence we could to bear on India to

try to prevent a war from developing. Chou said that this was a good thing, but he inferred that we might not be able to do too much because we were 10,000 miles away. China, however, was much closer. Chou recalled the Chinese defeat of India in 1962 and hinted rather broadly that the same thing could happen again. The Chinese detestation of the Indians came through loud and clear. Conversely, China's warm friendship for Pakistan as a firm and reliable friend was made very plain. The lesson that Chou may have been trying to make here was that those who stand by China and keep their word will be treated in kind.[60]

Yahya and his colleagues understood the Chinese position very well. At the same time, they also needed the US's support and arms supplies, not having fully converted their forces away from US arms. Even while he was setting up Kissinger's travel arrangements for the Beijing trip, Hilaly was also inserting into the exchanges the need for the US to pressure India into retracting its support of the Bangladesh movement and to 'stop saying in effect that a political settlement in East Pakistan has to meet with her [India's] approval.'[61] Hilaly suggested that Kissinger read Yahya's latest speech to the nation before coming to New Delhi and then Rawalpindi.

Kissinger was to confirm Pakistan's worst fears after his visit to Delhi. A handwritten note in Yahya's China file (on a Government House, Nathiagali letter-head) refers to Kissinger's statement that in Delhi 'he found a mood of bitterness, hostility and hawkishness and he came away with an impression that India was likely to start a war against Pakistan.' Pakistan's leadership heard this message but did not act to forestall that eventuality. They still thought that they could force the East Pakistanis to stay within Pakistan and, should war break out, that the Chinese and the US would stand by them. But they had to convince the world of their cause.

THE WAR WITHIN

Pakistan launched a publicity campaign to show the world that Bengali atrocities had preceded army action. Aslam Azhar of PTV was deputed to produce a colour documentary called 'The Great Betrayal' that used compiled newsreel footage and interviews to depict the violence of the Bengali insurgents on Bihari victims (non-local East Pakistanis who had fled from Bihar, India, at the time of partition). This film was widely shown in Pakistan to official audiences and sent abroad to missions to be used in their efforts to counteract the reports of independent journalists and observers. The effort did not succeed, however, since it was hard to determine with whom the responsibility for the dead bodies being shown lay. Indeed, by the summer of 1971 when Sheikh Mujib had been brought to trial at a jail on Jaranwala road outside Lyallpur (now Faisalabad), the government was hard pressed to find evidence to make its case against him. I (the author), Shuja Nawaz, then working for PTV, was deputed to take a copy of this film, a projector, and a projectionist, and proceed to Gujranwala railway station where a contact redirected us to Lyallpur. There we found ourselves headed to the jail which was guarded by soldiers of the Baluch Regiment commanded by a friend of my elder brother. I met with the attorney general who was prosecuting the case. He asked whether I could testify about the film. I replied that I had not shot or edited the film, and that the footage by itself could not specifically make the case about who had done the killing. Rather, the film could be edited in many different ways to tell different stories; that was simply the nature of film and film editing. The prosecutor was not happy with the answer and asked to see the film. The next day I was asked to go to the jail and wait, where I sat around in a room that had an itinerant population of lawyers from both sides, including A.K. Brohi who was defending Mujib. During a bathroom break, I ran into the presiding officer of the tribunal, Brigadier (later general) Rahimuddin Khan, commander 111 Brigade, Rawalpindi. My brother Asif was then his brigade major and getting ready to move to the border near Chamb. 'Arrye Shuja Mian! [Hey! Mr Shuja!] What are you doing here?' he exclaimed. When I explained my situation and my inability to present evidence, he muttered something under his breath and went away. He was a gentleman who played by the rules and was clearly quite uncomfortable with his assignment. Later that evening I was told to return to Rawalpindi and leave the film behind. I do not think it was ever used as evidence.

There was great uproar about killings during the period before the army action and immediately after it. Bangladeshi and Indian propagandists presented figures as high as three million killed.[62] Bangladesh had entered the Western pop culture scene as well, with John Lennon leading a special fundraising concert for Bangladesh with an eponymous title track. Meanwhile, leaks from the White House gave rise to articles by Washington columnist Jack Anderson about the Nixonian tilt toward Pakistan.[63] It would not be, till over three decades later that a West Bengali scholar, Sarmila Bose, would undertake a dispassionate examination of the killings. While blaming the Pakistan Army for allowing its soldiers free rein in killing individuals and losing discipline, she also pointed out that the killings and violence had many different faces:

> The civil war not merely between the two wings of Pakistan, but also within the territory of East Pakistan, between Bengalis and non-Bengalis, and among Bengalis themselves, who were bitterly divided between those who favoured independence for Bangladesh and those who supported unity and integrity of Pakistan.

Her case studies showed that 'brutalities were committed by all parties in the conflict and no party is in a position to occupy the moral high ground on this question without first acknowledging and expressing remorse for the inhumanities committed by its own side.'[64]

However, neither side has been willing to admit to them. I recall vivid descriptions of events involving the apparently indiscriminate killing of Bengalis by Pakistani soldiers under a schoolmate of mine. 'My men would slip away during the night to knock off Bengalis,' he stated. The very fact that these acts were countenanced by some officers was testimony to the breakdown of discipline of Pakistani forces, despite the issuance of written orders from General Niazi to guard against such excesses. (Others contend however that Niazi encouraged the army to knock off as many Bengalis as it could.[65]) A month after he had told us stories of indiscriminate killings by his soldiers, my schoolmate was back again in Rawalpindi from East Pakistan, having been seriously injured in the fighting there. He left the army in due course after being medically downgraded.

Whether 10,000, 100,000, or three million people were killed during the upheavals in East Pakistan in the first eleven months of 1971, it was not sufficient justification for the headstrong military calculations on both the Indian and the Pakistani sides which made war inevitable. For indeed war was becoming inevitable. And it would be costly.

NOTES

1. Brigadier A.R. Siddiqi. *The Military in Pakistan: Image and Reality* (Pakistan: Vanguard, 1996), p. 15.
2. Ibid., p. 25.
3. Ibid., p. 159. Brig. Siddiqi, who headed Yahya's PR operation had produced a plan for media management that included 'self-censorship' by the national press, no censorship of foreign media, and no personal projection of martial law or other government functionaries. The personal publicity issue gradually faded. But the media plan did cause endless confusion in the official media that was used to getting official press advice about what to project each day in the press or on TV in the evening. I recall as an English newsreader at PTV, Rawalpindi-Islamabad, on my first day after Yahya had taken over, the anguish of my news editor who tried calling the MD of the PTV to seek advice on the rank order of the evening news items. After having being blindsided by the news editor into taking a decision that day, the MD was found to be 'unavailable' on subsequent evenings! As a result the news editor had to rely on either calling his own news director to 'inform' him of the line up, thus shifting the blame upwards, or failing that to carry innocuous items, such as films of European yacht races instead of news of substance!
4. G.W. Choudhry, *The Last Days of United Pakistan* (London: C. Hurst and Company, 1974), pp. 50–51.
5. Interview with I.A. Sherwani.
6. These practices contrast with some earlier incidents involving allegations of foul play in the military. In one case that had Rawalpindi abuzz in the late 1950s, senior officers in Ayub's

regime reportedly were involved in the import of Burmese Teak wood for personal gain. When evidence of wrong doing emerged, the blame was laid at the door of a relatively junior officer who then reportedly committed suicide. In another case that made the rounds in private army circles, the commander of Pakistan's United Nations peacekeeping force in West Irian Jaya (now West Papua: Indonesian Papua Barat) was reportedly retired prematurely when evidence of looting by his troops was discovered. The hint of scapegoating in both cases remained strong. The only similarity between the earlier cases and the new situation in Ayub's and then Yahya's martial law regimes and their successors was that most such cases were 'resolved' within the military circles, without any public accounting or reporting.

7. 'General Yahya Khan and Gen. Abdul Hamid would slip out to Gen. Yahya's house in Harley Street, Rawalpindi, for the purpose of meeting some of their female friends. This house is reported to have been constructed out of funds provided by the Standard Bank, and had been taken on rent by the same bank and used furnished as a guest house.' *The Report of the Hamoodur Rehman Commission of Inquiry into the 1971 War,* (Lahore, Karachi, Islamabad: Vanguard), p. 291.

8. According to Major General Umar, Ataur Rehman Alvi of Standard Bank was 'handling political affairs directly on behalf of the President.' Cited in Hasan Zaheer, *The Separation of East Pakistan* (Pakistan: Oxford University Press, 1994), p. 112.

9. Affidavit in support of a Writ Petition no. 1649 of 1978 filed by General (retd) Agha Mohammad Yahya Khan vs. the Federation of Pakistan, 6 June 1978, attested by advocate Manzoor Ahmed Rana, oath commissioner, Rawalpindi. Reproduced by *Defence Journal* in facsimile December 2005.

10. Among the early entrants were the sons of senior current or former army officers, including Captains Jamshed Burki and Aftab Sher Khan.

11. Fazal Muqeem Khan, *Pakistan's Crisis in Leadership* (Islamabad, Karachi, Lahore, Pakistan: National Book Foundation, 1973), p. 40.

12. Interview, Lahore, April 2006.

13. Zaheer, *The Separation*, pp. 91–92 for a detailed account of the issues leading to the discord and dissolution of the federation on which this discussion relies.

14. Ibid., p. 95.

15. Ibid.

16. Rounaq Jahan, *Pakistan: Failure of National Integration* (Columbia University Press, 1972), pp. 25 and 62.

17. Siddiqi, *The Military*, p. 170.

18. Travelling around the Jhelum district, where our village Chakri Rajgan, is located during that election campaign, I often asked villagers this question and got the reply that they were voting for the sword. Why? 'Because Bhutto Sahib will bring us water taps' or 'Because Bhutto Sahib will give us a house'. Traditional politicians, including my own relative Raja Lehrasab Khan, whose family had controlled all elected positions in the area for as long as one could recall, failed to recognize this threat to the status quo. Indeed, he told me that Bhutto had approached him first to run on the PPP ticket but Lehrasab refused since 'I had given my word to Daultana's Council Muslim League.' Raja Lehrasab lost to Dr Ghulam Husain, a transplant from across the Jhelum River in Mandi Bahauddin.

19. Arnold Zeitlin, *The Sound of Thy Brother's Blood*, unpublished book manuscript, p. 158. Zeitlin, then an experienced young man, who had served in Africa and later was to serve in the Philippines, had a knack of getting around the country and winning the confidence of politicians of all hues. His ubiquitous presence and keen reportage led some to classify him as CIA spy, a charge pinned on most inquisitive foreigners. Later in his retired life, he was to help open a centre for training journalists in Pakistan.

20. Post operation report in GHQ about the situation in East Pakistan in 1971. Pakistan Army, GHQ Archives. Document number 3052, p. 7.

21. Post operation report in GHQ, number 3052, p. 9.
22. Zeitlin, *The Sound*, p. 164. The UK and US diplomats in East Pakistan were already estimating the Awami League getting 140 seats in East Pakistan.
23. Ibid., p. 172.
24. I was one of the English-language anchors of the broadcast from Rawalpindi-Islamabad TV, with Shoaib Hashmi (Faiz Ahmed Faiz's son-in-law and Lahore intellectual) and Ubaidullah Beg (former host of a popular quiz programme, *Kasauti*), both of whom handled the Urdu anchoring. We were astounded at the trust and rapport that we managed to establish with the audiences. To fill in gaps in our reporting, I had taken with me a book of elephant jokes that we shared piecemeal with the audience. Before the marathon broadcast ended we had started getting stuffed elephants and other notes and gifts from a grateful public. Professionally this was the high point of our careers in PTV news. I recall coming out at midnight for a smoke on the PTV lawn and seeing Gareth Gwenlan, then a BBC assistant producer (and later famous as producer of *Fawlty Towers*) who had been sent with another colleague to help train us in production techniques, standing, waiting for me to come out. He said he was so excited that he could not stay at home in Islamabad and drove during the night to be with us. The adrenalin kept us going non-stop for twenty-nine hours.
25. A.R. Siddiqi, *East Pakistan: The Endgame* (Karachi: Oxford, 2004), p. 50.
26. India's swift resort to this ban raised issues as to the nature of this hijacking. Pakistan believed that it was an Indian plot. India countered that the hijackers continued to live in Pakistan after this event.
27. Choudhry, *The Last Days*, p. 148.
28. I used to introduce the president's speeches and was standing by in the studio that evening to hook up to the live broadcast from the President's House, when I was told to read the president's statement in the first person, with a short introduction that ended with the words: 'I shall now read the president's announcement. I quote....' Halfway into the text I had to restrain myself from imitating the president's signature staccato delivery. Somehow I managed to complete the job without making a hash of it. Siddiqi also refers to the 'eerie touch' given to the announcement by the fact that a newscaster had to read the president's speech for him. Op. cit., p. 62.
29. Khalid Hasan's long essay 'Zulfikar Ali Bhutto' in his book *Rearview Mirror* cites this as the origin of the story. Also available on www.khalidhasan.net/longerpieces.
30. Sahibzada Yaqub Khan's name has undergone various changes over the years. In his interview with Larry Collins and Dominique Lapierre in *Freedom at Midnight* it appears as Yacoub Khan. In some of his later ambassadorial appointments, he used the hyphenated Yaqub-Khan.
31. GHQ report, Document number 3052, op. cit., p. 11. This operational order has Sahibzada Yaqub's signature.
32. Siddiqi, *The Military*, p. 60.
33. Yaqub came from the royal family of Rampur in India, where his father was prime minister and his uncle was the nawab, hence his honorific Sahibzada (scion of nobility). He had quit Rampur and all its riches for Pakistan at partition and fought against the Indian forces, which included his own brother, during the first Kashmir War.
34. Mahmud Ahmed, *History of Indo-Park War—1965*, p. 420.
35. Top Secret, Operation 'Blitz', Operation Directive, Document number 3050. Pakistan Army GHQ Archives.
36. Ibid.
37. Yaqub Khan's telegram to Yahya, dated 5 March 1971, cited in Altaf Gauhar's article 'How "Shera" turned into "Ghazi," *The Nation*, 25 January 1998.
38. It is hard to imagine a lieutenant colonel getting this much attention even for a military action. But the Bengali resistance used this title to demonize Tikka Khan. No contemporary record of this title is available from 1958. The background is as follows: Nowroz started an

armed struggle against Pakistan, but later surrendered to Tikka when Nowroz came to the army for negotiations. He and his followers, including his sons and nephews, were taken to Hyderabad jail, where his sons and nephews were executed for armed rebellion against the state. Rashed Rahman has a different origin for this title of 'Butcher of Balochistan': 'The *Parari* **Resistance:** The next rebellion broke out in 1962, starting from the Marri tribal area. The guerrillas chose for themselves the honorific *Pararis* (rebels). This guerrilla resistance spread to the other areas of Balochistan. By July 1963, the Pararis had established a number of base camps of varying size spread over some 45,000 square miles, from the Mengal tribal areas of Jhalawan to the Marri and Bugti areas. Consciously, the guerrillas in classic fashion avoided large-scale fixed encounters with the army. They harassed the government forces by ambushing convoys, bombing trains, sniping and raids on military camps. In retaliation, the army staged a series of offensives, reprisals and air bombardments whose main brunt fell on the people. This had the unintended consequence, as elsewhere in irregular wars, of expanding and consolidating support for the guerrillas. Atrocities by the army were widespread, earning General Tikka Khan, commander of the Balochistan theatre, the unflattering sobriquet of Butcher of Balochistan, long before he earned further such 'glory' in East Pakistan. The fighting continued until 1969, when Ayub Khan was removed and his successor, General Yahya, sued for a ceasefire with the Pararis. One Unit was dissolved and Balochistan province once again re-established.' See 'The Crisis in Balochistan' *South Asian Journal*, April–June 2005.

39. I recall sitting with him at the death of a fellow tribesman's mother in Rawalpindi and being regaled for hours about how he had personally done incognito comparison shopping in the bazaars, as the QMG, for bedding for soldiers.

40. Zeitlin, *The Sound*, quoting K.G. Mustapha, the editor of the English-language daily, *The Pakistan Observer*. Details of this night's operations are based on Zeitlin's account.

41. See Sarmila Bose, 'Anatomy of Violence: Analysis of Civil War in East Pakistan in 1971,' in *Economic and Political Weekly*, 8 October 2005.

42. Zulfikar Ali Bhutto, *The Great Tragedy*, a Pakistan Peoples' Party Publication, September 1971 (Vision Press), p. 50.

43. According to the uncorroborated story by his wife, Col. Janjua was asked to come to the office where he was shot 'in cold blood' by Major Zia.

44. Khwaja Shahid Hosain, director programmes at PTV and other senior broadcasting officials were in Dacca. Shahid Hosain recalled with a sense of schoolboyish glee his participation in identifying the location of the transmitter and then getting word that the mission had been accomplished.

45. In his later years, he was a major advisor to President Ghulam Ishaq Khan and the master of much political engineering at the national scale. In recent years he has became a champion of democracy and against all military rule, as evidenced in his numerous articles for the *Dawn* newspaper.

46. Bhutto, *The Great*, p. 51.

47. Ibid., pp. 78–79.

48. Lt. Gen. A.A.K. Niazi, *The Betrayal of East Pakistan* (Karachi: Oxford, 1998), p. 46. Little did Farman Ali realize that this diary would be captured by the Bengalis and later shown by Mujib to Bhutto. Also, in many ways, it appeared to presage the flag of Bangladesh, a red circle against a deep green background, with the red signifying the blood of the people who died in their war of independence from Pakistan. The Hamoodur Rehman Commission does not ascribe that sentence to Farman Ali, believing testimony from him and others that he was just making random notations of things that were said at a meeting. An Awami League leader was supposed to have uttered this threat at a public meeting earlier. Farman Ali was merely recording the words as he sat in a meeting.

49. Ibid., p. 50.

50. Ibid., p. 51.

51. In fact, he also had the wild idea of fighting his way through the Gangetic plains of northern India to link up with West Pakistan, over one thousand miles of hostile Indian territory and thus create a corridor between the two wings!

52. Lt. Gen. JFR Jacob, *Surrender at Dacca: Birth of a Nation* (Manohar, 1997), pp. 35–36.

53. Ibid., Appendix 6 quoting Manekshaw's interview with *Quarterdeck* (1996).

54. Ibid., p. 45.

55. Handwritten 'Record of a discussion between Gen. Sher Ali Khan and Henry Kissinger at the White House on Friday, 10 October, 1969'. From the personal China file of President Yahya provided in facsimile to me by my school mate Ali Yahya Khan, the president's son, in 1993. A published version of these papers, with a useful contextual note, subsequently appeared in Fakir S. Aijazuddin's *From a Head, through a Head, to a Head: The Secret Channel between the US and China through Pakistan* (Karachi: Oxford, 2000).

56. Memorandum of Conversation, The White House, Washington Top Secret/Sensitive, Meeting between the President and Pakistani President Yahya, 25 October 1970, The Oval Office. US National Archives. Reproduced by the National Security Archive, Washington DC.

57. Memorandum for the President from Henry A. Kissinger, subject: Chinese Communist Initiative, The White House, Washington. Op. cit. Hilaly was instructed to convey the message from China but not to give the original piece of paper. Kissinger attached a Note Verbale from Nixon to Chou proposing 'that representatives of our two governments meet together at the earliest possible moment, either in Rawalpindi or some other location, convenient to both sides to discuss the modalities of the higher-level meeting.'

58. Author's conversation with Mr M.M. Ahmad.

59. Top Secret/Sensitive/Exclusively Eyes Only Memorandum for the President from Henry A. Kissinger, 14 July 1971, The White House. My Talks with Chou En-lai. US Archives, reproduced by National Security Archive.

60. Top Secret/Sensitive/Exclusively Eyes Only, 14 July 1971, pp. 20–21.

61. Yahya China file. Op. Cit. Letter from Agha Hilaly to Dr Kissinger, 1 July 1971.

62. See, for example, Jag Mohan, *The Black Book of Genocide in Bangladesh* (New Delhi: Geeta Book Centre, 1971), Ministry of Information and Broadcasting, New Delhi, *Bangladesh Documents* Volumes 1 and 2, 1971.

63. Jack Anderson with George Clifford, *The Anderson Papers* (Random House, 1973), pp. 205–69.

64. Bose, *Anatomy*.

65. See, for example, Brigadier A.R. Siddiqi, *East Pakistan—The Endgame: An Onlooker's Journal 1969–71*.

And we are here as on a darkling plain
Swept with confused alarms of struggle and flight,
Where ignorant armies clash by night

– Matthew Arnold 'Dover Beach', 1867

Contrary to popular belief, 1971 witnessed not one but three major conflicts in the subcontinent: One was a civil war within Pakistan, with Yahya ánd his regime using military power to force the East Pakistanis to accept a united Pakistan. Another was a war with India, with Mrs Indira Gandhi's government taking advantage of the turmoil to launch an invasion of East Pakistan in support of Bengali freedom in November 1971, precipitating the third conflict: a Pakistani riposte from West Pakistan into Indian territory that began on 3 December 1971. With that move, Pakistan sought to forestall an Indian decision in East Pakistan and to draw international intervention into the conflict. The result for Pakistan was abject failure, as the military regime blundered from a muddled campaign in the Eastern Wing to a fruitless adventure in the west. Lack of a clear and attainable goal for the war in the west reflected another failure of command and execution. The regime also found itself politically outplayed by Bhutto in the West and the Awami League and India in the East. It started believing its own propaganda and deprived the West Pakistani populace of accurate information on the political state of East Pakistan. Before the year came to an end, Pakistan's forces in East Pakistan surrendered to a victorious Indian Army in Dacca (now Dhaka), East Pakistan became Bangladesh, Yahya and his coterie were ousted ignominiously, and Bhutto was handed the presidency and the mantle of CMLA by virtue of a *putsch* organized by relatively junior commanders, the first time that a military group in Pakistan forced a change over from a military to a civilian leader and also the first time a civilian had taken on both titles. A traumatized country was left to pick up the pieces after yet another military debacle.

The roots of this debacle lay in the inability of Yahya's martial law regime to see the need for political settlement rather than military action in East Pakistan. It failed to see that military action and prowess cannot be a substitute for political sensibility. Even Yaqub Khan's 'Operation Blitz' had missed out on this opportunity and stressed a military clean-up operation. Tikka's 'Operation Searchlight' merely brought that earlier thinking to fruition. His successor General Niazi's lack of understanding of the political sphere made him focus on the military solution alone to a problem that was at heart a political one.

Against this background, the Pakistan Army prepared to root out the Mukti Bahini,[1] the Bengali freedom fighters from East Pakistan, and secure the frontiers with India. It was a huge task, given the rambling 3000-mile highly porous boundary of East Pakistan with Indian territory on three sides and the Bay of Bengal to the south. Thus began a major civil war that eventually led to an all out war with India. Niazi's strategy was simple: fan out the solitary 14 Division from Dacca, the centre of gravity of East Pakistan, toward the borders in all directions, securing towns and cities and setting up a fortress defence, whose principal aim was to deny territory to the Mukti Bahini and their Indian sponsors. He had no air force to speak of: only one old squadron of aging F-86 Sabre Jets, on an old airfield in Dacca, without much radar cover. The assumption was that the Indians wanted the Bengali rebels to declare Bangladesh on land that formerly was East Pakistan, and then seek Indian help, giving India the diplomatic fig leaf it needed to cover up an attack on East Pakistan. So Niazi's main objective was to evict the rebels from East Pakistani territory and seal the routes of reinforcement and withdrawal of the Mukti Bahini.

The operation was designed to be implemented in four phases: first to clear all the border towns and cities, second to open the rail, road, and river systems, third to clear the interior and coastal areas of Mukti Bahini operations, and fourth to clear any remaining pockets of resistance.[2] The time frame for completion of these operations was 15 May, with the emphasis on 'speed and multi thrusts.' But this task was not within the capability of one division, so by April additional troops, 9 and 16 Divisions, were also moved from West to East Pakistan, although not with their full equipment. Major General Nazar Hussain Shah's 16 Division was given the north-west sector, including Rajshahi division, with orders to clear and hold the cities of Dinajpur, Rangpur, Bogra, and Rajshahi. Major General Shaukat Riza's 9 Division was responsible for the northern/central sector including Dacca and Khulna divisions. Major General Rahim Khan's 14 Division was given the area in the south and east, including Chittagong division and the Sylhet area. Niazi describes the situation in glum terms: 'We became like a foreign army in a hostile land. The Bengalis used to call us the 'Army of Occupation.' Mukti Bahini had the support not only of the local Bengalis, but of the whole of the Indian economic, political, and military set-up, in addition to advisers from Russia [perhaps a stretch of his imagination on the latter point, no evidence having been established that the Indians needed foreign advisers to help them at this stage].'[3]

The isolated and estranged Pakistani troops faced tough opposition, as the rebels, who had fled with their weapons fought with rifles, recoilless rifles, rocket launchers, and mortars. At places, the rebels resorted to minefields as well. The result was a messy conflict in which large segments of the local population, especially the highly vulnerable and targeted Hindus of East Pakistan, who were blamed by the military high command for fomenting separatist and pro-Indian views in East Pakistan, started fleeing into Indian territory. As a result of the desertion of Bengali troops and paramilitary forces, and of the influx of refugees into India, a Mukti Bahini force upwards of 100,000 was estimated by the Pakistan Army to have been assembled across the border in India.

By the end of April, Niazi was claiming victory in having cleared East Pakistan of most of the Mukti Bahini forces and opened up the 'river and sea routes' as well as rail communications. His bravado was reflected in the message he sent to GHQ on 17 May in which he claimed to have defeated the rebels in the towns and claimed around 30,000 rebels 'either killed or made ineffective, and the rest crossed over into India.'[4] In the process he had sent back Shaukat Riza to GHQ 'for inefficiency and buckling under stress of war conditions,' and replaced him with the newly promoted Major General M.H. Ansari. Riza had apparently disagreed with Niazi's strategy, and instead favoured a political solution to the East Pakistan problem. By the end of May, Niazi was boasting that the rebel resistance had been broken but also recognized the increased Indian support for the Mukti Bahini. He then asked for permission to enter Indian territory in hot pursuit to defeat the rest of the rebels on Indian soil, but General Hamid called him from Rawalpindi to say that both Hamid and Yahya were 'very happy with your [Niazi's] wonderful achievement. Don't enter Indian territory. I will discuss with you your future course of action soon.'[5] As Niazi resignedly states: 'That was that.'

THE US ASSESSMENT

While Niazi tried to gloss over his difficulties in the early stages of the operations, the US CIA was looking at the situation more critically. The CIA's 12 April assessment of the situation in Pakistan dealing specifically with the 'Conflict in Bengal' (note that they had not used the term 'East Pakistan'), stated that:

> The West Pakistani military leaders probably expected—or at least hoped—to destroy the Awami League (AL) and regain effective control of East Bengal in a matter of days, if not hours. They clearly miscalculated; most of the top AL leaders have been arrested, but lower level party leaders continue to be active throughout much of the countryside.[...] The 13,000 strong East Pakistan Rifles paramilitary force and the East Bengal regiments continue to resist the West Pakistani units in East Bengal; they are able to move fairly easily through most of the countryside.[6]

The CIA felt that the 'prospects are poor that the 30,000 West Pakistani troops can substantially improve their position, much less reassert control over 75 million rebellious Bengalis. This is likely to be the case even if the expeditionary force is augmented. For most of East Pakistan's residents, **the**

time has come for a separate Bengali nation.' [Emphasis added] The reasons for this gloomy assessment were succinctly put:

> Many years of economic discrimination and political repression by the west wing had made the autonomous Bangla Desh the choice of over 75 per cent of Bengali voters in the December 1970 elections. The refusal of Pakistan's military leaders to honor that choice and their attempt to terrorize the Bengalis into submission have almost certainly ended any general desire in East Bengal to see the Pakistani union continue.

The CIA confirmed the shipment of arms being trucked into East Pakistan from the Indian border and linked the continued resistance to the Pakistan Army to the quantum of support to the rebel forces from India. According to the CIA, the Indians felt that a 'successful Bengali insurgency would serve to weaken and discredit West Pakistan.' India had another incentive here as well: by supporting the moderate Bengali leadership of the time, India would forestall the emergence of a 'new extremist leadership...which would eventually take over the new country.' Such a situation would create severe problems for India, particularly in the Indian state of West Bengal, the home of 'several extremist Communist groups.' As a result, the CIA estimated clandestine Indian support although it did not rule out the possibility of 'deeper and deeper' Indian involvement and direct clashes with Pakistani forces. 'Even open military intervention by India could not be ruled out. India has sufficient forces to defeat Pakistani forces in East Bengal without drawing heavily on its troops on its other frontiers,' they claimed.[7] In making this assessment, the CIA anticipated a possible Pakistani attack on western India but were of the view that the Indians were better equipped to deal with such a situation (should it arise), than they were in 1965.

Discussing the stories of atrocities in Dacca and other places in East Pakistan, the CIA report came to the conclusion that 'no single Western country has much influence on the situation, but general Western disapproval may make the government in Islamabad less certain of the wisdom of present policies and more amenable to pressures for change.' It then proceeded to examine the various possibilities: a continued united Pakistan and an independent Bangladesh:

> The successful secession of the east wing would produce a severe psychological shock in West Pakistan. Indeed, President Yahya may well either resign or be ousted before the issue is decided in the east....West Pakistan could itself split into as many as four separate nations, though this contingency now appears unlikely....

The army is likely to remain a principal political factor in West Pakistan, though it may eventually turn over formal political power to some civilian

groups whose views are compatible with those of the military establishment....
The West Pakistani military machine's capabilities would remain—the army
would see to that.

LOCAL ASSESSMENTS

The Indian Army had meanwhile come to the firm conclusion that it should
support the Bengali freedom fighters but that this was not the right time for
an invasion of East Pakistan. Having been dissuaded by General Maneksaw
from an immediate invasion, Mrs Gandhi turned to the Border Security Force
(BSF) to see if they could undertake some incursions into East Pakistan. This
they did but with very mixed results, even seeking help once from India's
eastern command to extricate their forces that had found themselves
surrounded by Pakistan Army troops inside East Pakistan. As a result, on 29
April 1971, official responsibility for aiding the Bangladesh movement was
handed over to the Indian Army's eastern command, and the BSF was placed
under its control.[8]

In Pakistan, the NSC, under General Umar, was already predicting the
possibility of an Indian invasion given the heavy preoccupation of the
Pakistan Army with rebels in East Pakistan. It recognized the likely success
of such a venture because 'a large majority of the population of East Pakistan
had already been alienated.'[9] A subsequent ISI paper of June 1971 also hinted
at the possibility of war although it equivocated on whether India might opt
for an open conflict; in other words, if Pakistan could prevent the imbalance
of forces from going too heavily in India's favour, then India might be
dissuaded from going to war. But another June paper from the army's own
MI Directorate completely discounted the possibility of an Indian attack:
'India is unlikely to resort to all-out war with Pakistan but may embark on
[a] nibbling attack close to borders to support the rebels and occupy limited
territory.' The CGS, Gul Hassan, while generally agreeing with the MI's
assessment, noted that India could launch the trained Mukti Bahini after the
monsoon, and once the Pakistan Army was occupied with them inside East
Pakistan, 'the Indians could easily violate our borders and gain an easy and
confused victory.'[10] The danger signals were rife, but Yahya and his cohort
refused to take note of them. They still hoped to convince themselves, the
Bengalis, and world leaders, that they had East Pakistan under control and
could entice the refugees back to re-start the political process and keep
Pakistan whole.

WHITE HOUSE VIEWS

While the East Pakistan conflict was ensuing, Yahya continued to press US President Nixon and National Security Advisor Kissinger to release more military supplies for Pakistan, promising an amnesty and resettlement of Bengali refugees back in East Pakistan. Despite strong protests from India, both Nixon and Kissinger managed to find ways of obliging Yahya. In part, they did this in return for his help on China, but there was also a strong underlying distrust—even dislike—of Mrs Gandhi, who was often characterized by Nixon as a 'bitch.' Nixon also termed the Indians 'bastards' in his private conversations, often with Kissinger, who adopted the same term. This misplaced loyalty and friendship of the US leadership was to breed a false sense of security in Yahya's mind and may well have been the key factor in dissuading him from adopting a more conciliatory approach to the Bengali demands. Discussing a letter from Mrs Gandhi to Nixon in late May 1971 in the Oval Office, Kissinger urged Nixon to use a reply to Mrs Gandhi 'to bring pressure on her not to take military action' and to write to Yahya too, so that Yahya could then respond by 'listing all the things he's doing because he can't get any publicity here.'[11] The same day, Secretary of State William Rogers informed Nixon that the situation in East Pakistan 'is evolving to the point where we now believe it possible that it could touch off a war between India and Pakistan,' suggesting that the US try to influence Yahya to come to the realization himself that 'political accommodation' was needed to resolve the East Pakistan issue.

Later that afternoon at the Washington Special Actions Group (WASAG) meeting on Pakistan, chaired by Kissinger, and attended, among others, by General William Westmoreland, U. Alexis Johnson (Under Secretary of State), Richard Helms (Director of CIA), and David Packard (Under Secretary of the Defense Department), the group reviewed the situation in depth.[12] Before them was a map of the region showing troop deployments and reserves and their locations. Christopher Van Hollen of the State Department, a veteran of Pakistani affairs who knew the Pakistan Army well, summed up the Indian aims: 'Until March 25, India saw its interests served by a united Pakistan in which the Bengali element would be dominant. When the Pakistani military moved into East Pakistan, India's estimate of their own best interests shifted, and they now favour an independent Bangladesh under moderate leadership.' General Westmoreland spoke about his understanding from General Manekshaw, who was then visiting the United States, that the Indian military had had a sobering effect on Mrs Gandhi's initial desire for a 'lightning strike' into East Pakistan. Alexis Johnson doubted that such an attack would succeed. Westmoreland offered his assessment: 'I don't think Pakistan would attack in the West because they wouldn't want to take India on [on] two fronts.

Pakistan's logistic and supply support are marginal and their staying power is only about three or four weeks.' It was clear that the US was taking a more cool headed view of the situation than were Pakistan's military leaders or their analysts.

Indeed, Kissinger's own assessment of Yahya and his team left no doubt of where he stood intellectually, although this artful exponent of *realpolitik* continued faithfully to pander to Nixon's hatred of India and empathy for Pakistan. In a meeting on South Asia of the senior review group in July, Kissinger offered this unvarnished view of Yahya:

> On the Pakistani side, it is my impression that Yahya and his group would never win any prizes for high IQs or for the subtlety of their political comprehension. They are loyal, blunt soldiers, but I think they have a real intellectual problem in understanding why East Pakistan should not be part of West Pakistan. You will never get acceptance of the Awami League from the present structure. If India attacks, it will be in the next six months. The Pakistanis will not put the Awami League back in power in the next six months.[13]

Meanwhile, the White House and the Department of State were seeing the situation from opposite ends of a telescope. Even as late as August, Joseph Sisco of the State Department was declaring: 'I don't think the Indians will attack across the border.' He was of the view, rather, that the Indians would continue to support the Bengali fighters, and went on to add that 'in no circumstances will the Pakistanis initiate hostilities in the West.'[14] Nixon and Kissinger, on the other hand, were of the view that the Department of State was too cosy with India and too ready to see things from the Indian point of view. They tried to make up for this bias with their own tilt toward Pakistan.

Meanwhile in the subcontinent, the two adversaries India and Pakistan began strengthening their positions for the eventual conflict. Pakistan had sent 9 and 16 Divisions to supplement the traditional 14 Division that looked after East Pakistan. In light of the huge task given to the forces in that wing, two additional ad hoc divisions were raised and some of the existing troops were regrouped and their strengths supplemented. During the latter half of November, when the local situation seemed to be getting tenuous, five more infantry battalions were flown to East Pakistan. But, as Shaukat Riza asserts, some of these battalions comprised reservists who were too old and unfit for service, and when a contingent of them was sent by 14 Division to 202 Brigade, the brigade sent them back to Dacca.[15] With all the troops assigned, the Order of Battle of the Pakistan Army in the East wing was as follows[16]:

- Northwest Sector (Rangpur–Bogra): 16 Division
- Northern Sector (Mymensingh): 36 Division

- South Western Sector (Jessore): 9 Division
- Eastern Sector (Comilla–Chittagong): 39 Division
- North Eastern Sector (Sylhet): 14 Division

There were no real reserves for the East Pakistan theatre as a whole. The commander was expecting to shift troops around as needed. He had also planned for troops to fall back to secondary positions in the face of heavy odds. This assumption proved to be faulty since the communication infrastructure and logistics did not allow that to happen. Adding to that difficulty was Niazi's injunction that no unit would be allowed to fall back until it had suffered 75 per cent casualties![17] Regardless, given the overall strategy that East Pakistan by itself was indefensible and that its defence lay in the West, Pakistan's military commanders seemed to have adopted a haphazard and meaningless approach to provisioning for conflict in the East wing, diluting their strength in the West while committing more and more troops to a thankless task in the East.

INDIA'S PLAN OF ATTACK

During the summer, India began making preparations for intervention in East Pakistan, weighing carefully the implications of various actions. According to a secret US report, the Indian government held a high-level meeting in which the Indian Ministry of Home Affairs reported on the 'desperate' situation of the estimated 2.5 million refugees along the East Pakistan border, creating a potentially 'impossible burden on the Indian economy and infrastructure.'[18] The ministry suggested (in that meeting) that the Indian government press Pakistan to stop 'pressurizing East Pakistanis to flee' and 'force' it to repatriate refugees. The Ministry of External Affairs suggested that India should only recognize Bangladesh when 'India made the decision to risk military action against Pakistan for the liberation of the East.' It reported also on the 'extremely negative reaction' of third countries, especially Muslim countries to the East Pakistan situation and the 'wait and see' attitude of the major powers, notably the US and the USSR. The Defence Ministry, while 'stressing the preparedness of Indian armed forces and the weakness of Pakistani armed forces,' recommended against unilateral action at that point. It was unsure of China's involvement and aware of the willingness of some Muslim countries (Turkey and Iran) to help Pakistan. Further, the Indian military was not sure about its ability to receive military supplies from third countries (notably USSR) 'if India initiated what could be a long war.' Finally, they were wary of starting a war on two fronts 'which could create a **requirement for military occupation of all of Pakistan** [emphasis added].'

In light of these wary comments and concerns, the Indians agreed (at that meeting) to:

- Defer recognition of Bangladesh for the immediate future;
- Maintain military readiness;
- Push on the diplomatic front to force Pakistan to take back refugees, while hinting at Indian military action;
- Seek financial aid to help with the refugee situation, and;
- 'Release off-the-record press comments that India is reaching the point where some sort of action, possibly military, was possible if there was not immediate relief for the refugee situation.'

US sources within the Indian hierarchy reported that the opposition parties, both left and right wing, supported a tough line, including military action. Hoskinson remarked on India's 'sophisticated diplomatic and public relations campaign' and highlighted the fact that Mrs Gandhi was 'still moving with considerable restraint.' He suggested that this gave the US 'scope to reinforce this.' The Nixon White House did not oblige however, and the Indians prepared for action after the monsoon season.

Having decided to postpone full-scale military action in East Pakistan until sometime in November, Indian commanders had the time to get their formations into battle positions around their objective (see map 1971 war eastern front). Training could be completed and a strategic plan conceived. The COS of the eastern command, Lt. Gen. Jacob, came up with his four-point plan:

- Dacca was to be the final objective: the 'geopolitical and geostrategic heart of East Pakistan';
- 'Thrust lines were to be selected to isolate and bypass Pakistani forces';
- 'Subsidiary objectives were to be selected with the aim of securing communications centres and destruction of the enemy's command and control capabilities.' Niazi's 'fortresses' were to be bypassed and 'dealt with later.'
- 'Preliminary operations were aimed at drawing out the Pakistani forces to the border, leaving key areas in the interior lightly defended.'[19]

Jacob had begun planning for the attack even before orders came from Delhi and without bringing his Commander Lt. Gen. Jagjit Singh Aurora (whom he saw as being too busy directing the Mukti Bahini operations,) fully into the picture. He divided the theatre into four segments and the plan was to use forces accordingly:

- North Western Sector: 20 Mountain Division, plus 340 Mountain Brigade and an additional 71 Mountain Brigade Group, as needed.

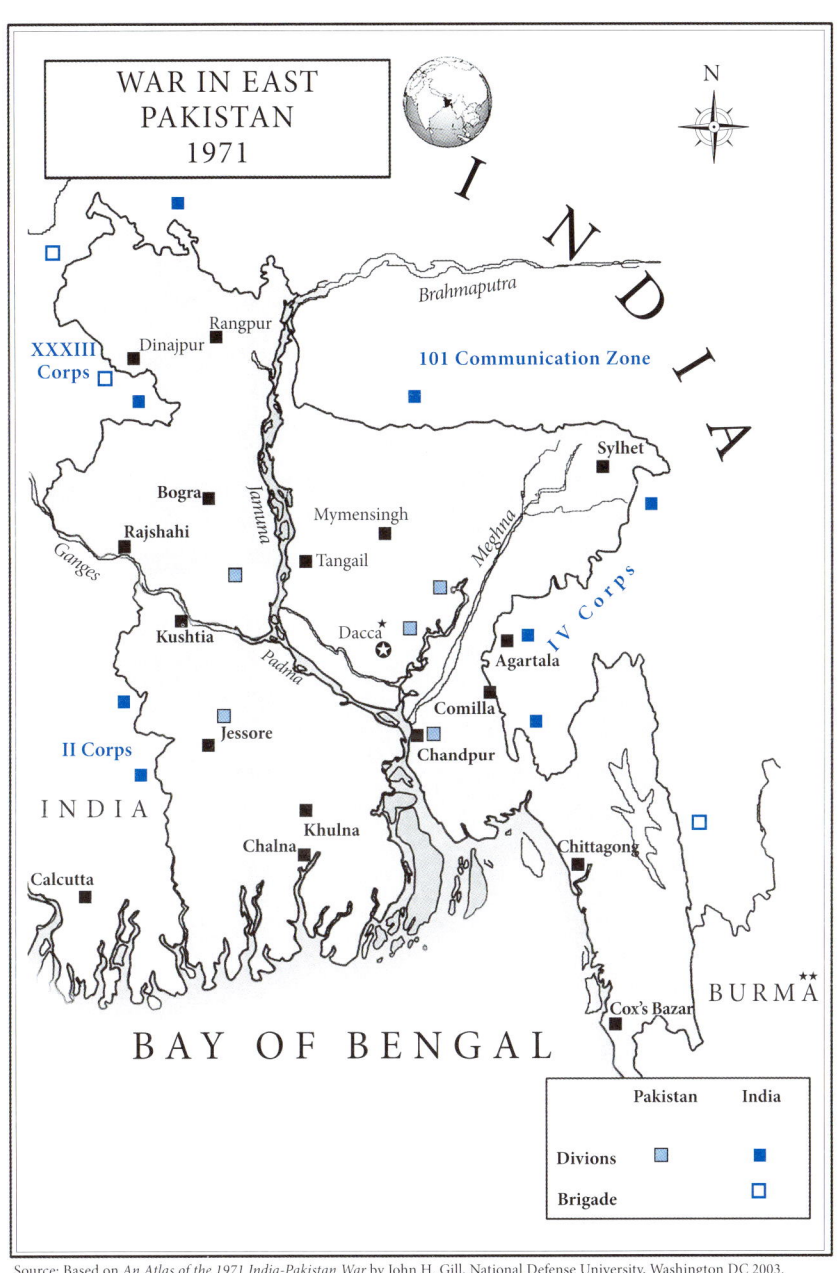

WAR IN EAST
PAKISTAN
1971

I N D I A

Brahmaputra

XXXIII
Corps

Dinajpur

Rangpur

101 Communication Zone

Sylhet

Bogra

Mymensingh

Jamuna

Rajshahi

Ganges

Tangail

Meghna

IV Corps

Kushtia

Dacca

Padma

Agartala

Comilla

II Corps

Jessore

Chandpur

INDIA

Khulna

Chalna

Chittagong

Calcutta

BURMA

Cox's Bazar

BAY OF BENGAL

	Pakistan	India
Divions		
Brigade		

Source: Based on *An Atlas of the 1971 India-Pakistan War* by John H. Gill, National Defense University, Washington DC 2003.

*Current spelling of capital of Bangladesh is Dhaka

**Current name of country is Myanmar

- Western Sector: 9 Infantry and 4 Mountain Divisions.
- South Eastern Sector: 23 Mountain Division, 8 Mountain Division (minus one brigade), and 57 Mountain Division. Headquarters IV Corps would command these troops.
- North Eastern Sector: 6 Mountain Division plus an additional brigade. The parachute battalion would be used for a drop on Tangail north of Dacca.

One month's supply of ammunition, stores, and supplies were to be readied for dissemination around East Pakistan. All seemed to be on track until General Manekshaw appeared on the scene at Fort William with his draft operational order. It then came to light that Manekshaw foresaw an attack to capture certain key towns in East Pakistan, such as Khulna and Chittagong rather than go for the heart of East Pakistan: Dacca. Jacob asserts that Dacca was not even mentioned in the objectives. An argumentative Jacob persisted on inserting the capture of Dacca as a priority. But Aurora sided with Manekshaw till as late as 30 November. The plans were subjected to war games, producing intense debates, particularly on the issue of capturing key towns on the road to Dacca from all directions. India had assembled three full corps plus an ad hoc command known as the 101 Communication Zone Area against Pakistan's actual three divisions (taking into account the reduced size of the ad hoc divisions). It had also strengthened its international ties by signing a 20-year 'Treaty of Peace, Friendship, and Cooperation' with the Soviet Union on 9 August, an act that technically ran counter to its professed non-aligned status but which basically formalized many of the current relationships between Indian and Soviet entities. Finally, the operation instruction was issued by Manekshaw on 16 August, and then all was set for the second war in East Pakistan, directly pitting the Indian and Pakistani armies against each other.

Interestingly, little such discussion was taking place in the Rawalpindi GHQ. Decisions were being made by the upper echelon of the army privately and often without even involving CGS Gul Hassan, who was responsible (in theory) for conveying orders to the field commanders. In fact, Yahya's headquarters seemed to be handling most of the orders to the field. As Gul Hassan asserts: 'I and my staff were tormented by the fact that we were kept totally in the dark because we did not know what, if any[,] action was being planned by our Government to counter the steps that India had embarked upon. The only news which trickled through to us was contained in our media, and that was so heavily sedated that it made the environment more morbid.'[20] Despite this, Gul Hassan did not raise a public fuss nor did he resign.

Gul Hassan, who had visited the East Wing to ascertain the situation on the ground, was not confident that Niazi's plan to fight at the border and then drop back to defend Dacca would work. The Indians would never allow that to happen, and given the terrain and the lack of air support, it would have been an impossible task for his forces to do so without being decimated in the process. But General Hamid continued to believe in Niazi's plan. The other option, of defending East Pakistan by launching a strike in the west, was available but Yahya continued to discount it. He told the British in September that he would not take pre-emptive action against India and reiterated his position in a conversation with US Ambassador Farland in October. He told Farland that 'this was the only sensible position.'[21] He may have been lulling the US into complacency, and in the process managed to do the same to himself and his immediate staff.

In September, Pakistan had already begun moving its forces in West Pakistan to the border with India. 111 Brigade, based in Rawalpindi, a part of the 23 Division of Major General Eftikhar Janjua, was ordered to move out to the Chamb area in September. It was given a series of contradictory instructions over the next few weeks, with orders to prepare to move to its forward positions and then pulled back again. At that point, India had not yet moved its regular formations from their Punjab cantonments, such as Jullundur. Pakistani prevarication and delay allowed them to bring their regular forces forward, displacing the much weaker BSF that confronted Pakistan along the western border during most of September.[22]

In the east, the government of India had taken a decision under the code name 'Operation Jackpot' to allow their army's eastern command to take charge of coordinating and supporting operations of the Mukti Bahini. General Aurora was given this charge. As a result, active operations began along the border with East Pakistan, to test the defences and to soften them up. The longer the Pakistani troops were engaged in battle, the harder it would be for them to fight when full-fledged war broke out. Pakistani reserves of both manpower and material were absent. As Shaukat Riza admits, this Indian approach succeeded: 'By November 20, we had lost most of the border outposts....Indian forces had established their forward bases inside our territory to facilitate offensive operations.'[23] They had the Pakistanis on the move and in an unready state when major Indian moves into East Pakistan began.

INDIA INVADES EAST PAKISTAN

On 19 November 1971, COS Hamid called Gul Hassan and told him to send a message to Niazi that the Indians intended to attack East Pakistan on Eid

Day (the holy Muslim festival), which was incidentally the very next day—20 November. He did not divulge the source but said it was 'reliable'.[24] The attack was to come from 'multiple directions with the main effort from the east (Comilla sector)'.[25] In fact, the Indian attack commenced during the night of 20/21 November and hit twenty-three salients. They quickly established control over areas in the Jessore, Rangpur, and Sylhet sectors. In other areas, the Pakistanis managed to hold on. Meanwhile at GHQ, Gul Hassan tried in vain to engage Yahya in the discussions about opening up of the western front. Yahya dismissed the idea because 'serious negotiations are in progress at this time and if we opened [up] a front in the West, these would be jeopardized'.[26] However, Yahya was in fact toying with the idea (of opening up the western front); on the one hand, he brushed off a foreign reporter's question about future plans, while on the other, at the inauguration of a Chinese plant at the Pakistan Ordnance Factories in Wah around that time, he said: 'In ten days I may be off fighting a war!'[27]

On 23 November, Yahya announced a national state of emergency at 1:00 p.m. (West Pakistan standard time), citing India's three-pronged attack against East Pakistan as the triggering event. At 6:00 p.m., at one of the regular media briefings that had been initiated by the ISPR Directorate, Brigadier A.R. Siddiqi announced that the Indians had attacked in force but that Pakistan had inflicted heavy casualties. He attributed the attack to India's 'desperate haste to capture a sizeable chunk of territory...for the proclamation of the mythical "Bangla Desh" Government'.[28] As Siddiqi was to acknowledge later on, these briefings were based on patchy information and little higher-level guidance—yet, they took on a life of their own, sometimes with comic effect. I recall that a day later, (on 24 November) he announced that Pakistan had destroyed two Indian tanks near Jessore. David Housego of *The Times* of London asked what type of tank it was, to which the deputy director intelligence replied he could not share that information, and, when pressed, cited security reasons. He refused to allow representatives of foreign media in East Pakistan to go see the destroyed tanks with the excuse that the Indians may have recovered them by then. At one point, Malcolm Browne of *The New York Times* piped up: 'Colonel! I was a tank driver and know that one has to identify a tank before shooting it. Did you by chance destroy your own tanks?' After some muttering among the briefers, came the answer: 'They were PT-76s.' The reason for the coy attitude was that Pakistan did not want to annoy the Soviets by mentioning arms that they had supplied the Indians. (The same day, 24 November, Pakistan called all reservists back into service. But no decision had been made yet to open the western front.)

Officially, India continued to deny that it had injected regular forces into East Pakistan. It attributed successes to the Mukti Bahini. But evidence of their presence began to mount. Heavy fighting took place around Hilli in north-western East Pakistan, for instance, and Pakistan TV cameraman, Raza Abbas, captured footage of Indian tanks that had been knocked out in the fighting there. This footage was aired on PTV in the 7:00 p.m. newscast (which I was delivering). India maintained that Pakistani forces took the offensive against Indian targets under the pretence of hitting Mukti Bahini camps inside Indian territory. It also alleged that Pakistan Air Force jets entered its air space on reconnaissance missions. On 21 November, India maintained that Pakistani troops 'supported by tanks and artillery, launched an offensive against the "liberated" territory around Boyra [an area where it said Mukti Bahini had set up camp inside East Pakistan]....The Indian Army mounted a local counter-attack, destroying 13 Pakistani Chaffee tanks and threw the Pakistanis back. It was at this battle that three intruding Sabre jets were brought down by a flight of Indian Gnats—and two of the pilots captured as they parachuted down on Indian territory.'[29] Following this incident, India took the decision to permit Indian forces to cross the border. The fighting escalated, with Niazi taking on the multi-pronged Indian invasion and gradually suffering loss of both land and manpower. By the time Niazi decided to defend Dacca, he realized that he had no reserves worth deploying, nor did he have the means to allow his battle-weary troops to begin a strategic withdrawal from their border outposts into the central triangle around Dacca. Niazi had no air cover, nor did his forces have the ability to ford the rivers and other water bodies that lay between the border and Dacca itself. Meanwhile in Rawalpindi, the GHQ was feverishly trying to cope with the escalating situation in East Pakistan. Its only trump card was an attack in the west.

Yahya felt he needed to get reassurance of their continuing support for Pakistan from the Chinese and sent a delegation comprised Air Chief Rahim Khan, Army CGS Gul Hassan, and a representative of the navy, to Beijing. At the last minute, he asked Rahim if he could include Bhutto in the delegation also, since he (Bhutto) knew the Chinese leadership quite well. Rahim recalls being somewhat surprised that Premier Chou En-lai thought that there would not be a war between India and Pakistan, and stressed the need for a political settlement. However, Chou was also open in his support for Pakistan and asked Rahim about the requirements of the PAF based on expected losses should a conflict erupt. Rahim estimated losing a plane a day and asked for twenty F-6s, (a Chinese variant of the MIG-19), adding that should war not take place, he would send the planes back. Chou readily agreed to providing the aircrafts.[30] (Remarkably, when Rahim re-visited China in February 1972, with Bhutto as president, Chou recalled their earlier exchange and told him that he had been correct in his assessment; Pakistan had lost twenty-six aircraft during the conflict). China expressed concern over the developing situation but at no point made any open commitment to come to Pakistan's aid in the event of an open conflict.

The overall situation was a cause of concern even in far-away Washington, as Nixon and his major advisers, Kissinger and Secretary of State William Rogers, met to review developments. Rogers commented that 'we have to face the fact that Yahya's position militarily is extremely weak,' to which Nixon responded 'He'll be demolished there.' Here was an opportunity for Nixon to weigh in and persuade Yahya to find a political solution rapidly, rather than risk defeat and potential dismemberment. Yet, as the conversation progressed, Nixon found himself committed to a policy of support for Yahya, whom he saw as 'a decent and reasonable man...[if] not always smart politically,'—due more, perhaps, to his dislike for Mrs Gandhi than his approval of Yahya. 'I think our policy wherever we can, should definitely be tilted toward Pakistan, and not toward India,' proclaimed Nixon.[31] The die was cast.

PAKISTAN ATTACKS

Meanwhile, Yahya was forced to confront the rapidly deteriorating situation in the East Wing. The CGS and the C-in-C of the Pakistan Air Force 'dragged him' to the GHQ operations room on 23 November to explain the conditions on the ground to him and to seek a decision to open the front in the west.[32] Even then he delayed matters, promising to make a decision by 27 November, which he did not do. Finally, a tentative decision was made on 29 November to open the western front but no date was set till the next day. Moreover, the decision was not conveyed to the forces on the Pakistan–India border till the evening of 2 December—when they were told that Pakistan would launch its troops on 3 December, the very next day! The naval chief was not even informed directly. He found out from the air chief, and his ships at sea heard about the attack on the radio! The Pakistani plan of attack was more pro forma than anything else. It was hinged on a pre-emptive air strike against Indian airfields.

3 December was the night of a full moon, an appropriate time for launching a madcap adventure that had no hope of success. Starting at 5:09 p.m. that evening, twelve Pakistani F-86 Sabres hurtled off the Peshawar airfield carrying two 500 pound bombs each. Six headed for Srinagar, six for Awantipura. A minute later, eight Mirage IIIEs carrying two 750 pound bombs each headed from Sargodha for Amritsar and Pathankot, accompanied by two F-104 Starfighters equipped only with their guns, to destroy the Amritsar radar. Two minutes later, two more F-104s took off from the same airfield to hit the Faridkot radar. Finally, at 5:23 p.m., eight Sabres headed from Murid airfield to drop their 500 pound bombs on Pathankot. In all, 32

aircraft out of an inventory of 278 fighting aircraft (this included Sabres, F-104s, Mirages, F-6s, B-57 Canberras and RB-57s, but not the two T-33 trainers) took part in the initial strike. Later that night, nine B-57s took off from the Mianwali airfield, heading for six Indian airfields bordering the Punjab; ten B-57s took off from Masroor base for six airfields in the Rajasthan sector, and a lone C-130 took off from Chaklala, Rawalpindi, to drop bombs on Srinagar airport. A total of 140 bombs of 500 pounds each were dropped during the night attacks. No damage assessment was possible.[33] In terms of both audacity and adequateness, this so-called pre-emptive strike was too little too late. Air Marshal Rahim Khan justified it in terms of safeguarding his assets; he did not wish India to come with its full force to destroy Sargodha, for example, and continue taking out Pakistani airfields one by one.[34] Compare this puny effort with the plans that the Israel air force crafted for their pre-emptive strike against the Egyptian air force in June 1967 in the words of the then head of the general staff division and later air chief and president, Ezer Weizman:

> The whole plan rested on total surprise: sending up a large number of planes from a number of bases and dispatching them, at low altitudes, stealthily. All those planes, taking off from different airfields, flying at different speeds, would get into formation as planned, and at precisely the identical moment, they'd arrive at nine Egyptian airfields....If the scales should tip against us, and we failed to destroy the Egyptian air force, only four planes were held in reserve for the defense of Israel's skies. Never has there been such an audacious attack, where everything was thrown into the balance.
>
> On the morning of 5 June, all we had were 196 operational combat planes, from Ouragans to Mirages. Dozens of planes were in the air in foursomes. Each foursome was headed for its own field, followed at precisely co-ordinated intervals, by additional foursomes.[35]

The result of this surprise attack by the Israeli air force was a complete success. Most of the Egyptian air force was destroyed on the ground, with very few losses for the invading Israelis, who relied not on bombs but on cannons and machine guns to do the damage.

That was not the story of the Pakistan Air Force's (PAF) strike that fateful evening when the western front was opened up. The PAF attack did not produce any significant success. Only the Amritsar airfield was blocked and only one of the radar targets was destroyed. Pathankot could not be attacked because of poor visibility. The only saving grace was that all PAF aircraft returned safely. This must have pleased the air chief and his planners, since the idea behind this venture was reportedly to 'coax the IAF [Indian Air Force] to hit out against PAF airfields, [after which] the PAF had hoped to cause unacceptable attrition on the IAF.[36] Pakistan managed to preserve its air force but failed to give any edge to its land forces in the ensuing war.

Even the US allies were taken aback at Pakistan's quantum of attack on 3 December. Admiral Thomas H. Moorer, the CJCS, told the WASAG meeting on 3 December, (held just three hours after the PAF's raid and the move by the Pakistan Army on the western front), that he was 'surprised that the Paks attacked at such a low level. In 1965, they moved much more strongly.' Henry Kissinger, the chair of the group, added: 'These aren't significant fields. That's [a] helluva a way to start a war.' Moorer filled in the details: 'One field had only 12 helos [helicopters] and 16 Gnats [fighter air craft]....There was a field not too far away with 82 aircraft on it, including 42 MIG-21s. They didn't go for them.'[37]

The manner in which the western front was opened and announced fits in with the generally confused state of higher level decision-making in Pakistan at the time. A small coterie of officers around Yahya and their civilian cheerleaders seemed to fall over themselves in proving their bravado and loyalty. Even the head of the ISPR, the official mouthpiece of the regime, did not know that war was imminent on 3 December. He received a call at his home from the defence secretary who told him about an announcement he had heard over Radio Pakistan that India had invaded West Pakistan. Radio Pakistan announced the news at 5 p.m. as did PTV. I was then a newscaster and producer with PTV. I was called from home to the Rawalpindi-Islamabad television station in Chaklala and told to be prepared to go on air as soon as transmission began. I made the announcement with a terse statement provided to me, which later sources (including Brigadier Siddiqi) confirmed was dictated by Information Secretary Roedad Khan. The statement contained was phrased so as to convey that Indian forces had attacked West Pakistan at 'various points'.[38] Apparently the thinking behind this subterfuge was to invoke US help, based, among other things, on the aide memoire of 6 November 1962 to Ayub Khan in which US ambassador McConaughy had promised to assist Pakistan 'in the event of aggression from India against Pakistan.'[39]

Siddiqi recounts the unreal level of confidence at the President's House when he asked about getting the president to approve the press release about the details of the Indian 'attack' so that Pakistan could 'justify the action taken.' In response to Siddiqi's request, Air Chief Marshal Rahim Khan thundered: 'What justification? Success is the biggest justification. My birds should be over Agra by now, knocking the hell out of them. I am only waiting for the good news.' It would be a long wait if he expected to hear that the IAF was out of commission! As it turned out, Siddiqi would not get his press release approved till just before 11:00 p.m., after which he proceeded to brief the 100 plus foreign media persons on the basis of what was clearly a fictional account—originally drafted by Gul Hassan and fine tuned by Siddiqi,—of what had occurred earlier that day. His press release ended with the ironically prophetic words: '1965 is repeating itself.'[40] Little did he know how far he was from predicting the end of this conflict. It would be much worse than 1965, which, after all, was a stalemate. 1971 would be a debacle for Pakistan.

A thousand miles away in the Indian eastern command headquarters, General Jacob got a call from the Army Chief Manekshaw at 6:00 p.m. Manekshaw told him that Pakistan aircraft were bombing Indian airfields in the west and asked him to contact and brief Prime Minister Mrs Gandhi, who was staying at the Raj Bhawan in Calcutta. Jacob asked Manekshaw if he could put his contingency plans for a full scale invasion of East Pakistan into effect and got the green light orally with the promise of a written confirmation to follow. He thought it appropriate to inform his Commander Aurora in the next office and requested Aurora to brief Mrs Gandhi. By 10:30 p.m., orders were ready and issued for the attack of Pakistani airfields in East Pakistan and an assault by Indian land forces. Aurora called for a bottle of whisky as his forces were launched on what they expected to be a short and decisive war.

Yahya made a spirited speech to the nation on 4 December, bringing a religious touch into his remarks: 'The Indian aggressors should know that they have to face twelve crore [120 million] Mujahids of Pakistan, imbued with the love of God and the Holy Prophet. The Indians know that in 1965, our brave forces had smashed them into pieces. But this time, God willing, we shall hit the enemy even harder than before.'[41] Yahya's propagandists chimed in with their own chorus. Z.A. Suleri of *The Pakistan Times* carried an editorial the next day that put a new spin to the misadventure: 'He [Yahya] spoke in the name of Islam....overnight the ethos is deeply Islamic....If crisis truly mirrors the condition and nature of a nation, today our character is transparently clear and no dust of controversy can blur its shining image.' The image he wanted to portray was that of a warring Muslim nation that would vanquish the 'perfidious' Indians. In that emotionally charged atmosphere, it was easy to distort reality.

ORDER OF BATTLE

As India and Pakistan hurtled into yet another conflict, the imbalance of their forces was striking, as was the huge gap between perception and reality on both sides (see map of 1971 war western front: overview). In terms of numbers alone, India's Army had 833,800 men, supported by 1,450 tanks and 3,000 artillery pieces. It had a huge reserve of men and materiel, and greater strategic and logistical depth. Thus, it could sustain losses and replace them. In contrast, Pakistan had a total army of 365,900 men, with 850 tanks and

WAR ON THE
WESTERN FRONT
1971

N

CHINA

AFGHANISTAN

JAMMU
AND
KASHMIR

NWFP

Peshawar
Islamabad
Rawalpindi

Srinagar

Lahore

Amritsar

Multan

Quetta

PUNJAB

COMMAND BOUNDARY

Western Command

New Delhi

BALOCHISTAN

IRAN

Southern Command

SINDH

INDIA

Karachi

GUJARAT

ARABIAN
SEA

	Pakistan	India
Division		
Armour		
Brigade		

Source: Based on *An Atlas of the 1971 India-Pakistan War* by John H. Gill, National Defense University, Washington DC 2003.
NORTH WEST FRONTIER PROVINCE*

800 guns divided between the two wings, with two of the divisions in the East carrying very basic arms and supporting equipment. In the air too, India had a marked advantage; with 625 combat and 450 transport and support aircraft. Pakistan had only 278 fighters and bombers in all. The Indian Navy also outnumbered Pakistan's tiny force, with twenty-one major battleships and an aircraft carrier, four submarines and a number of patrol boats.[42] Facing them were Pakistan's eight major battleships and a handful of patrol boats, plus four submarines (one of which, PNS *Ghazi*, sank off the south-eastern Indian port of Visakhapatnam, probably due to an accident while it was laying mines[43]).

The key numbers lay in the Order of Battle of the ground forces on both sides:

Formations	India	Pakistan
Commands	4	None
Corps	6	4
Armoured Divisions	1 (24 regiments)	2 (21 regiments)
Independent Armour Brigades	4	2
Infantry/Mountain Divisions	25 (285 battalions)	14 (171 battalions)
Independent Infantry Brigades	6	1
Para Brigades	2	1
Civil Armed Forces	88	51
Mukti Bahini Brigades	3 (approx 100,000 men)	

The civil armed forces were a rag tag bunch of ill-equipped and ill-trained men on both sides of the war, more of a hindrance than a help in most cases and, therefore, did not play a significant role in the conflict. But the critical imbalance of the total force structure was in East Pakistan where India had three corps arrayed against the one under-manned and under-equipped Pakistani corps; eight infantry and mountain divisions against four; twenty-three infantry brigades against thirteen; seventy-two infantry battalions against thirty-four; one para brigade against none on the Pakistani side, and, of course the 100,000-odd Mukti Bahini, who created difficulties for the Pakistan Army by infiltrating into East Pakistan and sabotaging installations. India also had a preponderance of armour strength with three regiments, equipped with Soviet amphibious PT-76s, compared with one on the Pakistan side and that too equipped with ancient M-24 Chaffee light tanks. It also had three independent squadrons to one Pakistan squadron. India also had the upper hand in terms of artillery and anti-aircraft weapons. Its biggest advantage, however, lay in the fact that it had a clear aim for its war effort: to capture and liberate East Pakistan. Its troops were trained and rested. On the other hand, Pakistan's troops in the East had an amorphous mandate: to keep India at bay. But they were fighting guerrillas in their midst and an enemy force at its borders. They were already fatigued and demoralized by the time full-scale hostilities began in the West and India commenced its attack on East Pakistan in earnest. Even the army in the West had been deprived of regular training and development in the previous years, as martial law duties and ancillary tasks deprived them of the chance to hone their military skills.

ENDGAME IN EAST PAKISTAN

India's strategic aim in the East remained clear: draw the Pakistanis out to the borders in all directions, engage them first with the Mukti Bahini and the BSF, and force them to commit resources to separate battles to preserve their lines of communication, thus diluting their strength and spreading them out. This would further make them incapable of falling back on to the centre in an orderly manner. The major attacks would then take place speedily from all four directions with a view to encircling Pakistani troops wherever possible and forcing them to surrender. The main target was Dacca, the centre of gravity of East Pakistan's defence. India's heli-lift capability would allow it to leap frog Pakistani defences and drop troops near Dacca, creating panic and eventually leading to the surrender of all troops in East Pakistan. India had conducted a masterly external manoeuvre, using its diplomatic skills to isolate Pakistan in world opinion and relying on the Mukti Bahini and the Bangladesh government-in-exile to create a difficult political situation for Pakistan.

By launching a counter-attack from West Pakistan to force India to withdraw forces from the East and also to bring international attention onto the conflict, Yahya hoped that he would then have time to work out some sort of devolution scheme with the East Pakistanis, but not with Sheikh Mujib and his party. This was a vain hope. The delay in launching the attack from West Pakistan, with Yahya and his cohort busying themselves with US–China relations and nursing the hope that Chinese and US pressures would force India to refrain from attacking East Pakistan—made the eventual attack lose both surprise and momentum. Moreover, Pakistan's restrictive war directive that forced it to defend every inch of territory in both East and West Pakistan made its task a huge challenge. It expected India to launch its main attack into East Pakistan along the Jessore–Dacca route, commencing at the border crossing from Bangaon in West Bengal to Benapole in East Pakistan and heading in a north-easterly direction toward Jessore and eventually to Dacca.[44] An auxiliary Indian effort was expected from the north-east in the Sylhet area, as was a para drop near Tangail, north of Dacca. Pakistani forces were supposed to fight for territory at the border, then drop back into fortresses and use them to interdict Indian movements through the gaps.

In the words of a later Pakistan National Defence College study of the war, 'the Indians planned and executed their offensive against East Pakistan in a textbook manner. It was a classic example of thorough planning, minute coordination and bold execution.'[45] The credit clearly goes to General Jacob's meticulous preparations in the Indian eastern command and to the implementation by his corps commanders, like Tappy Raina in West Bengal, who improved in the field and kept the momentum going. Having lured the Pakistani forces to the borders in the period 20 November to 3 December, they managed to isolate Pakistani defenders in their separate sectors, bypassing tough targets and hitting them from the rear. Pakistan's eastern command, meanwhile, stopped functioning as a cohesive entity controlling operations in the whole theatre. Each division was more or less left on its own. Strategy was not Niazi's forte. He was often described as more of a platoon commander, very deft in laying out lines of fire and defence for a platoon or a company, but no more.

India's 4 Division launched its offensive from the west into East Pakistan to capture Jhenida and Megura and then head toward Faridpur, while 9 Division was to cut the road to Jessore. The Pakistani 9 Division, under Major General M.H. Ansari, was defending this sector. Even while the ISPR spokesmen were informing the Pakistani and foreign media in Rawalpindi's Hotel Intercontinental briefing room that heavy battles were taking place and Pakistan was inflicting heavy casualties on the Indian attackers, the Pakistani 107 Brigade chose to give up Jessore without a fight and headed toward Khulna rather than Megura. Another brigade that was supposed to eventually fall back to Faridpur headed to Kushtia instead, linking up with troops of the 16 Division. Jhenida was surrendered on 6 December, and thus 9 Division basically held out with its remnants in the area west of Faridpur till 15 December.

In the north-west sector, India met very stiff resistance at Hilli as their 33 Corps with the 20 Mountain Division, two independent infantry brigade groups, one engineers' brigade, and two armour regiments came up against Major General Nazar Hussain Shah's 16 Division, with its 23, 34, and 205 Brigades, the sole 29 Cavalry Regiment, a field regiment of artillery, two mortar batteries, and a reconnaissance battalion. The heavily outnumbered Pakistani troops fought hard but eventually had to give up Hilli and fall back on Rangpur and Dinajpur where they held out till the end of the war.

In the eastern sector, Pakistan's 14 Division under Major General Abdul Majeed Qazi had a brigade each at Sylhet, Maulvi Baazar, and Brahman Baria. The 39 ad hoc Division under Major General A. Rahim Khan held the Comilla–Chittagong area with its two brigades. When India launched its attack with its 4 Corps, comprising 8 Mountain Division, 23 Mountain Division, 57 Mountain Division and Kilo Force (of Bengalis and other paramilitary forces), the Pakistani troops fell back in disarray and 'contrary to orders', 313 Brigade joined 202 Brigade at the Sylhet 'fortress.' As General Jacob writes: 'When we got radio intercepts confirming their move to Sylhet, we were very relieved. It meant, for all practical purposes, that two infantry brigades were out on a limb at Sylhet where they could be contained and their effectiveness neutralized.' After the war, while interrogating General Qazi, Jacob asked why he had moved his brigade to Sylhet. Jacob reports Qazi as having said that 'he (Qazi) was determined that he would not let us capture Sylhet.'[46] Niazi's fortress mentality had taken hold, preventing 14 Division and 39 Division from playing any role in defending the centre of gravity at Dacca. General Rahim Khan of 39 ad hoc Division was wounded in an air attack and got himself evacuated to Burma, the only senior officer who managed to survive capture in East Pakistan. (Later he was to become a senior official in the Ministry of Defence under Bhutto.)

The northern sector included, among other places, Dacca. Its defence lay in the hands of the 36 ad hoc Division under Major General Jamshed Ahmed with his two infantry battalions and a motley crew of civil armed forces. Against him was arrayed the curiously named 101 Communications Zone of the Indian Army with the 93 and 167 Brigade groups as well as some Mukti Bahini forces. Though heavily outnumbered, General Jamshed's forces fought a valiant rearguard action, holding out till 6 December when they fell back to their fortresses at Mymensigh and Jamalpur. There occurred one of those rare wartime exchanges between India and Pakistan commanders. Brigadier H.S. Kler sent a written letter by courier to Lt. Col. Sultan of 31 Baluch, the commander of Jamalpur Fortress, telling them his 'garrison has been cut off from all sides and you have no escape route. One brigade with full compliment (sic) of artillery had already been built up and another will be striking by the morning.' He told Sultan that forty air sorties had been allotted to Kler for the attack on Jamalpur and asked for an immediate response. The reply was quick and dramatically came wrapped around a bullet:

> I want to tell you that the fighting you have seen so far is very little, in fact, the fighting has not even started. So let us stop negotiating and start the fight.
>
> 40 sorties, I may point out, are inadequate. Ask for many more....Let me see you with a sten [a light submachine gun] in hand next time instead of the pen you seem to have so much mastery over.
>
> Now get on and fight.[47]

The troops of 36 Division kept fighting till they were ordered on 10 December to fall back toward Dacca, suffering heavily in that endeavour. On 11 December, India dropped a paratroop regiment at Tangail that linked up with 14 Corps and other forces to enter Dacca, provoking the surrender of Pakistani forces in East Pakistan. Jacob had allowed a CBS TV correspondent and others to see a whole brigade of paratroops at Dum Dum airport in Calcutta. When Niazi got these reports of troops emplaning, he panicked, and overestimated the number of troops dropped near Tangail. Yahya and Hamid had been feeding him a story about expected help from their allies. On 12 December, Gul Hassan was asked by General Hamid to convey a message to Niazi, which he did via telephone in Pushto, a language that Niazi did not understand but he found someone who did speak the language at his headquarters. Hassan told him: 'Yellow and White help expected from north and south shortly,' hinting at Chinese and American assistance that Yahya had been talking about. It transpired that this was a bogus message sent merely to keep Niazi's spirits up![48] To confound matters further, Hamid later denied being the requestor of this message.

The Indians had been intercepting these messages and also Niazi's frantic one that stated: 'Enemy heli-dropped approx one brigade south of Narsinghdi and landed one para brigade in Tangail area. Request friends arrive Dacca by air first flight 12 December.'[49]

Both Niazi and his commanders in Rawalpindi were living in their make-believe world. No such help was on the way.

THE FINAL WAR

Pakistan had a two-phase plan for its operations in the western theatre. In Phase 1, its formations from the north to the south were to attack with a view to protecting Pakistani territory, while forcing India to commit its troops, particularly to the northern Punjab and Kashmir. In Phase 2, a counterpunch was to be launched by 2 Corps in the area south of the Sutlej River, thrusting deep into the soft underbelly of the Indian Punjab and threatening its key towns as well as supply routes to Kashmir (see map Pakistan's proposed counteroffensive). With the capture of critical Indian territory, Pakistan's high command felt it could bring India to the negotiating table before East Pakistan fell. This did come to pass, as the attacks petered out along the ceasefire line in Kashmir and the border between the Indian and Pakistani Punjabs. The counterpunch never materialized and Pakistan's armoured strike force lay in its protective cover in the Changa Manga forest, never to do battle!

In Kashmir, 12 Division went on the attack into Poonch with its two brigades (2 and 26 AK Brigades) on the night of 3 December, breaking through the Than Pir ridge overlooking the Chandak bridge and the Chandak–Poonch road, and getting to within two to three miles north-east of Poonch. There they met an entrenched Indian force and the attack was brought to a halt within two days. South of them in Chamb, 23 Division went on the attack with the aim of securing the west bank of the Tawi River and thus preventing India from exploiting the Manawar–Tawi Gap that would give it rapid access to Gujrat and the GT road in Pakistan. 66 Brigade, 111 Brigade, and 2 Armoured Brigade were finally launched after weeks of frustrating wait. 111 Brigade was missing its regular commander, Brigadier Rahimuddin, who was at that time presiding over Sheikh Mujib's tribunal and the CO of 42 Punjab. Lt. Col. S.K. Tressler, was given joint command of the regiment and the brigade in the attack phase. Tressler had barely commanded his own regiment for one year. He was not ready for the dual responsibility and in fact got separated from his forces across the Tawi with his freshly minted aide, Second Lieutenant Raheel Anjum Malik, who had joined the newly-raised regiment directly from the military academy. They hid themselves in the tall grasses in a water-logged area, surrounded by search parties of Indian troops, who knew that the Pakistanis had been isolated, and finally made it back the next day. Eventually Brigadier Naseer Ullah Babar took over command of the brigade.

Under an ambitious commander, Major General Eftikhar Janjua, the division attempted to do more than it was commanded to do, capturing Chamb, and then heading across the river to Jaurian and Pallanwala. But before it took Pallanwala, it lost its commander in a freak accident when his helicopter struck a tree while landing and he suffered burns and internal injuries, dying soon after he reached Kharian hospital. The overall attack failed because the Indians anticipated it. The element of surprise had been lost. Further north, as they had done in 1965, the Indians quickly straightened the border in the frigid wastes of Kargil, occupying the high ground that allowed them to protect the road to Leh.

In the Sialkot sector, the Pakistani 1 Corps was instructed to defend the Ravi–Chenab corridor and prevent India from making for the headworks and main towns beyond the west bank of the Ravi River. As usual, both sides straightened out the border, occupying enclaves on either side of the river. 8 Division under Major General Abdul Ali Malik was in the Shakargarh area and rapidly advanced to clear the Dharam enclave on the west bank of the Ravi. (I was assigned to this formation during the early days of the war as a correspondent for PTV and interviewed six captured Indian soldiers. This event was captured by an ISPR photographer and found its way into newspapers and books on the war.) The Indians countered by occupying the Jassar enclave on the east bank of the Ravi. By 5 December, the Indians had launched their main offensive into the Shakargarh Bulge with a view to capturing Tanda, Marala, Sialkot, Pasrur, and Narowal, after which they were to head toward Wazirabad and Gujrat. They had immediate success in penetrating up to the Basantar Nullah and coming to the outskirts of Zafarwal, where Pakistan held out at the Bund (mud embankment). In doing so, they managed to occupy the northern half of the Pakistani Army, preventing it from contributing to any later development in the south. Before the fighting came to a stand-off, Pakistan had managed to lose a large number of tanks and troops as the 8 Armoured Brigade, under Brigadier Mohammed Ahmed, launched waves of tanks against Indian tanks in a hull-down position. 13 Cavalry lost many officers in the process and the Indians managed to deprive Pakistan of their equipment by launching anti-tank rockets against any Pakistani tank that was hit, so that it could not be recovered or repaired.[50]

In that early phase, there were limited incursions into Indian territory in the Lahore and Sulemanki sectors. A much larger and ambitious effort in the south failed miserably. This was the attack launched by Major General B.M. Mustafa's 18 Division which had apparently been cooked up between him and the COAS. The CGS, Gul Hassan, denies being part of this plan. It involved a bold move across open desert, without air cover, toward the Indian town of Jaisalmer in Rajasthan. The air chief, Rahim Khan, states that he was asked for air support and told the army that he did not have any bases close enough to provide more than perfunctory support. He thought the army would have 'their pants handed to them' by the Indians. Indeed that is close to what happened. The IAF had a field day, shooting up tanks like sitting ducks.[51] Indeed, some of the vivid scenes of that debacle were captured by a British ITN TV crew under Rowlinson Carter, that had managed to sneak out of Rawalpindi and head south. They came across the attack on a train loaded with tanks and captured the attack on film, only to be discovered by an officer who demanded the film. An alert cameraman had managed to change the film cartridge by the time the Pakistani soldiers came upon them and the infuriated major managed to 'expose' raw film rather than the film containing those scenes! After being berated, Carter was brought back to Rawalpindi, where he gleefully reported his adventure to me after sending the film off to ITN via Kabul.

Essentially, the war on the western front petered out within a matter of days. Brigadier Siddiqi recalls the Chinese military attaché on a visit to GHQ remarking to him that the fighting was more or less over after he saw the map showing Pakistani and Indian positions in the first week. Phase 2 of the Pakistan attack plan was never launched, because the Indians did not see the need to shift their troops from the south to northern Punjab and Kashmir. which would have left them vulnerable to a counterpunch by 2 Corps from the south. The Pakistani 2 Corps therefore waited in vain, as did the 1 Armoured Division. In fact, Pakistan managed to deplete 2 Corps by removing 33 Division and then dividing its troops between 18 Division in the south and 1 Corps in the north. On 14 December, 2 Corps was told to prepare to move to its forward positions. However, on 6:45 p.m. on 16 December, new orders came to wait for further instructions. The whole attacking caravan was dismantled and the equipment and weapons stored for safekeeping. The next day, the whole war was over. The ceasefire came into effect at 10:00 p.m. on 17 December. Another war was coming to an end for Pakistan, except that this time, it would be under circumstances that would continue to haunt the national psyche for decades to come.

SURRENDER

As early as 9 December, Governor A.M. Malik of East Pakistan had sent a signal to Yahya seeking an immediate ceasefire. Yahya replied that he left it to Malik and Niazi to decide what to do. As the war progressed and things heated up, Malik called a meeting at Governor's House at noon on 14 December. As usual, this message was intercepted by the Indians and General Jacob ordered an air strike on Governor's House, Dacca to help Malik make up his mind. The attack apparently had the desired effect. Malik offered his resignation to Yahya later that evening. Niazi meanwhile was on the phone with Hamid in Rawalpindi seeking help in expediting a ceasefire. Again the Indians listened in on the conversation.[52] Yahya then sent a message to Niazi praising him for having 'fought a heroic battle against overwhelming odds.... You have now reached a stage where further resistance is no longer humanly possible nor will it serve any useful purpose.' Yahya then informed Niazi that he was seeking UN help in brokering a ceasefire and to 'guarantee the safety of armed forces and all other people who may be likely targets of miscreants [the Mukti Bahini].'[53]

Niazi still believed that he had the forces to fight the Indians. But the advisor to the governor, Major General Rao Farman Ali had already been in touch with the UN seeking an end to the fighting. Farman Ali was eventually absolved of all responsibility for the debacle in East Pakistan by the Hamoodur Rehman Commission Report. Niazi served as a perfect scapegoat. His bluster and bravado made him an easy target. As late as 14 December, he sent another message to Yahya saying that his decision to fight it out still stood. That evening General Hamid called him to tell him that West Pakistan was in danger and that he should make arrangements to stop the fighting in the East, in other words, to arrange for surrender. Niazi believes that Yahya was too drunk to speak with him at that time. He alleges that an intoxicated Air Marshal Rahim Khan then came on the line to tell him to obey the orders to stop fighting. Niazi and Farman Ali then went to see Herbert Spivack, the consul general of the US in Dacca to present their terms for surrender. General Jacob heard about this visit but could not get confirmation from the US consul general in Calcutta. The US checked with Yahya through

Ambassador Farland and then asked its UN ambassador to pass Niazi's proposal that he had given to Spivack on to Bhutto so that Spivack could give it to the Indians at the UN. Bhutto chose not to do so. 'After confirming that Yahya wanted the message delivered, the Department [of State] instructed USUN [the US mission to the United Nations] to deliver the message to the Indian delegation with the caveat that the United States took no position on the contents of the message.'[54] Eventually on 15 December, Manekshaw received the message in Delhi and instructed Jacob on 16 December at 9:15 a.m. to go to Dacca and organize the surrender. Halfway there, in Jessore, he heard about Niazi's invitation to lunch.

Niazi had met up with the Indian General Nagra by the time Jacob arrived at the lunch meeting with the details of the surrender plan. At the ceremony, Jacob proposed that after the signing of the document, Niazi would hand over his ceremonial sword. Niazi said he did not have one but offered his pistol instead. At 4:55 p.m. on 16 December at the Race Course Ground, Niazi signed and handed over the instrument of surrender to General Jagjit Singh Aurora, following it up with the handing over a pistol. Much later, Jacob was to discover that the pistol apparently was not Niazi's own weapon but a messed up and dirty weapon probably taken from a military policeman![55] With that final dirty trick, Niazi had the last laugh, it seems. But it was an expensive one: Pakistan now had more than 90,000 persons, soldiers and others in East Pakistan, who were now prisoners of war in India, and would remain so for more than two years.

In Rawalpindi, a strange comic opera was taking place on 17 December. Yahya was getting ready to offer a new constitution for the country as part of a transfer of power package, devolving many responsibilities to both wings and to individual provinces. His statement was to be read by me on PTV at 7:00 p.m. Sitting in the hot studio lights, I waited and waited but no word came from the President's House. Finally, a colleague rushed in around 7:17 p.m. to say that the speech was cancelled on the orders of the secretary of the Ministry of Information, Roedad Khan, and I should hand over the text. Copies of the text of the constitutional plan had already been sent to foreign journalists but a courier was sent to get them back. Some journalists did not return their copies. Neither did I. To this day, there has been no coherent explanation for why this speech was written for release on that day, when Dacca had fallen. On reading the text today, it seems clear that it was nine months too late.

A NEW SOUTH ASIA

The map of South Asia had been changed dramatically by the events of 1971. India was triumphant and the regional hegemon. Pakistan had a new reality as a weaker state that it would find hard to accept. The echoes of this war would reverberate into the following decades. These were also the concerns that had bothered Pakistan's ally: the United States.

As early as 8 December, Henry Kissinger was lecturing his president and Attorney General John Mitchell in the Oval Office that: 'The Indian plan is now clear. They're going to move their forces from East Pakistan to the West. They will then smash the Pakistan land forces and air forces, annex the part of Kashmir that is in Pakistan and then call it off.' But his fears went beyond that to a potential Iranian position that West Pakistani instability 'posed a mortal threat to Iran.' Kissinger felt that the centrifugal forces in West Pakistan would be liberated, with Balochistan and the NWFP taking off on their own.[56] The CIA appeared to support this view, having received a report from a 'reliable source' the day before that indicated that Mrs Gandhi had spelt out the triple objective for Indian forces:

A. Liberation of Bangladesh
B. The incorporation into India of the southern area of Azad (Pakistani-held) Kashmir
C. The destruction of Pakistani armoured and air force strength so that Pakistan can never threaten India again.[57]

The CIA too predicted the downfall of Yahya. It also examined the possibility of NWFP and Balochistan becoming separate autonomous entities. On 12 December, another inside report from Mrs Gandhi's cabinet room confirmed the CIA's analysis. In Mrs Gandhi's words: 'India will emerge from the war as the dominant power in South Asia and also the Indian Ocean. China will respect India and may even decide to improve relations with India. On the other hand, Pakistan will lose its economic power without which it will not be able to support a large military complex. The current Pakistani military leadership will not be able to survive the military defeat.' Mrs Gandhi also expressed the hope that 'a new democratic Pakistan, based on autonomous republics, will emerge and that it will desire to have friendly relations with India.'[58]

Mrs Gandhi asked her defence chiefs to be ready to drive into Sialkot and then proceed as deep as possible, even up to Rawalpindi, with the aim of destroying Pakistan. The CIA managed to get actual minutes of this meeting and passed them to Washington urgently. Pakistan had in the meantime asked the US for three items: C-130 aircraft (possibly to evacuate its troops from

East Pakistan), F-86 aircraft, and ammunition for its 105mm guns. The US could not supply these items from its foreign military sales programme because of the embargo. Nixon asked Secretary of State Rogers to leave the room and then told his cabinet colleagues that the US would find another way to get these needed supplies to save Pakistan. Nixon then said he was going to ask the CIA station chiefs in Iran, Jordan, and Saudi Arabia to urgently approach the rulers of these three US allies to supply the weapons to Pakistan. The CIA station chief in Saudi Arabia contacted the head of the general intelligence department, Kamal Adham, and went with him to see Dr Rashad Pharaon, an advisor to the king, in Riyadh. The special and 'personal' Nixon request was conveyed to the king. All three CIA station chiefs were also asked to convey to the rulers that in a few hours' time, the US ambassador would probably arrive to warn them against any such help to Pakistan since that would infringe US laws against onward transmission of military supplies. Nixon's message was: 'Ignore the advice of the US ambassadors and do what the CIA station chief has requested!'[59] This last minute effort did not yield fruit.

Yahya had by then sent Bhutto to the United Nations to plead Pakistan's case with his customary eloquence and élan. Bhutto sought a meeting with Nixon but Kissinger managed to keep Bhutto away from Washington at that point. On 11 December, Kissinger and Bhutto spoke on the telephone and Kissinger conveyed to Bhutto the combined views of Nixon and Kissinger; that the two of them would press for an end to the fighting in the deliberations of the Security Council, even going to the extent of calling it a 'naked case of aggression.' But Kissinger prepared Bhutto for the eventuality that its resolution might be defeated. 'You have to decide whether you want to go to a simple ceasefire resolution, because it isn't that we don't want to help you, it is that we want to preserve you.' Bhutto expressed his thanks for Kissinger's efforts and promised also to make clear to the Chinese the nature of US support. 'I want you to know that it is deeply appreciated what you are doing, and we are eternally beholden....You will see the affects (sic) of that when this crisis is over how we will express our appreciation.'[60]

Just three days after that conversation between Bhutto and Kissinger, Yahya's 'friend' Ambassador Farland sent a long telegram to the Department of State, predicting the collapse of the Pakistan Army in East Pakistan and the likelihood that it would cease fighting in the West too. He saw Yahya being eased out and the 'rise to real power of Bhutto.' If Yahya chose to 'accept the loss of East Pakistan and to seek [a] way to halt further fighting in the west, such strategy would be difficult to swallow, but would preserve Pak army QUOTE fight another day UNQUOTE and would enable Pak army to retain to some extent its privileged position [and] control of media. Propensity of Paks to accept their own propaganda might ease pain of ignominious defeat in East Pakistan.'[61] Farland proposed to tell the Pakistanis, 'who have stumbled from miscalculation in March to misadventure in December,' that 'tossing good money after bad in taking on India in [the] West is [a] short-sighted folly.' and sought help in bringing the Chinese, the Iranians, and friendly Arab states to prevent Pakistan from pursuing hostilities in the west.

In the White House on 16 December, news of the Indians' unilateral ceasefire was welcomed by Kissinger in a telephone conversation with Nixon. 'We have made it!' he exulted as he and Nixon strategized on how to get credit in the news media for bringing the conflict to an end. 'Congratulations, Mr President!' said Kissinger. 'You saved West Pakistan!'[62] In the process, Nixon had managed to abet a huge change in Pakistani politics, bringing to power— in place of his friend Yahya—Zulfikar Ali Bhutto, a man whom he had considered a 'total demagogue.'[63]

Finally, the curtain fell on the year 1971—and Pakistan had lost more than half its country. It had 9,183 total casualties, against its estimate of some 30,000 total Indian casualties of wounded and dead. Pakistan had 3,132 officers, JCOs, and soldiers killed or missing, almost equally divided between East and West Pakistan (although lack of reporting from East Pakistan near the end of the conflict with India may have hidden some more Pakistani deaths).[64] And India had over 90,000 prisoners of war taken from East Pakistan.

WHY PAKISTAN LOST: A SECRET REPORT

The reasons for the debacle on the battlefield and the dismemberment of Pakistan have been the subject of many debates in the decades since 1971. Bhutto commissioned a group led by former Chief Justice, Hamoodur Rehman, to study the subject with the help of civilian and military advisors. Their monumental report never saw the light of day until it was leaked to the world by Indian media and then followed up by the Pakistani press more than twenty-five years later, allowing the government to declassify it. It is likely that the army did not want it to appear, fearing it would harm the institution's image even more. Bhutto too, although he came out lightly criticized, likely feared a backlash.

The Pakistan Army did commission its own review of the war by a team of eight officers (including one from the air force) immediately after the war, as early as 29 December 1971, but it was confined to the western front and kept strictly to purely military aspects of operations.[65] The unsigned report was presented on 31 January 1972, but it was not distributed widely. The authors of this report could not resist using hyperbole while describing the emotional impact of their three-week journey across the battlefields of a lost war:

> In our three weeks of incessant travel, we stood exposed to many ugly realities: close enough to be stared in the face.
>
> We saw effects and consequences of war in its many facets as an aspect of human behaviour: brutal, unforgiving, yet pulsating, demanding in skill, imagination and prowess; above all capricious—all at once.
>
> We witnessed chaos that spread on tractless (sic) sands. We heard stories of broken promises, near impossible tasks, inadequate resources aggravated by want of even a listening ear. We discovered staff duties [military processes] and battle procedures culled from decades of experience of fighting wars in all parts of the world and so assiduously taught in peace for application in war, mercilessly trampled at the feet of foretold results...Equally, we heard with choked throats innumerable acts of raw courage, superb leadership, defiant valour at all echelons of command.[66]

This was just the opening. The review was very critical and incisive since the authors believed 'that this Army has the courage to confess its short-falls and the supreme faith that we have the mettle of which soldiers are made of (sic). Give us the tools and leave us to train in our trade of arms, and then sooner than many faint hearts may think, we can deliver the goods—unfailingly and worthily to redeem the honour lost.' Unequivocally, the GHQ team declared that 'the war on the West Pakistan borders was started much too late to influence the battle of East Pakistan. By 3 Dec[ember] [19]71, [the]enemy had gained a firm foothold on the soil of East Pakistan, destroyed our air force in that sector and paralysed (sic) all communications in that wing....Had a more broad based policy formulation machinery existed, a timely and correct decision may have been taken which may have helped either to avert total disaster in East Pakistan or may have put us in a better bargaining position.' It is not clear if they were referring to a purely military machinery or a broader civil–military machinery. The truth is, however, that centralized decision-making within the inner circle around Yahya—excluding even key GHQ staff—and without any civilian input or oversight, allowed the military high command to make decisions without any basis in reality.

The gap between perception and reality is epitomized in General Yahya's statement to the Hamoodur Rehman Commission and in his deposition to the Lahore High Court of 1978. In those documents he maintains firmly that India launched the attacks on the western front on 3 December, and that 'with regard to the military defence of Pakistan, the strategy was framed with the proposition that fight shall take place with India on the borders of both wings. Our main aim was to continue fighting (sic). In furtherance of this we were about to launch another attack from West Pakistan.' He then blames Air Chief

Rahim Khan who purportedly 'betrayed and committed treachery by saying that he had no planes to fight with. Indira Gandhi had also declared a ceasefire at this juncture for the reasons unknown to the deponent [Yahya]. The deponent was told that we were left with fuel which is sufficient for not more than 12 days. [A] similar state of affairs was also disclosed about the ammunition. These were the circumstances which compelled the deponent to accept ceasefire and enter into negotiation.'[67]

This was the naive and incomplete analysis of the head of the state and the supreme commander of Pakistani forces in 1971. He failed to explain why Pakistan did not open the western front much sooner, nor did he explain why he failed to reach a political solution involving the Awami League, especially since in his deposition he goes to great lengths to blame Mr Bhutto for sabotaging all attempts to reach an accord with the Awami League and even delaying his return from the UN in New York. He also blames the 'Russians' for aiding India against Pakistan. His conclusion was, by any standards, startling: 'I can confidently say that no military historian would call this a military defeat.'[68]

It is significant that Yahya made no mention of the manner in which defence plans were formulated nor of the mechanisms that existed, at least on paper, for discussing and agreeing to a strategy of national defence. As combined C-in-C of the army and president—and therefore supreme commander—Yahya bypassed all formal decision-making systems. Instead, he and his inner circle of advisors came up with both political and military ideas and orders without the benefit of debate or input from relevant elements in the army, navy, and air force. Senior civilian officials from the ministries of foreign affairs and even defence found themselves out of the loop. Yahya could not tolerate disagreement with his views. Even his own principal advisor reportedly told the Hamoodur Rehman Commission that often Yahya would postpone decisions when faced with arguments that did not accord with his views, and then later on he would come up with whatever solution he felt comfortable with.[69] There was no coordination between the three armed services, compounded by their geographic separateness: the navy being in Karachi, the air force in Peshawar, while the army was headquartered in Rawalpindi. There was a JCSC and a Joint Warfare Directorate. But neither appears to have been actively involved in formulating decisions. The only JCSC meeting since July 1964 (a year before the previous war with India) had been held in August 1967!

The Defence Committee of the Cabinet, comprising the president and ministers involved with defence planning, existed on paper but had not met more than two times in the five years preceding the 1971 war. The last meeting had been in November 1968! Similarly, the Secretaries Coordination Committee on defence planning that afforded civilian officials an opportunity to contribute to the overall coordination of defence strategies and plans and produce a War Book had been largely dormant, the last update to the war plans being done in 1970. Finally, the NSC provided a potentially useful forum for assessing intelligence and giving direction to the various intelligence agencies. The president headed this body, set up in 1968, while the minister of home and Kashmir affairs was the vice chair. With Yahya otherwise pre-occupied and generally allergic to this formal decision-making apparatus, the NSC was left to operate under the direction of the president's aide, Major General Ghulam Umar. An atmosphere was created where Yahya only got news that he wanted to hear. No wonder he was to assert even as late as 1978 that Pakistan did not lose the war.

In fact, he would have been surprised to learn that his own GHQ staff contradicted Yahya's view within weeks of the end of the war. Criticizing the conduct of war, they stated that the 'war on the western front was delayed up to 3 Dec. 71 with no discernable (sic) advantage and once this front was activated, full weight of the offensive was not thrown into it when a sizeable (sic) part of the Indian Army was deeply committed in East Pakistan. It was limited to nibbling operations and the might of the Army was kept back for a more appropriate moment. The appropriate moment never came and the reserves never got launched.' Again the military's own analysts felt that had 'a suitable machinery existed at national level, these important decisions could have been taken in time and with a better understanding of the situation.'[70] The conclusions of the military's analysis was that: 'The causes of the disaster varey (sic) from running down of Army's professional efficiency by years devoted [to] involvement in martial law duties at the cost of military training, to inadequacy of resources, faulty policy formulation and unsound judgement (sic) and untimely decisions.'

A stinging indictment of the conduct of war from one brigadier came in a submission to the Hamoodur Rehman Commission.[71] Brigadier F.B. Ali, commander artillery of the 6 Armoured Division, sent his analysis of the debacle to the commission on 2 January 1972. He accused the military high command of not updating its war plan (which was based on a war solely on the western front), and failing to launch a full-scale offensive on the western front that would have led to loss of territory and forces by India in that theatre. He also pointed to the lack of 'foresight [and] imagination' on the part of the MO Directorate of the Pakistan Army's GHQ. The GHQ had created an Army Reserve North under Major General Muhammad Bashir Khan to oversee operations of, among others, 1 Corps (although Brig. Ali believes this was partly to keep an eye on the Bengali commander of 6 Armoured Division, Maj. Gen. M.I. Karim). 1 Corps sent numerous warnings after 12 December describing the deteriorating situation in its sector to the GHQ and asking for permission to move the 6 Armoured Division into action. All their messages were ignored. It was not until 6:30 p.m. on 16 December that permission was given for this move. But by then it was too little, too late. Brig. Ali also lashed out at General Irshad for 'unnecessarily' abandoning 'large tracts of our territory', and not making 'a single attempt to recover any of this territory, even though he had the mean[s] and the opportunity.' He cites a visit by General Hamid, the vice chief, in which General Hamid suggested to Irshad to 'use his reserve to make a flank attack on the enemy from the north of Zafarwal. This was never carried out.' Irshad also failed to concentrate his artillery and use it to good effect, according to Brig. Ali, ignoring General Hamid's suggestions also to do the same. Indeed. Brig. Ali sent a written complaint to Major General Muhammad Bashir Khan on 15 December, during the war, about the poor employment of artillery and suggested massing artillery to good effect in the 1 Corps sector of operations.[72] Nothing happened in response. Further, Brig. Ali stated to the Hamoodur Rehman Commission that the 15 Division 'took practically no part in the entire war, apart from abandoning the Phulkian Salient' to the Indians. He had also been the colonel staff of 18 Division in the south and had left it with a 'sound operational plan.' Instead, after he left, the division commander 'launched a hare-brained attack in impossible terrain. This met a severe reverse,'[73] adding to the litany of faults and failures of senior military leadership during the war.

While these criticisms by the GHQ team and individuals such as Brig. Ali, were never tested through an open inquiry or by giving the accused generals a chance of defending themselves, they were certainly not too far from reality. The aftermath of the war contributed to a general state of unhappiness that affected large numbers of officers. In the case of Brig. Ali, it led him to take actions against the military high command at the end of the war and in the year after it which left a mark on the history of the army.

A detailed analysis of the air, sea, and land operations by the GHQ's own team also lead to some broad conclusions that were devastating in that they focused on purely military aspects of the disaster. Air support was deemed inadequate and delays in provision of ground support for the Pakistan Army did not allow it to fight an effective defensive battle. 'Most of the formations have complained that it had taken 4 to 6 hours for their air requests to be met.' The critique did not spare the army's own operations.

A major drawback was the outmoded armour, with the M-series of US-made tanks seen as being 'not combat worthy due to their vintage.' Also, the lack of training of armour and infantry to fight as a cohesive team showed in almost all aspects. 'The war proved that we lacked knowledge of basic techniques and procedures involved' in tank-infantry cooperation, which had been the subject of much peace-time training. Commanders and staff at all levels in the army were unaware of the capabilities of armour. Senior commanders moved armour around from one sector to the other, creating inefficiencies and wear and tear on the equipment. Tanks were also overused for defence. Indeed, except for the Chamb sector where armour took part in the attack, Pakistani armour was primarily used to bolster defence rather than rely on anti-tank capabilities of the infantry for that purpose. Pakistan's artillery had also suffered since 1965, with cuts in manpower and communications systems in gun regiments. At the corps level, it was suggested that artillery advisors be separated from artillery commanders for better decision-making during wartime. The GHQ team suggested that at the army level, there should be artillery reserves built up at brigade strength to allow their deployment where needed rather than to deplete formations in the midst of their operations.

Finally, the GHQ team looked at the infantry, the largest element in the military's fighting force. It found that infantry had 'become wedded with concrete emplacement, minefields, tanks and DFs [Defensive Fire]. Once in these protected environments, it finds it difficult to come out to close with and destroy the enemy. We must get our infantry out of this mental and physical shape.' The infantry was ill-trained, under-equipped, and not ready for war. New battalions were sent into action within six months of raising. A minimum of nine months' training as a regiment was suggested before sending them into war.

No wonder then that the Pakistan Army failed to live up to expectations in its areas of expertise. The Hamoodur Rehman Commission tried to report on the broader issues involved in the debacle but the penetrating analysis of the GHQ's own team on the poor conduct of operations was not included in the commission's findings. As usual, a cloak of secrecy was placed over the Pakistan Army's shortcomings, whereas public discussion and debate would have allowed lessons to be learned and applied.

Bhutto too, had his hands full. He had to deal with more than 90,000 prisoners of war in Indian hands, a demoralized nation, and a shattered political system. While he may have wanted to put the army in its place, the last thing he wanted was to stir up more trouble within the military. His immediate aim was to consolidate power, an endeavour which led to the creation of another centralized system of command and control for the country's affairs and its people—a system that could not last too long before it fell prey to street unrest and, once again, to military intervention.

NOTES

1. This Bengali name for Liberation Force gradually emerged out of the 'Sangram Parishads' or resistance groups and the Mukti Fauj (Liberation Army) set up by Col. Osmany in East Pakistan and became the name of the Bengali freedom fighters.

2. Operation Directive issued by Lt. Gen. A.A.K. Niazi on assumption of command of eastern command. Secret situation East Pakistan, as presented to COS on 17 April 1971. Pakistan Army GHQ Archives. Also reported in Niazi, op. cit.

3. Lt. Gen. A.A.K. Niazi, *The Betrayal of East Pakistan* (Karachi: Oxford University Press, 1998), p. 61.

4. Ibid., p. 61.

5. Ibid., p. 63.

6. Secret CIA 'Subject: SNIE 32-71: Prospects for Pakistan', 12 April 1971. Declassified PA/HO Department of State, EO 12958, as amended 9 June 2005. Assembled by Centre for Indian Military History. This section is based on this document.

7. Secret CIA, 12 April 1971, p. 5.

8. J.F.R. Jacob, *Surrender at Dacca: Birth of a Nation* (New Delhi: Manohar, 1997), p. 38.

9. *Hamoodur Rehman Commission Report*, p. 177.

10. Ibid., pp. 178–179.

11. 135. Conversation between President Nixon and his assistant for National Security Affairs (Kissinger), Washington, 26 May 1971, 10:38–10:44 a.m. *US Foreign Relations, 1969–1976, Volume E7. Documents on South Asia. 1969–72*, released by the Office of the Historian.

12. 60. Minutes of Washington Special Actions Group meeting, Washington, 26 May 1971, 4:35–5:00 p.m. *US Foreign Relations*. Ibid., pp. 149–156.

13. *USFR 1969-1976, Volume XI*. 'Minutes of Senior Review Group Meeting' Washington, 23 July 1971, 4:10–5:30 p.m., p. 274.

14. *USFR 1969-1976, Volume XI*, p. 341.

15. Shaukat Riza, *The Pakistan Army, 1966–71* (Lahore: Army Education Press, 1990), p. 129. The Hamoodur Rehman Commission Report states 'three' battalions were sent on 26 and 27 November, p. 181.

16. I am indebted to a 1989 Military History presentation on the Indo–Pak War 1971 at the Pakistan Army's National Defence College, Rawalpindi, for much of these details, particularly the review of Land Operations by then Lt. Col. (later Brigadier) Mujtaba.

17. See the excellent exposition and maps in Lt. Col. John H. Gill, *An Atlas of the 1971 India–Pakistan War: The Creation of Bangladesh*, National Defense University, Washington DC, 2003. The Pakistan NDC 1989 Study also cites the injunction that 'The Pakistani troops were deployed close to the border and were not expected to withdraw till almost 3/4th of their strength was casualty.' Op. cit., p. 37.

18. Secret/EXDIS Memorandum for the WASAG Meeting on 26 May 1971 from Samuel M. Hoskinson to Dr Kissinger. Part of title and opening section (probably identifying source) redacted out. Declassified PA/HO, Department of State, E.O. 12958, as amended 9 June 2005. Assembled by Centre for Indian Military History.

19. Jacob, *Surrender*, p. 60.

20. Lt. Gen. Gul Hassan Khan. *Memoirs of Lt. Gen. Gul Hassan Khan* (Karachi: Oxford University Press, 1993), pp. 287–8.

21. *USFR 1969-1976, Volume XI*, p. 459.

22. Conversations with my brother, then Major Asif Nawaz, Brigade Major 111 Brigade.

23. Riza, *The Pakistan*, p. 131.

24. Gul Hassan, *Memoirs*, p. 320.

25. NDC study 1989, p. 37.

26. Gul Hassan, *Memoirs*, p. 322.

27. Shuja Nawaz, 'Threshold: The Making of a War in South Asia, November–December 1971', Master's Thesis, Columbia University Graduate School of Journalism, 1973.
28. Author's notes from Press Information Department releases and official briefings during that period form the basis of this and the following information about these afternoon briefings. They provided some comic relief at the time for the antsy foreign correspondents who had been gathering in anticipation of another Indo–Pak War but had been prevented from travelling on their own to the front lines. Many of them veterans of the Vietnam war coverage called the briefings, the Five o'clock Follies, like the US Military briefings in Saigon.
29. Major General D.K. Palit, *The Lightning Campaign* (New Delhi: Thomson Press [India], 1972), p. 72.
30. Rahim Khan recorded interview, provided to the author by Begum Mehrunnisa Rahim Khan. Gul Hassan, *Memoirs*, pp. 280–82 also records a summary of these discussions.
31. *USFR, Volume 1969–1976, Volume XI*, pp. 555–7.
32. Gul Hassan, *Memoirs*.
33. NDC Study 1989. Appendix A.
34. Rahim Khan recorded interview.
35. Ezer Weizman, *On Eagles' Wings* (New York: MacMillan, 1977), pp. 222–3.
36. NDC study 1989.
37. Minutes of WASAG Meeting, Washington, 3 December 1971, 11:19–11:55 a.m. Subject: South Asia. *USFR, Volume 1969–1976, Volume XI*, pp. 596–9.
38. We did not know at that time that in fact Pakistani aircraft had yet to take off for their Indian targets. I had spent that afternoon at a post-Friday prayers political rally addressed by Mr Bhutto in Liaquat Bagh, Rawalpindi, where I found myself taken to a seat behind him on the elevated dais by friends in the local PPP hierarchy. He spoke at length about the need to change over to civilian government in light of the crisis with India and his acceptance of the deputy prime minister's position under East Pakistani Nurul Amin. And he lashed out at the Western governments for not stopping Indian aggression in East Pakistan, addressing them in English through the cameras of the BBC and others pointed up at his dais. I returned with his party to the Hotel Intercontinental and then went home only to get a call to rush to the TV station. I recall making the announcement and then preparing for the next full English news telecast at 7 p.m. We were flooded with jingoistic statements from politicians, including Nurul Amin and called Bhutto to see if I could get a statement from him. He asked me to call back while he thought about it. When I called again he made a strong statement that it was now time for the military rulers to step aside and let the true representatives of the people take over. He also spoke harshly against India and its aggressive designs on Pakistan. I informed the TV bosses, sitting at the President's House at that time, of this around 6:30 p.m. and was told that we could not run such a statement. I said that Bhutto expected to see this in the line-up at 7 p.m., when I went on the air and if it was missing he would ask me why it had been pulled and by whom. They finally agreed to edit some of the more harsh criticisms of the military and I carried the item in my regular news broadcast at 7 p.m.
39. 191. Telegram from the Embassy in Pakistan to the Department of State. *US Foreign Relations, 1961–1963, Volume XIX*. Footnotes 6 and 7, p. 372.
40. A.R. Siddiqi, *East Pakistan—The Endgame: An Onlooker's Journal 1969–1971* (Karachi: Oxford University Press, 2004), pp. 201–202.
41. Radio Pakistan, 8 p.m. news read by Abdullah Ahmad. From the written records provided to the author by Khwaja Shahid Hosain.
42. Gill, *An Atlas*, pp. 13–14, except for the PAF strength which is based on the NDC paper of the Pakistan Army.
43. General Jacob quotes Admiral Krishnan, the flag officer C-in-C of the Indian naval command telling him on 3 December that fishermen had seen debris that they deduced was

from the *Ghazi* since signal intercepts had indicated it was entering the Bay of Bengal. Krishnan called it an act of God. It may have sunk on 1 or 2 December. 'Next morning, on December 4, Krishnan again telephoned asking me whether we had reported the blowing up of the *Ghazi* to Delhi. I said we had not as I presumed that he had done so. Relieved, he thanked me and asked me to forget our previous conversation. The official naval version given out later was that the *Ghazi* had been sunk by ships of the Eastern Fleet on 4 December.' Jacob, *Surrender*, p. 104. Later, Krishnan was one of the Indian officers caught in the celebrated photograph of the surrender ceremony at Dacca Race Course Ground, standing behind Aurora, with his peak cap at a rakish angel and showing chest hair.

44. This was the most obvious road route to the capital of East Pakistan and one that followed the track of the 'Asian Highway'. In 1970, I and another colleague from PTV had entered the Asian Highway car rally from Tehran to Dacca and this was the route designated for the rally to enter East Pakistan from the west. Unfortunately, India refused a visa to my co-driver a former naval officer and then engineer at PTV headquarters. So, we had to pull out of the race: an endurance rally that would have me driving by myself through India, into Nepal and back into India, without rest (before picking up my co-driver at Benapole!).

45. The following discussion relies heavily on this NDC study and General Jacob's account of the conduct of war in East Pakistan.

46. Jacob, *Surrender*, p. 118.

47. Riza, *The Pakistan*, p. 161.

48. Gul Hassan, *Memoirs*, p. 328.

49. Jacob, *Surrender*, p. 127.

50. I got most of his information first hand or from participants during that period. Our crew of two, myself and cameraman Amin Qaiser, came under air attack one day on the Zafarwal Bund while interviewing Brigadier Sher Ali Baz, whose troops held the Indians at bay at that juncture. We continued to shoot film as a coincidental flight of Pakistani Sabres attacked Indian positions in the foreground with napalm and bombs. Later, I was to interview in Sargodha at least one of those air force pilots, a 1965 war hero named Squadron Leader Cecil Chaudhry, whose plane was shot down by Pakistani reservists on his way back to Sargodha and who was 'captured' and then handed over to Pakistan army personnel.

51. Recorded interview, provided to the author by Begum Mehrunnisa Rahim Khan.

52. Jacob, *Surrender*, pp. 134–137.

53. Niazi, *The Betrayal*, p. 187.

54. *USFR, Volume 1969–1976, Volume XI*, p. 810. Item 300. Footnote 2.

55. Jacob, *Surrender*, pp. 144–148. For some reason Manekshaw had handwritten the time for the surrender as 16:31 hours. But the actual signature was put on the document at 16:55 hours, according to Jacob.

56. US *FR, 1969–1976, Volume E-7.*

57. CIA Memorandum on 'Implications of an Indian Victory over Pakistan,' 9 December 1971. Declassified PA/HO, Department of State. E.O. 12958, as amended 9 June 2005. Assembled by Centre for Indian Military History.

58. Priority Intelligence Information Cable, 12 December 1971. Number IN 491198 TDCS 314/13308-71. Declassified, PA/HO, Department of State, E.O. 12958, as amended 9 June 2005.

59. Conversation with former CIA officer.

60. Transcript of telephone conversation between Henry Kissinger and Z.A. Bhutto. 11 December 1971. *USFR, Volume 1969–1976, Volume XI*, pp. 777–8.

61. Confidential telegram from American Embassy, Islamabad, 14 December 1971 to Department of State.

62. Transcript of telephone conversation between President Nixon and Henry Kissinger, 10:40 a.m. 16 December 1971. Declassified, PA/HO, Department of State, E.O. 12958, as amended 9 June 2005.

63. *USFR, Volume 1969–1976, Volume XI*, p. 557.

64. Fazal Muqeem Khan, *Pakistan's Crisis in Leadership* (Islamabad, Lahore, Karachi: National Book Foundation, 1973. Appendix IV), p. 280.

65. Secret 'GHQ Report on Indo–Pakistan War December [19]71', Document number 3769/DA. Pakistan Army GHQ Archives. The report covered only 1 Corps, 4 Corps, and 12, 18, 23, and 33 Divisions, as well as the supporting role of the air force. Although the report was unsigned and does not contain the name of the officer involved in the study, subsequent inquiries by the author from officers involved in the 1971 conflict in the areas visited by the GHQ team indicate that the group was headed by Major General Azmat Baksh Awan, then commandant of the Command and Staff College in Quetta.

66. Secret 'GHQ Report on Indo–Pakistan War December [19]71.' Pakistan Army Archives. This section relies on this report.

67. Deposition by General Yahya Khan with a Writ Petition No. 1649 of 1978, 1 June 1978 before the Lahore High Court, attested by oath commissioner, Advocate Mahmood Ahmed Rana, Rawalpindi. Reproduced in *Defence Journal,* December 2005, Volume 9, No. 5.

68. Yahya's statement before the Hamoodur Rehman Commission. Included in Writ Petition, op. cit.

69. *Hamoodur Rehman Commssion Report*, p. 262.

70. GHQ report, op. cit. Subsection 'Causes of the Debacle'. Document number 3763.

71. Secret submission by Brig. F.B. Ali to the Commission of Inquiry, C/o The Supreme Court of Pakistan, 2 January 1972.

72. 'Immediate' note from Brig. F.B. Ali, 15 December 1971, to Major General Muhammad Bashir Khan, commander Army Reserve North. Number G-0113/10. From Brig. Ali's files.

73. Secret Submission by Brig. Ali to the Hamoodur Rehman Commission.

> I make a solemn pledge that I will serve you with all my heart and will, I will serve even if it kills me. I know what the people of Pakistan want…. I am simply nobody. I cannot be carried on a gun or a bayonet. I can only be carried in your heart. I will never deceive you. I will never betray you.
>
> – President Zulfikar Ali Bhutto[1]

Jinnah's Pakistan died with the signing of the surrender document in Dacca (now Dhaka) on 16 December 1971. With that signature, East Pakistan became Bangladesh. The mantle of leadership of Pakistan's West wing—the rump—was handed over to the leader of the PPP, Zulfikar Ali Bhutto, ostensibly by the army's CGS, Lt. Gen. Gul Hassan Khan and the air chief, Air Marshal Rahim Khan, but in reality as a result of a *putsch* by more junior officers headed by Brigadier F.B. Ali, who called for Yahya to step down.[2] Bhutto, both president and CMLA, picked up the pieces of Pakistan. Over the next six tumultuous years, he introduced his own brand of Islamic socialism, leavened with a heavy dose of feudalism and autocracy; negotiated successfully with India to agree on boundary lines in Kashmir and later the release of more than 90,000 prisoners of war from East Pakistan; regained lost Pakistani territories; placed Pakistan in a leadership position of the Third World and the Islamic world; gave Pakistan a new constitution that many of its politicians in the twenty-first century still hanker for; and launched Pakistan on the path to nuclear weapon status. That was the positive side.

On the negative side, Bhutto rapidly resiled from political agreements with opposition parties in the NWFP and Balochistan; survived a coup attempt by a group of unhappy young army officers in 1973 that saw him heading toward a civilian dictatorship; sent the army to fight an insurgency in Balochistan; emasculated the civil service; nationalized fledgling industries and commercial enterprises, and thus sank the economy; nationalized the missionary schools and colleges that had produced most of the leaders of Pakistani society till that point; created a paramilitary Federal Security Force (FSF) as a potential rival to the army; gave in to the Islamic opposition, banned alcohol, and declared the Ahmadi community 'non-Muslims,' handing the combined opposition enough weapons to magnify its political power and turn the army against Bhutto. In that short span of six years, however, the masses that supported him made Bhutto feel 'taller than the Himalayas' and then large numbers of them dropped him. More important, the army that facilitated his direct rise to the presidency dropped him in the end. Surging street protests, following a fixed election in 1977 that Bhutto did not need to fix, gave his opponents the weapon they needed to bring him down and paved the way for another martial law on 5 July 1977, leading the military government of General Ziaul Haq to revive murder charges against him, convict him, and sentence him to death by hanging.

In an action that scarred Pakistan's collective memory, at 2:04 a.m. on 4 April 1979, in Rawalpindi district jail, the Christian executioner, Tara Masih, pulled a lever on a specially constructed scaffold and Bhutto's by then frail body fell through a trap door.[3] A fearful military dictator had saved his own skin by executing an elected prime minister of Pakistan for the first time in the nation's history. With that event, Bhutto became an icon in the history and mythology of Pakistani politics, and became arguably an even more powerful force than when he was alive, and a constant thorn in the side of the Pakistan Army for decades to come.

It was ironic that a democratic upsurge in the ranks of the military, following the defeat in East Pakistan, led to the abrupt departure of General Yahya and his coterie from the corridors of power. On 17 December, Yahya had announced his acceptance of the ceasefire but the next day came news that he wanted to promulgate a new constitution. This galled a number of younger officers who were spurred to what their leader Brigadier Ali characterized as 'spontaneous action.' Relatively junior officers (some colonels and one other brigadier) in Gujranwala, led by Brigadier Ali, the commander artillery of 6 Armoured Division, tried to convince the GOC 6 Armoured Division, Major General M.I. 'Bachhu' Karim, to send a message to CGS Gul Hassan that they wanted a change at the top. Earlier, General Karim had called a meeting of his brigade commanders essentially to confirm that he, a Bengali, had their confidence. Brigadier Ali recalls stating that he told Karim: 'I have confidence in you but don't have confidence in anyone above you,' and asked that Karim convey these sentiments to the GHQ.[4] Karim hesitated. So Ali took matters into his own hands. With his CO's hesitating consent, Brig. Ali took over effective command of the 6 Armoured Division from General Karim. He then sent the colonel staff of the division, Col. Aleem Afridi, to GHQ in Rawalpindi with a message from the officers around him.

Gul Hassan recalls meeting Colonel Afridi who reported to him that a group, including Brigadier F.B. Ali, had met and conveyed their views to Major General Karim for onward transmission to GHQ. Their message, according to Brig. Ali was simple: 'Yahya must announce his resignation by 8:00 p.m. on December 19. Otherwise we will not be responsible for our actions.' According to Brig. Ali, Afridi found Gul Hassan somewhat subdued and packing his office when Afridi arrived with the message, perhaps expecting the end of the road for the entire higher command of the Pakistan Army. He perked up immediately when Afridi relayed the contents of the message. The group also had a list of generals whom they wished to see dismissed immediately, all from Yahya's inner circle. To this list, Gul Hassan is reported to have added the name of his GHQ colleague, Major General A.O. Mitha, the QMG under Yahya.[5] The implicit threat from Ali and his cohort was that the tanks would move down the GT road to Rawalpindi and effect a change by force if Yahya did not announce his departure as requested. Among the officers involved in this threat was Brig. Iqbal Mehdi Shah, who commanded an armoured brigade. Most of the rest were staff officers without any fighting troops under their command. Gul Hassan took Afridi to meet Hamid and then got Yahya to agree to announce that he would "quit as soon as it was possible for him to hand over to an 'elected representative of the people'".[6] That representative was Bhutto, then in New York.

The army high command went into panic mode. Major General A.O. Mitha, a close confidant of the president (and General Hamid) reportedly requested Brigadier Ghulam Mohammed of the SSG, the army's elite commando unit trained by the US and based at Cherat (not far from Rawalpindi), to move a company of commandos to intercept and hold up the expected armour column under Iqbal Mehdi Shah at a place called Taraki between Jhelum and Rawalpindi. Malik refused to do so because, as he told Mitha, he had no troops to spare, and reported the matter to Gul Hassan. Mitha also called Brig. Ali and, among other things, wanted to know if Hamid was acceptable as a replacement for Yahya. Ali said 'No.'[7] Yahya's departure was then announced.[8]

Hamid called a meeting on the morning of 20 December of all officers at the GHQ and tried to speak to them, perhaps with a view to ascertaining if they would accept him as a replacement for Yahya. His nervous speech was interrupted a number of times. He had to leave the room a few times to regain his composure. When he opened up the floor to questions, junior officers spoke with emotion about their lack of confidence in the military leadership. Some even asked for banning alcohol in military messes, a sharp turn from the culture favoured by Yahya and his team. Shaukat Riza states that a tape of this speech was played for Bhutto after he took over.[9] This was the first time that junior officers had forced a change in the top leadership of the Pakistan Army.

Against this backdrop, CGS Gul Hassan and the air chief stage-managed the transition, arranging to fly Bhutto back from New York and even sending a plane to Rome to bring him directly to Rawalpindi. Bhutto arrived late on 20 December and moved to the Punjab House where an impromptu swearing-in ceremony was arranged, with Bhutto signing the papers that would make him president of Pakistan. Standing to his right and handing him the pen to sign the document was super civil servant and future president, Ghulam Ishaq Khan. Looking on proudly to Bhutto's right were Ghulam Mustafa Khar and J.A. Rahim. Bhutto had met with Gul Hassan earlier and asked him to take over as army chief. Gul Hassan recalls turning down the offer at first and only accepting after Bhutto pressed him hard. In return, however, he asked to be allowed to keep his current rank of lieutenant general, to which Bhutto agreed. But the first fissure between these two erstwhile friends was to show in a matter of hours, as Bhutto informed the country in his long, passionate and extemporaneous midnight speech over PTV and radio that he had made Gul Hassan 'acting C-in-C,' adding that 'he should not expect that he will be promoted to the rank of a general merely because of this temporary arrangement.' When confronted on this by Gul Hassan later, Bhutto explained that Gul Hassan did not understand politics and that is why he had missed the point.[10] Not an auspicious start to the relationship.

Bhutto began his term as president and CMLA with his customary energy and speed. Following the pattern of previous martial law rulers, he issued orders for the dismissal of various key individuals and almost 1,300 civil servants. His cabinet included a strong representation of the founders of the PPP, many of whom had a strong socialist bent. He immediately began a series of reforms to change the political landscape, introducing new labour and education laws and began a series of public meetings, starting with a massive gathering at the National Stadium in Lahore that was festooned with blazing red banners with socialist slogans, including 'The People are the Fountainhead of Power.' In a live broadcast speech before the masses and a strong contingent of the diplomatic corps, he went after the 'robber barons' of Pakistani industry, using earthy epithets in the process.[11] A broadcast campaign was also launched against businesses that did not declare their full incomes and wealth or pay due taxes.[12]

Sensing a weakness in the military after its recent defeat, Bhutto also began a campaign to publicize the military's surrender ceremony in Dacca. The army opposed this campaign vigorously and the news reel film of the surrender was not shown again on PTV. Bhutto did not waver though in his criticisms, using the previous regime as a surrogate for the army as a whole in his public discourse. He could have sent home many of the discredited generals but chose to keep many of them while sending home some of the brighter ones, especially those who had opposed military action in East Pakistan. In the view of Brigadier Ali, the latter group included major generals Shaukat Riza, Ihsanul Haq Malik and Khadim Hussain Raja.[13] In August 1972, Bhutto retired Brig. Ali and five leading officers who had forced Yahya to resign, charging them with a conspiracy to prevent the elected representatives of the people from taking over in December 1971. Those who were forcibly retired included: Lt. Col. Muhammad Khurshid, Col. Aleem Afridi, Col. Javed Iqbal, Brigadier Iqbal Mehdi Shah, and Major General R.D. Shamim.[14] The latter was the GOC of 17 Division and had participated in the meetings organized by Brig. Ali. Soon the army began seeing Bhutto as a challenger rather than a saviour.

US Ambassador Farland meanwhile, was reporting to the White House in rather favourable terms Bhutto's rapid progress on various fronts in the first week of his rule. In a memorandum to President Nixon, Henry Kissinger summarized Farland's views:

> Bhutto has moved with extraordinary speed to solidify his control over West Pakistan and to set the stage for launching his political and economic reform program. He has been aided in this effort by the widespread demoralization both within the military leadership and the populace as a whole....In sum, Farland says, that Bhutto has taken over West Pakistan 'lock, stock, and barrel,' probably saving it from internal collapse in the process. On the other hand, it is not clear whether Bhutto will be able to rise above his reputation for unscrupulousness, vanity, an intense personal ambition to become a real statesman.[15]

Farland also reported that Bhutto had ordered a judicial inquiry into the causes of the military defeat. This Hamoodur Rehman Commission was originally supposed to report back in three months. However, it took some years for the report to reach the people of Pakistan, and even then, it was leaked, rather than released, into public view.

TENSION WITH THE ARMY CHIEF

Soon enough, Bhutto and his army chief, Lt. Gen. Gul Hassan Khan, were heading for a showdown. There were repeated and frequent instances of disagreement between them. Gul Hassan recounts numerous episodes where he felt that Bhutto was keeping tabs on his activities and trying to interfere in the internal affairs of the army. Bhutto's defence adviser, retired Major General Akbar Khan (of the Rawalpindi Conspiracy fame), also attempted to issue orders to military units to come to the aid of civil power in a reported police mutiny in Peshawar. Akbar Khan ordered the movement of artillery guns from Nowshera to Peshawar, which Gul Hassan brought to a halt. A similar mutiny in the Punjab also led to the demand for troops that Gul Hassan did not provide. Mustafa Khar, the chief minister of the Punjab, managed to bring things under control himself. Rafi Raza, the newly appointed special assistant to the president, recalls that Gul Hassan was generally uncooperative and said he could not spare troops since they were needed on the borders. Bhutto saw this as an attempt to destabilize his regime and Raza states that the 'incident also fixed in his mind the need for a Federal Security Force to deal with similar situations without recourse to the army.'[16]

Soon after taking over, Bhutto went on a tour of Algeria and Turkey and got a scare when his plane was asked not to proceed from Ankara till a message had been received from home. Rafi Raza recounts how they expected the worst: another army coup. It turned out to be something less dramatic:

the Soviet Union's recognition of Bangladesh. Still, nerves were on edge. At the end of January, Bhutto visited China and took along with him both Rahim Khan, the air chief, and Gul Hassan, the army chief. These three had been sent to China by Yahya during the period of conflict with India in 1971 soon after Bhutto had been named foreign minister, a trip that Yahya later asserted in his deposition to the Lahore High Court had allowed them to plot Yahya's ouster. Rahim Khan recounted that he was the real and original leader of this military team and Yahya asked him to take Bhutto along. Gul Hassan, on the other hand, recalled Bhutto as being the team leader. Neither of them referred to any discussion with Bhutto about removing Yahya. Regardless, the situation in January 1972 was quite clear. Bhutto was the leader now, and the respected friend of the Chinese leadership. He met Mao Tse-Tung and got a huge welcome despite the heavy snowfall that had restricted movement during the night before his arrival. After a successful press conference with Premier Chou En-lai, on his return journey from the Great Hall of the People down the wide expanse of Chang An avenue and then to the airport, Premier Chou insisted they ride together in an open car so that Bhutto could be given a 'proper send-off' by the people of Beijing. Wearing a Mao cap, President Bhutto seemed pleased with this gesture as he stood in the convertible car in the bitterly cold Beijing winter and waved to the thousands who lined the route of his cavalcade four deep, waving flags and banners.[17]

Bhutto had made up his mind to remove the men who he thought had brought him to power: Rahim Khan and Gul Hassan. As a replacement for the critical position of army chief, he first settled on Lt. Gen. Majeed Malik, but then appeared to doubt Malik's loyalty and settled on Tikka Khan, another Punjabi and a man who had proven that he could follow orders to the nth degree. As Bhutto explained to the Italian journalist Oriana Fallaci who challenged his appointment of Tikka as head of the army: 'Tikka was a soldier doing a soldier's job [in East Pakistan]. He went to East Pakistan with precise orders and came back by precise orders. He did what he was ordered to, though he wasn't always in agreement, and I picked him because I know he'll follow my orders with the same discipline.'[18] He was sure of his choice and of how he would dispatch Gul Hassan and Rahim Khan. 3 March 1972 had been declared a national holiday to celebrate the announcement of land reforms, and Bhutto invited Rahim and Hassan to the President's House, ostensibly for a meeting. Gul Hassan recounts that the earlier venue had been mentioned as Sihala, a small police training academy outside Rawalpindi, located on a route that was often the way-station for political detainees. When Gul Hassan demurred against bringing his secret maps to such an insecure location, he was asked to come to the President's House. Once there, Rahim and Hassan were informed that they both were being replaced.

Right after coming back from Beijing, Bhutto had asked the Foreign Secretary, Sultan Mohammed Khan, to see if the army and air chiefs could be placed in diplomatic assignments in 'some quiet places, where they would not be able to indulge in political scheming'. After some discussion, Madrid and Vienna were selected for Rahim Khan and Gul Hassan respectively.[19] At the President's House on 3 March, Rahim protested that there was no need for this drama and he would have gladly just resigned. 'Bhutto regretted what he had done; he said it was dictated by political necessity,' recalls Sultan Khan. Earlier, there had been a scramble to find a typewriter to produce the letters of resignation. All the stenographers had left for the day and the matter was ultra secret. Dr Mubashir Hasan recounts how a machine was finally found and he typed up the drafts which both Rahim and Gul Hassan eventually signed. Once the deed was done, Khar took them in his car, accompanied by Ghulam Mustafa Jatoi and hustled them to Lahore at breakneck speed. For the first time in Pakistan's history, the army and air chiefs had been kidnapped by the president! Bhutto was kind enough to send a written message to Mrs Rahim Khan that her husband was safe.[20]

Tikka Khan, meanwhile had no inkling that he had been tapped to be the next army chief. He had had a meeting with the president at 4:00 p.m. that afternoon and then left for his field post in Sahiwal. Dr Mubashir Hasan was deputed to go and inform him about his appointment and bring him back. Dr Hasan thus flew out on a small Cessna aircraft to Okara and then drove to Sahiwal Irrigation Department rest house where Tikka was bivouacked. A nonplussed Tikka received the news of his appointment with equanimity, threw his sleeping roll and suitcase on the plane, and accompanied by his aide-de-camp (who happened to be his son), returned to Rawalpindi with Dr Hasan to assume command.[21] A confident Bhutto took off almost immediately for a visit to Moscow and followed up on his tour later in the spring with a 22-nation trip to the Middle East and North Africa.

21 April 1972 was a distinct day in Pakistan's history. Bhutto took a formal oath as the president of Pakistan in the Race Course Ground in Rawalpindi under an interim constitution approved by the National Assembly. As usual, a military parade and air fly-by was arranged. But for the first time since Ayub Khan had taken over in 1958, the man taking the oath and the subsequent salute as president, CMLA, and supreme commander was not a military man but Zulfikar Ali Bhutto, the people's man. On a huge raised dais, he stood in front of a gigantic Pakistan flag, wearing a white suit, with a smaller Pakistan flag waving to his right and a newly designed presidential flag that he personally favoured (carrying a black scimitar on a yellow background) waving to his left.[22] A few steps behind him stood the newly minted chiefs of army, navy, and air staff. They were no longer to be known as C-in-C of their

services. Bhutto had changed their titles, after the removal of Gul Hassan and Rahim Khan, for their 'bonapartist tendencies.'

The military parades at the Race Course Ground were normally a well-run and disciplined affair. On 21 April, the civil and military elite were arrayed as usual on either side of the presidential dais. The soldiers on parade and their equipment were facing them at a distance, while deep in the distance were the masses, who had come to celebrate the first Pakistan Day after people's power had brought their leader to this dais.[23] An exultant Bhutto arrived in the ceremonial horse-drawn carriage formerly favoured by the British rulers, surrounded by the ceremonial president's bodyguards on their magnificent horses, carrying their lances in a vertical position, and resplendent in their scarlet coats and erect, golden turbans. Bhutto was clearly enjoying the panoply of this event. Soon after Bhutto took his oath and the parade began its march past the presidential dais, the crowds surged forward from their distant location, breaking down barriers and milling around the front of the dais. The discipline of the event broke down, as soldiers and tanks tried to march past the dais where Bhutto stood but were overwhelmed by the mass of people that flooded the field. Bhutto must have felt a certain amount of pride at this discomfiture of the military.

The previous month, on his visit to Moscow, Bhutto had been given a severe reprimand by Premier Alexei Kosygin about Pakistan's military action in East Pakistan and even about the appointment of Tikka Khan as the army chief, according to the Foreign Secretary, Sultan M. Khan. Responding to a conciliatory opening statement by Bhutto, Kosygin recounted how the Soviet Union had warned Yahya Khan that it would be catastrophic for Pakistan, but he continued to use force to keep the military in power. Kosygin warned that General Tikka Khan would be torn to pieces in Dacca. Then he continued to lambast Bhutto's choice of the new army chief: 'Your appointment of Tikka Khan as Army Chief of Staff has created a strong reaction with Mujib [who believes] that this means the end of all relations, and the Indian reaction is similar.' He also discussed a letter he had received from Indian Prime Minister Indira Gandhi in which she expressed concern that Pakistan was expanding its forces by four divisions even while India held a large number of POWs. But in addition, she reportedly offered 'to normalize relations with Pakistan in the political, economic, cultural and scientific fields. We wish to bury forever the senseless conflict about Jammu and Kashmir,' she said, and agreed to prepare for a summit to discuss these issues.[24]

PREPARING FOR THE SIMLA SUMMIT

In April, Mrs Gandhi sent a seasoned diplomat, D.P. Dhar, to begin discussions with Pakistan on preparations for a summit meeting that would eventually take place in Simla, the storied hill station where the government of British India used to go during the summer months. Bhutto began preparing for this encounter in earnest, seeking views from foreign leaders, especially during his 12 day-14-country tour of the Middle East and North Africa beginning on 29 May. At home, he sought to hear from various influential groups and invited them to visit him at the Governor's House in Murree, a hill station about 45 minutes' drive north of Rawalpindi. He also encouraged a national debate on the issue of talks with India and relations with 'Muslim Bengal.'

The Pakistan Army undertook its own exercise on what it wanted Bhutto to seek during his summit meeting with Mrs Gandhi. While Bhutto had spoken at length with his interlocutors about the Kashmir issue and the possible changes in the ceasefire line, transforming it into the Line of Control, he was apparently not as concerned about the issue of the POWs in India, including some 20,000 women and children. Sultan Khan recalls that when he was sent to Washington as ambassador after giving up his post as foreign secretary, this item was not in the five-point remit that Bhutto gave him. When Sultan Khan raised the issue of the POWs, Bhutto paused and then offered a lukewarm: 'There is no harm if you try to enlist support on their behalf.'[25] As he was later to explain to his daughter Benazir, Zulfikar Ali Bhutto had his reasons for this approach.

THE ARMY'S BRIEF FOR SIMLA

For the Pakistan Army, however, the issue of the POWs was closely tied to the key underlying issue: the recognition of Bangladesh. In a secret brief for President Bhutto, COAS Tikka Khan forwarded the army's views on the POW issue on 11 June 1972. Recognition of Bangladesh was the first item and the army's position could not have been clearer:

> A strong stand on this issue must be taken. Bangla Desh must not be recognized until firm international guarantees are given for the following: (a) Withdrawal of troops to the international border/ceasefire line. (b) Return of our POWs. (c) Dropping of the plan for the trials of so-called war criminals. (d) Proper treatment of Biharis [non-Bengali immigrants into East Pakistan following partition in 1947] and pro-Pakistan elements in East Pakistan. (e) Further meetings between East and West Pakistan to decide our future relationship.[26]

The army warned though that the 'proper political climate must be created so that people do not condemn the government's action.' It feared 'widespread agitations' if 'recognition is accorded without taking the people in confidence.' The army, like Bhutto, had learned the lesson of Tashkent and wanted to go well prepared into the summit. But the content and tone of the brief for President Bhutto was not that of a defeated force. Indeed, it favoured strong positions on a wide number of issues: repatriation of Bengali military and civil personnel from West Pakistan in exchange for their prisoners of war in India and Bangladesh, definition of the ceasefire line in Kashmir, and the exchange of captured territories. The army recognized that the 'bargain' of Pakistani POWs for Bengalis and Indians held in Pakistan 'would be in our interest as the number of PWs (sic) in India/"Bangla Desh" is much larger than the Bengali soldiers awaiting repatriation in Pakistan.' The army was dead set against the exchange of Biharis with Bengalis in West Pakistan: 'Unlike Bengalis in West Pakistan, the Biharis have a home in East Pakistan and they should remain there.' It was, however, willing to accept 'a few thousand' extreme cases where the Biharis have 'lost everything... and have nothing to fall back upon.' The brief also specified a schedule for a three-phase withdrawal of troops from the West Pakistan and Kashmir borders, with troops moving back within 3 to 5 days 1000 yards from their forward positions in Phase 1, de-mining and dismantling of defensive works in Phase 2, and returning to peacetime locations in the final phase within three months. It sought UN involvement for the withdrawals in Kashmir but direct Indo–Pakistan discussions for establishing the international boundary.

'As a principle, our approach to the problem should be that all withdrawal along the border and the CFL [ceasefire line] should be unconditional and also the whole [withdrawal from borders] issue should be treated as one. Separating the problem of international border and ceasefire line should be strongly contested by us,' stated the brief. It favoured a return to the old ceasefire line in Kashmir. While recognizing that the Indians held 5795.64 square miles of Pakistani territory in West Pakistan compared with only 110.35 square miles of Indian territory in Pakistani hands, the army took a strong position against any exchange of territory that might give the Indians a strategic or tactical advantage in future conflicts.

The army brief 'strongly rejected' trials of any of its POWs in Indian or Bangladeshi hands. It favoured immediate restoration of diplomatic ties with India as soon as agreement was reached on troops withdrawals and the repatriation of POWs, leaving trade negotiations with India and Bangladesh for later. On Kashmir its position was brief and unequivocal: 'We should not concede the Indian-held Kashmir to India. We should continue to insist that the Kashmiris have a right to self determination and India must give them this right. Pakistan could, however, agree to an (sic) arbitration on the question of Kashmir.'

Finally, the army insisted that President Bhutto tell the Indians 'that if they desire durable peace in this subcontinent, they should':

a. Withdraw their troops from all areas which are in their possession in both West Pakistan and Azad Kashmir.
b. Return all the Pakistani PWs held in India and so called 'Bangla Desh.'
c. Settle the Kashmir issue according to the wishes of her people.
d. Guarantee the safety and security of the Biharis and pro-Pakistan elements in East Pakistan.
e. Reduce the size of her armed forces to remove the fear of aggression in Pakistan.

The irony in the peremptory tone of the list and especially in the final demand was clearly lost on the army high command. This was not an army that had just lost a war. It sounded more like the terms of surrender offered to a defeated enemy. The brief was aimed as much at India as convincing Bhutto that if the Indian 'threat' remained at a high level, then 'obviously we will have to maintain a proportionately higher level of standing Armed Forces.' It conceded however that should India reduce its threat, the size of the Pakistan armed forces could be reviewed accordingly. Here, it cautioned Bhutto not to accept formation-level discussions of the relative size of forces, and instead to insist on the battalion/regiment level because the Indians were said to have a larger number of battalions in their brigades and divisions than did Pakistan.

SIMLA SUMMIT

Armed with his own strong views and the private and public views of opinion makers within his party and others on the political scene, Bhutto left for the Indian hill station of Simla on 28 June 1972 to negotiate post-war arrangements between India and Pakistan, which, in Bhutto's words, 'will be a turning point in Pakistan's history.'[27] Accompanying him on this historic journey was his young daughter Benazir Bhutto, freshly returned from her junior year at Radcliffe, the women's college at Harvard University. Bhutto wanted her to witness this event first hand. The savvy Bhutto gave his daughter strict instructions to control her demeanour: 'You must not smile and give the impression you are enjoying yourself while our soldiers are still in Indian prisoner-of-war camps. You must not look grim either, which people can interpret as a sign of pessimism.'[28] Four days of intense bargaining ensued, with Bhutto and Indira Gandhi failing to come to an overall agreement. Young

Benazir, the focus of much media attention, managed to control her emotions in public.

Finally, on 2 July, Bhutto decided that Mrs Gandhi would not come to an agreement and got ready to pack up and leave Simla. But he chose to use his farewell call on Mrs Gandhi to make a final plea on behalf of the people of both countries. His daughter recalls him saying that he had detected Mrs Gandhi's unease at the failure of the talks and spoke non-stop for half an hour, offering her a way out of their impasse. She did not disagree and said she would give her answer at dinner that evening. After dinner, the exchanges continued and a code was agreed on for the final solution: If agreement was reached, they'd announce that a boy had been born; if not, a girl. At 12:40 a.m. on 3 July came the words 'Larka Hai! Larka Hai!' (It's a boy! It's a boy!).[29]

Bhutto had pulled off a major coup, though negotiating from a weak position initially. He managed to get India to return all Pakistani territory, to restore trade and communications between the two adversaries, and convert the ceasefire line in Kashmir into the Line of Control. But he did not give way on Pakistan's stand on Kashmir. The only major issue on which he failed to get Indian agreement was the return of the 93,000 prisoners of war. However, he got India to guarantee that no Pakistanis would be subjected to war-crime trials and in fact, asked India to even take control of the few remaining POWs then in Bangladeshi hands. Explaining his strategy to his daughter, Bhutto stated: 'Prisoners are a human problem. The magnitude is increased when there are 93,000 of them. It would be inhuman of India to keep them indefinitely. And it will also be a problem to keep on feeding and housing them. Territory, on the other hand, is not a human problem. Territory can be assimilated. Prisoners cannot.'[30] He proved to be right. India managed to fritter away its battlefield victory on the field of public opinion in the aftermath of the 1971 war, even to the extent of alienating the Bangladeshis. All Pakistani POWs were eventually released in 1974, after Pakistan recognized Bangladesh. A triumphant Bhutto flew back to Lahore on 3 July and Rawalpindi the next day, declaring victory for the people of Pakistan and India. A day later, the National Assembly of Pakistan gave the Simla accord unanimous approval. He could now return to pressing domestic issues.

FISSURES AT HOME

Even before heading to India, Bhutto had crafted a deal with the opposition National Awami Party (NAP) and the Jamiat-e-Ulema-e-Islam (JUI) after protracted negotiations at the Flashman's Hotel, Rawalpindi, in March 1972. Under this 'deal', these parties were allowed to form coalition governments in the NWFP and Balochistan. This gave Bhutto some time to strengthen his position before challenging them. But even at that time, suspicion ran deep. Among others, the Baluch tribal leader, Sardar Khair Baksh Marri did not trust Bhutto at all, and stayed away from most of the discussions at the Flashman's Hotel. He predicted that Bhutto would find a way to renege on the deals.[31] Marri proved right. Within a matter of a year, Bhutto had dissolved both provincial governments and taken direct control of the two border provinces.

As he proceeded pell-mell down the path of reform and rebuilding the nation's confidence, Bhutto ran into troubles within his own team. The original socialists who had thought that they were the guiding force of the PPP and may have thought of him as a symbolic leader of their movement, found that Bhutto's practice of *realpolitik* allowed him to make deals with all sorts of parties and individuals, even if it meant forsaking some of the cherished principles of his comrades in arms. As he became more confident of his power, Bhutto exhibited signs of autocratic behaviour and tolerated no dissent. The first to feel his wrath was his erstwhile mentor J.A. Rahim, who left a reception at the President's House late in the evening of 1 July 1974 after making a disparaging remark about the feudal Bhutto, who had kept his guests waiting for dinner. Later that night, Rahim and his son Sikandar were both taken from their home, beaten up and taken into custody. Rafi Raza retrieved them and with help from Mubashir Hasan arranged for their departure from the country, for safekeeping.[32] Bhutto also distanced himself from Khursheed Hasan Meer, Sheikh Rashid, and Dr Mubashir Hasan, gradually easing them out of the inner circle. He identified Ghulam Mustafa Khar from southern Punjab and the youthful firebrand labour leader from Karachi, Mairaj Mohammed Khan, as his heirs apparent, only to have Mairaj arrested and mistreated. Khar was removed from his position as presidential favourite not long after, although he later managed to find his way back into Bhutto's favour.

BALOCHISTAN INSURGENCY

Even while he was realigning his political base, accommodating the many opportunistic politicians who had earlier hedged their bets but now saw in him a source of power, Bhutto concentrated on breaking up the hold of the coalitions of the NAP and the JUI in the NWFP and Balochistan. The capture of arms in a diplomatic shipment to the Iraqi embassy on 10 February 1973, alleged by the Pakistan government to be destined for Balochistan, and the subsequent death of Hayat Mohammed Sherpao, Bhutto's right hand man in the NWFP, in an explosion in Peshawar in February 1975, gave him his excuse. He dismissed the NAP–JUI provincial government in the NWFP, and banned the NAP the day after Sherpao's assassination. Thus he trashed the much-heralded Flashman's Hotel accord of 1972, giving credence to Khair Baksh Marri's deep-seated suspicions about Bhutto's true intentions regarding provincial autonomy. The Balochistan government resigned in protest, giving Bhutto an open field.

In pursuit of political supremacy in all provinces, Bhutto had to constantly challenge the NAP and specifically the Baluch leadership. He saw in the efforts of the NAP a repeat of the Bangladesh issue, a fear heightened by his knowledge that NAP had supported the Awami League in East Pakistan and that NAP supporters in Balochistan were fighting the Pakistan Army in the Pat Feeder area (south of Sibi) over the control of agricultural lands. This led Bhutto to declare that the provincial leadership of the Baluch sardars had failed 'to take effective measures to check large-scale disturbances in different parts of the province…causing a growing sense of insecurity among the inhabitants and grave menace to the peace and tranquillity of the Province.'[33] He thus managed to displace the NAP leadership from Balochistan and sent the Pakistan Army into the province, ostensibly with the aim of 'constructing roads, providing electricity and water to the poor Baluchis.'[34]

Bhutto thus invited the Pakistan Army back into the political process, a move that was later to haunt him. The minor Baluch leaders—those who could—took to the hills with their followers. The major sardars and other NAP leaders, including Khair Baksh Marri, were taken into custody by the government, charged with treason and subsequently brought to trial in Hyderabad. Support for their opposition is said to have come from different sources: the Afghan government of President Daud, (a long time supporter of NAP and proponent of the cause of an independent Pushtunistan), the Soviet Union, India, perhaps even distant Iraq that had long supported a free Balochistan movement in both Iran and Pakistan. Even more improbable was the recruitment by a Marxist by the name of Muhammad Bhabha—(the son of a member of the Communist Party of South Africa who had brought his family to Karachi to escape persecution)—of young men belonging to the upper-middle class, mostly from the Punjab to help lead the rebellion against Bhutto's regime. Some of these youngsters were at Cambridge University when they were recruited, hence their name: the London Group. Among them reportedly were Ahmed Rashid,[35] whose mother was formerly married to a leading Baluch Muslim League leader Qazi Isa, and who later became a well known journalist; Duleep 'Johnny' Dass, son of a retired senior air force officer, Air Commodore Balwant Dass; and Asad and Rashid Rahman, the sons of Justice S.A. Rahman of the Supreme Court of Pakistan.[36] Another partner was Muhammad Ali Talpur, the son of Ahmed Ali Talpur, a powerful Sindhi landlord, who later served as defence minister in Bhutto's government.

'Johnny' Dass was never seen again, believed to have been killed while in government custody in 1975, halfway through the insurgency.[37] The government also took into custody Najam Sethi, a Cambridge graduate and later one of the top editors of Pakistan and a minister in the caretaker government of Prime Minister Mairaj Khalid under President Farooq Leghari. Sethi was picked up in the Marri area in October 1975, kept in solitary confinement by the army for seven months, and then transferred to Hyderabad jail to join fifty-five other accused persons. Reports emerged from the Pakistan Army that these young men were involved in supplying, and helping motivate, train, and even lead some of the tribal insurgents into battle against the Pakistan Army in Balochistan. According to A.B. Awan, a former DIB, some of these young men had received training with the Palestine Liberation Organization in Jordan, others in India. A participant in the group states that this is not true but none of them is willing to provide further details of their recruitment and where they were trained. Awan also mentions some girls as members of this 'socialist cell,' a claim backed by a participant who said that none of the girls came to the hills. They were part of the study groups in London and Cambridge.[38] In Awan's view: 'Most of them [the young men who took to the hills] came back without making any contribution except that of providing some amusement for the tough Baluch fighters.'[39]

But the very fact that a group of middle and upper-middle class youth had chosen to leave their comfortable lives and become part of a revolutionary war against a perceived dictator made this a significant event. The fact that many of them came from the Punjab made it even more notable. As one participant put it, the main reason for going was 'the traumatic effect of the war in Bangladesh, the loss of half the country, and the issue of provincial autonomy, which this group saw as the key to keeping Pakistan together, which Bhutto and the Army were determined to undermine.'[40] The London Group wished 'to create a Marxist revolution in Pakistan and were not in favour of Baluch separatism, which some NAP leaders wanted and which, after the ceasefire, divided the group from the Baluch leaders.'[41] The young men and women had been influenced by the 1968 student movements in the United Kingdom and France, the anti-Vietnam War movement, and the anti-imperialist movements of Marxists theorists such as Che Guevara and Regis Debray, who believed that 'small groups of committed Marxists' could start a revolutionary movement without necessarily having a working-class or trade union movement to back them up. This led them into the hills of Balochistan, to align themselves with the forces of Mir Hazar Khan, a lieutenant of Khair Baksh Marri, who led the insurgency in the Marri area until 1976 when he left for Afghanistan but continued to direct actions from there.

The Pakistan Army had meanwhile profited from the gift of thirty Huey Cobra helicopter gunships from Iran, which was fearful of the potential spillover of the uprising in Pakistani Balochistan into Iranian Balochistan.[42] The army used these gunships against the people of the Marri tribe (including women and children) who had taken refuge in the Chamalang Valley on 3 September 1974. This action drew the Marri fighters down from their hideouts in the hills and a three-day battle ensued in which the heavily out-gunned Marris suffered grievously.[43] Even while he was planning the military action, Bhutto continued to meet Baluch leaders, such as Sherbaz Mazari, and encouraged him to speak with imprisoned leaders Khair Baksh Marri and Ghous Baksh Bizenjo at their jail in Sihala. Fighting continued in the barren wastes of Balochistan, with the tribesmen giving battle continuously despite the numerical and weapon superiority of the Pakistan Army. Finally, the Bhutto government issued a *White Paper on Balochistan* in December 1974, claiming victory, and stating that the army would withdraw. However, this withdrawal did not take place until well after the end of the Bhutto government. While the rest of the country may not have been aware of the extent and nature of the military action in Balochistan, large numbers of soldiers and officers of the Pakistan Army were closely involved in these operations and becoming aware of the fact that Bhutto was using the army for his own political purposes. More importantly though, they became increasingly aware of the key role being played by the army in propping up civilian rule.

A FAILED COUP

The army had by then shown some signs of its discontent with Bhutto's rule. With large numbers of Pakistani soldiers and officers still in Indian hands after the loss of East Pakistan, the army had time to assess the effects of the war on itself. The younger officers in particular, felt that the army high command had failed them miserably. Some of them had been part of the move that led to Yahya abdicating in favour of Bhutto in December 1971. However, a growing number of young officers (in both the army and air force)—many of whom had been highly decorated veterans of the 1965 and 1971 wars—saw a civilian dictatorship emerging under Bhutto. They also saw that Bhutto had made no attempt to rid the army of the 'rotten layer at the top.'[44] Indeed, he had promoted officers who had fled East Pakistan or had been part of the military action there. In August 1972, he had removed Brigadier F.B. Ali and others whom he accused of having tried to prevent the return of civilian rule in 1971. The young officers saw Pakistan heading toward another disaster and decided to do something about it. In 1972 and early 1973, a group of army officers led by Major Farouk Adam Khan started meeting to discuss the situation. Remarkably, their discussions did not focus on re-installing military rule. Instead, they were searching for a stable form of democracy. Among the participants in this group were my cousin Major Farooq Nawaz Janjua and other relatives, Major Nadir Parvez and Major Saeed Akhtar Malik (the son of the military hero of 1965, Major General Akhtar Hussain Malik).[45] In early 1972, Farooq Nawaz Janjua borrowed my commonplace folder of collected political quotations, (which included quotations from Thomas Paine and writings on freedom and democracy from Bertrand Russell and Félix Houphouët-Boigny), as well as my heavily annotated copy of Edward Luttwak's *Coup d'etat: A Practical Handbook*. These officers, many of whom had been platoon commanders or other staff at the PMA in Kakul, met regularly. At one time, they used the marriage of Farooq Nawaz in Jhelum for this purpose. A parallel group of officers in the air force under Squadron Leader Ghaus had similar ideas. They connected through Colonel Aleem Afridi, the man who had carried the message from Brigadier F.B. Ali to the GHQ demanding the ouster of Yahya in December 1971. Brigadier Ali was also brought into the picture as a senior officer who might be able to help make contact with other senior officers of the army.

In the process of expanding their circle, the group was penetrated by military intelligence. One member of the group, Lt. Col. Tariq Rafi, spilt the beans to senior army officers. The army chief, Tikka Khan became aware of the plot from a relative and fellow Janjua, Ahmad Kamal. Through the ISI, Tikka encouraged Rafi to continue participating in the dissident group.[46] Saeed Akhtar found out about the penetration. A meeting was held in Lahore on 24 March 1973 at which future plans were debated in light of this new information. Saeed Akhtar was of the view that it was too late to stop now and that the group ought to speed up its recruitment of senior officers to help effect the coup. Brig. Ali recalls telling the group that it would be best to go to ground 'for the time being.' He recalls that the younger officers appeared to have accepted his suggestion at the meeting. However, it appears that they changed their minds later on and continued with their plans.[47] Noting the increasing momentum of the group, the army decided to act. On 30 March, all the officers in the group were arrested.

Bhutto wanted to make an example of these rebels. They were subjected to vigorous interrogation. The army officers were kept at Attock fort while the air force officers were taken to the former US air base at Badaber near Peshawar. The story released to the public via the official media was that the officers were planning a coup to remove Bhutto and the entire military leadership and to install a government headed by retired Air Marshal Asghar Khan, the leader of the opposition Tehrik-i-Istiqlal party. Neither Brig. Ali nor Saeed Akhtar confirm this version, contending that the discussions were at too early a stage. No firm views had emerged on what to do nor what actions would follow a successful coup.[48] Bhutto, however, used the 'attempted coup' as a means of controlling the army's leadership by playing up the distrust of the senior officers by their younger colleagues.

A trial was set under a military tribunal at the Attock fort, (thus the name of the case): the Attock Conspiracy Trial. Bhutto needed the right officer to head the tribunal. He had been impressed by the obsequious manner of young Major General Muhammad Ziaul Haq, who had been the armour division commander in Multan. Zia had earlier served in Jordan with the Pakistan military advisory group in Amman and had reportedly been involved in planning the Jordanian army's actions against the Palestinians in the battles that gave birth to the rise of the Black September terrorist movement. He was sent back by Brigadier Nawazish, the head of the Pakistani contingent in Jordan, for having participated in that action against orders and in fact suggested that Zia be court martialled.[49] However, fellow armour officer, (at that time major general) Gul Hassan had managed to get Zia off the hook. After Gul Hassan became army chief, Zia was sent to Multan to command the armour division under the corps commander, Lt. Gen. M. Shariff. However, Zia maintained his contacts with the royal family of Jordan and hosted a visit of Crown Prince Hassan of Jordan. Bhutto first came into contact with Zia during the prince's visit and was affected by Zia's fawning manner and general demeanour.[50] Bhutto thus chose Zia to head the Attock tribunal. Among other things, this action gave Zia direct access to Bhutto. It is reported that he spoke with Bhutto regularly in the evenings to bring him up to date on the trial. The outspoken young officers provided much grist for the criticism of senior commanders of the Pakistan Army, something that must have pleased Bhutto in his effort to put the army high command in its place and also favoured Zia's own ambitions. Zia's own handling of the trial was described by both Brig. Ali and Saeed Akhtar Malik as 'fair',[51] and he allowed the officers ample opportunity to vent their feelings in the courtroom.

Rather than turning other army officers against the conspirators, the actions and words of the officer under trial made them into heroes among their younger colleagues. Frequent visitors to Attock fort and Campbellpur jail carried the message of discontent with the country's leadership back to the rest of the army, building a reservoir of distrust of the civilian administration. The harsh sentences that were inevitable further strengthened the army's unhappiness with Bhutto. And, to prevent officers of the army from meeting their imprisoned comrades, Bhutto had the convicted officers distributed across the country in distant jails.

This trial solidified Ziaul Haq's rise to power. When the time came to replace Tikka Khan in April 1976, Bhutto saw in Zia a potentially quiet and pliable army chief, one who came to Pakistan as a refugee from Indian Punjab and therefore had no ostensible tribal support or another base in the army.[52]

He pulled him up over the heads of six other senior generals and made him COAS on 1 March 1976. In doing so, he ignored (among others) Lt. Gen. M. Shariff, a highly professional Dehru Dun graduate and an apolitical soldier, who had been Zia's senior in Multan. Thus to legitimize Zia's promotion, Shariff too was elevated to a full four-star general and placed in the largely ceremonial position of chairman of the newly-formed JCSC, a new body that Bhutto had set up to better coordinate military policies. In doing so, Bhutto sealed his own fate, as the quiet Ziaul Haq, a personally pious individual, was miles apart from Bhutto's own line of thinking. When the time came, he would up-end Bhutto without any regret.

CHALLENGING THE ARMY

Very early in his tenure, Bhutto felt the need to have a military force of his own; one that he could employ as he saw fit without relying on the Pakistan Army. Gul Hassan's frequent demurrals in providing army soldiers to quell police revolts or civilian disturbances provided the impetus for the creation of a new Federal Security Force (FSF), a paramilitary organization, to be equipped and kept under civil control. Bhutto had already re-hired Said Ahmad Khan, a former IG police who had been dismissed by the Yahya regime, and made him his chief security officer, entrusting him with special jobs, some of which were beyond the pale of the law. When the FSF was created in September 1972, it was headed by a retired police officer Haq Nawaz Tiwana, with a budget of Rs 500,000. Soon thereafter, Tiwana was charged with murder by the governor of Punjab, Ghulam Mustafa Khar, for 'indiscriminate firing on an Opposition rally' on 23 March 1973, and removed.[53] Tiwana was replaced by another police officer, Masood Mahmud. Bhutto's finance minister, Mubashir Hasan describes Mahmud as 'an unprincipled, pompous, arrogant and unpopular officer who was known for his sadistic inclinations.'[54] Such a leader of the FSF would provide unstinted support to the prime minister. (Bhutto could not have known at that time that the same person would turn against him in the final murder case in which Bhutto was eventually convicted and hanged.) In August 1974, Bhutto sought to enlarge the FSF with another injection of Rs 130 million (Rs 13 crore). Mubashir Hasan challenged this in writing, asking to know the purpose for which the force was being created. He felt that if the aim was to catch smugglers, black marketeers, and other big criminals, then even Rs 200 million would be insufficient. He sought a meeting with Bhutto, who wrote back that he wished to discuss the 'financial and philosophical' issues with the finance minister. That meeting never took place. The FSF took on a special role as Bhutto's private military arm.

Another agency named the Federal Investigating Agency (FIA) was also set up, separate from the police, while an Airport Security Force (ASF) was also created. Bhutto also brought into his inner circle a senior police officer, Rao Rashid, who was designated special secretary and ended up providing him key political advice. When General Tikka Khan retired as COAS, he was appointed special assistant for national security. In effect, Bhutto had set up a system of intelligence-gathering and control parallel to that of the Pakistan Army, one that was reporting directly to him. A group headed by Rafi Raza was asked to review all these intelligence arrangements and advised Bhutto to revamp the system which it felt was inefficient and too devoted to reporting directly to the prime minister. Nothing came of those suggestions.[55] The army, however, kept a close watch on these developments and bided its time.

As a sop to the military, Bhutto increased the military pay scales and allowed the army to expand to make up for the loss of the forces that continued to be in Indian hands as POWs. He also expanded the defence horizons by enhancing Pakistan's international standing and using support from friendly Islamic nations to launch a nuclear weapons' programme.

THE NUCLEAR OPTION

About a month after taking power, on 24 January 1972, Bhutto gathered the country's fifty top scientists (including future Nobel Laureate, Abdus Salam), at a secret meeting in Multan at the home of local PPP leader, Nawab Sadiq Hussain Qureshi, challenging them to build a nuclear bomb that would help restore Pakistan's strength and reputation. This programme was to be seen eventually by many outside the country as an 'Islamic Bomb.' 'He had great charisma and he really moved those people,' Khalid Hasan, who attended the meeting as Bhutto's press secretary, said in an interview. 'They cheered him and they said they could do it. Everyone believed in Bhutto.'[56] In raising this challenge, Bhutto was merely repeating something he had hinted at in his own book *The Myth of Independence* (1967), and reviving a dream that interestingly had first been articulated by a small group of Muslim League students in Ceylon decades earlier. Former agent of the OSS, Edmond Taylor recounts picking up a propaganda sheet in the late 1940s with an editorial by Muslim students 'claiming for Pakistan (when it came into being) the right to manufacture atomic bombs for its defense.'[57]

Pakistan had in fact entered the nuclear age much earlier; in 1956, when the Pakistan Atomic Energy Commission (PAEC) came into being as a result of US President Dwight D. Eisenhower's 'Atoms for Peace Program,' under Dr Nazir Ahmed.[58] The initial work mostly focussed on fundamental research in high-energy physics. By 1961, the PAEC had set up centres in Lahore and

Dacca to conduct basic research. The next phase was the search for domestic sources of uranium. Uranium deposits were discovered in the Dera Ghazi Khan district in 1963.

In 1960, Dr Ishrat Hussain Usmani was appointed chairman of the PAEC. He helped lay the foundation of many of the key programmes and infrastructures that would later put Pakistan on the path of nuclear weapons. Among other things, he set up the Pakistan Institute of Nuclear Sciences and Technology at Nilore near Islamabad, (better known by its acronym as PINSTECH,) and the Karachi Nuclear Power Plant (KANUPP). The principal facility at PINSTECH was a 5MW research reactor, commissioned in 1965, and upgraded to 10MW under Chairman Munir Ahmad Khan in 1990, who took over from Usmani after the Multan meeting when Usmani reportedly balked at the idea of a weapons programme. A second research reactor came into operation in 1989 under Munir Ahmad Khan.

Initially, Usmani was lucky to have as the minister of natural resources and power a young Zulfikar Ali Bhutto, who supported these efforts and looked to China and (later) North Korea to provide help, particularly in the face of increased Indian rhetoric against Pakistan. Under an ambitious training programme, many bright young Pakistani scientists were sent abroad for training. Between 1960 and 1967, some 600 students were selected of whom 106 eventually returned with doctorate degrees.[59] By 1964, President Ayub Khan was expressing his concerns to the United States about an impending Indian nuclear programme.[60] In March 1965, an unusually prescient Bhutto was predicting to Patrick Keately of the *Manchester Guardian* that if India were to go nuclear 'then we should have to eat grass and get one, or buy one, of our own'![61] US nuclear historian George Perkovitch raises the possibility that fear of an Indian nuclear test as early as 1965 may have been a factor in Pakistan's decision to attempt a settlement of the Kashmir issue in 1965 by force. No doubt, it was Indian action that spurred Bhutto onward.[62]

Thus, Bhutto got into action immediately after taking over as president. As outlined by nuclear historian Carey Sublette:

> As soon as he had come to power, Bhutto had reached out to the rest of the Islamic world, particularly the nouveau riche oil states of the Middle East, for financial support. During 1973 and 1974, Bhutto held discussions with Libya and other states such as Saudi Arabia to line up financing for a nuclear weapons program. Bhutto and Libya's Colonel Qaddafi finally met and reached an agreement for a Libyan-financed Pakistani weapons program in February 1974 [Weissman and Krosney 1981; pp. 59–62].[63] In the early seventies, billions of dollars also flowed from Iran and Saudi Arabia to Pakistan, most of it for purposes other than the nuclear weapons program, but some of these funds were probably also diverted to support the pursuit of nuclear weapons.[64]

The Saudi ambassador to the United States and former intelligence chief, Prince Turki Al-Faisal, denies that any Saudi financing was provided for Pakistan's nuclear programme.[65] However, finance is fungible and it is highly possible for Pakistan to have benefited from both Libyan and Saudi financing at various stages in the development of its programme. I, the author, personally know of members of the PINSTECH team and staff of the PAEC who were posted to Libya for years at a time to benefit from relatively easy access to that country's financial resources, and Europe.

Bhutto's initiative served as a magnet for Pakistani scientists abroad, many of whom returned to their homeland to contribute whatever they could to the national nuclear development programme. Among the more celebrated names was that of Dr A.Q. Khan, who later earned the much debated sobriquet of 'Father of the Bomb.' But during those early days, there were conflicts within the nuclear team, between the PAEC scientists and people like Dr Khan, who came from outside the Pakistani nuclear establishment. At the Multan meeting, it had been decided to pursue both the enriched uranium and the plutonium paths to a nuclear weapons programme. A uranium refining plant was set up within the Chemical Plant Complex (CPC) at Dera Ghazi Khan. The CPC provided uranium dioxide for the Karachi reactor and uranium hexaflouride (or UF6) that eventually was to feed the Kahuta Enrichment Plant.[66] According to author M.A. Chaudhri, the PAEC team had already acquired a substantial amount of knowledge and technology for enrichment of uranium and even set up experimental centrifuge cascades based on an Italian design at a site in Chaklala. But the real impetus for pursuit of the enrichment route to nuclear weapons came with the arrival of Dr A.Q. Khan. This had been given special importance once India exploded its first nuclear device in the Rajasthan desert on 18 May 1974. Known as Pokharan-I—named after the location of the test site—and presented as a 'peaceful' nuclear explosion by the Indian government at that time, the 12 kilo-ton underground explosion[67] was marked by the code words, 'The Buddha is Smiling', sent from the site to signal its success. Pakistan now had some catching up to do.

The Pakistan Army was drawn into the programme when Bhutto asked the army chief, General Ziaul Haq to help the PAEC set up the Kahuta Enrichment Plant in 1976. Dr Khan had already arrived, carrying with him the plans for the Urenco enrichment centrifuges from the Dutch firm, Fysscish Dynamisch Onderzoek (FDO). The PAEC had done some preliminary work in selecting the site at Kahuta. The army was brought in to help complete the construction and get the project going at high speed. Brigadier Zahid Ali Akbar was designated by Ziaul Haq to head a special works organization to construct the facility. He completed a survey of the area and proceeded apace to set up the physical infrastructure.[68] Akbar noted the friction between the PAEC scientists and Dr Khan. At one point, Dr Khan informed Akbar that he had purchased tickets for himself and his family and was leaving Pakistan. Akbar then wrote a note on the subject to Gen. Zia and through him sought a meeting of the special cell that oversaw Akbar's work on the Kahuta complex. He proposed to Bhutto to give greater powers and autonomy to Dr Khan and his operation. 'We had never undertaken a project of such colossal importance. It was crucial that it be allowed to continue without any administrative or political bickering. For that it had to be autonomous,' recalls Akbar. If that could not be done Akbar asked to be relieved of his responsibility.[69] Bhutto agreed to his proposal. The Kahuta operation became autonomous, and Dr Khan was given free rein. This was a mixed blessing, in that it allowed Pakistan to speed up its acquisition of nuclear weapons technology but eventually also allowed the leakage of this technology to other countries. The army continued to be involved in the programme, providing security to the site and monitoring its activities on behalf of the COAS.

BHUTTO STRENGTHENS HIS POSITION

Soon after the Multan meeting, Bhutto took off on his journey to the Middle East and North Africa, preparing the ground for financial and other cooperation. Following the oil embargo and the surprising success of the Arab states against Israel in the 1973 war, the Arabs were flush with their windfall of oil revenues and willing to assert themselves on the global stage. Bhutto offered them an opportunity to coalesce their thinking against Israel and in favour of Pakistan's nuclear programme. He hosted the Islamic summit in 1974 in Lahore, showering his guests with great attention, even naming a huge stadium after Colonel Muammar Gaddafi of Libya. Bhutto also used that summit to recognize Bangladesh, thus setting the path for the return of the Pakistani POWs in India.

In 1973, Bhutto had managed an even greater domestic achievement: the drafting, and then approval, of a new constitution that transformed the country from a presidential system to a parliamentary one. With the approval by the National Assembly on 10 April 1973, and support even from members of the opposition who had earlier raised issues with aspects of the new law of the land, Bhutto became prime minister and chief executive with enhanced powers. The president was reduced to a mere figurehead, with Article 48 making the president wholly dependent on the advice of the prime minister. Bhutto's choice for president reflected his view of that slot: his choice was Fazal Ilahi Chaudhry, a member of the PPP and a minor player on the party's stage. Among the prime minister's prerogatives was the appointment of the three service chiefs and the CJCS. The constitution also made it a treasonable crime for anyone to usurp the powers of the prime minister. In September

1973, the parliament prescribed the death sentence for any act of high treason; a move meant to prevent military coups. The move was in vain, however, as later events were to show. Article 96 provided for a vote of no-confidence against the prime minister only if the resolution provided the name of the person who would replace the prime minister and was passed by a majority in parliament.

Although the opposition parties had tried their utmost to force Bhutto to concede greater autonomy to the provinces, the final shape of the 1973 constitution continued to maintain a strong centre. Defence, foreign affairs, currency, and communications, plus more than 60 other subjects were placed on the federal list, with another 47 on what was known as the 'concurrent list', where federal law would supersede the provincial laws.[70] This concession by the opposition was apparently given in return for the addition of Islamic provisions in the constitution, which officially made Pakistan an 'Islamic State'. It introduced a clause that only a Muslim could become the president or prime minister, and called for the set up of a 'Council of Islamic Ideology' that would embark upon the Islamization of laws for the next seven years. In effect, Bhutto set the stage for the Islamized government that was to follow his. In the waning days of his regime, Bhutto was to concede even more in this regard by banning alcohol and declaring the Ahmadi sect as non-Muslims.

Bhutto also strengthened his hold on decision-making related to defence matters. Having already reduced the former C-in-C of services to COS, he issued a *White Paper on Higher Defence Organization* in May 1976 that gave the prime minister ultimate authority on matters related to defence and national security. A Defence Committee of the Cabinet (DCC) would assist the prime minister in his deliberations, while a defence council headed by the defence minister would implement the DCC's decisions. Meanwhile, Bhutto continued to increase the strength of his newly-raised FSF from about 14,000 in 1974 to over 18,000 in 1976.[71] The Pakistan Army remained wary of this move. However, Bhutto temporarily managed to maintain support for himself within the army by increasing defence expenditures in nominal terms from Rs 3,725 million in 1971–2 to Rs 8,210 million in 1976–7.[72] Indeed, at a dinner given in Bhutto's honour at Quetta's Staff and Command College in April 1976, Bhutto's specially chosen COAS, General Ziaul Haq waxed eloquent about Bhutto's care and attention for the Pakistan Army:

> Those of us who are aware of the facts and figures are quite certain that the amount of attention which the Pakistan Army received since 1971 till to date has no parallel in the history of the Pakistan Army prior to 1971.
>
> With all this, Sir, I personally and on behalf of the army have nothing tangible to offer as yet. All I can say is that perhaps one day, by the Grace of God, while

you are still present, this Pakistan Army can show you that all the attention and affection that it received from you did not go to waste....

I am saying this in very simple and humble words from the bottom of my heart that we thank you, Sir, for all that you are doing and what you have done for us in particular.[73]

Zia probably meant every word that he uttered that evening. But he also knew how to get deeper into Bhutto's good books. Being a member of the armoured corps himself, when Zia was corps commander in Multan he proposed that Bhutto become the first civilian colonel-in-chief of the armoured corps, an honorary rank normally bestowed on very senior or retired officers from that arm of service. Part of the ceremony involves pinning the badges of rank on the shoulders of the person being honoured. Since Bhutto did not have a uniform, Zia had a special blue patrol uniform of the armour corps secretly stitched for Bhutto by Bhutto's tailor Hamid Khan in Karachi and brought to surprise him at Kharian, where the induction ceremony was to be held at the centenary celebration of the 11 Cavalry Regiment. The uniform, complete with the belts and the silver *toshadan* (pouch) that sets the armour uniform apart from the rest of the army, was left on Bhutto's bed in Kharian, a surprise that achieved its effect. Zia delivered another speech of fulsome praise at that investiture ceremony in Kharian, and was said to have overwhelmed Bhutto in Multan by searching for a copy of the Quran and swearing allegiance to him.[74]

HUBRIS

Even as Bhutto's hold on the country grew stronger, he was looking to build an even stronger political base for himself. In that quest, he shed many of his earlier supporters and brought into his administration remnants of the *ancien regime*—feudal landlords from the Punjab and Sindh and tribal maliks and sardars from Balochistan and the NWFP—largely men (and some women, including Syeda Abida Hussain of Jhang) who favoured a strong central government that provided them easy access to privilege and state resources. The media was brought under tighter control with the use of the Press and Publications Ordinance—so heavily favoured and used by Ayub Khan. Critics of the regime found themselves muffled or physically threatened. Even the puny English-language media were not spared. The Karachi weekly *Outlook* that had launched a campaign against Ayub Khan and suffered the consequences had begun re-publishing under Bhutto, but found that its relatively small quota of paper at officially controlled prices was reduced and then withheld. It had to purchase its paper on the black market. Government advertisements were also withdrawn, as were those of parastatal organizations such as PIA. Yet, the *Outlook* editor, I.H. Burney continued his independent commentary on the Bhutto regime until he was officially shut down. Bhutto realized soon after *Outlook* was shut down that he did not have an example of the 'free press' to point out to his foreign critics at news conferences. Emissaries were sent to Burney to persuade him to re-open the magazine and the regime even promised him additional paper and advertisements, but he refused.[75] Bhutto thus lost the support of the liberal intellectuals who had supported his rise to power.

Both PTV and the newly set up Pakistan Broadcasting Corporation (formerly Radio Pakistan) became personal publicity vehicles for the prime minister. Bhutto's every move was filmed and reported on. A special archive was set up for these materials. The Ministry of Information and its press and publications department spent great efforts to produce books of photographs of the prime minister's activities and even commissioned a coffee-table book from Stacey International,[76] materials for which were produced by the ministry staff. Soon, the sycophants around him and his media managers made it impossible for Bhutto to receive any but the most favourable comments about his government and himself.

Fuelled by this flood of praise and anxious to put his stamp on the country's politics for decades to come, Bhutto called for fresh elections in 1977. Rafi Raza was designated to manage this venture but accounts from both Raza and the information minister, Maulana Kausar Niazi, indicate that Raza's role was less critical than that of the so-called mini-cabinet that was set up to handle 'Operation Victory,' the code name for the election programme. This mini-cabinet included Rao Abdur Rashid (former IG Police and then Special Secretary), Afzal Saeed Khan, Vaqar Ahmed (a senior bureaucrat who was Cabinet Secretary), Saeed Ahmad Khan, Masood Mahmud (Director, FSF), Muhammad Hayat Tamman (Adviser for Public Affairs), Akram Shiekh (DIB), Saeed Ahmad Qureshi (Chief Secretary, Sindh), Brigadier Malik Muzaffar Khan (Chief Secretary, Punjab), Munir Hussain (Chief Secretary, NWFP), Nasranminallah (Chief Secretary, Balochistan), Major General Imtiaz Ahmed (Military Secretary to the Prime Minister), and Hamid Jalal (Additional Secretary in the Prime Minister's Secretariat and a former information official.)[77] In effect, the political workers of the PPP had been displaced by bureaucrats whose job was to deliver the elections results of Bhutto's choice.

While announcing the elections in January 1977, Bhutto promised 'a clean and fair election....I can assure you that we have the administrative ability to have a clean and a fair election,' he said.[78] Less than a year earlier, he had sent a scheme to Rafi Raza presenting a model based on how elections might be handled in his native constituency of Larkana for both the national and provincial assemblies so that it would be applied 'on a scientific basis for the whole country.' Among other things, the scheme assigned political roles to local officials, such as deputy commissioners and the superintendents of police, who would liaise with the president of the district committee of the PPP to ensure that analyses and instructions were consistently produced and followed.[79] In the detailed instructions issued with this model plan were forms that were to be used by district officials to vet candidates, to make sure that they were genuine PPP supporters. Bhutto did not wish to leave anything to chance.

Bhutto's information adviser, Pir Ali Muhammad Rashdi provides a good illustration of the overkill that ensued. Rashdi suggested, among other things, the setting up of surrogate candidates to run against PPP candidates should the opposition parties boycott the elections. 'Such surrogates should contest with *apparent seriousness* and when defeated by our official candidates, should be rewarded in some other way.'[80] The prime minister's special adviser, ex-policeman Rao Rashid took this idea a step further to explore with some opposition parties the idea of having surrogate parties that would run against the PPP to 'generate apparent but controlled heat in the elections to make it appear well-contested.' Bhutto approved this approach with a note: 'Please proceed along these lines.'[81] Rashdi referred also to the fact that the army had conducted the only fair elections in the country to date, referring to the 1970 elections. He wished that the 1977 election be seen to be fair too.

The opposition parties meanwhile, were thoroughly disheartened and disorganized. But, as Bhutto's stranglehold on Pakistani politics tightened, they were spurred into action. They coalesced into the Pakistan National Alliance (PNA), a hodgepodge of parties that represented a wide spectrum of views but tried to unite under an anti-Bhutto platform that used Islamic symbols and slogans to rally the masses against the PPP juggernaut. The PNA, however, faced a huge challenge. Bhutto himself was elected unopposed from Larkana. His opponent, Maulana Jan Mohammad Abbasi, was prevented from filing his nomination papers and reports arose that he had been kidnapped. On 20 January 1977, Bhutto's publicity machinery went into high gear, with the press information department's principal information officer calling senior correspondents to a briefing where they were told to 'link up the Prime Minister's unopposed election with his massive popularity and to highlight in their reports the services of the Prime Minister to the people of his constituency, the Province of Sind and the nation as a whole....The national press was advised to publish these reports prominently on front page...The newspapers were further advised to publish the latest official portrait of the Prime Minister in the centre of their front pages in 3 columns x 8 in[ches] size, with the caption: 'The Supreme Leader; The Undisputed Leader, the Great Leader.'[82]

The PPP put up candidates for all 200 seats in the National Assembly. Nineteen of them were elected unopposed before any vote was cast, 15 in Sindh and 4 in Balochistan. Eight seats reserved for FATA traditionally side with whichever is the ruling party. This left 3 seats to be contested in Balochistan, 115 in Punjab, 26 in NWFP and 28 in Sindh. The PPP only needed 101 seats to get a simple majority but it needed to win 105 out of the remaining 172 seats to get the two-thirds majority that would give Bhutto total control over the assembly and the ability to change the constitution. The PNA only fielded candidates in 169 constituencies, with some candidates contesting more than one seat. The nine parties of the PNA divided their tickets thus: Muslim League 36, Tehrik-i-Pakistan 23, Jamaat-i-Islami 31, Jamiat-ul-Ulema-i-Pakistan (JUP) 23, Jamiat-ul-Ulema-i-Islam (JUI) 24, Pakistan Democratic Party (PDP) 13, and the Khaksar Tehrik 2. The Muslim Conference was not given any tickets. By any math, the PNA's odds of winning were difficult at best. Even if they had won a simple majority, the wide and often conflicting range of views of this coalition (which Bhutto derisively characterized as 'a cat with nine tails,') would have doomed its operations. 'I do not think there was any need for resorting to rigging of polls. However, it was unfortunate that Prime Minister Bhutto himself was the first to make the incorrect move of getting himself elected unopposed,' states Kausar Nizai.[83] That set the tone for the rest of the election.

The PNA only garnered 36 seats to the PPP's 155, a result that even Bhutto might not have expected. Indeed, he was apparently embarrassed. He had invited his friend, US Ambassador Henry Byroade, to watch the election results come in with him at the PM House on 7 March 1977. The early results from Karachi went against the PPP, as did some results from Peshawar in the NWFP. But the Punjab results changed the picture entirely. 'Then [Bhutto] became absolutely quiet and started drinking heavily, calling Lahore and he said: "What are you guys doing?"... I saw Bhutto at 8 the next morning and he wasn't himself. He hadn't had any sleep, obviously drinking. He was just sad,' recalled Byroade.[84] Bhutto had a lot on his mind. Apart from the prospect of facing an Islamist-dominated opposition, he was fearful of the after-effects of such a lop-sided victory, especially on the rank and file of the Pakistan Army. The DG ISI, Major General Ghulam Jilani, had earlier sent him a conservative prediction of the election results. He had then followed it up with a secret missive addressed to Bhutto but copied to Ziaul Haq, the army chief, that referred to a poster in the army barracks in Multan that called for an 'Army Revolution' and linked it to the strong religious feelings of people in Multan, where the JI and the JUI had strong roots. Bhutto's reaction to that message was scrawled on Jilani's note. He drew attention to the heavy army concentration in Multan rather than the strength of the religious right. Quite rightly, he stated that 'such teachings become dangerous only when the chief of the army gives them *official blessings* and *respect*. This will boomerang.... That is why I told him [Zia] in my first letter that I do not want a "Mullah Army".[85] Little did he know that he had in fact created the conditions for just such an army under Zia. When Bhutto questioned some of Zia's actions, such as distributing copies of Quranic commentaries as prizes to soldiers who won debates, Zia responded diplomatically that 'Islam is not the private property of any individual,' but then he sent out a note to all units warning them that 'we, in the army, are not Mullahs[...] We are professional soldiers who have sworn not to get involved in any political activity whatsoever.'[86] He sent Bhutto a copy, to allay his concerns.

MARTIAL LAW IN THE CITIES

Faced with the overwhelming defeat by the PPP, the opposition alliance cried foul. As reports started emerging from the districts, it became clear that rigging had taken place at local levels. 'Polling places were alleged to have been closed for hours, ballot boxes removed at gun point, multiple voting confessed to, and marked ballots found on the streets,' according to an American observer.[87] Bhutto clearly had the military and civilian means to ride out the storm of protest. The opposition thus resorted to the time-tested method of street protests, using Islamic slogans as a cover for their activities. A general strike on 11 March succeeded in the major cities, testifying to the growing strength of conservative forces among the petit bourgeoisie. Next they announced a rolling series of strikes and demonstrations from 14 March onward. Bhutto resorted to another tested method of government in Pakistan: imposition of Section 144, which prohibited public assembly of five or more persons for political purposes. Meanwhile, he offered to sit down and talk with his opponents, while asking the election commission to investigate irregularities and even offering to set aside the provincial elections. Faced with an intransigent opposition, however, he ordered the arrest of leading PNA politicians. But the protests did not die down. Indeed, with every week, and especially on Fridays, when the faithful gathered for congregational prayers, the PNA used the assembled masses to carry out protest marches after prayers. Women with covered heads and sometimes carrying copies of the Quran joined the marches, making it difficult for the police to disperse the protestors with force.

Adding to Bhutto's woes was the series of strikes in Karachi and other cities that brought the economy to a standstill. Dissent began within the PPP itself, with Mubashir Hasan stepping down as secretary general of the PPP. Air Marshal Rahim Khan, whom Bhutto had sent into exile as ambassador in Spain, and Lt. Gen. Gul Hassan Khan, the former army chief and then ambassador in Greece, resigned their posts in protest, as did a number of senior foreign office officials posted abroad. April truly became the 'cruelest month' for Bhutto, as none of his attempts to placate the protesters succeeded. Even the strong arm tactics of his PPP and FSF troops failed to control the surging street protests. The official appropriation of the opposition's manifesto—by de-nationalizing small industries, prohibiting alcohol and gambling, and promising an Islamic system did not help Bhutto out of his hole. Neither did his attempt to appease the armed forces and the bureaucracy, with significant increases in their salaries, wrote Eqbal Ahmed.[88] Finally, on 22 April, Bhutto called out the army and instituted martial law in five cities. This martial law was only possible after a constitutional amendment was made by the Bhutto government. And it came over the head of the CJCS who had been left out of the discussions between Bhutto and Ziaul Haq on plans for its imposition.[89] The army now had a toe hold in the political system.

Earlier, Bhutto had been alarmed by an open letter sent by retired Air Marshal Asghar Khan, now a member of the PNA, to the three service chiefs asking them to rise against the Bhutto government. According to the BBC, 3000 copies of the letter were distributed to the armed forces. In this letter, Asghar Khan levelled a series of charges against Bhutto, starting with his alleged role in the break-up of Pakistan and ending with the charge of rigging the 1977 elections. 'Bhutto has violated the constitution and is guilty of grave crimes against the people. It is not your duty to support this illegal regime nor can you be called upon to kill your own people so that he can continue a little longer in office. Let it not be said that the Pakistan armed forces are a degenerate Police Force fit only for killing unarmed civilians....Answer this call honestly and save Pakistan,' stated Asghar Khan.[90]

Some differences had already arisen between Bhutto and his newly appointed army chief. Ziaul Haq protested when Bhutto told him that some generals had established links to the opposition and Zia asked that the civilian IB withdraw surveillance of army officers. Bhutto complied and replaced the IB chief. The army now clearly had the upper hand.

But the imposition of martial law in aid of civil power in selected cities brought the army face to face with the people of Pakistan, and especially the Punjab. A number of officers in Lahore refused to allow their troops to be used against civilians. Brigadiers Ishtiaq Ali Khan, Said Muhammad, and Niaz Ahmad asked to be relieved of martial law duties to avoid using force against civilians. Zia rushed to Lahore to meet them, accompanied by his military secretary, K.M. Arif. The officers 'told General Zia that their conscience forbade them to fire on the protesters agitating against election riggers and cheats.'[91] Zia had them dismissed from service immediately although Zia and his senior commanders had already discussed the elections and come to the same conclusions as these more junior officers about the nature of the election results. Ironically, Zia himself would disobey the constitution and his own oath in less than three months from then. A story made the rounds that some women protesters had gone to visit the home of one CO and gave him a gift of bangles—meant as an insult to his manhood.

Aware of dissent among the ranks, Bhutto had the service chiefs issue a statement of support, which said: 'We wish to make it absolutely clear that Pakistan Army, Navy and Air Force are totally united to discharge their constitutional obligations in support of the present legally constituted government.'[92] Again, the CJCS initially opposed this statement, but he was won over by the service chiefs, particularly Air Marshal Zulfiqar Ali Khan, who had been the person Bhutto had asked to get the statement issued. The reaction to this statement within the army was negative, and this was conveyed to Bhutto by the ISI. Ziaul Haq also had to follow up with a separate communication to the army explaining that it was not for the army to make statements on the legality of government. But Zia was weighing his options carefully, as the political maelstrom developed.

A FOREIGN HAND

Pakistan is a breeding ground for conspiracy theories. Tight control of the media by successive governments has made it ripe territory for the currency of rumours and insinuations, especially rumours involving a 'foreign hand' in the internal affairs of the nation. Bhutto too chose to blame 'foreign involvement' for the unrest and pointed the finger at the United States. Ever since his opposition to Ayub Khan, he had played the role of the *enfant terrible* against the United States, portraying himself as an independent nationalist who was the target of an international conspiracy. He saw his role as a leader of the Islamic World, and his conflict with the United States and other Western powers over the acquisition of nuclear technology as the grounds for accusing these countries of supporting anti-Bhutto forces in Pakistan. (France had bowed to US pressure and cancelled a deal to supply a reprocessing plant to Pakistan, and Bhutto's relationship with the United States had been running hot and cold in recent times.)

During the early days, Bhutto had played the US hand deftly, winning over Richard Nixon during his two trips to the United States, even though he failed to get any real military weaponry or other support after his 1973 visit. Indeed, in the last hours before he took off from New York at the end of his 1973 visit, he insisted on arranging a press conference so he could counter the general impression that had been created before his visit that he wanted more arms and in that sense his visit had been less than successful.[93] By 1975, the White House itself had gone through some soul searching. With Nixon and Kissinger gone, President Gerald Ford's national security advisor, General Brent Scowcroft drafted a memorandum that re-opened the flow of military supplies to Pakistan.[94] The memorandum, addressed to the secretaries of state and defense, and the director of the CIA, followed up on the 24 February public announcement to lift the embargo of US sales of lethal military equipment to both Pakistan and India. But the memorandum imposed certain conditions: all sales would be on a cash basis only—no grants or credits; each sale would be reviewed on a case-by-case basis; they would be consistent with US policy to promote normalization of relations between the two antagonists; and initially, the emphasis would be on purely defensive systems.

Pakistan was emerging from the Nixonian period of direct access to the White House. It had very few friends left in Washington. The few that were there, tried their best to help Pakistan. Among them, was General Scowcroft. 'In general, my feeling was that imposing equal embargoes on India and Pakistan after conflicts was in fact not equal treatment, because India had other access and indeed had an indigenous arms industry to a much greater extent than Pakistan. So that it was unilaterally punitive to Pakistan and that was the wrong way to go,' stated General Scowcroft in an interview with the author, as he recalled the origins of the 1975 NSC Memorandum in 2006.[95] 'US policy broadly tended to drive Pakistan toward nuclear weapons because the Pakistanis had relied extensively on the US to provide for their security... when conflicts with India led to embargoes, it undermined their confidence in that security relationship.' Pakistan began to think that 'it had to provide for its own security. The only way they could do it against a large power such as India was nuclear weapons,' said General Scowcroft. 'Our policy, however well intentioned, was wrong. Our policy to stop Pakistan enhanced their insecurity and acted as a perverse driver towards nuclear weapons.'[96]

Scowcroft tried to craft a memorandum that might favour Pakistan but Congressional pressure on the Ford administration forced it into providing both India and Pakistan with equal access. 'Congress was pro-India,' he stated, India being seen as a democracy. Bhutto's Pakistan failed to qualify as a democracy in American eyes. On his part, Bhutto had started seeing the US hand in the growing public unrest against him. He saw himself as the champion of the Muslim world and therefore a threat to the West. His nuclear ambitions fuelled the opposition to him in the US, he felt. The US in fact added to Bhutto's difficulties and suspicions by even denying him the sale of tear gas, an action that the PNA applauded. As was his wont, Bhutto went on a public offensive against the US again, deriding their attempts to get rid of him, especially after getting reports of a telephonic conversation in which a US staffer, Howard Schaeffer, at the embassy in Islamabad was heard saying to a colleague in Karachi: 'My source tells me the party's over.'[97] Standing in the National Assembly, Bhutto declared: 'Gentlemen! The party is not over!'

There was resounding applause from his supporters in the assembly. But the celebrations were to be shortlived.

Negotiations with the PNA became bogged down and the street agitation worsened. Even the army became concerned and readied its own 'Operation Fairplay' in case things got out of hand. Bhutto, by estranging the US, was no longer able to rebuild his military base. Additionally, by using the predominantly Punjabi military, especially in the Punjab, Bhutto was affecting the public's perception of the Pakistan Army as a saviour of the country. Bhutto got the reactions of the army's corps commanders directly in meetings that he arranged with them and Ziaul Haq. He also spoke with them directly when the negotiations with the PNA seemed to have run out of steam. His own intelligence chiefs, including the DG ISI, General Jilani, seemed to detect a stiffening of the army's posture and greater assertiveness in the commanders' meetings with the government.[98] Greater interaction and discussions between Bhutto and the senior army brass managed to convince them that Bhutto intended to take firm action against the opposition and might even use the armed wing of the PPP for that purpose. As always, the army feared that it would be forced to pull the chestnuts out of the fire for Bhutto, should his use of force backfire. A repeat of the Ayub Khan–Yahya conflict was developing.

Zia, aided by his local Corps Commander Faiz Ali Chishti, made contingency plans that they kept secret even from the CJCS, General Shariff. When the final negotiations between the PPP and the PNA deadlocked on 4 July, Zia took the decision after the 5:00 p.m. press conference of Nawabzada Nasrullah to take action.[99] But he held off for a few hours. At 1:00 a.m. on 5 July, after both Zia and Bhutto had gone back from a 4 July reception at the US ambassador's home in Islamabad, and soon after a press conference by Bhutto that he would meet the PNA again to resolve their differences, Chishti's soldiers went into action. In a well planned move, the 111 Brigade fanned out and secured key points, including the PM House, arresting ministers and even the military's own DG ISI, Jilani. The 111 Brigade's soldiers were the guards of the PM House in any case, so no fresh troops needed to be deployed to imprison Bhutto inside his home. No shots were fired.

Here is how then Brigadier Imtiaz Warraich, whose troops did most of the work in effecting the coup, described that night's work:

> On the fateful night at about 11:30 p.m., Chief of Staff 10 Corps personally came and conveyed the orders to me. There was a danger of civil war situation emerging, therefore, army had decided to intervene and take the higher political leadership both of Pakistan Peoples' Party (PPP) and the Pakistan National Alliance (PNA) into custody. Names of eleven leaders from PPP, mostly Federal Ministers and nine senior leaders from PNA were identified, who were to be brought to Officers Mess, Headquarters 10 Corps Chaklala....

When the task was accomplished by 03:30 hours and all leaders had assembled in Headquarters 10 Corps, the army chief General Zia spoke to the ex Prime Minister on [the] telephone that he had imposed Martial Law in the country therefore, Prime Minister would be escorted to Murree at seven o'clock in the morning. I may point out that during the whole operation no officer or troops entered the PM House and no disturbance was caused.[100]

After speaking to Bhutto on the telephone, (as narrated in the above account), Zia called up Gen. Shariff, woke him up and told him: 'Sir, I've done it!' 'Done what?' came the reply from the annoyed Sharif. 'Removed Bhutto,' replied Zia. 'Why are you calling me now?' asked Shariff. Zia told him that he (Shariff) had had experience with Ayub Khan and knew the next steps to take to put martial law into effect. Shariff slammed the phone on him.[101] Regardless, Pakistan was under military rule again and would remain so for over a decade.

Bhutto's fall from grace was aided by his own missteps: distancing himself from his original political core, taking on the army with his paramilitary organizations, and falling into the web of sycophants and unprincipled bureaucrats that made him oblivious to the reality around him. He also alienated the business and banking communities. Worse of all, despite having been genuinely elected by the people, he managed to acquire all the trappings and characteristics of the military dictatorship that he succeeded. When the time came for him to assert his power, he found out that the real power still lay with the army and it was not going to be used for political purposes. Zia may have been willing to support Bhutto to some extent, but when the discipline and integrity of the army was threatened, Zia decided to overthrow Bhutto. And once that act was done, there was no turning back.

NOTES

1. Extempore address to the nation, night of 20 December 1971. Press Information Department, Government of Pakistan. E.No 2559-R, issued 6:15 a.m., 21 December 1971.
2. Brigadier F.B. Ali interview and exchanges with author.
3. Translation of a chapter from Col. Rafi ud Din's Urdu book 'Bhutto kay akhri 323 din', www. chowk.com, July 2005. This district jail was a short distance from the President's House, the former home of the army chief, and also the author's home. During the night, its guards would strike the hours on an iron bar that rang loudly throughout the neighbourhood. On nights when hangings took place, one would often be woken up to the wailing of relatives, who then took the bodies home for burial. The jail was dismantled and replaced by a park that was named after Bhutto during the regime of his daughter, Benazir, but later re-named Jinnah Park. It is now being enhanced with a multiplex movie theatre.
4. Interview Brig. F.B. Ali.
5. Major General A.O. Mitha, Unlikely Beginnings (Karachi: Oxford University Press). Annex, letter from Col. Aleem Afridi testifying to this fact. Mitha also quotes an article by Brig.

F.B. Ali that Gul Hassan was clearing out his desk and looked very worried when Afridi arrived but regained his composure and good humour when he discovered that he was not the target of the movement by the younger officers.

6. Lt. Gen. Gul Hassan Khan, *Memoirs of Lt. Gen. Gul Hassan Khan* (Karachi: Oxford University Press, 1993), p. 342 and author's telephone interview with Brig. F.B. Ali.

7. Brig. Ali interview.

8. Richard Sisson and Leo F. Rose, *War and Secession: Pakistan, India, and the Creation of Bangldesh* (Berkeley: University of California Press 1990), p. 235.

9. Major General Shaukat Riza, *The Pakistan Army 1966–71* (Army Education Press, 1990), Chapter IX Epilogue.

10. Gul Hassan, *Memoirs*, p. 331.

11. He probably forgot that the speech was being broadcast live. PTV did not have a delayed broadcast mechanism at that time. Soon after Bhutto hurled abuse at the businessmen, he stopped and said 'Kaat do' (Cut it out!) 'Jazbaat mein keh gaya!' (That was an emotional outburst). But it was too late. Later re-broadcasts did not carry the offending words.

12. The author, as a PTV newscaster, was pressed into service to read in a heavy tone broadcast warnings to businessmen who did not declare their secret wealth.

13. Interview Brig. Ali. See also his article 'Conduct Unbecoming,' *Newsline*, Karachi, September 2000.

14. Ibid., interview Brig. Ali.

15. *USFR 1969–1976 Volume XI*, p. 872.

16. Rafi Raza, *Zulfikar Ali Bhutto and Pakistan 1967–1977* (Karachi: Oxford, 1997), pp. 159–160.

17. The author was a news and current affairs producer with PTV at that time and had been sent with a team headed by the director news and current affairs, M. Zubair Ali, to produce a documentary on China and to cover this visit for PTV as well as shoot film, on contract, for CBS News. President Nixon was due to visit Beijing in ten days time and CBS badly needed all the footage it could of Chinese leaders and sites for use in its coverage of that momentous event. Mr Bhutto also took with him his eldest son, Mir Murtaza Bhutto (who was a junior at the author's school and a member of his House at St. Mary's Academy, Rawalpindi). Also in the party was Sardar Khair Bux Marri, the impressive Baluch leader, whom Bhutto wished to wean away from his Soviet friends and expose to the Chinese. Mr Marri asked to remain behind in Beijing after the visit and returned with the PTV team a week later.

18. Oriana Fallaci, *Interview with History* (New York: Liveright, 1976), p. 190.

19. Sultan M. Khan, *Memories and Reflections of a Pakistani Diplomat* (London: The Centre for Pakistan Studies, 1997), pp. 421–22.

20. Mubashir Hasan, *The Mirage of Power: An Inquiry into the Bhutto Years, 1971–77* (Karachi: Oxford, 2000), pp. 82–3.

21. Ibid., p. 84.

22. Later he was persuaded to adopt the traditional presidential insignia and flag in place of his sword.

23. PTV cameras were covering the event 'live.' As a current affairs and news producer, I stood on a raised camera platform directly in front of the dais, helping with the live broadcast and taking photographs for my own collection.

24. Sultan M. Khan, *Memories*, pp. 426–27.

25. Ibid., p. 431.

26. Secret brief for the President-Summit Meeting from the COAS, forwarded by General Tikka Khan by hand to the DMO on 11 June 1972. Pakistan Army GHQ Archives. This section relies on this document.

27. Benazir Bhutto, *Daughter of Destiny* (New York: Simon & Schuster, 1989), p. 70.

28. Ibid.

29. Ibid., pp. 74–5.

30. Ibid., p. 75.

31. In many conversations with the author at that time at the home of Unver Isa, the son of Baluch Muslim League leader Qazi Isa, Sardar Marri told the author that he had known Bhutto since early childhood and could never trust him. Sardar Marri had the distinction of being one of the few Baluch leaders who managed to successfully resist the blandishments and temptations of different Pakistani rulers, starting with Ayub Khan. Later, he was to move to Afghanistan and even on his return continued to fight for Baluch rights, which his critics equated with the rights of Sardars to rule their tribes with an iron fist. Although educated at the Aitchison College in Lahore, Marri held strong feelings against the Punjabi elite that he felt ruled Pakistan for its own benefit, without regard to the need for a balanced federation of Pakistan.

32. Hasan, *The Mirage*, p. 255 and Rafi Raza, *Zulfikar Ali Bhutto*, p. 300.

33. From Bhutto's presidential proclamation of 15 February 1973, dismissing the government of Chief Minister Ataullah Mengal in Balochistan. Rafi Raza, *Zulfikar Ali Bhutto*, p. 269.

34. National Assembly of Pakistan Debates, 14 February 1974. Vol. I. No. 21 cited in Rafi Raza, *Zulfikar Ali Bhutto*, p. 271.

35. A common link for these young men was Cambridge University. Ahmed Rashid, a friend of mine, wrote to me from Fitzwilliam College at Cambridge that he was going into Eastern Europe to 'make a documentary' and then disappeared. The first I heard of him after that was when my elder brother, Asif Nawaz, told me that his military sources told him that Ahmed was with the Baluch insurgents, fighting under the *nom de guerre* Balach, the name of a legendary Baluch warrior.

36. Sherbaz Khan Mazari, *A Journey to Disillusionment* (Karachi: Oxford University Press, 1999), pp. 357–8.

37. Ibid., p. 358.

38. Background information from a participant in the group, who wished to remain anonymous.

39. A.B. Awan, *Balochistan: Historical and Political Processes* (London: New Century Publishers, 1985), pp. 299–300.

40. Anonymous original participant in the London Group, in direct communication with the author.

41. Anonymous original participating in the London Group.

42. Selig Harrison, *In Afghanistan's Shadow* (Washington, D.C.: Carnegie Endowment for International Peace, 1981), p. 37.

43. Mazari, *A Journey*, p. 363.

44. F.B. Ali, *Newsline*, op. cit., and conversations with Major Saeed Akhtar Malik.

45. General Akhtar Malik, as mentioned earlier, was a cousin of my father-in-law.

46. Hasan Abbas, *Pakistan's Drift into Extremism* (New York: M.E. Sharpe, Armonk, 2005), pp. 74–5.

47. Brig. F.B. Ali interview.

48. Brig. Ali and Major Saeed Akhtar Malik interviews.

49. Mitha, *Unlikely*, p. 321. Mitha recalls that General Yahya read out a message from Nawazish stating that Zia had disobeyed orders and participated in the attack by the Jordanian Armoured Division against Palestinian refugees and suggesting a court martial. Zia came to see Mitha who suggested he could not help him but that he should see the adjutant general. Instead Zia went to Gul Hassan who spoke to Yahya and bailed him out.

50. Benazir Bhutto remembers being introduced to Zia in early 1977 by her father and seeing him as 'a short-nervous, ineffectual-looking man whose pomaded hair was parted in the middle and lacquered onto his head. He looked more like an English cartoon villain than an inspiring model for the leader of the Pakistan Army. And he seemed so obsequious,

telling me over and over how honoured he was to meet the daughter of such a great man as Zulfikar Ali Bhutto.' Benazir Bhutto, *Daughter*, p. 87.

51. Interviews with Brig. Ali and Major Saeed Akhtar Malik, 2007.

52. Unlike many of the other senior commanders in the army who had been commissioned in the pre-partition British Indian Army at the IMA at Dehra Dun or from the Royal Military Academy at Sandhurst, (UK), Zia was trained at the Officers' Training School (OTS) at Mhow and commissioned in 1944. (GHQ Pakistan Army still has in its files the original form that accompanied him at Mhow, with a photograph of the young Zia pasted on it.) Dehra Dun and Sandhurst commissioned officers normally looked down their noses at OTS qualified officers, although their backgrounds tended to be similar in many cases. Zia, however, did not come from a military family. His father was a religious teacher. Zia himself remained a practising Muslim, a teetotaler, and a low-key individual in an army filled with many overtly ambitious officers. This stood him in good stead. His polite manner and indirect approach raised few hackles. In many ways, he represented the first generation of the post-colonial Pakistani officer.

53. Hasan, *The Mirage*, p. 268.

54. Ibid., p. 268.

55. Raza, *Zulfikar Ali Bhutto*, p. 302.

56. From Patriot to Proliferator: The myth of a Pakistani scientist as his nation's saviour long protected him. It took his peddling of atomic know-how to shred it. By Douglas Frantz. Times Staff Writer. *Los Angeles Times*, 23 September 2005. http://www.latimes.com/news/nationworld/world/la-fg-khan23sep23,0,7580622.story?coll=la-home-headlines.

57. Edmond Taylor, *Richer by Asia* (Time Inc. 1964), p. 170.

58. For this section, among others, I am indebted to the excellent historical work done by M.A. Chaudhri in 'Pakistan's Nuclear History: separating myth from reality' in *Defence Journal*, May 2006. www.defencejournal.com/2006-5/index.asp.

59. Carey Sublette 'Pakistan's Nuclear Weapons Program—The Beginning', www.nuclearweaponarchive.org/Pakistan/PakOrigin.html, last changed 2 January 2002.

60. George Perkovitch, *India's Nuclear Bomb* (Berkeley: University of California Press, 1999), p. 108.

61. Ibid., p. 108.

62. Ibid.

63. Steve Weissman and Herbert Krosney, *The Islamic Bomb: The Nuclear Threat to Israel and the Middle East* (New York: Times Books, 1981).

64. Sublette, 'Pakistan's Nuclear Weapons Program.'

65. Prince Turki al-Faisal, interview with author.

66. 'A Science Odyssey: Pakistan's Nuclear Emergence', Dr Samar Mubarakmand's speech, 30 November 1998, at Khwarzimic Science Society, Government College, Lahore, cited in M.A. Chaudhri, op. cit.

67. R. Chidambaram and Raja Ramanna 'Some Studies on India's Peaceful Nuclear Explosion Experiment', paper presented at International Atomic Energy Agency, Vienna 1975, IAEA/TC-I-14/19, IAEA, Vienna, p. 421. The 12 kiloton figure given by the authors of this paper made the Indian explosion the same size as the US bomb dropped on Hiroshima.

68. Lt. Gen. Zahid Ali Akbar, 'A.Q. Khan,' *The Nation*, Lahore, Pakistan, 18 September 2006.

69. Ibid.

70. Anwar H. Syed, *The Discourse and Politics of Zulfikar Ali Bhutto* (London: MacMillan, 1992), p. 175.

71. Hasan-Askari Rizvi, *Military, State, and Society in Pakistan* (London: MacMillan, 2000), p. 146.

72. Ibid., p. 147.

73. Zulfikar Ali Bhutto, '*If I am assassinated...*' (New Delhi: Vikas, 1979), p. 117.

74. As recounted by Major General (retired) Naseerullah Khan Babar, *Defence Journal*, April 2001. There are many such stories in circulation, although not all can be confirmed. Reports that Bhutto derisively referred to Zia as his 'monkey general' have not been corroborated. In fact, associates of both Bhutto and Zia say that Bhutto treated Zia with deference and respect and would never have demeaned him publicly.

75. Conversations with I.H. Burney. I wrote regularly from New York for *Outlook* and *Combat*, another Karachi weekly started by Yunus Said, a close associate of Bhutto whom he named as chairman of the National Press Trust. For some years I felt guilty as being the proximate cause of the ban on *Outlook*, when I wrote a piece that was critical of the rising military ambition of the Shah of Iran in the region. The Iranian government protested to the Pakistan Foreign Ministry and a reprimand was sent to me in New York, since I had previously worked for PTV, the government-owned TV network. I responded that I no longer worked for PTV and their rules did not apply to me. Soon after that incident *Outlook* was banned by the Bhutto government. I lost contact with Burney and only found out when he visited the US a few years later that I had nothing to do with his paper's demise.

76. *Pakistan*, Stacey International, London, 1977. Six officials were editorial advisers, and two of the four editors were also officials of Bhutto's information ministry. Although ostensibly a commemoration of the centenary of the birth of the founder of Pakistan, Mohammad Ali Jinnah, the book was heavily laced with Bhutto's view of Pakistan's history and displayed his photographs prominently, including a portrait by Yusuf Karsh of Canada. Ayub Khan was mentioned only in disparaging terms. Soon after the book appeared, Bhutto was toppled by Ziaul Haq and the volume was removed from circulation within Pakistan. The National Book Foundation bookshop stored all copies that it could retrieve in a room behind its bookshop in Rawalpindi.

77. Maulana Kausar Niazi, *Zulfikar Ali Bhutto of Pakistan: The Last Days* (New Delhi: Vikas, 1992), p. 43.

78. Zulfikar Ali Bhutto's speech to the nation, 7 January 1977. *White Paper on the Conduct of the General Election in March 1977*, Government of Pakistan, Rawalpindi, July 1978, p. iii.

79. *White Paper*, ibid., pp. 4–5.

80. Ibid., p. 14.

81. Ibid., p. 17.

82. PID report, reproduced in White Paper on elections, ibid., p. 145.

83. Niazi, *Zulfikar Ali Bhutto*, pp. 68–71. The seat allocation figures are from the same source.

84. Stanley Wolpert, *Zulfi Bhutto of Pakistan: His Life and Times* (New York: Oxford), p. 279.

85. Wolpert, *Zulfi Bhutto*, p. 281.

86. Ibid. From General Ziaul Haq's note No. 4852/320/PS-1b, 5 February 1977 and kept in the Bhutto Family Archives.

87. M.G. Weinbaum, 'The March 1977 Elections in Pakistan: Where Everyone Lost', *Asian Survey*, July 1977.

88. Eqbal Ahmed, 'Pakistan: Military Intervention', *Le Monde Diplomatique*, October 1977.

89. General K.M. Arif, *Working with Zia* (Karachi: Oxford, 1995), pp. 71–72.

90. Niazi, *Zulfikar Ali Bhutto*, p. 79.

91. Arif, *Working*, p. 73.

92. Ibid., p. 74.

93. I produced coverage of his visit for PTV while on leave from *The New York Times* and was at the airport with him when the well-connected Pakistani press counsellor, Iqbal Butt, was asked by Bhutto to set up this press conference at very short notice. Butt called his friend Abe Rosenthal at *The New York Times* (whom he had befriended in New Delhi many years earlier) to get a reporter sent in at that late hour. Poor M.A. Farber was called in

from his home in New Jersey late in the evening. Another reporter from Reuters showed up as did a few others from the wire services, giving Bhutto a chance to state that he never intended to ask for weapons during this trip, with his usual confidence and eloquence.

94. National Security Decision Memorandum 289, 24 March 1975. Box 1. National Security Decision Memoranda and Study Memoranda. Gerald R. Ford Library. Also available on the web at www.fordlibrarymuseum.gov/library/document/nsdmnssm/nsdm289a.htm.

95. Interview with General Brent Scowcroft, Washington DC, 3 March 2006.

96. Interview with author.

97. Dennis Kux in his *United States and Pakistan: 1947-2000* (Washington, D.C.: Woodrow Wilson Centre, 2001), pp. 229-30 presents the US side of the intercept, stating that it was an innocuous response to a query from a journalist in Karachi who had heard that Bhutto was forcibly detained at the US embassy.

98. Here I am indebted to the inside information from General K.M. Arif in his *Working with Zia*, (Karachi: Oxford, 1995), pp. 80-88. Arif was later to become vice chief under Ziaul Haq.

99. Lt. Gen. Faiz Ali Chishti, *Betrayals of Another Kind: Islam, Democracy and the Army in Pakistan* (Rawalpindi: PCL Publishing House), pp. 63-71.

100. Interview with Imtiaz Warraich by A.H. Amin for *Defence Journal*, October 2001.

101. As recounted by Gen. Shariff to his colonel staff, my brother Asif Nawaz at JCS HQ.

Pakistan, which was created in the name of Islam, will continue to survive only if it sticks to Islam. That is why I consider the introduction of [an] Islamic system as an essential prerequisite for the country.
                              – General Ziaul Haq's first speech after the coup, 5 July 1977.

After launching a coup against Zulfikar Ali Bhutto, Mohammad Ziaul Haq, once an obscure general known for his personal piety, religiosity, and humility, turned into a ferocious instrument of change for Pakistan. His regime was to be the longest military rule in Pakistan's history with far-reaching effects that still haunt the body politic of Pakistan. It witnessed the emergence of the lower-middle class, the rise of Islamists in the military, and state sponsorship of militant Islamic (largely Sunni) sectarian groups, (which provoked a Shia backlash and spawned sectarian warfare). His regime also saw the maturation of the country's nuclear technology, the intrusion of the military into almost all sectors of the economy, and a growing Culture of Entitlement, reflected in state-endorsed asset accumulation and corruption in both the civil and military environment. The resulting stunting of political activity and discourse left the country teetering after Zia's sudden departure from the scene, when his airplane crashed in the Bahawalpur desert on 17 August 1988. Externally, Zia inherited a country under intense external pressure, faced with the growing military and nuclear power of India to the East (which threatened to negate Pakistan's efforts to resolve the Kashmir dispute in its favour). It also witnessed the demise of the monarchy in Afghanistan and the subsequent Soviet invasion of December 1979 that thrust Pakistan into the frontline of the war against the Soviets, and a massively popular religious revolution in Iran in the same year that energized the small but organized Shia community in Pakistan. The imposition of martial law by Zia was meant to be short lived. Swearing by the Muslim's credo of *La illah illallah Muhammadur Rasul Allah* (There is no God but Allah and Muhammad [PBUH] is his Prophet), he promised elections within 90 days. But like other dictators before and after him, he gave up on that promise.[1] He was to return to this religious theme later on. On 1 September 1977, he announced in a press conference:

It is not in the Quran nor has it been revealed to me that elections will be held on October 18 and nothing will happen thereafter....In my opinion the Presidential System, which is closer to Islam, is more suitable for Pakistan. I will put it up to the National Assembly on October 28 and leave the decision to the next government....My Government is an interim government....This country can be kept together by the armed forces and not by politicians.[2]

As a result, the army, instead of entering politics temporarily, was drawn into civilian affairs for almost a decade, distracting it once more from its professional duties, training, and operations, and weakening it as a military institution. The dynamics of governance under a dictatorship led Zia to rely on a cohort of like-minded and pliable officers whom he would rotate out of office periodically, before they struck roots or gained too much influence. He plied these officers with gifts and favours, producing a new crop of millionaire generals who became part of the vested interest group that ran the country for over a decade. The Culture of Entitlement that Yahya's brief regime had introduced became entrenched, and a new norm for self-aggrandisement and wealth creation from official sources was created. Similarly, Zia used Islam with a cynical disregard for its principles of honesty and selflessness: talking of a *Nizam-e-Mustafa* (the rule of the Prophet Muhammad [PBUH]) while using state-collected wealth taxes, (known as *zakat)*, as largesse for political purposes. The immediate beneficiaries of these actions were the mullahs and the religious parties, specifically the Jamaat-i-Islami, which for the first time in Pakistan's history found itself in partnership with the government.[3] Among other things, Zia ordered his military commanders to select and appoint *Nazim-us-Salat* or prayer leaders in their areas of control, who would ensure that people performed their daily prayers according to the prescribed ritual. Military commanders were also encouraged to join communal prayers with their men, and within the army's assessment procedures a new section was added to the annual confidential report of officers that dealt with their moral and religious behaviour.

By the time of Zia's death, the country was in a state of political paralysis, with the army calling all the shots. Civil society was riven by sectarian violence in the Punjab and the NWFP (between the Shia and Sunni sects), ethnic conflict in Sindh (between the Mohajirs—descendants of refugees from India—and the local Sindhis). The active involvement of the army high command and intelligence services, particularly the ISI, in the conduct of the Afghan war, the ISI's direct and unfettered access to overseas financing from the US CIA and private and official Saudi sources, and involvement in the making and breaking of domestic political parties and alliances, had changed the equation between the civil and military. This involvement and financial autonomy of sorts also gave the ISI a permanent role in foreign policy. No longer would the military cede to the civil its constitutional role as guardian of the ideology of Pakistan. Instead, the army was to take on the twin mantles of guardian of both the territorial and ideological frontiers, a role that it was to jealously guard in the decades that followed.

Zia's successes were mixed. Ceding the economic management to a group of conservative and careful bureaucrats, his regime insulated Pakistan from many of the borrowing excesses of other Third World economies in the 1980s. As a result, Pakistan saw steady growth rates and a guarded return to free-market economics after the deep nationalizations of the Bhutto era that had left the business community disheartened or forced into exile. But the regime did little to turn back the nationalizations of Bhutto: perhaps the bureaucrats were loath to give up their expanded controls. Yet, the inflow of arms and drug money to finance the Afghan *jihad* produced its own blowback effects. Drug use skyrocketed in Pakistan. Drug smuggling became a major activity, drawing into its trap even the military, whose National Logistics Cell (NLC) trucks carried arms from the port of Karachi to the north and eventually to the Afghan frontier and sometimes were commandeered by corrupt officials to carry heroin down to the airports and the seaport.[4] Meanwhile, the Pakistan Army grew in size and influence, as a new corps was added, headquartered in Quetta, to counter the Soviet threat from Afghanistan. Zia took on the mantle of CMLA and later also of president, but retaining his uniform and position of the COAS simultaneously. This move in particular drew his senior military officers into the political arena and expanded the role and stature of the ISI. The consequences reverberated in Pakistan's history for decades.

Zia's regime was a watershed for Pakistani politics. He was the first COAS who represented the post-colonial officer class. He came from a humble non-military background and had joined the army, as many others did in the 1940s, as a means to upward mobility. He also represented the conservative values and ritualistic religiosity of the urban lower middle class. However, he did not have a clear political agenda for the country; his agenda was merely to survive and retain power, and he was to use religion as a powerful tool in that regard. In the end, Islamization was the legacy he left Pakistan.

DISTINCT PHASES OF ZIA'S RULE

Zia's first moves were tentative, as he was trying to gauge the political situation to see how best to cover up his illegal usurpation of power. The first phase of his rule was therefore marked by attempts to provide legal cover for his actions and to remove Zulfikar Ali Bhutto from the scene, either virtually or literally. Article 6 of the 1973 constitution spelt out clear punishment for any extra constitutional moves to replace the duly elected president and prime minister:

> 6. High Treason: (1) Any person, who abrogates or attempts or conspires to abrogate, subverts or attempts to subvert the Constitution by use of force or show of force or by other unconstitutional means shall be guilty of high treason.[5]

So Zia needed a strong justification for his actions:

I want to make it absolutely clear that neither I have any political ambitions nor does the army want to be taken away from its profession of soldiering. I was obliged to step in to fill the vacuum created by the political leaders. I have accepted this challenge as a true soldier of Islam. My sole aim is to organize free and fair elections which would be held in October of this year [1977].[6]

Initially, he asked Bhutto's president, Fazal Ilahi Chaudhry to stay on in his post and act as the constitutional head of state, retaining only for himself the role of CMLA and chief executive (reprised later by General Pervez Musharraf some twenty-two years later). A military council was set up, comprising the chairman JCSC (Zia's senior, General M. Shariff), Zia himself (in his role as COAS), and the chiefs of the air and naval staffs (Air Chief Marshal Zulfiqar and Admiral Sharif respectively). In fact, General Shariff was asked by Zia to chair the meetings of this body in deference to his seniority, producing the anomalous situation under which Zia as chief executive and CMLA outranked Shariff, and the council recommended actions that Zia as the chief executive would later decide upon. Often helping the deliberations of this body was the bureaucrat chosen by Zia to become the secretary general-in-chief, Ghulam Ishaq Khan, and Zia's own military COS. But this artificial construct did not sit well with the emerging one-man rule of Zia and this body became 'dormant,' according to a close Zia confidant.[7] The emphasis shifted first to the martial law administrators conference, comprising the four provincial martial law administrators, the chairman of the JCSC, the deputy/vice COAS, the DG ISI, and senior military officers holding political or bureaucratic posts. This became the effective instrument for Zia's exercise of power until he replaced President Chaudhry on 16 September 1978.

A key question that arose immediately after the Zia coup was how to dispose of Mr Bhutto and his PPP. While initially leaning toward a free political campaign, Zia was soon confronted with the fact that the PPP retained popular support and might be returned to power if elections were held in short order. Zia's own situation was precarious, given his usurpation of power. For the first two years of his regime, he was pressed into actions that allowed him to remove Bhutto from the scene, provide a legal cover for his actions, and begin a process for the Islamization of Pakistani society. The second phase began with the Soviet invasion of Afghanistan in 1979 and included the surreptitious acquisition of nuclear technology to move Pakistan toward weaponization of its nuclear programme. The final phase of his regime ran concurrently with the second phase from March 1985 onwards, when party-less parliamentary elections were held and Zia selected Mohammed Khan Junejo to become prime minister. While on the surface this indicated a move to civilian rule, Zia retained martial law until he was forced to remove it by Junejo. Zia had made a vague promise to remove his uniform by 1990, but that was not to be. He died in his uniform. two years before that deadline was up.

SEARCH FOR LEGITIMACY

Zia's first legal challenge grew out of the petition of September 1977 filed by Begum Nusrat Bhutto against martial law, accusing Zia of treason under Article 6 of the 1973 constitution. However, Zia's laws (continuation in force) order of 5 July suspended the constitution while retaining its political framework. This produced the ironical situation under which the Supreme Court continued to function even while the constitution which gave it authority was in abeyance. Harkening back to a tradition of the judiciary under times of stress that began with the dissolution of the National Assembly in 1954 by then Governor General Ghulam Mohammad, the Supreme Court invoked the Doctrine of Necessity to give Zia legal cover for his action in a landmark decision on 10 November 1977. 'By accepting the doctrine of necessity, they had, in effect, undercut their own authority, making martial law superior to the Constitution,' observed one foreign scholar.[8] This action by the court allowed Zia additional leeway to amend the constitution, which he was to do in March 1981 through the issuance of another PCO crafted by his legal team headed by Sharifuddin Pirzada. This PCO comprised different parts of the 1973 constitution, which were selectively used to justify the one-man rule and ensure that neither the political system nor the judiciary would change its mind about supporting Zia's regime. All judges were asked to take a fresh oath under the PCO. Those that refused were sent home. Gauging the latent strength of the PPP to be a clear and present threat, Zia postponed first the 1977 elections and then also the 1979 elections, after seeing the results of the local bodies which came out in favour of the PPP's surrogates.

To control the political parties, he issued fresh rules that required all parties to be registered with the election commission with details of their manifestos, officials, and financial records. Any party that did not do so was disqualified. In Pakistan's disorganized political system which relied on feudal landlords and hereditary leaders, this created serious hurdles for many parties. But Zia was not taking any chances. In October 1979, he banned all parties, prohibited public gatherings, and introduced strict censorship of the press. He was clearly confident that he could rule the country with the help of his military officers and senior bureaucrats. The latter group was essentially running the ministries in the absence of civilian ministers. The bureaucracy revelled in this situation, being free of political control and being able to get action on its proposals from a ready and responsive military establishment.

But first Zia had to deal with Bhutto. As he put it, he was surprised to find out that Bhutto was still confident about coming back to power. Indeed, Bhutto told Zia at their meeting after Bhutto had been detained and sent to the Governor's House in Murree, that 'if you need any help, you can count on my support. Once the dust settles, we could run the country together.'[9] Zia released Bhutto, only to find out that Bhutto's popularity was still high. After his release, Bhutto began drawing huge crowds at rallies where he berated the military take-over. In the meantime, Zia had had access to the files and records of the former prime minister and deemed the written record to contain enough culpable evidence of high-handedness and corruption of power to justify initiating legal proceedings against Bhutto. Zia was given a keen instrument by a former colleague of Bhutto. Ahmad Raza Kasuri, a PPP parliamentarian who had broken with Bhutto, alleged that an attack on his motorcade in Lahore on 10 November 1974 that led to the death of his father, had been planned and executed by Bhutto's henchmen at the latter's behest. He filed a fresh police report naming Bhutto as the man behind his father's murder. Zia used that case to imprison Bhutto and put him on trial. A string of willing informers, including the hand-picked head of Bhutto's FSF, Masood Mahmud, testified against their former boss and named him the originator of the idea behind the fatal ambush.

On 18 March 1978, the Lahore High Court unanimously convicted Bhutto and sentenced him to death by hanging. The matter was eventually brought to the nine judges sitting on the Supreme Court. One of the judges soon retired, another suffered a medical disability and could not continue. The remaining seven heard the appeal, including a marathon presentation by Bhutto listing his role and accomplishments on behalf of Pakistan. Finally, on 2 February 1979, the Chief Justice Anwarul Haq delivered the court's split judgment, upholding the death verdict for Bhutto and the other four defendants, with three justices siding with the chief justice and three disagreeing. The deed was done. The court rejected the review appeal filed on 24 March 1979. Mercy appeals to the governor of the Punjab, General Sawar Khan, were immediately rejected and the petition sent on to General Zia as the final arbiter of Bhutto's fate. His position on the case was already spelt out: 'If the Supreme Court says: "Acquit him," I will acquit him. If it says: "Hang the blighter," I will hang him.'[10]

Some thirty clemency appeals came from foreign governments and dignitaries. But, the popular saying in Pakistan at that time was that there was one grave: either Bhutto would fill it, or Zia. Bhutto had no power; Zia did. The other service chiefs rejected the appeals for clemency, as did the federal cabinet. Zia went through the motions of seeking their advice, assuring them that their views meant a lot to him in making the final decision. Finally, he presented the clemency issue to the martial law administrators' conference on 24 March. Only one participant suggested waiting for the elections so that the new government could decide on this matter. The majority upheld the verdict. On 1 April, Zia read the summary prepared by the law division in favour of the Supreme Court verdict and wrote: 'Petition is rejected.'[11]

Last minute efforts by Begum Nusrat Bhutto to meet Zia and personally seek clemency also failed. She approached Lt. Col. Rafiuddin, the commander of the 27 Punjab Regiment that guarded Bhutto in his specially strengthened jail compound in Rawalpindi district jail, after she and Benazir Bhutto had had their last meeting with Z.A. Bhutto, and asked him to arrange a meeting with Zia.[12] Rafiuddin approached Brigadier Khwaja Rahat Latif, the sub-martial law administrator, but he was only reprimanded in turn for speaking with her. Begum Nusrat Bhutto and her daughter also requested that they be allowed to accompany Bhutto's body to Larkana, their preferred resting place for him, after his execution. Earlier Rafiuddin had surreptitiously confirmed their wish (that Bhutto be taken to Larkana for burial), but that request too was denied.

On 4 April 1979, soon after midnight, an emaciated and weak Bhutto, who had not been eating for some time before his execution, was taken in the middle of the night on a stretcher, his hands bound in front of him, and made to stand on the gallows. His hands were then cuffed behind his back. His last words, according to Rafiuddin, were an incomplete phrase: '*Yeh Mujhe...*' (Rafiuddin surmises that he wished to say '*Yeh mujhe takleef dey rahey hai*'—This is hurting me).[13] Later, many stories were to emerge about Bhutto's last days and hours.[14] Brigadier Rahat Latif quotes the jail superintendent as saying that Bhutto asked for the removal of the mask from his head before being executed. General Chishti blames Zia, his erstwhile partner in the coup d'etat, for trying to pin the blame for the hanging on him and even linking him to stories that Bhutto was mistreated and physically abused in jail. Chishti maintains that he was not part of the martial law set-up, and was therefore unconnected with the hanging. Even Colonel Rafiuddin was the object of accusations that he had beaten Bhutto in an effort to seek a confession from him before his death. This story was later appropriated by the British-Indian writer Salman Rushdie in his novel *Shame*, about a Zia-like dictator in a Pakistan-like country.[15] Earlier in the night, a distraught and obviously disoriented Bhutto had spoken out his younger daughter Sanam's name twice and then mumbled: 'Pity.... My wife left.' (The military had set up an elaborate listening system in the rooms where Bhutto was incarcerated, according to Col. Rafiuddin.) When informed of his execution date and time, (according to Rafiuddin), Bhutto felt that his lawyers had messed up the case and his party had betrayed him.

A forlorn Bhutto was to die. But his death was to haunt Zia's remaining days in power. Zia was never able to set up a political system that was based on free and fair participation of the electorate, nor could he accept the idea of civilian control over the military. All his subsequent days were spent in grudging concessions to civilian partners and increasing isolation from his colleagues in the military, as his cohort either retired or moved on to civilian positions. Fresh waves of junior generals moved into the GHQ of the Pakistan Army, many of them selected more for their lack of political ambition and professionalism, or for their apolitical stance, rather than on the basis of closeness to Zia himself.

The reaction to Bhutto's hanging was muted in Pakistan. The PPP had been beaten into submission and was itself split. The other opposition parties had been made complicit in the Zia decision by virtue of his (Zia's) consultations with their leaders—who had their own fears of the PPP as a force that might rise again. With Bhutto out of the way, Zia could now concentrate on other matters at hand.

THE AFGHANISTAN IMBROGLIO

The Pakistan–Afghan relationship had never been warm. Indeed, Afghanistan had cast a vote against Pakistan after the latter's independence in 1947 when it sought membership of the UN. From time to time, the Afghan government had raised the cry for 'Pushtunistan', or land of the Pushtuns, which claimed all the territory in Pakistan up to the right bank of the Indus River (since the latter was in fact a majority Pushtun area). Afghanistan had never recognized the Durand Line—the border between Pakistan and Afghanistan—drawn as part of an agreement signed on 12 November 1893 between the King of Afghanistan, Abdur Rahman, and Sir Mortimer Durand, the foreign secretary of the colonial government of India, on the grounds that it split tribes and their territories. Being a landlocked country, its nearest sea port was Karachi in Pakistan and most of its trade and necessary supplies came overland from Pakistan via the Khyber Pass near Peshawar, or the Khojak Pass near Chaman and Quetta in Balochistan. This did not prevent Afghanistan from fomenting tribal unrest in the border region. Indeed, a small scale Afghan-inspired invasion in 1960 in the Bajaur Agency, north of Peshawar, elicited a heavy Pakistan Army attack that routed the tribal insurgents. Pakistan, facing a hot border against India, did not wish to be drawn into a military tussle on its western frontier. Indeed, soon after independence in 1947, it had withdrawn most of its regular forces from the seven tribal agencies in the NWFP of Pakistan (from north to south: Bajaur, Mohmand, Khyber, Orakzai, Kurram, North Waziristan, and South Waziristan,) that were collectively known as FATA. Of these, only the Orakzai Agency did not share a border with Afghanistan. Pakistan's federal government gave FATA a degree of autonomy and a separate legal framework by the name of Frontier Crime Regulations (FCR) that distinguished it from the legal and political system of Pakistan, and relied on the tribal leaders to use their own customs and the jirga system to help maintain order in conjunction with the government's 'political agents'. In return, the government made regular payments to the tribal Maliks, according to their perceived stature in the community. This gave the area a semblance of stability.

In Afghanistan though, the heavy hand of the monarchy under King Zahir Shah was creating fissures. The Farsi-speaking elite surrounding the king had created a huge economic and social gap between itself and the masses. Afghanistan also began relying increasingly on the Soviet Union for military support and economic assistance. The US, meanwhile, was relying on its string of allies—Pakistan, Iran, and Turkey,—as a bulwark against Soviet aims. The education and training of Afghans in Moscow led to the creation of a growing number of leftists and socialists in the urban educated classes. Leading this movement was the Marxist Peoples Democratic Party of Afghanistan, or the PDPA, born in 1965 and then split in 1967 into two factions, both called PDPA but one known as *Parcham* (The flag) after the name of its newspaper and headed by Babrak Karmal, and the other known by its newspaper *Khalq* (The People) and headed by Nur Muhammad Taraki. Soon these two parties went into open opposition against the king who shut down their newspapers and political activities. Sensing the weakness of the monarchy, the king's cousin and minister of defence, Mohammad Daud, engineered a coup on 17 July 1973 with help from some elements of the Parcham group and the military while Zahir Shah and his coterie were on holiday in Italy.

A shrewd Daud began purging the Marxists and opening up relations with Iran and the United States while at the same time stoking the fires of Pushtunistan, much to the alarm of Pakistan. Daud's modernist reforms alienated an embryonic Islamic movement within Afghanistan which was operating under the leadership of scholars and spiritual leaders such as Burhanuddin Rabbani, Sibghatullah Mojaddedi and Abdul Rabb-ur-Rasul Sayyaf, who had been educated at al-Azhar University in Cairo and been strongly influenced by the Muslim Brotherhood. They had taken up opposition first to Zahir Shah and then to Daud. The United States welcomed and encouraged Daud's foreign policy moves, seeing his actions, particularly in warming up to US ally Iran, as 'significant contributions to the improvement of regional stability—thereby helping to fulfil another principal U.S. objective.'[16] Pakistan, meanwhile, saw an opportunity as Daud cracked down on the Islamists, forcing many of them to flee across the border into Pakistan. In addition to the major leaders, the militant refugees included young Islamic radicals such as the Kabul University trained engineer Gulbadin Hekmatyar, who had been imprisoned in 1972 for two years for his anti-government activities in Kabul.[17] Pakistan not only gave these Islamic radicals succour, it also provided assistance to them in their efforts against the Afghan regime of Daud. In preparation for heightened activity on the Afghan frontier, the Pakistan government set up an Afghan cell in the Foreign Office in 1973 that continued to operate till 1976, under the guidance of Prime Minister Bhutto and his Foreign Minister, Aziz Ahmed. The work of this cell slowed down in the final years of the Bhutto regime, but new events in Afghanistan brought it back to life.[18] The cell continued to meet monthly under General Ziaul Haq's regime till his death in 1988, and after that, as needed.[19] The ISI and the Frontier Constabulary that patrolled the border began intelligence operations in Afghanistan and the border region while supporting the young rebel exiles.

But events in Afghanistan were to begin a cycle of upheaval and violence that was to grip the region in a major war for more than a decade. On 27 April 1978, following massive protests against Daud's regime, the military in combination with the by-now united PDPA, overthrew and executed Daud, ushering in the openly socialist Saur (April) Revolution, with Taraki, Hafizullah Amin and their Khalq allies in control. A Treaty of Friendship signed with the Soviet Union in December 1978 further strengthened the belief that the Soviets had had a hand in spurring the revolution and led to the infusion of Soviet military and civil advisors into Afghanistan. The Islamic leaders in Afghanistan fled to Pakistan to join the growing number of Afghan dissidents gathering there, including by now Yunus Khalis and Sayyid Ahmad Gailani. The nucleus of an Islamic coalition in exile began to emerge in Pakistan, and it began to garner the attention and support of the Pakistani authorities. The downward spiral in Afghan politics accelerated, leading to frequent internecine clashes in Kabul. An open rebellion fomented by the Islamic exiles in the western city of Herat in March 1979 drew the attention not only of the United States but also of the Soviet Union. In Washington, Zbigniew Brzezinski (National Security Advisor) warned President Jimmy Carter of the danger posed by the Soviet Union's strong presence in Afghanistan and its potential influence in the region as well as on access to the warm waters of the Persian Gulf.[20] He was not the only one to raise this warning.

According to Prince Turki Al Faisal, on a visit by Daud to Saudi Arabia in 1977 when he met both King Khalid and then Crown Prince Fahd, the Saudis warned Daud against the communists. Daud reassured them that he was very much in charge and would initiate some action against them soon. 'Apparently they ate him for breakfast, before he ate them for lunch!' said Prince Turki.[21]

ENTER THE SOVIETS

The new duo of Taraki and Amin began to break up. Taraki and his Soviet supporters became disenchanted with Amin who, as defence minister, had been unsuccessful in combating the rebels operating in the country and from Pakistan. Amin, sensing a change of heart on the part of the Soviets, pre-empted the split by arresting and then executing Taraki after the latter's return from the Non-Aligned Summit in Cuba in August 1979. The Soviets continued their pretence of working with Amin but realized soon after that he had lost control of the countryside to the rebels. They air-lifted and pre-positioned two battalions of their own troops at a base near Kabul in the first week of December 1979, and on 24 December their forces, massed along the border with Afghanistan, crossed the Amu Darya (river), ostensibly to help restore order at the request of the Afghan leadership. Other troops flew into Bagram and Shindand airbases. Amin was assassinated. Babrak Karmal, who had earlier been exiled as ambassador to Prague, was flown in as the new head of state. Soon, some 85,000 Soviet troops were assembled in Afghanistan, comprising some 60,000 infantry and 25,000 artillery, signals, construction, border or security unit, and air force personnel. When compared with the 250,000 troops used by the Soviets to invade and secure Czechoslovakia in 1969, it raised the possibility that the troops were meant more to prop up the puppet Karmal regime than fight a war inside Afghanistan. The numbers of Soviet forces remained more or less static through the mid-1980s.[22] Most of the troops were confined to the Kabul area.[23] The 1500-mile border with Pakistan, with its numerous routes of ingress and forbidding terrain, remained largely porous and unprotected.

With the arrival of Soviet forces close to its border, the political geography of the region had suddenly changed. Pakistan was now a frontline state against the Soviets. Its major allies were to be the Saudis and the United States, in that order. US National Security Advisor Zbigniew Brzezinski favoured covert support for the rebels who had begun receiving Pakistani aid. He got President Jimmy Carter to sign a secret memorandum allowing such assistance. Speaking to *Le Nouvel Observateur* many years later in 1998, Brzezinski stated:

> According to the official version of the story, the CIA began to assist Mujahideen in the year 1980, that is, after the invasion of the Soviet army against Afghanistan on December 24, 1979. But the truth that remained secret until today is quite different: it was on July 3, 1979 that President Carter signed his first order on the secret assistance to Kabul's pro-Soviet regime opponents. That day I wrote a memorandum to the President in which I told him that that assistance would cause the Soviet intervention (...) we did not force the Russian intervention, we just, conscientiously, increase[d] the intervention possibilities.

[...]That secret operation was an excellent idea. Its objective was to lead the Russian to the Afghan trap[...] The very same day the Soviets crossed the Afghan border, I wrote the following to President Carter: 'This is our chance to give Russia its Viet Nam.'[24]

But the road to Kabul lay both literally and figuratively through Islamabad. First the United States had to surmount its own erected barriers to friendship with Pakistan, having imposed sanctions for its nuclear ambitions on its erstwhile and soon to be future ally. Adding to the general unhappiness in Washington with Zia's Pakistan was the terrible incident of 21 November 1979, when an irate mob of students angered over unsubstantiated reports that the United States had been involved in the takeover of the mosque in Makkah, stormed the US embassy in Islamabad and torched it, killing two Americans and two Pakistani employees. Zia had been on a photo opportunity bicycle tour of Raja Bazaar in neighbouring Rawalpindi that day and the military failed to react with alacrity to this attack. The US government soon evacuated its embassy staff and US civilians from Pakistan, bringing relations to a new low between the two states.

But soon after the Soviet invasion of Afghanistan, *realpolitik* took over. President Carter telephoned Zia to talk about the Afghan situation and promise aid. The British Foreign Secretary, Lord Carrington descended on Islamabad in January 1980, as did the secretary general of the Organization of the Islamic Conference (OIC). Zia's initial response to Carter was lukewarm; he dismissed the first offer of $400 million as inadequate, calling it 'peanuts' while speaking to journalists on 18 January 1980, (perhaps without realizing the import of that snub on a US president who had once been a peanut farmer in Georgia). Despite this official reaction, some covert aid did begin to flow from the US to the rebels via Pakistan, matched with financing from the Saudis. Zia and his colleagues assessed the various options before them and chose to take up the most dangerous route available: open opposition to the Soviet invasion in the diplomatic chambers of the world while providing covert support to the Afghan opposition operating from Pakistani soil. The Zia government did this despite clear and unambiguous threats from the Soviets, starting with Foreign Minister Andrei Gromyko's statement of 12 February 1980 that Pakistan faced a grave risk by allowing itself to be used as a 'springboard...against Afghanistan.'[25] Zia even refused to raise the issue of aid during a visit to the White House at the invitation of President Carter, and when Carter brought up the issue of F-16 fighters that Pakistan had earlier sought, Zia's response was very blasé: he stated that the matter could wait till after the US presidential elections that were surely keeping Carter busy at that time.[26] Perhaps informing Zia's intransigence was the cold calculation that to invade Pakistan, the Soviets would need a much larger force and would face a well-developed and trained Pakistan Army. But the possibility remained that the Soviets might use Afghanistan as a way station to head through western Iran to the Persian Gulf. The Iranian Revolution of Ayatollah Khomeini in 1979 had created turmoil within Iran, leaving its armed forces incapable of providing any resistance against a huge and determined foe such as the Soviets. So, Pakistan had little choice but to take on the Soviets in Afghanistan. But it suffered heavily for its principled stance.

Within months of the initial troubles in Afghanistan, some 400,000 refugees trekked across the border into Pakistan. By the time the exodus was over, some 4 million refugees had settled into makeshift camps in Pakistan and started permeating into the heartland.[27] Such refugees have been a part of the history of the Indian subcontinent for a long time. Each time Afghanistan had a violent change of regime, the deposed rulers and their supporters would exit to the area that is now Pakistan. Many of them never returned, marrying into the local tribes and families. But this time the flood of refugees was huge, and Pakistan did not have the capacity to cope with the social, economic, and political fallout of this large influx of refugees. Apart from disrupting the social and political fabric of the tribal areas, the refugees brought their blood feuds and rivalries as well as links to the poppy-growing culture of Afghanistan that suddenly made Pakistan a major pipeline for heroin to the West. Not only that, the relocation of heroin factories to the tribal region on the Pakistan side of the border made Pakistan the single largest supplier of heroin globally, exporting mainly to Europe and America, where they 'captured 50 per cent of the market.'[28] *The Politics of Heroin* author McCoy estimates that from 'zero heroin addicts in 1979, numbers rose to 5,000 users in 1980, 70,000 in 1983, and then in the words of Pakistan's own Narcotics Control Board, went 'completely out of hand' to over 1.3 million addicts in 1985.[29]

As the fighting against the Soviets escalated and arms supplies began arriving from the West, the Middle East and even China, a new 'Kalashnikov Culture' was born in Pakistan. Even the ISI was not immune to the temptations of making money from the misuse of the arms supplies for the Afghan jihad. Arif Ayub, who was director for the Afghan desk in the Pakistani Foreign Office and later an ambassador to Afghanistan, cites the black market rankings of weapons as follows: 'Russian weapons were the most expensive, followed by East European, Chinese, and Middle East (Egyptian) weapons.'[30] The first director of the Afghan bureau of the ISI, a brigadier, was moved out in 1983 following the 'Quetta incident' in which three Pakistani officers had been caught colluding with Afghan commanders and accepting bribes for giving them arms above their quota.[31] The three officers were court martialled. (Brigadier Mohammad Yousaf was then selected to take over the Afghan bureau.) But some of these smuggled arms continued to be sold in the local market, with the prices of AK-47s, for example, fluctuating widely in line with the arrival of new shipments. Under the then DG ISI, Lt. Gen. Akhtar Abdur Rahman, a no-nonsense officer with a singular vision of fighting the Soviets and driving them out of Afghanistan, there were few audit controls or checks in place. He brooked little interference—even from the Americans—in the internal operations of the ISI's Afghan activities, keeping them from the prying eyes of CIA and even congressional inquiries. It was left to his successor, Lt. Gen. Hamid Gul, to set up a system of controls and audits that would account for the weapons and the cash in the pipeline. As Gul told Senator Gordon Humphrey, who sought details of the operations: 'I've got my orders from my government and you don't direct me, my affairs, my business, how I conduct it. However, as far as accounts are concerned, you can take the account books. The books are open.'[32] Militarily, Pakistan had to expand its forces to deal with a second western front. Its troop count rose during the period after the Soviet invasion of Afghanistan by some 12 per cent to 478,000 in 1982, while its defence spending increased by some 168 per cent from $713 million in 1974 to $1.86 billion in 1981.[33] It reorganized the forces that had already been deployed in Balochistan (to fight the insurgency there during the Bhutto period) into a new corps based in Quetta, with a defensive posture in case the Soviets decided to give Pakistan a bloody nose for supporting the rebels in Afghanistan.[34] In time, this corps received some of its weapons from those supplied by United States, including 'some 200 14.5mm machine guns, RPG-7s, and SA-7s.'[35]

Immediately after the Soviets rumbled into Kabul, Prince Turki recounts how the Saudi king received a call from President Zia, who wished to send General Rahman to the kingdom to brief its leadership. Thus, maintains Prince Turki, the Pakistan–Saudi nexus was established against the Soviets well before the United States got into the act with Zbigniew Brzezinski's visit to the region in February 1980. The establishment of a direct link between the Saudis and the ISI was a significant break from the Saudis' prior relationship with Pakistani intelligence, which, according to Prince Turki, up to that point had been mainly with the civilian intelligence bureau.[36] Soon, vast amounts of official funds began flowing from Saudi Arabia to Pakistan, largely through official banking channels and also through private banks such as the Bank for Commerce and Credit International (BCCI); later the subject of inquiries in the West. Contrary to some stories in Western media about suitcases of cash being carried by Prince Turki's agents to Rawalpindi and being nearly discovered by Pakistani customs agents on arrival, Prince Turki maintains that only official channels were used for these transfers.[37] Private Saudi money was also encouraged and these flows used various channels, including the informal network of *Hundi* agents and the *Hawala* system under which funds were delivered speedily and efficiently to specific recipients merely on oral instructions and the use of simple code words. This system, which had been in use for remittances by workers in the Middle East to their relatives in Pakistan, allowed some Saudi financing to bypass ISI controls and reach favoured rebel leaders—more often than not the leaders of the Sunni Mujahideen, such as Gulbuddin Hekmatyar.

Once the financial and supply networks had been set up, the ISI, and not the Pakistan Army, took on the principal role for the execution of the covert war against the Soviets. This gave the ISI an autonomy and financial strength that it had not possessed before, creating a bit of friction between the army and the ISI. Traditionally, the ISI had been regarded as a backwater by professional army officers, most of whom were loath to serve in it. Even those who were posted to it sought early rotation out of it for fear that they would be seen as 'spooks' and unreliable by their military colleagues and seniors. Most ISI officers were shunned by their army peers, even socially. The ISI was set up originally as a counter-intelligence agency, dealing with external threat analysis and occasional operations. It liaised, for example, with the intelligence agencies of Iran and Turkey. Military Intelligence (MI), located in the army's GHQ in Rawalpindi, had the major role of providing support to the military's activities, even in neighbouring countries. Until the 1980s, MI retained its purely military emphasis. The ISI, however, had been inducted into the business of domestic political analysis, starting with the Yahya regime's elections of 1970. It began making efforts to link up with elements in political parties, in particular the Islamic parties (such as the Jamaat-i-Islami), with a view to using them as a foil against the populist parties such as the PPP, the National Awami League, and the NAP. But these connections were less partnerships and more a principal-client arrangement. Zia's Islamist leanings gave these links greater import. But within the army, the fear arose at the outset of the Afghan war that the role of the ISI would be counter-productive. Following the age-old dictum that the best intelligence is policy neutral, the military leadership, even around Zia, was critical of the ISI's new role.

General Arif, Zia's COS, writes: 'Military operations and military intelligence are two different subjects, even though they go side by side. In all armies of the world, they are handled by separate departments, under specialized military experts.'[38] The combining of these two elements under ISI for the purposes of conducting the jihad against the Soviets in Afghanistan was seen by Arif and others as problematic. However, the Islamist duo of Zia and Rahman were able to take advantage of this enhanced role of the ISI for pushing through an agenda of their own. Zia insisted that the Mujahideen forces be combined into a smaller, more efficient central group. The normally fractious tribal leaders of the Mujahideen were reluctant, but Zia, working through Rahman and even Prince Turki, managed to threaten and cajole them into forming a seven party alliance in 1984, representing different geographical and sectarian elements. His main leverage came from his ability to withhold financial and military support from those that did not play the game.

Based in Peshawar, the seven party alliance comprised four fundamentalist parties headed by Hekmatyar, Khalis, Rabbani, and Sayaf, and three moderate parties headed by Gailani, Nabi, and Mujaddadi. A subsidiary office operated out of Quetta to the south, where party representatives were based and established contacts with their field commanders in the Kandahar and western Afghan regions. The ISI set up a system of rationing support to them according to their operational effectiveness, although soon it became apparent that some were being favoured on ideological grounds, for being 'more Islamist' and potentially more pro-Pakistan. By 1987, the four fundamentalist parties (headed by Hekmatyar, Rabbani, Sayaf, and Khalis respectively) were each getting close to a fifth of the total stocks of military supplies, totalling some 67 per cent of all aid, with Hekmatyar's group getting the largest share. The leaders were then responsible for supplying their field commanders. However, after repeated complaints from the field commanders of leakages *en route*, the ISI instituted a system of providing some supplies directly to the field commanders for specific operations. One major of the ISI was deputed to try to track the 55-odd bases close to the border that were used as jumping-off points for the six major Mujahideen supply routes into Afghanistan. These routes ranged from Chitral in the north that supplied northern Afghanistan and the Panjshir Valley. through the Parachinar parrot-beak that intruded into Afghanistan. and then through Waziristan south to Chaman in Balochistan. Another indirect route to Herat was through Iran.[39] Ayub of the Foreign Office calculates the division of supplies and financing as roughly one-third each to Hekmatyar and Rabbani (including Ahmed Shah Massoud), and one-third distributed among the rest. He attributes this more to Zia's own bias in favour of the Islamists because of his alliance with the Jamaat-i-Islami.[40] Regardless, the majority of the aid went to the Sunni fundamentalists, who also received direct infusions of cash from Saudi sources. These are also mainly the Pushtun groups. Another factor that may have skewed the distribution in the favour of these groups was that many of the operating officers of the ISI liaising with the Mujahideen were Pushtuns themselves.[41]

The Afghan bureau of the ISI was the focal point of the anti-Soviet war in Afghanistan. It had three branches: operations, logistics, and psychological warfare. A separate department was created to handle food and clothing for the Mujahideen, purchased with CIA funds, while another supplied food and material to the Afghans who remained in their own country, with a view to retaining a local Afghanistan-based network of support for Mujahideen operations. Earlier attempts to use the Afghan refugees in Pakistan for jihadi operations had been hindered by 'rampant corruption within the Pakistan-staffed Commissionerate (sic) of Afghan Refugees (CAR).' Much of the money for supporting the Afghan refugees ended up being diverted, leading to great unhappiness among them with their Pakistani hosts.[42] The Afghan bureau, in short, undertook to provide for the refugees and to train and equip the Mujahideen forces, churning out over 80,000 warriors between 1982 and 1987, and even taking on the risky task of selecting 'volunteers,' often Pushtuns from the regular Pakistan Army who were fluent in Pushto or Dari (Afghan *farsi*) and were infiltrated into Afghanistan to guide the Mujahideen and help them use unfamiliar weapons systems effectively. Such soldiers were under strict instructions not to reveal their identity. If they were captured, Pakistan would deny that they were from the Pakistan Army.[43]

With the change in the US presidency from Carter to Ronald Reagan, the war effort got a fillip. This time Zia was ready to accept an enhanced US aid offer. Direct collaboration between the CIA and the ISI also increased, particularly between the CIA Director William Casey, an ex-OSS officer in the Second World War days, and Akhtar Abdur Rahman. Casey was a man on a mission and he found resonance in the focused thinking of Rahman and his colleagues. Being from the private sector, Casey was not risk-averse and, according to Pakistani sources, even encouraged the Pakistanis to get the Mujahideen to hurt the Soviets inside their territory by launching attacks north of the Amu Darya. By keeping the Pakistan Army disassociated from the efforts of the ISI, a measure of deniability was maintained. The CIA also succeeded over time in making some direct contributions to their own favourite commanders, including Abdul Haq, as did the Saudis. Among the conduits were Saudi charities, including those run by a young Osama bin Laden. The easy manners and affability of Prince Turki won over the ISI officers, whom he saw frequently. He was to build personal relationships with all the heads of the ISI over time, showering them with gifts and attention. A favourite gift of his adorns the homes of various retired ISI DGs and former COASs: a piece of ornate gold thread calligraphy on the black cloth that is used to cover the Holy Kaaba in Makkah each year. In addition, medical facilities were provided to those Pakistani generals who needed treatment abroad. Hamid Gul acknowledged that the Saudis had provided him this facility. The CIA did not shrink from direct bribery also, either directly or through cut-outs. Hamid Gul recounts an effort by the CIA station chief in Pakistan to get his son Omar into Texas A&M University after finding out that Omar had applied to Michigan. Gul says he refused to accept this bribe and was told: 'But this is a small service that we can give. And we did this for all the children of Akhtar Abdur Rahman.'[44]

Other sources of finance for the education of senior generals' children also emerged. A mysterious character who developed close ties to both Zia and Lt. Gen. Faiz Ali Chishti was Dr Saad Gabr. He was of either Egyptian or

Moroccan origin and had set up an Institute of Ummah Islamic Studies in North Hatley, Ontario, Canada and associated with it Joanne Herring, a socialite and friend of Zia from Houston, Texas. (Herring was later named by Zia as Pakistan's honorary consul.) Chishti was inducted into the board of the institute on Zia's suggestion. Gabr tried to get Pakistan not only to give him financial backing but also to allow him to set up an export promotion scheme for Pakistani products. He also managed to get close to Zia and to Rahimuddin. Chishti asserts that Gabr offered to employ his (Chishti's) son, Irfan at the institute at $700 a month. 'He was already paying Faaiz, Lt. Gen. Rahimuddin's son, six hundred and twenty-five dollars a month, as agreed by the President,' Chishti recalls. Chishti says he declined the offer.[45]

The British and French were also entering the bribery game by getting into the good books of Ahmed Shah Massoud, the Tajik commander, who reported to Rabbani in Peshawar. They bypassed the Pakistani ISI to set up direct arrangements with him. The Saudis were doing the same with Hekmatyar, the most active of the Peshawar Seven. But, even as these connection games were being played, at the ground level, the Soviets were finding themselves outfought by the rag tag Mujahideen, whose main advantage was their knowledge of the territory and their simple credo of faith, which armed them in a 'holy war' against the 'infidels' from the north. The Soviets' tactics also contributed to their own discomfiture. They ensconced themselves in their secure bases in and around Kabul and only exited to launch sporadic attacks, leaving the countryside effectively in the control of the Mujahideen. The Soviets had the advantage in the air, with their helicopters and airplanes, but only until the US Congress, under goading by a maverick representative from Texas named Charlie Wilson, managed to browbeat his colleagues to increase the quantum of aid exponentially and include in it a ferocious new weapon that changed the whole face of the Afghan War: the shoulder-fired Stinger missile. A US army report on the use of the Stinger in the Afghan conflict came to the conclusion that it 'changed the nature of combat' and was 'the war's most decisive weapon.' It attributed some 269 downed aircraft in 340 firings to the Stinger; a great success rate for any weapon of that type.[46] Thereafter, the Soviet military machine was effectively blunted and casualties mounted.

Soon after President Ronald Reagan took office in January 1981, the US opened up the taps for aid flows to Pakistan, crafting a $3.2 billion plan for the next five years. This was not the 'peanuts' that Carter had offered earlier. Pakistan was now suddenly in the catbird seat, calling the shots on other issues too, such as the return to democracy (deemed 'your internal situation' by Secretary of State Alexander Haig[47]) or Pakistan's nuclear ambitions (put on the backburner for now), although there were some difficulties over the delivery of the forty F-16s sought by Pakistan to improve its defence posture against India.

The covert aid via the CIA continued to flow at speed. Through all these exchanges, the Pakistan Army was not deeply involved in the exchanges. The ISI took the lead. Zia would often meet US visitors alone or sometime bring in his ISI Chief Rahman. Meanwhile, the Foreign Office did its best to have a hand in the making of foreign policy but often had to concede to Zia's personalized form of governance and the ISI's upper hand in managing the situation on the ground in Afghanistan. Zia kept Foreign Minister Agha Shahi and the mandarins in the Foreign Office on tenterhooks by threatening every now and then to cement a formal alliance with the Americans that would have jeopardized Pakistan's newly-acquired status in the Non-Aligned Movement. Eventually Zia replaced Shahi with his own former military boss and armour commander, retired Lt. Gen. Sahibzada Yaqub Ali Khan, a seasoned diplomat who was well-respected in Washington, Paris, and Moscow; all posts where he had represented Pakistan. Yaqub's arrival meant that the Foreign Office's voice was once again heard, because of his previous relationship with Zia, and most decisions on Afghanistan were taken by consensus within the government. Indeed, one foreign service officer who sat in on the Afghanistan discussions involving Yaqub and retired Lt. Gen. Fazle Haq (who was governor of the NWFP), states that these two were 'quite contemptuous of Akhtar Abdur Rahman and his 'Sergeant Major briefings.'[48]

The Soviets meanwhile started off by taking a lenient view of Zia's strategy, blaming the Americans for pushing him into the war against them in Afghanistan. The short-lived general secretary of the communist party, Yuri Andropov summed up his view of the situation in Afghanistan in a speech to the central committee of the party in January 1983 thus:

> The Afghan question is being actively used in the struggle against détente. The Afghan revolution needed assistance, and it has received it. However, the situation in Afghanistan and around it still remains unstable. There are some possibilities that opened up with the beginning of the negotiations between Afghanistan and Pakistan. During the meeting in November with President Zia ul-Haq, I tried to make him understand that the political settlement of the Afghan problem, and subsequently the possibility of Soviet troop withdrawal from Afghanistan, depends on the position of Pakistan to a decisive degree. The Pakistani President expressed understanding of the Afghan problem in his rhetoric, and even assured me that they were already half way to its solution. However, many signs show that the Americans have tied Islamabad's hands quite well.[49]

Following Andropov's death and that of his successor Constantin Chernenko, the eventual consolidation of Gorbachev's power allowed the Soviets to take a harder line—and as their casualties mounted in Afghanistan, their view of

Zia changed to one of an implacable foe who needed to be neutralized. At the meeting of the secretaries of the central committee of the Soviet communist party on 15 March 1985, following Chernenko's death, Gorbachev spoke about his meetings with various foreign leaders who had come to Moscow:

> President Ziaul Haq of Pakistan….is one cunning politician. He constantly wanted to assure us of his friendly feelings, his good neighbourliness, and that he himself was a victim of a situation where there were about three million so-called Afghan refugees in Pakistan. In general, it was pure demagoguery with the perversion of a facts….We pointed out to the President of Pakistan that somebody would like this bleeding wound to remain [open] for long years to come. But then the question emerges: in what kind of situation would Pakistan and its leadership find itself then? I told Ziaul Haq directly….you are a military man yourself and understand very well that we know in the most precise way what is going on in Pakistan right now, where and what kind of camps are functioning that train the *dushman* ['enemy' in Farsi, and used by the Soviets to refer to the Mujahideen], who is arming the bandits, and who is supplying them with money and all other necessities. Thus, overall, we put quite serious pressure on Ziaul Haq, and he left the room clearly unhappy.[50]

They took the battle into Pakistan, using the Afghan intelligence agency 'Khad' and surrogates such as the Al Zulfikar Organization (AZO), a revolutionary group headed by Murtaza Bhutto, (the son of the slain Pakistani Prime Minister Zulfikar Ali Bhutto), who first obtained refuge and support in Kabul and then in Damascus, both Soviet allies. At least one missile attack on Zia's aircraft at Chaklala airport in Rawalpindi was attributed widely to Al Zulfikar, known in Pakistan Army circles by its initials 'AZO'. Murtaza had also travelled to India to seek support for his efforts. On the early morning of 7 February 1982, two AZO agents, Aamir and Faisal, waited in a city park that lay in the flight path of aircraft from the Islamabad airport at Chaklala, and took aim at Zia's Falcon aircraft as it took off from the east–west runway. With Faisal providing cover with a Kalashnikov, Aamir locked on to the Falcon through the eyepiece of his SAM-7 anti-aircraft missile. Once the light turned green, (indicating the missile had locked onto the aircraft,) he fired it and then took off with his colleague shouting: 'Run Aamir, It's a hit!' But his amateur training had deprived him from staying locked on to the target and he did not even have the goggles that would have saved his eyes from the smoke of the missile as it took off. He averted his eyes at the last second. The errant missile missed as the Falcon's pilot saw the rising missile and took sudden evasive action.[51] Subsequent attempts on Zia also failed, in Pakistan and in India.

The only successful operation of the AZO that garnered headlines was the hijacking on 2 March 1981 to Kabul of a PIA aircraft on a domestic flight that took off from Karachi. The aircraft was carrying, among others, a retired army officer, Tariq Rahim who was once an ADC to Zulfikar Ali Bhutto and who had come to Pakistan for the burial of his father from his foreign service posting in Tehran. The plane was supposed to be taken to Damascus but ended up in Kabul because of lack of fuel. There in Kabul, Rahim, who apparently was seen by Murtaza as a traitor to Z.A. Bhutto, was shot on 6 March by one of the hijackers named Tipu.[52] The flight then took off for Damascus the next day. The hijacking ended that day, after Zia agreed to release some fifty-four PPP supporters in Pakistani jails.

SECURING THE HOME FRONT

All military rulers desperately seek legal cover for their extra-constitutional actions, while deep down they understand that the only course of their legitimacy is the power inherent in their military command. Zia was no exception. His military colleagues favoured the idea of holding elections and transferring power to the elected representatives of the people. Zia himself favoured the idea of a referendum that would give a semblance of legality to his rule and allow him to stay in power. His handpicked assembly, the so-called Majlis-e-Shoora or advisory gathering, also favoured elections. As usual, Zia went through a process of consultations, while keeping his own preference alive and close to his chest. Surprisingly, his legal wizard Sharifuddin Pirzada initially opposed a referendum, thinking that there was no need for it since the Supreme Court had validated Zia's takeover on the basis of necessity. Zia met a stream of objections to this idea from his own military commanders. At one formation commanders' meeting, various officers conveyed to him the 'shame that many officers feel in wearing their uniforms in public', since the masses had come to associate the army with dictatorship and harsh Islamic justice. Many of these officers were sub-martial administrators, who had to deal with summary punishments meted out by military courts, which included public floggings and lashings. Zia allowed these comments to be aired, but ignored them.[53]

Zia finally managed to have his cabinet approve the referendum plan in November 1984. An election cell was set up in the martial law secretariat and headed by Lt. Gen. Syed Refaqat, who was 'borrowed' from the JCS HQ for the purpose.[54] In a speech to the nation on 1 December 1984, Zia spelled out the referendum plan and said that a 'Yes' vote would mean that the people had confidence in him and he would stand elected as president for another five years. But the question that was put to the people was not so direct. Rather, on 19 December, the people of Pakistan were asked to respond to a question that was carefully crafted to ensure victory for the only person whose name was on that referendum:

> Do you endorse the process initiated by the President of Pakistan, General Muhammad Ziaul Haq, for bringing the laws of Pakistan in conformity with the injunctions of Islam as laid down in the Holy Quran and Sunnah [Traditions] of the Holy Prophet (peace be upon him), for the preservation of and further consolidation of that process, and for the smooth and orderly transfer of power to the elected representatives of the people?

The only options were 'Yes' and 'No'. According to the government, some 60 per cent turned out to vote and a huge majority approved Zia's plans and thereby 'elected' him as president for another five years. Other estimates of the turnout were a fraction of these numbers. Whatever the case 'really' was, Zia thus became a civilian president but retained his uniform at the same time. He now began distancing himself from his military colleagues. Even the martial law administrators meetings became few and far between, as did his visits to the GHQ of the Pakistan Army. Increasingly he was now a loner, surrounded by a circle of political engineers whose major aim was to ensure that he, and as a result they, remain in power for as long as possible. With the benefit of 20/20 hindsight, even his close military colleagues were later to have a different view of the situation. 'A faulty democratic system with its built-in checks and balances, is, in the long term, better than a seemingly benign one-man rule, in which the process of accountability has no place,' wrote General Arif.[55] When Zia offered a peace pact to India's Prime Minister Indira Gandhi, a senior civil servant remarked sarcastically: 'He needs to offer a peace pact to his own countrymen first!' Zia increasingly saw himself as the *Amir ul Momineen,* or leader of the faithful, who did not need a parliament to help him run the country. Even within the army, he failed to give leeway to his vice or deputy chiefs to run the military in his absence, often encouraging corps commanders and other senior officers to disagree with the vice or deputy chief and deal directly with Zia himself.[56]

His Byzantine manner of rule became evident in the wake of the referendum and the general elections of 1985, when he had to select a prime minister. Even one of his closest military colleagues termed him 'devious.' After proposing that three names would be presented to the National Assembly, he began meetings with groups of parliamentarians, having told his staff that he would ask each group to vote on a paper ballot containing three names. Yet when he met the groups, only one name was presented (orally) to them: Mohammad Khan Junejo of the Pakistan Muslim League from Sindh. His COS, Major General Malik Abdul Waheed, recalls the surreal meeting that ensued between Zia and Junejo. Zia warmly welcomed Junejo in his office on 20 March at 8:00 p.m. and told him that he planned to nominate him as the prime minister of Pakistan. A grim-faced Junejo did not thank the president, but instead immediately asked: 'When do you plan to remove Martial Law?' Zia tried retrieving the situation by saying that martial law would now support the prime minister, but the damage had been done. A few days later, on 23 March 1985, Zia presented Junejo's name to the till then party-less assembly for ratification. Junejo sailed through, but his new-found strength allowed him to alter the relationship with the president. In time, political parties were revived, and Junejo was to proudly announce that martial law would be lifted.

Junejo began by refusing to accept all of Zia's nominees for cabinet posts, acceding only to Yaqub as foreign minister and Mahbubul Haq, first as minister for planning and development and later as finance minister. He also got rid of Lt. Gen. Mujibur Rehman, the secretary of the Ministry of Information. Many other military officers were sent home. Junejo also spoke publicly about reducing the perks and privileges of the senior military brass, threatening at one stage to remove their large staff cars and putting them in the domestically produced Suzukis (mini-cars produced by the Japanese firm, Suzuki). This suggestion provoked a riposte in the newspaper *The Muslim* on 28 June 1987 from retired Lt. Gen. Ejaz Azim, who had clearly been encouraged by Zia to write an article that defended the senior leadership of the military. 'Any attempts to sow doubts in the minds of our soldiers regarding the quality of their Generals, to my way of thinking, does not serve the best interests of the country,' wrote General Azim.[57] A rejoinder came from 'Watchman,' a former army captain, in the *Dawn* on 8 July: 'What General Azim is really saying is that Generals are a group apart and that any criticism of their conduct is by definition grossly unpatriotic....this is a very thin-skinned breed of men...And...the future of the country rests on very unstable foundations. If the leading lights of the military can take offence at such slight cause (sic), their reaction in case of a more radical shift in the country can easily be imagined.'[58] The lines were drawn.

Adding to the rough sailing for Zia's regime was the growing public discontent with his harsh Islamic rule. The imposition of the mandatory *zakat*—the Islamic wealth and welfare tax—and its use by Zia to fund mullahs and various activities that were outside the pale of welfare, (including sending favoured individuals for Haj—the pilgrimage to Makkah—free of cost), did not go unnoticed by the people. The Shia community—a minority, but a powerful one—was also up in arms against this tax, since it did not conform to their sect's jurisprudence. Following their protest, the Shia were exempted from paying this tax, and thus so were all the others who simply declared that they belonged to the Shia *Fiqh-e-Jafria* simply to avoid paying the tax. Public spectacles such as lashing of persons convicted of 'anti-social' behaviour added to the general discontent, even among the military officers, who saw themselves being tarred by the same brush that painted Zia as an ideologue and fundamentalist. Zia also instituted the Hudood ordinance, which imposed severe restrictions on women and their status in society, and would remain in place for decades to come. Even the Jamaat-i-Islami, Zia's early partner in politics, ended up parting ways with him and siding with the Movement for the Restoration of Democracy (MRD), an alliance of political parties that decided to agitate against Zia's martial law government. According to a former member of the Islami Jamiat-e-Talaba (IJT), the student wing of Jamaat-i-Islami:

> The Jamaat's Karachi organization, led by Prof. Ghafoor and Syed Munawwar Hasan, was never comfortable with Mian Tufail Mohammed's alliance with Ziaul Haq. By the time of the 1985 election, the Karachi leaders were being openly critical of Zia but the Punjab leadership remained positive about Zia, having supported him in the referendum. The Jamaat never went fully with the MRD, but this internal division gave the impression that Jamaat had gone with [the] MRD. For his part, Zia responded by orchestrating things so that all Karachi Jamaat leaders lost their seats while the Punjab crowd got in. Of the 10 seats in the NA won by the Jamaat that year, only 2 were from Karachi, marking the beginning of its decline and MQM's rise in Karachi. The internal division in the Jamaat ended only when Mian Tufail Mohammed completed his term as Amir in 1986, and was succeeded by Qazi Hussain Ahmed.[59]

Only the PPP—now headed by Benazir Bhutto—remained somewhat aloof. Bhutto had been released from prison and had left the country in 1983 to seek medical treatment abroad for an ear infection. She bided her time, stirring up opposition to Zia's regime from her base in London. In August 1985, she returned home to bury her younger brother Shah Nawaz and was re-arrested in Karachi. She returned to France on 3 November 1985 to take part in the proceedings of the court investigating her brother's death in Cannes.

Martial law was lifted on 30 December 1985. Junejo had managed to push Zia enough to get this done. The time was ripe for Bhutto to return 'home', as she put it. 'Home' meant the length and breadth of Pakistan,' she wrote in her autobiography.[60] She prepared for her journey by travelling to Washington to garner support and publicity. Then, on 9 April 1986, she took a flight from London to Dhahran in Saudi Arabia and connected to a PIA plane to Lahore. Accompanying her was a horde of party faithfuls and foreign journalists. Landing in Lahore at 7:00 a.m. on 10 April 1986, she was greeted by a crowd estimated at a million that had been gathering since the night before to welcome her back. It took her ten hours to move from the airport to the Minar-i-Pakistan (a tower commemorating the birth of the idea of Pakistan), only 10 miles' distance, as the crowd swelled to a million or even more.[61] Many Pakistanis, who had stayed away from the recent elections, now had an excuse to gather again and show their political will. But Zia was not done. There was still some muscle-flexing to come.

ENDGAME IN AFGHANISTAN AND AT HOME

Zia and his chosen prime minister were on a collision course. They clashed on policies and appointments. Junejo had misgivings about the close relationship between Yaqub Khan and Zia and did not trust Yaqub to follow through on Junejo's wishes to engage in fruitful discussions with the Soviets in the ongoing talks on Afghanistan in Geneva. The ISI had its own angle in these exchanges, seeking to ensure that Afghanistan came under a Pushtun who was aligned with Pakistan more than with any other country in the region. (This was primarily why they had favoured the fundamentalist Gulbuddin Hekmatyar, even when regular army officers in the border region were suspicious of his aims and aspirations.[62]) Zia wanted to call all the shots and keep things under his direct control. With the Soviets under increasing military pressure, helped by the increasing foreign aid to the Mujahideen and the induction of the deadly Stingers that negated their air advantage, various schemes were hatched to allow them to withdraw from Afghanistan. The UN special representative, Diego Cordovez had also been active in trying to broker a settlement in the Geneva talks. In October 1987, the US oil tycoon, Armand Hammer arrived in Pakistan carrying a proposal that involved using the former Afghan King Zahir Shah, now in Italy, to return and help serve as 'political glue' for an interim Afghan government. General Rahman had by that time been promoted to CJCS.

Rahman's successor was Major General Hamid Gul. Gul, Yaqub, and Zia met Hammer and worked out an arrangement under which the Soviet puppet Najeebullah would be removed and the former king would step in—without the Peshawar-based Mujahideen leaders. This offered the Soviets a way to save face as well as a way out. Junejo learned of the agreement after the event, and the fact that it was authored by Zia and Yaqub irked him immensely. For him this meant that Yaqub had bypassed him yet again. So Yaqub had to go.[63] Deprived of the presence of Yaqub, who had in fact supported the Geneva Accord track, Junejo was left to fend for himself against the ISI and Zia. An unequal contest, as events were to indicate.

Junejo also was asserting his authority in appointing senior military officers and approving their promotions to three and four-star ranks. He would withhold action on individuals till those whom he wished to promote were also promoted. Among the beneficiaries of this stance was Lt. Gen. Shamim Alam, later CJCS, whose promotion came about on Junejo's insistence, but only after a Zia favourite, Major General Pirdad Khan, was promoted. Junejo had sat on Pirdad's promotion to lieutenant general till Zia agreed to Alam's promotion. Gradually, relations between Zia and Junejo soured. Among those blamed for this situation was General Refaqat, the president's new COS. Zia was told that the prime minister had ordered surveillance of him by the civilian IB. The ISI under General Hamid Gul may have been mentioned as the source of purloined photos taken by IB operatives, allegedly of cars entering the President's House. Regardless of the realities on ground, perceptions of a chasm between Zia and Junejo fuelled real tensions between them. Soon after Junejo arrived back from a visit to the Philippines on 19 May 1988, Zia announced that he had dismissed him at a hastily convened press conference organized by General Refaqat on three hours' notice.[64] His rationale, in his broadcast speech to the country the next day, was 'rampant corruption, nepotism, and maladministration, finally leading to a complete breakdown of morality and law and order in the country'.[65] He also blamed Junejo for not facilitating the move toward Islamization. According to Arif, the president ordered the head of the Signals Corps to confiscate all the recording equipment of the IB once Junejo had been dismissed. This equipment was released later without any screening.

In all this, the army high command was kept in the dark. The VCOAS, General Mirza Aslam Beg, was simply told by Zia that he was dismissing Junejo. Beg's views were not sought. Even Hamid Gul was not privy to the plan, according to his later conversation with General Arif. Zia had truly become a one-man administration, aided only by his immediate team. The corps commanders were not given a detailed explanation till early July 1988, well over a month after the prime minister's dismissal. One reason for this may have been Zia's busy schedule. The other more basic issue was the increasing gap between Zia and his generals in terms of age and service group. His latest crop of corps commanders had been approved by Junejo before the latter's dismissal, and included officers who were colonels when Zia took over in 1977. While they showed their obedience to his position, it is not clear that they shared his vision or felt they owed him undying loyalty.

CHANGES IN THE ARMY

Zia had tried hard to change the ethos of the army, making Islamic ritual and teachings part of the army's day-to-day activities. He had changed the motto of the army from Jinnah's 'Unity, Faith, and Discipline' to '*Iman, Taqwa, Jihad fi sabeelillah*' (Faith, Obedience of God, and Struggle in the path of Allah) soon after taking over as COAS in 1976. Apart from encouraging commanders to join their troops in congregational prayers and elevating the status of the regimental *maulvis* or religious teachers (though not without resistance from some old guard officers[66]), he allowed members of the fundamentalist Tablighi Jamaat to preach at the PMA. It was routine for Tablighi Jamaat representatives to deliver the *khutba* (sermon) after Friday prayers at the PMA in Kakul till 1984. (In 1985, the new commandant, Major General Asif Nawaz, forbade the Tablighis' entry, stating: 'This is a military academy, not a seminary!'[67]) But given the changes in demographics of the newly inducted cadets, Zia's actions had created a different breed of officers. Recruitment data from the GHQ of the Pakistan Army indicate that since the 1970s recruitment moved from the traditional districts to new cities.[68] With increased urbanization and the inflow of remittances from overseas workers to their families in the countryside, many newly rich rural people migrated to the fringes of smaller towns and cities. The expansion of cities, particularly in the Punjab, created a new base for recruitment to the volunteer army: the children of the lower-middle class, akin to Zia's own background, who chose the military because of its economic and social advantages rather than military traditions. A telling piece of information from a former member of the IJT confirms that the Jamaat-i-Islami took advantage of the changing demographics and nature of the army by sending out directives to its members to try to sign up for the army by taking the Inter Services Selection Board examinations.

Zia's senior commanders were generally a compliant lot. However, not all of them came from the same background as him, and held their own counsel in private. Some of them had grown up in the English-speaking missionary school atmosphere and represented old military families or tribes. The army they entered still had old British-style messes with alcohol and formal dinner nights. Zia, who had always maintained his religion and avoided alcohol, did not quite fit in with that crowd—but they obeyed and tolerated him because he was now their senior. Senior commanders generally began following the rituals of Islam, at least while around him. Some of them had genuinely become practicing Muslims during this time. Others still retained a certain independence. By the late 1980s, Zia had had to promote officers to corps commanders who were much junior to him—and apolitical, so that he could keep them away from the business of ruling the country, which was solely his domain now. Most of the senior generals in Zia's last four years had been commissioned in the mid- to late 1950s, well over ten years after his own entry into the army in 1944.[69] He did not treat them as colleagues but as very junior acolytes. As a result, his meetings with corps commanders were devoid of the conversations and debates that occurred in his early days as CMLA; they became one-sided. For example, at promotion boards, he would simply approve some individuals without waiting for or seeking comments from others. The generals knew better than to challenge him.

To fortify his position, Zia had married his son to General Rahimuddin's daughter. Rahim came from a celebrated family in Muslim Hyderabad Deccan in India. His wife was the niece of an Indian President, Zakir Hussain. Other marriages produced a coterie of power around him. One of General Akhtar Abdur Rahman's sons married another of Rahimuddin's daughters, while another married the daughter of Lt. Gen. Zahid Ali Akbar, a contender for the post of COAS, or at least VCOAS. Zia had good reason to feel secure and supremely confident, the blind spot of all dictators.

Zia had also opened up new avenues for the army officers and soldiers to profit by virtue of their positions. By setting up a new and different type of military arrangement with Saudi Arabia, he had sent a contingent of the Pakistan Army to be located at Tabuk in Saudi Arabia, ostensibly to provide training but in fact to protect the kingdom from any attack from the north (by Iraq or Israel). Another, private explanation, was that the force was set up to protect the royal family in case of an uprising. The Pakistani armour brigade, named the 12 Khalid bin Waleed Independent Armoured Brigade Group after the legendary Islamic warrior, was in Saudi Arabia from 1982 to 1988. Initially, the protocol established it for three years. It was then extended for another three years at the Saudis' request, according to a general who served in it. The brigade was reactivated during the first Gulf war of 1990, for which Pakistan sent its troops again. The rotations allowed more officers and soldiers to benefit from the experience, and of course, from the extra pay and allowances given to them (which included the chance to perform the pilgrimage to Makkah, a major benefit for any Muslim). A small contingent was kept at Riyadh to liaise with the Saudi Ministry of Defence. By 1983, about 20,000 Pakistani troops were based in Saudi Arabia, or roughly 5 per cent of the total Pakistan Army.[70] By the time the arrangement ended in 1988, Pakistan had rotated some 40,000 troops and officers through the Saudi base. But there were some tensions in negotiating the arrangements, as the Saudis were sensitive about having Shia troops. Pakistan took a firm stand on the issue by not following that Saudi injunction but it created some dissonance and eventually the brigade was wound up. This overseas brigade supported by Saudi money allowed the Pakistan Army to expand its own numbers when these troops eventually returned. But this move had its downside too:

> The sending of two batches of officers and men to Saudi Arabia in 1982 and 1985 seriously undermined armoured corps efficiency. Two classes were created in both within the officers and the rank and file. The incentive to somehow go to Saudi Arabia created unpleasant situation in many units in terms of class rivalry, favouritism and even further dilution of uprightness and soldierly forthrightness and simple approach towards regimental soldiering. Only individuals gained while the military spirit of the army described by Clausewitz as the most important foundation of an army was eroded. This was followed [after Zia] by other carrots that made people more money minded and calculating like secondments to Somalia, Bosnia etc.[71]

The Zia period also saw the army's deepest penetration of the civil sector till then. At the level of the central government, by one estimate, roughly one-fourth of the 35–40 senior bureaucratic slots were occupied by senior military officers. Many retired generals held ambassadorial posts, including in key slots such as Moscow and Washington. Army officers were also increasingly being appointed to lower level positions in the bureaucracy. In the provinces especially, as martial law continued to be in place during the first seven or so years of the Zia regime, military (largely army) officers retained the top positions. At one point all governors in the Punjab, Sindh, the NWFP and Balochistan were retired generals. Often the former corps commanders in individual provinces were made governors. But the emplacement of army officers continued down to the district level. In a structure similar to the shadow government of the military in Indonesia under Suharto, the army had appointed officers to dog and shadow civilians at all levels of the administration. While the induction of army officers into the civil was not a new phenomenon, (indeed it began under Ayub Khan), the normal rules and quotas for such induction were ignored by Zia's regime. He realized that his only constituency was the army, and chose to strengthen it at all levels.

Zia also had a way of co-opting individuals (both in the civil and military) in a manner that was unprecedented. He would telephone subordinates, even those well below the command level, and try to find ways of 'helping' them out. A favourite tactic of his was to encourage his GSOs to ask for favours, such as subsidized plots of land in burgeoning Defence Housing Societies, or trips abroad, or medical treatment (often at the Cromwell Hospital in London that had been set up by the BCCI of Agha Hassan Abedi, a close confidant of Zia). A special favour that he dispensed freely was all-expense-paid trips by generals and their wives to Saudi Arabia for *umra* (the off-season pilgrimage to Makkah) or for Haj. While Muslims are enjoined against going on these pilgrimages with any other than their own resources, this was a favour that no one seems to have refused!

Within the army, Zia found some opposition. At least two times attempts were made to oust him, once by a militant Islamic group headed by a major general, and the second time reportedly by junior officers who were said to be linked with the rebels headed by Murtaza Bhutto and trained in India. The first was the Tajammal Hussain Malik Conspiracy Case in which the ISI reportedly became aware of a plot to assassinate President Ziaul Haq and then launch a bloody coup to depose the current government and install an extreme Islamic government in its place. The attempted assassination and coup was to occur on 23 March 1980 during the annual Pakistan Day parade. The alleged masterminds behind the coup were Major General Tajammal Hussain Malik, his son, Captain Naveed, and his nephew Major Riaz, a former MI officer. 'ISI decided against arresting these men outright because they did not know how deep this conspiracy went and kept these men under strict surveillance. As the date of the annual parade approached, these men were arrested along with quite a few high ranking military officers. The officers involved were set free after General Zia ul-Haq's death.[72] Several army officers were arrested on 3 January 1984, for hatching a conspiracy against the Zia government in connivance with India. (The case is known as the Attock Conspiracy case-II). Many of these officers were freed because of lack of evidence, and a few were sentenced to jail.[73]

SEEDS OF CORRUPTION

While Zia himself led a generally pious and simple existence, his relatives and others around him took full advantage of his power and his tendency towards nepotism. According to his military secretary (then brigadier and later major general) Mahmud Ali Durrani, 'He was a very religious man but his understanding of religion was extremely limited[...] His understanding was what his parents [had] taught him or [based on] the madrassah he attended[...] He was genuinely religious. I've seen him stand and say his prayers all night. However, he used religion for his personal benefit.' This personal religiosity is attested to by Zia's college-mates at St. Stephen's College in New Delhi. One of them, Ramesh Mukehrji, recalled that his first glimpse of Zia was 'offering *namaaz* [prayers] in the corridor of the hostel.' When Mukherji asked him: 'Why do you pray so often?' Zia replied: 'Because my father asked me to do so.'[74] Durrani contends that Zia's personal religiosity was not an act. Others support that contention and point to his humility also. But he used Islam for political purposes and condoned malfeasance.[75] Clever operatives often chose to approach his wife and played on his penchant for Islamic symbolism and rituals. In one case, Zia even suggested his brother-in-law as governor of the Punjab. To gain his favour, senior government and military officials and their wives began hosting religious gatherings at their homes and inviting Zia or his relatives and religious speakers or divines whom he favoured.

The BCCI's banking operation also took off during Zia's regime, adding to the growing hints of corruption in his regime. Though headquartered in different locations around the world, to avoid regulation by any single jurisdiction, it managed to infiltrate Zia's inner circle. In its initial period, BCCI had the Bank of America as a shareholder. Zia's son, Ijazul Haq, a graduate of Southern Illinois University in the United States, was hired by the Bank of America in 1978 and later was promoted to vice president and regional manager in Bahrain. Similarly, BCCI managed to employ the sons of current or retired senior intelligence, civil service, and military officers, and gain favoured access through them. It even set up a foundation in Pakistan that was chaired by Ghulam Ishaq Khan even after he became president of Pakistan. Among those who were offered money by BCCI was Mahbub ul Haq, who told me that he had been offered $25 million to set up a think-tank in Pakistan. After Bhutto's execution, Pakistan had become isolated internationally. BCCI stepped in and helped it meet its foreign exchange shortfall with a $100 million loan to the Rice Corporation. It also was reported to have secretly lent the State Bank of Pakistan $25 million to bolster its reserves so that it could get access to loans from the IMF and the World Bank.[76]

Abedi liked to 'collect' senior officials. BCCI also set up an overseas publishing operation headed by former senior civil servant, Altaf Gauhar and run by him and his family members. This included a magazine *South* that reportedly soaked up some $50 million during its operations before folding up. It provided generally positive coverage of Zia's regime until after his death when Gauhar's son Humayun, in the October 1988 issue, criticized Zia for 'thwarting the democratic process with lies and deceptions to perpetuate his rule.'[77] According to a *Wall Street Journal* front page article: 'In one example of the BCCI's patronage, the Bank's Dubai branch in May 1985 issued a check personally payable to Gen. Zia for 40 million rupees, the equivalent of nearly $3 million at the time. A copy of the check doesn't indicate whether the funds were intended for personal use or, as government officials now suggest, for religious purposes.'[78] BCCI also had other uses: it acted as a conduit for the flow of funds from the CIA and other sources to the Afghan jihad, and was alleged to have provided some financing for the purchase of parts for Pakistan's nuclear programme.[79]

Zia's family name was also dragged into the drug trade, when a dogged investigator in Norway asked Pakistan's FIA to arrest three men: Tahir Butt, Munawar Hussain and Hamid Hasnain. The prosecutor identified the three as 'standing behind the drug traffic from Pakistan to Norway.'[80] Hasnain was the vice-president of Habib Bank in Rawalpindi. When police picked him up, they found in his briefcase personal bank records, including checkbooks, for President Zia, his wife, and their daughter. The suspect was characterized as 'virtually the adopted son' of president and Begum Zia and had ready access to their home. An angry Begum Zia called from Egypt (which she was visiting at the time), to ask why Hasnain had been detained. Zia's son, Ijazul Haq, while acknowledging that he knew Hasnain as his and his family's banker, denied vehemently these characterizations of Hasnain by Lawrence Lifschultz for *Newsline*.[81] At a meeting with Zia, the local officials reportedly explained to him the extent of the evidence and the Norwegian government's strong interest in the case. The case proceeded, and all three were convicted. Later, according to a BBC TV programme *Panorama,* a Japanese drug courier named Hisayoshi Maruyama was arrested in Amsterdam in 1983 with 17.5 kilos of heroin. He was alleged to have links with one of the major drug dealers in Pakistan and also had access to Zia's home since he reportedly treated Zia's handicapped daughter, operating as a doctor with a bogus medical degree.[82] Zia, the consummate family man, allowed numerous such individuals to take advantage of him. As time went on, the negatives were piling up against him.

UNCLE SAM'S PRESSURES

A major factor in the decline of the US–Pakistan relationship was Pakistan's secret nuclear programme. Zia had decided that he would brazenly lie about Pakistan's nuclear ambitions and did so on numerous occasions, denying that Pakistan was seeking nuclear weapons. Yet, evidence was mounting of Pakistan's attempts to acquire nuclear technology to enrich uranium, and its alliances with China and other countries to use their resources or facilities towards that end. Two Pakistanis had been apprehended in Canada while attempting to send to Pakistan material acquired from the United States. In July 1984, another three Pakistanis were caught in Houston for illegally trying to export similar equipment. Yet, even when President Ronald Reagan wrote to Zia in September warning him of the risks inherent in such a course of action, Zia's response was noncommittal and evasive. Apparently resorting to a form of behaviour normally associated with minority Muslims in hostile societies and known as *Taqiya* (dissimulation), he was more direct in responding to Senator Daniel Patrick Moynihan: 'we are nowhere near it [a weapon stage]. We have no intention of making such a weapon. We renounce making such a weapon.'[83] He even misled his friends. When Congressman Charlie Wilson—the man whom he credited with giving Pakistan and the Afghan resistance the weaponry they needed to defeat the Soviets in Afghanistan—brought a passel of key US legislators to Pakistan, Zia blatantly lied to them too. At the end of a dinner for them, behind closed doors, locked from the inside by his ADC, he said he would: 'speak from [his] heart', and then proceeded to tell his American guests that 'his country's nuclear program was exclusively for peaceful purposes. He asked that they accept his word: Pakistan had no intention of building a delivery system.'[84] Remarkably, Zia was to state openly in a moment of candour to a visiting US delegation that had come to apprise him of the dangers of pursuing the nuclear option, that Islam allowed him to lie for a good cause![85]

But the tide was turning against Pakistan in the US Congress even at that stage. As the Senate discussed a new six-year aid package of some $4 billion, Senator John Glenn of Ohio added an amendment that required the president to certify annually that Pakistan did not possess, nor was proceeding towards, a nuclear weapon. In the face of opposition from the White House that would place it in a bind in the support for the Afghan war, a slightly looser language was suggested for the amendment that Pakistan did not posses a nuclear weapon and that US assistance was helping its non-proliferation aims. Senator Larry Pressler, a Republican from South Dakota, was commandeered to launch this resolution that was then passed, attaching his name to the history of US–Pakistan relations for years to come. Another hurdle was erected by Congressman Stephen Solarz of New York, whose amendment demanded that the president certify annually that Pakistan was not importing nuclear technology from the US. Failure of the US president to provide a waiver would bar aid to Pakistan. These two amendments represented the looming threat and control of the US over Pakistan's aid programme. This threat would not be exercised until after the Reagan years, when President George H.W. Bush refused to certify the foreign aid package and Pakistan was struck from the recipients' list.

BRASSTACKS

The Pakistanis themselves did not help matters at all. Faced with a potential threat to their eastern frontier from perennial opponent, India, who had assembled a huge force to conduct a war game called Brasstacks in January 1987, Pakistan felt it had to respond with alacrity. It moved forces into position to counter-attack Indian Punjab through its soft underbelly of the Sutlej–Beas gap and checkmated the Indian move. The Indians' aim in launching Brasstacks was to test their ability to mobilize forces and launch an offensive against Pakistan using their strike corps. According to the Pakistan Army's information on the exercise, it was also to 'test operational planning and reaction to the use of limited tactical nuclear weapons by the enemy [Pakistan] to blunt the offensive of the strike Corps.'[86] Brasstacks was divided into four sub-exercises, starting off with a war game in New Delhi from 21 to 25 July 1986, followed by another war game conducted by western command from 10–14 November 1986. The third phase, extending over November–December 1986, involved setting up standing operating procedures and drills, and formulating concepts related to specific areas such as communications, electronic warfare, amphibious operations, etc. The culmination of the operation was the final phase in which troops of both southern and western commands were used in two separate exercises, involving land, air, and even naval forces, in support of a deep penetration of Pakistan.

The area chosen for the exercise was Rajashtan, and the manoeuvres were to be on an East–West axis, coming close to the Pakistan border near

Bahawalpur, Marot, and Khairpur. According to Indian documents (which Pakistan managed to acquire), the idea was to capture Pakistani territory up to the Ravi River in a two-phase operation (first to the Sutlej and then to the Ravi River), bringing Pakistani reserves to battle at a place of India's choosing and thus to ensure their destruction. What made the Pakistanis nervous and forced them to counter with their own troop movements into the relatively undefended underbelly of the Indian Punjab was the fact that India partially mobilized its reserves, reactivated forward air bases, cancelled training courses, and also inducted the 6 Mountain Division into the Jammu area, while issuing instructions to formations to 'be ready for assigned operational roles at short notice.'[87] If Brasstacks was to be a precursor to an Indian attack into Sindh, it did not happen. However, the two nations had come close to a war, and the situation was only defused after Zia resorted to his famous 'cricket diplomacy' by going to India to watch a cricket match between India and Pakistan.

To further show off its nuclear potential Pakistan orchestrated a leak through Dr Abdul Qadeer Khan, the head of the Kahuta enrichment facility, to a respected Indian journalist, Kuldip Nayar, confirming that Pakistan had a nuclear weapon. When the story broke, there was the immediate and obligatory denial and retraction; and the intermediary, the editor of *The Muslim* (an English daily), Mushahid Hussain, ended up losing his job. Ironically, Zia himself was to tell *Time* magazine a month later: 'You can write today that Pakistan can build a bomb whenever it wishes.'[88] The US avoided opening up this issue in public, given the state of the Afghan war at that time. Further complicating the situation were the later revelations of more Pakistani-sponsored attempts to acquire nuclear technology in the United States. But Reagan stood firm in sticking to the letter of the Solarz amendment and issued his waiver in 1987.

The US was now seeking to find a way for the Soviets to exit Afghanistan peacefully. Pakistan, meanwhile, wanted to ensure that it got a compliant and acceptable Afghan government installed. Suspicion of each other reigned supreme among these two allies. The ISI wanted to keep the CIA in the dark about their conduct of operations and to strengthen the hands of their favourites; people like Gulbadin Hekmatyar. The CIA, meanwhile, sought to bypass the ISI and make direct contacts with the Mujahideen. Within four days of the signing of the Geneva Accord that led to the Soviet withdrawal— on 10 April 1988 at 9:35 a.m., to be precise—an explosion occurred in the secret ammunition storage dump at Ojhri Camp, near the boundary of Rawalpindi and Islamabad. (This storage dump was presumably being used to stash ammunition that was to be supplied to the Mujahideen). This was followed by an even bigger blast at 9:45 a.m. registering an intensity of 3.8 on the Richter scale. A rain of missiles and fire descended on the twin cities. By the time it ended, some 100 persons were dead and 1,100 injured,[89] including a celebrated politician and ex-air force hero, Khaqan Abbasi. The blast served to add to the tensions between General Zia and his civilian Prime Minister Junejo. An inquiry commission was set up, headed by the corps commander of X Corps, Lt. Gen. Imranullah Khan. Needless to say, this army officer's report, which was never made public but was leaked out in dribs and drabs, attributed the blast to an accident in mishandling of weapons that were being loaded for dispatch to the Mujahideen. But there was no unanimity on this. Immediately recriminations were made about the event and its subsequent inquiry, with the demands being made that Akhtar Abdur Rahman be held to blame for having sited the ammunition depot in such a vulnerable location in the centre of the city. Others sought to blame the DG ISI Hamid Gul, who was ready to accept the responsibility. The handling of the Ojhri investigation created further problems for Zia's relations with Junejo, and in fact culminated in the exit of the latter.

Whether the Ojhri blast was an accident or not, enough evidence pointed to either the Soviets or the United States as having caused it. Among many others in Pakistan, Brigadier Yousaf of the ISI notes that it may have been in the US's interest to allow the Soviets to make 'an uninterrupted retreat' from Afghanistan. The US did not wish the Mujahideen to have an unequivocal victory. To bolster his argument, he points to the lack of alacrity with which the US re-supplied the weapons lost in the Ojhri blast. Fresh supplies did not arrive from the United States till December 1988.[90] Brigadier Yousaf maintains that he and General Rahman had formulated a plan for laying siege to Kabul and bringing it down, thus winning the war in Afghanistan as a whole. But Rahman was posted out of the ISI before this could happen. Fate overtook both, generals Zia and Rahman.

A FATEFUL AIR CRASH

On 17 August 1988, General Zia, accompanied by a host of senior officers of the Pakistan Army, including the CJCS, Akhtar Abdur Rahman, as well as the US ambassador in Islamabad, Arnold Raphel and the defense attaché, Brigadier General Herbert M. Wassom—descended on a desolate bit of desert between Multan and Bahawalpur called the Tamewali firing range. They had been invited to observe the tank trials of the latest American battle tank, the M1/A1 Abrams. The US was pressing hard for Pakistan to acquire this tank, a deal that would have tied Pakistan to the US spare parts' pipeline for years to come. Major General Mahmud Ali Durrani, the GOC of the 1st Armour Division stationed at Multan and a former military secretary to Zia, had been instrumental in arranging the tank trial on behalf of the Armoured Corps

Directorate and getting it on Zia's agenda. General Rahman had found out about the event and sought an invitation first from Durrani and then from the VCOAS, General Mirza Aslam Beg, who reportedly told him that a different demonstration would be held to which he would be invited.[91] But Rahman's name was on the VIP list sent by the CGS, Lt. Gen. Mian Muhammad Afzaal, who too was to attend the tank trials. The US ambassador had asked on 9 August to attend the demonstration and was invited by the military secretary to the president, Brigadier Najeeb. A number of other generals were also invited to attend. The commander of the Bahawalpur Corps, Lt. Gen. Muhammad Shafiq, was asked to arrange a presentation on the status of his newly formed command. The programme was set at least five days before the event and, according to Durrani, the manifesto showing the names of the people travelling to Bahawalpur was ready and fixed days before the event. Both Raphel and Wassom were to go to Bahawalpur with Zia, although their own aircraft also went to Bahawalpur. General Beg flew there in his own small jet propeller plane. Zia and his generals took a helicopter to Tamewali.

The tank trial was a shambles. The 55-ton M1/A1 behemoth, designed for the cleaner climes and hard surfaces of Europe and North America, did not fare too well in the desert of the Tamewali. A film of the trials shows the tank trying to fire on the move and from a stationary position, surrounded by clouds of dust.[92] But the movement of the tanks was seriously constrained by the fact that its engines sucked up the fine dust of Tamewali and clogged its filters, jamming the Chrysler turbine engines. The most pathetic sight was of the tank trying to climb up a dirt ramp built at the site, getting stuck, and then sliding sideways off the ramp like a drunken sailor. Clearly, this was not the tank for the Pakistan Army. The VIP visitors returned to Bahawalpur. Zia attended the presentation by General Shafiq, and then, following *zohr* prayers, had lunch before heading to the airport.

Zia's aircraft was another US product: the redoubtable and seemingly indestructible C-130 Hercules, a cargo plane that had become a worthy successor to the famed DC-3 of Second World War fame and beyond. First introduced into the US Air Force inventory in 1956 as the C-130A, an upgraded version—the C-130B—came into service in 1959, and the last plane in that series was delivered in 1963. Zia would often use the C-130B, designated Pak One, with another C-130B designated Pak Two as a stand by. It was equipped with a roll-on VIP capsule that provided a comfortable, air-conditioned ride and some soundproofing.

17 August was a clear and sunny day in Bahawalpur when Zia and his party arrived at the airport at 3:30 p.m. Zia, as was his wont, invited other senior officers who had come to see the trials to jump into his aircraft. A number of them, including the CGS Afzaal, who was due to take a PIA flight from

Multan to Islamabad later that day, took him up on his offer. So did Major General Muhammad Hussain Awan, who commanded the 23 Division in Jhelum. The only one who did not choose to ride with Zia was Beg, who had his own plane standing near the president's C-130 but who was to admit later that had the president asked him one more time he would have jumped in. Beg was the last to shake Zia's hand before the latter climbed into his plane. Pakistan Air Force C-130B, serial number 62-3494, from the PAF's 35th Air Transport Wing, based at Chaklala, rumbled off from runway 26 at 3:46 p.m. carrying Zia, Rahman, Ambassador Raphel, General Wassom, and twenty-seven others. Visibility was five miles, good. The weather was clear, and the outside temperature was a toasty but dry 37 degrees centigrade. There was a light south-westerly breeze. Nothing unusual to see or report. A small Cessna had earlier completed a precautionary flight over the airport to ensure that there was no untoward activity or any lurking anti-aircraft weapons in sight. The other aircraft took off shortly and headed in their own directions. Zia's plane turned onto its course for Islamabad—out of sight of the air controllers at Bahawalpur, one of whom called Wing Commander Mash'hood Hassan, the pilot of Zia's plane, to confirm his position. Back came the reply: 'Pak One, Stand by.'[93] Those were the last words from Pak One.

Then, based on eyewitness accounts, in the clinical language of the subsequent official report: 'The aircraft was observed to be very low over the Sutlej River and varying about the pitch axis in an up and down motion. Some motion was also noted in yaw and roll. The pitching continued to worsen, according to witnesses, until a steep dive, steep climb, and near vertical dive resulted in the aircraft impacting the ground at approximately 1551E [3:51 p.m.]. The impact [angle] with the ground was estimated to be approximately 60–65 degrees.'[94] The crash site was barely 7.5 nautical miles from Bahawalpur airport. There were no survivors. All that was left was a mystery as to how and why the crash occurred. Within those five fateful minutes, Zia and his top military leadership had been eliminated and an era in Pakistan's history came to an end.

Meanwhile, Zia's VCOAS, Mirza Aslam Beg, was flying back to Rawalpindi with Hamid Niaz (MGO), Jehangir Karamat (DGMO), and Brigadier Ejaz Amjad. Beg's pilot Colonel Minhaj heard about the crash from a helicopter pilot headed for Multan who had landed at the crash site. General Shamim Alam, who was a passenger on one of the two helicopters headed for Multan, reported to Beg from the site of the crash that 'there is nothing left.' Beg and his fellow passengers had seen a column of smoke when they left Bahawalpur 'some 8 to 10 minutes' after they had taken off but paid no attention to it. Now they turned back, circled over the crash site, and after some internal discussion about going back to Bahawalpur, decided immediately that Beg was needed in the GHQ. Recounting that journey to army officers at the GHQ a few days later, Beg spoke emotionally of his anguish and the conflicting thoughts that raced through his head during that one-hour flight back to Rawalpindi.[95] According to Zia's close aides, Beg and Zia did not have a warm relationship. Beg was constantly being undermined by Zia through his direct communications with corps commanders and others who were supposed to report to Beg.

After arriving in Rawalpindi and consulting with his MGO Niaz, General Imranullah Khan, the corps commander X Corps (based in Rawalpindi), Imtiaz Warraich of the JCS HQ, General Karamat, and the ISI chief, Hamid Gul, Beg and his colleagues 'unanimously' decided not to impose martial law but to follow the constitutional route. The army brass decided to inform the air chief and the vice chief of naval staff (who was sitting in for the naval chief while the latter was abroad). The chairman of the Senate, Ghulam Ishaq Khan, next in line of succession after Zia, was 'invited' to come to GHQ around 7:30 p.m. (an action that effectively established the rank of the army above the civil,) where he was told that he would take over as the next President. Ishaq in turn made Beg the COAS.[96]

On the day of the crash, a thousand miles away, I (the author) was visiting my brother, then Lt. Gen. Asif Nawaz, in his home at Flagstaff House in Clifton, Karachi, where he was corps commander of V Corps. He first learned of the news of the crash from a police source. Immediately thereafter, he called his colleague Gen. Shafiq at Bahawalpur and asked if there were any instructions to go on alert. Shafiq was blasé in his response, saying: 'He's gone. That's it.' Sitting next to my brother as he slammed his telephone down in anger, I heard him mutter: 'He's not pushed! Something's not right.' Something was surely not right. But Pakistanis did not know about it from their own government until three hours after the crash. Indeed, although Beg was to assert that he informed his corps commanders and formation commanders while *en route* to Rawalpindi, they did not hear about it till much later. For that period, Pakistan did not have a head of state or government, since Zia had not named a prime minister to replace Junejo. It was not till later that night that Ishaq informed Pakistanis of the changes in their government and imposed a state of emergency in a televised address. The elections of 16 November promised by Zia were still to take place. But questions still remained about how Zia and Rahman had died and who was behind it.

THE IMMEDIATE AFTERMATH

Pakistan is known to be a Petri dish for conspiracy theories. The crash provided much fodder for speculation and discussion in the drawing rooms of the country and in streets and homes country-wide. The general assumption was that this was not an accident. If it had been one, the pilot or co-pilot would surely have screamed: 'Mayday!' Who was behind the crash? The list of suspects was large: the Soviets and their Afghan allies, still smarting under their losses in Afghanistan. If not the official Soviet and Afghan intelligence services, then at least a renegade group that was trying to salvage something out of the detritus of Afghanistan's lost war. The Indians, who saw Zia as an implacable foe and an Islamist who would never relent in his Jihad against them in Kashmir and in fomenting trouble among the rebellious Sikhs in eastern Punjab. The Israelis, who did not wish another nuclear power to emerge in the greater Near East. The Americans, who saw Zia's Islamicism and quest for nuclear weapons as a dangerous development. Domestically, the Shia community, who had been outraged at the murder of their revered leader Arif Al Hussaini and had threatened revenge. (Zia, being the ally of Sunni Saudi Arabia, was being identified as behind that murder). Within the army itself, there had been earlier attempts to get rid of Zia; after all, he had been blocking the rise of many others by staying in the dual driver's seat: that of army chief and president.

Beg sought to allay the fears of his senior military brass by convening a meeting shortly after the crash at the Ayub Hall near his office. Speaking in chaste Urdu, a visibly distraught and emotional Beg began with a prayer for the departed and then began recounting the events of 17 August. He started by labelling the crash a conspiracy and said they would find out whose conspiracy it was, how many 'of our own people were involved,' adding parenthetically that 'you cannot have a conspiracy without our own people' and promising that 'we will find them and bring them to justice.' He then turned to the events of 17 August. He said he came to many decisions during that flight back from Bahawalpur but then decided that he needed to take his colleagues' advice before acting. Although the Pakistan Army is a disciplined force and respects seniority, Beg probably understood that he had not established himself as the leader of the pack. Zia had not allowed that to happen. Beg referred respectfully to Zia as the 'Shaheed President' deeming him a martyr, (technically correct in orthodox Islam, since anyone who dies in an accident is considered a martyr and given instant access to heaven). After deciding on handing over titular power to the civilians under former super-bureaucrat Ghulam Ishaq Khan, Beg suggested a cabinet meeting that would be attended by the three service chiefs. He said that he recognized that it was 'illegal', but thought it necessary to show the country that the military was behind the change. The cabinet meeting ratified five decisions:

- Ishaq would be the acting president;
- The cabinet would remain and help run the country;
- The rule of law would be maintained;

- A state of emergency would be proclaimed to tackle any problems rapidly;
- An emergency council would be formed, including the senior ministers, the chief ministers of the four provinces, and the three service chiefs.

Beg then addressed the question of who might be behind the crash. His focus was on the Soviets and on India, and the 'threats against Pakistan from two sides.' He cited a statement by a Soviet spokesman of 13 August that threatened Pakistan if it did not 'change its attitude' toward Afghanistan, then 'Russia and Afghanistan would have only one option: to take retaliatory action against Pakistan.' Then he referred to the statement by the Indian Prime Minister Rajiv Gandhi 'from the tall ramparts of the Red Fort' in Delhi on 15 August, India's Independence Day, that 'if Pakistan does not stop aiding the Sikhs, then India will be forced to take action against Pakistan. I hope that Pakistan realizes its mistakes otherwise we will make such a move that Pakistan will regret its actions.' He then reverted to the conspiracy theory, stating that 'unless our own people are involved, no one can damage our country.'

Beg underlined the importance of following the constitutional path and of having civilian rule, which were the impetus behind the decisions of 17 August. He said he wanted to consult his corps commanders, so he called them to Rawalpindi for a meeting (here he misspoke during his GHQ talk, citing a meeting on the 'night of 16th and 17th' when he meant the 18th and 19th). The meeting lasted into the night, ending around 2:00 a.m. on 20 August, (the day that Zia was to be buried). This meeting resulted in major decisions on four main points:

- Supremacy of Islam;
- Obedience of law and justice;
- Support for the freedom war in Afghanistan;
- Democracy till 16 November 1988, when elections were slated, and the installation of a new government after that.

INVESTIGATION: A CUL DE SAC

In the days immediately after the crash, hectic activity took place to decide, among other things, where Zia was to be buried. (His COS, General Refaqat was asked by President Ishaq to select a spot, and he suggested the Faisal Mosque in Islamabad.) There was also a demand for an investigation from the public and from within the army. Beg had promised that there would be one. But there was no evidence of the army conducting a detailed investigation on its own. Instead, the US offered to help: a joint team of the Pakistan Air Force and the US Air Force was authorized by Air Marshal Hakimullah to:

- Inquire into the circumstances under which Hercules C-2130 aircraft S No 62-3494 crashed on 17 August 1988;
- Assess the extent and cause of the damage;
- Apportion blame, if any;
- Make recommendations to avoid recurrence of similar nature.[97]

Lacking an ambassador on the spot, and recognizing the need for one immediately in this sensitive period and super sensitive slot, the US acted with alacrity. Robert Oakley, who had been serving at the White House in the NSC and had been involved in South Asian affairs, was asked to pack two suitcases and told: 'Well, you go. Be the new ambassador.'[98] And so he left. 'Initially, we, like Pakistan, thought that there was something suspicious there. So we looked at everything as best we could internally and externally. And all of our intelligence assets were put to look for what might be behind this because we feared [that] this is part of a bigger attack upon Pakistan, just as most Pakistanis thought it was too,' Oakley recalls. In fact, Secretary of State George P. Schultz, assured the Pakistani president and the army chief, (according to Oakley,) that 'all of our intelligence assets are focused upon the threat to Pakistan. And if we find out anything, we'll let you know.' But he added that: 'We found nothing, which was a pleasant surprise.' When asked about the role of the FBI, he appeared to have suffered from a memory lapse after all these years. About the 'long arm law' that allowed the FBI to investigate the deaths overseas of American citizens, Oakley said: 'At that stage it didn't exist.' In fact, the law was in force at that time. The 1984 Comprehensive Crime Control Act authorized the FBI to investigate international terrorism cases where Americans were taken hostage. A 1986 Omnibus Diplomatic Security Antiterrorism Act broadened the FBI's extra-territorial responsibilities to include terrorist incidents in which an American is assaulted or murdered.

The US charge d'affaires in Islamabad, Beth Jones, recalls accurately that the FBI law did exist and that in her view the FBI needed to be involved. She also recalls that Oakley agreed with that. But Oakley's recollection is that the FBI was initially asked and 'they said no.' Jones is very specific about how the US side handled the matter. She states that the first CENTCOM commander, Marine General George B. Crist, said that since a military officer had been killed, it was the military's jurisdiction and not that of the FBI. Jones recalls that later on, the FBI was called in and they sent their agent in charge of the Athens office, but by then it was too late.[99] General Crist, now retired in Florida, does not recall details of what transpired at that time except that

Richard L. Armitage (Assistant Secretary of Defense for International Security) may have been involved in the decision. According to Crist, Armitage was apparently making decisions from the Pentagon on this matter at that time.[100] Armitage recalls that there 'was a lot of confusion' about the investigation. There were also allegations swirling about the involvement of the Afghan secret police, Khad. He believes that the Pakistanis wanted to handle the investigation themselves. Reports also emerged about the frequent failures of this type of aircraft, leading to crashes. The Pakistanis, according to Armitage, wanted to take the lead and the US conceded. He did recall speaking with the FBI and testifying before a House committee to that effect.[101] The close collaboration between the US and Pakistan militaries, which remained a cornerstone of the US–Pakistan relationship, may well have helped snuff out the detailed examination of the evidence at that time.

There were also concerns on both sides about the precarious situation in Pakistan. Oakley recalls that the US 'sent warnings to everybody, which is the way the United States acted at that stage certainly. Be careful! Don't try to take advantage of the situation in Pakistan because the United States is looking after it.' In his view:

> From our[the US's] point of view, there were two extremely important things. One was to find out all we could possibly find out about who and what was behind it. And the second one was to make sure that the confidence between the United States and the President and the Chief of the Army Staff and others was not upset. I think, actually, from that point of view it came out pretty well because of the way we conducted the investigation and the fact that, for once, we were able to keep it from being public until the investigation was completed, despite the screams from Washington saying, 'You hide things from us.'

Against this background, the joint air force team undertook its inquiry of the crash, focusing primarily on the technical aspects. Their findings were unequivocal and unanimous, although the US tried to put a different spin on the results, trying to establish that a technical malfunction may have caused the crash. They examined the possibility of weather, fuel contamination, an external missile attack, an internal fire or explosion, equipment malfunction, and structural failure in flight before coming to the conclusion that none of these had been a factor that caused the airplane to evidence the dolphin-like movement known as 'Phugoid,' where the 'dead-stick control' of the aircraft pulls the plane up automatically each time it goes into an uncontrolled dive. This yo-yo motion was reported by eye witnesses on the ground.

The team hypothesized that the control problems leading to the crash could have been caused by either 'a mechanical or hydraulic fault in the aircraft systems,' or was 'induced by the pilots either voluntarily or involuntarily.' Their investigations and tests at the Lockheed simulation centre ruled out the first. The only other cause left was sabotage. This could have been effected in one of four ways: by deliberate or mechanical interference with the flight control centre, physical interference with the controls in the cockpit, incapacitation of the pilots at the controls—either singly or simultaneously as a result of a criminal act, or by the use of explosive devices to achieve either of the first three. Available evidence ruled out the first, but an experienced hand could have contaminated the elevator boost package—a remote possibility, but one that the team could not rule out. Although lacking a cockpit voice recorder, the possibility of physical interference with the controls could not be ruled out either but the team thought it was improbable given that there are more than two persons in the cockpit whom an intruding hijacker would have to overpower in the short span of some two minutes before the impact. As for the final possibility, incapacitating the flight crew, the board felt that it was possible.

The likely methodology used to incapacitate the pilots could be gleaned from the declassified summary of the report of the Board of Enquiry that was officially released to the press in Pakistan a couple of months after the accident. Detailed articles appeared a few years later in a local weekly.[102] The story of the investigations conducted by the board in Pakistan, which pointed to sabotage as a cause of the crash of the ill-fated plane, unfolds as follows.

One of the most experienced member of the joint team, Group Captain Zaheer Zaidi, and his colleagues collected the first batch of samples from the crash site and delivered them, within thirty hours of the accident, for analysis at the Electron Microscope Laboratory (EM Lab) of PINSTECH, Islamabad.[103] By the morning of 19 August preliminary evidence indicating foul play had been obtained in the form of surface deposits on the inner side of the edges of a huge hole in the aft cargo door. These deposits contained high concentrations of unusual elements antimony (35%), phosphorus (34%), as well as other suspect elements. The fuselage does not contain these elements which are essential components of detonators. Subsequent examination of samples from other areas of the plane revealed significant amount of the unusual elements on the surface of a section of the cargo hold floor as well as on the area behind the pilot's seat in the cockpit.

To confirm or refute the suggestion that the accident could have been due to mechanical malfunction resulting from a faulty hydraulic pump, and to exclude some of the other possibilities, the pumps, filters, etc., from the plane were analyzed at the EM Lab. No problem was detected with the pump pistons and nothing abnormal was discovered with the particles usually found in used hydraulic fluid or on the filters. The likelihood of mechanical failure was thus ruled out.

Samples of tests conducted of various explosives at Pakistan Ordnance Factory were also analyzed in the EM Lab. Relative concentration of various elements in these tests and its comparison with that in samples from the plane enabled the identification of detonators possibly used on board. Burnt mango peel and mango seeds found some distance from the crash site had also been provided for analysis. A surface deposit with potassium content up to 84 per cent was found on the mango seeds while antimony up to 65 per cent was found on both sides of the mango peel. It was known that two crates of mangoes had been loaded aboard the aircraft as a gift for the president. The final conclusion of the Board of Enquiry was that low intensity detonations from explosives hidden in the mango crates could have been used to release a gas that rendered the passengers and the pilots unconscious resulting in the crash of the plane.

The actual methods to incapacitate the flight crew could have ranged from the 'very simple to the ultra sophisticated.' The simple techniques would have left physical traces that they did not find. Hence, the board pointed to the possibility that some 'specialist organization well-versed in carrying out such tasks and possessing all the means and abilities for its execution' was behind this event: Detecting such an act of sabotage is very difficult. But the board came to the conclusion that

> ...a chemical agent may well have been used to cause incapacitation of the flight deck crew. The chemical agent could have been packaged in innocuous containers such beverage tins, gift parcels, aerosol cans, thermos flasks etc and smuggled on board without arousing suspicion. The activation of these gases during flight, either manually, remotely or automatically would result in the insidious incapacitating of the flight deck crew.[104]

The board was unable to pinpoint the types of chemicals used and their exact application. Since no autopsies were performed, they could not pursue this approach. They did point to the presence of 'high levels of potassium on a mango seed and antimony and chlorine on the mango peel'. The cockpit-supporting rod also had high levels of phosphorous and antimony, and the aft cargo door area had high levels of phosphorous, antimony and sulphur. Further the alcohol, tobacco and firearms (ATF) laboratory report states that traces of PETN, (pentaerythritol tetranitrate) which is a secondary high explosive, were found on the butt end of the emergency escape hatch rope near the aft cargo door. Although the ATF discounted a high explosion, the presence of PETN 'is unusual', especially in the presence of the other chemicals such as antimony and phosphorous. A strong possibility arose that someone could have caused an explosion to release a gas that would have incapacitated the crew rapidly. One form of such a gas is VX, a nerve agent that is normally in liquid form but becomes a gas when exposed to oxygen. It is ten times more toxic than Sarin (another nerve gas), and kills almost immediately if just a drop comes into contact with a person's skin or is inhaled. It basically seals the central nervous system, causing convulsions, paralysis and death.[105] If an agent like this had been used, it would have resulted in the instantaneous freezing of the pilots and other crew members with their hands locked on the controls, causing the yo-yo movement of the C-130 that was observed by witnesses on the ground.

Another method of incapacitating the crew would involve painting the surfaces of the controls inside the cockpit with a psycho-active drug similar to the drug Ecstasy sold on the US narcotics market, an action that would take no more than a minute or two, and could have easily be done during the stop over in Bahawalpur, when there was much activity in and around the aircraft. Workmen had serviced the VVIP capsule, repaired a cargo door, and otherwise been in the aircraft. According to the *Defense and Foreign Affairs Weekly*, 'a top level chemical warfare expert ...revealed to the *Weekly* that the chemicals which apparently caused the crash of the Lockheed C-130 in which then President Zia ul-Haq was killed were related to the type of chemicals which officials from the West German firm, Imhausen, have been charged with selling illegally in the United States....The drug, 3-methyl-tentanyl, was probably placed on the controls and headsets used by the aircrew. 3-methyl-fentanyl, which is 3,000 times more powerful than heroin, was probably put on to the controls and headsets in a dose sufficiently diluted to allow an elapse of time before fully disorienting the aircrew. The drug permeates the skin.' Imhausen had been charged with setting up a pharmaceutical plant in Libya but the report in the *Weekly* said that 'the Libyan plant had the capacity to make such designer drugs as MDMA [Ecstasy], but there was no evidence to suggest that the drugs used to assassinate President Zia came from that facility.'[106]

It was no surprise that the joint Pak–US air force team came to the simple conclusion that the most probable cause of the accident was a 'criminal act or sabotage perpetuated (sic) in the aircraft leading to the crash of the aircraft.' What was surprising, however, was the subsequent effort of both the Pakistan government and the US government to prevent any detailed examination of the evidence or of persons associated with the aircraft, its security, or possible motives behind the crash. The US CENTCOM and State Department prevented the FBI from coming into the picture but did not appear to investigate the deaths of its own ambassador and general. The fear may have been that of finding incriminating evidence which would implicate a country in the region or even one of the superpowers of the time. A strange footnote to this whole episode was the accusation by the US ambassador to India, John Gunther Dean, a respected foreign service veteran: 'Dean thought that plot to rid the world of General Zia bore the hallmarks of Israel, or specifically the Israeli intelligence agency, Mossad.'[107] Dean came back to Washington and tried to push his theory. He was instead declared mentally incompetent, lost his medical and security clearances, and ended up resigning from the Foreign Service at the age of 62. He was then forbidden from going back to India, sent to his home in Switzerland for six weeks, and only then was he allowed to go to pack his belongings in New Delhi. Even today from his home in Paris, Dean still persists in his suspicions. An intriguing possibility exists of the Mossad or even the CIA launching a false flag operation to kill Zia, using Pakistani collaborators (the insiders that General Beg alluded to) as witting or unwitting agents. When they ended up killing the US ambassador and a general, there was no other way for the US except to seal the investigation. Even today, as Barbara Crossette (formerly of *The New York Times)* informed me, the US National Archives has not declassified some 250 pages related to the crash. Why?

The range of suspects was wide. But nothing much was done to pursue them methodically. The matter was handed over to a senior policeman, F.K. Bandial, rather than the ISI or MI to pursue. A judicial inquiry commission was also set up and produced no results. No one appears to have wanted to upset the status quo. When General Zia's son sought to get the inquiry opened up, he received a letter from Bandial offering to send someone to interview him. Ijazul Haq did not respond to that request. The sons of General Akhtar Abdur Rahman tried pursuing the matter also, but reportedly were dissuaded from doing so by their US contacts. The US behaviour was strange in that it tried to present the crash as a mechanical failure of the aircraft to the press and to paint the joint team's findings as those of the government of Pakistan alone.

Many questions still remained. Why did the three member judicial commission, headed by Supreme Court Justice Shafi-ur-Rehman, constituted in 1992 by Prime Minister Nawaz Sharif to probe further into the issue not reach a conclusion? Was it due to the in-camera testimony of Group Captian Zaidi who may have expressed his suspicions and apprehensions? The commission by the witnesses was also told that because of a 3 x 2 meter oval hole in the aft cargo door, that indicated that the plane may have been hit by a missile was not further pursued as no corroborating evidence was found on the outer surface of the hole by the EM Lab. The commission instructed one of the explosives experts to physically examine the door and report if it was possible to discern that the plane was hit by a missile or it crashed because of an explosion within. The cargo door, weighing 2,200 kg was not found among the debris of the plane so securely stored in Multan. Why were half-hearted and innocuous efforts made to delay the provision of results of analysis by the EM Lab to the board members? Why was Group Captain Zaheer Zaidi relegated to the position of base commander of the miniscule PAF base at Lower Topa immediately after the enquiry, then sent on deputation to the navy and finally retired in 1991?

Even the Pakistan Army seemed to have lost its desire to pursue the matter. General Beg's own inquiry was buried. The sixth meeting that year of the JCSC was held on 22 October 1988, (the first one since the death of Zia). It began with a 'recitation from Holy Quran followed by its translation,' and then surprisingly it moved immediately to item 1-A: 'Re-employment of retired armed forces officers in civil departments.'[108] Business as usual! This was the first meeting that General Beg attended as army chief, and the first that Admiral Iftikhar Sirohey chaired. Despite Beg's emotional promise to the GHQ officers to hunt down the perpetrators of this crime, there was no item on the agenda to discuss the circumstances of Zia's death, nor any follow-up investigations. No motion was presented to pursue an investigation or bring the perpetrators to task.

Over time, the new President Ghulam Ishaq Khan and the army chief, Mirza Aslam Beg settled into their posts. Elections were held, and the daughter of Zulfikar Ali Bhutto, the young Benazir Bhutto, was elected prime minister. 'I do not regret the death of Zia,' she told *The Economist.*[109] She did not have much incentive to find the culprits, especially if it created waves for her fledgling administration. She had her own battles to fight—of which there were to be many.

NOTES

1. Many of his hastily announced measures were withdrawn or amended in the early days of Zia's regime, leading to the popular redefinition of his title of CMLA (chief martial law administrator) as 'Cancel My Last Announcement'.

2. Lt. Gen. Faiz Ali Chishti, *Betrayals of Another Kind: Islam, Democracy and the Army in Pakistan* (Rawalpindi: PCL Publishing House), p. 135.

3. Shahid Javed Burki, 'Pakistan Under Zia, 1977–1988,' *Asian Survey*, Vol. XXVIII, No. 10, October 1988. Burki, a senior World Bank official at the time, was a confidant of Zia and an economic adviser to the general. He had written a critical history of the Bhutto years. Zia invited him to write Zia's biography but then delayed the venture, suggesting that it would be best left for the period after Zia left office.

4. Lawrence Lifschultz, 'Bush, Drugs and Pakistan: Inside the Kingdom of Heroin,' *The Nation*, 14 November 1988, p. 477. Lifschultz also cites *The Herald* of September 1985: 'The drug is carried in NLC trucks, which come sealed from the NWFP [North West Frontier Province] and are never checked by the police. They come down from Peshawar to Piri, Jungshahi, Jhimpir where they deliver their cargo, sacks of grains, to government godowns [depots]. Some of these sacks contain packets of heroin.' See also Alfred W. McCoy, *The Politics of Heroin* (second revised edition, Lawrence Hill Books, 2003), pp. 466–87 for a detailed review of the drug trade in Pakistan resulting from the Afghan War.

5. *Constitution of the Islamic Republic of Pakistan 1973*, Mansoor Book House, Lahore, pp. 18–19.

6. *The Pakistan Times*, 6 July 1977, quoting Zia's speech of 7 p.m. the previous evening on the assumption of power.

7. General K.M. Arif, *Working with Zia: Pakistan's Power Politics 1977–1988* (Karachi: Oxford, 1995), p. 110.

8. Louis D. Hayes, *The Struggle for Legitimacy in Pakistan* (Lahore: Vanguard, 1986), p. 261.
9. Arif, *Working*, p. 113. See also Chisti, *Betrayals*, p. 18 for a detailed report of that and subsequent meetings between the two.
10. Gavin Young, *The Observer*, 1 October 1978.
11. Arif, *Working*, pp. 200–201.
12. See Colonel Rafiuddin, *Bhutto key Akhri 323 din (Bhutto's Final 323 Days)* (Lahore: Jang Publishers), pp. 114–115.
13. Once the executioner had done his duty he descended to the area below the gallows to straighten the body. Rafiuddin recalls remembering that Bhutto had said in his cell that night that he wished the army soldier guarding his room, Havildar Mehdi Khan of 27 Punjab Regiment, to receive his watch. A debate ensued among the jailers about who ought to get the watch but Rafi insisted it be returned to the family and also asked for the wedding band that he had seen Bhutto fiddle with. The ring was not to be found. So, Rafiuddin asked that the executioner Tara Masih be searched. Sure enough the ring was produced from his pocket and later handed over with the watch and other belongings to the family by the army. Rafiuddin, *Bhutto*, p. 126.
14. One detailed account of that period and Bhutto's final hours is by Brigadier, later Major General, Rahat Latif, entitled *...Plus Bhutto's Episode: An Autobiography* (Lahore: Jang Publishers, 1993). Latif was not present inside the jail at the time of the execution and relies on second-hand accounts by jailers. He too was accused of having beaten Bhutto and denies that in this book.
15. Rushdie, a friend of the author since the 1960s, even gave the offending tall colonel my first name, in his inimitable fashion!
16. United States Department of State, Afghanistan in 1977: An External Assessment, 30 January 1978. Cited in The National Security Archives' AFGHANISTAN: THE MAKING OF U.S. POLICY, 1973–1990 by Steve Galster, 9 October 2001. http://www.gwu.edu/ ~nsarchiv/NSAEBB/NSAEBB57/essay.html#docs, accessed 23 February 2007.
17. Brigadier Mohammad Yousaf and Major Mark Adkin, *The Bear Trap: Afghanistan's Untold Story* (Lahore: Jang Publishers, 1992), p. 40.
18. Arif, *Working*, pp. 306–307.
19. Arif Ayub, former director Afghan desk, Ministry of Foreign Affairs.
20. Galster, 'Afghanistan: the Making of U.S. Policy, 1973–1990.'
21. Interview Prince Turki Al Faisal, Washington DC.
22. Yousaf and Adkin, *The Bear*, p. 46.
23. Out of a total of four MRDs (Motor Rifle Divisions) of 11,000 each and one and half AADs (Air Assault Divisions), one MRD and AAD were based in Kabul, plus a Guards Air Assault Division at Bagram outside Kabul, providing a mobile reserve. ISI sources, Pakistan. Yousaf and Adkin, *The Bear*.
24. 'The Outrageous Strategy to destroy Russia' by Arthur Lepic. See: http://www.voltairenet. org/article30038.html accessed 23 February 2007.
25. Arif, *Working*, p. 315.
26. Dennis Kux, *The United States and Pakistan 1947–2000* (Washington, D.C.: Woodrow Wilson Center Press, and Baltimore and London: Johns Hopkins University Press, 2001), p. 254.
27. Arif Ayub, former director Afghan desk. Ayub cites the high birth rate of the refugees in Pakistan that accounts for some 3 million refugees in 2007. Well after many had returned home to Afghanistan. A figure of 3 million is mentioned in 'The Effect of the Afghan Refugees on Pakistan' by Grant Farr in *Zia's Pakistan: Politics and Stability in a Frontline State* edited by Craig Baxter (Westview Press. 1985), p. 97.
28. McCoy, *The Politics*, p. 480.
29. Ibid.
30. Arif Ayub, e-mail exchange, 24 April 2007.

31. Yousaf and Adkin, *The Bear*, p. 20.

32. Interview with Lt. Gen. Hamid Gul.

33. 'The Military and Security in Pakistan' by Rodney Jones in Baxter, *Zia's Pakistan*, p. 73.

34. My brother, Asif Nawaz, promoted to brigadier at that time, was posted to help raise this new headquarters under Lt. Gen. Jamal Said Mian in Quetta and remained there till he was posted as the GOC 7 Division in Peshawar.

35. Yousaf and Adkin, *The Bear*, p. 102 and conversations with my brother, Asif Nawaz, then a brigadier in Quetta.

36. Turki interview.

37. In his magisterial survey of the war on terror, *Ghost Wars* (New York: Penguin Press, 2004), p. 71, for example, Steve Coll, cites a very specific story of a Saudi agent Ahmed Badeeb who arrived at Karachi airport carrying a suitcase filled with $1.8 million cash to be delivered to President Zia in Rawalpindi. Very improbably, no one met the agent at the airplane in Karachi. He was left to fend for himself with inquisitive customs officials while General Akhtar Rahman and others reportedly waited to receive him in Rawalpindi. For anyone who has dealt with Pakistani bureaucracy, this story does not ring true, since even the lowliest foreign visitor has protocol arranged for him to make it through customs and immigration without any let or hindrance. Coll, who had travelled in the region, ought to have been aware of these procedures. Prince Turki flatly denies that any such incident occurred. It is likely that Badeeb conflated another experience involving private cash transfers with an official trip to Pakistan.

38. Arif, *Working*, p. 319.

39. Yousaf and Adkin, *The Bear*, pp. 105–110.

40. Ayub, op. cit.

41. Among them was a celebrated descendant of the former Afghan King Abdur Rehman named Yahya Effendi, whose parents had settled in Rawalpindi.

42. Yousaf and Adkin, *The Bear*, p. 29.

43. Conversations with various ISI veterans.

44. Hamid Gul interview.

45. Chishti, *Betrayals*, p. 191.

46. David B. Ottaway, 'Stingers Were Key Weapon In Afghan War, Army Finds,' *The Washington Post,* Wednesday, July 1989, p. A2.

47. Kux, *The United States and Pakistan*, p. 257.

48. Foreign office staffer.

49. Speech by Andropov, 4 January 1983, VA-01/40473, Bundesarchiv-Militärarchiv, Freiburg; translated by Svetlana Savranskaya.

50. Minutes of the Conference of the Secretaries of the CC CPSU, held in the office of CC CPSU General Secretary Comrade M.S. Gorbachev, 15 March 1985. http://www.gwu. edu/~nsarchiv/NSAEBB/NSAEBB172/Doc5.pdf last accessed on 8 March 2007.

51. Raja Anwar, *The Terrorist Prince* (Lahore: Vanguard Books. Translated by Khalid Hasan, 1998), pp. 134–135. The major runway used for landing aircraft at Chaklala ran East-West and normally landings and take-offs were in an East-West direction, making Zia's aircraft a predictable target.

52. Anwar, *The Terrorist*, pp. 95–115.

53. Source: then Major General Asif Nawaz, GOC, 7 Division, Peshawar.

54. Arif, *Working*, pp. 228–9.

55. Ibid., p. 230.

56. Interview with his director general martial law and chief of staff, Major General Malik Abdul Waheed.

57. Lt. Gen. (retd) Ejaz Azim, 'Unfair Criticism of Generals Deplored,' 28 June 1987, *The Muslim.*

58. Islamabad Diary, 'Don't Put them in Suzukis' by 'Watchman, *Dawn,* 8 July 1987.

59. Former member of the IJT, who wished to remain anonymous.
60. Benazir Bhutto, *Daughter of the East: An Autobiography* (London: Hamish Hamilton,1988), p. 271.
61. Ibid., pp. 278–9.
62. As early as 14 August 1982, Gulbadin Hekmatyar had tried to align himself openly with the Jamaat-i-Islami to help organize a march through Peshawar with the Jamaat on the occasion of Pakistan's Independence Day, ostensibly to celebrate the birth of Pakistan. My brother, then Major General Asif Nawaz, was the GOC 7 Division and ex-officio sub-martial law administrator under Governor Fazle Haq. I was visiting him at that time. On 13 August, he was told about these plans in the early afternoon and also of plans by the PPP to also take out a procession, ostensibly for the same reason: to celebrate Pakistan's birthday. Sensing the possibility of a clash, General Asif Nawaz called Hekmatyar to his office and asked him if he knew who was allowing him to stay in a safe and secure Peshawar suburb. 'The army' replied Hekmatyar. General Nawaz then threatened to deport him to the border region if he interfered in Pakistani politics from where he told Hekmatyar, the Soviets could easily come and lift him away. A check-mated Hekmatyar withdrew from the procession. Other leaders of the various parties were detained for the night. No untoward events occurred the next day.
63. Riaz M. Khan, *Untying the Afghan Knot: Negotiating the Soviet Withdrawal* (Durham and London: Duke University Press, 1991), pp. 226–7.
64. Arif, *Working*, p. 391.
65. *Dawn*, Karachi, 31 May 1988 cited in Arif, *Working*, p. 391.
66. Two now retired generals recounted how they had to deal with the *maulvis* in their commands to avoid interference in their operations. In one case, the religious teacher had decreed that it was un-Islamic to wear shorts. So afternoon sports were cancelled till the new commander arrived and sarcastically told his officers in front of the *maulvi* that television was forbidden too, since it too was un-Islamic! This provoked a huge outcry. The *maulvi* was then summoned and told that he would be required to attend physical training as a full member of the regiment and would be expected to accompany the troops on all field exercises and battles. The other case involved the *maulvi's* fundamentalist sermons after Friday prayers. The commander in this case asked for advance drafts of the sermons, an arduous task for the *maulvi* who was used to extemporaneous sermons and who sought to be excused from doing that work. Soon after that the commander gave a list of prescribed subjects on which sermons could be delivered. The army currently has a list of approved topics that are used for regimental sermons.
67. I was visiting PMA, Kakul when this occurred.
68. Data provided by GHQ, Pakistan Army to the author.
69. See also the very useful chart showing the ranks and generational gaps in Stephen P. Cohen, *The Pakistan Army* (Berkeley: University of California Press, 1984), p. 56.
70. Rodney W. Jones in Baxter, op. cit., p. 74.
71. Maj. (Retd.) Agha Humayun Amin 'Handling of Armoured Corps as a Case Study, Part II,' *Defence Journal.* Issue Number, 3-4-1979, Vol. 5, Karachi, 1979.
72. Brigadier Syed A.I. Tirmazi (1985), *Profiles of Intelligence* (Combined Printers. Library of Congress Catalogue No. 95-930455).
73. 'Purging Pakistan's Jihadi Legacy' by Syed Saleem Shahzad, Asiatimes Online, 22 December 2004. http://www.atimes.com/atimes/South_Asia/FL22Df03.html accessed 2 March 2007.
74. 'Zia, The Stephanian' by a special correspondent, *News India*, 4 November 1988, p. 18. This article also contains a rare photograph of Zia as a young man being made up to play the role of a *fakir* in a college play. His college mates also recall that he and two of his platoon mates in the 9th University Training Corps were rated the best turned out cadets. D.P. Basu recalls that Zia 'used to be very particular about attending the parade which used to be held at 7 a.m. in Red Fort even in winter.'

75. On the moral front, the military regime continued some of the worst practices of the previous regimes, including surreptitious audio and video recordings of political opponents' most private moments. Senior military officers with access to these videos would then deride the subjects of their surveillance as being immoral or corrupt, while they saw nothing wrong in their own actions.

76. Peter Truell and Larry Gurwin, *False Profits: The Inside Story of the BCCI, the World's Most Corrupt Financial Empire*, New York: Houghton Mifflin, 1992, pp. 80–81.

77. Ibid., pp. 91–93.

78. Thomas Petzinger Jr. and Peter Truell, 'Patronage Banking: BCCI Makes its mark through intimate ties to Pakistani leaders,' *The Wall Street Journal*, 23 October 1991, p. 1.

79. Truell and Gurwin, *False Profits*, p. 144.

80. Lifschultz, '*Bush, Drugs and Pakistan*', p. 492.

81. 'Its an absolute lie!', Ijazul Haq interview by Lawrence Lifschultz, *Newsline*, July 1990, p. 74.

82. Lifschultz, '*Bush, Drugs and Pakistan*', p. 494.

83. Kux, *The United States and Pakistan*, pp. 276–7.

84. George Crile, *Charlie Wilson's War* (New York: Grove Press, 2003), p. 481.

85. Interview with Richard L. Armitage, who was at this meeting.

86. Pakistan Army GHQ document on Brasstacks and Zarb-e-Momin.

87. Pakistan Army GHQ document.

88. Kux, *The United States and Pakistan*, p. 285.

89. Arif, *Working*, p. 386.

90. Yousaf and Adkin, *The Bear*, p. 223. Zia's former COS, Major General Malik Abdul Waheed, also stated that although he did not have direct evidence he believed that the US must have been behind this sabotage of the weapons pipeline to prevent the Mujahideen from winning a clear victory. Interview with author.

91. Arif, *Working*, p. 405. Arif notes that Beg's recollection is at variance with the GHQ records. Other details form author's interview with Durrani.

92. I was shown this film by a defence attaché at the Pakistan embassy in Washington after the event.

93. Edward Jay Epstein, 'How General Zia went down,' *Vanity Fair*, June 1989, pp. 42–60 contains one of the best reconstruction of events related to the crash published in the West. Arif, *Working*, pp. 397–409 provides very useful additional details but no clear idea of who may have been behind the crash.

94. Government of Pakistan accident investigation report prepared by the Pakistan Air Force Board of Inquiry, headed by Air Commodore Abbas H. Mirza, and including PAF's Air Commodore Muzammil Saeed, Group Captain Zaheer H. Zaidi, and Wing Commander Sabahat Ali Mufti, and the US Air Force Technical and Advisory Team headed by Colonel Daniel E. Sowada, and including Lt. Col. Bruce Blocher, Major William Rouse, Captain Stuart Takahara, Captain Dennis Simonson, and Captain William Callahan. Text contained in message from Ambassador Robert Oakley in Islamabad to Department of State. Photo copy provided to author.

95. Videotape of General Beg's talk after the crash before the officers of the Pakistan Army GHQ. Translated from Urdu to English by the author.

96. Arif, *Working*, p. 402.

97. GOP and US Air Force report, op. cit.

98. Interview with Ambassador Robert Oakley.

99. Interview with Ambassador Beth Jones.

100. Telephone conversation with General George B. Crist, 8 March 2007.

101. Interview with Robert L. Armitage.

102. *Takbeer*, Karachi, issues of 20 August 1992 and 19 August 1993. The likely source may have been Group Captian Zaidi, who is reported to have confided to associates that the crash

had been caused by 'our own people' and then covered up. The *Takbeer* report also stated that the aft cargo door had disappeared, and along with it the evidence of an explosion inside the aircraft or from outside (if there was a simultaneous rocket fired on the aeroplane).

103. Khan A. Shoaib, PAEC, who headed the research at that end. This sub-section profits form his recollections and records provided to the author directly.
104. GOP and US Air Force Report, op. cit.
105. www.mayoclinic.com/health/infectious-disease/MH0027, accessed 12/19/2005.
106. *Defense and Foreign Affairs Weekly*, 13-19 March 1989. Alexandria VA.Volume XV. Number 10. Page 1.
107. Barbara Crossette, 'Who Killed Zia?' *World Policy Journal,* New York. Fall 2005. Vol 22, Issue 3, pp. 94–102. Crossette a veteran foreign correspondent with experience in South Asia was a colleague of mine when I started at *The New York Times* in 1972.
108. Secret. Joint Staff Headquarters: Minutes of the 6/88 meeting of the the Joint Chiefs of Staff Committee held at JSHQ on 22 October 1988. Pakistan Army GHQ Archives.
109. 20 August 1988, p. 27.

15 | The Troika's Musical Chairs

The trouble with military rule is that every colonel or general is soon full of ambition.

– General Yakubu Gowon of Nigeria[1]

Democracy is not something you put away for ten years, and then in the 11th year you wake up and start practicing again. We have to begin to learn to rule ourselves again.

– Chinua Achebe[2]

After eleven years of continuous dictatorship, Pakistan, like many African and Asian nations, had to re-learn the ways of democracy. Unfortunately, the class monitors were the army and the bureaucracy—two institutions that had known little else than autocratic rule for the most part—and often saw the will of the people as something to be feared because it was unpredictable and unmanageable. In less than five years after General Ziaul Haq's death, the country would see two prime ministers come and go, and two army chiefs as well. In the eleven years that Zia ruled Pakistan with an iron fist, and installed his carefully selected candidates in the Senate and the National Assembly as well as in other leading positions, the military–bureaucracy alliance had seen its heyday. It would have a difficult time adjusting to civilian rule.

Upon Zia's death, the supreme bureaucrat Ghulam Ishaq Khan found himself in a position to be president with the super powers granted by Zia's 8th Amendment to the constitution that effectively changed the parliamentary system to a presidential one. However, despite the fact that the new army chief, General Mirza Aslam Beg, decided to give Ishaq the role of acting president, he was not about to give up his own ambitions nor his interest in running the country. The president, the army chief, and the prime minister would become the troika that would run Pakistan's fissiparous politics for the next eleven years, till the cycle repeated itself with another coup d'etat in 1999. The result of this delicate balancing act was a political game of musical chairs as presidents, prime ministers, and even army chiefs came and went. The poor people of Pakistan had to re-learn democracy over and over again. Amazingly, they never lost hope.

Zia had promised to hold elections on 16 November 1988, and the new president and the army chief stayed with that timetable. The Senate meanwhile remained intact, populated by a compliant lot that had its allegiances cemented to the ruling Zia-ist clique. Sensing the potential of the hitherto suppressed PPP of Benazir Bhutto, the army high command and the ISI under Lt. Gen. Hamid Gul found it necessary to shore up the opposition and especially the Muslim League in the key province of Punjab, the largest and economically most prosperous part of the country. According to some reports, Gul travelled to Lahore, the capital of the Punjab, to help cobble together a coalition under the umbrella of the Islami Jamhoori Ittehad (IJI, or the Islamic

Democratic Alliance), led, among others, by Zia's chosen young Punjabi politician, the affable Mian Mohammad Nawaz Sharif.[3] The titular head of the IJI was a PPP turncoat, Ghulam Mustafa Jatoi, one of the famous 'uncles' (or veteran colleagues of her father) that Benazir Bhutto had let go from her party on her return to Pakistan from exile. The aim of the ISI was to present a counter weight to the PPP in the Punjab, its traditional stronghold.

Sharif had been handpicked by Zia's Punjab governor, a former ISI chief, Lt. Gen. Ghulam Jilani Khan, first to be finance minister in the province, and then chief minister. He represented a new breed of businessman-cum-politician, but with a strong conservative bent, ideally suited to reflect the needs of the growing urban populations of the Punjab and to undermine the support of both the left and the right, including the Islamic parties. The ISI chief and his deputy, Brigadier Imtiaz Ahmed (known because of his feline eyes as 'billa'), reportedly geared up the IJI with threats that Bhutto would roll back the nuclear programme and damage the planned jihad against Indian occupation of Kashmir.[4] Sharif acknowledges the forces behind the formation of the IJI in terms of political needs, 'It was the need of the hour that all the critical forces get together and fight elections jointly. And we of course, were keen that we join hands with other like-minded parties and forge an alliance. So that I was forced because [of] this...desire...on all sides [to join the IJI]. All the parties...felt that the elections must not be fought separately. We were keen to fight this election...under an umbrella of an alliance. So that is how the alliance came into being, and I think the alliance did well.'[5] He did not wish to discuss the role of the ISI or other individuals in this venture.

While concerned about the prospect of Ms Bhutto coming into power and exacting revenge on Zia's legatees, the US ambassador Robert Oakley pressed for free and fair elections in his frequent exchanges with General Beg and President Ishaq. So whatever fix was put in by the caretaker had to be surreptitious and well within the means of the ISI. The United States suspected that attempts might be made to postpone the elections or not hold them at all. Even as the airplane carrying Secretary of State George Shultz and ambassador-designate Robert Oakley flew toward Islamabad for the Zia funeral, this was a thought that raced through their minds. In Oakley's words:

> One of our objectives discussed on the plane flying out to the funeral was: let's do everything we can to make sure the elections are held. And they're held properly and there's no screwing around. Now this required a couple of things. It required Beg not only going along with it, but it required Beg overruling General Hamid Gul and building up the IJI...[with]...help...[from] Mr\[Husain] Haqqani, [a well known journalist and recently recruited advisor to Sharif] who was sent down to Lahore to work with Nawaz Sharif to create this IJI. And I'm told that Gul said to Beg, 'No, we can't have elections. We're not ready yet. And the PPP's going to win

so let's postpone the elections.' And Beg said no. And Beg sent word to the chief justice separately....Ghulam Ishaq Khan also sent word to the chief justice that 'in making your decisions, we think it would be a good idea to have the elections.'

Beg and the President weren't talking to each other at that stage. At least they weren't talking to each other on this [matter]. I was talking to both of them. And [as a result]...they both said, 'We think the elections should go ahead.'[6]

Benazir Bhutto, while acknowledging that civilian operatives may have been co-opted to work with the ISI and the Pakistan Muslim League (PML) to help form the IJI as a counter to her PPP, discounts the role of the civilians: 'I draw a distinction between the civilian operatives and between members of the armed forces who are there to uphold the constitution and were asked to commit extra-constitutional acts, because of the abuse of office by the head of the ISI and others.'[7]

The elections went off without any major incident. But the result may not have been what the army or Ishaq expected. It was also remarkable, if Oakley's information about Gul's prediction to Beg is correct, that the ISI was actually correct in predicting the results in favour of the PPP unless a strong IJI were set up. (It was probably one of the few times that the ISI got the results right up to that point.) There were three major winners: the PPP won 38.5 per cent of the votes for the National Assembly, garnering 93 seats out of the total 207. The first-past-the-post system allowed it to pick up seats even if its total vote count was not so much bigger than its rivals. The IJI came a close second, with 30.16 per cent and 55 seats. The new force, the Muhajir Qaumi Mahaz (MQM, or the Refugee National Front), came in with only 13 seats, mainly from Karachi and Hyderabad in Sindh, enough to give it a key role in a coalition.[8] Both Jatoi and Mohammad Khan Junejo, (who headed Nawaz Sharif's PML,) lost their seats, allowing Sharif to take up the leadership of the IJI. Sharif managed to garner a huge win for the PML in the Punjab and eventually became chief minister of that key province. Thus, Sharif had a strong hand to play in the subsequent political poker. In the provincial elections that followed, the IJI took the Punjab. PPP candidates became chief ministers of Sindh and the NWFP. Benazir Bhutto had a victory of sorts but not a real mandate. The president bided his time, as behind-the-scenes efforts commenced, to see what kind of coalition might emerge that could be to his and the army's liking. He waited a full ten days before finally conceding that Benazir Bhutto could form the next government. But much happened in that period that was to affect not only her ability to govern but also the chequered history of Pakistani politics in the next decade.

Elizabeth ('Beth') Jones, who had been in Pakistan for only two weeks before the Zia crash as the Deputy Chief of Mission (DCM) but had been introduced by Ambassador Arnold Raphel to many senior Pakistanis in that short period, suddenly found herself as the US charge d'affaires. One person that she met and kept up with was Zia's COS, Lt. Gen. Syed Refaqat. She recalls Refaqat saying to her that Zia's plan had been to issue a decree before the elections that would require that nobody could become prime minister unless he (or she) had received at least 5 per cent of the vote from each province. Refaqat said 'we knew that she [Benazir Bhutto] wouldn't get 5 per cent from Balochistan,' and would thus 'prevent her from becoming prime minister.' But with Zia gone now, Refaqat said 'that plan wasn't going to work now.' The day after the elections, Jones spent the day going around the key offices: the Foreign Ministry, GHQ, the ISI, and she recalls that in her meetings, very senior Pakistani officials were saying to her: 'We didn't vote for her [Bhutto]. We didn't want her as the prime minister of Pakistan. But we are so proud of Pakistan[…]and we are going to help her succeed.'[9] Once he was settled in, US Ambassador Oakley too was determined to help Bhutto succeed 'to the point that the embassy was writing white papers for her at his direction,' recalls Jones. Yet, attempts were made at the highest levels to curtail Bhutto's powers.

Oakley again gives a ring-side description of the machinations that occurred:

> Then you had the negotiations about whether she'd be allowed to take office. It was a gentleman's understanding […] or gentlewoman's understanding that she wouldn't get involved in the nuclear program […] Or army promotions and assignments or Afghanistan. Those things were sort of left to the president and the chief of the army staff. Because you had this peculiar situation: Zia had been, in essence, the president, the prime minister, and the chief of the army staff. So he had all the levers of power. And no one had made a provision for what happens if he dies. How much of a voice on which issues is that of the president, how much of the prime minister, and how much of the chief of the army staff. No one knew the answer to those questions.[10]

Assistant Secretary for International Security at the Pentagon, Richard L. Armitage, was sent with Assistant Secretary of State of the Near East and South Asia, Richard Murphy, to Pakistan to help ensure that there was a smooth transfer. They met Beg, who assured them that he would pose no obstacles to Bhutto forming a government but his concern was that she might interfere in army promotions. Murphy and Armitage then met Bhutto and conveyed the results of their meetings to her, including Beg's concern. 'I got it!' said Bhutto, according to Armitage.[11]

Bhutto maintains that she 'won the elections outright' given that she got most of the minority, women, and the FATA candidates behind her.[12] But, she maintains that efforts were made to break her majority. The ISI approached Makhdoom Amin Fahim of the PPP and told him that if he defected with ten PPP members, he could be the next prime minister. She stated that other parties were invited to the presidency to see if they could form a majority large enough to put up a prime minister. Of course, there was still the open question of the acting president himself, since he had to be elected formally. Bhutto recalls a meeting she held at Dr Niazi's home in Islamabad, attended by her senior colleagues, where they debated the issue of the next president. She favoured putting forward the name of Malik Qasim. According to her, the view presented by Dr Niazi and Iftikhar Gilani was that the PPP had too slim a majority to take on Ghulam Ishaq Khan in the presidential elections. 'He's a man who'll play by the rules,' and so these two proposed that the PPP support Ishaq. 'That was a wrong calculation,' as later events proved, she said. In the end, she said she agreed to support Ishaq but maintains that this was for the sake of a 'national consensus' and because the PPP had a 'narrow majority.' The army, she said, later tried to 'peddle' the notion that she agreed to terms for becoming prime minister, including Ishaq as president, and ceding control over Afghan policy and army promotions. 'Absolute rubbish!' is Bhutto's characterization of these conditions. In fact, she recalls that after hearing the issue of Afghanistan and the imminent Soviet withdrawal, 'I volunteered to keep Sahibzada Yaqub Khan.' But, she maintains, there was never any discussion of the other issues. Beg threw a private dinner for her and her family, a sort of 'get to know you' event. The only matter that he brought up was the fear among some in the army that she might seek revenge. The other issues were never brought up directly, nor did she receive a briefing on the nuclear programme, on which she confirms that only Oakley briefed her on what the US knew about it.[13]

A contrary view emerges from Admiral Iftikhar A. Sirohey, the CJCS, based on a report given to him by Beg of his meeting with Bhutto after she called on him at the GHQ. According to this version, Beg was opposed to Bhutto, and had promised Zia's widow that neither Bhutto nor Junejo would succeed her late husband. He reiterated this at a meeting at the President's House after the elections. On 24 November 1988 at a meeting of the JCSC, Beg informed the committee of his meeting with Bhutto where 'she agreed to five points which he had asked for'. The points were: (a) no change in the Afghanistan policy; (b) no change in nuclear policy; (c) no change in defence policy; (d) no meddling in the administrative set-up of the civil service; and (e) General Zia's family will not be harassed.[14]

Sirohey reports that President Ghulam Ishaq Khan had not been party to this agreement between Beg and Bhutto.

It was against this uncertain background that 35-year old Benazir Bhutto ascended to the office of prime minister on 2 December 1988, occupying the position that her father had held before he was removed by Zia's coup and executed. It was a bittersweet moment for her and her mother when she was sworn in, but one they had been awaiting for many years. At the same time, having grown up in a hurry, she fully understood the fact that she was not an independent agent in the ruling Troika. The limits had been set for her. Among other things, she had been told that the Afghan War was at a critical stage (following the Geneva Accords), and it was necessary for continuity's sake that Sahibzada Yaqub Khan should stay on as her foreign minister. She had also agreed to support the candidacy of Ishaq for president when the new assembly convened.

The euphoria of becoming prime minister was thus short-lived for Benazir Bhutto. Soon, she was trying to assert her position on the issues that had been deemed *verboten*. As Ambassador Oakley recalls: 'She began to push, wanting more of a voice on the Afghan war. And we were pushing her to do more on the nuclear program, to try to slow it down....[...]She was getting briefings from us on what was going on...and pretending like she couldn't do anything about it. At the same time, she wanted to avoid a confrontation on that issue, I think, at all costs.'[15] That meant that she was having to walk a tight rope.

From all accounts, while not warm, her relations with both Ishaq and Beg were proper and not combative in those early days. Bhutto recalls a friendly Beg in those early days.[16] Yet rumours started circulating that the army and Beg did not want to show her respect and that Beg would not even wear his army cap when he met her since that would mean he would have to salute her. Soon things were to go off kilter, partly because of Bhutto's own mistakes and partly because the opposition to her and her party was so well-entrenched in the Ziaist system that she had inherited.

BEG'S ARMY AND HIS ROLE

Beg saw his own role in those early days as that of a 'referee' trying to keep calm on the political playing field and ensuring that differences between the two leading parties and their leaders were resolved inside the assembly and not on the streets; otherwise, the army would be unnecessarily drawn into the squabbles.[17] But Beg found himself increasingly drawn into the public debates and could not resist speaking out at almost every opportunity that he got. Beg represented the new Pakistan Army. He was the first army chief commissioned after Pakistan came into being and did not come from a military background, having been born in Azamgarh in the former United Provinces of British India. He had participated in the Pakistan Movement as a young student and was committed to an independent and strong Pakistan, especially relative to India. As a *muhajir* (or refugee) from India, Beg almost had to prove to his largely Punjabi and Pathan colleagues in the army that he was at least as patriotic as them, if not more. In fact, like many other refugees from India, he evinced a deep suspicion of the Indians and believed that the

'Hindus want to dominate other religions.'[18] On the military front, he continued to see India as the main enemy and readily cited the war directive that enjoined the Pakistan Army to defend every inch of Pakistani territory. The outwardly calm Beg believed in an aggressive defence, of 'keeping my options open. If it suits me, I'll strike deep.'

A soft spoken, deceptively slight man who had once been a commando and trained by the Americans during the early days of the SSG as a 'stay behind' guerrilla in case the Soviets overran Pakistan, Beg had a mind of his own and was not afraid to speak out. As a colonel in East Pakistan in 1971, he wrote a report to his CO on the deteriorating political situation in the East wing and was sent back to West Pakistan for his outspokenness, (thus escaping captivity as a POW). Later, as a corps commander in Peshawar in 1986, he delivered a talk at the Staff College in Quetta, arguing against a two-front situation for Pakistan because of its stance on Afghanistan. He favoured defusing the western border to better protect the eastern one against India.[19] He had kept a low profile during Zia's regime and now saw an opportunity to shape the army and the country according to his vision. As a former member of the SSG and a trained commando, he was likely to leap into issues without much fear or concern about the consequences. The news media had a field day with him, ambushing him at all times and at all functions, and he was happy to oblige them with his ready expositions.

Beg moved rapidly to publicize the work and workings of the army in a media policy that was dubbed *Glasnost*, after the opening of the Soviet system under Gorbachev. This was a change from the highly closed information policies of the Zia regime and even though he had inherited the corps commanders from Zia, most of them were far junior to Zia and closer to Beg's age and service group, commissioned in the mid-1950s, and were children of an independent Pakistan. The army had by then become a far more professional force than the one that Pakistan inherited at independence, with officers being made to go through a series of rigorous training courses and selection boards before they were promoted. No senior officer could rise up the ranks without having been through the Staff College in Quetta or the War Course at the National Defence College (NDC) in Rawalpindi. Even the Staff College course had been revamped and updated, especially after a detailed critique of the army's training programme in Stephen Cohen's book *The Pakistan Army*. Many officers had been sent to overseas staff colleges or taken specialized courses in the United States, Germany, Turkey, Australia and other places (although US training had been discontinued under sanctions for some time). Some fifty officers were sent overseas each year, and according to Beg, 'more than 60 per cent of them top their courses. The remaining are near the top.' Officers were also encouraged to undertake language training and sent abroad for immersion courses, for example in German, allowing them to access professional materials in foreign languages with ease.

The modern Pakistan Army under Beg also saw itself as much more professional than the civilian administration, where Beg saw 'the most accommodating officers…and sycophants' being promoted. In the army on the other hand, he was proud to point to a system of selection that sifted the better officers and allowed them to rise to the top. Only 7 per cent of lieutenant colonels made it to brigadier, only 17 per cent of brigadiers made it to major general, while only 2 per cent made it to lieutenant general. Beg took pride in the fact that for promotions to be effected, forty general officers looked at the promotion list and even if one person raised an objection, a person's chances of getting promoted were damaged. (However, while this system may have worked for the uniformity and discipline of the army, it also encouraged risk-averse behaviour and conformity to the 'staff solution' rather than creative thinking at the upper echelons.) Beg also took pride in what he saw as an 'army system of command' that was superior to that of the Pakistan Air Force and Navy, where he said that a new air or naval chief brought along a new team to run the force each time. Beg claims that he did not change any commander when he took over, not even his ADC. Here, he may have been rationalizing the status quo since none of the corps commanders had been selected by him and he could not remove them without causing ripples. Beg did not have much of an opportunity to make changes until late in his three-year term; (corps commanders normally stayed for only four years in their three-star rank of lieutenant general). However, the intensive training and exposure to both military and political issues made the senior officers of the army under Beg aware of developments around them and, consequently, made them more prone to take action on political matters. Corps commanders meetings presided over by the army chief included briefings on political issues by the DG ISI. Beg had also inherited many of the practices and rules of the Zia period. But one practice that he removed was the reference in the officers' annual confidential reports, to their views and behaviour with respect to religion.

ZARB-E-MOMIN: A NEW APPROACH?

To make his mark on the army and to put the fledgling government of Bhutto in a place where it could not withdraw support for the army's aggressive new strategies, Beg introduced a series of war games and studies to show how Pakistan could go on the offensive against India. He tasked his DGMO, Major General Jehangir Karamat, to come up with the operational plans for this approach. As Karamat explains it, each holding corps was to create local reserves as part of their defensive plans (to stabilize threatened sectors). It was also to create strike forces to undertake offensive operations in selected sectors. This planning was executed through plans drawn up in the GHQ and matured through a series of planning exercises, war games, and map exercises over a period of time.[20] 'The logic behind General Beg's thinking was to send a message to the Indians that Pakistan had the capability and resolve to carry out effective defence against Indian aggression and carry the fight into Indian territory,' recalls Karamat. 'We had also created the impression through carefully orchestrated activities that the victorious fighters from Afghanistan would be organized into Pakistan-officered brigades and used in Kashmir. Remember that the Indians had just extricated from a disastrous intervention in Sri Lanka and faced the Sikh insurgency with fears of [the latter] linking up with Kashmir through Pakistan.' But Karamat believes that 'there were misgivings about the feasibility of these plans. Holding Corps were reluctant to shed forces and resisted Army offensive plans, but these were brushed aside.' However, Karamat maintains that the overall strategy seemed to have worked to deter India.[21]

In fact, what Beg was doing was to clothe the current thinking of the Pakistan Army in a new doctrine. Since the Pakistan Army had always relied on offensive ripostes as a part of its overall defence plans, his 'Offensive-Defensive' plans were nothing new. The only new thing was the ability of the army to conduct a massive exercise to see if it could use a strike corps effectively in establishing a bridgehead and breaking out in an offensive manoeuvre. Moreover, Beg's idea of creating 'strategic depth' by allying with Afghanistan and Iran appeared to run counter to every policy of the Pakistani government's war directive, which insisted that the army defend every inch of the border. The idea of Pakistan allowing India to occupy key cities near the border such as Lahore, Gujranwala, Gujrat, Bahawalpur, Rahim Yar Khan and areas in Sindh, and then retreat for 'strategic depth' to the wilds of Afghanistan or the desert of eastern Iran, was beyond the pale. Once India had these key sites, it would be 'Game Over' for Pakistan! But, the army high command—being a disciplined lot—did not challenge its chief.

In this context, Beg invited Prime Minister Benazir Bhutto to a war game in which some of his assumptions were floated and tested out:

> General Beg called me for a briefing of war games. And in the briefing of war games—at that time, you remember the Kashmir insurgency was not in such a peak...he said to me about 'Blueland' and 'Redland' (sic) [normally this was Foxland in Pakistan Army war games parlance]—this was India and Pakistan fighting each other out (sic), and how Blueland takes Srinagar because Blueland has the support of 100,000 battle-trained Afghan Mujahideen, the Kashmiri Awam (general population) who are against the Indians, as well as the Pakistani Army.

And he said that if I gave the go-ahead, I would wear the…Crown of Glory and of
Triumph.[22]

With reference to the quote above, Bhutto recalls: 'I thought, it's not going to
turn out as I'm hearing it. So I gave the impression that I'm not very happy
with this presentation. I don't believe it's the right presentation.' And she left
it at that. In hindsight, she justifies not taking a stronger stand against such
thinking because she was new to governing and military matters and felt even
then that by bringing her into these war games, the army might be seeking
blanket approval of their operational plans, something that she believed could
only be approved by the political leadership of the country.[23] Here she may
have been confusing war games with operational plans, while understanding
correctly that the results of war games fed into the planning process.
Understandably then, when Bhutto was to publish details of this encounter
in an updated version of her autobiography, Beg responded with his own
version of what had transpired, noting too that the GHQ recorded all these
sessions and a perfect record would exist there. According to Beg:

> After listening to the presentation, she remarked: 'Can you capture Srinagar?' I
> said: 'Yes, if you place the resources at our disposal.' She did not answer. I tried to
> look into her eyes to find out if she was really serious, but she had lowered her gaze
> and offered no comments.[24]

Regardless, Beg's thinking and the army's war games culminated in a plan for
a massive military exercise in November–December 1989 named *Zarb-e-
Momin* (Strike of the True Believer), conducted in central Pakistan, where the
Punjab plains debouch into the desert of Sindh. As usual, the exercise
involved two forces: Foxland (the adversary, a thinly disguised India) and
Blueland (the homeland: Pakistan). Lt. Gen. Zulfiqar Akhtar Naz was
commanding Foxland and Lt. Gen. Alam Jan Mahsud the Blueland forces.
Foxland was located in the corridor between the Chenab and Ravi rivers
(facing east to west), and between the Indus and Jhelum rivers in the corridor
between Mianwali and Khushab (facing north to south). Blueland was to the
south in the same corridor. The aim was for Blueland to defend against a
two-pronged attack by an adversary that outnumbered it roughly in the same
ratio as India to Pakistan; in an area that had varied terrain, (both desert and
plains), and in offensive actions that involved water crossings; through the
establishment of a bridgehead over the combined Jhelum and Chenab rivers
near Shorkot. One reason for choosing the location was to ensure that this
exercise would not be seen as threatening to India, as Brasstacks had been
when India conducted it in Rajasthan near the Sindh border in 1987. *Zarb-
e-Momin* involved some 200,000 men from four corps, including an armour

division and seven infantry divisions, plus independent armour and infantry brigades and collaboration with the Pakistan Air Force.[25]

The whole exercise was based on Beg's concept of offensive-defence; that is, mass mobilization and rapid and aggressive movement of forces in a riposte into enemy territory. Among other things, he had requisitioned tractors on which he mounted guns and covered with thin metal sheets, ostensibly to provide protection against ground fire. These tractors, carrying troops, were supposed to be able to traverse the desert with ease, forgetting that they had no protection at all against enemy fire. One armour commander recalls having asked Beg before the exercise for armoured personnel carriers so infantry could travel at speed and keep up with armour during an attack mode. Beg promised the commander that he had a solution. The commander was astounded to see the jerry-rigged tractors show up!

Beg claimed that 'our Armed Forces are fully tuned to fighting an offensive-defence, with well-tested concepts and strategies, even in an environment where they may be outnumbered.'[26] To show off this change in attitude from the previous battles of holding formations, foreign military attachés, including the Indian defence attaché, were brought in, to observe the exercise as was a mini-army of media to publicize the war game. Unfortunately, the home side 'lost' some of the encounters and the exercise was wound up rapidly. Regardless, the army had certainly made its point to the public, and to India, that it was ready for an offensive. US Ambassador Oakley recalls offering Beg a critique that a US colonel, who had observed the exercise, had prepared. The offer was spurned by Beg, and Oakley later passed on that report to General Asif Nawaz.[27] This critique, among other things, pointed to pervasive confusion during the period between H-Hour and the subsequent attack, when the Pakistan Army, despite meticulous planning, tended to lose control of the battlefield due to lack of current and useful information. The result was confusion. The post-exercise debriefing by the Americans also focused on the lack of delegation to junior officers, including young captains, subalterns, JCOSs and NCOs. It pointed out to the wasteful employment of relatively senior officers, for example, majors leading patrols and not being able to visualize the battle in the medium-term, i.e. 24 or 36 hours hence.[28]

TROIKA EMERGES

As the VCOAS to Zia, Beg had had little input into nuclear policy or command and control, since these were areas that Zia had kept for himself—and now, Beg had an opportunity to extend his own control into these realms. After Zia, President Ishaq had inherited the mantle of control of the nuclear issues. Soon after being elected, Bhutto, who had been kept in the dark about these issues, sought to regain her control of the nuclear programme as the head of government. She asked for briefings and was told they would be given but never were. Finally, she got impatient and called a meeting with Munir Ahmed Khan, the chairman of the PAEC, and Dr A.Q. Khan, the head of the Kahuta enrichment project—the latter of whom was supposed to report to her anyway. Beg found out after the meeting was called and telephoned her in a panic. Sensing the opportunity to re-open the issue, Bhutto then invited the President and the army chief to arrange a meeting with them so they could speak about nuclear command and control.[29] In fact, Bhutto claims to have inaugurated the nuclear command and to have authored the first nuclear doctrine for the country:

> I called it the 'Benazir Nuclear Doctrine' or the 'PPP Nuclear Doctrine'—because it was evolved in our time. And under that nuclear doctrine, although we had the capability to put together a bomb, [so as] to give the international community confidence, we decided not to put together the components of the bomb. We decided not to shape metal. We decided not to enrich Uranium to 92 per cent although, at that time…we agreed to go down to 60 per cent.[30]

Until that point, the president had been solely in charge of the nuclear programme. Not even the army chief was part of the control mechanism. Army Chief Beg got his hand in the control system after Bhutto's initiative. Thus was laid the foundation of a new system of government in Pakistan known as the 'Troika', providing a modicum of checks and balances to the political system but always keeping the main three actors on the political scene: the president, prime minister, and the army chief on the alert. But this was not to assure stability, as individual subjects provided an opportunity for the principals to air their differences, sometimes publicly. The untrained and young prime minister found herself tested a number of times, as she and her similarly unpractised colleagues proceeded to take on the entrenched bureaucracy and politicos.

Adding to Bhutto's difficulties was the growing perception that the new regime was reverting to the ways of the older one: charges of nepotism and graft dogged her brief reign. Early on, Bhutto took off for an *Umra* that had to be transmuted by her staff into an official visit so she could be seen to have been received by the Saudi king, an important symbolic issue for her audience at home. One of her senior advisors, former UN Ambassador Iqbal Akhund, pithily characterized these types of junkets that had first been made common by Zia as 'expense account piety.'[31] Plane loads of officials would accompany the president or the prime minister to Saudi Arabia to wash off their sins. In a political system that thrived on access to governmental resources, the new leadership of the PPP found it easy to divert resources or seek special treatment for its favourites. Reports circulated of ministers seeking cuts from foreign aid agencies and awarding contracts to friends and relatives of the Bhutto family 'to make up for their suffering' under the previous regime. Within a year, the public media had caught on to these financial shenanigans; the culmination of which came in the form of a cover story of *The Herald* in August 1990 with the headline: 'Take the Money and Run!' (The 'run' part was referring to the dismissal of her government, which had transpired just days before the publication of the article.)

From the outset, the ISI and MI both had their eyes on the Bhutto family, as did the not-so-loyal opposition in the Punjab government of Chief Minister Nawaz Sharif, which tried its utmost to topple the PPP's central government. Major differences arose in the handling of foreign policy and domestic matters, pitting Bhutto against first the president and then the army chief.

AFGHANISTAN: WITHDRAWAL PAINS

Bhutto knew that the Soviets planned to withdraw from Kabul in February 1989. However, no one knew what would happen in Afghanistan once the Soviets departed. While there appeared to be general unanimity in Pakistan for a smooth succession and the emergence of a friendly Afghan government, the Soviets, even in their final days, insisted on the Afghan leader Najeebullah playing a role, however diminished, in the new government. The seven Mujahideen leaders each wanted to have a major share of the government in Kabul and their tenuous unity showed signs of conflict, with Gulbadin Hekmatyar, earlier the favourite of the ISI and the Saudis, breaking openly with the rest. Bhutto wished to bring the pro-Iranian chieftains of north-western Afghanistan into the equation. The ISI continued to favour the more radical right-wingers that had proved themselves as more 'effective' in operations. The field commanders also wanted to have a say in the new system, but their Peshawar-based leaders insisted that they would decide on how the successor government would be shaped. Pakistan pressed the various Mujahideen factions for the formation of an Afghan interim government (AIG), with ministries doled out according to the relative strength of the participating seven members of the Mujahideen alliance. But it chose not to offer the AIG formal recognition. Only the Saudis were quick to recognize this entity. The United States, meanwhile, seemed willing to withdraw from the scene now that the Soviets had left, but wished also to rub the Soviets' nose in the dirt.

At a meeting attended by Bhutto and the US Ambassador Robert Oakley in Peshawar, (but importantly not by any Mujahideen leaders,) a plan was discussed to establish a foothold in Afghan territory to give the AIG firm status in its homeland. Jalalabad, the key way-station between Peshawar and

Kabul, was selected as the target: the hitherto guerrilla warriors of the Mujahideen were entrusted with the job of taking the city after laying siege to it; a change from their hit-and-run tactics to conventional warfare. Recollections vary about who came up with the Jalalabad plan. For their part, both Oakley and Bhutto recall Hamid Gul as being the enthusiastic proponent of the plan. Gul, however, says that Oakley wanted Jalalabad to set up the Afghan government. Bhutto, on the other hand, recalls Gul telling her that 'Jalalabad will fall within a week.'[32] He promised that with the supply lines cut from Kabul, the garrison at Jalalabad would crumble. This appeared to be at odds with the historical realities of Afghanistan whose centre of gravity has always been Kabul. A footnote to this operation was the inclusion in the battle for Jalalabad—unbeknownst to most participants at the Peshawar meeting— of a young Saudi financier and Islamic militant named Osama bin Laden.

Despite the high hopes of the ISI chief, the plan to take Jalalabad failed miserably. The Mujahideen could not fight a set-piece battle. They were not united, and proved vulnerable to bribery. In fact, the Soviets managed to push through a series of convoys from Kabul to Jalalabad, aided most probably by Mujahideen commanders who had been bribed. The fighting continued for months and further exacerbated the acrimony between Bhutto and the ISI chief, despite his attempt to work with her on the Afghan issue in the first few months of her government. She had known that Gul had worked against her prior to the elections. And she was informed that Brigadier Imtiaz Ahmed, the person in charge of internal political issues at the ISI, was coming up with ways of throwing the PPP out of power. She managed to get Imtiaz removed from the ISI, much to Gul's unhappiness. Bhutto was also told that Gul was behind the *fatwa* (religious edict) issued by a leading cleric in Saudi Arabia to the effect that a woman could not head a Muslim country, and that an effort was underway to have scholars debate the same issue at the OIC. While these domestic issues were swirling, Gul had come up with a proposal for a confederation with Afghanistan that Bhutto did not approve of. Bhutto now strengthened her resolve to move Beg from his powerful post. She faced opposition to her Afghan policies from elsewhere too. After the Soviet foreign minister had come to Islamabad carrying a proposal that would allow Najeebullah to remain for a transitional period of six months, a plan that she favoured, she was told by Gul, 'You cannot deny us the drive into Kabul in victory to pray at the Kabul mosque.' President Ishaq too was a fervent proponent of jihad and took a hard-line position in internal debates as well as with US visitors.

Bhutto recalls that she received reports that Gul and the ISI were behind attempts to have her removed and perhaps even behind an abortive attempt to assassinate her at Lahore airport (though this was not confirmed or proved). Finally, fearing that Gul might overturn her government while she was out of the country, just before she left on a visit to Turkey in May 1989, Bhutto agreed to Gul's removal from the ISI. Although she did arrange a farewell dinner for him to soften the blow, the relationship ended on a less than cordial note. Beg then moved Gul to be the corps commander in Multan. The Afghan jihad meanwhile descended into chaos and confusion, with individual warlords and commanders trying to establish their control over resources and positioning themselves for the eventual fall of Kabul. The AIG was ineffective at coordinating a coherent policy. Within Pakistan, the Foreign Office attempted to bring some order to the negotiations with the Soviets, even while the ISI and the army chief took a stronger stance, hoping for a military victory.

MISSTEPS

Having removed Gul, Bhutto turned her attention back to the ISI. She had set up a committee to review the role of the intelligence services in Pakistan—especially their role under a democratic set-up. Headed by Air Chief Marshal Zulfiqar Ali Khan, the four-person committee looked at the ISI, the IB, the ASF and the provincial 'special branches' of the police. Ironically, it was her father who by decree had ordered the ISI to set up a political wing and to review domestic political developments for the prime minister, a role for which the ISI had not been well-equipped. Over time, however, the ISI broadened its role and became a pervasive force in Pakistani politics that could even force the hands of its own benefactors or sponsors, army chief and prime minister included. Bhutto now tried to take control of the ISI, which, as an inter-services entity, properly came under the aegis of the CJCS. Then, in a move that did not win her any friends in the military establishment, she chose to bring back retired Lt. Gen. Shamsur Rahman Kallue, a quiet gentleman unsuited for the rough and tumble of intelligence and politics, and asked him to take over as DG ISI. In doing so, she failed to understand the culture of the Pakistan Army. Kallue was a course mate of Beg from the 6th PMA course, but the two did not get along. He was a friend of the prime minister's advisor, General Imtiaz Ali, also a course mate of Beg, who did not get along with the latter either.[33] Though trying, on the one hand, to bring in Kallue to diminish the role of the army chief—(who would normally have put forth a candidate or panel of candidates for the opening, but this did not happen, in part because of Bhutto's unfamiliarity with these norms)—Bhutto did not know that retired officers lose their clout and cachet and do not have a network among the new senior commanders of the army, who resent the presence of the former in policy-making roles. The ISI was suddenly cut off from the Pakistan Army. The MI Directorate at the GHQ, under Major

General Asad Durrani, became the eyes and ears of General Beg as well as a counter-force to the ISI in the political arena. Among the many moves Beg made was the creation and strengthening of the 202 Survey Section in Sindh 'to keep the army informed of all the happenings [in the province],' because the ISI and the IB did not keep the army informed.[34] Needless to say, the hapless Kallue—whom critics (including the US Ambassador and much later even Bhutto), farcically dubbed 'no clue,'[35]—found himself isolated and ineffective.

Bhutto was relying for military advice on two other retired generals: her father's military secretary, Major General Imtiaz Ahmed, and Lt. Gen. Naseerullah Babar, a 1971 war hero. She believed that the army respected their views. This was not the case, however. Their lack of constitutional knowledge may have led her to her second clash with the army and the president. In a move that she perhaps thought would render General Beg ineffective, she tried to promote Lt. Gen. Ahmed Kamal to the position of chairman of the JCSC while sending home the incumbent Admiral Iftikhar A. Sirohey, the former naval chief, who had succeeded Akhtar Abdur Rahman. Kamal had been recommended by both Babar and Imtiaz. Bhutto states that Beg was brought into the plan and agreed to it, only to resile later. Her reasoning for Sirhoey's removal was that his three years were up since he had been a four-star admiral and naval chief for that long and that an executive order of her father had fixed the service tenure of service chiefs at three years. She believes that Sirohey and Hamid Gul went to complain to President Ishaq and made the argument that if the prime minister were to make this change, they would all lose control. She believes that Beg was then brought in and forced to change his mind.

Beg had forewarned Sirohey as early as December 1988 about the prime minister's idea of replacing him.[36] On his part, Sirohey kept the president aware of all subsequent developments. By July 1989, he had found out that a panel of candidates, including the Air Chief Hakeemullah, Admiral Y.H. Malik, and Lt. Gen. Ahmed Kamal, had been identified as his replacement. In August, Sirohey heard from the prime minister's adviser on defence, Major General Imtiaz, that the prime minister 'wished him to thank me [Sirohey] for all the assistance and support I had rendered to her and the government. She had been pleased to permit me to proceed on retirement from 14 August 1989.'[37] She also offered to accommodate him in any other position of his choosing. Sirohey reported this to the president who then called the adviser and asked him to rebut a report about Sirohey's departure that had already been leaked to the press. Ishaq gave them a deadline for the rebuttal, but the rebuttal did not materialize because the prime minister was reportedly 'out of contact' in interior Sindh. President Ishaq asserted his right under the 8th Amendment of the constitution to appoint the chairman of the JCSC. He was of the view that Sirohey's new position started the clock anew and that he would therefore not retire until September 1991. Checkmate. This matter was never fully or openly resolved, and rather, poisoned the atmosphere between the prime minister and the president as well as the army chief and the chairman JCSC. According to Bhutto:

> In the press, they'd fomented that I had planned to make Beg the chairman, joint chiefs of staff, and I had planned to make General Imtiaz, the retired general, the chief of the army staff. And that was all rubbish. There was no such plan. Everybody was on board. It was all very clear in the files and very clear in our briefing: Beg was consulted. They had agreed that Kamal would be a good choice for chairman, joint chiefs of staff. And the file was moved accordingly. But after the file was moved, it was Sirohey who went to the president and Hamid Gul who went to the president. And then Beg was called by the president. And then the next thing I knew, Beg had taken a political somersault.
>
> [...]After that, my relations with Beg broke. It went from worse (sic) to worse after that. After that, he backed the no-confidence move against us, which failed. After that, he called my parliamentarians to the frontier and tried to get them to destabilize the frontier assembly. After that, he became part of the Ishaq–Gul combine to overthrow the democratically-elected government of the people of Pakistan.
>
> He was kept totally in the dark, because when...our government was overthrown, he was under the impression that there would be no clear-cut majority and that the votes would be divided three ways between the PPP, the PML-N and others. So, obviously he had been misled into backing the dissolution of the government. He thought he'd be the King's player (sic). He didn't realize that actually Nawaz Sharif would be given a two-thirds majority. I don't think Ishaq realized either what would happen.[38]

US ambassador Oakley recalls that Bhutto believed that 'foreign (and especially US) support would keep her in office no matter what, right up until the last minute.' And she did not think that her defence advisers were a liability. 'In the middle of the Sirohey crisis, she told me in apparent sincerity that these two [Babar and Imtiaz] had excellent relations with the entire army leadership and keep her fully informed, so there could be no surprises or problem.'[39]

SINDH SQUABBLES

A lot more happened in the interim. Beg and the prime minister also clashed openly on the policy towards the state of lawlessness in Sindh, where the PPP had originally formed a coalition with the MQM. But gradually things fell apart, as the two partners tried to access scarce state resources for their own benefit. Open hostility developed between the MQM and the PPP across the province and especially in Karachi and Hyderabad. President Ishaq began to voice his own concern about these developments. The PPP government sought help from the army in the name of 'anti-dacoity' (robbery) operations to restore order in Sindh. According to contemporary reports, the army commanders told the government that if the army was to operate, it would need to clean up interior Sindh as well as Hyderabad and Karachi. The army insisted that it be given a free hand to operate under the rubric of Article 245, which protected the army from any legal challenge in the pursuit of its duties in aid of civil power. Moreover, the army wished to operate throughout Sindh rather than just in designated areas and major cities, largely dominated by the MQM. Here, the corps commander V Corps, Lt. Gen. Asif Nawaz, took a firm position (supported by his division commanders), suspecting that a number of PPP provincial ministers were harbouring the criminal elements or actively supporting them, 'You gentlemen, from top to bottom, are immature and cannot run a government,' he is reported to have said to certain functionaries of the erstwhile Sindh government.[40]

The MQM leader, Altaf Hussain, had established himself in a section of Karachi named Azizabad, and erected gates on the major access roads to this locality. In effect, he had challenged the writ of the government in that area. The PPP government instructed the army chief to have the gates demolished. General Beg telephoned Lt. Gen. Asif Nawaz, and conveyed the orders to demolish the gates. General Nawaz refused to do so, explaining to Beg that once the gates were demolished, the PPP supporters would rampage through Azizabad and then the army would need to 'clean up the mess'. He managed to dissuade Beg, thus protecting the MQM base.[41] Within the MQM, there was strong suspicion that the corps commander, Lt. Gen. Asif Nawaz, was against them, and that this reflected a traditional Punjabi attitude of condescension towards the refugees, who were often labelled in derogatory terms as 'tiliyer,' 'Hindustanis' or even among army circles as 'pajamawallas.'[42] The MQM chief Altaf Hussain himself bore a deep wound from his days when he had tried out for the Pakistan Army and been rejected after being ragged as a 'refugee'. He referred to this slight often, not recognizing that Beg too was a refugee and had stated that he never was discriminated against. Yet, it was General Nawaz to whom both the MQM and the PPP turned on 11 February 1990 to effect an exchange of political prisoners that both sides had taken during their urban battles. The exchange took place in the corps headquarters, putting the army front and centre as a neutral but key player in Sindh. Asif Nawaz, until then a quiet and reclusive professional soldier, thus came to be known on the national stage. Beg up to that point did not know the MQM leadership well and had to be introduced to them by Nawaz during his visits to Karachi. Beg is said to have gradually built up his own direct relationship with the MQM, but he did not try to influence General Nawaz in any way to favour the MQM against the PPP.

Things came to a head between the army and the PPP government after the flare-up on 27 May 1990 at an MQM-dominated locality called Pucca Qila in Hyderabad, the major city in Sindh. One Sunday, after rising political temperatures between the Sindhis and the Muhajirs, fighting erupted in Pucca Qila resulting in some 30 deaths and another 350 in Karachi as the violence spread to the south.[43] According to the refugees, the police, under orders from the PPP-dominated Sindh government, attacked Pucca Qila, choosing a time when Beg was out of the country and the corps commander of V Corps was on a tour of the border area. Even the GOC of the division in Hyderabad, Major General Javed Ashraf Qazi, was on a tour of China. The troops of the Hyderabad division were also in Chor in the desert on military exercises. In short, the PPP appeared to have acted without consulting the military. The IG police organized an attack on Pucca Qilla which was seen as a hiding place for weapons used by the MQM, although the army had told the police that there was no weapons dump there.[44] When the MQM retaliated, according to Maj. Gen. Qazi, 'the police took off', not only vacating Pucca Qilla but also leaving the entire city unprotected.[45] Once the situation got out of hand, the army was called in. The army got the Muhajir and Sindhi population's leaders to meet, and arranged to have the displaced Sindhis brought back to their homes.

But the recriminations began and continued to bedevil the relations between the army and the PPP government. The MQM felt that the PPP government had sponsored a campaign against them and appealed to the president for help. The army had to restore not only law and order but also attempt to build confidence between the communities—and began to feel frustrated. 'We'd arrest them [criminals] and then hear that they had been released, sometimes on the orders of the minister for jails of the province!' said Major General Qazi. Some individuals were arrested two or three times and released each time. At one point, the Interior Minister, Aitzaz Ahsan was reported to have gotten into an argument with Corps Commander Lt. Gen. Nawaz over a list of 'terrorists' that the PPP wanted picked up. Nawaz refused to do so, stating that the PPP government was trying to 'use' the army to 'crush its political opponents.'[46] In fact, Ahsan claims that the corps commander's hands had been tied by General Beg after the former had agreed to support a policy action in clearing up some 'terrorist' cells in university hostels. Nawaz promised Ahsan that he would solve the problem in his own way without seeking the constitutional protections that General Beg was demanding. In this instance, he placed his soldiers in the pickets and on patrol duties around Karachi, thus freeing the 'Civil Armed Forces to provide the necessary back-up to the police as it entered the hostels.' As for the newspaper reports of a slanging match between the two, General Nawaz sent Ahsan a faxed note 'repudiating the story,' following which the newspaper corrected its story.[47]

ARMY PROMOTIONS

The prime minister added to her difficulties with the army by taking the advice of her military advisers on yet another move. In June 1990, she sought the extension of Lt. Gen. Alam Jan Mahsud, a Pathan who was then commanding the corps in Lahore, possibly with a view to having him succeed Beg when the latter's term as COAS ended in August 1991. Beg read this as interference in the promotion system of the army and an abrogation of his prerogative. He finessed the issue by sending Lt. Gen. M. Ashraf Janjua to take over the Lahore corps. General Mahsud, a thoroughly professional soldier without any overt ambition, was given his customary farewell dinners and left the army quietly. The DCM at the US embassy, Beth Jones, recalls getting a call from General Babar—Bhutto's special adviser—asking her if she could arrange a phone call from the US president so that Bhutto could get the president's support for her choice of army chief. Jones told him that arranging a call was one thing, but that if the government of Pakistan were then to release a statement that the president supported Bhutto's choice of army chief, 'the White House, the State Department and the embassy would deny that.'[48] There was a subsequent phone call, but the issue of the army chief was not aired, according to Jones. The cumulative effect of the young Bhutto's struggle with the well-entrenched army chief on the one hand, and the elderly and well-experienced president on the other, produced a result that was to presage seemingly regular upheavals in Pakistani politics.

At the 21 July 1990 meeting of Beg with his corps commanders, the army high command decided that the Bhutto government was no longer acceptable. Beg conveyed these views to President Ishaq, who had been collecting his own list of issues with the prime minister. A month later, Ishaq acted. Invoking his enhanced powers under the 8th Amendment, Ishaq dismissed the Bhutto government on 6 August 1990, charging her with corruption, inefficiency, and misconduct. He then proceeded to call for new elections to be held on 24 October 1990 under a caretaker prime minister. For that role, he chose Ghulam Mustafa Jatoi, a former PPP loyalist who had joined the opposition and lead the IJI in the run-up to the 1988 elections.

Bhutto's regime had never been able to establish a firm foothold. Confronted with growing US disenchantment with Pakistan's nuclear programme and the United States' desire to exit rapidly from Afghanistan once the Soviets departed, a hostile opposition party in control of the influential Punjab province, and deteriorating relations with the army chief and the president, Bhutto was unable to establish her writ. Yet, she managed to gain a fair amount of support in the United States, and raise the confidence of even General Beg to the level that he asked her to get Pakistan additional F-16s during her 1989 visit to Washington DC, which she did manage to do, promising the Americans cash payment for the additional planes. But the nuclear issue and the Pressler Amendment, which would automatically freeze all aid to Pakistan if it crossed the nuclear weapon enrichment threshold, hung over Pakistan's head and was the subject of frequent reminders from both US ambassador Oakley and his deputy, Beth Jones. Jones recalls being a frequent visitor to the president's office in Islamabad, reminding him that if Pakistan chose to further enrich uranium to weapons grade then the US president would not be able to issue a waiver and the Pressler Amendment would kick in stopping all aid to Pakistan. Personally, both Oakley and Jones were opposed to the Pressler Amendment. Jones gave Ishaq a chronology of all the meetings they held with Ishaq warning him at different stages. 'Both Bob [Oakley] and I were extremely resistant to the Pressler Amendment. It was completely stupid and counterproductive...made it impossible [for us]...It cut off all relations with the Pakistani military for a decade.'[49]

The nuclear issue also created some excitement during May 1990, when tensions between India and Pakistan arose out of the upsurge of nationalistic violence in Kashmir and Pakistan's subsequent support for the 'freedom movement'. The US believed that both countries were on the brink of war and a nuclear exchange might be in the offing. Deputy Director of the CIA, Robert Gates, was sent to both Pakistan and India to quieten things. Bhutto was on a Middle East tour when he arrived. The Pakistanis denied any preparation for nuclear war. In fact, President Ishaq vigorously countered Gates's 'frank' comments in which he had told the Pakistanis (including General Beg, who sat silently throughout the meeting) that the US had war-gamed the matter and calculated that Pakistan would lose a war with India, and the latter would end up occupying Pakistani territory. Ishaq said that 'if war games could decide the outcome of wars, none would ever have been fought.' Ishaq's response to threats of freezing US aid was emphatic, 'The truth is that the US too often used its aid as a lever. We did not succumb in the past and we will not give up our principles for the sake of American aid or fear of war.'[50]

The ISI had already started using its experience and resources from the Afghan jihad to begin helping the Kashmiri uprising against Indian control in Kashmir. India, of course, felt that Kashmir was an integral part of the union and saw this as interference in its internal affairs. Part of the Pakistan Army calculus in supporting the Kashmiris was that it would drain Indian military resources and force them to cut back on their troops facing Pakistan across the international boundary; a calculus that was to be repeated and become the basis of many an ill-planned venture against India in Kashmir in later years. Bhutto was not part of the initial planning for the Kashmir operation that was conceived and executed by the ISI. Indeed, at a meeting that she called to discuss the Kashmir situation, she was advised by the Foreign Office as well as the military, through its DGMO, Jehangir Karamat, that the army did not favour a military solution to the Kashmir situation.[51] Bhutto called a meeting of all parties to discuss the Kashmir issue on 4 February but she could not preside over it since she was in hospital recovering from the birth of her child. Chief Minister Nawaz Sharif 'spoke sensibly' on the topic, according to Akhund.[52] However, the next day, Sharif issued a call for a strike in support of Kashmir. Sharif, himself of Kashmiri origin, spoke vigorously of fighting for Kashmiri 'independence'. His colleague, Sheikh Rashid, declared publicly that he was sponsoring a training camp to help support the Kashmiri jihad.[53] The growing intrusion of Pakistan into the Kashmiri uprising provoked US congressional attention. Congressman Stephen Solarz called a hearing on Pakistan's support for 'terrorism,' putting Pakistan under scrutiny and further reinforcing the view widely held in Pakistan that with the Afghan war winding down, the United States would yet again abandon Pakistan.

The US was also watching the disintegration of the Bhutto government from within. Charges of corruption involving her husband, Asif Ali Zardari, surfaced often. At one point, one of Bhutto's senior aides went to Beth Jones at the US embassy and asked for her help in raising the issue of Zardari's alleged corruption with PM Bhutto, since her colleagues could not raise it. Jones refused. Jones also recalls senior PPP ministers coming to her to explain how they needed to make deals in a hurry, related to contracts for oil exploration, for example, knowing that they did not have much time in government. The Canadian ambassador also told Jones of direct approaches to him of a similar kind. 'It could have been such a good thing for Pakistan,' says Jones ruefully, of the first Bhutto stint in office.[54] Thus, despite efforts by the United States, and even by the international financial community— including IMF Managing Director, Michel Camdessus, who had told his senior staff: 'We must help this lady!'—Bhutto found herself fighting for survival barely twenty months after she had taken office. Arrayed against her was not only the political establishment but also the military whom she had antagonized.

In 1989, a group of retired ISI officers were implicated in a plot code-named 'Midnight Jackal' to subvert parliamentarians from the PPP and bring about the fall of Bhutto's government through a no-confidence vote in the National Assembly. Bhutto maintains that she got reports of these efforts and that the finances were coming from Saudi Arabia, so she dispatched an emissary to King Khalid to check the veracity of this claim:

[He] said, 'no.'

I said, 'You call me your daughter. If there are any problems, tell me.' And he sent me a message back...'I said you are my daughter and you are my daughter. I would never do it. Your father was like a brother to me. I respected him. I said that his murder was unjust. I said it then. I told Zia, and I am telling you. I said you are my daughter. I would not do it. And I have not done it. But they are private groups.'

One of his advisors told my emissary that the private group is the Bin Ladens. So we knew. And why did we get suspicious? Because the ten million dollars arrived in mango crates. So my own political supporters turned around and said, 'Why would mango crates come from Saudi Arabia? Date crates would come from Saudi Arabia.' If they'd sent it in date crates and not mango crates, maybe we wouldn't have known the money had come.[55]

Regardless of where the money came from, whether it was Bin Laden or other sources, Midnight Jackal failed and finally Ishaq had to dismiss Bhutto's government. However, other resources were then tapped to ensure that she did not get re-elected. Ishaq's surreptitious plan had been repaired and even when Bhutto sent an emissary, Happy Minwalla, to inquire if a move was afoot against her, the president told Minwalla that he had 'no intentions of doing anything against the constitution,' a white lie that helped him keep the lid on his moves. Roedad Khan, an eminent civil servant, who had been pressed back into service with Ishaq, writes about the fears that Bhutto would get wise to their plans. But she was apparently convinced by Ishaq's assurance to Minwalla. In the end, Ishaq did what he promised: he used the constitutional powers that he had inherited from Zia to dismiss Bhutto and call for fresh elections.[56] Even when Bhutto telephoned him that fateful evening of 6 August 1990 to ask him the reasons for his actions, Ishaq told her to listen to his six o'clock address to the nation.[57] A two-panel cartoon in *The Frontier Post* captured her brief tenure very nicely: it showed in 1988 a car, minus tyres, raised on a pile of bricks. Ishaq is handing over a key to Bhutto, saying 'Drive it!' The next panel for 1990 shows Bhutto having put the rear wheels on the car and proceeding to put the front wheels on, but Ishaq is standing in front, saying: 'Stop it now!'[58]

ELECTIONS 1990

One of the first steps after Bhutto's removal was the appointment of a new DG ISI. Beg sent his DG MI, Major General Asad Durrani, to take over from Kallue. Durrani continued to hold both intelligence posts for some time (later he was replaced as DG MI by Major General Javed Ashraf Qazi, a future DG ISI under General Abdul Waheed). Beg was determined to help Bhutto's main rival, Nawaz Sharif of the Muslim League, and his IJI colleagues win the impending elections. He sought local financing too and got Rs140m from Yunus Habib of Habib Bank and later Mehran Bank in Karachi. This amount was deposited in the ISI's accounts and then disbursed by its new DG, Durrani, to opponents of Bhutto before the 1990 elections. Durrani later provided an affidavit listing the recipients of money from the ISI following a case registered by retired Air Marshal Asghar Khan against General Beg, General Durrani, and Mr Habib on the 'criminal distribution of the people's money for political purposes.'[59]

As reported by the leading newspaper columnist, Ardeshir Cowasjee, based on the Durrani affidavit:

> Nawaz Sharif received [in rupees] 3.5 million, Lt. Gen. Rafaqat [of President Ghulam Ishaq Khan's election cell] 5.6 million, Mir Afzal 10 million, Ghulam Mustafa Jatoi 5 million, Jam Sadiq Ali 5 million, Mohammad Khan Junejo 2.5 million, Pir Pagaro 2 million, Abdul Hafeez Pirzada 3 million, Yusuf Haroon 5 million [he confirms having received this for Altaf Hussain of the MQM], Muzaffar Hussain Shah 0.3 million, Abida Hussain 1 million, Humayun Marri 5.4 million. Aslam Beg, under oath, revealed the existence of a political cell within the ISI, whilst strangely clarifying that though he was aware of the distribution of funds, he was never personally involved.
>
> Further names of anti-PPP politicians who received payments from the ISI during the run-up to the 1990 elections rigged in favour of the IJI and Nawaz Sharif were later revealed [in rupees]: Jamaat-i-Islami 5 million; Altaf Hussain Qureshi and Mustafa Sadiq 0.5 million; Arbab Ghulam Aftab 0.3 million; Pir Noor Mohammad Shah 0.3 million; Arbab Faiz Mohammad 0.3 million; Arbab Ghulam Habib 0.2 million; Ismail Rahu 0.2 million; Liaquat Baloch 1.5 million; Jam Yusuf 0.75 million; Nadir Magsi 1 million; Ghulam Ali Nizamani 0.3 million; Ali Akbar Nizamani 0.3 million.[60]

Accompanying the above-mentioned affidavit was a photocopy of a letter dated 7 June 1994, from Durrani to then prime minister (for the second time) Bhutto from his post as Pakistan's ambassador to Germany. This letter lists additional 'embarrassing or sensitive' information in the shape of amounts that were given to former PPP stalwarts Hafeez Pirzada, Sarwar Cheema, and Mairaj Khalid. Durrani wrote that 'the remaining 80 million were either deposited in the ISI's 'K' fund (60 m[illion]) or given to director external intelligence or special operations (perhaps the saving grace of this disgraceful exercise. But it is delicate information.)' Cowasjee notes that that in the margin of this paragraph is a comment 'by the writer in his own hand [saying], 'This is false. The amount was pocketed by Beg (Friends),' referring to the think-tank that General Beg was planning to set up after retirement.[61] Other recipients of the Habib funds included the election cell in the office of the president. Durrani maintained that the operation had Ishaq's blessings and 'the whole-hearted participation of the caretaker PM [Jatoi]' and that the military high command was aware of it. Beg was to assert later on that he had briefed Prime Minister Nawaz Sharif and his successor as COAS, General Asif Nawaz, about these funds, but this clarification was offered in April 1994, more than a year after General Nawaz had died. Beg did not mention receiving any funds for FRIENDS, nor why the army would accept donations from a private banker when it had resources from the state as well as its own foundations to look after its troops' welfare.

The caretaker government of Prime Minister Ghulam Mustafa Jatoi, a former PPP stalwart, launched investigations into corruption of some of the PPP ministers and even Bhutto herself. While a laudable goal in any administration, such actions were seen by external observers as being one-sided. The US envoy, Robert Oakley, who by then had acquired the reputation of speaking his mind and had been dubbed 'viceroy' by some in Pakistan, spoke out against such actions. In a speech in New York, he warned against singling the PPP out for such inquiries: 'In my view, if there is to be "accountability" for those holding political office, it should not start from the November 16 1988 elections which brought in the PPP, but should also include the 1985–1988 period when the IJI parties and politicians ran the government.'[62]

PRIME MINISTER NAWAZ SHARIF

Not surprisingly, the IJI,—with an IJI caretaker prime minister and pro-IJI ministers in power—was swept into power in November 1990, capturing 105 out of 216 seats in the National Assembly and control of all four provincial governments. The Pakistan Democratic Alliance (PDA), headed by the PPP, won 45 seats, the second largest bloc in the assembly. Thus, Bhutto was elected leader of the opposition. Despite loud complaints by Bhutto and others about irregularities, the election observers from the National Democratic Institute for International Affairs, funded by the US Congress, gave the results its seal of approval, though with some reservations: 'Notwithstanding serious irregularities in certain constituencies, the IJI would have obtained the largest number of seats in the National Assembly.'[63] As one overseas commentator for Oxford Analytica puts it: 'The victory of the IDA [the English initials of the IJI], with 105 seats (a gain of 50), had been anticipated; but the extent of its success is a surprise.' Among the factors contributing to the defeat of the PPP and its loss of some 48 seats in the assembly were:

- Bhutto's failure to bring about any major social or economic reforms;

- Her inability to strengthen her support base in Punjab, which has 60 per cent of the country's voters, compounded by her constant conflict with Nawaz Sharif, the leader of the IDA
- Although there was no firm evidence of massive vote rigging, the caretaker government certainly used its power and resources to influence voters against Bhutto. Ishaq and Beg spoke against her.
- The IDA, albeit a motley coalition of parties, was able to field a single candidate in every constituency against the PPP, which in the past was the main beneficiary of split votes.[64]

The caretaker Prime Minister, Jatoi, having done his duty, was dispensed with in the National Assembly as he vainly tried to become the regular prime minister. Nawaz Sharif had been pre-ordained for that role. As Admiral Sirohey notes: 'As far as the JCSC was concerned, Mr Nawaz Sharif was the next prime minister…. There was a very fortunate situation for the country when there was harmony between the President, the Prime Minister and the armed forces.'[65] The following two-and-a-half-years would prove how poor Sirohey's judgment was on political matters.

Sharif swept into the capital, flush with his success at the polls and having secured his base in the Punjab, where his brother Shahbaz Sharif was an activist chief minister. The PPP had been sidelined for the time being. He was the first businessman-cum-chief executive with a platform that was pro-business. He also believed that he had a mandate from the people that allowed him to re-shape the economy and Pakistani politics. Very quickly, he brought into play a series of privatizing moves that garnered the support of the business community and began opening up Pakistan's highly controlled bureaucrat-run economy. His own family had suffered at the hands of the earlier nationalizations by Z.A. Bhutto. Their Ittefaq Foundries had been taken over and the family had to seek political and business refuge in the United Arab Emirates where they had to borrow to start afresh. He was determined to recreate his business empire again and also to empower the new and rapidly rising urban population that had brought him to power in the 1990 elections. He did not fully comprehend or support the nature or the role of the troika that had been formed after Zia's death. He felt it was loaded against him as the prime minister.

In Nawaz Sharif's view: 'If the president thinks that he can dissolve the assembly, he has the power to dismiss the government….He has the power to do—to appoint the governors…the chief of army staff and the others….the chief executive [the prime minister] who has the mandate of the people, who is responsible for delivering the goods to the people…is very heavily dependent on the president…. And if the president wants to blackmail the chief executive or the prime minister, he can do so. So [when] they are referring to that [system as a] troika it cannot be called a troika. It was a sort of understanding…a tacit understanding between two people: the president and the chief of army staff, versus the prime minister.'[66]

Upon coming into office, Nawaz Sharif recognized that the president had inherited certain powers and areas of primary responsibility from Ziaul Haq: foreign policy, especially on the Afghan issue, nuclear matters, and Kashmir. He believed that the army wished to keep three things with them: Afghan policy, Kashmir policy, and the nuclear policy. Sharif ran into rough waters when he tried to assert himself. For instance, Beg came into his office recognizing the supremacy of the civil in his Order of the Day issued to all troops. Yet, Beg believed himself to be ordained with the power to help the civil decide political matters, and he had the military man's typical disdain for the politicians' ability to take tough decisions or resolve national issues amicably. Ishaq, a stickler for rules, understood the powers of the president all too well and largely shared Beg's poor opinion of politicians. Ishaq generally found himself siding with the army when he had issues with Sharif. On the Kashmir issue, however, Ishaq and Sharif shared a common goal. They saw the fight for Kashmir to be a jihad that was incumbent on Pakistanis and supported whatever trouble they could foment in Kashmir for India, even if it meant using the Islamic radicals from the North West Frontier region or the newly freed-up fighters that had waged the successful jihad against the Soviets in Afghanistan.

Sharif also came into the PM office in the wake of a sudden US decision on 9 October 1990 to impose sanctions on Pakistan for pursuing its nuclear enrichment programme. Some $600 million of US aid were halted because the US believed that Pakistan had enriched its uranium to weapons' grade. Helping in this decision was the fact that Pakistan had lost its strategic value to the US after the Soviets pulled out of Afghanistan. Despite last minute efforts by the US administration in Washington to persuade Congress to delay imposing sanctions until after the installation and settling-in of a new government in Pakistan, US lawmakers were in no mood to compromise. All aid ceased and even the F-16 fighter jets that Pakistan had started paying for were impounded and parked in a dry desert base in the hinterland. US officials advised Pakistan to continuing paying for them to keep the deal alive whenever relations thawed. That thaw did not occur for some years. But the sanctions did not deter Pakistan. If anything, as later events were to prove, they further strengthened the view in Pakistan that it needed to ensure its own security by acquiring nuclear weapons. As President Bush's national security advisor was to state, the US pushed Pakistan in that direction.[67] So, the new prime minister had his hands full from the outset, dealing with issues at home and abroad.

TENSIONS WITH BEG

Beg was content to have his own former DG MI, Asad Durrani—now in the ISI—keep the military informed. Though the DG ISI titularly reported to the prime minister, Durrani in fact did not win Sharif's confidence and kept any criticism of him that occurred in the inner circles of the army high command away from Sharif's ears. In time, this led to a parting of ways. As Beg entered his third and final year as army chief, he was also looking to the future. He prepared a paper on the higher command of the armed forces that suggested further strengthening the role of the CJCS. Among other things, this paper suggested giving the chairman the control over the army's budget and its senior promotions, both key elements in the power pack of the army chief. Ishaq appeared to understand the implications of these suggestions and did not act immediately on them. But he was forewarned of Beg's intentions.

Sharif and Beg also crossed swords on the issue of the coalition fight against Iraq's invasion of Kuwait. When the US and its allies put together 'Operation Desert Storm' to free Kuwait, Pakistan was asked to participate and to send troops to Saudi Arabia. Nawaz Sharif consulted the army chief who agreed to Pakistan's participation in the war.[68] Pakistan did agree to send some troops to defend Saudi Arabia but not to participate in any hostile actions outside its borders. Beg, who was attuned to the popular views of the Pakistani street, saw Pakistanis generally opposing any US-led invasion. The right-wing religious parties were on the rampage, now asking for a jihad against the Americans. Many of them offered to send their followers to defend Iraq against the US invaders. Following a visit to Multan where he had been energetically discussing Pakistan's role in the coalition, he went to a war game organized in Gujranwala on 16 January 1991. There, a paper was presented by his head of the air defence command, Agha Masud, which advocated a different tack and presented a grim view of the invasion. The co-authors of this paper were General Javed Nasir and General Hamid Gul, according to Beg's personal secretary at that time, Brigadier Ziauddin Khwaja. Even as allied air and land troops easily broke into Kuwait under the rubric of Operation Desert Storm, the paper talked of the strength of the Iraqi forces and their ability to send back 'body bags' that would break the US spirit at home. Beg took up that refrain and spoke against the plans for a US-led invasion. In a speech on 2 December at the Pakistan Ordnance Factory at Wah, Beg spoke of the 'strategic defiance by the people of Iraq against the "strategic military intimidation" by the powers that be' [the US and other coalition forces.] He then went on to prescribe a similar strategic defiance for Pakistan by establishing 'an understanding with Iran and Afghanistan.'[69] His speech at Wah and a subsequent one at Quetta on 16 December, in which he talked of Pakistan building a 'viable deterrence [meaning nuclear], which is meaningful, real, and visible' got immediate accolades from a leading pro-Iranian commentator and Beg associate, Mushahid Hussain (later a founding director of Beg's foundation FRIENDS, and after that, a member of Nawaz Sharif's own inner circle, before joining Sharif's opponents in another military government). Hussain, the former editor of *The Muslim*, wrote that 'these views are bound to find resonance among the Pakistani people since they reflect popular aspirations for a foreign policy which is independent both in form and content and seeks to promote the national interest divorced from the crutches of the United States, which, in the popular perception, is seen as the best friend of the Muslim world's worst enemy, Israel.' Hussain went on to praise Beg's break with the Americans and conclude that 'Pakistani leaders have been willing to sacrifice the national interest at the altar of the American connection.'[70]

On 28 January 1991, soon after the US invaded Kuwait to 'liberate' it and carried the war to Iraq itself, Beg defined the Gulf War as 'a Western-Zionist game plan to neutralize the Moslem World'.[71] Speaking for about half an hour to some 600 officers of the Pakistan Army at a Sunday gathering at the army's GHQ, he said that the United States of America will meet the same fate in this war as the Soviet Union had to face after its intervention in Afghanistan. Referring to Iran and Iraq as 'two giants' who were seen by the West to pose a threat to Israel, 'Iraq,' Beg charged, 'was encouraged to invade Kuwait, which provided enough justification for initiating this war.' He predicted that the war would be a long one, lasting into the summer months, with the US forces being bogged down in land warfare after little initial success of the air effort. He suggested a 'strategic consensus' of regional countries against this war to provide a meaningful deterrence.[72] Beg's perspective was at sharp variance from the government's policy and its active participation in the coalition effort. Pakistan heard immediately from the Saudis through diplomatic channels that because of Beg's opposition to the coalition's plans against Iraq in Kuwait they would want Pakistan to bring back the soldiers that Pakistan had sent there.[73] Beg also had a soft spot for Iran and maintained close ties to its leadership. At the same time, he began propounding his philosophies of 'strategic depth' and 'strategic defiance', borrowing to some extent these concepts from his former DG ISI and current corps commander, Hamid Gul. The idea behind these doctrines was that Pakistan could tie up with Afghanistan and Iran to be able to fall back into their territories in case of war with India.[74] Even in his last few weeks in office, he was entertaining visiting delegations from Iran and discussing collaboration with them. The incoming chief, Lt. Gen. Asif Nawaz, sent a message to Beg through the DG MI, Major General Qazi, that he hoped no firm commitments were being made since he planned to review all such activities upon taking over in August. To drive the point home, General Nawaz arranged a separate meeting with the Iranian visitors to make sure they understood that Beg was a lame duck.[75]

This public break on the Gulf War with the prime minister did not sit well with Sharif nor with the United States. In fact, Sharif recalled that: 'I didn't like that statement of General Aslam Beg because it clearly came into clash with...a declared policy of the Government of Pakistan.... I was very upset at that time.... of course, the (sic) history also proves that [the] policy pursued by the Government of Pakistan was the right policy and that [the Beg] policy...that statement and that thinking, that ideology was incorrect.... Had we followed the policy of General Aslam Beg—we were doomed!'[76]

SELECTING A NEW ARMY CHIEF

By the time the dust settled on 'Desert Storm' and Kuwait was liberated, the rift between Beg and Sharif widened. Ishaq too had become wary of this seemingly delayed but overtly ambitious streak of his army chief. Rumours began flying that Beg did not wish to leave when his term expired on 16 August 1991. Contenders began to emerge for the post of Beg's successor and also for the post of CJCS, both of which were to fall vacant the same day. Among the issues being bandied about was whether a Punjabi army chief would be recommended to the appointing authority, the president, by a Punjabi prime minister or whether the best person would be selected regardless of ethnic origin. The senior-most serving officer at that time was Lt. Gen. Shamim Alam Khan, whose promotion to lieutenant general had earlier been effected by Prime Minister Junejo during his tiff with General Ziaul Haq. He was followed in seniority by the Karachi corps commander, Lt. Gen. Asif Nawaz. It was widely rumoured that Beg's own choice of army chief was Lt. Gen. Hamid Gul, who was then a corps commander in Multan.

Shamim Alam was one of nine sons of an Indian survey officer in the corps of engineers during the Second World War, all of whom ended up joining military service. All nine rose to high ranks and most of them were awarded high battle honours. One of the brothers, Brigadier Zahir Alam Khan, helped in capturing Sheikh Mujibur Rahman when the army moved against the Awami League in Dacca (now Dhaka) on 25 March 1971. Shamim Alam was educated at Lawrence College and then Government College Lahore, and was a cavalry officer. He won a Sitara-e-Jurat in the 1965 war as a commando with the SSG. He was trained at Staff College at Camberley in the United Kingdom, saw action again in 1971 in Chamb with 28 Cavalry, and had attended the war course. He was also an instructor at the NDC, commanded an armour brigade and then the 1st Armoured Division before being sent to GHQ as VCGS. He later commanded an infantry division and then II Corps as a lieutenant general. He had a stint at GHQ again as the CGS before being sent to command the Bahawalpur Corps.[77] All in all, a brilliant career.

Asif Nawaz belonged to a military family of the Janjua Rajput clan from Jhelum, which had sent soldiers into various armies since time immemorial and had been fighting other tribes in the Potohar plateau, including the Gakkhars, who dominated the region. His father, Raja Abdul Ghafoor Khan, and uncles had served in the army. His grandfather had risen to the rank of honorary captain in the British Indian Army. He joined the army straight after high school at St. Mary's Cambridge School in Rawalpindi and after initial training at the Joint Services Pre-Course Training School in Kohat, arrived at the PMA in Kakul from where he was selected as the top cadet in his intake (the 15th PMA regular course) to go to the Royal Military Academy in Sandhurst, United Kingdom. He was there from 6 September 1955 to 20 December 1956 and then was commissioned into the Pakistan Army with his PMA course on 31 March 1957 into 5 Punjab Regiment, (Field Marshal Ayub Khan's regiment and also of his adoptive father Brigadier Muhammad Zaman Khan, who had looked after him since infancy), joining the regiment in Dacca, East Pakistan (now Dhaka, Bangladesh), then commanded by Lt. Col. A.A.K. 'Tiger' Niazi. He missed action in the 1965 war, being in the ISI as a young captain in Karachi. He was selected for service with the British Army on the Rhine in West Germany, where he served in 1969 as a company commander with the Gordon Highlanders and then in the United Kingdom with the Green Howards in York. He took his Staff College Course and then the War Course and in between served as brigade major of 111 Brigade in the Chamb sector in Kashmir in the 1971 war against India, then taking over as CO of his Sherdils in the Fazilka sector during the war. Later he served at corps headquarters in Multan under fellow Sherdil, General M. Shariff, and moved with him to JCS HQ as his colonel staff before being promoted to brigadier, when he helped launch a new corps headquarters in Quetta. He commanded 7 Division in Peshawar from 1982–85 and then took over as commandant of the PMA before being promoted to lieutenant general as commander V Corps in Karachi in May 1988 (among the last senior army appointments approved by Prime Minister Junejo), where he came into the spotlight as a tough but fair officer who could handle the hurly burly of politics with equanimity. Ishaq had dealt with him during the Bhutto period. Nawaz and Beg had clashed on a number of occasions on policy issues, specially related to the problems in Sindh, where Nawaz favoured a political solution and quiet diplomacy, while Beg favoured army action and aired his views often in the public.

The third and junior-most contender was Hamid Gul, whose grandfather had been in the army but his father did not join. He entered PMA in the 18th regular course and was commissioned into 19th Lancers. He held choice instructional appointments and then was selected to go to Staff College, Camberely (UK). He saw action in 1965 but his brigade was never launched during the 1971 war in the 'offensive that never came.' As he put it, 'we were in the assembly area when we were pulled back. What a bitter period of our history that was.' He was COS of a corps, then commanded an armoured brigade, and the 1st Armoured Division before moving to GHQ as director MI under General Beg, who later sent him as DG ISI. There, he claims to have created the IJI, the alliance of parties that opposed Bhutto's PPP in the 1988 elections. Bhutto removed him from the ISI and he was then sent to Multan as the corps commander. An unabashedly ambitious, intense, and eloquent person with detailed views on almost any topic that he is faced with, he favoured a strong army involvement in Pakistani politics and alliances with Afghanistan that would afford it 'Strategic Depth.' This was consonant with Beg's views. Gul also had close relations with Sharif, having installed him at the head of the IJI and supported him with ISI funds and resources. Ishaq showed Gul the document that had been given to him by Ambassador Oakley of the Gujranwala presentation of 17 January 1990 and that had scribbled across it 'from HG to AB.' He denied that he had authored it, pointing to the bad English of the text as not his style. But he says that Ishaq told him he would have difficulty making him chief and that Oakley used to refer to him as 'Saddam Gul.' According to Gul six names were sent up to the president through the prime minister, without any change. He says his name was on the top. Asif Nawaz was at the bottom. He also states that even Gulbadin Hekmatyar met Ishaq and recommended that Gul be made chief.[78]

Ishaq was aware of the machinations going on behind the scenes. He wished to avoid a direct confrontation with Beg and acted swiftly, after Asif Nawaz had been brought from Karachi to the GHQ as CGS in May 1991. Within a month, on 11 June, even as the rumour mills of Rawalpindi and Islamabad were abuzz with talk of a potential coup by Beg, Ishaq announced that Beg was retiring and would be succeeded by Asif Nawaz as army chief, while Shamim Alam Khan would become CJCS. Ostensibly, he acted in order of seniority. In fact, Ishaq had conducted a series of interviews with key military and civilian persons to seek their views on what qualities they were looking for in the next chief. General Rahimuddin Khan, biased in favour of Nawaz, who had been his brigade major and subsequent friend, says he told Ishaq that the army needed a strong leader who could inspire it and who was apolitical.[79] Beg's personal secretary, later Lt. Gen. Ziauddin, described Nawaz as an 'imposing personality.'[80] Apparently, that is what Ishaq was looking for someone strong enough to lead the army and give it direction, without getting ambitious about political affairs.

Nawaz Sharif denies Gul's claim that six names were sent up. He says there were only three names: Shamim Alam, Asif Nawaz, and Hamid Gul. Sharif says he favoured Shamim Alam, being the senior-most. He says he did not have time to discuss the issue either with his own colleagues or with Ishaq. This claim is hard to believe, given that Sharif and his colleagues spent a lot of time discussing the army, the presidency, and their relations with both institutions.[81] In Sharif's view, the powers to recommend the COAS to the president 'are that of the prime minister. But he [Ishaq] felt that this is his exclusive domain, and...why should he discuss this matter with the prime minister. So, he was keeping all these secrets very close to his heart. So I went to him and I said the time was approaching him for a new chief of army staff to be appointed...in my view we should go for the senior-most and that is General Shamim Alam. [But] he said, "No I have already decided on General Asif Nawaz and therefore he will be the new chief of army". That settled things.

Ishaq wanted to do everything publicly, to show that a smooth transition was taking place in the army's high command. Therefore, a parade was organized at the Army Hockey Stadium in Rawalpindi, attended by Ishaq, Beg, and the incoming chief. Soldiers from Beg's former regiments, 16th, 30th and 36th Baluch Regiments, 20th Sindh Regiment, and the SSG marched past (in the case of the SSG commandos, they hopped past, shouting Islamic battle cries). Beg took the farewell salute, flanked by Prime Minister Nawaz Sharif to his left and President Ishaq to his right. Ishaq praised Beg while recognizing that Beg's 'frank comments sometimes caused misgivings', but that at heart Beg had sincerity of purpose and consideration for the national good.[82] His successor, Asif Nawaz, stood one step behind them. A few senior politicians and row upon row of soldiers filled the stadium. This parade was the first such ceremony for the Pakistan Army.[83] Beg was to retire to his 12,000 square-foot new home opposite the Army House in Rawalpindi and become active in politics in due course, starting a political party of his own that never gained traction. He was a frequent speaker on public issues and foreign policy, but did not attract a following from either end of the political spectrum.

The day after the parade, a small private ceremony was organized in the lawn of the Army House by its staff and military guards. The COAS's flag was raised at one minute past noon and General Asif Nawaz officially took over as COAS, surrounded by family and very close friends. Although he had selected Brigadier Sikander Shami, another Sandhurst graduate and son of a celebrated hero of the 1965 war with India, to be his personal secretary, he temporarily retained Beg's personal secretary Brig. Ziauddin Khwaja before promoting the latter to major general and posting him to Lahore.[84]

A FRESH START

The next morning, General Nawaz drove into the GHQ for the first time as the army chief. A splendid guard of honour led by a nervous young captain of his parent regiment, 5 Punjab, welcomed him to his new job. He began by issuing his Order of the Day, a customary message to the officers and troops of the Pakistan Army that presented his views on the nature and role of the Pakistan Army. After the customary and obligatory seeking of 'Allah's blessings and guidance from the Quran and Sunnah', he praised the army that in his view had 'the best fighting men in the world. Few would know this better than me, for I was born and bred within the environments of this Army, and have had its culture thoroughly imbibed and nurtured within my soul.' But very quickly he got to the heart of the matter:

> ...as the democratic process has now taken hold, I would like it to be clearly understood that the Army must have nothing to do with politics. Let the elected representatives do their job, while we concentrate on acquiring ever greater professional excellence. Remember, soldiering is a fulltime profession that is very demanding and does not brook half-hearted measures.

He ended with the gist of his message:

> We must avoid involvement in politics and devote ourselves to our profession. Let us consolidate our gains and develop realistic and implementable doctrines, organizations and systems that make optimum use of available resources.[85]

Briefly put, he was clarifying for his colleagues in the military a shift in approach and leadership from Beg's grand designs and political adventurism. However, as events unfolded, he was drawn into the political maelstrom. In fact, as he was meeting his senior colleagues at the GHQ to chart a new direction for the army, a few miles north at Faisal Mosque, Prime Minister Nawaz Sharif was standing shoulder to shoulder with Ijazul Haq (the late dictator Ziaul Haq's son), proclaiming Zia a *shaheed* (martyr) and claiming that uncovering the elements behind Zia's death was now his 'prime mission in life.' They were marking the third anniversary of Zia's death. Nothing came of Sharif's promise though, and the comradeship between Sharif and Ijazul Haq would end with a parting of ways, when the junior Haq tied his fortune to another military ruler in 1999.

In discussing with my brother the draft of his Order of the Day, I had pushed for a public and highly visible move against corruption in the army as a signal to the rest of the political system, even sending him a draft to that effect. He countered that, 'I have only three years. If I get involved in this, I will not have time for anything else. You don't know what sort of army I have inherited!' He was also careful not to overemphasize the role of religion, so that the army could focus on its military training and activities.

THE CORPORATE ARMY

On becoming COAS, General Nawaz not only commanded some 520,000 soldiers and officers. He was also chief executive officer (CEO), so to speak, of a huge industrial conglomerate with an annual turnover (in 1991) of 12–14 billion rupees, ranging from small arms, ammunition, electronics, and telecommunications to banking, breakfast cereals, cotton ginning, plastics, real estate, automobile engineering, cooking oil, and transportation of goods, among other things. The largest private conglomerate at that time, the Crescent Group, only had an annual turnover of six billion rupees.[86] As the army chief, General Nawaz directly controlled the appointment of persons to head the operations of entities such as the Frontier Works Organization, the Special Communications Organization, and the National Logistics Cell (NLC—responsible for transportation across the country, having started during the Afghan jihad to carry US supplies from Karachi to the north). He also appointed persons to run the Fauji Foundation and the Army Welfare Trust, set up to benefit ex-servicemen. Another group of entities came under the administrative control of the government's Defence Production Division (DPD). These included the Pakistan Ordnance Factory at Wah and the Heavy Defence Industries at Taxila as well as the Heavy Rebuild Factories (also at Taxila). While the COAS did not actually control the operations of these entities under the DPD, he appointed the officers who ran them, and the army was the main customer of these enterprises.

While there was some initial justification for the army to be involved in running enterprises that provided it secure material and weapons, the spread of the army into other areas created a 'crowding out' effect, taking away resources and opportunities from other competing governmental and private activities. The army received preferential access to state controlled resources and were not subject to the tight constraints and scrutiny that the market imposed on private entities. Pakistan Railways, for instance, suffered as the NLC took on the job of transporting items up and down the country. The same was true in banking and consumer goods. By definition, the senior managers of these enterprises were not trained managers of private enterprises. They had to learn on the job, translating their military leadership skills to the world of commerce, with very mixed results. However, these appointments gave the army chief a good lever to use in shuffling and rewarding individuals as needed. Senior army officers vied with each other to get plum appointments so they could double dip with their military pensions and benefits as well as the generous perquisites that came with their new jobs as heads of army-controlled enterprises.

Among the most visible results of the military's intervention in the marketplace were the rising numbers of Defence Housing Authority (DHA) schemes that had sprung up in and around the military cantonments across the country. By placing the logistics and military lands and cantonments under the respective corps commanders, General Ziaul Haq had created a new way of involving serving officers in commercial ventures. Heavily subsidized plots garnered multiples of their purchase price on the free market. Over time, a secondary market developed for the files of these plots in prospective DHA schemes, with bidding wars carried out by private brokers, pushing prices higher and higher. This behaviour shifted the purpose of the DHA away from providing adequate post-retirement housing for army officers, to purely commercial ventures that competed with the private sector. The army became involved in acquiring land, ostensibly for military purposes, and then turning it into lucrative housing schemes. The Ministry of Defence, which had been responsible for releasing state land to the military or reacquiring it in case the army did not need it, gradually lost all control of that process during the Zia era. Even if he wanted to, General Nawaz would not have the time or energy to turn back the clock on these ventures. The 'Culture of Entitlement' that Zia had nurtured had taken root. It had become normal for senior army officers to own multiple plots of land in cantonments at inflated values, and for these officers to be accommodated in well-paid jobs in army-controlled enterprises, or failing that, in the foreign service as ambassadors. The new chief would create huge waves if he tried to turn back this tide. But he had other issues that weighed even more heavily on his mind.

THE POLITICAL DIMENSION

The appointment of the new army chief was an event of some significance; over time, the post had taken on greater heft. 'The army chief acquired salience in Pakistan's body politic because of the chronic political instability and fragmentation of the political process. The political elites were so weak and divided that they could not sustain the principle of civil supremacy over the military,' wrote a leading military analyst, Dr Hasan Askari Rizvi, immediately after Asif Nawaz had been named the new army chief. Because of the weakness of the politicians, Rizvi believed that the army leadership became more involved in political matters, autonomous in its decision making, and resentful of any civil interference in its matters. Finally, politicians began cultivating the military brass to gain advantage over their political opponents.[87] Rizvi warned Nawaz Sharif 'not to alienate the generals while stay[ing] in command of prime ministership—a dilemma that post-martial law regimes often face.'[88]

The new troika had one celebration early in its tenure. With the Soviet withdrawal from Afghanistan in February 1989, fighting for Kabul had intensified. Eventually, the city fell to the rebel Mujahideen, who formed a new government. A triumphant meeting took place in Peshawar, at which the army chief, the prime minister, US ambassador Robert Oakley, and Sharif's new ISI chief, Javed Nasir sat down to plan an entry into Kabul.[89] Eventually, the party, including Prince Turki Al-Faisal of Saudi Arabia, took off for Kabul in a C-130 aircraft that came under fire as they flew into the city. As they crossed into Afghan air space, the ISI chief yelled out a Islamic battle cry, startling the other passengers. An exultant Sharif could lay claim to having fulfilled his mentor Zia's promise of liberating Kabul. Afghanistan was freed of the Soviets and the fighting now began among the Afghans, the results of which struggle were to haunt the region for decades hence.

Other international issues that hung over the new army chief were Pakistan's relations with India, the United States, and Iran. Coming from a post-independence generation, General Nawaz took a pragmatic view of the hostility toward India. He recognized that the Kashmiri struggle for their rights needed Pakistan's continued support. But he saw opportunities for better understanding with the Indian military to reduce tensions across the border, and invited Indian retired military officials, including the hawkish former army chief, General K. Sundarji, to visit him at his home in Rawalpindi.[90] He was invited by the Indians to visit but they made the mistake of announcing this in the parliament before the invitation had reached Pakistan and been approved by Prime Minister Sharif.[91] After Indian COAS, General S.F. Rodrigues insisted that he come, 'even for a tennis match,' evoking memories of General Zia's 'cricket diplomacy' of earlier years, General Nawaz sent him a light-hearted message through the Pakistan defence attaché in New Delhi, Brigadier Jamshed Gulzar: 'I don't play tennis, but I did box for Sandhurst!' That settled the issue. Privately, he talked about the possibility of engendering greater confidence by having both sides move troop formations an agreed distance away from the international boundary, as a precursor to talks between the political leaders. This led to a private warning conveyed from senior US officials through me (the author) that the new chief needed to be careful that he did not 'get too far ahead of the public opinion on Kashmir and related issues.'

As far as the United States was concerned, the relationship between the Pakistan Army and Centcom was strong, despite the ups and downs of political relations. General Nawaz had a strong and informal relationship with the Marine, General Joseph Hoar, who had succeeded Norman Schwarzkopf of Desert Storm fame as the third commander of Centcom. Nawaz encouraged Hoar to visit Pakistan and even travel around the country. One such visit was to Balochistan where Hoar was hosted by corps commander Lt. Gen. Abdul Waheed, laying the ground for a good relationship between the two later on. General Waheed told me soon after he succeeded General Nawaz that he was grateful for this accidental introduction to Hoar, whom he had taken on a shooting trip. But the nuclear issue and terrorisms continued to bedevil relations between the US administration and the Pakistan government. General Nawaz was determined to help Pakistan come out from under the threat of being listed as a terrorist state. When the US approached him informally to see if Pakistan might make soldiers and officers available to help the US in its peacekeeping role for the United Nations in Somalia, he was quick to respond that the proper channel for this request was through the prime minister. However, the Pakistan Army was ready to do what it could to help, if it were given the right equipment for the job.

The first contact was made with me in Washington by Under Secretary of State Frank Wisner, who said that President George Bush wanted to get Pakistan's okay before he went to spend Christmas 1992 with the US forces in Somalia. I relayed this message to General Nawaz and the latter's positive response back to Wisner. Next, I heard from Ambassador Oakley who wished to talk about modalities. I raised the issue of equipment. He said that the Department of State lawyers had ruled that because of the embargo against Pakistan, the United States could not provide any equipment directly to Pakistan. First, I suggested the possibility of using the US reserves that were left in Saudi Arabia after Desert Storm. The second approach we talked about was to have the US supply the equipment and transportation for the United Nations that could in turn use it to bring the Pakistanis to Somalia. The equipment finally came from US stocks in Italy. Eventually, this is how the US got out of its own legal bind. I suggested that a direct call from President Bush to Prime Minister Sharif, who had not been honoured by such a communication up to that point, would be greatly appreciated. It was.

Soon after taking over, General Nawaz visited Iran. Earlier, in the waning days of the Beg tenure as army chief, he had had some discussions with visiting Iranian delegations that had been talking to General Beg about collaboration at different levels. During his October 1991 visit to Tehran, he recalled President Hashem Rafsanjani taking him aside after the formal meetings and asking him: 'When could we expect to receive the technology that your predecessor had promised us?' General Nawaz says he knew instantly that this was a reference to nuclear collaboration and feigned complete ignorance. He promised that he would go back and check with the president and prime minister and follow up. General Nawaz told me that on his return he met the president and prime minister together and told them about this. He asked if they had authorized General Beg to make any promises to Iran. Both said they had not. Therefore, he did not follow up on the matter with Iran.

Beg's DG MI, then Major General Javed Ashraf Qazi recalls General Nawaz meeting a delegation sent by Iranian minister, Mohsen Rezaie to meet General Nawaz with a view to seeking Pakistan's help for Iran's nuclear programme. General Qazi recalls vividly that General Nawaz told the delegation: 'Pakistan's nuclear programme is not for sale and no country on earth should think of acquiring the technology from Pakistan because Islamabad has made it a policy decision not to take part in proliferation of the technology since Pakistan has attained it for its own exclusive use.'[92]

DIFFERENCES EMERGE

In the meantime, the deceptively mild-mannered prime minister with a long memory was rankled by the seriousness with which the president was taking his extraordinary powers under the 8th Amendment. Sharif believed that the president was bound by whatever advice the prime minister gave him. Ishaq Khan did not agree. The latter had already chosen the new COAS, going against Sharif's choice. Sharif began to make some moves to remove the 8th Amendment but failed to gain enough leverage in the assembly. This created further tensions between him and Ishaq Khan. Sharif also found that he and the new army chief thought differently on most matters. Having grown up in the business community, Sharif believed in the give-and-take of the marketplace. Personal relationships were important to him and to his father, Mian Muhammad Sharif, known to the public as 'Aba-ji' (the polite equivalent of 'Daddy', by which both Nawaz Sharif and his brother Shahbaz referred to their father). One of the first actions that the Sharif family initiated was a gathering arranged by the patriarch of the family where he sat down his two sons before the new army chief and told General Nawaz in Punjabi, their common tongue: 'These two are your younger bothers. If they misbehave, just tell me and I shall fix them!' The general was not used to such informality and may have appeared stand-offish. Later, his taciturn responses at the breakfast meetings that the prime minister would invite him to, also did not add to building confidence between them. Sharif began cultivating other generals in the army, using, among other things, family or tribal connections to reach out to them. In one case, he was reported to have given the brother of the corps commander in Lahore a lucrative license for an industrial unit. This led to the corps commander being summoned for a dressing down by the new chief.

Reports started coming in to the COAS that the prime minister had gifted new BMW cars to some generals. This created alarm in the mind of Asif Nawaz. One day, he was visited by Shahbaz Sharif, who brought over the keys to a BMW, and said: 'Aba ji has sent as a gift for you.'[93] General Nawaz refused with thanks. Later, when he went to call on the prime minister in Murree, he found out for himself that these reports about the BMWs were accurate. According to him, as he prepared to leave, the prime minister accompanied him to his car, surrounded by colleagues. 'What car are you using?' asked Sharif. 'A Toyota Crown,' replied General Nawaz, pointing to the old model he had used for his visit. 'This car does not befit you,' said Sharif in Punjabi, their shared language, and signalled to a colleague who trotted off and drove back a new BMW sedan that had been clearly waiting for that moment. Sharif presented the keys to the BMW to General Nawaz, saying: 'This is the car that you deserve.' General Nawaz recalls being momentarily frozen by the audacity of this action. Quickly, he dropped the keys back into the prime minister's hand, and said: 'Thank you very much. Sir! I am happy with what I have,' saluted him, and drove off.[94] What the prime minister probably thought as a friendly gesture was not seen as such by the army chief, who felt that it was a public demeaning of his office and a crude attempt at bribery. The disconnect between these two members of the troika grew worse over time.

Sharif describes Asif Nawaz as a 'headstrong individual, who did not consider the Prime Minister as (sic) the Prime Minister.' in other words he showed no respect to the civilian head of government.[95] Sharif also states having received reports that General Nawaz was meeting politicians and complaining that the government was not operating well, with a view to creating a lack of confidence in the Sharif government. General Nawaz talked with me (the author) about meetings with members of Sharif's own cabinet, some of whom would come to see him at Army House to complain about Sharif and seek the army chief's help in toppling Sharif. He would tell them that if they were unhappy, they needed to change things within the political system. Among the PML leaders who came to see him with this message were Pervez Elahi, Malik Naeem (whose own brother was a general in the army), and Sheikh Rashid. In the meeting with Elahi, during which Elahi bemoaned the loss of the 'protecting hand' of General Ziaul Haq and the hijacking of the PML by the Sharif brothers, and suggested the army chief needed to support a change in the civilian leadership, General Nawaz said to him: 'If you are waiting for a signal from me to do something then you will be waiting for a long time! You politicians need to handle these things by yourselves.'[96] One famous female Punjabi politician, who was later given a senior diplomatic assignment, even complained to General Nawaz that the Sharif brothers were 'blackmailing' her since she had accepted cash from them which she had used to persuade an opponent to concede an election to her in her political constituency. She said to General Nawaz that the Sharifs were using that incident against her to get her to do their bidding.[97] No doubt, some of these same politicians were going back and telling Sharif stories about General Nawaz.

Then, there was the old habit of drawing the army chief into areas that were not in his orbit. Ziauddin, the former personal secretary to Generals Beg and Nawaz, who was then a major general and heading an army division in Lahore, recalls being asked by Chief Justice Naseem Hasan Shah about a case that had been launched against Ghulam Ishaq Khan: 'What does the army chief want?' Ziauddin contacted General Nawaz who told him to tell the chief justice, 'Do what is right.'[98]

Two other events alarmed General Nawaz and contributed to the widening of the gap between him and the prime minister. First, he got word that the prime minister had said that 'some of our people should also be promoted within the army.' This echoed Benazir Bhutto's statement that had created ripples within the Beg army headquarters earlier. The army had increasingly become a self-contained corporate entity that did not brook any interference from any external quarter. Yet, when I asked him about the brothers of both Malik Naeem and Chaudhry Nisar who were serving officers, General Nawaz told me that he intended to promote both 'since they are both good officers.'[99] He had tried to raise the issue of changing a number of senior officers whom he had inherited from Beg but the president had dissuaded him, wondering why he seemed to be in a hurry to make these changes. Yet, he did the best that he could, including sending the DG MI, Major General Qazi to become MGO. Qazi's remit was clear cut: clean up the corruption and the mess in purchasing supplies for the army! He also planned to change the Islamist corps commander in Rawalpindi for having allowed a maverick major general to launch an unauthorized attack in 1990 in the Kargil area that resulted in the loss of many lives.

Nawaz Sharif believed that as prime minister he had the right to appoint anyone to any position in the army. But he insists that he made no such move during Asif Nawaz's tenure or even later during the Musharraf period. Another report that reached General Nawaz was a conversation between Sharif and his confidants, which included the IB Chief Brigadier Imtiaz Ahmed, who was alleged to have said in response to Sharif's complaints about the 'headstrong' army chief that he would 'make a Gul Hassan out of him!' In other words, he would be able to remove the army chief easily, following the example of the senior Bhutto, when he had the army chief Gul Hassan and the air chief Rahim Khan abducted to Lahore and then replaced. Others who were reported to have turned against Nawaz included the prime minister's close confidant, Chaudhary Nisar Ali Khan, an erstwhile supporter of Asif Nawaz. General Nawaz, who believed in coming out in the open with his innermost thoughts sometimes to the level of political indiscretion, repeated this threat at a formation commanders' meeting and asked them rhetorically: 'Will you let someone do this to your chief?'

The ISI head, General Durrani, recalls being alarmed at this statement and worried that it would further poison relations between the army chief and the prime minister, when one of the hundred plus officers at the meeting carried the story back to Sharif. He states that he did not wish to add to the mistrust between the two, and when Nawaz Sharif asked him later if there was any interesting news out of the army meetings, he said 'No.' Within a matter of days, he states that he heard from the army chief that the prime minister wished to change the DG ISI, as he had 'lost confidence in him'.[100] The prime minister then moved quickly and in a meeting with the army chief informed him that he had decided to appoint Lt. Gen. Javed Nasir as the new head of ISI. Nasir, a born-again Muslim with a rakish past, had once been the engineer-in-chief at GHQ. Sharif had not asked for the traditional panel of names from the army chief and acted without any consultation. A member of the proselytizing Tablighi Jamaat, Nasir had become a devout Muslim with a flowing white beard. He did not look at women and would turn his face away if a woman entered the room. And he had no background in intelligence work. General Nawaz was surprised and annoyed by the manner in which the new ISI head had been appointed. Now he would have to contend with a hostile ISI supporting the prime minister against him. The pressures continued to mount on the army chief to launch a coup from both inside the army and from political circles. He was determined to resist them.

US VISIT

They even followed him to the United States in January and February 1992, when he was the first senior Pakistani official to visit the US after the imposition of sanctions and while Pakistan was under the threat of being declared a terrorist state. During that visit, Nawaz met, among others, Secretary of Defense Richard Cheney, Deputy Director of the CIA Richard J. Kerr, and officials at the NSC in the White House, as well as members of Congress and the Centcom head, General Joseph Hoar. He also held a background luncheon meeting with the publisher of The Washington Post, Katherine Graham, and her senior editors and reporters, to explain Pakistan's nuclear policy and reassure them that Pakistan would safeguard its nuclear assets.[101] During his meeting at the CIA, he bluntly raised with US officials the question of a coup. 'Do you want the army to intervene?' he asked. 'Because those are the signals that you keep giving me!' He did not get a clear reply. During the same trip, he was approached by Yusuf Haroon, member of a leading Pakistani business family and former vice president of Pan American airways, who came from New York to visit him at my home in Alexandria, Virginia, to persuade him to consider a coup, which Haroon contended would be supported broadly and for which the latter would help clear up any legal issues and garner US support. A disappointed Haroon was later to ask me to help persuade General Nawaz to act.[102] Despite his estrangement from the prime minister, General Nawaz said he did not wish to pursue the extra-constitutional path. When asked much later whether he knew of any plans of a coup, Prime Minister Sharif categorically denied that he had any evidence that General Nawaz planned to upend the government.[103]

It was during the US visit that General Nawaz managed to make one personnel change at home that had been a source of concern to him. He had been very wary of his senior-most corps commander, the former head of the ISI, Lt. Gen. Hamid Gul; especially so when he was out of the country and Gul could act in his stead as the temporary army chief. He was also aware of the fact that Hamid Gul had political contacts, despite being a corps commander. Gul had, for instance, been calling journalists and briefing them during Bhutto's short-lived regime. He also felt that Asif Nawaz was open to the idea of a roll-back of the nuclear programme that the Americans were seeking. Gul had been a candidate for the post of army chief (which Nawaz finally got), and he held a grudge against the Americans who he felt had opposed his appointment. Pakistan was determined to develop good relations with the United States again and to avoid being labelled a terrorist state. To neutralize Gul, Asif Nawaz decided before leaving for the United States in January 1992, to move him to the Defence Production Complex at Taxila. He instructed the new corps commander in Lahore, Lt. Gen. Jehangir Karamat, to go and relieve Gul at short notice. While he was in the United States, he received a call from his CGS, Lt. Gen. Farrukh Khan, that Gul had refused to take up his new assignment. Gul had apparently spoken with the prime minister and understood from him that the prime minister would support him. Gul then telephoned his wife to inform her that he would not be moving. MI intercepted his calls and reported them to the army chief.[104] When the CGS called him at my home in Virginia, General Nawaz instructed the CGS to place Gul at the disposal of the Ministry of Defence; and if he did not go, he would stand retired. That is what happened in the end.

By the summer of 1992, General Nawaz felt himself isolated from the prime minister. He had not yet been able to establish a relationship of trust with the president either. He arranged through a common friend, Shahid Javed Burki, to convey to the president that he needed to meet him, and the need to establish an understanding on how to deal with a recalcitrant prime minister. He also feared that Sharif might seek to remove him and wanted Ishaq's reassurance on that issue.[105] Burki met the president the same evening and brought back word that the army chief need not worry about being removed from office. Ishaq also agreed that they should meet. General Nawaz did not wish to suggest a coup but a smooth in-house change within the prime minister's party, if that would help calm things down. This was the gist of a single sheet aide memoire that he carried to his subsequent meeting with Ishaq and brought back from the meeting.[106] (He suspected, as he had told Burki earlier before Burki's meeting with Ishaq, the president's office and home were bugged and his documents were not safe either.) Subsequently, the president developed a better understanding of the army chief's position and they established a good rapport.

SINDH LIGHTS THE FUSE

The issue that really ruptured relations between the army chief and the prime minister was the policy on Sindh. The PML had formed an alliance with a former partner of Bhutto's PPP—the urban-based MQM, which had gained in strength after Bhutto's fall and had challenged the army too on occasion. Starting life as an urban-based political party that filled a vacuum in Pakistani politics, the MQM had become a militant group that relied on near-fascistic discipline and enforcement to keep its members in check. It was alleged to have begun operating a parallel government in Karachi and in other urban centres of Sindh. Meanwhile, both the MQM and governmental agencies were pressuring the PPP and harassing their members in the cities and the countryside. Even the US Congress took note of this and the Congressional Human Rights Caucus wrote to Sharif to complain about it, while praising the efforts of General Nawaz to restore order in the troubled province. 'We have been encouraged by the release of hundreds of political prisoners, including members of the opposition political parties. We have also received positive reports that the army, under the leadership of the new Chief of Army Staff General Asif Nawaz, has taken significant steps to suppress terrorist activity within the urban centers of the country.'[107] That may have further exacerbated the prime minister's concerns about the COAS.

The army had also encouraged the formation of a rival faction of the MQM to counter the central role of Altaf Hussain's MQM, prompting Hussain to leave the country for the United Kingdom. As the law and order situation worsened in the province, the government had sought the military's help in quelling it. The army acted swiftly against the troublemakers, including the MQM. This created a serious problem for the government, leading Sharif to think that the army had done it on purpose to weaken his coalition. But once the job was done, the army wanted to quit its operations in Sindh. This did not sit well with the prime minister.

On 5 June 1992, Prime Minister Sharif lauded army personnel for killing nine terrorists in Tando Bahawal near Hyderabad. According to local police, they recovered two Kalashnikovs, a shotgun, thirty-six hand-grenades and other explosives. But following an expose by a Pakistani journalist for the BBC, in a stunning reversal of position, the Pakistan Army announced on 13 June that the people killed on 5 June were not terrorists but innocent *haris* or poor peasants. The army revealed that its investigation, ordered by the army chief General Nawaz into the incident, led it to believe that the peasants had been picked up by a detachment under a Major Arshad Jamil and murdered in cold blood. The alleged purpose of this action was to terrorize some women who had initiated legal action against one of the major's local friends. There was no firefight nor were any weapons recovered from the scene. Because of this incident, General Nawaz immediately removed the local division commander and some subordinate officers, and Major Jamil and his accomplices were brought to trial. Jamil was eventually sentenced to death and hanged on 28 October 1996. The accomplices were given life sentences. The Pakistan Army, by carrying out an open inquiry and sharing its results, had acted swiftly to right a wrong, winning the approval of the public.

As *The Friday Times* editorial in the wake of this incident put it:

> Gen. Asif Nawaz, Chief of Army Staff, has been better than his word. For the first time in living memory, army heads have rolled for an anti-public act—a Major General, two Brigadiers and one colonel were sent packing and a major will most certainly face a court martial for the Tando Bahawal tragedy. The COAS has now moved into second gear and demonstrated his resolve to be ruthlessly fair. The dreaded terrorist wing of the MQM was defanged in the blinking of a fearful dusk in Karachi last Friday....This is certainly the Pakistan Army doing its duty in Karachi.
>
> Here is the army chief's philosophy: Violence is not the way for political parties or groups to settle political differences; ordinary citizens are tired of being coerced, intimidated and surrounded by fear; political factions are a fact of life, they should live amicably with one another; the army will not take sides.[108]

Within three weeks, the army chief and his colleagues presented the president and the prime minister their report on Sindh, with a view to extricating their forces from the province. At a four-hour meeting in the GHQ, attended by the president, the prime minister, the ministers of defence, interior, the chief minister of Sindh, the CJCS and the air and naval chiefs, General Nawaz notably did not ask for additional legal cover under Article 245. Rather, he stressed the need for an immediate political and social programme in support of the military's 'Operation Clean-up'. He presented a list of seventy-two 'big fish' whose arrest could bring normalcy to the province of Sindh. The corps commander V Corps, Lt. Gen. Naseer Akhtar, outlined details of an alleged plan by the MQM of establishing a separate 'Urdudesh' or 'Jinnahpur'. But he distinguished between the criminal elements of various organizations and political parties, and the majority of Sindhis, whether Urdu-speaking or native Sindhis, who were 'law abiding and patriotic citizens.'[109] This presentation clearly alarmed Prime Minister Sharif and his colleagues, who felt that the army had overstepped itself and was threatening the government's coalition with the MQM.

Rumours of an impending army coup started circulating in the capital. One story that emerged from a pro-Sharif senior intelligence official involved the 111 Brigade, which guards the capital and the homes of the president and prime minister. The brigade was reported to have moved out 'with arms and live ammunition' and was seen approaching Rawal Lake and Nilore Road near Islamabad. This was around the period in December 1992 when the PPP had promised a Long March on the capital and the government suspected that the army chief, via the MI, had signalled to the PPP to proceed. The Sharif government was also keeping tabs on a leading journalist, Maleeha Lodhi, who visited Army House frequently and was suspected of being a PPP supporter and stoking the army chief's anti-Sharif mood. She was the subject of some brazen and even scurrilous attacks via rumour and innuendo by the IB. A senior official close to the prime minister, who wished to remain anonymous, says he called the Rawalpindi corps commander, Lt. Gen. Ghulam Mohammed, a religious holdover from the Beg era and asked him about the troop movements. GM, as he was known, said he would call him back later. This official suspects he immediately called Asif Nawaz, because he tried GM's number again and found it to be busy. A little while later, he says that the army chief had called him directly and said: 'Why did you call GM?' The official explained the reason and his information that the army was on the move. General Nawaz then reportedly said: 'Will you inform the PM?' 'No,' replied the official.[110] However, no action was taken by the army that night. A previous DG ISI, Asad Durrani, when asked about this incident, was incredulous. 'It also does not make any sense. If you want to take over, you don't have to go and deploy yourself around Rawal Lake. 111 Brigade sends a couple of companies, they go and take over the PM House. In fact, the units are already there doing the guard duty.'[111] Even if true, there is no evidence that the army did anything threatening that night. But the atmosphere was tense as 1992 came to a close.

Asif Nawaz met twice with his senior corps commanders in Rawalpindi during December 1992, after an overseas trip to Poland. After one of the meetings he arranged a smaller gathering at his home, and invited a handful of corps commanders. Among them were Generals Karamat, Naseer Akhtar, and Muhammad Tariq. None of them recalled any talk of a coup at that meeting.[112] Tariq, however, does remember that Javed Nasir telephoned Karamat in his room at the mess where he was staying, before and after the meeting at Army House, perhaps to get details of what transpired. Karamat confirmed this. So the level of suspicion was very high, even among the corps commanders. Hassan Abbas quotes Yusuf Haroon as stating that a coup was discussed at a meeting in the corps commander's home in Lahore days before General Nawaz died, and word of it leaked out.[113] General Nawaz did not travel to Lahore in that period. The meeting where he met with a small group of corps commanders had taken place in Rawalpindi at Army House. Despite repeated questioning from each of them individually, none of the corps commanders recalls any mention of a coup at this dinner.[114] Among other things, General Nawaz had his impending visit to the United States on his mind. We spoke about his plans on the telephone when he was at a stopover in Geneva after a visit to Poland, and I was in Vienna, Austria. During that conversation, he acknowledged that, 'things are fine with the prime minister. It's some people around him that are causing problems.' Yusuf Haroon also reported to Mushahid Hussain that General Nawaz had a coup in the offing and that he had spoken with the general about it during his Washington trip. He also told Hussain that he had come to Pakistan during the summer of 1992 to 'plan the new cabinet under General Asif Nawaz.' Hussain also recalls hearing from Prime Minister Nawaz Sharif about a conversation he had with Nawaz a few days before his death, during which the general seemed stressed out. He had told Sharif that he was under 'great pressure,' but reassured Sharif of his good intentions.[115]

During this period, Nawaz was apparently under great pressure from those who saw martial law as inevitable and, according to one political analyst, Nasim Zehra, these people 'offered a task-list to the general. Banners appeared on the walls of Lahore and in parts of Rawalpindi and Islamabad, which read "*Asif Nawaz Aao, Mulk Ko Bacchao!*" (Asif Nawaz, Come Save the Country!).' Zehra quoted a 'concerned' retired general saying at that time: 'I am worried. It is in such times when politicians come running to you to convince you that you must save the country. Many of us fall prey to the temptation.' But, Zehra concluded: 'Clearly Asif Nawaz did not.'[116]

General Nawaz also was concerned deeply about the growing sectarian violence in the country, especially in the Punjab. In an earlier conversation with me, he stated that roughly 300,000 civilians were under arms in Pakistan at that time and worried that if they were to unite, the Pakistan Army would not be able to handle the ensuing violence inside its borders. He talked with me about the possibility of disarming the sectarian militias, such as the ultra-orthodox Sipah-e-Sahaba and other Jhang-based entities. There were reports from some of his colleagues subsequently that he had in mind an operation sometime in 1993 to that end. During his tenure, he had managed to dissociate the army from the Islamist parties and continued to try to reduce the influence of the Islamists inside its ranks.

The army chief was preparing for his second visit to the United States, to take place in early February 1993, when he suffered a heart attack while exercising one morning at Army House on his treadmill. He was rushed to the hospital after some attempts to make him comfortable at Army House, but despite all efforts to resuscitate him, he passed away in the afternoon on 8 January 1993, barely one year and five months after taking over as army chief. A fitting tribute to him came not only from the local media, but also from Western media.

The New York Times obituary the next day was headlined 'Champion of Democracy'. The British newspaper *The Independent* obituary said:

> The last of the Sandhurst-trained generation of Pakistani officers, Nawaz was known as a 'soldier's soldier' who had no political ambitions. His aim was to keep the army out of politics and restore the military's credibility both at home and abroad after long bouts of martial law. During his short 16 months in office, he was instrumental in trying to restore Pakistan's relations with the West, after Washington cut off all aid to Islamabad because of its nuclear program. As a strong believer in liberal values, he was trying to improve the military's relations with India and take Pakistan out of the dead-end legacy of Islamic fundamentalist rhetoric led by his two predecessors, General Ziaul Haq and General Aslam Beg.... Unlike so many of his predecessors, Nawaz was incorruptible.[117]

The Frontier Post called him a 'post-cold war warrior', and specifically on his handling of the explosive Sindh situation, stated:

> When assigned the job of bringing the law and order situation under control in Sindh, a mess created by civilian components of troika and various agencies, the army under him adopted an admirable course of 'even-handedness' to the dismay of the rulers in Islamabad. By doing so the army got unprecedented support from all sections of the people in Sindh, especially from the alienated Sindhis, and its legitimacy and neutrality was restored in the eyes of the people.[118]

As this and other newspapers noted, General Nawaz's death created a vacuum in Pakistan at a time of high political tension at home and abroad. His death did not bring to an end the struggle between the army and the prime minister nor between Sharif and President Ishaq, as later events were to prove. Moreover, General Nawaz's death was to play a major role in those events.

SELECTING A NEW CHIEF

Even as the previous chief was being buried and mourned by a stunned nation, jockeying began for his replacement. The senior-most corps commander, Lt. Gen. Muhammad Ashraf Janjua, who had earlier suffered a reprimand at the hands of his fellow Janjua, Asif Nawaz, took over as acting chief. Many considered him a favourite of Sharif. Meanwhile, Ishaq wished to promote Lt. Gen. Farrukh Khan, the CGS, to army chief. Farrukh Khan had been a close confidant of Asif Nawaz and was a mild mannered individual who would be seen to carry forward General Nawaz's policies. But Nawaz Sharif bitterly contested Ishaq's plans. The two had an acrimonious exchange, following which Sharif's advisor, Chaudhry Nisar, came to see Roedad Khan, the president's advisor, and asked him to see if Ishaq could select anyone other than Farrukh since Sharif felt that Farrukh had been behind all the prime minister's problems with Asif Nawaz. Finally, the president called Lt. Gen. Saranjam Khan from GHQ and asked him to call Lt. Gen. Abdul Waheed to come and meet the president. Ishaq had selected Waheed, also known by his tribal name as Abdul Waheed Kakar, then corps commander in Quetta and getting ready to retire.[119] Kakar had not gotten along with Beg and had been 'exiled' to Quetta by Beg.[120] Of course, in Pakistan's conspiracy-prone atmosphere, the first comments that arose were that Ishaq had selected a fellow Pushtun to strengthen his hands against the Punjabi prime minister. Neither Ishaq nor Sharif realized at that point the import of this choice.

NOTES

1. General Yakubu 'Jack' Gowon was a course mate of my elder brother Asif Nawaz from 6 September 1955 to 20 December 1956 at the Royal Military Academy at Sandhurst (UK) and a teammate on the Sandhurst boxing team. Asif Nawaz was in Ypres Company (New College) while Gowon was in Normandy Company (Victory College). They both were commissioned in December 1956 from Sandhurst. My brother was then ranked number one in his 15th PMA course that was commissioned in early 1957, because of having gone to Sandhurst. On his return from Sandhurst, he joined 5 Punjab Regiment, the Sherdils, commanded by Lt. Col. A.A.K. 'Tiger' Niazi in Dacca, East Pakistan (later infamous for his disastrous tenure as a general in the same location in 1971). Gowon progressed rapidly through the Nigerian army and made it to colonel when a coup on 29 July 1966 occurred. The coup leaders named him to head the government. He soon became a general while my brother was still a captain.

2. http://www.brainyquote.com/quotes/authors/c/chinua_achebe.html accessed 16 November 2007.

3. Among the techniques reportedly used by Gul and Sharif to keep these meetings hidden was the designation of the encounters as meetings between Hamid Gul and Husain Haqqani, a former *Far Eastern Economic Review* correspondent, who had signed up to be an advisor to Sharif and later became his official media advisor. Haqqani later was to switch over to Benazir Bhutto, who made him ambassador to Sri Lanka. Some observers of the

scene accord Haqqani a prominent role in the formation of the IJI and in the Sharif government's operations. Bhutto however disagrees saying that the civilians, like Haqqani, did not carry any clout and that it was the 'uniform' of the army officers of the ISI that swayed most politicians to go against her party.

4. Husain Haqqani, *Pakistan: Between Mosque and Military* (Washington, D.C.: Carnegie Endowment for International Peace, 2005), p. 202. Haqqani cites how Gul persuaded the Jamaat-i-Islami head Qazi Hussain Ahmed, to join the coalition against the PPP. He does not mention his own role in this period.

5. Interview with Prime Minister Nawaz Sharif.

6. Interview with Ambassador Robert Oakley.

7. Three-part interview with Prime Minister Benazir Bhutto, starting in Washington DC and ending with two sessions in Dubai.

8. Saeed Shafqat, 'Pakistan under Benazir Bhutto', *Asian Survey*, Vol. XXXVI, No. 7, July 1996, p. 659.

9. Interview with Ambassador Elizabeth ('Beth') Jones.

10. Oakley interview.

11. Interview with Richard L. Armitage, former Assistant Secretary of Defense for International Security, 1983–9, and Deputy Secretary of State, 2001–5.

12. Interview with Bhutto. This section relies on her responses during this interview.

13. Interview with Prime Minister Bhutto.

14. Admiral Iftikhar A. Sirohey, *Truth Never Retires* (Lahore: Jang Publishers, 2000), p. 367.

15. Oakley interview.

16. PM Bhutto interview.

17. Interview with General Mirza Aslam Beg.

18. Beg interview.

19. Mary Anne Weaver, 'Letter from Pakistan,' *The New Yorker*, 14 November 1988.

20. E-mail exchange with General Jehangir Karamat. April 2007.

21. Exchange with General Jehangir Karamat.

22. Interview with Benazir Bhutto, summer 2006. I had asked her about this episode and a later one involving General Pervez Musharraf. Later she included a version of this exchange in a revised edition of her autobiography *Daughter of the East* that included an additional chapter updating her life as a prime minister. Army officers maintain that war games are just that. They test assumptions and individuals have roles assigned to them to play out to the best of their abilities. All armies use this technique to learn from these brain-storming sessions and refine their actual operational plans. War games should not be confused with actual operational plans.

23. Benazir Bhutto interview.

24. General Mirza Aslam Beg, 'The Rejoinder to Benazir Bhutto,' *The Pakistan Observer*, 12 April 2006.

25. Presentation by ISPR Directorate, courtesy of Brigadier Riazullah, DG ISPR.

26. 'Deterrence, Defence, and Development' *Defence Journal*, July 1999.

27. Oakley interview.

28. I am grateful for this detail to a Pakistan Army major who attended the US debriefing in the field.

29. Bhutto interview.

30. Bhutto interview.

31. Iqbal Akhund, *Trial & Error: The Advent and Eclipse of Benazir Bhutto* (Karachi: Oxford University Press, 2000), p. 89.

32. Bhutto interview.

33. Interview with Lt. Gen. Ziauddin Khawaja, who was private secretary to Beg.

34. Interview Lt. Gen. Javed Ashraf Qazi, later director MI and DG ISI.

35. Interviews with Oakley and Bhutto.

36. Sirohey, *Truth*, pp. 379–80.
37. Ibid., p. 385.
38. Bhutto interview.
39. Private correspondence from Ambassador Robert Oakley to Shahid Javed Burki, 15 April 1992.
40. Quote from *The Herald*, March 1990, p. 44.
41. Conversation with General Asif Nawaz.
42. The first term refers to a weak local blackbird, the second to the origin of the refugees from India, also known as Hindustan, and the third to their habit of wearing form fitting white pants or pajamas as opposed to the traditional *shalwar* (baggy pants) worn by the Punjabis.
43. Shafqat, *'Pakistan Under Benazir Bhutto,'* p. 662. The GOC Hyderabad, Major General Qazi states that the number of killed was less than ten and the figures were highly exaggerated. Ms Bhutto asserts that the total number of deaths could be not corroborated and was 'normal' for the area.
44. Interview with Lt. Gen. Javed Ashraf Qazi at that time major general and GOC of the army division in Hyderabad. He was also responsible for breaking up a major operation of the Al Zulfikar Organization (AZO), the group headed by Ms Bhutto's brother Mir Murtaza Bhutto. Some sixty members of the AZO were eventually discovered and picked up. This event may have brought him to the notice of General Beg who eventually brought him to GHQ as the director, MI in place of Major General Asad Durrani. The AZO operated independently of PM Bhutto's government. The army conducted this operation without informing the prime minister until well after it had been completed.
45. Interview Lt. Gen. Qazi.
46. *The Herald*, July 1990, p. 31.
47. Aitzaz Ahsan, 'A man and a general,' *The News*, Lahore, 22 January 1993. In this eulogy, published after the death of General Nawaz, Aitzaz Ahsan stated that by disengaging the army from political concerns, General Nawaz 'has left it in politically competent hands. The torch has been passed on with the ease of a relay race in an athletics competition. There will be no controversy or debate, because he established the tradition of civilian competence.'
48. Interview with Beth Jones.
49. Ibid.
50. Akhund, *Trial*, p. 234.
51. Report from a senior Foreign Office official, who remarked that Karamat, normally a quiet man was uncharacteristically blunt in his assessment of the situation and in his assertion that the army was not prepared to go to war with India.
52. Akhund, *Trial*, p. 209.
53. Ibid.
54. Beth Jones, op. cit.
55. Bhutto interview.
56. Akhund, *Trial*, pp. 306–307. This action was taken within days of Iraq's invasion of Kuwait, which helped Pakistan avert the full concentration of the United States on this action in Pakistan.
57. Roeded Khan, *Pakistan—A Dream Gone Sour* (Karachi: Oxford University Press, 1998), p. 109. The author, now a popular pro-democracy columnist, claims 'There was no deception plan'.
58. Feica Cartoon, *The Frontier Post*, 8 August 1990, p. 7.
59. Ardeshir Cowasjee 'We Never Learn from History 2,' *Dawn*, 4 August 2002. Cowasjee, a columnist wrote a series of articles exposing Beg's role in this affair and wrote also that Beg had not rebutted his facts nor challenged them in court.

60. Ardeshir Cowasjee, 'Take the money and run: why this prevarication?' *The Daily Times*, Lahore, 22 January 2006.

61. Cowasjee, 'We Never Learn from History 2.' FRIENDS was the acronym of General's Beg think-tank that was officially inaugurated on 21 August 1991 three days after he retired but for which he had begun collecting support before he left the army. I recall being told about this enterprise while Beg was still COAS by Mushahid Hussain, the Pakistani journalist and now politician, who told me that Beg was destined for great things and he had joined the Board of FRIENDS. This was before Beg retired from his post and Mushahid found his vocation in politics under first Nawaz Sharif's Muslim League and then his opponents' Muslim League during the Musharraf regime. Hussain remains on the Board of FRIENDS.

62. Speech by Ambassador Robert B. Oakley at the Asia Society, New York, 11 September 1990.

63. '1990 Pakistan National Assembly Elections', Executive Summary. National Democratic Institute for International Affairs, Washington DC, January 1991.

64. 'Bhutto's Defeat', Oxford Analytica, Friday, 25 October 1990.

65. Sirohey, *Truth*, p. 445.

66. Interview with Prime Minister Sharif.

67. Interview with General Scowcroft.

68. Interview with Prime Minister Nawaz Sharif.

69. 'Defence forces should be able to act as deterrent—Beg', *The Nation*, Lahore, 5 December 1990.

70. Mushahid Hussain, 'Towards a made-in-Pakistan worldview.' *The Nation*, Lahore, 16 December 1990.

71. 'Gulf Predicament', Oxford Analytica. Tuesday, January 1991.

72. Mariana Babar, 'Iraq to prove Afghanistan: Beg sees game plan in allied action. Germany, Japan to emerge new power centres.' *The Nation*, Lahore, 29 January 1991, p. 1.

73. *Ghadaar Kaun? (Who's the traitor?)* Nawaz Sharif's story in his own words, a book length interview with Sohail Warraich. (Lahore: Sagar Publication. 2006), p. 94.

74. Hamid Gul was shown a copy of the paper that found its way to the US ambassador Robert Oakley who showed it to him. Gul denies that he was connected to the paper, arguing among other things that it was poorly written in English that he would have never used. Interview with author.

75. Interview with Lt. Gen. Javed Ashraf Qazi.

76. Sharif interview.

77. Interview with Brig. Zahir Alam Khan, *Defence Journal*, April 2002.

78. Interview with Gul.

79. Conversation with the author.

80. Ziauddin Khwaja interview.

81. In the days and weeks leading up to the selection of the new chief, various groups were trying to decipher the signals and trying to align themselves with whomever they saw as the eventual winner of the derby. Sharif's own senior advisers apparently had their own favourites too. Two of them, Chaudhary Nisar Ahmed and Malik Naeem may have conveyed to Asif Nawaz that they had been lobbying for him with the prime minister. Sharif denies that he discussed the issue with his colleagues. On the day the announcement was to be made by President Ishaq, Asif Nawaz was called to meet him. On his return from the presidency, he telephoned me in the United States to tell me that he had been named the next chief and stated that 'I want you to remember Nisar and Malik Naeem, for helping make this possible.' Nisar's father Brigadier Fateh Khan had been a senior military man himself.

82. *The Muslim*, 16 August 1991, p. 10.

83. Ishaq created confusion about the name of the new chief by referring to him often as 'General Asif Nawaz Janjua,' using his tribal surname name that the general did not use but other members of his extended family did. In Pakistan's still rather feudal society, many newspapers had started referring to him as General Janjua.

84. A simple handing-over ceremony of the armband was done in the central corridor of Army House. Zia who later came to fame as DG ISI and temporarily as General Pervez Musharraf's replacement in October 1999 had expected that because of tensions between his former boss and General Nawaz, he might be sent to Siberia. He was pleasantly surprised with the outcome. The author recorded these events and the formal guard of honour the next day on film and video tape.

85. Order of the Day by General Asif Nawaz, COAS, Pakistan Army, 17 August 1991. Issued in both English and Urdu. This was read out to all troops.

86. M.A. Niazi, 'COAS as CEO': Pakistan's military-industrial complex,' *The Nation*, Lahore, 22 June 1991.

87. Hasan Askari Rizvi, 'COAS and the political process,' *The Nation*, Lahore, 14 June 1991.

88. Ibid.

89. At this meeting, while discussions were at their peak, Javed Nasir turned to General Nawaz and whispered that it might be good to arrange a cricket match. A bizarre suggestion, given the setting. It turned out that he was trying to get the prime minister and the army chief together and suggested a friendly cricket match between their teams. General Nawaz recalls telling him to shush!

90. A family photo of General and Mrs Sundarji with General and Begum Asif Nawaz at Army House was carried in the posthumous first volume of General Sundarji's autobiography completed by his wife. General K. Sundarji, *Of Some Consequence: A Soldier Remembers* (New Delhi: Harper Collins, 2000).

91. Pakistan's newly arrived deputy high commissioner in Delhi, Shahid Malik, had played a keen role in generating the invitation to the army chief. He was holding the fort as the acting high commissioner, awaiting the arrival of the regular ambassador, Riaz Khokhar, from Islamabad.

92. Interview with General Qazi and article 'Gen. Asif had refused nuclear assistance to Iran, says Javed' by Muhammad Saleh Zaafir, *The News*, 14 February 2004.

93. Recounted by General Nawaz to Shahid Nawaz.

94. As recounted to the author by General Asif Nawaz.

95. Sharif, *Ghadaar Kaun?* p. 93.

96. Recounted by Shahid Nawaz, who was then living at Army House, Rawalpindi.

97. Conversation with General Asif Nawaz. This politician had switched political parties earlier and was to switch yet again after the Sharifs were overthrown by another military coup.

98. Ziauddin interview.

99. Conversation with author.

100. Interview with General Asad Durrani.

101. Katherine Graham arranged this meeting through me and it was held after the end of General Asif Nawaz's official programme. Pakistan's ambassador to the US, Abida Hussain, was not at the interview and complained the next day when she read the story in *The Washington Post*. General Nawaz assured her that he had the president and the prime minister's blessings to discuss these matters during his visit.

102. General Nawaz stayed at our home after the official portion of his visit was over. Yusuf Haroon's exact words to the author on the way back to the airport were 'You need to feed your brother some raw meat!' to embolden him to act.

103. Interview with PM Nawaz Sharif.

104. Interview with General Qazi.

105. The author was instrumental in setting up this contact.

106. That aide memoire may have been based on a hand written suggestion that Asad Durrani had prepared and given to him earlier and that he had shown to his son-in-law Salman Shah. The army chief's personal secretary, Brigadier Shami, at one point had mentioned to the author that he had personally typed the one page memo at his home, to keep it from being leaked. When asked to confirm this in a formal interview some years later, he said he did not recall that event.

107. Letter from the Congressional Human Rights Caucus, signed by the two co-chairmen. One of them Congressman Tom Lantos of California was instrumental in pushing this line of thought in exchanges with Pakistan.

108. 'Put Pakistan first', *The Friday Times*, 25 June–1 July 1992, p. 1.

109. 'Army presents list of 'big fish' wanted in Sindh', *The News*, Islamabad, 21 July 1992.

110. Interview with a senior official of Nawaz Sharif who did not wish to go on the record.

111. Interview with Lt. Gen. Asad Durrani.

112. Interviews with General Jehangir Karamat, Naseer Akhtar, and Lt. Gen. Muhammad Tariq.

113. Hassan Abbas, *Pakistan's Drift into Extremism* (Armonk, NY: M.E. Sharpe, Inc, 2005), pp. 149–150.

114. Interviews by author.

115. Communication from Mushahid Hussain.

116. Nasim Zehra, 'Late Asif Nawaz Janjua: The "straight" soldier,' *The Frontier Post*, Peshawar, 12 January 1991.

117. Ahmed Rashid, 'General Asif Nawaz,' *The Independent*, 11 January 1993, p. 21.

118. 'General Asif Nawaz: a post-cold war warrior'. *The Frontier* Post, Lahore, Editorial, 10 January 1991.

119. Roedad Khan, *Pakistan—A Dream*, pp. 114–115.

120. In his conversation with me within a couple of days of being named COAS, General Waheed used the Punjabi term '*Khudda Line*', meaning dead-end to describe his posting to Quetta by Beg.

Politics is not an end, but a means. It is not a product, but a process. It is the art of government. Like other values, it has its counterfeits.

– Calvin Coolidge (1872–1993), US President[1]

General Abdul Waheed, who took over as COAS following the sudden death of General Asif Nawaz on 8 January 1993, was largely unknown outside the army. But he was soon to establish his presence in both the army and the political sphere, during a period of some tumult. A gruff professional soldier who spoke his mind and had gotten in trouble with his previous chief, General Mirza Aslam Beg, he was preparing to head into retirement when he was picked by President Ghulam Ishaq Khan without the advice of Prime Minister Nawaz Sharif and over the heads of other contenders, and made the army chief.[2] Waheed had the wherewithal and the inclination to keep the army on the professional path of his predecessor.

But Waheed had no illusions about his abilities in the political arena, confiding to me soon after taking over that he lacked his predecessor's knowledge of the political system and ability to handle conversations with the Americans. He was willing to learn, however, and was known as a decision maker, unafraid to tackle the seemingly intractable issues that came with his job as a member of the troika running the country. He was no Islamist and in fact posed a threat to the rising number of Islamists within the army. But above all, Waheed was a nationalist, who saw no harm in putting Pakistan's interests ahead of even his country's closest allies, such as the United States.

His sudden ascension to the post of COAS ushered in an era of considerable political turmoil both internally and externally, as the army became embroiled in resolving political problems between the president and the prime minister and eventually, within six years, took over yet again. Like his predecessor, Asif Nawaz, whom he called 'my brother,'[3] Waheed was under considerable pressure to impose martial law as the internal political situation deteriorated. However, he chose not to impose martial law, and managed to find a civilian solution under the aegis of the army, eventually choosing to retire rather than accept an extension of his term that was offered to him by an appreciative Benazir Bhutto.[4] Waheed remarked that General Nawaz may have been 'preparing me for this job' because he introduced him to the Centcom Commander General Joseph Hoar and the new US Ambassador John Monjo when Waheed was commanding the XII Corps. Indeed, Ambassador Monjo recalls being told by General Nawaz to plan his introductory visit to Quetta only after making sure that Waheed was there.[5]

True to form, the new COAS acted quickly to put his own imprint on the senior commanders of the army. With the retirement of Lt. Gen. Muhammad Ashraf Janjua from the Lahore corps, Waheed moved the Adjutant General, Lt. Gen. Humayun Bangash, a close confidant of General Nawaz, to Lahore and promoted Major General Ziaullah to lieutenant general and Major General Moinuddin Haider to lieutenant general and adjutant general of the Pakistan Army. (Zia had been approved in the final board presided over by General Nawaz before his death.) Haider had arrived back in Pakistan three days after General Nawaz's death after reviewing the troop needs and logistical requirements of the UN Peacekeeping force in Somalia. Within the next year or so, Waheed was to change a number of corps commanders and other senior officers to put his own choices in their stead. Some felt that he was trying hard to put his own mark on the army by removing some of 'Asif Nawaz's boys.' Regardless, he had taken charge of the army and would brook no interference from the civilians.

RELATIONS WITH THE UNITED STATES SLIDE

An immediate item on the new COAS's agenda was the upcoming trip to the United States by his predecessor that had been slated for the first week of February 1993 and for which much of the groundwork had been done. Pakistan had managed to avert being classified a terrorist state the previous year after General Nawaz's visit to Washington, but remained on the watch list. It was critical for Waheed to reinforce the points made by the previous COAS to establish his own relationships with senior officers of the Pentagon and the Department of State. Moreover, a new Democrat administration had taken over in Washington under a youthful Bill Clinton. It was important for Waheed to make a strong first impression on his counterparts there. Immediately after he took over, he raised with me the issue of this visit and expressed his concern that he was not yet prepared for such an endeavour, not having had any exposure to such activities in his previous role as a corps commander in Quetta. I tried to impress upon him the importance of being the first major foreign military official to meet the new Clinton administration in Washington and advised him that the Indian COAS was due to visit the United States a little later. General Waheed decided against going to the United States in February, thus missing out an opportunity to imprint the minds of the new leaders in Washington with his ideas. By the time he arrived in Washington later in the year, the Indian COAS had already been there.

The Democrats under President Bill Clinton had a strong pro-India bias and were very suspicious of Pakistan and its activities in Kashmir as well as in the nuclear field. This suspicion continued to bedevil relations between them and Pakistan for the next eight years of the Clinton era, while relations with India improved considerably. The Clinton administration resembled the Carter regime in its missionary zeal to reduce nuclear proliferation and support democracies around the world. Waheed meanwhile had decided to pursue the nuclear enrichment programme come what may, and was prepared to do his best to keep the Americans guessing about Pakistan's actions and intentions. His own suspicions about the negative attitude of the US administration was strengthened by the formation of a new bureau of Near Eastern and South Asian Affairs in the Department of State, which lumped India and Pakistan in the same office. Pakistan feared it would get second-class treatment from the Americans. The renewed focus on terrorism and Pakistan's support for the Kashmiri militants also put Pakistan on the verge of being classified a terrorist state. The activist role of the right-wing DG ISI, Lt. Gen. Javed Nasir, did not help matters with the US either.

THE ISI'S ISLAMIST BENT

A bearded, fire-and-brimstone spewing Islamic warrior, who had been a course-mate of General Hamid Gul at the PMA, Lt. Gen. Javed Nasir turned to religion in a serious way in 1986. Now, he was keen to find ways of supporting Islamic causes anywhere in the world. Earlier, he had been key in setting up arrangements to arm and support Bosnian Muslims, in collaboration with Iran.[6] He saw opportunities to hurt India not only in Kashmir but also in other regions. Among his many ventures was the provision of weapons to the Arakanese Muslims who inhabit the area bordering Burma's frontier with Bangladesh and were fighting for an independent enclave.[7] Washington was aware of many of his actions, and was especially annoyed when Prime Minister Nawaz Sharif sent them a message that he would crack down on extremist elements—as if to throw the US off scent. This was the second such letter that Prime Minister Sharif had sent a US president. An earlier 'extraordinary' missive to President George H.W. Bush had also been greeted with extreme scepticism, provoking a private communication from former US ambassador Robert Oakley to the then army chief, warning of the consequences of 'lying to the president of the United States.'[8] The DG ISI was reported to have established contacts with Tamil extremists and set up a gun-running operation and other fund-raising activities in Bangkok. A major US television news network was investigating the ISI's links (during Nasir's tenure) with the militant group Al Fuqra's representatives in the United States.[9] Most of the information about the ISI's dangerous and expanded role was conveyed from the United States to COAS General Waheed through back channels. Acting on this and other information, Waheed persuaded the prime minister to remove Javed Nasir and replaced him with a former DG MI, Lt. Gen. Javed Ashraf Qazi.

General Qazi describes a strange non-military atmosphere at the ISI when he arrived to take over on very short notice. The corridors were filled with bearded officers in civilian *shalwar kameez*, many of them with their *shalwar* hitched up above the ankle, a signature practice of the Tablighi Jamaat to which the former DG Javed Nasir belonged. He was shown the 'strong room' that once had 'currency stacked to the ceiling' but was now empty as adventurist ISI officers had taken 'suitcases filled with cash' to the field, including to the newly independent Central Asian states, ostensibly to set up safe houses and operations there in support of Islamic causes. There were no accounts nor any receipts for these money transfers. As a result, the government and the ISI had no claim to any of the properties that were acquired by individuals allegedly on its behalf. Most officers were absent from their offices for extensive periods, often away for 'prayers.' Among the first instructions that the new DG ISI issued were related to the mandatory wearing of uniforms by all army officers at the ISI. Gradually, the practice of inordinate and long attendance at prayers also disappeared. General Qazi also wound up the maverick operations in South East Asia and began a process of rotating out the extremist elements from the ISI and transferring them back to the army where they would not be able to spread their militant gospel. He also dissolved the Bangkok operation.[10]

Qazi says he found the ISI lacking command and control. Brigadiers had become used to interacting directly with DG Javed Nasir, bypassing the major generals. Ad hoc decision-making prevailed. There was a huge commitment to Afghanistan, very little on India. The jihad in Kashmir had been 'privatized'; handed over to freelancers who gave a bad name to Pakistan. The previous DG used to spend a lot of time with the prime minister's party (the PML) or at the PM House. Waheed asked Qazi to revamp the ISI. He took out many operatives from Afghanistan and sent home many of the Afghan war veterans. He says he shifted the emphasis in Afghanistan from trying to manage events to information gathering. But it is not clear if the ISI managed to dissociate itself from interfering in Afghan matters. To open up the ISI's work, Qazi invited foreign military attachés to visit Azad Jammu and Kashmir, the portion that was under Pakistani control. In Kashmir, the ISI managed to get a ban on all organizations except those that were purely Kashmiri, especially to put an end to support for those organizations that were being operated by retired military officers. The Hizbul Mujahideen, he maintained, was a purely '100 per cent Kashmiri' outfit. The other operation they supported at that time was the Kashmiri Lashkar-e-Tayyaba, later to acquire some repute as a 'terrorist' organization. Qazi says he saw the political role of the ISI's internal wing limited to informing the government but not to get involved in politics. This seems to be the stance taken by many ISI chiefs, ex-post. His critics blame him for eviscerating the operational heart of the ISI. But both he and Waheed understood the importance of staying clear of the US's gaze and rebuilding relations with the only remaining superpower. Relations with the

US were already strained. There was almost no cooperation with the CIA. 'No one ever visited us from the CIA during my tenure,' confirms General Qazi.

The Pakistan–United States relationship was on the decline, as the Pressler Amendment cut off all aid to Pakistan. Even the US AID director was asked to slowly wind up his operations. Ambassador John Monjo recalls that painful parting of ways, tinged with a certain awkwardness. An example was that of Pakistan returning six leased US frigates that the US had no need for and that were destined for the scrapheap. Pakistan was persuaded to send the frigates not back to the United States but to Singapore, where they were broken down, according to Monjo.[11] Despite these difficulties, Monjo and Waheed acknowledge that they managed to work together on many issues, including support for the US-supported operations of the United Nations in Somalia, where, incidentally, the US forces suffered a public humiliation at the hands of the Somalia 'technicals', and where Pakistani forces had to step in and rescue the embattled US troops. When the US decided to pull out, it asked Pakistan to stay behind to manage the transition. Monjo and Waheed worked together on that effort, and Pakistani forces provided cover to the US, allowing it to exit Somalia safely.

THE TROIKA CRUMBLES

Even while he was shoring up external relations, Waheed had to contend with emerging fissures in the relationship between President Ghulam Ishaq Khan and Prime Minister Nawaz Sharif. Waheed's appointment had in fact added fuel to the fire. Sharif felt slighted that Ishaq had not consulted him nor given his preferences due weight in the selection of the new army chief.[12] Sharif also began preparing to cut Ishaq's powers by repealing the 8th Amendment in concert with the PPP. Prime Minister Sharif began making overtures towards Benazir Bhutto and her party: he released Bhutto's husband, Asif Zardari, on bail and allowed him to go to London where Bhutto had delivered a child. Sharif also started speaking out in the National Assembly on the need to re-examine the 8th amendment. He set up a parliamentary sub-committee to examine this issue, effectively polarizing the ruling party between his group and that of the president.

Presidential advisor Roedad Khan commented on 'the impatience shown by Nawaz Sharif in getting himself nominated for the post of President of the Pakistan Muslim League' following the death of the previous party president and former Prime Minister Mohammad Khan Junejo on 21 March 1993.[13] Four cabinet members, including the president's son-in-law, resigned because of the split within the PML. The prime minister and the president began avoiding each other, even at social functions that both attended. As the relationship within the Troika deteriorated, elements of the PPP approached Ishaq to see if he might align himself with the PPP and engineer the removal of the prime minister. Roedad Khan states that the president authorized him to tell Farooq Leghari and Aftab Ahmed Sherpao of the PPP that Ishaq supported a no-confidence motion against Sharif. According to Roedad Khan, Ishaq did not wish to use his powers to dissolve the assembly one more time, having had to suffer single-handedly the criticisms following the Bhutto government's dismissal in 1990.

Sharif, aware of the machinations of the PPP and the president, chose to come out in the open. He went on air on 17 April at 8:15 p.m. and delivered a hard-hitting speech, lashing out at Ishaq and accusing him of attempts to subvert the political system. He spoke about 'a lot of pressure, threats, intimidation and blackmail, all of which were aimed at forcing me to step down' and outlined plans (allegedly made by Ishaq) to subvert his government and that of the Punjab. He vowed not to dissolve the assemblies or to resign.[14] The gauntlet had been thrown! Roedad Khan was at dinner with Waheed at that time, and reports that Waheed was alarmed by this 'declaration of war' on Sharif's part but was consoled by the fact that the 8th Amendment might give them a way out of this crisis without the army having to be drawn into another martial law. He gave Roedad permission to convey the army's support for whatever constitutional measure the president took to resolve the situation.[15] The president had been advised earlier by his legal and political aides to secure a certain number of resignations from the assembly and thus precipitate a crisis that would allow him to dismiss the assembly. He chose not to take that approach. But the Sharif speech managed to tip the balance.

The day after Sharif's speech Ishaq went on air to announce that he was dismissing the government and calling for fresh elections under a caretaker government headed by another Punjabi politician, Balkh Sher Mazari from Dera Ghazi Khan. His charge sheet included misconduct, maladministration, corruption, and failure to pursue actively an investigation of the death of the previous army chief, General Asif Nawaz.

SHARIF RETURNS TO POWER...BRIEFLY

Much to President Ishaq's horror, the Supreme Court of Pakistan for once stood its ground and declared the dismissal of Prime Minister Sharif illegal. It did not accept a plea from Ishaq for a review of the decision either. Sharif was reinstated on 26 May 1993 and the battle between the prime minister and the president was joined anew with the army chief as an interested observer, fearful that he might be asked to pull the political chestnuts out of the fire. Within two days, a triumphant Sharif had won a vote of confidence from the

National Assembly with 120 votes, after Bhutto's PPP boycotted the emergency session of the parliament. The battle was won, but the war continued. Sharif struggled to establish his writ at the centre and in the Punjab, and he was unable to convince Ishaq to dissolve the provincial government. A stalemate ensued that Sharif tried to break by taking on extraordinary powers authorized by a resolution of the National Assembly to take over direct control of the province. The Chief Minister Punjab, Manzur Wattoo, refused to yield. Sharif tried to get the Rangers (normally used for border security work) to help take over the government in Lahore but the army chief checkmated the move, since Rangers were commanded by an army officer.

General Waheed tried to come up with a solution that would lead to fresh elections. Another suggestion was made to the president by a group of Islamic party representatives (the Islami Deeni Ittihaad led by Maulana Samiul Haq), that involved new elections without Ishaq in place. According to this scenario, Ishaq agreed to step down if Sharif did so too.[16] The view from the army side was somewhat different. Waheed and his corps commanders had discussed the issue too and apparently under Waheed's guidance decided that both Ishaq and Sharif had to go to clear the decks. This would lead to fresh elections and perhaps new faces. Waheed then began a quick series of shuttle visits, first to Sharif and then to Ishaq. He was accompanied by General Ghulam Muhammad (Corps Commander X Corps, Rawalpindi), and Lt. Gen. Javed Ashraf Qazi (DG ISI). In these meetings, he sealed the arrangements. According to General Qazi, Sharif was concerned that Ishaq might renege and tried his best to persuade Waheed to remove Ishaq. Waheed explained that he would be going to Ishaq right after meeting Sharif and would make sure he was resigning too, but that Sharif had to resign as well. As they left the meeting, Sharif trotted up to General Qazi and held him back, saying to him in Punjabi: 'Make sure you don't forget to take care of us! These two Pathans [Ishaq and Waheed] may gang up on us.'[17]

The army chief, who had had no liking for politics, was now forced to play the kingmaker. Both Ishaq and Nawaz Sharif agreed to resign on 18 July 1993 and fresh elections were slated for 16 November, with a caretaker government to be formed, headed by a neutral individual. The army, as usual, did not trust the civilians to come up with truly neutral names, but it had to rely on their advice. General Qazi was entrusted with the job of finding the right candidate and getting approval from all sides.[18] A large number of names came up, including politicians, judges, military officers, and bureaucrats. Almost the entire list of 80-odd names was rejected by all sides: Ishaq, Sharif, and now Benazir too. Finally three economists' names emerged for consideration. These included A.G.N. Kazi and Mahbub ul Haq. Haq was rejected by Benazir because he had served under Sharif. She also said no to Kazi. The major focus settled on the third economist, Moeen Qureshi, a senior Pakistani official at the World Bank who had by then retired and formed his own investment firm 'Emerging Markets' in Washington DC with support from global insurance giant AIG. Qureshi however, was fighting cancer at the time, and when approached on the matter, he initially refused to take up the post. Qureshi had a quiet demeanour and had managed to maintain his distance from the Pakistani community in Washington enough to escape being categorized in one group or the other. He had had a stellar career first at the IMF and then at the World Bank, where he had served as head of the Bank subsidiary, the International Finance Corporation, and later was senior vice president of the Bank Group. He was widely respected and seemed to be everybody's choice.

When Qureshi had said no, General Qazi began searching for his back-up candidate. This was Justice Mohammad Haleem, who had been chief justice of Pakistan in 1981–89, and provoked no objection from any of the three parties. Haleem was travelling in interior Sindh at that time. Word was sent out by General Qazi to his ISI staff in Karachi to contact him and bring him to Islamabad. Meanwhile, frantic efforts were made to contact Qureshi again to see if he could be persuaded to change his mind. A key contact was made by Saeed Sheikh, a Washington-based US businessman and friend of Nawaz Sharif, who managed to convince Qureshi, then in Singapore, to change his mind and accept the job. A relieved General Qazi then contacted his people in Sindh to make sure they had not yet broken the news to Justice Haleem. He found out, to his relief, that the good Justice had not been located as yet. Instructions to bring him to Islamabad were withdrawn.

Frantic efforts were then made to bring Qureshi from Singapore to Pakistan. A formal *sherwani*—the traditional black frock-coat worn for special occasions in Pakistan—was stitched for him (with help regarding size and measurements from his brother, Bilal Qureshi). Sharif went on air to announce the dissolution of the assembly. Ishaq's concession speech could not be broadcast till 2 a.m., at which time, nobody was awake. The *sherwani* was carried to Qureshi's airplane as he landed. Qureshi was sworn in the same night on 18 July, minutes before midnight. The deed was done. The army had brokered yet another change of government.

A BUSY INTERREGNUM

Prime Minister Qureshi quickly formed a cabinet of businessmen and technocrats and even commandeered a friend and colleague from the World Bank, Shahid Javed Burki, to advise him. The DG ISI was involved in checking and clearing the names of the ministers and provincial chief ministers for the new prime minister.[19] Qureshi's principal aim was to restore balance to the political system and arrange a free and fair election within the three months stipulated by law. But he ran into a thicket soon after taking over, when he announced that his team had uncovered a huge back-log of unpaid or written-off loans taken out by important figures in Pakistani politics. Confronted by this, he felt he had no option but to investigate this matter and to publish the names of the defaulters, many of whom happened to be members of Sharif's party. Understandably, Sharif cried foul and suspected the worst: that the Qureshi government would help his opponents win the elections.

Qureshi also undertook to reform some aspects of the government, including a far-reaching effort to give the State Bank of Pakistan autonomy from the Ministry of Finance, so that the Bank could play a key independent role in monitoring and regulating the economy and act as a check to any free wheeling actions of the government and its Ministry of Finance. Burki was the principal architect of this reform. This activism provoked protests from some politicians who felt that the caretakers were going beyond their remit, which was simply to hold elections. But the army was behind the new regime and helped it stay firmly on course.

ELECTIONS 1993

The elections were held as scheduled on 24 and 27 October. As General Qazi told me: 'The ISI did not take part in the election process. It was absolutely free and fair.' Indeed, he says he personally took leave and spent those days in Murree. While this hands-off approach is hard to prove, given the traditional ISI involvement in the political process, it may not have overtly tried to manage elections across the board. Reports of managing some individual races did emerge. Qazi says that the ISI had not offered any assessment of expected results. It was resigned to either side coming in.[20] The final results were a narrow win for the PPP, with Sharif blaming the caretakers for tilting in Benazir Bhutto's favour by publicizing the list of defaulters on governmental loans. Bhutto had 86 Muslim seats to Sharif's 77 out of the 217 contested seats (207 Muslim, 10 non-Muslim) that were filled by direct election; 20 seats were reserved for women, who were chosen by elected members. Bhutto managed a comfortable margin but did not have a mandate. The Islamic parties did not even manage to get into double figures as a group. And the MQM did not figure at all.[21]

General Waheed suggested either a coalition government or at least a president from the other party, to effect reconciliation. Bhutto resisted the idea of a coalition because she thought Sharif would not accept the second slot. Sharif refused this idea of a coalition too but favoured the idea of a Muslim League president. Qazi states that Waheed suggested keeping Waseem Sajjad on and asked Qazi to take Sajjad to meet Bhutto the next day. But before that could happen, Qazi heard from Bhutto who asked him to check out that morning's *The Nation*, a pro-Sharif newspaper that discussed this arrangement. Sharif had been briefed about it the day before and when confronted by this leak said he may have been followed to the meeting by a reporter. Bhutto then backed out of the arrangement and began looking for fresh candidates, finally settling on her own party stalwart, Farooq Ahmed Khan Leghari. She sought General Qazi's advice between Leghari and Aftab Ahmed Sherpao. Qazi said he preferred Leghari, who eventually won over Sajjad.[22]

BHUTTO REDUX

Bhutto's second term as prime minister was marked by a more careful handling of her relations with the army and the intelligence services. She found in the new ISI head a more accessible individual, and he in turn served as a useful conduit between her and the COAS, Waheed. She faced some immediate issues and some unexpected challenges, as events beyond Pakistan's western borders again embroiled her in global issues. Bhutto needed to win back the US's friendship, re-open Pakistan's access to the US weapons' system, and regain control of the F-16 fighters that Pakistan had paid for but which were still under US embargo. Here she had a little help from the new American president. In the words of Robin Raphel, the newly named Assistant Secretary of State of South Asia, 'Clinton was mesmerized by Benazir Bhutto.'[23] But nuclear proliferation was the stumbling block, and the US had to be persuaded to ease sanctions. In return, Pakistan, and specifically the Pakistan Army, agreed to play a role in providing support to many US-sponsored initiatives across the globe which demanded troops. Pakistan sent a contingent to Somalia and to Bosnia, and provided troops to UN Peacekeeping forces in Haiti as well. The army also maintained very close and warm relations with the US Centcom, many times effectively bypassing government-to-government channels. It also increased its support for US anti-terrorism activities and in 1993, the Pakistan Army found and helped capture the mastermind of the failed attack on the World Trade Center in New York; a man named Ramzi Yousef. He was handed over to a grateful United States for trial.

The proliferation issue was a concern to Pakistan itself. Even as early as the first term of Nawaz Sharif, his ISI chief, Lt. Gen. Javed Nasir says that he had reported to the prime minister about the suspicious and money-making activities of Dr Abdul Qadeer Khan, the head of the uranium enrichment effort that was at the heart of Pakistan's nuclear weapons system. Nasir says he compiled a dossier of 23 properties owned by A.Q. Khan in and around Islamabad and presented the list to Nawaz Sharif but Sharif ignored the issue and refused to take any action against the man. Khan complained to the president about Nasir's actions against him at that time. Nasir says he also complained to Sharif about Dr Khan's frequent overseas trips. He says he suspected earlier that Khan was 'selling documents' to others, and so he (Nasir) went to the then COAS, General Asif Nawaz, to suggest that Dr Khan be asked to store all his top secret documents at the Military Operations Directorate of the GHQ. Orders were issued but Dr Khan delayed in complying, and then complained that they were 'too sensitive'. Nasir also states that he reported to Prime Minister Sharif that the Iranian foreign minister had met Dr Khan and also reported to Ishaq about Khan's overseas trips that included sites as far apart as China, Iran, Syria, and Algeria. Ishaq, who ran the nuclear programme, having inherited that role from his predecessor, was ready to curb Khan's work.[24] During Bhutto's term, the army chief, General Waheed, also had some suspicions about Khan's activities, and recalled that he appointed Major General Ziauddin Khwaja, an engineer by training, 'to keep an eye on him.'[25] Ziauddin confirms this and also confirms his own participation in numerous exchanges with the United States on nuclear issues during this period. He was then in charge of Combat Development at GHQ, and closely allied with the nuclear programme on behalf of the army.[26] The army, meanwhile, while profiting from the nuclear programme and its leveraging potential in terms of acquiring additional weapons systems from other countries, was, for the time being, content to let Ishaq manage the programme.

DEALING WITH UNCLE SAM

Bhutto's ISI chief, General Qazi, also recalls that Bhutto kept the Army Chief and the ISI chief fully in the picture on dealings with the United States, and thus the three had a 'uniform' view and response to efforts by the US to halt and roll back Pakistan's nuclear efforts. None of them trusted the United States explicitly, although Bhutto took the softer approach to keep the US pliable. ISI had gathered information about the Dubai activities of A.Q. Khan and his attempts at forming a network of agents. When confronted about these activities, Khan said that he needed a clandestine network to bypass the US's controls on access to nuclear technology.[27] Waheed had decided that the nuclear programme was none of the US's business and that Pakistan would press ahead with its enrichment programme regardless. However, Waheed found it heavy sailing when he had to deal with the new crew that the Clinton administration had brought into play. The ex-journalist turned diplomat, Strobe Talbott, who was named Deputy Secretary of State by fellow Rhodes Scholar Bill Clinton, found himself confronting a no-nonsense military man when they met in Islamabad for the first time. Talbott had been on a visit to India and had become enamoured by Indian democracy vis-à-vis the mongrel political system of Pakistan, with its heavy dose of military control. Waheed reportedly told Talbott that 'his [Waheed's] country…was not going to accept a moratorium when everyone knew that India was hell-bent to produce as much fissile material as quickly as possible for its own bomb programme. As for our offer of relief on the Pressler Amendment, he said naturally [that] Pakistan wanted delivery of the planes it had bought 'and paid good money for—but not on your terms.' Mimicking the look of a man being hanged…he added, 'We will choke on your carrots!'[28]

When carrots did not work, Talbott resorted to playing the heavy. At the beginning of one meeting during Waheed's visit to Washington, he began the meeting by leaning across the table and abruptly snapping at Waheed: 'General! You have been lying to us!' (Referring to Pakistan's continuing efforts to enrich uranium). Waheed turned beet-red in anger and would have responded in kind had Ziauddin, who was sitting next to him, not slipped him a hastily scribbled note stating: 'Don't reply. He's trying to get you angry!'[29] Waheed ignored the insult but stuck to his guns. More than following national policy, he was asserting the army's critical role in ensuring an adequate nuclear defence against India. Immediately after that meeting, Ziauddin flew back to Pakistan because a US team was due to meet Prime Minister Bhutto. They were surprised to see him sitting across the table at their meeting with Bhutto. The army wanted to ensure through Ziauddin's presence at the meetings—with Bhutto—that Bhutto was not cajoled or bamboozled into agreeing to anything that the military found unpalatable. The Americans also had their eyes on neighbouring India and its position on nuclear weapons and missile tests. Waheed had been warned by his experts that the US might wish to take a look at Pakistani facilities under the pretext of helping Pakistan safeguard them. 'If they step inside the doors they will know what we are doing!' he was warned. So he stonewalled the Americans.[30]

The United States wanted Pakistan and India to follow a path of 'strategic restraint' (according to Robert Einhorn, a key policy-maker on the nuclear issue in Washington during that period), in order to control both the number and the long-range capabilities of missiles. It sought to set benchmarks, such as no more tests, no more fissile material for India, control missile capabilities, and export controls. India did not like the limits they had put on missiles. Pakistan proposed to discuss the full range of issues, bilaterally. But India rejected that idea, since it did not wish to tie its hands with China, another perceived threat.[31] India, on the other hand, did not wish to discuss Kashmir in any but bilateral channels. It refused intercession by the United States or the United Nations.

Einhorn maintains that in the early Clinton years, the US–Pakistan relationship was marked by 'mistrust' and that Pakistanis viewed the US as an 'unreliable security partner.' The manner in which the United States dropped Pakistan after the Afghan war had tremendous effects in Pakistan, in his view. 'A number of pathologies resulted, including the growth of a militant culture in Pakistan' said Einhorn. In return for re-opening the F-16 issue, the US sought a formal commitment of restraints on nuclear technology and missile development from Pakistan. But Pakistan said it was already practicing restraint. This, according to Einhorn, was the context of General Waheed's comment about choking on US 'carrots.'[32] On its part, the US suspected Pakistan was not telling the truth on a number of things. Yet, when Bhutto made her visit to Washington, she managed to open the doors to more military purchases from the US. However, on the home front, there was trouble brewing.

AN ABORTIVE ISLAMIST COUP?

Early in her second term, Bhutto's administration was shaken by the news that the army intelligence had uncovered a plot in September 1995 involving nearly 40 army officers, including Major General Zaheer ul Islam Abbasi, Brigadier Mustansar Billa, Colonel Azad Minhas, and others, to overthrow the government and the senior leadership of the army. The aim was to capture and eliminate the military eldership during a high-level meeting at GHQ on 30 September and declare Pakistan an orthodox Islamic state.[33] Abbasi was the man who had been removed from his command in the Kargil area of Kashmir by General Asif Nawaz and given a non-operational desk role at GHQ after having undertaken an unauthorized and costly foray into Indian-held territory in 1990, losing many men, including a brigadier. Abbasi would have been fired had it not been for the reported intervention of another member of the Tablighi Jamaat, General Javed Nasir. When the news of the attempted coup got out, Abbasi was court martialled and sentenced to jail. Meanwhile, the army clamped down on release of details of this incident, believing that it was an aberration, and that the army had in place sufficient measures to weed out the militant Islamists in its ranks. It refused to face the reality that the army officer corps was increasingly coming from urban centres where there was a strong Islamist current, and that the army's own population after all mirrored the increasingly conservative bent of the country's general population.

Bhutto herself also tried to downplay this incident since it came just before the US House and Senate were due to take up a bill passed by the Senate the previous month that would reopen military sales to Pakistan for the first time in five years under an amendment introduced by Senator Hank Brown of Colorado. That bill would allow Pakistan to receive $368 million of military equipment it had bought in 1990, but which had been withheld because of the Pressler Amendment.[34] Eventually, the Brown Amendment was passed, after Bhutto's very successful visit to Washington in early 1995, and Pakistan added to its military arsenal three Orion anti-submarine aircraft, air-to-air and surface-to-surface missiles, radar equipment, and parts for Cobra helicopters. Moreover, it reopened the possibility of millions of dollars of direct US economic assistance. But this economic assistance ran aground, with increasing US concerns about Pakistan's missile imports from China and growing support for the Kashmiri insurgency against Indian rule, as well as the rise of a new, more virulent form of Islamic fundamentalism in Afghanistan, which some suspected was spawned by Pakistan's ISI.

RISE OF THE TALIBAN

Things had not been going well for the clap-trap government of the Mujahideen in post-Soviet Afghanistan. Internecine warfare continued and individual warlords held sway in their regions, imposing undue taxes on the common people. Intra-state commerce was severely curtailed. In a sharp reaction to this state of affairs, there was an organic growth of an opposition movement led by a group of *talibs*, or students, from the religious madrassahs that had opened across the border in Pakistan during the war, (and later also in Afghanistan).[35] A local Kandahari leader named Mullah Omar led a group of his followers in the summer of 1994 to forcibly take over the roadside tax-collection posts set up outside Kandahar, following an incident on 20 September 1994 involving the rape and murder of some Herati boys and girls who were travelling through the area and had been accosted by the bandit Mujahideen at a post some 90 kilometres north of Kandahar. Omar was a Ghilzai tribesman and a veteran of the anti-Soviet campaign (during which he had lost an eye). This added to his charismatic appeal to the masses, who sought to overthrow the regime that had succeeded the communists and free themselves of the yoke of rapacious tax collectors. Omar ousted the Mujahideen involved in the Herati family's massacre, and helped bury the dead.[36] His numbers grew and he began moving north and eastwards towards Kabul, where a shaky coalition supported by the troops of Ahmad Shah Masood, the Tajik leader, maintained a tenuous hold. Large numbers of locals, largely Pushtuns, the single-largest tribal group in Afghanistan's crazy quilt of tribes and ethnic groups, joined his crusade. They took control of large swathes of territory without a fight.

At that time, Pakistan was trying to open a land route to Central Asia. The Interior Minister, General Naseerullah Babar, had sent a convoy of trucks to make the trek from Quetta through Kandahar to Turkmenistan. Local warlords, not the Taliban (plural of *Talib*), ambushed and captured some of the trucks and held them hostage. According to the DG ISI, General Qazi, Babar asked for the ISI's help in contacting the Taliban and getting his trucks released. The ISI still maintained ties in Afghanistan and managed to contact Mullah Burhanuddin Rabbani, subsequently the President of Afghanistan, and Mullah Ghaus (killed later in Mazar-i-Sharif) and arranged a meeting with General Babar. The JUI leader, Maulana Fazlur Rahman, also wanted to be in that meeting but was turned away. Thus, the ISI helped arrange the release of the trucks. A grateful Babar promised to provide help to the Taliban, later taking undue credit for having helped create them. Major General Afzal Janjua, a former senior ISI official, states unequivocally that the 'Taliban were not a creation of Pakistan,' but acknowledges, as do others, that Pakistan found it expedient to collaborate with them as they gained strength, and provided support, as needed, to dislodge a pro-India Tajik-dominated regime in Kabul.[37] It is clear though that Pakistan's help was critical for the Taliban's initial success. General Qazi states that Pakistan had access to a huge cache of weapons that had been stored inside Afghanistan since the war against the Soviets. The 'Pasha Dump' near Kandahar was in 17 tunnels and had enough supplies to equip a corps, according to him. Pakistan made these available to the Taliban, giving them a tremendous boost. 'The only thing they demanded from us was petrol and food. Never asked for money,' recalls Qazi. The ISI, he maintains, had only a liaison function, perhaps a politic understatement. The Taliban also managed to get support from Prince Turki Al Faisal of Saudi Arabia through the General Intelligence Directorate.[38]

After defeating the forces of Gulbadin Hekmatyar in the south (whose forces were besieging Kabul from that direction), the Taliban started making inroads against the coalition government of President Burhanuddin Rabbani, capturing regional centres and moving toward Kabul, sometimes by making deals with local warlords. According to Ambassador Arif Ayub, Rabbani provided 'three million dollars in cash' to the Taliban 'through Mullah Naqibullah, Rabbani's ally and Governor of Kandahar. (However, only two million dollars were passed on to the Taliban as Naqibullah decided to keep one million.)'[39] The Taliban's inexorable advance continued and was aided by a swelling of their numbers with fresh recruits from within Afghanistan and from the refugee camps and madrassahs in Pakistan. The ISI advisers did what they could to provide training and other support—but at heart this was a popular uprising that was fuelled by the wish of the Afghan people to restore order and stability to a society wrecked by years of foreign occupation and then rapacious Mujahideen warlords.

Finally, on 27 September 1996, the Taliban entered Kabul. Rabbani and his cohort fled to the north. The Taliban picked up the former dictator, Najeebullah from the United Nations compound (where he had taken refuge since 1992), and shot and then hung Najeebullah in front of the presidential palace. Wild West justice had arrived in the Wild East, with a vengeance. This was a preview of what was to come in the next four years, as the Taliban imposed a severe form of Islamic rule, based on unbending interpretations of Islamic laws, including corporal punishment and public executions for all kinds of offences, including social ones. They reduced women to second-class citizenship, refusing to let them function in public, go to school, or participate in the economy or politics—which provoked a fresh flow of refugees to Pakistan. Despite all these negatives, the United States saw in the situation an opportunity for oil distribution from Central Asia via Afghanistan and pushed for support to an American oil firm, UNOCAL, which began making contacts with the Taliban government with official US backing. Among the consultants to UNOCAL was Zalmay Khalilzad, an Afghan emigrant, who had become a US citizen and conservative scholar (later ambassador under President George W. Bush). This US interest in helping Afghanistan and then hoping to use it as a transit point for oil and gas from Central Asia had been evident even during the earlier regime. Now it intensified.[40] Pakistan and the Saudis provided additional help to Afghanistan under the Taliban, with Pakistan refurbishing the telephone systems and even hooking up Afghanistan to Pakistan's domestic phone system so that a call from Quetta to Kandahar was treated as a local call! The dream of Generals Beg and Hamid Gul of a unified Pakistan and Afghanistan seemed to have arrived. But, as usual in such patron–client relationships, the ISI and the Pakistan government found their Taliban pupils becoming increasingly independent and uncontrollable. The Bhutto government itself was divided internally and with the army on how to approach Afghanistan.

Bhutto also had other things on her plate, including a rising chorus of complaints about corruption in her government, involving, among others, her husband Asif Zardari, whom she had named Minister of Investment. She had her own man as president, but he too was showing signs of independence and sending her constant notices about issues that he found needed her attention.

A NEW ARMY CHIEF

Bhutto relied heavily on support from the army chief, General Waheed, but his time was up in January 1996. Bhutto felt strongly about Waheed:

> I wanted Waheed to continue..... I found him to be a very shrewd person and a brilliant strategician or tactician,...And he was [a] totally non-interfering Army Chief. Many attempts were made to politicize him. All sorts of malicious, poisonous letters were circulated to provoke him into acting against the political government. But he did not do so. He was an honourable man. He spoke bluntly.... So I wanted him to stay on for a year. Unfortunately, he did not want to continue.[41]

Yet, despite her efforts to persuade him to stay on, he refused to accept an extension and retired on time—a highly unusual action by an army chief in Pakistan, and perhaps the first time that anyone had taken that stance.[42]

Regardless, as soon as it became clear that Waheed was going home on time, the horse race for his succession began. As usual, it was marked by a lot of public debate and acrimony. Stories started appearing about one candidate or the other and his antecedents. Among the leading candidates were CGS Lt. Gen. Jehangir Karamat, Lt. Gen. Javed Ashraf Qazi (former DSG ISI and then Commander 30 Corps in Gujranwala), Lt. Gen. Nasser Akhtar (former Corps Commander V Corps in Karachi), and Lt. Gen. Mohammad Tariq, another corps commander. Among other things, tribal loyalties started playing a part. General Qazi's powerful Awan tribal network wanted one of their own to be selected. Karamat did not have a tribal network to lean on. Akhtar was supposed to be a favourite of Asif Zardari with whom he had built good relations while in Karachi. Tariq recalls he was asked to come to Islamabad and wait at a private house there for his interview with the prime minister, but it never materialized.

Bhutto states that she favoured Qazi, with whom she had had a good relationship when he was at the ISI.

> Javed Ashraf Qazi was the person that I proposed should be made Chief of Army Staff after Waheed refused an extension. Farooq Leghari was vehemently opposed to him. So then the next choice that we came up with was the second—I was toying between Karamat and Naseer Akhtar. Farooq Leghari opposed Naseer Akhtar on the grounds that the MQM were opposed to him because of the operations that had taken place in Karachi. And Farooq Leghari proposed that we should go with General Tariq. I liked General Tariq, but when I looked at the list of seniority, and we had had all that [to worry about].... I didn't like to go down so deep, although I personally liked Tariq and would have been happy with him, but I thought superseding so many generals and then retiring them was not right. And so then I said that 'well, we should go for Karamat.'

Farooq said, 'No…he's retiring.' And I said, 'No, Farooq. You've said, "no" to Javed Ashraf Qazi. You said, "no" to General Naseer Akhtar. If…General Tariq was [ranked number] two or three, I'd happily make him. But he's number five.' And I said, 'The army already has difficult perceptions about us. Let's not worsen it.' So then I moved a file promoting General Karamat. And Farooq agreed to make him chief.[43]

Karamat believes that his selection was primarily based on Leghari's and Waheed's preferences and that Bhutto had no real role in this.[44] However, the day he got a call from Legahri's office to set up a meeting with the president, he recalls getting a call from Maleeha Lodhi asking to meet her immediately. They met at a small restaurant, Pappa Salli's, where Maleeha told him that Bhutto wanted to let him know that she had suggested his name to Leghari. This break with protocol appeared to reflect the desire of the prime minister to establish an alliance with the new army chief. Following that Karamat got another call, this time from Asif Zardari. After getting permission from Waheed, he met Zardari at the Bhutto family friend Dr Zafar Niazi's home and was told the same thing that the prime minister had said. Later in the evening, when he met Leghari, the president told him that this was a joint decision: 'I suggested your name. The Prime Minister agreed and so did the army chief.'

A RIFT AND A SEPARATION

The selection process of the new army chief reflected not only the highly personalized decision-making process behind the scenes but also magnified the growing differences between Leghari and Bhutto, as reports of corruption in the government mounted. Meanwhile, the law and order situation in Sindh worsened and Karachi was once more in the grip of extreme violence. Sectarian divisions also emerged as Shia and Sunni groups battled it out in a Lebanese-style proxy war, supported by foreign financial help from both Iran and Saudi Arabia. Leghari tried to keep the government on its toes by sending the prime minister periodic missives pointing out to shortcomings in her performance. In turn, he believes the government deployed the IB to keep tabs on Leghari and his family. But apparently the MI was keeping tabs on the prime minister.[45]

The Byzantine intrigues continued behind the scenes. Even years later, the memories and the feelings ran strong. According to Bhutto, Leghari was told by a religious woman whom he visited in Dubai that, 'God has chosen Farooq Leghari, so he doesn't need to respect Benazir Bhutto.… [Then] in August 1996, Jehangir Karamat sent me a report.… in which he said that Hamid Gul told him that the president wants to get rid of the prime minister. Now, what was the president doing becoming bosom buddies with Hamid Gul?....' Earlier that year, she recalls a visitor who told him that General Mahmud [Ahmed then DG MI] told him that, 'either the president gets rid of the prime minister or the army gets rid of the president.' And in January, 1996, when she was flying to inaugurate Akora Dam in Balochistan a journalist named Azhar Sohail called her and came up in the plane to her and said, 'Prime Minister, I was called by DG MI General Mahmud. [He] said, "Azhar Sohail, you leave the prime minister and you accuse her of corruption, and if you don't we'll sort you out when we overthrow this government".'[46]

Bhutto reported these machinations to the army chief and advised him to get the DG ISI Lt. Gen. Nasim Rana to remove a major general from the ISI who was reportedly 'conniving' against her government. But Karamat dismissed these ideas. In her view, Karamat 'was a good man, but he did not stand up to the President of Pakistan in his illegal dealings or others who were using the President of Pakistan's weakness.' Eventually, she says she confronted Leghari, 'So I went to the President, and I said, 'What corruption? You are worried about corruption?' He said, 'No.' I said, 'You're worried about governance?' He said, 'No.' Because Karamat told me. Now I didn't know who to believe, the Army Chief or my own President.'[47] What she did not realize was that both the president and the army chief had started keeping her government at arms length by that time. It was just a matter of time.

She believes that the plan was to remove her around the time of her brother's killing. Mir Murtaza Bhutto had returned to Pakistan, provoking a rift within the Bhutto clan, as he reasserted his right as the son of Zulfikar Ali Bhutto to head the PPP. But the military was suspicious of his contacts and had been monitoring his earlier trips to India and alleged links to the Indian intelligence service, RAW (Research and Analysis Wing). There was also a reported rift between Asif Zardari and Murtaza Bhutto. On 20 September 1996, when Murtaza was coming home to his home in Clifton, Karachi, his caravan of vehicles was stopped by the police, and a fire fight ensued in which he was mortally wounded and lay dying on the street for quite some time before being taken to a hospital. But it was too late. The last of the Bhutto males had been killed in an encounter shrouded in mystery, and rumours swirled about who was behind that event.

Leghari assured her of his loyalty when she met him after this tragedy. That was too much for her at that time. She broke down in tears.[48] Leghari had some history in his dealings with Bhutto. As a member of her party, he regretted that even in her first term she delayed allowing him to run for chief minister of Punjab. By the time she decided to let him run, it was too late to create the right conditions, he said, although it was evident that the PPP did not have the votes in the Punjab to fill that slot. He lost, and eventually found himself appointed first as minister for water and power and then finance minister. Leghari recalls that they had differences even during her first term on the issue of corruption in government involving her husband. When Iftikhar Gillani and Aitzaz Ahsan came to him in Spring 1990 to say they had heard that Ghulam Ishaq was getting ready to turf out their government, they persuaded Leghari to accompany them to meet Bhutto and explain the reasons behind the expected move. Her first reaction was negative. 'You are listening to my enemies!' she said. Later she relented and asked for advice on how to proceed. They advised her to reshuffle the cabinet and fire corrupt ministers. She wanted to delay the move till after the budget. In the meantime, Leghari says that he ran afoul of her in the case of an appointment of a 'corrupt' official as head of Karachi Electric Supply Company (KESC) which took place in Leghari's absence. (The 'corrupt official' was once Zulfikar Ali Bhutto's class fellow at Berkeley). The two had a bitter exchange, with Leghari telling Bhutto that this would affect her reputation, and offering to resign. Leghari says that he found out later that there was a $400 million power sector loan from the Asian Development Bank (ADB), and Bhutto was directly involved in changing the consultant for the ADB loan. He states that he heard (during a trip to the World Bank) that Zardari and Bhutto were allegedly getting a chunk of this loan, and warned her against this action. She took the item to the Economic Coordination Committee and tried to barrel it through but Leghari objected publicly.[49] Two weeks later, their government was thrown out.

Once back in power, Leghari asked for the Finance Ministry rather than the Foreign Ministry that she offered him. Bhutto supposedly responded with, 'I know why you want to be finance minister. You want to keep a check on us!' She used retired General Asad Durrani to plead her case at Maleeha Lodhi's house in Islamabad, where Bhutto was formulating her cabinet. General Javed Ashraf Qazi was acting as a go-between and also a link to General Waheed. Leghari agreed eventually to be foreign minister and says he took the oath of office. But the presidential election was due immediately. The PPP tried to get Waseem Sajjad to be the joint candidate of the PPP and the Muslim League, but Nawaz Sharif balked at the suggestion. Eventually, on the advice of others, including Nawabzada Nasrullah, Sherbaz Mazari, and Akbar Bugti, Leghari was made candidate for president and elected. He resigned from the PPP in a show of neutrality and, without consulting her, announced the need for both the leading parties to join to remove Article 58(2)-B, which gave the president undue powers.

Leghari states that he started receiving reports of corruption, including the purchase of the so-called 'Surrey Palace' by Asif Zardari, through an agent. He recalls that he was kept informed also by General Qazi of the ISI and General Waheed and later by General Karamat. He says he never detected any divergence in what they told him and what they conveyed to Bhutto. The troika seemed to be stable. But the president still retained his powers to dismiss the government and was constantly asked when he would exercise that power. In one instance, in March 1996, he told Zahid Malik, a journalist with ties to the establishment, that he would use those powers if there was a need to protect the country, but that he had no intention of doing so at the moment. Then he became aware of some shady business deals involving the disposal of a gas field by the Bhutto government and fought against it. This soured relations no end. Compounding the problems between them was the appointment of new judges, proposed by the PPP that Chief Justice Sajjad Ali Shah, her own appointee, had turned down. Bhutto and her colleagues wanted to have the chief justice thrown out. Leghari says he counselled against it. Bhutto put pressure on him to do so. Leghari then said he would launch a reference to the Supreme Court on this issue. Eventually she agreed to abide by the chief justice's decision. But the hurt remained.

The other bone of contention was Bhutto's brother, Murtaza. Zardari and Bhutto came to see Leghari to complain about Mir Murtaza Bhutto whom she suspected of harbouring ill will toward her and her husband Asif Zaradri. Leghari advised them to settle their differences. But he recalls that they went away with a visible disappointment at the outcome of the meeting.[50] He maintains that all the police officers in Clifton where Murtaza Bhutto lived were 'hand-picked by Benazir and Asif Zardari.' Even Shoaib Suddle, the deputy IG Police had his place right in front of Murtaza Bhutto's home. The Station House Officer who was alleged to have later killed Murtaza reportedly shot himself in jail with his own revolver, according to Leghari.

Against this background and in light of the deteriorating situation, Leghari and Karamat began to see eye to eye (but separately) on the case against Bhutto. Leghari states that Karamat never directly complained against Bhutto. Karamat tried to get Bhutto to meet Leghari and resolve their differences, but she refused, deriding Leghari and his civil servant aide.[51] Leghari says that he tried up to the last minute to save her despite information from various sources of the precarious economic situation. She sent three ministers to talk to Leghari (Rao Sikandar Iqbal, Khurshid Shah, and Naurez Shakoor) and find out why Leghari was angry with her. He said he was trying to save her but she was not controlling Zardari. Leghari was also approached by Nawaz Sharif,—accompanied by Abida Hussain, Chaudhry Nisar, and others—to ask Leghari to dismiss her. Sharif complained about the economy and corruption. Leghari urged a bipartisan approach on economic issues and told them that whenever there were elections, he would promise a 'free and fair elections'. He asked Sharif to call on Bhutto and work things out with her. At that point he says he had not thought of dismissing the Bhutto government nor had he discussed the issue with the army chief. But four or five days before he decided to dismiss her, he told Karamat that he was planning to dismiss Bhutto's government because 'We had reached the point of no return.'

Mounting national and international discussion of corruption involving the Bhutto family, especially her husband, Asif Zardari, began creating waves. *The New York Times* ran a special expose on her family fortunes.[52] A US congressional report on graft cited the 'Asif Zardari Case' as an exemplar of corruption around the globe.[53] Leghari says he also 'found to [his] horror' that the PPP government was misstating Pakistan's foreign exchange reserves at that time, some $300 million less than the official figure of some $625 million and the economy was 'bleeding $40–45 million a day'.[54] This became the primary cause of the dismissal of Bhutto's second government, but not one that he could state publicly since it would cause a run on the economy. Leghari called Karamat, who told him that it gave them no time! But Leghari persisted and dissolved the government on 5 November 1996.

ANOTHER INTERIM PRIME MINISTER AND ELECTIONS

Leghari says he chose a PPP veteran, Malik Mairaj Khalid, as the caretaker prime minister without consulting Karamat. However, he did get feedback from the army on some cabinet members: Mumtaz Bhutto and Khwaja Tariq Rahim, about whom the army had some doubts. Subsequently, he says, there was some criticism of the cabinet from 'journalists who were close to the military.' One person whom Leghari personally selected was Shahid Javed Burki, an old friend from the World Bank, who became adviser to the prime minister on finance. As the minister responsible for accountability, he selected Najam Sethi, a crusading journalist from Lahore. He also asked Pakistan's ambassador to the United States, Maleeha Lodhi, to stay on. The DG ISI Nasim Rana gave his input into the cabinet choices. General Karamat would convey the views of the corps commanders and principal staff officers to Leghari, who would often manage to debate him out of his objections. Leghari says he found out that the senior commanders were making fun of Karamat about his inability to carry their views successfully before the president. He therefore suggested that Karamat arrange a meeting for Leghari with the senior military commanders. At the meeting, Leghari spoke about the elections, ministers, and corruption. He felt that he had carried the day. There were only a few questions. Later, former caretaker Prime Minister Moeen Qureshi told him that he had mishandled the army by forcing his views on it. Qureshi said that he used to put his ideas to General Waheed and let him present them to the army high command. The senior commanders thought they were hearing Waheed's own ideas and rarely objected!

Chief Justice Sajjad Ali Shah told Leghari within ten days of the government's dissolution that, 'One group of corrupt people will go, another will come in.' He advised against elections and suggested that 'people' meaning the army 'will be very happy—do a referendum. Extend this interim government by two years.' He felt that this time was needed to complete accountability. The cabinet also had a strong lobby for extension. But it did not get extra time. However, the caretakers did manage to buy some economic breathing room for Pakistan through the frantic efforts of Burki and Salman Shah (by then Chairman of the Privatisation Commission), who jetted around the Middle East and China to borrow funds at short notice and get some financial reforms in place.

The election on 3 February 1997 allowed Sharif to come back into power with a clear majority and a mandate. His PML won 137 seats out of the 217 reserved for Muslim candidates. The PPP only managed to get 18 seats, while the MQM got 12 seats and the Awami National Party 10. The Islamic JUI only got 2 seats. There were 21 independents. In addition, Sharif's PML took over all the provinces except Balochistan. He could call his shots now.

NAWAZ SHARIF REDUX: FRESH BATTLES

One of the first major steps that Sharif took was to finally remove the irritant of the 8th Amendment that gave the president the powers to dismiss governments and assemblies. Mustering his forces in the National Assembly, he quickly put forward and approved the 13th Amendment to the constitution, which annulled the 8th Amendment and gave the prime minister the power to appoint the heads of the armed services. Before doing this, Sharif asked both the army chief and President Leghari if they had any objections to the move. Both said they had no objections. The deed was done. But many feared that Sharif would become a civilian dictator and use his enhanced powers to remove all opposition to his government. The setting up of an accountability group (the Ehtesab Bureau) under a family friend was a clear indication of things to come.

Sharif also took on the judiciary that he felt had been against him, turning down the nominees of Chief Justice Sajjad Ali Shah for elevation to the Supreme Court and only allowing their promotion after pressure was applied on him. Sharif persisted in his efforts to remove the chief justice. Leghari recalls Sharif coming to see him in the company of Shahid Hamid, (erstwhile friend of Leghari who had appointed him as governor of the Punjab but now had been won over by Sharif), to ask him to remove the chief justice. Sharif said that Hamid would make the case against the chief justice. Leghari said to Hamid, 'Why didn't you tell Nawaz Sharif my expected answer. It would be the same as Benazir Bhutto's time: No!' Hamid retorted, 'At that time the judges were united. Now they are divided. We can do it!' Leghari states that he warned against this move and even told Sharif that the chief justice thought highly of him. But Sharif was not deterred.[55] He managed to get the army chief's acquiescence and then instigated a revolt among the judges against the chief justice, who in the meanwhile, dismissed as unconstitutional another Sharif amendment that would make it illegal for any member of the National Assembly to break ranks with his party in assembly voting. When Sharif criticized this move in parliament, the chief justice filed a case of contempt against the prime minister. The army chief was brought into this battle to calm things down and both he and the DG ISI, Lt. Gen. Nasim Rana, acted as go-betweens. A meeting was arranged by Leghari at which all principals were brought together. General Karamat started by asking the chief justice whether he would withdraw the contempt case. Leghari recalls the chief justice's face turning red. 'How can you interfere with cases?' asked Shah. 'I came here at the request of the President, not to decide cases!' Leghari tried to calm things down by suggesting that the country needed stability, not another upheaval, and suggested a delay of two weeks in the contempt case. This cooled down the chief justice, and he agreed. Sharif then pleaded, 'Show mercy!' To which Shah retorted, 'I am the Chief Justice not for mercy but for Justice!'

Having won a reprieve, Sharif used the time to get the Balochistan High Court on 26 November 1997 to file an appeal against the original appointment of Sajjad Ali Shah as chief justice. Leghari found out and told Karamat that Shah in turn was getting ready to restore Article 58(2)b, giving the president the power to dismiss governments. Leghari says that at that point he told the army chief that he would leave his office. Later that night at 10 p.m., Leghari says he got a call that Sharif wanted to meet him along with the army chief. Both of them arrived at midnight, accompanied by the chairman of the Senate Waseem Sajjad—the man who would become president should Leghari quit—Law Minister Khalid Anwar, veteran politician Ilahi Bux Soomro, and the ISI chief, Lt. Gen. Rana. Leghari had his civil service aide Shamsher Ali Khan by his side. Sharif asked Khalid Anwar to present the case against the chief justice and presented a judgment that they wanted Leghari to sign, dismissing Justice Shah. 'Even if the judgment is mala fide?' asked Leghari, referring to his information that suitcases of money had been taken to Balochistan to obtain this judgment against the chief justice by his fellow judges. Leghari warned that the country was heading for disaster, and ended with, 'I'm tired of this.' Waseem Sajjad then interjected, 'I am a constitutional lawyer and fully agree with the advice of the Law Minister for removal of the Chief Justice.' Leghari then summed up his position, 'I've come to a conclusion that will solve this problem. I'll resign tomorrow. Waseem Sajjad has no qualms of conscience. He'll do what you want.' Soomro then asked, 'Why should you resign for the sake of a mad old Sindhi judge?' Karamat also added, 'No sir! You cannot resign. Pakistan is going through a difficult and sensitive period.' General Rana echoed those sentiments. By then it was 4 a.m. Leghari suggested that he wanted to sleep on it and intended to go to the office at 9 a.m. and resign. Soon after the others left, Leghari says he was handed a note from General Karamat who was the last to leave. Karamat had given it to the military secretary to the president, Brigadier Ghazanfar, asking him to deliver it after they had departed. It read, 'If you resign then I'm also resigning tomorrow.'

Leghari says he waited for a while to allow Karamat to get home and then called him, warning against Karamat's resignation. Using a local term connoting extreme danger, Leghari said to Karamat that if he resigned then Sharif would have total power and it would be like giving 'a monkey a razor'. Karamat requested Leghari in turn to wait for another meeting in the morning before taking any decision. Karamat arrived the next morning with the chief justice, who said this was his battle and there was no need for the president to resign. That day the PML supporters stormed the Supreme Court. The army chief, who states that he had been forewarned about some sort of a demonstration at the Supreme Court and the use of Punjab House as a marshalling point, did not provide protection when approached by the chief justice, stating that all such requests had to come from the Ministry of Defence. Karamat told Sharif about this and was assured that the prime minister would ensure peace. When this did not happen, Karamat decided not to get into the situation.[56] The chief justice in turn restored the 8th Amendment. Leghari had by then become aware of the likelihood of impeachment, given Sharif's huge majority. He then decided to resign but Karamat came back with the DG ISI this time to plead with him again not to do so. Karamat said that Sharif and company would ruin the country. But Leghari persisted and announced his resignation on 2 December 1997, one year before his term was up. In the interest of maintaining the system in place, Karamat had allowed the prime minister to bludgeon his path to acquisition of power in a manner that emboldened Sharif. Karamat was not aware of the implications of this new-found confidence till it was too late. A new chief justice was appointed, a compliant Waseem Sajjad became acting president until Sharif presented an even more compliant Justice Rafiq Tarar to become his rubber-stamp president. Sharif had bought himself some security within Pakistan. But he did not have control over the external front. Soon he was facing another crisis that would test his mettle.

TESTING TIMES

Pakistan's relationship with India had been sliding, as the Kashmiri conflict escalated with a rise in anti-Indian jihadi activity and the resulting Indian counter moves. Both sides had also been engaging in a missile race, as they developed or bought foreign weapons systems that would give the capability of striking each other's major cities. Under Bhutto and then Sharif, Pakistan had acquired missile technology from both China and North Korea. General Karamat confirmed that during Bhutto's tenure and following a visit by her to Pyongyang, Pakistan had made a deal 'on a cash basis' to get the SA-16 missile from Korea, adding to the Green Arrow missiles from China.[57] Neither of these missiles was of strategic significance: the SA-16, was a surface to air missile (range 10 km) and the latter (Green Arrow) an anti-tank missile (range 3 km). Bhutto also recalls making a special trip to Pyongyang, but insists that it was at the request of the International Department of the PPP and tacked on at the end of a visit to Beijing. Both deny unequivocally that Pakistan traded nuclear secrets for weapons from North Korea, as they would be expected to do. But Pakistan did benefit from these purchases and relationships. Nevertheless, the liquid propellant Ghauri missile produced by Dr A.Q. Khan Research Laboratory (KRL) was reportedly an upgrade of the North Korean Nodong missile. The solid fuel (one stage, and subsequently two stage) Shaheen missile fabricated by National Development Complex, initially under the PAEC, is said to be a much-improved long range version of the Chinese M-11 missile.

Pakistan and India had and continue to spurn the Nuclear Non-Proliferation Treaty (NPT) considering it discriminatory since it divides the world into nuclear haves and have-nots. Both have also not signed Comprehensive Nuclear Test Ban Treaty (CTBT) although Pakistan does maintain an observer status at Comprehensive Nuclear Test Ban Treaty Organization (CTBTO) since it has committed itself to the establishment of two international monitoring stations on its soil. The two countries had thus prepared the ground literally and figuratively for the development and testing of their nuclear weapons for which they could not be held accountable on legal grounds. Indian army personnel had begun digging tunnels and preparing shafts at Pokhran in the Rajasthan desert for a possible potential nuclear test as early as August 1995.[58] Pakistan had 'cold tested' (triggering the explosion of natural rather than enriched uranium and thus avoiding a chain reaction) their nuclear device in March 1983 in the Kirana Hills near Sargodha. This was done under the guidance of Dr Ishfaq Ahmad, who was primarily responsible for the classified programme of PAEC as member (technical). Dr Ahmad later on, in 1991, assumed the charge of chairman of the organization. The first cold test was followed by 'about two dozen cold tests over a number of years. In July 1990 even a 'nuclear aerial device' was cold tested dropping it from a modified F-16 aircraft. KRL carried out the first cold test of its nuclear device in March 1984.'[59] The Pakistan Army had assisted Dr Ahmad in the early 1980s in the search for a site for testing of nuclear weapons and settled on Chagai in the Ras Koh Hills of Balochistan. However, it was in 1991 that the Chagai site began to be prepared in detail, with advice from Dr Samar Mubarakmand, chief scientist of PAEC, keeping in mind the technical necessities of a nuclear test. The Chagai site had a 1 km long, 4m x 3m, horizontal tunnel, with an overhang of 700m of solid rock. A second site in the Kharan desert, 150 km away, was an L-shaped shaft 120m deep with a 70m horizontal arm.[60]

A secondary site was at Kharan that had a vertical shaft, enough to accommodate another device. The mountain they chose had at least 400 feet of solid material above the horizontal tunnels they dug for the test. The PAEC, rather than the KRL headed by the celebrated Dr A.Q. Khan, took the lead since their weapon design had beaten out Dr Khan's design and had passed the cold test.[61] Preparations continued for the real test of the nuclear weapon on both sides of the border and to develop missiles that would be capable of carrying them to the other side. By December 1995, a leading US analyst was alerting the US congress to the importance of these threats in the subcontinent, 'It is not surprising that we view the nuclear capabilities—and the associated ballistic missile programmes—of India and Pakistan with considerable concern and as the regional issue of greatest importance,' Bruce Riedel (Deputy Assistant Secretary of Defense for Near Eastern and South Asian Affairs), told the House International Relations subcommittee on Asia and the Pacific, even as he tried to justify the sale of equipment and spare parts to Pakistan.[62]

India had also gone through a political upheaval, with the relatively conciliatory Congress Party government of I.K. Gujral having been replaced by the much more jingoistic and belligerent Bharatiya Janata Party (BJP) with its extreme right-wing component led by L.K. Advani, a rabid anti-Pakistani Sindhi refugee. As US nuclear expert George Perkovitch documents in detail in his magisterial book on the development of the Indian nuclear weapons programme, the BJP party leadership kept the decision close to its chest and was waiting for an opportunity to proceed with another series of tests.

The successful test of the KRL-designed missile named Ghauri by Pakistan on 6 April 1998 from the Tilla Jogian firing range in Jhelum district gave them the excuse. Prime Minister Vajpayee gave the go-ahead for the Indian nuclear weapons test at Pokhran. In doing so, he was bolstered by some cold calculations that had preceded this action. In Indian governmental as well as academic circles, much thought had been given to the idea of open weapon testing. Both the United States and the Soviet Union had at one time toyed with the idea of using nuclear explosives for peaceful purposes such as for digging canals, harbours and reservoirs. However, the former had given it up in 1977 and the latter in 1988 due to concerns arising from radioactive contamination. India had tried to get away with its nuclear test of 1974 by dubbing it as a Peaceful Nuclear Explosion. But it could have by no means justified another nuclear explosion for ostensibly peaceful purposes in 1998 when others had already abandoned it. By 1996, a study of the potential effect of a weapon test had examined in some detail the economic fallout from such tests. 'If India were to conduct another peaceful nuclear explosion (PNE) in its desire to keep its 'options open,' there is no doubt that economic threats will be made against India by the US and its allies. Technology controls will be intensified. Foreign assistance may be suspended.' But, after examining the after effects of a test and the state of the Indian economy with its improved imports-to-debt ratio and substantial foreign exchange reserves of some $20 billion, the study had concluded, 'India need not worry about any negative fallout on its economy due to the US and its allies' reactions and counter-measures in case it decides to renew its nuclear testing.'[63]

India's relatively closed economy and less dependence on the United States for military and economic aid also prevented it from suffering from any sanctions over the short term. Pakistan, on the other hand, with its fledgling and relatively open economy and high dependence on the United States and the West in general, was highly susceptible to pressures. There is no evidence that Pakistan had conducted any serious economic analyses of the results of going public with a nuclear weapon. Its economy had been sliding downwards through the periods of successive political turmoil and mismanagement, with external debt mounting, production declining, and inflation on the rise. It also faced huge balance of payments deficits that made it a perennial client—and hence prisoner—of the IMF, an institution that was known to favour US direction and could effectively shut off its spigot of financial aid at the US's bidding.

On 11 May 1998, India tested three nuclear weapons at Pokhran, following it on 13 May with another two tests. This was greeted with great public acclaim at home and was presented overseas as India's attempt to counter China and Pakistan's aggressive designs. US intelligence had failed yet again to predict the test. Pakistan was also caught unaware but rested in its confidence that it too had started making preparations. Now it was time to decide whether to follow suit or not. The Indian gambit was to force Pakistan either to acknowledge that it had been unable to weaponize its nuclear programme or to go for a test and suffer the consequences of its action. Either way, relative to India, Pakistan stood to lose.

The Pakistani leadership moved into action stations on hearing of the Indian test. Sharif was in Central Asia when the India blast occurred. He says that he decided immediately that Pakistan needed to respond in kind, and called General Karamat from there. Karamat says he advised against any precipitate action and suggested that they discuss the pros and cons upon the prime minister's return, 'The Foreign Secretary was on an open line. He tried to give me [the] green light—I had to be non-committal. I wanted them to do the math and be clear on what they were getting into. We also wanted and got—a decision after full deliberation—absolutely essential for posterity', says Karamat. The decisions Sharif 'took on his own will haunt him and us forever—Taliban recognition, freezing accounts etc.' The decision to test was made by the Defence Committee of the Cabinet (DCC) after a very comprehensive discussion and, at Karamat's insistence, a presentation from the finance minister on the post-test economic situation. He says that he had wanted Mueen Afzal, the secretary general of finance to do it and had had a discussion with the latter, but they did not allow Afzal to attend the meeting. 'I was not doing all this because I did not want to test but because I wanted a fully debated and considered decision. I got it.'[64] Sharif says he insisted that they proceed with plans to test and over-ruled Karamat, who feared that the US would retaliate against Pakistan with sanctions. He recalls that both Karamat and the naval chief opposed the tests, while the air chief supported the move.[65]

On his return, the prime minister convened the DCC, including his foreign minister, finance minister, the foreign secretary, and the three service chiefs. Contradicting Sharif's memory of that meeting, Karamat says that the three service chiefs went into the meeting in full agreement. 'Can anybody believe that the three service chiefs would get into a DCC with such an agenda without making sure that they were all on the same page? I was CJCSC and made sure that we had a pow wow to get our thoughts clear. There was never any difference in the opinion of the service chiefs—they all wanted to test. They all knew that under US law sanctions are mandatory after such an event—we wanted the PM and others to understand this and we wanted an assurance that budgetary constraints post event would not lead to a degradation of operational capacity—especially in Kashmir. We got this assurance. This was what it was all about. As far as preparing for the test was concerned—that was underway the moment the Indians tested—we knew exactly what had to be done and were doing it regardless of what was going on in different circles.'[66] A surprising attendant at the DCC meeting was the Minister for Religious Affairs, Raja Zafar ul Haq, a one-time lawyer from Rawalpindi, who represented the prime minister's contacts with the religious groups that were clamouring for tests.

The chairman of the PAEC, Dr Ishfaq Ahmad, was in the United States and immediately headed home. But in that first meeting, Dr Mubarakmand (Member Technical of the PAEC) stood in for him and when asked if Pakistan could respond to the Indian tests with tests of its own, is reported to have said that it would take the PAEC ten days to test its nuclear weapons. The next day, Dr Ahmad, back from the US, met the army chief and the prime minister and reaffirmed that pledge with the words: 'Mr Prime Minister, take a decision and, Insha Allah, I give you the guarantee of success.'

The Pakistani public was in a state of shock because of the Indian nuclear tests. The popular reaction was that Pakistan should respond with its own tests as soon as possible. It was felt that if Pakistan did not test now it would never be able to do so in the future. Dr A.Q. Khan had claimed as early as 1984 that Pakistan had assembled one or more devices[67] while Foreign Secretary Shahryar Khan had announced in 1992 that 'the capacity is there,... his country possesses elements which, if put together, would become a device.'[68] Pakistan had all along maintained a position of deliberate ambiguity regarding its nuclear capability. As the government delayed a decision regarding the ending of this state of ambiguity with a nuclear test, people became restive and some even began to doubt if the country did, indeed, have such a capability.

Sharif was under great public pressure at home to respond to the Indian test. He was also under external pressure not to do so, and thus stood to reap the benefits of economic and political help. Among others, President Bill Clinton of the United States spoke with him at least four times during this period to dissuade him from testing. 'Clinton...tried to dissuade me but when he saw that I was not coming around to his way of thinking, he offered me an economic package of $5 billion,' Sharif recalled in a later interview. When Sharif balked at accepting the offer, Clinton threatened him with sanctions.[69] But the chorus at home was closer at hand and louder, despite the potential fallout, both political and economic. The governor of the State Bank, a former senior IMF staffer, Mohammed Yaqub, had for his own reasons fought against the provision of foreign currency accounts (mainly US dollars) for Pakistanis that was a huge callable burden on the central bank, a financial Sword of Damocles that could fall at short notice and bankrupt the country's reserves. Yaqub saw any sanctions as an opportunity to wipe out this potential foreign exchange debt to Pakistanis by seizing it through force majeure and offering to pay back account holders in easily printable local rupees.[70] He suggested to the Finance Minister Sartaj Aziz a scheme for paying back residents of Pakistan with such accounts at a premium exchange rate and arranging a different method for non-residents. Aziz apparently did not carry these ideas forward as suggested. Neither Aziz nor the Secretary General Finance, Mueen Afzal, reportedly opposed Sharif's desire to proceed with the test, regardless of the economic consequences, although all must have known that Pakistan was facing a severe financial crisis, with dwindling reserves and a potential default against its obligations to foreign debtors should it face sanctions after going openly nuclear. But Gohar Ayub Khan states that Chaudhry Nisar Ali Khan, Sartaj Aziz, Mushahid Hussain, and Begum Abida Hussain, all opposed tests by Pakistan at the first meeting of the DCC. Two days later, a majority of the members favoured the decision of the prime minister to proceed with the test![71]

Publicly, Pakistan played coy during this period, leading many to speculate that the prime minister, who was not known for making tough decisions rapidly, had managed to avoid this one too and thus saved Pakistan from the aftershocks of testing. But his nationalistic pride was being underestimated by commentators. 'On 18 May 1998 Dr Ishfaq Ahmad was informed by Prime Minister Sharif of the government decision to carry out the test.'[72] The scientists and engineers of PAEC had, in any case, started preparations for the tests immediately after India had tested its devices. The tunnels which had fallen into a state of disrepair were urgently readied but there was no time to replace the rickety cages used for descent into the vertical shaft at Kharan. 'On May 19 two teams of 140 PAEC scientists from various classified groups of PAEC left for Chagai by air while some members left by road with the equipment. Dr Mubarakmand, whose group developed the diagnostic capabilities, led the team of scientists who carried out the tests. Diagnostic cables, telemetry system and other equipment were made ready. The subsystems of devices, transported from Rawalpindi in an aircraft, were assembled in the five 'zero' [detonation] rooms in the tunnel at Chagai (the sixth device was subsequently assembled on 29 May in the 'zero' room at the horizontal end of the L-shaped shaft). Dr Mubarakmand certified assembly of the devices in his presence. Total simulation of the test was carried out from the tele-command centre. On 25 May army *jawans* [soldiers] started sealing the tunnel.' International spy satellites recorded the events at Chagai in detail, down to the pouring of concrete at the tunnel mouth. It was only a matter of time before the cement was to dry.

On 28 May 1998, Pakistan responded to the Indian tests with five tests at Chagai. At 3:16 p.m., Muhammad Arshad, the young man who had designed the trigger mechanism and therefore had been selected for this job, pushed the button.[73] Within thirty seconds, the black granite of the Ras Koh Hills at Chagai turned white as a result of the tremendous heat of the explosion. Pakistan had matched the Indians five to five. 'Today we have settled a score!' declared Prime Minister Sharif,[74] who now had the monopoly of being a national hero. Two days later, Pakistan exploded another (that is the sixth) device of an advanced design in the secondary site at Kharan and could at last state that it had topped India (or equalled it, counting the 1974 test). The US failed to detect that test.

The PAEC's Dr Mubarakmand explained the reason for the six tests, 'We were aware that PAEC scientists were getting the opportunity to carry out the test after more than a decade of cold tests and it was felt that we should make the best use of it. The tunnel at Chagai and the shaft at Kharan had provision for six tests, therefore, stocks of six different designs, sizes and yields were picked up. All the devices were based on PAEC design, which had been earlier tested in cold tests.'[75] The announced yield of the five tests conducted at Chagai was 25–36 kilo tons, 12 kilo tons and three devices in the sub-kiloton range, while that of the Kharan test was 12 kilo tons. These were comparable in yield to the six tests conducted by India from 1974 to 1998. International monitoring stations of CTBTO and other seismic stations have reported lower yields for the tests conducted by India and Pakistan and have also disputed the number of devices tested by the two.

After the Chagai tests Dr A.Q. Khan could not resist calling a press conference of his own to declare that he had succeeded in exploding the nuclear devices. He failed to tell his correspondents that he had initially not been invited to the test. This was due to intense rivalry between PAEC and KRL as to who would conduct the nuclear tests. PAEC rather than the KRL headed by the celebrated Dr A.Q. Khan took the lead since their weapon design had beaten out Dr Khan's design and had passed the cold test. PAEC which had a much more broad based nuclear programme also had the additional advantage that 'the tunnel at Chagai was developed by its engineers and scientists. It had greater experience in carrying out cold tests and claimed wide capability in carrying out hot tests of different yields and designs.'[76]

> A shorter and exclusive DCC meeting convened between May 15-18 had decided to give a matching response to India and assign the task to PAEC. As the news that PAEC had been asked to prepare for the tests travelled to KRL, a furious Dr Khan protested to Chief of the Army Staff, General Jehangir Karamat who, in turn rang up Prime Minister Nawaz Sharif. It was decided, as a compromise, that members of KRL will be associated in the team preparing the site.[77]

Dr A.Q. Khan and four senior scientists from KRL arrived at the test site along with Dr Ishfaq Ahmad and Maj. Gen. Zulfikar Ali (Chief of Combat Development at GHQ), twelve hours before the detonation of the devices on 28 May 1998. Soon after the series of tests, senior members of the PAEC team returned to a memorable welcome in Islamabad. The army, which was responsible for the logistics, delayed the return of the KRL team and held them up at Quetta. They were so much out of touch with what was going on that, after the test at Kharan on 30 May, Dr A.Q. Khan issued a statement that two devices had been tested. The Pakistan Foreign Office had to step in to issue the correct news that only one device had been detonated.[78] Nevertheless, Dr A.Q. Khan was to gradually arrogate for himself the title of 'Father of the Bomb' and his legend grew. As did his ability to act autonomously on behalf of his country and himself.

AL QAEDA RAISES ITS HEAD

A rather telling conversation took place after the blast, as Sharif called President Clinton to tell him that he had 'conducted the atomic blasts.' Sharif recalls that Clinton regretted this action but told Sharif: 'My hands are now tied,' meaning that he had to impose sanctions on Pakistan. However, Sharif says that Clinton told him that he appreciated that Sharif had been straight with him (Sharif used a cricketing metaphor: 'played with a straight bat', that Clinton is unlikely to have known about or used). 'I said "thanks"....after that President Clinton became my friend. He often called me.' During one of these exchanges, Sharif states that Clinton told him that he had been informed that some people were planning a large-scaled attack of destruction against the United States and that Osama Bin Laden and his people were a part of this plot and had the support of the Taliban. 'He attacked their bases in Afghanistan, on which I complained to him and asked him why he did it. I used to explain to him that whatever action he took should be done after deliberation.'[79] But Sharif appears to be conflating in hindsight later events, since the Al Qaeda attacks on US embassies in East Africa did not take place till August 1998 after which the US launched retaliatory missile attacks on alleged Al Qaeda targets in Afghanistan.

ANOTHER BATTLE

As Sharif attempted to establish total control over the government and the country, he found Army Chief Karamat lacking the desirable enthusiasm for his various ideas. Among the many steps that Sharif took was the 15th Amendment which would enforce Islamic Law throughout Pakistan and raise the government's actions in that regard beyond the reach of the courts. Hassan Abbas, the author and former police officer, refers to this as Sharif's dream of a 'caliphate.' But the Senate managed to thwart the passage of this bill, which had sailed through the National Assembly earlier in August.[80] Sharif wanted to use the army to run civil administration also, drawing it closer into his embrace. Karamat recalls being bombarded with new ideas of army involvement in civilian administration at almost every meeting he held with Sharif. He says that he would agree to 'think about' the individual issues and then put them on the back burner since Sharif would no doubt have new ideas to launch at the next meeting and was unlikely to follow up on the earlier ones. Among the suggestions that came from Sharif was to use the army to patrol the GT road, conduct surveys of schools to determine how many were actually operating with staff, and helping the Water and Power Development Authority (WAPDA) monitor its customers' meters to ensure there was no pilferage. Karamat did not agree to most of these suggestions, although his successor did. Karamat may have underestimated the memory of the prime minister, who may have been keeping a tally.

A rejuvenated Sharif began to spread his wings. This time his target was the army chief, General Karamat. Sharif had his eyes and ears within the GHQ and may have felt that Karamat did not have the full support of all his corps commanders. There are different views on this score. Any chief can change his corps commanders at any time. And he is not bound by their views; the army is not a democracy. Recounting that period, Sharif says he felt 'strongly that Government and politics is the affairs of the politicians and political parties. And the Army has no...business to interfere with the affairs of Government.'[81] As a result, in his view, Karamat had intruded into the affairs of the government by suggesting, in a speech on 6 October 1998 at the Naval Staff College in Lahore, the formation of a NSC to provide stability to the political system. This topic had been discussed publicly in various fora but the army chief's support gave it new life. Karamat's speech was met with a positive response from political parties as well as the press.

Sharif took umbrage at these developments. He stewed over it overnight and then asked Karamat to come meet him. Sharif wanted Karamat to issue a clarification that the latter said he was unable to do, since he had told the prime minister all the things he stated in his speech many times before. He maintained there was nothing new in his speech.[82] According to Sharif: 'I have great regards for General Jehangir Karamat, but...when he stepped out of his domain, I had to talk to him, and I said, "This is not on. We can't accept it".' Recounting the meeting some eight years later, Sharif portrays his angry reaction to Karamat's speech vividly, with staccato sound bites:

> Everybody thought that the Prime Minister's position had been undermined exactly by the statement of the Chief of Army Staff. I also felt the same and so I spoke to him I said, 'Jehangir Sahib, this, is none of your business to give a statement like this. Do I ever give a statement as far as the Army's concerned? Or the Army's policies are concerned? Does the Prime Minister ever interfere into the affairs, or meddle into the affairs of the Army? I don't do that. [Addressing the interviewer] You must be knowing that the Prime Minister has all the powers to devise the policies that he thinks is right for the Army. He can even give out...a... directive to the Army that all the promotions starting at Second Lieutenant to the General and all the postings and transfers will be done after seeking the approval of the Prime Minister. And this will have to be implemented. But has he ever done that?[83]

Clearly, Sharif had a long list of issues in his mind. Karamat does not recall this voluble rhetoric from Sharif at the meeting. He recalls Sharif telling him that the 'government had been undermined....This is a very difficult situation.

This will now be discussed in parliament whether the army chief should be saying these things or not.' He sought a solution. Karamat says he told him to issue a statement that the army chief has said nothing new. But Sharif was not having any of that. 'Somebody had worked him up' recalls Karamat. 'This has gone too far' said Sharif. 'We'll have to discuss this.' So Karamat said: 'You need not discuss this. I'll leave.' Sharif's demeanour changed dramatically, recalls Karmat. Suddenly he was relaxed and he readily accepted this offer from Karamat. Karamat believes that Sharif or people around him were in touch with people in the army and this may have given Sharif a little extra confidence in dealing with the army chief in a peremptory manner.[84]

Karamat also ascribes the origins of this action to earlier events. The prime minister had been briefed at GHQ on the law and order situation. He did not react during that meeting, but sent an emissary later to see if the army could be deployed for law and order. Shahbaz Sharif also came back with the suggestion to get help with WAPDA's survey, which Karamat did not support. Karamat told Shahbaz Sharif about reports coming from all parts of the country about law and order and corruption. This may have spooked the prime minister about the army chief's possible motives for highlighting problems.

Karamat met the prime minister and his brother two days before his Naval War College speech. Among the issues he raised was the selection of the next chief. Sharif said that matter was entirely up to the prime minister and he did not wish to discuss it with Karamat. 'That was a rude shock to me,' recalls Karamat. He suspects that Sharif may have wanted even at that time to go down the ladder to make someone very junior the next army chief, perhaps even Lt. Gen. Ziauddin. And he was to find out later that Sharif suspected that Karamat might support Lt. Gen. Ali Quli Khan as the new chief, something he says he may well have done. Sharif offered to issue a notification retiring Karamat from the COAS position so that he would be left solely with the position of CJCS—he had been holding the two positions concurrently at the time. Karamat responded that he needed to be sure of who the new chief would be before he agreed to move upstairs to chairman. Sharif was not pleased with this reply. As Karamat left, he recalls Shahbaz Sharif saying to him that the meeting had not gone well. He wanted to see if he could sort things out with his brother, the prime minister. Karamat went back to his home and thought hard about the situation. He then decided to use the Naval War College to make a firm statement.[85] That provoked the break and Sharif got Karamat to take early retirement, two months before he was to retire. Thus, Sharif got his chance to appoint someone who he thought would be a more pliable army chief.

APPOINTING A NEW ARMY CHIEF

After Karamat's departure, Sharif had a choice of five leading candidates. The senior-most was Lt. Gen. Ali Quli Khan, the son of Lt. Gen. Habibullah Khan Khattak, and former DG MI under General Waheed. Ali Quli was seen by some conspiracy theorists as favoured by Waheed, a fellow Pathan, who was alleged to have delayed making him a lieutenant general so that he would retain his seniority when Waheed's successor's term expired in January 1999. A Sandhurst-trained officer then serving as CGS, he was known to be professional and tough. However, Sharif had memories of the MI operating against his interests during the Waheed period. Next in line was Ali Quli's course mate, Khalid Nawaz, who was serving as MGO. The next two, Lt. Gen. Salahuddin Tirmizi and Lt. Gen. Pervez Musharraf, were at par, according to Prime Minister Sharif and his Military Secretary, Brigadier Javed Iqbal. Both had the same 'score' in terms of their Annual Confidential Reports (ACRs), including some black marks (that Sharif studiously avoided discussing even years after the event).[86] About Musharraf, then commander of the strike corps at Mangla, Sharif recalls that his 'ACRs said very clearly that he is not fit for the appointment of Chief of Army Staff.'[87] Moreover, the 'agencies' (short-hand for the ISI and other intelligence outfits) had reported that he was not 'suitable' for the post. They reported that Musharraf was a person who was 'quick in taking action and could be easily roused....Takes actions without deep thought.'[88] The fifth candidate was Lt. Gen. Ziauddin Khwaja,[89] then adjutant general at GHQ and previously a corps commander.

On 7 October 1998, Sharif chose Musharraf to be the new army chief, replacing Karamat. Ali Quli and Khalid Nawaz sought early retirement after being superseded, following a tradition of the Pakistan Army. This would be Sharif's most fateful decision, as later events were to prove. However, with hindsight, Sharif now admits that he acted in 'haste' and that he was given 'wrong advice'. Specifically, he points to Lt. Gen. (retired) Iftikhar Ahmed Khan, the defence secretary, and his brother and the prime minister's close aide, Chaudhry Nisar Ali Khan, who had some personal difficulties with Ali Quli Khan. Sharif claims that he was told that 'he is on so and so's side and he is related to so and so.'[90] Ali Quli's sister, Zeb, was married to Gohar Ayub Khan, a member of the prime minister's party. Thus, Sharif settled on Musharraf, a Mohajir from north India and therefore not likely to have strong tribal or clan affiliation in the army. Musharraf also had close relations with General Iftikhar and through him had met his brother, who had the prime minister's ear, although he contends that he was completely surprised by his selection. He recalls Sharif telling him: 'One of the reasons why I have selected you is that you are the only lieutenant general who never approached me, directly or indirectly, for this job.'[91]

The army was stunned by the resignation of Karamat. Musharraf states that 'there was even greater resentment in the army than I had imagined over General Jehangir Karamat's forced resignation' at the hands of 'an overbearing Prime Minister with a huge parliamentary majority...[who] had been busy gathering all powers in his office.'[92] Addressing his first corps commanders conference at GHQ on 17 October, Musharraf explained the circumstances surrounding Karamat's departure, even reading out a paragraph from a letter written by Karamat to the adjutant general citing his reasons for resigning. He said that 'the ex-COAS took a decision which was in the best interest of the country.' The minutes of that meeting note that 'he [Musharraf] further emphasized, (sic) that he understood the state of shock created by the suddenness of the change, however, the incident is now part of history and there should be no further discussion on the subj[ect].' Musharraf then pointed to 'attempts by vested interests to exploit the sit[uation]. Their aim is to belittle the army and to create a rift between the Govt. and the Army.' He sought 'complete unity and cohesion' to counter these moves.[93] He dilated on the 'political instability and uncertainty' in Pakistan, the 'growing threat of subnationalism and smaller provinces agitating, the economic catastrophe due to sanctions and shadow of debt-servicing default [and] social unrest.' On the external front, Musharraf felt there was 'no serious external threat to Pakistan. Indian Army is, however, carrying out exs [exercises] close to our border and we shall take appropriate safeguards.'[94]

Musharraf then outlined for his colleagues a set of ten broad policy guidelines dealing with issues as well as codes of behaviour. Right after the first guidelines dealing with 'focus on professionalism and readiness,' he highlighted for his senior commanders that there would be 'No change in policies on Kashmir, LOC [Line of Control] and Working Boundry (sic) etc.' Significantly, Kargil was not mentioned. He ended with guideline number 10: 'Everyone to stay away from politics and politicians. Only the COAS will interact with the Govt. to present the army's view pt (sic). He will indeed discuss all matters with his subordinate commanders to form opinion on national issues.'[95] Here he was echoing the words of earlier chiefs, especially General Asif Nawaz, who had told his corps commanders that he would act as a buffer between them and the politicians. Even General Nawaz believed privately that they would still talk politics in their smaller groups and out of his ear-shot. The key points that emerge from this record of Musharraf's first GHQ meeting with his corps commanders is the absence of any talk about planned actions in Kashmir, specifically in Kargil, and indeed of Kashmir as a growing issue of concern.

Sharif took advantage of the new appointment to get the army to commit to helping WAPDA in checking its electricity meters and to do a study of 'ghost' schools in the Punjab. Musharraf was ready to oblige, even though he noted that the prime minister was trying to influence promotions in the army. Their working relationship was good, but a storm was to brew between them that grew out of military action in Kargil. Within barely one year of his appointment, Musharraf and Sharif were at loggerheads and Sharif would end up losing out, sending Pakistan back to a state of military rule and political uncertainty.

NOTES

1. *Have Faith in Massachusetts*. Houghton Mifflin. Chapter 12. Cited in *Columbia World of Quotations 1996*.
2. General Waheed belonged to a well known family of Peshawar and was educated at the celebrated Edwards College in that city. Despite an early set back when he was held back for one term at the PMA, (a point that his detractors continuously reiterated), there had been a steady rise in his military career, joining the Frontier Force Regiment after being commissioned from the PMA in the 19th PMA Long Course in 1959, and doing so well in the entrance examination for the Staff College that he was selected to go for the Staff College in Canada. He had fought in the 1965 and 1971 wars and was wounded in the Battle of Chawinda during the 1965 war. He served under General Rahimuddin as COS of the XII Corps in Quetta, commanded a division in Sindh, and later was adjutant general at GHQ in Rawalpindi, before being sent to command the Quetta corps himself.
3. Conversation with author soon after he was nominated COAS.
4. Interview with Prime Minister Benazir Bhutto.
5. Interview with Ambassador John Monjo.
6. The arms shipments were sent on a C-130 and were approved by the COAS, General Nawaz. Nasir is also alleged to have sent shipments to Bosnia via Malaysia, according to General Jehangir Karamat in an interview with the author. It is also plausible that the United States was aware of these shipments and looked the other way since it allowed the Bosnians to defend themselves against well armed Serbian forces. See also 'Ex-ISI Chief Reveals Secret Missile Shipments to Bosnia defying UN Embargo', in *South Asia Tribune Publications*, Issue No. 22, 23–29 December 2002.
7. Interview with Major General Afzal Janjua, ex-ISI Directorate.
8. Ambassador Robert Oakley's telephone call to author 1992.
9. ABC TV's investigative unit was pursuing the story that reportedly linked faxes from Javed Nasir's office to Al Fuqra, a group established by Sheikh Mubarik Ali Gilani in New York in 1980. Gilani was the person that *Wall Street Journal* reporter Daniel Pearl was reportedly going to meet when he was kidnappped and later killed in Pakistan in February 2002. The producer came to see me to ask about my brother's death and the investigation. But by the time they were trying to pull together the story on Prime Minister Sharif's government, Sharif had been displaced. The story lost its appeal.
10. Interview with Lt. Gen. Javed Ashraf Qazi.
11. Monjo interview.
12. Interview with Prime Minister Nawaz Sharif.
13. Roedad Khan, *Pakistan—A Dream Gone Sour* (Karachi: Oxford University Press, 1997), pp. 117–118.
14. 'Nawaz sees conspiracy to undermine his govt,' *The News*, 18 April 1993, p. 1.
15. Roedad Khan, *Pakistan—A Dream Gone Sour*, p. 122.
16. Ibid., pp. 132–133.
17. Interview with Lt. Gen. Javed Ashraf Qazi.

18. This is largely based on interviews with General Qazi, but supplemented by conversations with Sartaj Aziz and Saeed Sheikh of Bethesda, MD.
19. Interview with Lt. Gen. Javed Ashraf Qazi.
20. Ibid.
21. *Political Handbook of the World 1992,* (Binghamton, NY: CSA Publications, 1992).
22. Interview with Lt. Gen. Javed Ashraf Qazi.
23. Interview with Robin Raphel.
24. Interview with Lt. Gen. Javed Nasir.
25. Interview with Gen. Abdul Waheed.
26. Interview with Lt. Gen. Ziauddin Khwaja.
27. Interview with Lt. Gen. Javed Ashraf Qazi.
28. Strobe Talbott, *Engaging India: Diplomacy, Democracy and the Bomb—A Memoir* (Washington, D.C.: Brookings Institution Press 2004), p. 32.
29. Interview with Lt. Gen. Ziauddin Khwaja.
30. Conversation with General Abdul Waheed.
31. Interview with Robert Einhorn.
32. This section is based on the Einhorn interview.
33. Hassan Abbas, *Pakistan's Drift Into Extremism: Allah, The Army, and America's War On Terror* (M.E. Sharpe, 2005), pp. 132–133. Abbas contends that Abbasi had support from the Rawalpindi Corps Commander Lt. Gen. G.M. Malik. Major General Irshadullah Tarar states that General Asif Nawaz had told Gen. Malik that he would be sent home, i.e. forcibly retired. But before that could be effected, General Nawaz died. (Interview of Gen. Tarar with author).
34. John F. Burns, 'Pakistan Arrests 40 Officers; Islamic Militant Ties Suspected,' *The New York Times,* New Delhi. 16 October 1994.
35. See Ahmed Rashid, *Taliban: Militant Islam, Oil and Fundamentalism in Central Asia* (Yale University Press, 2001), and Kamal Matinuddin, *The Taliban Phenomenon: Afghanistan 1994-1997* (Karachi: Oxford University Press, 1999). The Talibs existed even during the anti-Soviet jihad as a component of the Harakat-e-Inqilab-e-Islami of Nabi Mohammmedi and the Hizb-e-Islami of Yunus Khalis, which were part of the seven *tanzeems* or organizations of the Islamist warriors who had fled the communist regime of Afghanistan and sought refuge in Pakistan.
36. Matinuddin, *The Taliban*, pp. 25–26, citing Colonel Imam of the ISI who was consul general for Pakistan in Herat at that time. Imam, whose real name was Syed Sultan Amir, was posted to Herat from 1992 to 2001 and helped the Pakistan Foreign Office on matters dealing with Kandahar because most of the Mujahideen commanders had been trained by him during the war against the Soviet Union. 'Imam' was the standard radio call sign of the commander of any Pakistani detachment or regiment. He himself was trained as a ranger at Fort Bragg in the United States.
37. Interview with Major General Afzal Janjua.
38. Interview with Lt. Gen. Javed Ashraf Qazi
39. Ambassador Arif Ayub. Written exchange with author.
40. See Ahmed Rashid, *Taliban*, for a detailed treatment of the emergence of UNOCAL as a player in Taliban dominated Afghanistan.
41. Interview with Benazir Bhutto.
42. Farooq Leghari has a slightly different take on this. He recalls Waheed saying he would get back to them about an extension but never did. Leghari states that Waheed never actually refused the extension. Interview with author.
43. Interview with Benazir Bhutto.
44. Interview with General Jehangir Karamat.
45. Leghari interview.
46. Bhutto interview.

47. Ibid.
48. 'He said to me that, "You are my leader.... You are my sister. The question does not arise that I would ever dismiss your government. I would resign; I would not dismiss your government." And then when I said, "No." He turned around and he told me, "BB, you don't believe me because your brother let you down. But this brother won't let you down". Ibid.
49. Leghari interview.
50. Ibid.
51. Karamat interview.
52. John F. Burns, 'Bhutto Clan Leaves Trail of Corruption in Pakistan,' *The New York Times*, 9 January 1998.
53. Asif Ali Zardari Case History, US Minority Staff Report for Permanent Subcommittee on Investigations Hearings on Private Banking and Money Laundering: A Case Study of Opportunities and Vulnerabilities, 9 November 1999, pp. 22–28.
54. Leghari interview.
55. Bhutto interview.
56. Karamat interview.
57. Ibid.
58. George Perkovitch, *India's Nuclear Bomb: The Impact on Global Proliferation* (Berkeley and Los Angeles: University of California Press, 1999), p. 365.
59. Shahid-ur-Rehman, *Long Road to Chagai* (Islamabad: Print Wise Publication 1999), pp. 80–82
60. *Pakatom*, PAEC, Islamabad, 28 May 1999.
61. M.A. Chaudhri, 'Pakistan's Nuclear History: Separating Myth from Reality,' *Defence Journal*, May 2006, Vol. 9, No. 10.
62. 'India, Pakistan Nuclear Programs, Missiles Top Concerns.' Testimony to the House International Relations Subcommittee on Asia and the Pacific by Deputy Assistant Secretary of Defense Bruce Riedel, 6 December 1995.
63. Dr G. Balachandaran, 'India's Nuclear Option: Economic Consequences,' *Strategic Analysis*, May 1996, Vol. XIX, No. 2.
64. Written exchange with General Jehangir Karamat, April 2007.
65. Nawaz Sharif, *Ghadaar Kaun?* (Who's the traitor?) (Lahore: Sagar Publication, 2006), pp. 125–126.
66. Written exchange with General Karamat.
67. Shahid-ur-Rehman, ibid., p. 80.
68. *The Washington Post*, 7 February 1992.
69. Sharif, *Ghadaar Kaun?*, p. 127.
70. Conversation with Mohammed Yaqub.
71. Gohar Ayub Khan, *Glimpses into the Corridors of Power* (Karachi: Oxford University Press, 2007), p. 297.
72. Shahid-ur-Rehman, ibid., pp. 7–12. This paragraph relies on Rehman's monograph, courtesy of Dr Khan A. Shoaib.
73. Chaudhri, 'Pakistan's Nuclear History.' [Article quoted earlier.]
74. John Ward Anderson and Kamran Khan, 'Pakistan Sets Off Nuclear Blasts,' *The Washington Post*, 29 May 1998, p. 1, cited in Perkovitch, op. cit.
75. Shahid-ur-Rehman, ibid., p. 11.
76. Ibid., p. 10.
77. Ibid., p. 11.
78. K.A. Shoaib in written exchange with author.
79. Sharif, *Ghadaar Kaun?*, p. 127.
80. Abbas, *Pakistan's drift*, pp. 164–165.
81. Sharif interview.
82. Karamat interview.

83. Sharif interview.
84. Karamat. Communication with author.
85. Karamat interview.
86. The army's ACRs use the Designation V for Vices to note any commentary on individuals. Not all commentary is actually written down. Sometimes the army chief would call in a general and warn him against certain unacceptable moral behaviour.
87. Sharif interview.
88. Sharif, *Ghadaar Kaun?*, p. 135.
89. He normally went by just his given name: Ziauddin. But his father used the last name Khwaja. He was erroneously called Ziauddin Butt by the media and even his own army colleagues, who linked him to Prime Minister Nawaz Sharif, a fellow Kashmiri. Ziauddin denies that he had a relationship of any sort with the Sharif fmaily. But General Karamat recalls warning him 'for his own good' about visiting the Sharifs in Lahore.
90. Sharif, *Ghadaar Kaun?*, p. 134.
91. Pervez Musharraf, *In the Line of Fire* (New York: Free Press, 2006), p. 84.
92. Musharraf, *In the Line*, p. 85.
93. Secret 'Mins/Decisions of 60th Corps Comds Conf held at GHQ, Rawalpindi on 17 Oct 98. General Headquarters, GS Brach (SD Dte). Copy number 24. Dated 27 October 1998.
94. Secret 'Mins/Decisions,' 27 October 1998, p. 3.
95. Ibid., pp. 5–6.

17 | THE LIBERAL AUTOCRAT

I shall be an autocrat, that's my trade; and the good Lord will forgive me, that's his.

– Catherine the Great

This is not martial law, only another path towards democracy. The armed forces have no intention to stay in charge any longer than is absolutely necessary to pave the way for true democracy to flourish in Pakistan.

– General Pervez Musharraf, Chief Executive of Pakistan,
speech to the nation, 17 October 1999, 8:30 p.m.

General Pervez Musharraf, the so-called 'reluctant coup maker'[1] of 1999 was to take on the mantle of the 'liberal autocrat'[2] soon after taking over the country. But he too failed to match his stated intentions with his actions and soon got embroiled in political games, much like many of his predecessors. This was the cause of his eventual difficulties. He was a sharp and intelligent officer who impressed most of his superiors and had a rich military career, as an artillery officer, a commando, staff officer, and then commander of troops. Born in Delhi, he moved with his family to Pakistan after independence and spent his early years in Turkey, when his father was posted at the embassy in Ankara, and held all the right appointments, brigade major, regimental commander, brigade commander, and staff appointments at GHQ and the NDC before being promoted to major general and then lieutenant general. Apart from the Staff College and the War Course at the NDC, he also attended the Royal College of Defence Studies in the United Kingdom, where he was highly regarded. He was not risk averse and ready to stick his neck out when needed. He had a certain wild streak in him and critics pointed to his rakish attitude that often got him into trouble and accounted for some of the written and spoken critiques of his personal behaviour. Even Prime Minister Nawaz Sharif admitted to some pause in selecting him as the army chief when confronted with such reports.[3] But Musharraf was a determined nationalist and ambitious. His orientation was more worldly than many of his colleagues and it is a wonder that he survived through the Ziaist Islamist period without running foul of General Ziaul Haq's moralistic approach to personnel management.

As the new army chief, Musharraf hit the ground running and established a good rapport with the prime minister while asserting the army's pre-eminence in a growing number of areas. His support for the Kargil adventure and removal of a pro-Sharif general would eventually lead to a break between the two. After Sharif's ham-handed, though entirely legal, attempt to remove Musharraf from office while he was on his way back from a visit to Sri Lanka, Musharraf's generals launched an illegal coup that dropped Sharif from grace. Following a period of international isolation for his military rule, Musharraf found himself rehabilitated after the terrorist attack on the United States of

11 September 2001. His immediate U-turn and ready alliance with the West against his erstwhile allies, the Taliban of Afghanistan, thrust him onto the global stage as a key partner of the United States in its global 'War on Terror'. Despite many attempts by terrorist groups to assassinate him, he managed to survive and strengthen his hold on the political system, effectively transforming Pakistan's parliamentary political system into a de-facto presidential system. Wearing both his uniform and his civilian suits, he epitomized the 'liberal autocrat,' that he was, espousing his own form of 'enlightened moderation.' He survived by using his military power and his civil authority to force his views or to make deals and manipulate the polity of Pakistan to his advantage for the second longest tenure of any military ruler.[4] His liberal instincts, for example, against many restrictive Islamic laws, often ran against the hard wall of political reality and he was forced to compromise and to re-group frequently. But many saw him as a well-intentioned man who took on the impossible task of transforming a flawed social and political system—which he called 'sham democracy'—into his own form of controlled democracy.

In many ways, Musharraf was an anachronism in the twenty-first century, a military ruler in a world that had moved on to democracy, with all the noise and confusion of the latter.[5] He felt strongly that whenever he left office, particularly once he shed his military rank, the country would revert to its Hobbesian state of political anarchy and would need to begin anew the passage to democratic norms. Meanwhile, there would be tumult on the national stage as well as at the global level. And he was at the centre of it all.

THE KARGIL BATTLE

Within weeks of taking over, Musharraf faced a military decision that would prove to be a key tipping point in the benighted democratic experiment in Pakistan. His local commander in the remote, desolate, and frigid waste of the Kargil sector in Kashmir, Major General Javed Hasan, presented a plan to take advantage of the winter lull to 'straighten' out the Line of Control (LOC) between Indian troops and Pakistan's army in the disputed territory of Kashmir. The aim was to gain the military upper hand by dominating the Kargil heights, thus threatening the main Indian supply route, National Highway 1A, linking Srinagar to Dras, Kargil, and Leh. They had not presented this plan to the previous chief, General Jehangir Karamat, who would have rejected it, based on his knowledge of earlier such episodes when he had been DGMO.[6] The Corps Commander X Corps, Lt. Gen. Mahmud Ahmed and General Musharraf signed off on the plan and got the prime minister involved in the idea of raising the temperature of political discussions on Kashmir with India. This precipitated a military confrontation that eventually led to US intervention in the dispute and the eventual withdrawal of Pakistani troops from their advance positions across the LOC in Kargil. This severely wounded Musharraf's relationship with the prime minister and set back the nascent peace process between India and Pakistan. It also became a key factor in the eventual military coup that ousted Nawaz Sharif on 12 October 1999.

Before understanding the nature of the Kargil conflict of 1999, it is important to bear in mind the history and topography of that location. The Kargil conflict was not the first major Indo–Pakistan battle for that space on the Kashmir border. In fact, one of the first actions in the 1948 Kashmir War was the securing of the Kargil heights by Pakistani forces. In subsequent wars, in 1965 and 1971, Kargil was again the object of desire because of its commanding position on the border between Indian- and Pakistani-controlled Kashmir. It was eclipsed somewhat by another even more remote and frozen wasteland, the Siachen Glacier, further to the north and east of Kargil, near the Chinese frontier. Siachen is reputed to be the longest glacier in the Karakoram Range, and at 70 kilometres, it is the second longest in the non-polar regions of the world, extending from a height of over 11,000 feet at its mouth to over 18,000 feet at its source. With temperatures of minus 50 centigrade, it became truly the highest and coldest battleground[7] in the world when, following disputes about maps which showed Siachen to be in Pakistan territory, India launched Operation Meghdoot (named after a Hindu divine cloud messenger) on 13 April 1984, and took most of the glacier's 2,300 sq. km.[8] The Pakistani troops—who were planning to race toward Siachen at the time but were held back because the local commander wanted to wait for warmer weather—were beaten back. One Pakistani commander described that attempt to retake Siachen as 'extreme infantry operations.'[9] Subsequently, both sides battled on the roof of the world. An apocryphal story on the internet and even in the official Indian report on Kargil has a young Pervez Musharraf leading an attack by the commandos of the SSG on Siachen in 1987.[10] In fact, he had served in the area as a captain earlier on but in 1987 he was a brigadier commanding the artillery for the armoured division in Kharian. However, he had observed the 1984 Siachen operation from the vantage point of the Military Operations Directorate at GHQ, and, like many of his colleagues, memories of that strategic loss haunted him.

Having lost parts of Siachen, Pakistan sought to gain the upper hand elsewhere on the LOC in Kashmir, even while it maintained pressure on India in Siachen. Kargil offered a good target since it overlooked Indian National Highway 1A connecting Srinagar to Dras (through Kargil), to Leh in Ladakh. Its heights, though not easy to traverse at 10–18,000 feet—and as frigid as

Siachen—were relatively easier to access from the Pakistani side, with steeper inclines on the Indian side. Even so, it was not an easy trek. The main road that allowed supplies to be brought close to the battle zone was only a Grade 2 track that ran parallel to the LOC and permitted limited mobility. Most of the supplies had to be transferred on to mules or porters' backs in maximum 40 pound loads and then taken to the forward positions, a distance of some 108 miles that needed eight days and nights of travel in winter. The Burzil Pass that allowed easier access was only open three months of the year. Many supplies had to be dropped by air. Even large helicopters found it hard to operate at those temperatures and heights. Only small helicopters could be used to carry supplies in slings, if the weather permitted. The casualties in the Northern Areas ran into the hundreds every month, mostly due to the weather. Holding a 480 km front was not an easy task for either the Pakistanis or the Indians. There were gaps that could be filled or exploited at all times.

Among the many attempts to gain advantage at Kargil was a failed attempt in 1990 by the Force Commander Northern Areas (FCNA), Major General Zaheer ul Islam Abbasi, a dedicated Islamist who had earlier been expelled from India as defence attaché after being implicated in a botched attempt to gather information from a double agent. The FCNA designation was used to comply with the Suchetgarh agreement after the 1971 war with India that prohibited the induction of fresh forces into the disputed territory of Kashmir. This is why the commander was not called GOC, which was a regular Pakistan Army designation. The force under him was composed of former Northern Scouts and other paramilitary troops under the rubric of the Northern Light Infantry (NLI), generally recruited from the region but commanded by Pakistan Army officers. The Pakistan Army regularly rotated officers into the FCNA and the NLI to provide them battle inoculation. A special clasp could be added to the defence medal worn by those who had served in Siachen on or after 1984. The FCNA in fact equalled a regular division with three brigades including one that was responsible for the Siachen Glacier. Without clearance from the army chief General Mirza Aslam Beg, Abbasi launched an attack on the LOC and then managed to leave his men isolated and under severe Indian counter attack. The local Brigade Commander, Brigadier Masood Navaid Anwari, decided to take it upon himself to carry supplies by helicopter to the front and was shot down and killed.[11] In all, Pakistan lost some 50 men and 10 officers in that encounter.[12] Abbasi was removed from command by the new chief, General Asif Nawaz, who also intended to remove the Corps Commander X Corps, Lt. Gen. G.M. Malik from his post. (As mentioned earlier, Abbasi later was implicated in a coup against the army high command and Prime Minister Benazir Bhutto, and sent to jail. He is now a free man and active in a religious missionary group in Rawalpindi.)

The effect of Ziaist Islamic teachings had taken hold by that time and continued to influence military behaviour into the next decade, according to a former FCNA commander, Major General Irshadullah Tarar. 'Cold military logic,' he said, had been replaced by Islamic slogans and prayers. Rather than subjecting plans to military critiques and precision, they were often prefaced with phrases such as: 'By the Grace of God, we will put 10,000 rounds over there and *Inshallah* the enemy will be routed!' Plans were discussed to use Mujahideen from Afghanistan in Kashmir, for instance, without subjecting them to military or logistical analysis. 'You cannot quantify God's Grace,' said Tarar.[13] When mistakes were made—for example when an officer and his men who were dropped on a remote mountain peak were lost,—rather than investigate why that happened, General Malik was heard saying at the corps commanders' meeting in October 1992: 'They were lucky they embraced *Shahadat* (martyrdom)', and left it at that.[14] Tarar also recalled that the general impression was created that the Indian Army would not fight. Indeed, an all-out war scenario was war gamed in GHQ in 1990 under General Beg at X Corps HQ. Tarar, who was attending for his corps commander, Lt. Gen. M. Tariq, demurred, because he said he felt the Pakistan Army was not prepared for it. This may be the incident that Prime Minister Benazir Bhutto attended and recalled in an interview with the author in 2006 (and subsequently in her revised autobiography). During that encounter, she had held her fire on the questions but, according to her, failed to be convinced of the plans.

RASHOMON EFFECT

Regarding the 1999 Kargil battle, there are clearly many sides to the story: the Indian side, the Pakistani side, and within the Pakistani side, the story told by General Musharraf and his colleagues on the one hand and by Prime Minister Sharif and his colleagues on the other. There is a veritable 'Rashomon Effect', with all the participants having a different perspective on the same set of events.[15] Kargil proved to be a case study in this regard.

Benazir Bhutto recalls a presentation during her second term, when she was invited to a war game at Joint Staff Headquarters, chaired by Air Chief Marshal Farooq Feroze Khan. The two competing 'army' commanders were the then DGMO, Major General Pervez Musharraf, who was commander of Blueland (the home side) and Air Marshal Ayub Mir, the Foxland (enemy) commander. Bhutto recalled, after being asked about it in an interview in the summer of 2006,[16] a Kargil-type of operation in Kashmir being discussed at this war game:

I was given a presentation by Pervez Musharraf, who was DGMO. And he gave me the same 'Blue Land-Red Land (sic)' theory and about how the war would break out and we would lose Sindh, we would lose Punjab up to Rahim Yar Khan, but we would win Kashmir.

Now, I agreed with him that we would end up losing Sindh and Rahim Yar Khan because he explained how we would be cut off. But I didn't agree with him that we'd end up winning Kashmir. This was supposed to be hypothetical, but…I never took anything that was said to me as hypothetical without giving a response that tomorrow would be factored into any real situation.

So then I put him through a series of questions, which I hadn't put to Beg [when an earlier suggestion had been put to her to reopen the Kashmir front] because that time…I didn't have the same confidence. But this time I had a little bit more confidence. So [this time] I put him through [a grilling]. I said, 'Then what will happen, once you take Srinagar?' So he said, 'Then we put the flag of Pakistan on the Assembly of Srinagar.' And I said, 'And then what will happen after you put the flag on Srinagar?' He said, 'Then you'll go to the United Nations and tell them we've taken Srinagar.' I said, 'And then what will happen when we tell them that we've taken Srinagar?' He said, 'Then you'll tell them, 'change the geography of the map.' So I said, 'And then what will happen?' So then he stumbled, he said '—what do you want me to say? What's happened, we've won.' So I said, 'No General, if I say that, they will tell me, 'go back.' They will tell me, 'Withdraw from Srinagar. Don't only withdraw from Srinagar, but withdraw from Azad Kashmir too.' Because under the United Nations resolution, first the plebiscite—we have to withdraw even from Azad Kashmir where the plebiscite has to be held. So the map won't be changed in that way.'

So maybe I should just have said…'no, this is not something we want.' But I didn't want the military people who were there to think that I was—they were always accusing me of being soft on India—stopping them from conquering Srinagar because I was soft on India. I wanted them to see that I was opposed to this idea on the concrete grounds that it was not a political reality to think that you could go into Srinagar and put a flag…because there were other international treaties and United Nations resolutions that could also be brought into force and a particular power situation in the world.[17]

Musharraf has a much more succinct recollection of that encounter, which he said took place in the context of the Indo–Pakistan situation at that time:

In that presentation I told her [Prime Minister Bhutto] that the time window for the resolution of Kashmir dispute is short. Because, with passage of time, the India–Pakistan equation, military equation and economic equation is going against us….she minded that a lot.

I told her that with time, the differential is increasing and the window will close. Therefore, if at all, we have to do anything, we should be planning to do it in a short while. Otherwise we lose the opportunity…. It was just that I had a more proactive view on what we should be doing in Kashmir and she did not like that.

She held totally defensive: 'let's sideline the issue altogether. Don't bother about it'.... So she took offence to it. And I did reply again, I said, 'I personally think that time is not on our side. Time is in the favour of India.' There was no Kargil type of situation discussed....

I said only that the Mujahideen were doing something over there. My view was if we are bringing about qualitative enhancement and quantitative is all in our hands, in the government's hands, as far as Mujahideen are concerned. You can send them arms etc. whenever you like. Qualitatively, that is all that I said, but I didn't give her...give ANY kind of a plan of action, military action. That was not the mandate [of the war game].[18]

While Bhutto is correct to see the danger of hypotheticals leading to real events, there is a difference between a war game and an operational plan. The army conducts war games on all sorts of scenarios: some plausible, others not. And the Blueland and Foxland commanders do not have a fixed script to follow. They do their best to present their ideas in light of the situation and on the basis of whatever information they have. It is not clear if Kargil actually emerged out of those war games. But, it is clear that the Pakistanis had been smarting after Siachen and were constantly on the lookout to raise the temperature in Kashmir. Kargil offered the Pakistan Army that opportunity.

PERSONALITIES AND PLANS

What happened at Kargil in 1999 may also have had its origin in the coming together of a number of personalities. The FCNA commander, Major General Javed Hasan, had recently come back from the United States, where he had served as defence attaché. He seemed to have a good sense of what American thinking was at that time and pushed the idea of a 'tactical' operation that would help raise the Kashmir issue's profile internationally and bring the Americans on board.[19] The Commander X Corps was Musharraf's fellow artilleryman, Lt. Gen. Mahmud Ahmed, based in Rawalpindi but responsible for the Northern Areas as well. Mahmud Ahmed, who later formally joined the Tablighi Jamaat, was educated at the prestigious Lawrence College, Murree, and known as an erudite and scholarly individual. Among other things, he had been working on an magnum opus on the 1965 Indo–Pakistan war that took him over eighteen years to complete. The CGS, Lt. Gen. Mohammad Aziz Khan, had served in the Kargil area as a brigade commander and then as commander of FCNA as well as in ISI dealing with Mujahideen operations. He too was highly religious, indeed one of the few brigadiers during the late 1980s who sported a flowing black beard. (Later he was to trim it back to regular spade-shape.) He knew the terrain and the troops well. One of the local brigade commanders at Kargil at the time was Salahuddin Satti, later corps commander X Corps and CGS at GHQ. The DGMO, Major General Tauqir Zia, was the odd man out initially, since he had doubts about the end-results of the Kargil plan. He went along with the plan. (Among his more difficult later jobs was to stonewall the Indian DGMO during their weekly telephone calls every Tuesday, when the latter asked him about events in Kargil.) At the ISI, a Sharif appointee, Lt. Gen. Ziauddin, says he too had some questions about the plan. His head of operations, Major General Jamshed Gulzar had served as defence attaché in India in 1992 and also as brigade commander 111 Brigade in Rawalpindi before that. Gulzar's job was to manage the Mujahideen in the Kargil sector. The fact that Sharif, Ziauddin, and Aziz were all of Kashmiri origin is also cited by some critics of the Kargil adventure as a contributing factor. But Musharraf, Ahmed, and the rest were not Kashmiris and had a major say in what was planned and executed.

This confluence of senior officers who had served in the Northern Areas produced a plan to take advantage of the winter months, when India normally lowered its guard at the LOC, to infiltrate at five points into what they effectively called 'No Man's Land', the areas that were not occupied by the other side, and set up bunkers or stone shelters called '*sanghars*' at about 108 spots along the 480 km front.[20] The Mujahideen would offer a cover for these operations. Aziz and Mahmud presented this plan as an opportunity not only to take the upper hand in the Kargil sector but also perhaps to repay the Indians in their own coin for their capture of Siachen in 1984. According to General Karamat:

> Kargil came up several times. The Dras–Kargil Road was an interdiction target for indirect artillery fire. During my tenure, Indians interdicted Neelam Valley Road, cutting off AJK [Azad Jammu and Kashmir]. We had a major planning conference to develop a response. We decided to construct a bypass and continue interdiction on Dras–Kargil Road. This did not work and Indians continued. In the next conference we considered physical interdiction of the road but decided the consequences would create problems for locals and hamper covert operations in IHK [Indian Held Kashmir] (the freedom struggle was in full swing). We decided to move heavy weapons forward and carry out interdiction with direct fire. This was enormously effective. The Indians got the message and backed [off] on Neelam Valley Road. In any case, we had decided to develop an alternative route for logistics into AJK—this was completed.[21]

By constricting Highway 1A, the Indian major supply route—(there was another more difficult supply route for Dras)—the Pakistani generals hoped to keep the counter-attack down. If the Pakistani troops were able to hold out through the summer months, Pakistan would have a controlling hand in the negotiations on Kashmir in general once the next winter set in. These were the assumptions, at least. A senior officer of the Joint Chiefs headquarters, who attended a briefing for the prime minister and senior cabinet members, was alarmed at the heroic assumptions that counted on India's inability to bring up supplies quickly in support of a rapid and heavy counter attack. 'They seemed not to have done a thorough Staff Check,' he said. In fact, Pakistan had no information on Indian reserve stocks in Leh or beyond. A staff check is normally a testing of assumptions by brain storming from the enemy's perspective. This officer then commissioned privately a staff check by two colleagues who were given 36 hours to come back with 'what they would do if they were the Indians'. He got his answer back the very next day. 'We can bring in our [i.e. the Indian] reserves and artillery,' they told him, reporting from the Indian point of view. Pakistan eventually would have to contend with a heavier counter attack than anticipated. 'The traffic through Kargil started moving once the initial shock was over and the Indians deployed in strength.... our conclusion was that utilizing the capacity of the large Indian Transport Command and moving loaded trucks at night through Kargil, the Indians could build up enough supplies to last them the next winter even if we continued to hold the heights.' This officer was reluctant to try to stop the momentum of this train that seemed to be heading to a wreck, especially since he had seen the prime minister and his colleagues seem to acquiesce to the plans with only some minor questioning. His conclusion was that 'if this staff check had been carried out during the planning process, and the right conclusions drawn, then the military aim of interdicting the Kargil road would have had to be modified to actually severing the road. But that would have had far-reaching strategic effects. If Pakistan had cut the road physically, the Indians would have launched a counter thrust elsewhere in Kashmir and the conflict would have escalated. This was contrary to the political aim and Kargil may have been called off.' But that was not to be the case. The momentum for action was carried forward by the generals, with the prime minister and his coterie acquiescing.[22]

The ingress began under 'Operation Badr' (named after the site of the famous early battle of Prophet Muhammad [PBUH] against heavy odds) in February 1999, and the construction work on the *sanghars* and supplying of food and weapons continued surreptitiously till the spring, when Indian patrolling resumed. From all accounts, this began as a localized tactical operation that took on larger proportions as the fighting began, and escalated, some months later. The NLI managed to progress some 5-9 km across the LOC, according to Indian reports. A parallel Mujahideen operation was launched, probably in the northern segment of the front, with a fair amount of radio traffic in local languages, to provide cover for the operations of the NLI and the Pakistan Army. There was a broader Kashmir plan at work that had been presented and discussed by the army chief with the prime minister and his key aides in early 1999, although interestingly, even after all the subsequent public spats about who said what to whom and when, not one of the participants will talk openly about that aspect of the discussions. A key participant confirmed this to the author but refused to elaborate on the broader Kashmir plan. One aspect of this plan may have been the use of reinforcements from Afghanistan. Mullah Mohammad Rabbani, the Afghan president at that time (Mullah Omar being the real power but functioning as an *Eminence Grise*), was asked by Pakistan to provide 20–30,000 'volunteers' for the Kashmiri jihad. He startled the Pakistanis by offering 500,000![23] This kind of thinking was misdirected, according to Major General Tarar, since these Afghans had no experience nor training to fight at altitude, nor did they have the languages that would allow them to operate in Kashmir.[24]

By all accounts, including the assessment by the Indian army chief, General V.P. Malik, and the official report from India, The Kargil Review Committee Report, the Kargil infiltration plan was a resounding success in terms of its surprise effect. Indian intelligence totally failed 'to anticipate or identify military action of this nature on the border by the Pakistan Army.'[25] Part of the success of the Pakistanis was due to the use of FCNA troops rather than moving Pakistan Army troops into the region, which might have been observed by Indian agents. Further, FCNA troops, by virtue of their location in the Kargil sector, did not need acclimatization, critical for entry into the rarefied atmosphere of the Kargil heights. India had also underestimated the total number of regiments under the FCNA to be 13, rather than 15.

The first indication to the Indians that Pakistan had managed to successfully penetrate the open areas around the LOC was given on 3 May 1999 'by two 'shepherds'....(both occasional sources of 121 Brigade [of the Indian Army]), in the general area of Banju in the Batalik sector.' This prompted aggressive patrolling by the Indian Army and further intrusions were detected. Some advance patrols were ambushed. 'By 17 May 1999, there was increasing evidence that armed intruders had occupied the heights in the gaps between the Indian defended areas in all sub-sectors of the Kargil sector in various strengths.'[26] Meanwhile the Indian army chief, General Malik had taken off on 10 May for a visit to Poland and the Czech republic and despite talking on the telephone with his colleagues frequently about the developing situation, was assured that everything was under control. The Indians failed to identify the nature and extent of the intrusion. And they had trouble identifying the troops and determining whether they were Pakistan Army or Mujahideen. Indeed, even after his return, when he raised the issue about the faulty intelligence of the RAW and the civilian IB, the secretary of the NSC secretariat, Satish Chandra, shushed him with a whispered: '*inki bhi laaj rakhni hai*' (we have to save their honour too).[27] The Pakistani deception plan apparently had succeeded beyond measure. It was not till they recovered the identity cards and diaries of the Pakistanis that the Indians were able to establish the presence of Pakistan Army regulars, something that Pakistan refused to acknowledge.

Another key piece of evidence was an Indian intercepted telephone conversation that involved Generals Aziz Khan (in Rawalpindi) and Musharraf (in Beijing) on 26 and 27 May that established that they knew about the activities in the Kargil sector and wanted to make sure they were ascribed to the Mujahideen. They also had misgivings about Prime Minister Sharif's position and discussed briefing him and reminding him of earlier briefings.[28] Musharraf was also concerned about the effect of what was now a growing battle with rapidly deployed Indian forces on the counter attack, on the newly launched peace initiative of Prime Minister Sharif with his counterpart, the new Prime Minister of India, Atal Behari Vajpayee of the BJP. Vajpayee had visited Lahore and issued a joint declaration with Sharif on 21 February 1999 vowing to work toward 'peace and stability between their countries.'[29] But Musharraf welcomed the increased international attention to the conflict and the calls for an end to the fighting. As he was later to write in his autobiography, he was pleased that the Indians had failed to detect no more than three of the five major intrusions into their areas.[30]

The Pakistani Foreign Minister, Sartaj Aziz, was due to arrive in New Delhi soon after Musharraf's second conversation with Aziz Khan. Aziz recalls the hostile atmosphere when he eventually landed at New Delhi airport on 12 June and was surrounded by an army of journalists, all wishing to know how and why Pakistan seemed to be sabotaging the peace process.[31] Every Indian newspaper it seemed carried the Musharraf–Aziz Khan telephone conversation and highlighted the segment in which Musharraf tries to ensure that Sartaj Aziz does not concede any withdrawal by the Pakistanis in Kargil. Aziz says he felt 'humiliated' by having his hands tied behind his back. He believes that the Kargil operation was planned well before January and well before the Vajpayee visit and links it to the 1994–96 Neelam Valley artillery attack by India. 'I don't think they realized the full implications of these plans.' He recalls a first briefing on 12 March and then 17 May, after the intrusion had become public. The 12 March briefing he said was 'partial, because they never mentioned the army crossing the LOC. Only the mujahideen were mentioned.' The 17 May briefing by Jamshed Gulzar at ISI headquarters, he said, elicited many questions from himself, Majeed Malik, and others.

In fact, Nawaz Sharif had visited the Northern Areas with Musharraf and had been briefed on the local situation on 29 January. Another briefing was given in the Northern Areas in Kel on 5 February that dealt with the interdiction taking place in that sector from the Indian side of the LOC.[32] Ziauddin recalls suggesting to Musharraf in the early spring that the principal staff officers and the corps commanders needed to be brought into the picture. He says that Musharraf asked the CGS to arrange such a meeting and it took place. (This meeting must have been held after 11 March 1999, when the 61st corps commanders' conference was held at GHQ. Neither Kargil nor Kashmir was on the agenda of the 61st conference. But Musharraf did stress the need for 'Sanctity of Discussions,' that is whatever is agreed in the meetings becomes the singular view in the army. No dissent. And he also emphasized 'Consensus on National Issues,' including Kashmir, Afghanistan, Nuclear, and Internal Security between all tiers 'Armed Forces, Foreign Office and Govt.')[33] The culture of GHQ demands that the chief speaks and everybody else listens. If the Kargil plan had been presented by the corps commander to his fellow commanders, without an introduction of support from the president, the COAS, and the CGS, it may well have been shot down as impracticable over the long term. Once the COAS has signed off on the plan and it is discussed at the corps commanders' meeting after the event, no one in his right mind will challenge the chief. There is great emphasis on being a team player and not rocking the boat. The only General, Tariq Parvez, who tried to second guess the decision got fired, as described below.

Ziauddin maintains that as far as the need to bring the prime minister on board is concerned, local actions, such as Kargil, are within the purview of the local commanders and stayed within the army's chain of command. There was no need, in his view, to openly bring the prime minister into the plan. But he believes also that once the secretary of the Ministry of Defence, a retired general, who was known to have the ear of the prime minister, was briefed, then it could be assumed that Sharif knew what was happening. In any case, both sides routinely made small ingresses along the LOC.[34] The real issue this time was, as another senior retired general stated, the Pakistanis went in too far.

It was at the 17 May briefing that General Ziauddin of the ISI recalls a discussion of the Kashmir operations in general and Kargil in particular. He recalls the presence of former CGS and retired Lt. Gen. Majeed Malik and the Secretary of Defence, retired Lt. Gen. Iftikhar, both of whom took part in the discussions. The briefing map indicated the location of the 108 bunkers that Pakistan had occupied or constructed, and the briefing stated that the 'Indians could not oust us.' At the end of the briefing, there was a suggestion (reportedly by General Mahmud Ahmed) for a 'dua' or prayer for the success of the venture.

Before they dispersed, Zia recalls Nawaz Sharif stating: 'This is a military operation. All I can say is that…there should be no withdrawal, no surrender of any post because that will greatly embarrass us.' He asked if 'we could hold on.' Both Aziz Khan and Mahmud Ahmed said they could. In assessing the Indian reaction, they talked about the possibility of attacks across the international boundary, but also thought that the Indians would be unable to counter-attack in force. Zia believes that the prime minister left 'everything to the army to decide.' Yet, surprisingly for him, he actually 'asked questions', as did Majeed Malik. The DGMO, Tauqir Zia, responded to their concerns. So, in Zia's view, Sharif was fully in the picture from that point on. Zia also states that Mahmud used to take maps to the PM House to brief him as posts fell. According to Zia, the prime minister had the authority to order a halt to the operation at any point if he had serious doubts. But he did not.[35] This is damning testimony from a man whom Sharif was later to appoint Musharraf's replacement and who was then under threat of a court martial and under house arrest for almost two years on Musharraf's orders.

Sartaj Aziz maintains that Shireen Mazari's book on Kargil was written with the help of the army's paper and briefings, and mixes up the details and the dates of the various briefings to exonerate Musharraf. He also states that the army had failed to fully assess the results of the super-nationalistic BJP's electoral victory in 1998. Indeed the BJP was to eventually translate its earlier success into a major forty-seat majority in the October 1999 national elections. In his view, 'the Indians overreacted' after the BJP win. The army failed to take into account all the implications of this strong reaction, he said. They assumed that this was a local action that would remain at a low profile and soon winter would set in again and Pakistan would remain in its advance positions.[36] The Indian army chief also assumes something similar and states that the milder winter in 1999 meant the thaw came sooner and the intrusions were discovered earlier than Pakistan expected.

Once discovered, the intrusions became the subject of extensive Indian operations. Heavy artillery and air attacks ensued, inflicting serious damage on the relatively exposed *sanghars*. The defenders had some initial success against Indian air attacks, shooting down aircraft and helicopters. But then they began running out of ammunition and food supplies. Re-supply in that terrain was difficult at best. Between May and July, the Indians gradually got the upper hand, using their numbers to great advantage. They even blockaded Karachi with their navy, in case the conflict erupted into an all-out war. At that point, Nawaz Sharif decided to take matters into his own hands and pressed the army for more details. The army gave more briefings. But as time went by, the ground situation went against Pakistan. An agreement could have been worked out between India and Pakistan even in June without having to go to Washington, according to Sartaj Aziz. In that sense, he says, 'Kargil was an unmitigated disaster' for Pakistan.

Vajpayee had authorized the Indian Foreign Minister Jaswant Singh to explore an agreement on Kashmir with Sartaj Aziz. They had met in March 1999 during a foreign ministers' meeting at Nuwara Eliya in Sri Lanka. The two met privately on a bench overlooking a lake, without any notes or other participants, and made great progress on issues, identifying issues on which they had unacceptable options as well as those that had a common good.

Singh said he wanted to avoid division on the basis of religion. He was open to the idea of geographic division, coming closer to the ideas of the Kashmir Study Group.[37] They agreed to continue their exchanges privately in the months ahead, using Pakistan's high commissioner or ambassador to India, Ashraf Jehangir Qazi, as the contact. The fall of the BJP government in India on 17 April, and then the Kargil adventure, put an end to that initiative, says Aziz. Later when he met Vajpayee, he says the latter 'had tears in his eyes.' He said to me: '*Sartaj Sahib! Yeh aap ne kya kiya?*' (Mr Sartaj, what did you do?) Aziz believes that the military coup put an end to the idea of progress on Kashmir with India.[38]

HEADING TOWARD WASHINGTON

After the turbulent month of May 1999, with increasing Indian military pressure, the relationship between Sharif and Musharraf became strained. Sharif could not bring himself to come out in the open in opposing the army chief. But, in hindsight he maintains that he was 'hoodwinked' by the army. Sharif says that he was told, even on 17 May, that it was the Mujahideen doing all the action, not the Pakistani troops. He says that the situation eventually became so bad on the ground that the army chief came to see him, and asked him to pay the Americans a visit: 'Musharraf told me to go. [He said to me,] 'Sir, you have to go there [to Washington]. Pull him [Clinton] into it'. Sharif recalls that 'All our supply lines were disrupted. Our *jawan's* were shouting, "if you cannot send us rations at least send us ammunition!"'

Musharraf, when asked about this in 2006, had a diametrically opposite recollection of the situation on the ground:

> Now, that was a time when the nation needed strength and unity between the military and the political, and decide whether we should come back or not. Because we had actually caught the Indians by their throat. There were five ingresses, they did not even touch three of them. They recaptured 60 per cent of one. [In] the other, they took 5, 10 per cent. So we were really sitting in a good position.[39]

Musharraf has covered this period in some detail in his autobiography. But it is useful to hear his unvarnished words from our interview on what happened before Sharif raced off to Washington after speaking a number of times with Clinton. Sharif had called Clinton on 2 July, the day he met Musharraf and heard his presentation before the DCC, and again on the 3rd, the day after the DCC meeting. Recounting the DCC meeting, Musharraf said:

> So it was 2nd July...[at] the conference—DCC meeting,...including air chief, [and] naval chiefs...I personally on a map gave [a] complete one hour briefing—for 49,

50 minutes—the exact military situation, all possibilities, and our responses and I finally came out [and] I told him that as far as military is concerned I can assure you we are quite okay. And whatever their [Indian] offensive, they are really bleeding a lot. Their casualties are in the thousands. 1,700 surely we know.... So we are quite all right.

Now take a look at the political side. Now over and over, he wanted to ask me, 'Should we withdraw or not?' I said, 'Look...'

> SN [Shuja Nawaz]: He actually asked you that.
> PM [Pervez Musharraf]: Yes. I refused to answer that. I told him, 'Mr Prime Minister, I have told you the military position. I am the army chief and the chairman. I have told you the military position and I told you that militarily, we'll stand. Let me assure you that in all contingencies, we're all right. Now whether to withdraw or not is a political decision and I'm afraid you will have to take that decision.' And not once, but three times he wanted to fire a gun on my shoulder. I could see that probably he wants to because of the American pressure.
>
> So we dispersed. We decided to meet again Monday to decide. I went off to Murree for a weekend. At night—Saturday night 10 o'clock I received a phone call saying the prime minister wanted to speak with me. And he said, 'I am going. I'm going to the United States.... Please meet me at Chaklala airport.' I drove through the night to Chaklala airport. And again he was asking me, 'Should we withdraw or not?'....I told him 'I have given you a complete analysis. I have given you the military analysis. It is your decision now; [it's] a political decision.'
>
> So he went [to Washington]. He decided to withdraw. I personally would not blame him for [that decision]....it is a decision he took. But what I would like to say is that even before this, there was a malicious campaign against the army in the papers and I am almost sure that he was orchestrating it. And I went and told him also, that: 'look, at this juncture you should not create differences between the army and government. This creates a very wrong image nationally. And our unity at this hour, where we should show unity against India, that is disturbed. How are these people writing?' So this is what I said to him. But [he was] always very pleasant: 'Who writes these things? These are very bad people. Who writes such things. They should not be written', and 'Don't worry'.[40]

Musharraf could have taken a firmer position against the withdrawal but apparently did not. Uncharacteristically, if his account is to be believed, he allowed Sharif to make his decision to go to Washington and seek Clinton's help in arranging a ceasefire and withdrawal of troops from the forward lines. On his part, Sharif had taken an indirect approach yet again with yet another army chief, while apparently harbouring deep distrust about the army chief's aims. And so Sharif headed West at short notice, on a PIA flight to New York, which was diverted to Washington.

THE CLINTON MEETING

When Sharif arrived in Washington after 'inviting himself' (according to Bruce Riedel, who was the note taker in the subsequent one-on-one meeting with Clinton and the author of a detailed paper on that encounter)[41] he was received at the airport by Saudi ambassador Bandar bin Sultan, who then briefed his American friends about Sharif's demeanour. The US team saw that he was 'extremely nervous' and 'anxious' [...] Carrying a great burden. Very worried about where things were going' on Kargil. Specifically, Riedel described in an interview that he discerned that Sharif was concerned about the escalation of Kargil into a national conflict with India that Sharif wanted to avoid at all costs. He was also looking ahead to a difficult situation with his own army after the Kargil situation. 'The army wanted to show some accomplishment for Kargil. Sharif said to the President, in effect, "I'm in a box. I need your help!" To which the President replied: "You have put me in a box. There's no simple way out!"' The US had been alarmed by the fact that not only had Sharif invited himself to come to Washington at short notice but he also brought with him, in an unusual move, his family. It was almost as if he did not think it would be safe to go back if his mission failed.[42]

Interestingly, Sharif's own recollection of the trip to Washington is at a sharp variance from that of Musharraf and indeed the US version. In an Urdu interview he gave to a Pakistani journalist that was compiled into a book, he states that he called Clinton and asked to meet him in Washington. Clinton said he would need to rearrange his schedule and call him back. Sharif says Clinton called him back and so Sharif made his plans to leave for Washington.[43] Musharraf, he says, showed up at the airport as he was leaving for the United States, to plead with him to extricate the army from Kargil, where the Indians had begun to make progress.

In the one-on-one exchange with Clinton, (which Clinton insisted be recorded by Riedel) Sharif did not contest the basic issue in Kargil: that Pakistan had, in fact, crossed the LOC, which was the US's understanding. Sharif did not challenge that nor did he dispute the Pakistan Army's involvement. The US did not distinguish between regular army and army-controlled elements. Riedel conceded that the White House 'was aware' of the intrusion before May but it was only in May that the US became aware that 'the situation was getting dangerously out of control.' In their view, Musharraf may not have drawn all the right conclusions about Kargil and did not have all the answers. 'This was a gamble,' said Riedel. The White House was also aware of Centcom Commander Anthony Zinni's attempt to intercede and get Pakistan to the talking table but Riedel stated that Zinni did not arrange the Blair House summit. That summit emerged out of Clinton's direct conversations with Sharif prior to his dash to Washington DC in which

Clinton laid down the parameters: a clear commitment on withdrawal from the LOC, before Sharif could come to Washington.

Zinni had arrived in Pakistan on Clinton's instructions on 24 June and spent two days there telling the Pakistani leaders: 'If "you don't pull back, you're going to bring nuclear war and annihilation down on your country. That's going to be very bad news for everybody." Nobody actually quarrelled with this rationale. The problem for the Pakistani leadership was the apparent loss of national face. Backing down and pulling back from the Line of Control looked like political suicide.'[44] He suggested a meeting with President Clinton. 'That got Musharraf's attention, and he encouraged Prime Minister Sharif to hear me out.' Zinni recalls that Sharif had not be willing to meet him and when he left Musharraf's home on his last evening and headed back to the hotel, he had not yet heard from Sharif about a possible meeting and was prepared to leave without seeing him. Musharraf called Zinni in his car as he was returning to his hotel to say that Sharif had been approached by Musharraf and had agreed to meet Zinni. Musharraf said he would meet up with Zinni at the Prime Minister's place. At the meeting, Sharif asked a 'lot of questions'.[45] He also recalls that 'Sharif was reluctant to withdraw before the meeting with Clinton was announced...but after I insisted he finally came around. He ordered the withdrawal. We set up a meeting with Clinton in July.' Zinni also noticed that in all the meetings with Sharif, Musharraf did not utter a word.[46] If Zinni is correct, then both Musharraf and Sharif shaded the truth, since Musharraf knew about the US suggestion for a withdrawal and abetted Zinni in making the argument for it before Sharif. He should also have been aware of an offer of a meeting with Clinton and that Sharif had agreed with Zinni to order a withdrawal before he left for Washington. In fact, Zinni recalls stating that he wanted some sort of proof that the Pakistanis were preparing to withdraw before Clinton would finally agree to a meeting. This, he said, happened soon after he got back to Washington and when the US satellites observed activity on the Pakistani side indicating that they were getting ready to move back from their forward positions. He says he then gave the green light to the White House.[47] Musharraf's autobiography suggests he was not a party to Sharif's plans. The Rashomon Effect again?

Riedel felt that Sharif came on his own volition and not because Musharraf sent him. The US did not want to put Sharif in a position where he could not deliver what he promised. Regarding Sharif's statement that he went to Washington at the army chief's behest, Riedel said: 'Perhaps. But I don't buy it.' However, he does challenge the veracity of Musharraf's assertion in the latter's autobiography that Pakistan did not have any 'deliverable nuclear weapon system' at that time to challenge the US assertion that Pakistan was getting ready for a wider conflict. Calling that 'misleading his reader in the extreme,' Riedel elaborated that 'if that is the case, as General of the army, what in the world were you doing! If you had a "hollow deterrent" then you were truly crazy to have embarked upon this [attack on Kargil].'[48]

At the White House, Clinton told Sharif that the Americans were aware of preparations for getting the nuclear weapon system into action. There was no specific reference to any base or any activity. He was referring to 'extremely reliable information that we had that nuclear weapon systems were being prepared, and this was highly abnormal; in our judgment it represented a ratcheting of readiness to use them. Sharif did not argue against this, rather, he responded: "I assume the Indians are doing the same." But when Clinton said: "Even if one of those weapons was used, [...]" Sharif completed his sentence for him: "...it would be a catastrophe."'[49] An angry Clinton was losing his patience with Sharif, who the US side felt had arrived in Washington with a brief that 'was confused and vague on many details but he seemed a man possessed with a fear of war.'[50] Clinton asked Sharif to take a break and talk with his advisers. After that break, he presented Sharif with a draft statement that drew also from the 'non-paper' that Sharif had brought with him and that would signify a Pakistani agreement to withdraw from the LOC. The statement also referred to the restoration of the Lahore peace process with India and reaffirmed Clinton's long standing plans to visit South Asia. Sharif insisted on adding a sentence that 'the President would take personal interest to encourage an expeditious resumption of the bilateral efforts (i.e. Lahore) once the sanctity of the LOC had been fully restored.' Clinton agreed but told Sharif that he intended to tell the press that this language meant 'a Pakistani withdrawal.'[51]

Thus, Sharif did emerge the next day for the photo opportunity at the White House, with an agreement that would end the Kargil conflict in due course. He stopped in London and Riyadh *en route* to Pakistan. But clearly, he knew that the army chief would not be taken with his action, even when he went on air on 12 July to tell his countrymen that the 'Mujahideen' would withdraw from the LOC. 'While there is no doubt that the Kashmiri Mujahideen through their sacrifices and battle successes wrote out a new chapter in their freedom struggle, the situation on the diplomatic front became so complicated that it was no easy task to straighten it out or control its adverse fallout,' he told his countrymen. 'It is true that the Mujahideen were present on several Kargil heights but it was part of their long freedom struggle and inseparable from it....Once the Mujahideen had succeeded in drawing world attention to Kashmir, it is understandable that they would wish to disengage.'[52] He did not refer to the Pakistan Army's involvement in the affair. In retrospect, a senior army officer deemed this 'a major international error. While it served its purpose in the initial stages of the conflict, once it became obvious to the international press that Pakistani regular forces were operating in Kargil, we should have accepted it. By not doing so we were labelled as liars and every statement we subsequently made was suspect.'[53]

That speech would not paper over Sharif's differences with Musharraf.

FEAR AND CONSEQUENCES

The US was anxious to receive a special emissary from Sharif to follow up on issues that the US had promised to pursue in support of the Lahore process. 'After this near death experience, Clinton, who was a born optimist and a born peacemaker' wanted some good to come out, says Riedel. But he recalls that things did not seem to be going well in Islamabad and for weeks they heard nothing. Finally, Shahbaz Sharif, the prime minister's brother, arrived in September. He met F. Karl 'Rick' Inderfurth, the Assistant Secretary of State of South Asia, and Riedel. But his remit was different. On behalf of Nawaz Sharif, Shahbaz wanted a public statement from the US against a coup, something that the US found hard to construct in the abstract. But they did provide a tepid statement from the State Department: 'Concerns in Washington about the stability of the Pakistan government of Prime Minister Nawaz Sharif resulted in an unusual statement by an unnamed US State Department official warning that the US would "strongly oppose" any attempt by 'political and military actors' to take power unconstitutionally. The remarks, originally quoted by the Reuters news agency on Tuesday, have since been confirmed by other senior State Department officials.'[54]

That statement did not do the trick; especially when things within Pakistan had taken a turn for the worse between Sharif and Musharraf, even while both tried to put the best spin on events. As reported in *Dawn*:

> Chief of Army Staff General Pervez Musharraf on Thursday dismissed reports of differences with the government as disinformation. 'There is no misunderstanding between the government and the army,' Gen. Musharraf told reporters at a reception marking the national day of Saudi Arabia. He refuted reports that he was planning to quit amid an alleged rift with the government over the handling of the recent Kashmir conflict with India.
>
> I am going to complete my tenure,' he said. Mr Musharraf was speaking after chairing a meeting of top military commanders. It followed an unusual warning by the United States on Monday against any 'unconstitutional move' to remove the government of Prime Minister Nawaz Sharif. The US statement was issued after talks between Sharif's brother Shahbaz Sharif and US officials in Washington last week. 'I don't think there is mention of the army' in the US statement, the COAS said.[55]

Surprisingly, Musharraf recalls that in the post-Kargil period, Sharif was unduly friendly towards him. Yet, Musharraf kept hearing stories that Sharif was looking to replace him as army chief and perhaps even move him upstairs to CJCS. He was holding that chairman's slot in an acting capacity at that time. Around the same time, Musharraf detected that one of his corps commanders, Lt. Gen. Tariq Parvez (known to all and sundry as TP), of XII Corps in Quetta seemed to be having second thoughts about the Kargil situation. At a meeting at GHQ, TP spoke critically about the planning and execution of Kargil. Musharraf says he challenged him on the spot by saying: 'If you are saying that [so] that the prime minister knows, let me tell you that I will tell him your views myself.' Musharraf says he suspected that TP was getting through to the prime minister through his relative Raja Nadir Parvez, a former officer and war hero and a member of Sharif's ruling party,—and ascribed this to TP's ambition.[56] Later, there was a report that TP had repeated his criticism of the Kargil action in a talk to his officers in Quetta. Musharraf spoke with Shahbaz Sharif and told him that he needed to speak with the prime minister about this situation and said that he wanted to get rid of TP. He also conveyed through Shahbaz that he did not want to become chairman if it meant giving up his job as army chief, suggesting that they could appoint anyone else as chairman. According to Musharraf, Shahbaz came to see him the next evening, accompanied by Chaudhry Nisar Ali Khan, and assured him that he would take care of it.[57]

The next day, Musharraf had lunch with Sharif, who asked him, 'Who is this TP? You should remove him. You were correct, he should be removed.'[58] He then issued a notification through the president on 29 September appointing Musharraf formally as chairman (and concurrently army chief). Soon after that Musharraf says he heard from Sharif that he was going to perform *Umra* (optional Muslim pilgrimage to Makkah that can be performed any time of the year) and asked if Musharraf could accompany him. Since Sharif was leaving from Lahore, he asked Musharraf and his wife to join them there for dinner the evening prior to departure. There, at the Sharifs' Raiwind estate, Musharraf recalls a tableau that had been repeated earlier with previous chiefs, including General Asif Nawaz:

> It was very pleasant. Here, Aba Ji [Nawaz Sharif's father] is telling me, that 'You are like a son to me. These two don't dare say anything against you. If they do, tell me.' So Nawaz Sharif says, 'Why should we do this? He is like a brother to us.'[59]

Then there was an exchange of gifts and the two families went to Makkah to get their sins absolved at official expense.

WHOSE COUP?

Within a month or so, however, Nawaz Sharif was to make his move against his 'brother' while Musharraf was out of the country in Sri Lanka on an official trip. Musharraf was due to arrive back on 12 October. His flight was delayed, but when they came close to Pakistan, the captain of the aircraft was informed that they could not enter Pakistani airspace and needed to go to a neighbouring country, with the exception of Dubai (for which no reason was given). Short of fuel, the plane was diverted eventually to Nawabshah. But then events on the ground overtook this saga in the air and Musharraf's generals acted in his absence; they took Sharif into their control and got the plane to land at Karachi. Musharraf has a detailed account of this in his readable autobiography. Some other details emerged from conversations with Lt. Gen. Mahmud Ahmed, the corps commander in Rawalpindi, and the man who masterminded the operation against Sharif that evening.

Sharif had decided to remove Musharraf from command of the Pakistan Army and replace him with Lt. Gen. Ziauddin of the ISI, a man whom he had selected against Musharraf's wishes to join the ISI earlier that year. Musharraf had wanted to make Ziauddin his CGS. Most people believe that Sharif was either related to Ziauddin or found in him a kindred spirit, both being of Kashmiri origin and many, even in the army mistakenly referred to him as Ziauddin Butt, a Kashmiri name that he does not use, to link him to Sharif. Ziauddin maintains that he had never met Sharif nor his father before he was interviewed for the ISI job. The other candidate for the job was Aziz Khan, a former ISI officer and another Kashmiri. He also states that he was asked to come to the PM House and informed of the decision to remove Musharraf and make him (Ziauddin) the new chief. A written order was shown to him. Ziauddin says he told the prime minister that such an appointment could only be made with the president's approval. The President, Rafiq Tarar, a Sharif favourite, was only too willing to comply and immediately signed the paper that was sent to him.[60] Sharif then is reported to have borrowed extra 'pips' or badges of rank from his own Military Secretary, Brigadier Javed Iqbal, and put them on Ziauddin's epaulets. An announcement was then sent to radio and television. Ziauddin then began calling GHQ and other posts and informing people of his new position and making his own appointments to senior slots. But he did not take into account the antipathy toward Sharif that existed among the senior brass of the army, including his fellow Kashmiri Aziz Khan, whose primary loyalty lay with his chief, Musharraf.

Later, Lt. Gen. Mahmud Ahmed would state unequivocally that:

If General Musharraf had not been changed that evening...then 12th October would have been another day like 11th October before, like 10th October was, like 9th October was. In other words, notwithstanding the uneasy, so-called uneasy relationship between the army and the political government of the time, the army would not have taken over for any reason but for this, which was a political decision on the part of Nawaz Sharif.

In fact, ever since July that year when Mr Nawaz Sharif went to the United States...tension between the Army and the government of the time...was very high. In fact, this tension had existed before that. And this tension in fact began to even out as time went by so that August was less tense.... General Musharraf's relationship with the Prime Minister became a little more easy in August and it was even easier—even better in September. So that if Mr Nawaz Sharif had not taken the critical decision of changing Musharraf on 12th October, and if he had continued with his own government and not changed the chief of army staff prematurely, then I suppose the relationship would have improved with the passage of time, rather than worsening.[61]

Mahmud and Aziz Khan, the CGS, were playing tennis in Chaklala, when they heard that the army chief's plane had been delayed and that an announcement of a change in command had been broadcast.

General Aziz and I—we were together when we heard the news....this was a very critical decision and it could not be left at that. The change of command at that time was very critical, especially from the point of view of the fact that Indians were deployed, the...tension was high along the border, not in Kashmir only, but also along the border. Therefore this would not have been allowed to go unchecked. I then ordered the 111 brigade commander [Brigadier Salahuddin Satti] to move in and to contain the Prime Minister's House where they were living...and to prevent the change in command.'

He then contacted Lt. Gen. M.H. Usmani, the corps commander V Corps in Karachi, who then coordinated the activities at Karachi airport to allow the army chief's plane to land. Mahmud meanwhile took matters into his own hands in Rawalpindi:

I moved into the Prime Minister's house at about 8–8:30 [p.m.]. And when I met Mr Nawaz Sharif, the first question I asked him was about General Musharraf's arrival and his plane, and why it was delayed and that he should order the concerned authorities to allow the plane to land. But in the meantime, they had...taken the necessary steps to safeguard the landing of the aircraft in Karachi.[62]

The Hollywood-style drama in the air ended in the middle of the evening and a visibly rattled Musharraf took charge of the country, going on the air in his military uniform to announce that he was taking over the government. As former US ambassador, Robert Oakley was to say on Public Broadcasting Service's News Hour that evening: 'When one deals with the army recklessly in Pakistan, one usually pays the price.'[63] Moving with deliberate speed, Musharraf took on the relatively neutral title of Chief Executive and decided to keep the constitutional head of state, President Rafiq Tarar, in place, even while suspending the constitution and curbing Tarar's powers.

In his more considered televised speech on 17 October 1999, he explained the rationale behind the coup and outlined his goals:

My dear countrymen. The choice before us on 12th October was between saving the body—that is the nation, at the cost of losing a limb—which is the Constitution, or saving the limb and losing the whole body. The Constitution is but a part of the nation therefore I chose to save the nation and yet took care not to sacrifice the Constitution. The Constitution has only been temporarily held in abeyance. This is not martial law, only another path towards democracy. The armed forces have no intention to stay in charge any longer than is absolutely necessary to pave the way for true democracy to flourish in Pakistan.

Ever since 12th October I have deliberated, carried out consultations and crystallized my views about the future course to be adopted. I wish to share these with you today.

My dear countrymen, our aims and objectives shall be: (1) Rebuild national confidence and morale. (2) Strengthen the federation, remove inter provincial disharmony and restore national cohesion. (3) Revive the economy and restore investor confidence. (4) Ensure law and order and dispense speedy justice. (5) Depoliticize state institutions. (6) Devolution of power to the grass roots level. (7) Ensure swift and across the board accountability.

Good governance is the pre-requisite to achieve these objectives. In the past, our governments have ruled the people. It is time now for the governments to serve the people. The government I plan to institute shall comprise: Firstly (sic)—The President. On my request, President Rafiq Tarar has very kindly agreed to stay. Second—A National Security Council headed by the Chief Executive with six members. These members will be Chief of Naval Staff, Chief of Air Staff, a specialist each in Legal, Finance, Foreign Policy and national affairs. A think-tank of experts shall be formed as an adjunct to the National Security Council to provide institutionalised advice and input. Third—A Cabinet of Ministers who will work under the guidance of the National Security Council. Four—The Provinces to be headed by a Governor, functioning through a small provincial cabinet. All these appointments shall be made purely on the basis of professional competence, merit and repute.[64]

Familiar words to those Pakistanis who had survived previous martial law governments. The intentions were unobjectionable but the ability to deliver would be a challenge. He made progress on the first, third, and to some extent the sixth objectives of his regime. But the rest would elude him, as Pakistan degraded into worse religious and sectarian violence; and terrorism, both domestic and imported, became an increasing threat.

Behind the scenes, he had already attracted legal and financial wizards to prepare for the task of governing ahead and to remove legal obstacles as rapidly as possible. Citi-Banker Shaukat Aziz was busy compiling lists of potential members of the cabinet to offer to the new chief executive.[65] Legal guru Sharifuddin Pirzada was to come up with a new PCO to allow the government to function under legal cover and to indemnify the coup makers who had after all breached the constitutional provisions against coups and could have been charged with treason. Musharraf characterized his generals' actions as a 'counter-coup' against Sharif's coup against him. (Information received by the author from senior civil servants at that time indicates that the army had begun investigating corruption and the financial situation of the country in the months leading up to the coup, so there may well have been some contingency plans prepared for a coup.)[66] Why did the army not mount such an action when Karamat was dismissed by Sharif? General Mahmud's answer was that Karamat had only a few months left in his term. Musharraf was being sent home prematurely.[67] Eventually, Musharraf would cover himself legally by a series of measures: through a Supreme Court judgement of May 2000, the LFO of 2002, and by amending the constitution through the 17th Amendment. Among other changes in the constitution, the omnibus amendment ensured that anything that the government did during and after the coup of 1999 could not be challenged in a court of law. The detail and scope of the changes were breathtaking. It indemnified the general and his regime against any legal charges for all their actions.

But a key element of the new amendment was wrought and passed after a Faustian bargain with the Islamic parties, under which Musharraf was allowed to retain concurrently his posts of COAS and president of Pakistan, notwithstanding a law that did not allow anyone in the 'service of Pakistan,' that is holding a public office, from standing for elections unless a period of two years had passed. For the first time, Pakistan's constitution was amended with reference to a single individual and his job. As later events proved, this arrangement was susceptible to successful challenge and just such a challenge would lead to political turmoil in Musharraf's Pakistan in the waning months of 2007.

THE AYUBIAN ERA: TAKE TWO?

While Musharraf did not want to be compared to any previous dictator or autocrat, the new government's path most resembled, in many ways, the one chosen by Pakistan's first military ruler, Ayub Khan, in 1958. Musharraf, however, did not wish to repeat any of Ayub's mistakes. But, in fact, he managed to do just that. History began repeating itself. Leading politicos were either banned or otherwise removed from the political scene. Nawaz Sharif was packed off to exile in Saudi Arabia under an alleged 'secret' agreement that would prohibit him from returning for ten years. That agreement did not last, as the Saudis, apparently with Pakistani approval, allowed Sharif to exit their kingdom for the freer climes of the United Kingdom in November 2005. The National Accountability Bureau (NAB), a successor to Sharif's Ehtesab Bureau and Ayub's EBDO, and headed by an army officer, implicated Benazir Bhutto and her husband in numerous cases, in addition to the ones that Sharif had instituted against Bhutto's husband, Asif Zardari. Zardari stayed in jail, even as his wife established a base in Dubai and garnered support for herself around the world, till his eventual release on bail for medical reasons, allowing him to move to New York.

Musharraf wanted to create the strong impression that his regime would eliminate corruption from the scene. In a startling revelation to bolster his own image in that regard, he released a list of all property owned by him and his family. He listed five housing plots (two in Karachi, including one in which his house was being built, one each in Rawalpindi, Peshawar, and Lahore). He also listed agricultural land in Bahawalpur, his parents' house in Islamabad, his daughter's house in Karachi, and two other plots (one in Eastridge, Rawalpindi, and one in Gwadar).[68] In doing so, he gave credence to the criticism of the Culture of Entitlement that allowed senior army officers to purchase valuable urban land at throwaway prices on the instalment plan, something that was not available to others in the country. But his action also reflected how far the Moral Compass had shifted over the decades, as acquisition of so much property was not considered unusual.

The new military regime went through the same phases as previous regimes, seeking to legitimize the extra-constitutional takeover by seeking approval from the Supreme Court and then through a referendum under a PCO that replaced the constitution:

> The electorate was asked for its 'Yes' or 'No' to the question: 'Do you want to elect President General Pervez Musharraf as President of Pakistan for next five years for the survival of local government system, restoration of democracy, continuity and stability of reforms, eradication of extremism and sectarianism and for the accomplishment of Quaid-i-Azam's concept?'

The PCO barred court, tribunal or any other authority from calling in question the validity of any of its provisions or of any action based on it. However, the order was challenged in the Supreme Court of Pakistan, which dismissed all petitions saying the order was valid under the PCO.[69]

The referendum on 30 April 2002 was held amidst complaints from political parties and human rights groups that it was flawed legally and logistically. However, the Election Commission declared that 71 per cent of registered voters had gone to the polls and 97.5 per cent of them had given Musharraf a 'Yes' vote. Musharraf later was to apologize for irregularities at the local level but saw the result as a validation of his take-over. He then assumed the title of President of Pakistan, while retaining his uniform as army chief.

A new system of grassroots democracy was introduced, involving local elections and administrators called 'Nazims', much like the Basic Democrats of the Ayub period. The role of the major regular political parties and the bureaucracy was thus further curtailed, as new actors emerged. Musharraf also fostered the arrival of a new generation of legislators by adding a graduation clause to the election rules that allowed only those who held an undergraduate degree from an accredited college or university to run for national office. The flaw that he allowed to creep into the process was to allow religious institutions that were not integrated into the education system to issue their own certificates that were given equivalent status to undergraduate degrees from regular schools. Thus, Musharraf, the avowed modernist, helped create a legal foothold for large numbers of Islamists to enter parliament.

Musharraf also gathered around himself the rump of the Muslim League which represented the people who did not stay with Sharif. This became, once again, a congeries of opportunists and turncoats from both Sharif's Muslim League faction and Bhutto's PPP. This group was largely Punjab-centric. He rationalized that decision in his memoir thus:

> I needed a national political party to support my agenda. I had the option of forming a new party, but decided...to revive the Pakistan Muslim League (PML), the party of Quaid-i-Azam Mohammad Ali Jinnah that had led us to freedom to our own country.[70]

Musharraf chose the name PML (Q) after Quaid-i-Azam, on the advice of his 'old and trusted friend' from his Forman Christian College days in Lahore, Tariq Aziz. Aziz, in turn, introduced him to his own friends and reported benefactors Chaudhry Shujaat Hussain and his cousin Chaudhry Pervez Elahi, members of what used to be Sharif's PML, who quickly defected to Musharraf's side to form the so-called King's Party. Musharraf did not see it contradictory to state in his memoir in this regard, that. 'I was not trying to play politics.'[71]

But in a move that broke with the Ayubian tradition and seemingly went against Musharraf's own political inclinations and instincts, he allowed the ruling Muslim League to align itself with a coalition of the Islamic parties that fought the 2002 elections under the banner of the Muttahida Majlis-e-Amal (MMA or United Action Front). For the first time in Pakistan's electoral history, the Islamist parties jointly won 18 per cent of the seats in parliament and won control of the NWFP, making it a breeding ground for religious extremism, aping the fundamentalist leanings of their Afghan neighbours, the Taliban. This was the Musharraf regime's unintended consequence of trying to ensure that neither Sharif nor Bhutto's party won a sizeable chunk of the electorate. In the process, he managed to effect something that even General Ziaul Haq, the arch conservative and Islamist, could not: a louder voice and bigger presence for the extremist Islamist groups in Pakistani polity. Musharraf's favoured PML (Q) won the majority, and a Baluch leader, Zafarullah Khan Jamali, was sworn in as prime minister. The PPP became the largest opposition group in the assembly but the leader of the opposition, Maulana Fazlur Rehman, was named from one of the Islamic parties, the JUI.

Another major difference from the Ayubian model was the massive induction of the military into civil administration and commerce. More than 1,000 officers were brought into senior positions in the civil administration, academia, foreign service, and even civil service training institutions after Musharraf took over. While no official data are available, many individuals have managed to pull together lists of military personnel inducted into the civil service and in government-owned corporations or parastatal organisations. One such article provided the following detail:

As many as 104 serving and retired Lieutenant Generals, Major Generals or equivalent ranks from other services are among the 1,027 military officers inducted on civilian posts in different ministries, divisions and Pakistani missions abroad after Oct 12, 1999 military takeover.

The number of army Brigadiers or their equivalent ranks from the Navy and Air Force is even higher at 160, according to an annexure placed before the Senate library. There have been 14 ambassadors and a high commissioner from the military ranks during this period....

The range of fields where military officers are working on civilian posts encompasses every sector of human endeavour including communications, education, diplomacy, water and electricity management, information, post office, jails, local bodies, think-tanks, industrial production, shipping, minority affairs, population welfare, health, agriculture, railways, highways, housing, labour and manpower, social and women development, law and justice and sub-sectors of sports from cricket to hockey.[72]

This recruitment and installation of military officers into the civilian sector ensured the continued loyalty of the military, giving Musharraf, who continued to wear his hat as army chief concurrently with his new office of president under the Supreme Court order that legalized this dual office system till 2007. Indeed, he had tasted opposition from within the army on the issue of holding dual offices at a corps commanders' meeting in December 2003, when a number of commanders suggested that he appoint a new army chief and thereby restore the dwindling prestige of the army, rather than continuing to hold both offices. However, at a much larger formation commanders' meeting the next April, an allegedly orchestrated movement was launched to persuade him to change his mind about shedding his uniform in the interest of the stability of the country. He then offered to take their advice under review. Soon, the offending corps commanders who had raised the original issue were moved from their slots. This allowed him to move newer and more compliant officers into senior slots.[73]

Like Ayub, Musharraf now saw himself aligned with a faction of the PML, except this time around, the League was led by a staunchly conservative dynasty from Gujrat led by Chaudhry Shujaat Hussain. The prevarications of this group prevented Musharraf from getting the National Assembly to pass a Women's Rights Bill till 2006, something that he had promised soon after he took over.

With the troika now replaced by an inherently unstable one-legged stool in the shape of the army chief-cum-president—(and eventually a technocratic prime minister, former Citi-Banker Shaukat Aziz)—elected in August 2004, Musharraf's Pakistan did not have a long-term sustainable political structure. Gradually, he had to confront the possibility of allowing the previous political parties and their leaders to return home and participate in the political process. Those moves created their own disruptive dynamics, as Benazir Bhutto came and took a confrontational position after landing in Pakistan in October 2007. Nawaz Sharif tried to re-enter some weeks later, under the cover of a Supreme Court order that declared his exile illegal, but was bundled off with Saudi Arabian help to Jeddah to complete his ten-year exile that he was alleged to have agreed to when he left the country originally.

Musharraf could point to some economic progress under his regime. Earlier, Sharif had introduced privatization and the ascendancy of the business class—a good start for the hitherto moribund government-controlled economy, but he had allowed it to be tainted by corruption. Musharraf's regime continued the pro-business trend, under his finance minister and then Prime Minister, Shaukat Aziz. Its economy began growing at a rapid pace, hitting 7 per cent average GDP growth. Pakistan managed to escape the strictures of the IMF and began attracting investment flows from expatriate Pakistanis and the Middle East. It benefited enormously from the flow of US aid following the global 'War on Terror' launched by the United States following the attacks on its soil by Osama Bin Laden's Al Qaeda from bases in Afghanistan. But Pakistan also attracted the unwanted interest of the world in its nuclear programme after news broke of the sale of nuclear technology and know-how by Dr A.Q. Khan, the self-styled Father of the Pakistani Bomb.

TRADING WITH THE TALIBAN

As discussed earlier, successive governments in Pakistan have maintained a deep interest in maintaining close ties to Afghan regimes, especially to counter Indian influence in the Central Asian region. The ISI maintained its own contacts and operations in Afghanistan and Central Asia, relying on the Islamist networks that created and sustained the 'jihad' against the Soviet Union in Afghanistan. Gradually though, the ISI lost its hold on the antediluvian Taliban regime, which, according to former DG ISI Ziauddin, 'lived in the 14th century'.[74] Ziauddin would know, since he was continuing the tradition of active ISI involvement in Afghanistan, even after the Taliban had established their control. Among other things, he was also involved in finding a suitable longer-term arrangement for the country in the wake of the Soviet departure. In that quest, he met the former king Zahir Shah, living in exile in Rome, and Zahir's son-in-law. He says he found the king reluctant to re-enter Afghan politics, given his age. Ziauddin also met Mullah Omar, the wily Taliban leader, who had quickly established himself not only as a political leader but also as *Amir-ul-Momineen* (the Leader of the Faithful, i.e. the Muslims).[75] Omar established himself by an elaborate public spectacle before some 1,500 mullahs in early 1996 during which he removed the robe reported to be that of Prophet Muhammad (PBUH) from its place in a shrine at Kandahar and donned it before his followers. He thus gained legitimacy in the eyes of his followers, and replaced the rule of the Mujahideen with a harsher and stricter application of orthodox Islam, the likes of which had not been seen anywhere else, even in Wahabi Saudi Arabia.

The ISI did not have a great deal of leverage over the Taliban once the latter established themselves, but they did have key contacts and used them effectively. One element was the outpouring of support from religious schools or madrassahs on the Pakistan side of the Durand Line border with Afghanistan. Many of these schools had been the breeding ground for the Taliban leadership and rank and file during the period of the Soviet War and later. The Islamist parties in Pakistan also established direct contacts with the Taliban, sending delegations to Omar. According to a contemporary witness, Kathy Gannon of the Associated Press, the ISI 'used Pakistani mullahs…to mould and manipulate Mullah Omar. Additionally, the ISI recruited Afghans trained at Pakistani madrassahs to infiltrate Mullah Omar's inner circle.'[76]

The Pakistan Foreign Office was also concerned at the increasingly radical and extremist views of the Taliban leadership and tried at one time to influence Mullah Omar directly. Ambassador Arif Ayub, who was on the Afghan desk, recalls one early meeting that they arranged with Omar. In the meeting, retired Lt. Gen. Moinuddin Haider, the then interior minister, wanted to dissuade the Taliban from blowing up the Buddha statues at Bamiyan, a decision that the Taliban had made following the imposition of UN sanctions. Aziz Ahmad Khan, additional secretary (Afghanistan) and Ayub were present at the meeting as well. They carried with them a copy of the Quran to show Omar a quotation that had been suggested by President Tarar, containing advice about not abusing the non-believers since they would just abuse back. They tried to explain to Omar that some of his actions were not according to the Quran. 'Where in the Quran are these forbidden?' asked Omar. They produced a copy of the Quran to show him. But the mandarins in the Foreign Office had unthinkingly used an English translation of the Quran to make their argument. When they presented the translated copy to Omar, who could not read it, he dismissed it with a curt: 'This is not even written in Arabic!'[77] The second argument used by Haider was that even the legendary Afghan warrior king, Mahmud of Ghazni, who was known as 'But Shikan' or Destroyer of Idols, did not destroy the statues, so why should Mullah Omar bother about them? Omar explained that Mahmud of Ghazni did not have any dynamite, otherwise he too would have blown up the statues. Haider's third argument was an article in The Nation (of Lahore) of that day describing how Amr Ibn Aas, the first Muslim governor of Egypt, had protected all the Christian statues. He added that Omar could perhaps follow the policies of his namesake. Mullah Omar responded contemptuously that the person's name was 'Amr' not 'Omar.' For good measure, Mullah Omar also addressed a letter to the Pakistani President Musharraf advising him to introduce Islamic laws in Pakistan. According to Ayub, 'Haider took all this surreal nonsense in stride and never lost his equanimity or sense of humour. He told us on the journey back that something similar had happened to a vet who was trying to blow through a tube some mixture into the throat of a buffalo, but unfortunately for the vet the buffalo blew first!'[78]

Omar continued with his policies of severe public punishments even for minor offences, confining of women in homes, eradication of the poppy crops that provided many Afghans with their incomes, and bans on music and dancing, both key ingredients of Afghan culture. Over time, Afghanistan became a closed society, concealed behind the veil of radical Islam. A kind of false security was introduced in Afghanistan though, as crime rates plummeted, probably because of the most vigorous corporal and often capital punishments for minor offences. In Kandahar, for example, for the first time in living memory, no one could carry a weapon inside the city. All the weapons were deposited in a central armoury and individuals given a token in lieu of the weapons.[79]

Afghanistan had drawn the diaspora of former Mujahideen fighters from across the Islamic world. Among them was Osama Bin Laden, the Saudi who had rebelled against his motherland for harbouring foreign infidels in the Gulf War, and sought refuge first in Sudan and then Afghanistan. Having arrived at the fag end of the Afghan war when he was involved in the battle for Jalalabad, Bin Laden had made good contacts, especially in the Khost province. He hooked up with the Taliban after they captured Jalalabad from the Northern Alliance-dominated government in Kabul. Gradually, Bin Laden attracted a coterie of zealots from among other countries and regions such as Egypt, Syria, Iraq, Libya, Morocco, Central Asia, and South East Asia. This was the birth of a new organization named Al Qaeda, or the Base, the fundamental root and rallying point of activist rebellion against 'un-Islamic leaders' in the Muslim world and foreign interests, especially the United States, which was portrayed as the arch enemy of Islamic people. Training camps were set up to provide soldiers for various Islamist rebellions around the globe, especially after the United States' retaliatory cruise missile attacks following the 1998 bombings of its embassies in East Africa by Bin Laden's operatives. After that attack, Mullah Omar found it easy to connect to the activities of Bin Laden, who also provided support to his Afghan hosts, in cash and kind. In fact, and contrary to the general impression that Omar and Bin Laden had an earlier connection from the jihad against the Soviets, the two had fought in different sectors: Bin Laden with the Tajiks (of what ended up being the Northern Alliance), while Omar fought in the south. By 2001, the movement had not only trained some 20,000 recruits but also produced an *Encyclopedia of Jihad* that found its way in May 2001 to the headquarters of the CIA in Langley, Virginia, courtesy of Kathy Gannon.[80] Far from being a scholarly volume, this book turned out to be a handbook of terrorism.

Following the 1998 attack, the ISI was tasked to help separate Omar from Bin Laden. Ziauddin recalls going to meet Omar and asking him to send away his dangerous guest. In the quest to finding the key to their relationship, Ziauddin says he spoke to Mullah Omar about getting rid of Bin Laden. He found Omar reluctant at first but found some give in his position later on. 'He is like a bone stuck in my throat, I can't swallow it nor can I get it out!' explained Omar. When Ziauddin asked Omar whether it was the money that Bin Laden gave the Taliban that made Omar 'beholden' to him, suggesting that, if that was the case, alternative sources of financing could perhaps be found. Omar responded in Pashto: *Da mata ywa rupay na rakarray de!* ('He hasn't given me even one rupee!' using the name of the Pakistani currency that many Afghans had gotten used to.) 'My people will lynch me if I hand him over. He is a hero!' But, Ziauddin says he managed to convince Omar to seek a legal way out of these constraints. Omar agreed to the possibility of a trial with four judges, one each from Afghanistan, Pakistan, Saudi Arabia, and a fourth neutral Muslim country. But other external events prevented this from taking place.

At around the same time, the ISI had worked with the US in setting up a 60-person commando team, whose men were trained in the United States and whose main aim was to find and capture Bin Laden.[81] This team, which had been deployed near the Afghan border, reportedly melted away during Musharraf's successful coup against Sharif on 12 October 1999, when, according to Steve Coll, Ziauddin tried to enlist the unit's support in protecting Sharif against the army.[82] This may be a good story but highly improbable, given that a whole brigade of the Pakistan Army was already deployed in Islamabad and Rawalpindi, and Sharif and Ziauddin were both taken into custody within hours of the announcement that Musharraf had been replaced. How could 60 men take on a brigade that was already in position?

The US had itself been negotiating directly with the Taliban on Bin Laden and for business deals connected with opening up oil routes from Turkmenistan and other Central Asian countries. US Ambassador William Milam, Under Secretary of State, Thomas Pickering, and Assistant Secretary Inderfurth had all met different Taliban officials or spoken with them on the telephone in 1998 and 1999.[83] The results were negative, as the Taliban stonewalled all those initiatives. CIA efforts to track down and capture or kill Bin Laden had also failed. The Saudis, who had been involved in Afghanistan for many years, ever since the jihad against the Soviets, had also tried their hands at brokering a peace deal among the Afghan factions first, and then after the Taliban emerged victorious, with Mullah Omar, to get Bin Laden. Prince Turki Al Faisal, the head of the Saudi General Intelligence Directorate and a frequent visitor to the region, had been involved in all these efforts. First, he had crafted a peace plan that got support from the United States, Pakistan, and the Taliban. This was based on an arms embargo, a national army from all factions, and collection and destruction of excess arms. But it foundered on the lack of support from Russia and Iran. According to Turki, Iran had a vested interest in Afghanistan on behalf of the Hizb-i-Wahadat, the Shia group, and had its revolutionary guards in Mazar-i-Sharif as well as Bamiyan, the two strongholds of the Hizb-i-Wahadat. Turki also met Rabbani, the deputy of Mullah Omar, in Islamabad and enlisted his support. But when Iran and Russia failed to sign on, the plan was scrapped.[84]

Once the Taliban had established control, Turki came back again through Pakistan, spoke first with Lt. Gen. Nasim Rana of the ISI and then met Mullah Omar in June 1998 to negotiate a handover of Bin Laden. Omar 'agreed in principle but wanted a *fatwa* (religious edict) to absolve him' of his responsibility to protect his guest as a Muslim. 'We agreed to form a joint committee to find a religious way out for Mullah Omar,' says Turki. Omar's personal advisor Mutawakkil visited Saudi Arabia and expressed support for the idea, but after the August attacks on the US embassies in East Africa things slowed down. Turki says he went back to meet Omar in September 1998, in the company of General Rana of the ISI, and this time 'Mullah Omar refused—not only to deliver him, but he also refused to admit that he had agreed in the first place! He simply said there was a mistake in translation and that he had never made that commitment.' Turki challenged him on that, provoking an angry Omar into leaving the room in a huff and dousing his head with a bucket of water to cool himself down, before returning. Turki and General Rana relied on a Pakistani officer from the ISI for interpretation.[85] According to ISI sources, the meeting ended with Omar verbally attacking the Saudis, thus angering Turki, who left the meeting in a huff, predicting rather presciently that Afghanistan would suffer for this action.[86]

9/11: A CHANGED WORLD

Afghanistan's tragedies have a way of becoming a boon for Pakistani dictatorships. The Soviet invasion of Afghanistan brought General Ziaul Haq in from the cold, from being a tin pot dictator, the object of US sanctions, to being the US's favoured ally in the jihad against the Soviets and the instrument of change in the region. General Musharraf, who too had been given the cold shoulder by the US, even to the extent of having a hurried and hidden meeting with President Bill Clinton after Clinton's long and publicly successful visit to India, would find himself front and centre again. (Although, Clinton had a positive impression of Musharraf: 'He was clearly intelligent, strong and sophisticated.'[87]) From not even being allowed to publicly shake Clinton's hand in his own capital city of Islamabad, he would find himself feted and eulogized at the White House by Clinton's successor, President George W. Bush. From being a dictator, part of a dying breed on the world map, Musharraf was to become the voice of moderation and a potential 'anchor of stability' (to borrow President Richard Nixon's words for both the Shah of Iran and President Ferdinand Marcos of the Philippines) in a region of instability.

11 September 2001 was to change not only the history of the United States, but that of Pakistan and Afghanistan as well. Its after-shocks were felt in the Middle East, specifically in Iraq. On that day, 18 young men, largely of Saudi origin, plowed two separate passenger aircraft into the World Trade Center in Manhattan (New York City), and another into the Western face of the Pentagon in Washington DC. The attackers were soon identified as members of Al Qaeda, who had been to Afghanistan and had been sent by Bin Laden

on their suicide missions. With the collapse of the Twin Towers in Manhattan, a new phase began in US–Pakistan relations. Musharraf became a central figure in the ensuing drama.

Musharraf's key advisor and the new DG ISI, Lt. Gen. Mahmud Ahmed, was on a ten-day visit to the United States at that time. He was due to leave for Pakistan on the evening of 10 September, but because of a request for meetings on the Hill he stayed on. That morning, Ahmed was at a breakfast meeting with Congressman Porter Goss (later Director of the CIA) and his colleagues on the House Intelligence Committee on Capitol Hill when their meeting was interrupted with a note from an aide, followed soon by another one. The meeting was hastily adjourned. According to Ahmed, they scrambled out of the office and watched on television the 'dreadful nightmare' of the attack on the World Trade Center and then on the Pentagon. He then hurried back to his hotel, the Four Seasons in Georgetown, past the Department of State, and heard on the cab's radio that the State Department had also been struck, which was not correct. (He preferred staying there rather than at the nondescript hotels near the CIA's Langley, VA headquarters.) He tried contacting CIA Director George Tenet but could not get through.

On the morning of the 12th, Musharraf met Tenet, who was in a 'state of shock'. He was then invited to meet Deputy Secretary of State Richard Armitage, Assistant Secretary Christina Rocca, and a few others at the Department of State. He was accompanied by Ambassador Maleeha Lodhi, and the Deputy Chief of Mission, Zamir Akram. Armitage, whom Ahmed later described as a 'big, hulking bully', was beside himself. Ahmed said that his feeling was that they wanted 'to get back to those who perpetrated this!' He noted a lot of 'anger, frustration, and resentment' in Armitage's demeanour.[88] Armitage made it clear that Pakistan needed to show which side it was going to be on. When Ahmed started to recite the history of US–Pakistan relations, Armitage interrupted him: 'History begins today!' Ahmed was not used to be spoken to in this manner. He seemed visibly shaken.[89] As they exited the room after the meeting had concluded, one of the US officials (not Armitage) came to Ahmed and said: 'By God! They are thinking of using the nukes.' Ahmed recalls that 'he did not say against whom. [...]But the feelings were so high.' When queried about the likely target, he said it was most likely Afghanistan, not Pakistan. The discussion at the State Department had been mainly on what position Pakistan should take. 'We took the position that having been a victim of terrorism itself, Pakistan would take a position against terrorism. We'd fight terrorism.' There was no mention of Afghanistan at that time since it was not known who had committed the act. In fact, the Afghan government was being quoted as criticizing the terrorist acts. He denies that he was asked to make a commitment. He spoke to General Musharraf on the 12th and conveyed his thoughts on the meetings. He also gave Musharraf a gist of what had happened during his ten-day stay in the United States. Ahmed states (in his interview with the author) that he was not ready to respond immediately to the US demands. In fact, when Armitage gave him a list of US demands on the 13th, Ahmed was seen by other participants in this meeting as demurely saying: 'This is fine!' after scanning the document to which Armitage responded that he might want to check back with his president on it.[90]

In his memoir, Musharraf quotes Ahmed as saying that Armitage had said that 'not only that we had to decide whether we were with America or with the terrorists, but that if we chose the terrorists, then we should be prepared to be bombed back into the Stone Age.'[91] This reference became the headline-grabbing introduction to Musharraf's autobiography in the United States in September 2006. Based on my two separate conversations with Ahmed on this point, it is clear that Ahmed did not convey this message to Musharraf in those words and that Musharraf may have conflated different parts of the conversation he had with Ahmed into this dramatic statement. No other participant in those meetings has confirmed the Musharraf account. Armitage, a man who is unafraid to speak his mind and has a Marine Corps sense of integrity and bluntness, also categorically denied this on US television and in an interview with the author. He further elaborated that he met President Musharraf at Blair House during the latter's visit to Washington (after the White House meeting of Bush and Musharraf but before he had officially launched his book) and told him that he had not made that statement to Ahmed.[92] Musharraf and he parted as friends (with Musharraf telling Armitage: 'Tony Zinni said you were a good fellow!'), but Musharraf did not retract that statement about the bombing of Pakistan during his book tour nor did he mention that he had met Armitage and discussed this issue when he was asked about the quote in subsequent media appearances. A participant at the corps commanders' meeting of 13 September recalls that Musharraf did not ascribe the 'Stone Age' threat of the United States to Ahmed. Rather he referred to a conversation with a 'friend from New York' who had alleged contacts with high level officials in the United States and who conveyed this threat to him. Musharraf apparently had made up his mind on this issue.[93]

Musharraf had also been at the receiving end of calls from Secretary of State, Colin Powell, who asked him to choose sides but did not launch any threats. Based on that, he says that he analyzed the situation 'military-style' and took the decision in the 'best interests of my country' to go with the United States against his erstwhile allies, the Taliban. Why he 'war-gamed the United States as an adversary' is unclear, since Pakistan was not the direct target of any immediate US military action.[94] However, Pakistan did have a lot to lose by prevaricating or going against the United States, and would have been ostracized economically and politically. He also saw an opportunity to use the global War on Terror to move against similar elements at home, and he says he was determined to stay this course, even if the mullahs came out on the streets. As a result, when US Ambassador Wendy Chamberlain brought him a copy of the official list of seven demands, he was prepared to agree. The US asked Pakistan to:

1. Stop Al Qaeda operatives at its border and end all logistical support for Bin Laden;
2. give the United States blanket overflight and landing rights for all necessary military and intelligence operations;
3. provide territorial access to US and allied military intelligence and other personnel to conduct operations against al Qaeda;
4. provide the United States with intelligence information;
5. continue to publicly condemn the terrorist acts;
6. cut off all shipments of fuel to the Taliban and stop recruits from going to Afghanistan; and,
7. if the evidence implicated Bin Laden and Al Qaeda and the Taliban continued to harbour them, to break relations with the Taliban government.[95]

In effect, the United States wanted *carte blanche* to proceed against whomever they thought had attacked it by establishing extra-territorial rights in Pakistan, among other things. No government in Pakistan, or for that matter in any other sovereign nation worth its salt, could have acceded to all these demands. The United States was not perceived very warmly in the streets of Pakistan at that time, especially since it had abandoned Pakistan with the Afghanistan problem and over three million Afghan refugees after the Soviets departed. Musharraf says he did not agree to all these demands, especially the second and third ones. The third was especially problematic, since it demanded access to Pakistani bases. But later evidence indicates that Pakistan has managed to provide the United States with bases for more than 'logistic and aircraft recovery,' as Musharraf defines the demand in his memoir.[96] Private conversations with Pakistani officials indicate that Pakistan allowed small groups of US Special Forces personnel into its operational territory in Waziristan to help with anti-insurgency operations and also allowed use of a SSG satellite training camp at Tarbela, a camp that was once used for training Kashmiri jihadi groups. In the words of one former senior intelligence officer, the Americans 'now are everywhere', although he may be overestimating their presence as 'one to three regiments.'[97]

Regardless, as the 9/11 Commission Report states:

Pakistan made its decision swiftly. That afternoon, Secretary of State Powell announced at the beginning of an NSC meeting that Pakistani President Musharraf had agreed to **every** [emphasis added] US request for support in the war on terrorism. The next day, the US embassy in Islamabad confirmed that Musharraf and his top military commanders had agreed to **all seven demands** [emphasis added]. 'Pakistan will need full US support as it proceeds with us,' the embassy noted. 'Musharraf said the GOP [Government of Pakistan] was making substantial concessions in allowing use of its territory and that he would pay a domestic price. His standing in Pakistan was certain to suffer. To counterbalance that, he needed to show that Pakistan was benefiting from his decisions.'[98]

GOODBYE TO THE TALIBAN

Before he broke with the Taliban, Musharraf made some last minute efforts to see if he could persuade them to give up Bin Laden and thus avoid direct US intervention in the region. Pakistan was one of only three countries that had recognized the Taliban regime: Saudi Arabia and the UAE being the other two. And even this recognition had come on the initiative of the DG ISI Nasim Rana who persuaded Prime Minister Nawaz Sharif to do so after the Taliban had captured Mazar-i-Sharif in May 1997, against the advice of then army chief Jehangir Karamat.[99] Pakistan had little choice in keeping diplomatic relations with Afghanistan. Pakistan was its land-locked neighbour's lifeline to the world and it shared a substantial proportion of the tribal population with Afghanistan. Even in the worst of times, when Afghanistan actively propagated anti-Pakistan separatist movements in the NWFP or provided succour to rebels fighting the Pakistan Army in Balochistan, Pakistan maintained its ties with Afghanistan. Now, the situation was getting very difficult. Musharraf dispatched his intelligence chief, Mahmud Ahmed, to meet Mullah Omar and see if he could be persuaded to hand over Bin Laden or at least eject him from Afghanistan. While identified as an Islamist, Mahmud says that 'we were not obsessed with Mullah Omar', and there were misconceptions about 'our nurturing them'. He concedes that after 9/11, Pakistan had to change its stance toward the Taliban. Before the US bombing of Afghanistan on 7 October 2001, Ahmed made 'three or four trips' to Afghanistan to meet Omar and see if he could persuade him to release some UN workers who had been taken hostage and also get him to send Bin Laden out of the country. He says he saw his mission as one to prevent hostile actions against Afghanistan, to safeguard Pakistan's interests, and protect it from the after effects of a US attack.[100]

In that quest, Ahmed met Mullah Omar a number of times and found him very sceptical of the US allegations linking Bin Laden with the attacks on US soil. Omar insisted there was no proof, and was unwilling to hand over Bin Laden 'or any Muslim' to any non-Muslim. He was open to let Bin Laden go to other countries or to hand him over to Muslim countries. 'I gave my word to Osama Bin Laden! As a Muslim, I cannot break my word! Either he should die or I should die!' asserted Mullah Omar to Ahmed. At that point, the US was not interested in any Afghan trial of Bin Laden, they wanted possession, Ahmed told him. But Ahmed was also facing a quandary. He says he 'didn't try to persuade' Mullah Omar to do anything against his beliefs. 'I am a Muslim,' stated Ahmed in his interview with the author. 'Why would I go against another Muslim?' In his assessment, the US had 'strategic designs for the region' that included stopping the 'religious revolution from spreading. [...]But the real reason, he felt, was economic: [to] prevent exploration and exploitation of fossil fuels from Central Asia.'[101] The result was that he warned Omar about the impeding US attack but did not try to push him to concede anything. These meetings always involved Pakistani interpreters and sometimes Foreign Office representatives. Their gist was soon carried to Musharraf and the Americans, who too had their suspicions about Ahmed's loyalties.

According to Paul R. Pillar, who was the CIA's Chief Intelligence Officer for the Near East and South Asia from 2000 to 2005, the United States' thinking on the Taliban at that time was similar to Pakistan's apparent stance. In other words, they would have preferred to have continued dealing with the Taliban, 'however reprehensible' that was, because the policy 'priority was to get Bin Laden.' At a White House meeting that he attended earlier in 2001, he states that the 'overwhelming view was: let the Taliban alone, provided they give up Bin Laden.' But they had their suspicions about Ahmed's loyalties, and thus about the extent that Ahmed would try to persuade Omar to give up his guest.[102]

The Americans had been particularly rough with Ahmed the previous year when he visited Washington and met Under Secretary of State, Thomas R. Pickering. Pickering recalled: 'I delivered a very tough message to him: if you are not helping us with the Taliban and they are our enemies, then we will have to consider you an enemy...[He] didn't like that very much and it caused quite a bit of stir.' Pickering said that the US was aware of 'his Islamist credentials, background, interest...and at the same time we felt we had to approach him directly since he was in charge.'[103] Shortly after the US attack on Afghanistan commenced, Musharraf removed Ahmed from his position as DG ISI, giving him a civilian job, as head of a military-owned corporation, from which he retired in 2005.

Pakistan's worst fears about the US attack were soon realized. The United States forged a coalition with the Tajik-dominated Northern Alliance, comprising forces of General Rashid Dostum and the late warrior Ahmed Shah Massoud. The Northern Alliance had close links to India, among other things, and represented a minority tribal group in Afghanistan, whereas Pakistan had a large Pushtun population. The largely Pushtun areas of Afghanistan in the south and east came under heavy air attack, and the US forces attempted to destroy whatever little infrastructure remained of the

Taliban government, and to encircle Osama Bin Laden, sub-contracting some of the fighting to Afghan fighters. In the process, they made the mistake of using non-local fighters from the north and the north-east of Afghanistan in the key siege of Tora Bora, (in the areas bordering Pakistan), where Bin Laden was supposed to have taken refuge in a series of tunnels that dated from the anti-Soviet jihad that his own people had helped dig and stock over the years. Tribal loyalties and resentment against these 'intruders' from the north and north-east prevented the latter's successful deployment. That, combined with the ill discipline of the Afghans contracted to capture Bin Laden, meant that he slipped out of that cordon, and escaped, most probably to the rugged mountains in the northern border regions of Pakistan around Dir and Bajaur. The US lack of understanding of local systems and relationships stood in the way of its efforts to capture Bin Laden. The paucity of boots on the ground, and among those the relatively small numbers of trained Special Forces personnel who were fluent in Pushtu or Dari, the local languages, contributed to the failure of the US to capitalize on its overwhelming air superiority. As a result, the Taliban escaped in droves into Pakistan, where they melted into their own fellow tribesmen in the FATA (see map of FATA: 'The new battleground'), comprising seven tribal agencies on the Pakistan–Afghan border that functioned autonomously of Pakistani laws. Afghanistan's problem became Pakistan's problem and remains so to this date.

Suddenly, Musharraf became party to an attack on a Muslim state and was designated a target of Al Qaeda and Afghan Taliban militants. As a result, he was the subject of repeated assassination attempts, most of which were linked to Afghan suicide bombers. His Prime Minister, Shaukat Aziz, was also targeted. The Pakistan Army, however, was ill-prepared to tackle this new kind of low-intensity conflict that slipped across its western border, first into the NWFP and Balochistan, and then into Pakistani cities. Al Qaeda operatives hid in the border regions that already had a substantial foreign militant population subsequent to the Afghan war against the Soviets. Many of them had married into the local tribes and were protected by them. The conventional army of Pakistan, equipped with tanks, artillery, and supported by aircraft was unable to operate against the insurgents, who were not in uniform or occupying fixed defences, and were well equipped for guerrilla warfare and had the support of the local population. The insurgents' first line of attack was the Frontier Constabulary or the Frontier Corps (FC) who normally patrolled the border region and kept the peace among warring tribes. The FC and other paramilitary troops were not equipped with armoured vehicles or personal protective armour. The army continued to send them in sweeps but they were vulnerable to mines and hidden attacks, and their losses mounted. The only successes were largely on the basis of intelligence intercepts by Pakistan and the US that allowed them to apprehend some lower level members of Al

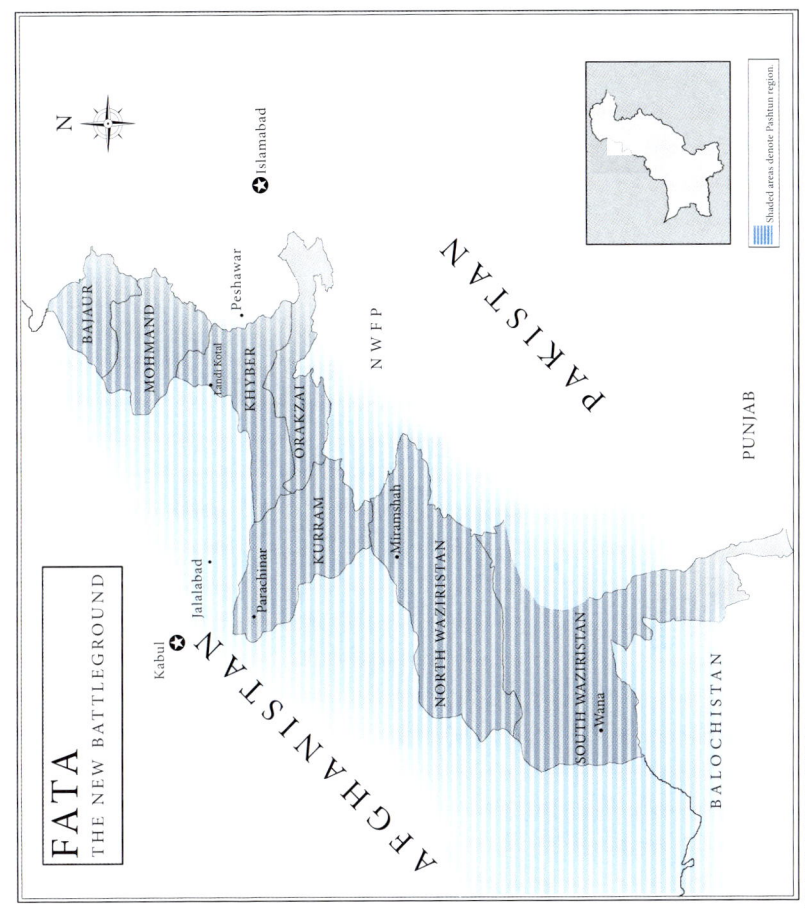

FATA
THE NEW BATTLEGROUND

N

Kabul
Jalalabad

AFGHANISTAN

BAJAUR

MOHMAND

Landi Kotal
KHYBER

ORAKZAI

Parachinar
KURRAM

Mirumshah

NORTH WAZIRISTAN

SOUTH WAZIRISTAN
Wana

BALOCHISTAN

Islamabad

Peshawar

N W F P

PAKISTAN

PUNJAB

Shaded areas denote Pashtun region.

* Federally Administered Tribal Areas

Qaeda. But, ironically, each such success created opportunities for further recruitment of the disaffected youth of Pakistan to the cause of the insurgents. Pakistan received, on average, some $1.2 billion annually during the period after 9/11 from the United States for the 'War on Terror' as reimbursement for its use of forces in the border regions, among other things. But the US did not impose conditions or benchmarks for the use of these funds, and little of this money was seen as improving the personal armour or fighting capability of the army and Frontier Constabulary in the border area in a counter-insurgency mode. Pakistan's ill-equipped forces suffered heavily and were forced to regroup. It was only in late 2007 that the US began to focus on large-scale development in FATA, an approach that ought to have been aggressively followed from the outset.

Musharraf's policy of hobbling the two major political parties of Pakistan, Sharif's PML and Bhutto's PPP, had given the Islamic parties a free reign which they had successful exploited through electoral wins in the NWFP and Balochistan. As a result, the 'enlightened moderation' that Musharraf espoused was offset by the increasing 'Talibanization' of large chunks of Pakistani territory in the provinces bordering Afghanistan, allowing Taliban supporters to infiltrate into Afghanistan almost at will. Policing the 100-mile rugged frontier became difficult. Pakistan pushed some 80,000 troops into the region initially, raising it to over 100,000 in 2007, but they were not enough to do the job of blockading the border, and their losses mounted; close to 800 troops were killed. One reason was the low number of coalition forces on the other side in Afghanistan: only some 40,000, of which half were US troops. A misguided US attack on Iraq soon after the Afghan invasion had meant that the US was unable to deploy the necessary forces in Afghanistan. Special Forces personnel who were earlier deployed in Afghanistan say that they were re-deployed to Iraq just as they were gaining some traction in Afghanistan.[104] Rather than examine its own mistakes in this conflict, the US found it expedient to attack Musharraf's lack of effort in sealing the border and encouraged the newly installed US-sponsored Afghan President, Hamid Karzai, to criticize Musharraf regularly. Musharraf, quick to take offence, especially from a weaker neighbour and a leader who had throughout the Soviet War sought refuge in Pakistan (reportedly under the ISI's care), responded with anger and harsh words on the occasion. However, he also used his back channels to convey to Karzai that confrontation with Pakistan would not suit his interests. Pakistan had a sizable Pushtun population and Musharraf would be constrained to meeting their needs before he met Karzai's. Musharraf sent a trusted former SSG commando colleague and senior ISI general to Kabul to speak to Karzai, as a precursor to his own visit. The effort provided some temporary respite.[105]

By 2007, from being President George W. Bush's 'buddy' and a much-lauded ally in the US War on Terror, Musharraf found himself as the object of severe attacks in the US Congress and administration. Talk about alternatives to Musharraf began seeping out of Washington think-tanks and congressional offices, as lawmakers in that city chafed at unending demands for money to be spent on Iraq and Afghanistan. They demanded results, and focused on Musharraf as the ally who, in their view, was not doing enough for the United States. Musharraf thus faced a new and distant opposition in the halls of the US Congress, a difficult one to assuage. Congressional pressure was eventually to force the US administration to put pressure on Musharraf not only to show results in the fight against terrorists on the border but also to concede political freedoms at home.

ON OTHER FRONTS

For a military man who believed not only in 'unity of command'—a mantra that allowed him to rationalize his single-man presidential form of government even while the country had a parliamentary system of government in place,—Musharraf did not display a unity of focus on his political aims. Like previous rulers, both civil and military, he showed a schizoid approach on a number of issues. The major one involved relations with the Islamists. Rather than keeping the traditional Army–Mullah relationship of patron and client, he unwittingly gave the Islamists political and legislative respectability by allowing them to run for office in a field devoid of the major political parties: Sharif's PML and Bhutto's PPP. While battling internal terrorism and militancy on the one hand, he allowed the ISI and other agencies to keep open ties to Islamist groups which could be used to pressure India on Kashmir. The assumption was—as his CGS, Aziz Khan pithily put it in his (intercepted) telephone conversation with Musharraf during the Kargil affair—that the army had them [the militants] by their '*tooti*,' a term implying either the throat or, in the vernacular, their private parts. This turned out to be untrue. The militants, even those that were banned, re-emerged in various guises and formed new alliances with other groups, even with Al Qaeda, and helped set up attacks not only on other sectarian groups in Pakistan but also specifically on Musharraf. Miraculously, he managed to escape death a number of times. Musharraf now found himself in a war at home against his former Islamist allies, as the activities of the Islamic militants seeped into the settled areas of Pakistan, such as Swat, from the FATA bordering Afghanistan. He was forced to rely on the regular army to quell these uprisings, raising the possibility of unhappiness within the army's ranks at having to fight their own countrymen.

Musharraf's reform agenda for government had included reducing the size of government. While a noble objective, he found out that accommodating a large number of disparate groups under the large tent of his favoured PML (Q) meant that his prime minister had to accede to breaking up the ministries into new ones. So, rather than a dozen ministries that might have helped regulate the affairs of state, Pakistan suddenly had a plethora of ministries, ministers, and parliamentary secretaries. The cabinet of Prime Minister Aziz had 32 ministries, with 37 ministers at the federal level, 24 ministers of state, 2 advisors with the rank of federal ministers; that is, 63 ministers in all, plus 42 parliamentary secretaries, 46 chairmen of standing committees, and 4 chairmen of special committees.[106] In other words, anyone who needed to be fitted in was accommodated! To operate the government in a manageable manner, Prime Minister Aziz relied on a smaller group of ministers. However, these key individuals were often at loggerheads with each other, since some of them included people with diametrically opposed views and backgrounds, and others had prime ministerial ambitions themselves. The way Musharraf was said to define the division of responsibilities was to separate 'governance' from the rest of the 'political system'. A commission to reform government and improve governance, headed by the highly successful governor of the State Bank of Pakistan, Ishrat Husain, was set up. It proposed some changes in the operational aspects of government but did not focus on the nature or size of the cabinet.

ECONOMIC PROGRESS

One of the biggest challenges faced by Musharraf when he took over was the sorry state of the economy. Pakistan's foreign exchange reserves at the time were around $300 million, with foreign direct investment (FDI) around the same figure. Relative political stability, the inflow of remittances from expatriates after 9/11, the opening up of the economy to private foreign investment, all contributed to a healthier economy, with foreign exchange reserves rising to around $13 billion. Workers' remittance rose from $1.1 billion in 2000 to $4.3 billion in 2005. FDI meanwhile rose to $2.2 billion, according to the World Bank. A key role in this was played by the steady management of money supply and interest rates by the State Bank, giving businessmen some sense of stability. According to the government, the GDP rose from around 4.1 per cent in 2000 to 7.8 per cent in 2005. Military spending though showed a decline from 4.1 to 3.4 per cent of GDP.[107] But the US and other financial assistance following Pakistan's alliance with the United States in the 'War on Terror' yielded immediate gains; between 2001 and 2006, some $10 billion had come in through open channels to Pakistan.

According to the Congressional Research Service (CRS): 'Pakistan is among the world's leading recipients of US aid, obtaining more than $2.6 billion in direct US assistance for FY 2002–FY 2005, including $1.1 billion in security-related aid. Pakistan also received billions of dollars in reimbursement for its support of US-led counter terrorism operations.'[108]

There was no unanimity among economic analysts on the causes of past development or prognosis for further economy growth. A leading Pakistani expatriate economist, Parvez Hasan, noted that the path to growth had been laid in the Sharif period by opening up the economy to the private sector and foreign investment. But he had some words of cautionary advice:

> Pakistan has been able to avoid disruption to economic growth, despite major economic shocks [such as the earthquake that devastated large parts of Northern Pakistan in 2005], because of adequate level of foreign exchange reserves and large foreign investment flows related partly to rapid privatization. However, the current account balance of payments deficits, after official transfers, increased to $5 billion in 2005–06, and the July–October 2006 data suggest [it] could grow to $6.0 billion or over 4 per cent of GDP in 2006–07, if the recent decline in international oil price is not sustained. Meanwhile, inflation though stable at around 7–7.5 per cent is stubbornly high.[109]

One of the major economic shocks that Hasan alludes to was a natural disaster that leveled large tracts of mountainous areas and destroyed the livelihoods of millions in 2005. The Pakistan Army played a major role in getting aid to the survivors and helping rebuild the area despite huge losses to its own infrastructure and manpower in the region. However, critics maintained that the army was slow to react and not well equipped for the task. US assistance and aid from other donors in cash and kind helped Pakistan weather that storm. An interesting aspect of the relief work was the emergence of many Islamist organizations, including some that had been banned, such as the Jamaat-ud-Dawa, that established relief operations and won many adherents to their cause in the process. An embarrassed government could not shut down their operations but saved face by stating that they were restricted to the earthquake zone and for relief work only. Meanwhile the price of oil on the world markets continued to climb, forcing Pakistan's economy into a corner.

OPENING DOORS TO INDIA

The positive side of the earthquake, however, was the closing down of most Kashmiri militant training camps in the affected areas and the re-opening of the border between Pakistani- and Indian-controlled Kashmir, although in fits and starts. Musharraf could take some credit for this move. He had launched his first peace initiative after a trip to India in 2001, when he showed the Indian public that he was open to change in the frigid relationship between India and Pakistan. Despite his failure to get an Agra Declaration issued by himself and Prime Minister A.B. Vajpayee, he persisted in his efforts to get the two warring neighbours to the table, instead encouraging parallel Track 2 diplomacy (former military and civil leaders) and using other back channels, whenever they became useful.

Despite these efforts, in 2002, Indian and Pakistani troops came to face each other at the border, as a tense world watched these two regional nuclear powers, fearing a conflict that might get out of hand. This confrontation was sparked by a series of attacks by Kashmiri militants belonging to the Lashkar-e-Tayyaba and Jaish-e-Mohammed, two groups that had lines of communication and support within Pakistan. The militants carried out attacks on individuals and targets in Kashmir and then a brazen attack on the Indian Parliament on 13 December 2001. As Steve Coll reported in *The New Yorker*:

> Little was known about the attackers, but India suspected the Pakistan government and its Inter-Services Intelligence (ISI) agency was behind the attack. Since the late 1980s, ISI has covertly funded and armed violent Islamist groups in Kashmir. By 2001, two of the larger jihadi groups— Lashkar-e-Tayyaba and Jaish-e-Mohammed—had developed ties to Al Qaeda. After the December 2001 attack, Indian President Atal Behari Vajpayee ordered the Indian military to mobilize for war. India and Pakistan's looming confrontation became the first nuclear crisis of the 21st century and it posed a very modern problem—the impact of state-less religious networks with millenarian ideas.[110]

Indian military officials sought to respond, on the assumption that the militants had Pakistani backing. Some 700,000 Indian troops were placed in Kashmir and the Indian Air Force was poised on Pakistan's borders. The Indian Navy moved into battle positions in the Arabian Sea. Pakistan moved its troops to the borders too. On the Pakistani side, the government appeared to have understood the importance of reining in the rogue elements that were bent upon sabotaging the nascent peace process with India. Pakistan promised to shut down training camps and other such facilities. On the Indian side, a major push for de-escalation came from the growing and influential expatriate Indian community that was investing heavily in India and warned the prime minister of the consequences of jeopardizing their efforts with a security situation that precluded Indian Americans from staying on in the country after a security alert had been issued by the United States government. Richard Armitage was sent by the US government to help both sides see reason. Among other things, the US was still committed to its war in

Afghanistan and did not want to see its regional efforts being overtaken by a war in the subcontinent that might even expand into nuclear conflict, with disastrous consequences for the region and the world. After ten months of tensions, the situation calmed down enough for the two sides to disengage and then resume their talks.

Musharraf made other efforts to present new ideas and 'out of the box' solutions to the dispute. But the schizoid approach to Kashmiri militants and to keeping the religious right on his side seemed to hobble his efforts. He could not make any serious headway in opening borders to normal traffic with India or encouraging trade to the extent that it would create large groups of vested interests on both sides of the border. Visa restrictions were discussed at the level of the Foreign Offices of both sides, and a trickle of improvements occurred. Without major leaps over the hurdles of history, Musharraf failed to achieve the breakthroughs that he sought, although some traction on both sides of the border on a geographic splitting of Kashmir was evident during 2007.

Musharraf also opened another front in Balochistan, against a recalcitrant and elderly Baluch tribal leader, Sardar Akbar Khan Bugti, who had retreated to the hills with his armed band of followers and continued to snipe at the military presence in Balochistan. Bugti wanted Balochistan to get a greater share of its natural resources, such as gas, and also of the benefits of opening up a new port at Gwadar. This was a reprise of the 1970s demands of the Baluch leaders. According to former President Farooq Leghari, he had warned the government about the presence of the armed Baluch tribesmen who had come even into his own territory in the borderland of Punjab and Balochistan. Leghari also suggested to Musharraf, who was on a flight to inaugurate the port of Gwadar, that a substantial proportion of the jobs at the port could be reserved for Baluchs and trainings schools be set up to prepare them for those jobs. Musharraf listened to Leghari but did not act on his advice. Instead, when Bugti took to the hills, Musharraf sent the army after him, finally cornering him in a remote cave. When army officers entered the cave to talk Bugti into surrendering, they apparently tripped a booby trap charge that blew up the cave and killed Bugti and the officers. The Baluch now had one more cause to oppose the central government in their province. Musharraf had forgotten the traditional British aphorism on how best to deal with these tribes: 'Honour the Baluch!' And as Mohammad Ayub Khan, Pakistan's first military ruler, wisely observed: 'With the Balochis (sic) we have to be generous and let them run in the manner they understand, provided the *sardars* behave themselves and remain loyal. I am very glad to hear that the Baluch possess some admirable qualities. Kindness can, but money cannot buy him and also he has an acute head instinct and is devoted to the leader of the clan.'[111] The unhappy Baluch, resentful of what they saw as an overbearing army presence and action in their territory, provided the Taliban a ready home in Quetta and its environs when the US military action pushed them out of Afghanistan.

THE NUCLEAR BAZAAR

Musharraf's path toward history-making actions was strewn with many obstacles: some of his own causing and others that he inherited. One such inheritance was the presence of a man named Dr A.Q. Khan, the Pakistani metallurgist, who had come to serve Pakistan during Zulfikar Ali Bhutto's period and brought over the designs of uranium processing plants that allowed Pakistan to move towards making a nuclear weapon. Part brilliant and hard-working scientist, part patriot, and part self-serving, publicity-seeking egomaniac, Dr Khan brought more than his knowledge and the blueprints for making a cascade of centrifuges that would allow Pakistan to enrich uranium on its own. He also carried with him a network of contacts and friends that he gradually expanded to help Pakistan bypass the strict sanctions against nuclear proliferation in general and Pakistan in particular.

The uranium enrichment project in Pakistan had been initiated by the PAEC in February 1975 on the suggestion of Dr Abdul Qadeer Khan who was then employed at the URENCO uranium enrichment plant at Almelo, The Netherlands. Dr Khan himself joined the project in January 1976. The fledgling institution, then known as Engineering Research Laboratory (ERL), seceded from the PAEC in July 1976, and was later on named Khan Research Laboratory (KRL). While PAEC continued on a low key programme of nuclear fuel reprocessing for the separation of plutonium, KRL went full speed ahead on the enrichment route. Prime Minister Zulfikar Ali Bhutto very cleverly diverted the attention of the world from the enrichment project by publicly stressing upon the reprocessing efforts.

As a favourite of Ziaul Haq, A.Q. Khan had set up his autonomous operations and accounting systems and expanded his operations to provide Pakistan the capability of buying and reverse engineering weapons systems from around the world. As different DGs of the ISI attest, they became aware that he was skimming profits for himself and had accumulated a vast personal fortune and set up safe-houses in Dubai and other locations where he could secretly meet his colleague and plan his operations.[112] Consecutive governments allowed him to operate with impunity, while allowing him to portray himself as the Father of the Bomb, a title to which he had only partial credit.

The idea of supplying nuclear know-how to other countries appears to have occurred quite early to Dr A.Q. Khan. The topmost technical echelon at KRL, other than Dr Khan himself, comprised scientists and engineers transferred from the parent organization, PAEC. The first inkling came in 1986 when two of these senior scientists approached President Ziaul Haq and reported that Dr Khan was considering providing sensitive information to a Muslim country.[113] These complaints were ignored and the matter was given an ethnic colour and attributed to professional rivalry between these scientists and Dr Khan as well as between PAEC and KRL. The two scientists were transferred back to PAEC and one of them still occupies a very high position in the organization.

Among Khan's foreign network were the Libyans and the Koreans. He also made contacts with the Iranians and at a late stage with Saddam Hussain's Iraq, though with much less success in the case of Iraq. His secret activity continued unabated, till the stopping and search of a ship, the *BBC China*, in October 2003 by Italian coast guard cutters as it headed for Libya. On board they found 10,000 centrifuges of the P-2 design (P-1 and P-2 being successive Pakistani designs). The shipment had originated from Malaysia from Scomi Precision Engineering that had made the centrifuges on the orders of a Sri Lankan associate of Khan named Buhary Sayed Abu Tahir. Tahir operated through a cutout, SMB Computers of Dubai. Discovery of this shipment led eventually to the unravelling of the Khan empire, as the Libyans, under increasing sanctions and pressure from the United States, came clean, giving up all their documents and materials acquired from Khan. In return they were given a free pass on their own links to past terrorist activities, and the trade and travel ban against them was lifted by the United States. The world media went on a feeding frenzy against Khan and Pakistan. *TIME* magazine splashed him on its cover, an honour denied till that time to Musharraf or even the elder Bhutto. But this time the headline next to a grim-faced Khan was 'Merchant of Menace.'

The ability of Khan, a metallurgist, to portray himself as nuclear scientist and to claim credit for producing Pakistan's nuclear weapons, was breathtaking. Even more so was the scope of his international network and how long it operated without being busted:

> Starting with the stolen centrifuge designs from the Netherlands, and augmented by weapons designs from China, the syndicate also included engineering assistance from Britain; vacuum pumps from Germany; specialized lathes from Spain; furnaces from Italy; centrifuge motors and frequency converters from Turkey; enrichment parts from South Africa and Switzerland; aluminium from Singapore; and centrifuge parts from Malaysia, all orchestrated from an administrative hub in Dubai.
>
> Despite mounting evidence, however, it is unlikely that the full extent of the network that International Atomic Energy Agency (IAEA) Director General Mohamed ElBaradei dubbed 'the nuclear Wal-Mart', will ever be fully known.[114]

In September 2003, in New York the CIA Director, George Tenet, revealed to Musharraf the evidence of Khan's dealings, including the transfer of centrifuge technology to Iran. In October, Deputy Secretary of State, Richard Armitage, presented further evidence against Dr Khan in a meeting with Musharraf in Islamabad. This led to the speedy winding up of the Khan network. Musharraf ordered the heads of military's Strategic Plans Division and ISI to investigate the American evidence against Khan. The ISI collected its information about the Dubai activities of A.Q. Khan and confronted him. But, Khan said that he had needed a clandestine network to bypass the US controls on access to nuclear technology.

The A.Q. Khan affair is documented in detail in the recently published dossier of The International Institute of Strategic Studies (IISS).[115] According to this publication, Khan's contacts with Iran date from the mid-1980s and extended into the following decade. He provided Iran with centrifuges, technical designs, components and a list of suppliers. IAEA inspectors later identified the Iranian gas centrifuges as P-1 (Pak-1) type, the model developed at KRL in the early 1980s. It was alleged, and later confirmed, that Iran also received designs for the advanced P-2 version centrifuges as well.

In December 2003, Libya announced that it had a nuclear weapons programmes, based upon equipment purchased on the black market, which it was abandoning. The Libyan gas centrifuges components were found to be very similar to the one used by Iran. Even the design of a nuclear device was found among the documents. In a written confession in 2004, Khan also admitted to supplying North Korea with about two dozen centrifuge machines together with sets of drawings, sketches, technical data and depleted uranium hexafluoride gas.

Khan admitted to transferring technology and information to Iran between 1989 and 1991, to North Korea and Libya between 1991 and 1997 and additional technology to North Korea until 2000. The centrifuges sold to Libya were produced in Malaysia, Turkey, Europe and South Africa and trans-shipped through a front company in Dubai. Though the network comprised members from Dubai, Germany, Malaysia, Sri Lanka, Switzerland and Turkey, investigations focused on Pakistan because the actual equipment, or its design, and the leader were from Pakistan. As a consequence a number of employees of KRL were investigated by the Pakistanis. Beginning with two directors (in December 2003) at least 26 individuals, including three KRL DGs and two retired brigadiers, were interrogated. However, less than half of those detained were formally arrested and most of those jailed, except Mr Mohammad Farooq, responsible for procurement at KRL, were released by July 2004.[116] The identities of those put under some form of continued 'house arrest', other than Dr A.Q. Khan himself, have not been made public.

That the activities of Dr A.Q. Khan went on undiscovered for such a long time is not surprising. In addition to his expertise in the enrichment technology, Dr A.Q. Khan was a very good manager and task master in the context of the Pakistani environment. He provided excellent technical facilities and working conditions in the laboratory and unmatched salaries and personal benefits as compared to other institutions in the country. While the employees worked with dedication and diligence it also ensured absolute loyalty, from the lowest to the highest level, to Dr Khan. Even if some of them had got a whiff of the proliferation activities they would have kept quiet.

Dr A.Q. Khan was also a shrewd public relations manager and had established a very good relationship with the local media. He used the media to gradually build his status as a hero in the eyes of the people; his name became synonymous with the nuclear programme of Pakistan long before the weapons were even tested. His reputation was often exploited by the government since he was encouraged to issue statements about the indigenous nuclear capability at times when the country felt threatened by the build-up of Indian conventional forces on the border. The image he had so carefully cultivated stood him in good stead when he was accused of nuclear proliferation. He had become virtually untouchable and President Musharraf and his government could take only limited action against him for fear of adverse public reaction.

The A.Q. Khan affair proved to be a nightmare for the government of Pakistan and the army. The IISS report talks of some gray areas, speculating on 'the past Pakistani governments' knowledge of and even involvement in A.Q. Khan's secondary proliferation activities.' It further states that 'Khan probably had some signal, if not explicit permission, from his superiors for nuclear cooperation with Iran. However, no evidence has yet emerged that a clear directive was ever given to Khan to provide nuclear technology to Iran.' Critics noted that virtually all of Khan's overseas travels, to Iran, Libya, North Korea, Niger, Mali, and the Middle East, were on official Pakistani government aircraft. The centrifuges provided to North Korea were probably also transported in unmarked containers on PAF planes. Complicity of General Mirza Aslam Beg, COAS at the time, has also been alleged. It is even being suggested that Musharraf had agreed to arrest Dr A.Q. Khan only after striking a secret deal with Richard Armitage in 2004 that his army generals involved in illegal nuclear trade would not be touched and that he himself would be accepted by the Americans to rule Pakistan in his military uniform.[117]

Without supporting evidence of any type these allegations remain in the domain of wild speculation. The government of Pakistan has firmly denied the involvement in the proliferation activities of any person other than some of those interrogated. The free hand that Dr A.Q. Khan enjoyed was due to the remarkable degree of authority and autonomy given to him by successive Pakistani governments, partly because of the highly sensitive nature of his work, partly because he had to covertly obtain materials and equipment from abroad for the county's nuclear programme, and partly because of the aura of technical achievements he had built around himself.

Musharraf was suddenly caught in the vortex of this story. Rightly, questions were asked whether Khan operated on his own or with the Pakistan government's consent. Suddenly, all leaders, past and present, both military and civil, denied any knowledge. Suspicions? Yes—but knowledge? No! Or they blamed each other for having allowed this to happen. The ubiquitous ISI and the army that had tried to keep track of Khan during Aslam Beg, Asif Nawaz, Abdul Waheed, and Jehangir Karamat's tenures as COAS could not explain how the scientist could not only have made the deals but also shipped documents and materials on Pakistani aircraft to distant sites. The head of security at the KRL at Kahuta was a retired brigadier. But he too seemed to have not seen anything untoward. One reason for this may have been that Khan knew how to grease palms. The other was more realistic: he found ways through his network of providing Pakistan with weapons systems that it could not acquire openly. Hence, the army benefited from that access to military technology. Khan had reportedly built a public relations network and empire within Pakistan with paid informers and journalists who built up his name and defamed others, as needed. His story had attained folkloric status. Even tough military generals like Mahmud Ahmed of the ISI thought he was a national icon and an Islamic patriot.[118]

Musharraf went on air and announced that he had pardoned Dr A.Q. Khan because he was a national hero but placed him under protective custody. He refused to allow the IAEA or the United States to talk to Khan even after the Iranian authorities, under their own pressure from the IAEA inspectors, divulged that the traces of enriched uranium that the IAEA found in their equipment may have been from parts that came from Pakistan. Suddenly memories and talk of General Aslam Beg's references to Iranian offers to buy the bomb from Pakistan came to the fore. Beg, of course, denied any such thing. But the evidence was coming too close to the army. For it seemed likely that either the army was complicit in Khan's activities or it had been derelict in its security and surveillance duties and allowed such a large hijacking of national secrets and resources to take place for personal gain of one or more individuals right under its nose. Musharraf, like his predecessors, was loath to let the stain creep on to the army. After all, he had once proclaimed at the 25th anniversary celebrations of the KRL that Khan was a 'giant of a man...the man who would give Pakistan a nuclear capability single-handedly.' And referring to Khan and his cohort, he called them 'Mujahids [Holy Warriors]' who 'have put Pakistan in the exclusive nuclear club. They have made Islamic nations proud.'[119] This may explain his action on Khan. And this was the stuff that gave strength to Pakistan's critics for making an 'Islamic Bomb'.

Not surprisingly, the United States let the matter lie for the moment, knowing that it needed Musharraf more than it needed Khan at that time. After all the 'War on Terror' was in full swing and Musharraf was a keen ally. Lucky Musharraf had dodged another bullet! Then in 2005, former Dutch Prime Minister Ruud Lubbers disclosed in a newspaper account that:

> The CIA asked the Netherlands not to detain Pakistani scientist Dr Abdul Qadeer Khan for stealing nuclear secrets from a Dutch facility...Speaking on Dutch radio programme Argos..., Lubbers said the Dutch authorities held off from taking action against Khan in 1975 and 1986 because the US security agency wanted to gain more information about the scientist's activities....He told the radio station that when [he was] Minister of Economic Affairs in 1975 he discussed the Khan case with US officials. The Americans, Lubbers said, suggested blocking Khan's access to Urenco [the firm where Khan worked] would be sufficient. As Prime Minister in the mid 1980s Lubbers again raised the issue as the CIA had been monitoring Khan for 10 years, without any obvious breakthrough in the investigation. Again the Americans did not want action taken against Khan, Lubbers said.[120]

The BBC reported that 'According to Mr Lubbers, US intelligence wanted to find out more about Mr Khan's contacts while he was working as an engineer at the top secret Dutch uranium enrichment plant at Almelo.'[121]

This hands-off approach was confirmed by the Dossier[122] prepared and released in the United States on 8 May 2007 by the IISS of London. Its principal author, Mark Fitzpatrick, confirmed that 'No doubt the CIA was aware of Khan's activity', hazarding the guess that they did not wish to jeopardize their investigation of their whole network by exposing their knowledge at an early stage.'[123] Another cause could have been the US's need to maintain ties with Pakistan, then a frontline ally in the war against the Soviets in Afghanistan. In 2005, the US was in another war in Afghanistan, and Pakistan, this time under Musharraf, was an ally yet again. Checkmate. The CIA Director, George Tenet, also explains in his memoir that 'there is a tension when investigating these kinds of networks. The natural instinct when you find some shred of intelligence about nuclear proliferation is to act immediately. But you must control that urge and be patient, to follow the links where they take you, so that when action is launched, you can hope to remove the network both root and branch, and not just pull off the top, allowing it to regenerate and grow again.'[124] The US's inaction had allowed the Khan network to flourish for another ten years before the Libyans pulled the curtain aside to reveal its existence to the world.

THE ENDGAME?

As he entered his eighth year at the helm of affairs in Pakistan, Musharraf exuded confidence. His relations were still apparently good with President Bush. He had made himself a name on the regional stage and in the Islamic world, espousing his 'enlightened moderation' approach even as he supped with Islamic dynastic rulers and ultra-conservatives, who brooked no domestic opposition. He had allowed the operation of a relatively free media though, like Ayub Khan before him, he had found a new weapon to control the emerging broadcast and computer-based media with a new version of Ayub's Press and Publications Ordinance. His PEMRA (Pakistan Electronic Media Regulatory Agency) was very effectively using its power to grant licenses for broadcasting operations to shut off any dangerously negative views. No criticism of the army was brooked. The short-term nature of the broadcasting licenses allowed the government to use PEMRA to keep everyone in check with just a telephone call.[125] There were no incriminating written directives or press briefings to contend with, as Ayub had found to his discomfiture. In some cases, as in the government's attempts to control the Dawn Group of newspapers, official advertising, which forms the bulk of print advertising and which is supposed to be doled out to media on the basis of audited circulation reports, was stopped from appearing in some papers. This deprived them of a large portion of their advertising revenue.

Musharraf had correctly diagnosed the military–civil relationship in Pakistan in his autobiography when he cautioned against military rule:

> First, whenever the army gets involved with martial law, it gets distracted from its vital military duties. Military training and operational readiness suffer. Second, when we superimpose martial law and place the military over the civilian government, the latter ceases functioning (sic). When martial law is later lifted, the civilian functionaries remain ineffective. Their growth is stunted. Last, I learned that whatever the law, civil or military, the poor are always the victims of oppression.[126]

But he seemed to forget his own analysis when confronted with challenges to his rule and to the super imposition of the military on civilian administration. This conflict between his intentions and actions confounded his allies and opponents alike and it thrust the army deeper into discussing political matters and pre-empting the decision making authority of the civilian cabinet that Musharraf had set up. Often, meetings of corps commanders preceded cabinet meetings and the latter only rubber-stamped the decisions that had been discussed and approved by the corps commanders under Musharraf's guidance and control.

Increasingly, Musharraf, who liked to cast himself as aloof from and allergic to politics, seemed to be caught up in the machinations of his political party supporters, as they orchestrated huge rallies and used official resources and connections to produce large gatherings wherever he appeared. Too often, Musharraf donned the civilian garb of run-of-the mill politicians, sporting the ridiculous headgears or other accoutrements associated with politicos on the campaign trail. For indeed there was a campaign in the offing. 2007 was the year of decisions: would he retain his uniform or doff it by the year's end, as stipulated by the 17th Amendment. Increasingly, he thought he was getting the best intelligence from his trusted sources but his advisors were trying more and more to second-guess him. He had no deputy to rely on, since he believed in unity of command, military style. No two swords in one scabbard for him. In the political sphere, he could have allowed his technocratic Prime Minister to emerge from under his shadow and into his own right as a politician and allowed him to form his own group of urban and urbane politicians. But he did not. In the army, he kept the Vice Chief, and others, all very competent military officers, on a tight leash. Musharraf had learned the lesson of Zia and not allowed too much distance between himself and the GHQ.

But, Musharraf could not fight time. As he grew older and remained COAS, his immediate military colleagues became much younger than and distant from him. Gradually, as he allowed or forced his original military cohort to depart, he had to promote new, much younger generals in their place. By April 2007, he was promoting lieutenant generals from among those who had been commissioned from the Pakistan Military Academy in 1972, eight years after he had graduated himself and roughly twenty courses his junior. In the army, a gap of two courses is an unbridgeable chasm. The one-legged stool of the general-cum-president becomes weaker when it has to rely on a cohort that is in a different intellectual and age group altogether. While he did his best to promote only those whom he knew or thought he knew, it was impossible for him to be on the same page as all his generals. Army discipline being what it is, his conferences at GHQ could not be anything but monologues, with generals nodding their agreement with the chief and no one stepping out of line. This is the malaise of military leaders everywhere, not just in Pakistan. As a contemporary critique of the US military indicated:

> The system that produces our generals does little to reward creativity and moral courage. Officers rise to flag rank by following remarkably similar career patterns. Senior generals, both active and retired, are the most important figures in determining an officer's potential for flag rank. The views of subordinates and peers play no role in an officer's advancement; to move up he must only please his superiors.[127]

By trying to select pliable clones, a leader who brooks no dissent renders himself vulnerable to the unexpected event or to individuals who cloak their inner selves. Bhutto discovered this with Ziaul Haq. As 2007 progressed the question that remained for Musharraf was whether he would surmount the bounds of history and reinvent himself to be able to remain in power and to transform Pakistan into a progressive and modern country under a new 'French-style' presidential system that he favoured, or see his plans run aground:

> I feel that even if we adopt a presidential system, we will still have to modify it to suit our environment, to have checks…. So I think it cannot be a total adoption of the American presidential system. One should look at the French presidential system. Over there, there is a sharing of powers between the president and the prime minister. One could even then see if there is power sharing, whether we call it the presidential system or we call it the parliamentary system and give some authority to the president. So maybe…this needs to be discussed with legal experts. But as far as presidential system *versus* parliamentary system is concerned, both can be non-functional, both can be functional. You have to have checks and balances in each to make them functional.[128]

Would he turn to the centre once again, and ally himself with the very parties whose leaders he had hounded out of Pakistan? Or, would he stay the course and be surprised by events beyond his control, shed aside by a fickle ally such as the United States, and undermined by the very forces of Islamism that he helped foster for so long in the name of political expediency? Finally, there was always the unexpected event—or one that spiralled out of control—such as the summary removal and reference against the sitting Chief Justice Iftikhar Muhammad Chaudhry that grew into a national movement and provided a magnet for all kinds of opposition to Musharraf's regime.

Another event that threatened the government's writ was the taking over of the Jamia Masjid also known as the Lal Masjid or Red Mosque in Islamabad by members of a radical Islamist group. The *burqa*-clad women and their male colleagues, who established control over the Lal Masjid and the associated women's seminary Jamia Hafsa, could not be evicted from the centre of the capital despite the government's protracted negotiations. The negotiations were headed by the PML (Q) leader Chaudhry Shujaat Hussain and ironically by the Minister for Religious Affairs, Ijazul Haq, whose father, General Ziaul Haq had supported the religious leaders of the Lal Masjid with moral and material support. The wags in Islamabad said that the government was scared of the 'men in black' (lawyers wearing their black jackets) and the 'women in black' (the black *burqa*-clad women who took over the mosque.) This confrontation was eventually to end in bloodshed as the army had to go in with force, killing one of the clerics and numerous fighters inside the mosque complex who had clearly been brought in from other jihadi groups to defend it against any attack. This episode exposed the continuing nexus between elements inside the army and its intelligence services with the religious extremists whom they saw as potential allies against India in Kashmir and in the future in Afghanistan. These extremists responded with sporadic violence throughout the country but there was no widespread street unrest. This final action against the extremists gave Musharraf an opportunity to marshal the forces of moderation in the country that demanded an end to condoning of radical extremism among the clerics. But he was caught up in the maze of politics and could not match his actions to his words.

Musharraf had the tendency to take upon himself the brunt of criticism rather than let the prime minister handle it at the level of government and thus build up the parliamentary system of the country. He felt he could surmount all obstacles with grit. Like Ayub, Yahya, and Ziaul Haq, Musharraf found himself increasingly isolated from trusted friends or allies who could give him contrary views without fearing for their jobs. Like them, he felt he had all the knowledge and the information needed to make good decisions on all topics. But the laws of autocratic rules deemed that not to be so. Over time, he did not have the kind of control that he thought he had, nor the information that might allow him to alter course radically.

This was reflected in his dismissal of the Chief Justice of the Supreme Court, Iftikhar Muhammad Chaudhry, in March, on the advice of the prime minister and with information allegedly provided by his intelligence services. The charges against the chief justice were patently minor and of little consequence. The Men in Black—(the lawyers)—turned out in force all over the country in killing heat and pouring rain to protest Musharraf's decision. Ordinary citizens supported them en masse. Slogans of 'Go, Musharraf, Go!' rang out. One young boy was heard yelling 'Go, Musharraf *Chaetii* Go!' using the Punjabi word for 'quickly'. There seemed to be no support for Musharraf's actions from anyone other than the army, whose corps commanders were induced to issue a statement that they supported the government. Eventually a Supreme Court bench of 13 judges headed by Justice Khalilur Rehman Ramday overturned Musharraf's decision with a 10 to 3 majority, reinstating the chief justice, and forcing the government to accept defeat in the name of an independent judiciary.

This historic decision was to reverberate into the latter part of 2007 with major after-shocks, as he launched his own 'second coup' on 3 November 2007 as the COAS, to remove the Supreme Court and set aside the constitution. He then muzzled the broadcast news media and imprisoned large numbers of supporters of the PPP and other parties that opposed him. (Interestingly the Islamic parties sat out the political struggle, biding their time.)

Musharraf himself remained super-confident and focused on what he saw as his role in Pakistan's history: to restore democracy, with whatever military force he could muster. The inherent paradox of his approach escaped him and he saw a continuing role for himself at the helm.

A candid Musharraf, ever the optimist, had earlier ended his conversation with the author on a positive note, conveying his view of Pakistan's place in a changing world environment, filled with terrorism, uncertainty, and fickle allies:

> It's a challenge and an opportunity. If we can't handle ourselves well, then we are ditched. But if we can, then we have our significance.... I am...very much an optimist....We have our own power. We have...all the resources, we have all the capability. Earlier, we could not manage. [Now] if we can manage our resources and capability, we have tremendous potential.

That has been the hope and the prayer of Pakistan since its painful birth in 1947. But the 'we' that Musharraf used needed to include all Pakistanis—not just the army, acting on their behalf. To grow politically and flourish economically, the country did not need another systemic upheaval or military intervention.

But his 'second coup' of 3 November 2007 upset all those plans. Even though he announced fresh elections for January 2008, and both former prime ministers Benazir Bhutto and Nawaz Sharif returned home to tumultuous welcomes, the downward slide of yet another autocratic regime in Pakistan had begun by the end of November 2007, as internal and external forces gathered momentum to force Musharraf to shed his uniform and eventually to quit the scene. A new and compliant Supreme Court exhumed the Doctrine of Necessity to validate yet again Musharraf's extra-constitutional actions. Musharraf bowed to internal and external pressure and finally doffed his uniform on 28 November in an emotional ceremony, installing General Ashfaq Parvez Kayani[129] as the 14th COAS and prepared to take the oath of office as the president the next day as a civilian. But public unrest simmered and eventually grew, as did foreign opprobrium. Paradoxically, the domestic and external attention focussed yet again on the Pakistan Army to resolve the many wars within and thus to help the country return to the path of democracy that Musharraf had once promised.

NOTES

1. A title coined for him by columnist Nasim Zehra.
2. This was the description of Musharraf by the *Newsweek* editor and commentator Fareed Zakariya.
3. Interview with Prime Minister Nawaz Sharif. Sharif came from a middle class background with strong conservative values. Yet, he liked the good life himself and even countenanced the use of surreptitious information gathering on his opponents and the use of smears, blackmail, and even physical violence by the IB, against noted journalists Maleeha Lodhi and Najam Sethi. However, he drew the line on one occasion. DG ISI Lt. Gen. Javed Nasir recounted an incident when he took some hidden camera photos of opposition leader Benazir Bhutto to show to Sharif. He refused to see them, asking Nasir: 'Do you have sisters?' When Nasir acknowledged that he did, Sharif replied: 'Then you wouldn't want such photos of your sisters to be shown around.' Nasir says he destroyed the offending photos.
4. After General Ziaul Haq's eleven years as COAS and President of Pakistan. Earlier, Ayub Khan had shed his rank of C-in-C of the Pakistan Army after taking over as President and CMLA in 1958, though many regarded his period as military rule, since he promoted himself to Field Marshal, a rank that does not retire.
5. Pakistan ranked with countries like Fiji, Bangladesh, Thailand, Myanmar (Burma), and Libya in 2007. Even quasi military rulers, like Hosni Mubarak of Egypt, were few and far between. This was a huge shift from the 1960s and 1970s, when 'Brazilianization' (a term coined by Fred Halliday of the London School of Economics for military rule) of countries was so much the norm in the developing world, with close to fifty countries under military control.
6. Confirmed by General Karamat to author in e-mail exchange.
7. *TIME* magazine, 31 July 1989. Cover story.
8. Pervez Musharraf, *In the Line of Fire* (New York: Free Press, 2006), pp. 68–69.
9. Interview with Major General Irshadullah Tarar, former Force Commander Northern Area, 1990.
10. Both B. Raman, an Indian analyst, and Selig Harrison, a US analyst, have picked up and recirculated this erroneous information. See, for example, http://www.saag.org/papers/paper66.html (accessed 17 November 2007). More recently a new book *Deception: Pakistan, the United States, the Secret Trade in Nuclear Weapons* by Adrian Levy and Catherine Scott-Clark (Walker and Company, New York, 2007) also carries this story.
11. Brigadier Anwari was under posting as DMO at GHQ at that time and I had an interview set up with him during my visit to GHQ that summer of 1990, when we heard that he had been killed in a helicopter crash at the Kashmir border.
12. Tarar interview.
13. Ibid.
14. Major General Tarar attended that meeting for his corps commander Lt. Gen. Tariq.
15. Rashomon refers to the award-winning 1950 film by the Japanese director Akira Kurosawa in which a woman is raped and her husband is killed. The film depicts the story from four different viewpoints of participants in that crime. The name has entered scientific research into the effect of perception of memory and how different individuals experiencing the same event can produce equally plausible but different stories about what they saw. See for example Karl Heider, 'The Rashomon Effect: when Ethnographers Disagree,' *American Anthropologist*, March 1988. Vol. 90, No. 1, pp. 73–81.
16. Interview with Prime Minister Benazir Bhutto.
17. Ibid.
18. Musharraf interview.

19. Interview with Lt. Gen. Javed Hasan. He is an extremely articulate officer, who later on headed the NDC and then, after leaving the army, the Pakistan Administrative Staff College in Lahore.

20. This and much of the following information is gleaned from separate interviews and conversations with Generals Musharraf, Ziauddin, Ahmed, Hasan, and others, who did not wish to be identified. The official viewpoint is given in President Musharraf's autobiography and in Shireen M. Mazari, *The Kargil Conflict 1999: Separating Fact from Fiction* (Islamabad: Institute of Strategic Studies, 2003). Her account is based on officially supplied briefings and presentations from the Pakistan Army and presents the official view that in Kargil Pakistan was simply reacting, though pre-emptively, to India's aggressive intentions along the LOC.

21. E-mail to author 27 May 2007.

22. Conversation with a member of JCS HQ staff, who wished to remain anonymous.

23. Ziauddin interview.

24. Tarar interview.

25. General V.P. Malik, *Kargil: From Surprise to Victory* (India: HarperCollins, 2006), p. 78, and *From Surprise to Reckoning: The Kargil Review Committee Report* (New Delhi: Sage, 1999), para 13.1.

26. Malik, *The Kargil Review Committee Report,* pp. 98–100.

27. Malik, *Kargil: From Surprise,* pp. 105–11.

28. Ibid., Appendix 2, pp. 407–14.

29. Text of the Lahore Declaration and the Joint Statement of Prime Ministers A. B. Vajpayee of India and M. Nawaz Sharif of Pakistan. 21 February 1999. Malik, ibid., Appendix 1, pp. 401–06.

30. Musharraf, *In the Line,* p. 96.

31. Interview with Sartaj Aziz. This section relies on his recollections.

32. Mazari, *The Kargil Conflict,* p. 57.

33. Secret Minutes and Decisions of the 61st Corps Commanders Conference held at GHQ, Rawalpindi on 10 and 11 March 1999, dated 27 March 1999. Pakistan Army GHQ Archives.

34. Ziauddin interview.

35. Ibid.

36. Interview with Sartaj Aziz, Foreign Minister of Pakistan.

37. A US-based group headed by M. Farooq Kathwari, an émigré Kashmiri who studied in Rawalpindi, Pakistan, and then moved to the United States to become Chairman of Ethan Allen, a major furniture and home furnishings company. The KSG includes many leading US academics and former diplomats.

38. Sartaj Aziz interview.

39. Musharraf interview.

40. Ibid.

41. Bruce Riedel, 'American Diplomacy and the 1999 Kargil Summit at Blair House.' Policy paper series for the Center for Advanced Study of India at the University of Pennsylvania, 2002.

42. Riedel interview.

43. Sharif, *Ghadaar Kaun?* pp. 142–153. Sharif gives a verbatim recollection of his conversation with Clinton, emphasizing that he sometimes called Clinton 'Bill' and sometimes 'Mr President' who in return called him 'Nawaz' or 'Mr Prime Minister.' His account does not convey any of the panic that Riedel's account from the White House side indicates was his state of mind at that time.

44. Tom Clancy with General Tony Zinni (retd) and Tony Kolz, *Battle Ready* (New York: G.P. Putnam's Sons, 2004), p. 347.

45. Interview with General Anthony Zinni.

46. Ibid.
47. Ibid.
48. Riedel interview.
49. Ibid.
50. Riedel, 'American Diplomacy,' p. 11.
51. Ibid., p. 13.
52. Government of Pakistan website, http://www.pak.gov.pk cited in http://www.acronym.org. uk/dd/dd39/39kash.htm accessed on 28 April 2007.
53. Written comments from senior Pakistan Army officer.
54. K. Ratnayake and P. Symonds, 'US concerns over political stability in Pakistan.' 24 September 1999. http://www.wsws.org/articles/1999/sep1999/pak-s24.shtml accessed on 27 April 2007
55. *Dawn* news wire service, 23 September 1999. http://www.lib.virginia.edu/area-studies/SouthAsia/SAserials/Dawn/1999/25sep99.html#coas accessed on 27 April 2007
56. Musharraf interview.
57. Ibid. This whole segment is based on this interview.
58. Ibid.
59. Ibid.
60. Ziauddin interview.
61. Interview with Lt. Gen. Mahmud Ahmed.
62. Ibid.
63. Public Broadcasting Service's News Hour with Jim Lehrer, 12 October 1999.
64. 2ww.fas.org./news/Pakistan/1999/991017_mushraf_speech.htm. Accessed on 27 April 2007.
65. Although in an interview with the author, Aziz maintains that he had never met Musharraf before he was contacted to come and become the Finance Minister.
66. Army officers had sought this information surreptitiously from senior officials of the finance cadre.
67. Mahmud Ahmed interview.
68. 'Musharraf declares family assets'. *Dawn*, 3 November 1999. Based on a press release from the ISPR Directorate.
69. Human Rights Commission of Pakistan. http://www.hrcpelectoralwatch.org/referendum. cfm accessed on 27 April 2007.
70. Musharraf, *In the Line*, p. 166.
71. Ibid., p. 167.
72. Nasir Iqbal, '1,027 civilian posts occupied by servicemen,' *Dawn,* 3 October 2003.
73. Information in the preceding paragraph based on exchanges with a former corps commander who was present at these GHQ meetings. He wished to remain anonymous.
74. Ziauddin interview.
75. Ibid.
76. Kathy Gannon, *I is for Infidel* (New York: Public Affairs, 2005), p. 42.
77. Ambassador Arif Ayub.
78. Ambassador Ayub e-mail.
79. Ziauddin interview.
80. Gannon, *I is for Infidel*, p. 87.
81. Ziauddin interview.
82. Steve Coll, *Ghost Wars* (The Penguin Press), p. 479.
83. Interview with Thomas R. Pickering.
84. Interview with Prince Turki Al Faisal.
85. Ibid.
86. Coll, *Ghost Wars*, p. 414.
87. Bill Clinton, *My Life* (New York: Alfred B. Knopf, 2004), p. 903.

88. Mahmud Ahmed interview.
89. Interview with another participant at the meeting of Ahmed and Armitage on 12 September 2001.
90. Conversation with another participant at that meeting.
91. Musharraf, *In the Line*, p. 201.
92. Interview with Richard Armitage.
93. Conversation with a former corps commander.
94. Musharraf, *In the Line*, p. 201.
95. Thomas H. Kean, Chair and Lee H. Hamilton, Vice Chair, *The 9/11 Report: The National Commission on Terrorist Attacks Upon the United States* (New York: St. Martin's Press, 2004) pp. 473–74.
96. Musharraf, *In the Line*, p. 206.
97. Conversations with Pakistani officials and former intelligence personnel.
98. Kean and Hamilton, *The 9/11 Report*, p. 474.
99. Exchange with Karamat.
100. Mahmud Ahmed interview.
101. Ibid.
102. Interview with Paul R. Pillar.
103. Interview with Pickering.
104. Private conversations with Special Forces and Navy Seals who operated in Afghanistan and then Iraq.
105. Interview with a former colleague of Musharraf.
106. http://www.na.gov.pk/ministry.htm accessed 30 April 2007
107. http://devdata.worldbank.org/external/CPProfile.asp?PTYPE=CP&CCODE=PAK accessed 30 April 2007.
108. K. Alan Kronstadt, *Pakistan-U.S. Relations*, Updated 9 May 2006, Foreign Affairs, Defense, and Trade Division, Congressional Research Service. The Library of Congress.
109. Dr Parvez Hasan, 'State and Pakistan Economy: Where have we come from? Where do we go? Pakistan Society of Development Economists. Paper Presented at the 22nd Annual General Meeting and Conference, Lahore, 19–21 December 2006.
110. Steve Coll, 'The Stand off,' *The New Yorker*, 13 February 2006.
111. Craig Baxter, ed., *Diaries of Field Marshal Mohammad Ayub Khan 1966–1972* (Karachi: Oxford University Press, 2007). Entry for Sunday 15 January 1967, p. 49.
112. Interviews with former DGs of the ISI.
113. This information comes from Khan A. Shoaib of the PAEC in a written communication to the author.
114. 'New Players on the Scene: A.Q. Khan and the Nuclear Black Market' by Colonel Charles D. Lutes, e-journal. http://usinfo.state.gov/journals/itps/0305/ijpe/lutes.htm accessed on 30 April 2007.
115. *Nuclear Black Markets: Pakistan, A.Q. Khan and the Rise of Proliferation Networks —A Net Assessment*, IISS, London, May 2007. This section is based on this report.
116. Khan A. Shoaib (ex of PAEC) to author.
117. *Deception: Pakistan, the United States, and the Secret Trade in Nuclear Weapons*, Adrian Levy and Catherine Scott-Clark, Center for Strategic and International Studies, Washington DC. Sept 2007, pp. 356, 378.
118. Mahmud Ahmed interview.
119. '25 years of Excellence and National Services', brochure produced by KRL Laboratories. 31 July 2001.
120. 'CIA asked us to let nuclear spy go, Ruud Lubbers claims', ANP, 9 August 2005. http://www.globalsecurity.org/org/news/2005/050809-khan-cia.htm accessed 8 May 2007.
121. 'CIA let Atomic expert go' BBC News, 9 August 2005. http://news.bbc.co.uk/2/hi/europe/4135998.stm accessed 8 May 2007.

122. *Nuclear Black Markets: Pakistan, A.Q. Khan and the Rise of Proliferation Networks—A Net Assessment*, IISS, London 2007.
123. Author's exchange with Mark Fitzpatrick after launch of IISS Dossier, op. cit., in Washington DC, 8 May 2007.
124. George Tenet with Bill Harlow, *At the Center of the Storm* (New York: HarperCollins, 2007), pp. 282–83.
125. This was confirmed by army officials who were aware of cases where they did not want certain programmes to air and asked PEMRA to make the call.
126. Musharraf, *In the Line of Fire*. p. 65.
127. Lt. Col. Paul Yingling, 'A failure of generalship,' *Armed Forces Journal*, May 2007. http://www.armedforcesjournal.com/2007/05/2635198 accessed 30 April 2007.
128. Musharraf interview. Musharraf's legal advisor, Sharifuddin Pirzada asked for and received a copy of the French constitution from a US business contact.
129. Kayani, commissioned in 1971 from the PMA, Kakul in its 45th regular course, was very junior to Musharraf (who was commissioned in 1964), reflecting the gap between Musharraf and his senior officers. Kayani was seen as a temperate influence on Musharraf even when he was DG ISI and had a more worldly view than many of his colleagues, having been trained in the United States.

18 | TODAY AND TOMORROW

Over the years, the Pakistan Army has been regarded, with some merit, as a highly disciplined and trained force, relying on volunteer recruitment. The Pakistani population traditionally has shown great respect, even adoration, for its soldiers and officers. Many youth voluntarily sign up for service in the army as officers or soldiers following family or tribal traditions, or, recently, as a means of upward social and economic mobility. Its soldiers and junior officers have time and again shown their abilities on the battlefield. The leadership of the army has, however, let the forces and the country down repeatedly. Gradually, instead of respect, feelings of fear and loathing have pervaded the political discourse on the army and its role in the country's polity. Are these well-founded? In 1965, in the middle of a war against India, songs about '*Ae watan ke sajeele jawaano; meray naghme tumhare liye hain*' (O' splendid soldiers of the homeland, my songs are for you!) were in vogue.

In the late 1980s, as dictator fatigue set in during the Zia period, many army officers refrained from going out into the public in their uniforms. In the 1990s, resentment of the military took on an economic garb, as the army was seen encroaching into the commercial life of cities and even farms, provoking a pun on the name of a well-known corps commander, linking him to shady land deals in Lahore cantonment. In 2007, the country saw the jarring banners carried by lawyers who were protesting the removal of a chief justice by the military ruler of Pakistan: '*Ae watan ke sajeele Genrailo; saaray ruqbey tumhare liye hain!*' (O' handsome generals of the homeland, all the plots are just for you!). This negative perception and reference to the most visible and talked about aspects of military rule and operations: foremost of which is the creation of residential Defence Housing Societies throughout the country for military officers, which yield huge windfall profits when individual officers sell their plots—reflects one of the many challenges to the army today. The army is perceived to be in charge…everywhere.

In the words of a popular local Punjabi poet, Ustad Daman, soon after Pakistan's first national martial law in 1958:

> *Aj Pakistan diyaan Maujaanh hee Maujaahn*
> *Jithay vekho, Faujaahn hee Faujaahn*
>
> *Now each day is fair and balmy,*
> *Everywhere you look, the army!*[1]

A NEW BATTLEGROUND

An army ill-equipped and untrained for low-intensity conflict suffered heavily at the hands of well-trained guerrillas that melt into the population. And increasingly, its association with the American superpower that is driving the war against the Taliban in Afghanistan pitted the army against its own tribes, and by 2007 with Islamic militants inside the settled parts of the NWFP in Swat. The United States began putting pressure on Pakistan to do more to plug the gaps in the porous and rugged 1,350 mile border with Afghanistan, something that the US and NATO forces had failed to do from their side of the divide. The army had to move front and centre in the fight against terrorism on the border and inside the country, a role for which it was not properly trained nor equipped.

Successive government in Pakistan allowed the unruly situation in FATA to develop over its sixty years of existence by retaining the anachronistic system of autonomous tribal government for the tribal areas rather than amalgamating them into the rest of the country and developing the region economically and politically. The legacy of General Ziaul Haq's Islamization that fed the rise of the mullahs as a counterpoint to the tribal leadership has further created a dissonance in the society of the FATA, giving the mullahs the upper hand. Pakistan found itself taking on a policing function on behalf of the United States along the long and rugged Afghan border. Its forces were not trained for counter insurgency warfare nor equipped with the modern protective gear or technology that would allow them to operate at night or with rapid mobility. The US failed to set benchmarks for progress in this new battleground, relying instead on a system of reimbursement for payments to Pakistan for its efforts in FATA. It was only some six years after the events of 9/11 that the US and Pakistan began discussing economic and social development schemes. The US produced a plan for $750 million to be spent on developing FATA but by the end of 2007 it was still waiting for approval in the US Congress.

There was also a lack of trust on both sides as Pakistan expected the US to decamp from Afghanistan as it had done in the past, leaving Pakistan to deal with a hostile tribal force on both sides of the border with Afghanistan. Pakistan also was wary of the government in Kabul that the US had propped up after evicting the Taliban since it considered the Kabul government of Hamid Karzai to be heavily biased in favour of the Northern Alliance and not representative of the Pashtuns who traditionally ruled Afghanistan. Some twenty million Pashtuns inhabited the borders regions straddling the Durand Line, with Pakistan having a slight edge in numbers over Afghanistan (see map of FATA). Understandably, Pakistan exhibited a schizoid approach toward the Afghan rebels, doing just enough to keep things under control on its side of the border. But this was not to last, as the Pashtun militants came under the influence of the Taliban from across the border and gradually expanded their network inside FATA. The terror network struck back not just in FATA but also against the army inside Pakistan proper, with a new weapon:

suicide bombers. The front line Frontier Constabulary and Frontier Corps, staffed by tribesmen from FATA, suffered major losses and often surrendered rather than fight their fellow tribals. The militants then spread into the settled areas, strengthening the simmering insurgency in Swat and sent its suicide bombers into the cities of Pakistan. Among its major target was President General Pervez Musharraf himself.

Pakistan, with or without Musharraf, faced a long war against terror and militant Islam within Pakistan, a war for which it did not seem to be ready. And its military leaders struggled to understand their country's polity and its future needs.

An insight into the minds of the senior officer cohort that was well represented in the leadership of the Musharraf regime when he took over in 1999 is available in internal studies done at the NDC in the late 1980s:

> Pakistan's political history has been considered as being unmistakenly (sic) stamped with rank authoritarianism. Throughout the political history of Pakistan, our policy has remained unchanged in terms of families, organisations and interests. Political figures have changed but the interests, origins and behaviours have been the same and personal. Class interests have always taken precedence over the national interests....To remedy all these we have to ensure that the present democratic system [Benazir Bhutto's rule] must be allowed to function without interruption. The nation must achieve their political objectives through this process of democracy otherwise our problems will further compound (sic) by increased dissension, fragmentation among provinces, political agitations, violence, emergence of centrifugal forces and secessionist tendencies, lack of economic progress and decline and erosion of the national WILL.[2]

But this introspection is not confined to the civil system alone. Rather it is also aimed squarely at the lack of military leadership which is described in another senior officer's paper as 'inept and weak....We have no vision and perspective of the future and thus live on a day-to-day basis.' (The roots of this poor leadership can be traced back to Ayub Khan's role in institutionalizing the appointment of sycophantic and sometimes incompetent officers to the highest ranks who would not buck the trend or question any of his actions.) Describing the need to examine the impact of the national environment on the military's leadership, this senior officer goes on to decry the lack of adherence to the Islamic ideology that led to the creation of Pakistan, a materialistic attitude among society in general, rampant corruption, and a passivity among the general populace that is furthered by authoritarianism. He does not hold back on criticism of the military leadership either, citing the lack of creativity because of the bondage of standard operating procedures, sycophancy, conformity and careerism. The latter is held responsible for three major weaknesses of the military leadership:

- Centralization of command: which is alien to manoeuvre warfare and curbs initiative
- Lack of delegation of authority: similar to centralization, and
- Zero risk syndrome: which creates a risk averse culture.[3]

Interestingly, the much trumpeted hallmark of military rule and the presidential rule of General Musharraf was 'unity of command', which allowed him to exercise total control and run the government by fiat. As in the case of previous military rulers of Pakistan, he failed to recognize that this concept of leadership works well for the military but creates serious problems in running the much more complex network of civilian and political institutions that form a national polity.

AN ARMY UNDERGOING CHANGE

The conditions that led to the weaknesses of the military system described above are not just societal but also arise from the recruitment patterns of the Pakistan Army that define the nature of its officer class and other ranks (soldiers). Traditionally, the army was a predominantly Punjabi force. In British India, three districts: Campbellpur (now Attock), Rawalpindi, and Jhelum dominated the recruitment flows that helped India send some 2.5 million soldiers to fight in the Second World War on behalf of the British Empire. The NWFP gradually began supplying troops and officers, as settled areas Pushtun tribesmen joined the military. Sindhis and Baluchs largely stayed away from formal military recruitment because of their powerful local tribal systems that did not permit individuals to sign on with any force other than their own. Although some attempts were made to extend recruitment into the urban areas of Sindh and Balochistan and bore some fruit over time, in the first few decades of Pakistan's independence, the army remained largely a Punjabi–Pushtun enclave. Indeed the appellation PM (Punjabi Mussulmans) used by the British continued to be used till the 1990s, even though the profile of the army had changed somewhat. Throughout, the Pakistan Army has remained a volunteer force.

By 1990, the percentage representation in the Pakistan Army as a whole (officers and other ranks or soldiers), was as follows:

Punjabis	65 per cent
Pushtuns	14 per cent
Sindhis and Baluchis	15 per cent
Kashmiris	6 per cent
Minorities	0.3 per cent[4]

Since then, with the provision of waivers for both physical and educational qualifications, recruitment has been increased from the formerly less well-represented areas. Based on separate GHQ data for soldiers and officers, Punjab shows an overall decline in recruitment of soldiers from 63.86 per cent in 1991 to 43.33 in 2005, with Central Punjab outpacing Northern Punjab, the traditional recruitment ground, by 7,500 to 5,000 recruits in 2005. Southern Punjab had 1,800 recruits. Recruitment from the NWFP and FATA increased from 20.91 to 22.43 per cent, Sindh rose from 8.85 to 23.02 per cent—with rural Sindh accounting for the majority of the recruits (5,095 to 2,500 in 2005)—in Balochistan, it rose from 0.49 to 1.52 per cent in 2005 with 200 urban to 300 rural recruits in 2005, and in Azad Kashmir and the Northern Areas, recruitment rose from 5.86 to 9.70 per cent.[6]

Looking at the officers commissioned into service during the period 1970–89 in comparison with 1990–2006, we also see a change in the relative share of different parts of the country. The Punjab rose marginally from 66.46 to 66.93 per cent, but within the Punjab there are notable changes in the home districts of the officers, shifting to the more populous and emerging urban centres of Central and even Southern Punjab. This is in line with rapid urbanization trends nationwide. These bigger cities and towns are also the traditional strongholds of the growing Islamist parties and conservatism, associated with the petit bourgeoisie. The Zia period (reflected in the statistics for 1980–89) shows a sharp bulge in all cases, as the army became a visibly more lucrative and attractive profession for the urban youth and a means for upward social mobility.

Numbers of Officers Commissioned from Selected Districts of the Punjab and Sindh (by decade)

District	1970–79	1980–89	1996–2005
Attock	17	242	175
Chakwal	15	165	277
Faisalabad	41	403	233
Gujranwala	16	269	181
Jhelum	36	442	262
Jhang	2	138	56
Lahore	86	877	774
Multan	23	227	227
Rawalpindi	88	1338	1373
Sialkot	30	357	283
Hyderabad	4	82	63
Karachi	25	364	396
Larkana	0	10	36

Source: Pakistan Army GHQ, 2006.

The importance of the bulge in the Zia period is also underscored by the fact that the officers who joined in that decade are now poised to rise into the general officer category. In January 2006, for example, out of approximately 804 officers granted commission in the army during 1978 to 1979, 29 brigadiers, or roughly 3.6 per cent of the original intake, were recommended for promotion to the rank of major general by the Army's Selection Board presided by General Musharraf.[7] This is what is known in the army as the '*Zia Bharti*' or Zia's Recruits, a cohort that is generally more conservative than preceding promotees. When the current group of senior lieutenant generals retires, most of whom were commissioned in the late 1960s and early 1970s, the Zia Recruits will take over the running of the Pakistan Army. Apart from being inducted into the army during the middle of Zia's Islamist ethos and official fostering of religious ideology and dogma, this group suffered at the hands of the US and Western European embargo of aid to Pakistan. Not only was it deprived of advanced overseas training during its formative years, this officer cohort was denied exposure to the world outside till late in their careers, by which time their worldview had been formed and in many cases, become entrenched.

THINKING OF MILITARY OFFICERS

The current cohort of senior army leaders in Pakistan represents the last group of officers who were able to take advantage of overseas training in their early years and were exposed to wider external influences. The effects of such training and exposure are reflected in some of its thinking on national issues. Again, a glance at selected writings by officers who made it to the senior-most ranks of today's Pakistan Army reveals a relatively liberal slant but always with a strong nod to Islamic values. One especially interesting study produced at the NDC in the late 1980s was a contribution by an officer who became a four-star general in recent years. Assessing Pakistan's broader economic and social development needs, he presented a series of 'recommendations [that] are pragmatic and realistic.' These include reversing the 'policy over the years [in which education] has suffered due to low priority, inadequate financial allocations and absence of prudent and a realistic approach.' He recommended the increase of spending on education from 2.2. per cent of GNP (sic) to 5 per cent over the next decade, with increased emphasis on teacher training and female education at all levels. And, anticipating the moves of the current Musharraf government, he suggested '*madrassahs*' or religious schools be integrated into the education system, while making religious education compulsory so that it is 'based on the study of the Quran to understand its meanings in the correct perspective.'

Of particular interest in this wide-ranging survey of Pakistan's development needs is a frank assessment of the failure of government and politics and a degradation of societal mores. This future general identified many causes of political instability since independence. Among them, of note were:

- In post-partition Pakistan, no attention was paid to the development of peoples' institutions at grass roots levels, consequently it gave rise to an oligarchy stemming basically from land holding individuals, the businessmen and educated bureaucracy, who were not interested in any development other than their own. Unfortunately this oligarchy still forms the bulk of our political elite.
- The history of constitution making in Pakistan has been a turbulent one. Firstly, we delayed the formulation of the constitution, once formulated we displayed a lack of respect for it.
- Our failure to hold regular and fair elections has resulted in a political immaturity even after over forty years of our existence.
- Because of generally inept political leadership, particularly in our formative years, the Army gradually began to play a more active role in politics which culminated in military takeovers.
- Frequent military takeovers, periods of martial law and the resultant erosion of democratic values has been one of the main factors for our political fragility, and a tendency towards authoritarian rule influenced primarily by our colonial legacy and our cultural milieu has also been a causative factor for imposition and sustenance of military rule.[8]

While impressive in its analytical sweep, the paper from which these points were taken reflects not only the well-grounded training and development of the senior military echelon, but also an underlying disdain for the civilian and political infrastructure. Ironically, it could also serve as a critique of the current dispensation in Pakistan, where a military regime persisted in civilian garb and where the army had penetrated civilian society and government. The army trains officers not only to become better military officers but, as they rise in rank, also to discuss and tackle wider societal issues. This broader training is not very profound, more often than not it involves hit-and-run presentations by 'experts' and some limited reading materials that are available at the NDC and other training institutions. Only recently has the army started sending officers for advanced studies abroad in non-military subjects. Yet, in comparison with the very limited training and career development of the civil servants, the army feels confident that it has the wherewithal to handle any type of administration, even if outside its military orbit. (See attached Box on selection procedures and career development and training of army officers.) This self confidence is an important factor in assessing civil–military relations in Pakistan and understanding why the army dominates the landscape.

TRAINING IN THE ARMY

Having inherited a well-established system of training and career development from the British Indian Army, the Pakistan Army has continued to develop and fine tune its system of training of officers and soldiers. Special attention is paid to selecting and preparing officers for their duties over time. This system of training allows the army to prepare its officers and men for their professional duties and gives them an edge in terms of their exposure to ideas and thinking on broader national and international issues over their civilian counterparts.

A battery of education, intelligence, and medical tests, followed by interviews help select individuals first for evaluation by the Inter-Services Selection Board and then for training as officers at the PMA. Roughly 325 cadets out of more than 4,000 applicants make it to the PMA in Kakul. Another 200 or so are selected for the Junior Cadet Academy, to prepare them for eventual induction into the officer training programme of PMA that has two intakes every year and commissions them every six months after a training period of two years. Induction of specialists in the medical, engineering, communications (signals), remount, and veterinary branches, is in addition to the PMA intake.

Once in the army, officers undergo periodic training at one or more of some nine major training institutions that include the generally well known Staff College at Quetta and the National Defence College at Rawalpindi. The training path is determined in part by the specialization of the individual officers but almost all of them have to undergo basic training in tactics, followed by the Junior Staff Course after 4–6 years of service. As they enter mid-career stage (6–10 years), officers are prepared through additional training to command a company, followed by the Staff College, which is filled through a tough examination on a competitive basis. Leading candidates are selected after interviews to attend foreign Staff College courses to broaden their horizons and training opportunities. Those who fail to make it to Staff College are often directed toward Logistic or Intelligence courses during their 12–16th years of service. Staff college graduates are given choice appointments, often as brigade majors and then as COs of their regiments. After this they are prepared for higher command through the War Course or advanced logistics and management courses. Brigadiers attend the National Defence Course which is designed to inculcate strategic thinking and planning.

Some 150–200 officers are sent for training overseas, either on staff courses or for specialized training in their respective arms of service. Almost an equal number of foreign officers are trained at Pakistan Army institutions, allowing a cross fertilization of ideas and experience. A sizable number (more than 25) of officers are sent for post-graduate training abroad. About 60 officers, JCOs, and NCOs are provided post-graduate training opportunities inside Pakistan. Officers belonging to specialized branches such as engineering and medical services, are also sent for higher training abroad. In addition, individual officers are encouraged to undertake language instruction in key foreign languages inside Pakistan as well as abroad. Some 80 officers may be undergoing language training in Arabic, Chinese, French, German, Hindi, Persian, Turkish, Russian, or Japanese at any point.

To broaden the experience of officers, adventure training is also encouraged, involving gliding, sea diving, trekking, skiing, and hang gliding, among other pursuits. A limited number of officers are also allowed study leave to pursue their own educational interests either in Pakistan or abroad.

Very strict developmental planning is done for officers at each stage of their individual careers, and promotions are based on the basis of annual evaluations as well as review by special boards composed of senior officers. The military secretary's branch is responsible for career planning and preparing the selection boards. It also handles the selection of candidates for induction into the civilian sector against a quota for the armed forces.

The military budget that once was subjected to scrutiny by the civil through a well-established system of powerful financial advisors and the Ministry of Defence, started becoming a black box once the army attained a position of power, starting with Ayub Khan's elevation to minister of defence in 1954. Once martial law was introduced in 1958 and Ayub Khan took over as president, the relevance of civil scrutiny became obsolete, as far as the military was concerned. The military share of the budget has ranged from 30–40 per cent, but it is still kept as a one-line item that is not subjected to any detailed examination or debate in the National Assembly. The share of defence in the consolidated budget for FY 2005/06 was Rs 223.5 billion (although this may well be understated because huge portions of military-related expenses are hidden in other sectors[9]), compared with Rs 275 billion for social sector development expenditure and net lending as a whole out of a total budgetary expenditure of Rs 1282.9 billion. Expenditures on education account for no more than 1.6 per cent of GDP and on health for 0.5 per cent (compared with defence spending at 3.4 per cent, mentioned above).[10] Internally, the army has a well-developed system of budget formulation that builds up its requirements from the users at the formation level and then aggregated before being submitted to the government for approval. The major segments of expenditure are: equipment (including maintenance and repair), reserves of supplies and ammunition, salaries and provision of housing, rations, medical services, etc. Pensions were removed from the defence budget, following the lead of India and transferred to the civil side, but recently this move was reversed to get a better idea of total defence spending.

The Pakistan Army is also associated with a wide range of commercial activities that it uses to raise funds for its own internal use. The challenge for the army is to make them publicly transparent in terms of financial reporting, and to create distance between their operations and the military high command. For example, if they are to function in the competitive marketplace, then the routine appointment of senior army officers to head and operate these enterprises should be discontinued and the firms be subject to market forces. The Turkish experience with import substitution activities of military enterprises suggest that it might be better to divest such firms to the private sector. While the dictates of national security demand that Pakistan not become over-reliant on foreign suppliers (the memories of past embargoes and their looming threat cannot be ignored), it is critical not to overreach in terms of creating import substitution industries for military purposes and only to concentrate on key items, and thus to reduce the economic costs of such activities.

The army also needs to re-examine its wide and apparently expanding perks and benefits that provide a cradle-to-grave system of healthcare as well as long-term employment for its members, especially the senior officers. In a developing country which does not reward its civil servants well nor its educationists, a jarring reminder of the relative affluence of senior military officers is the series of army messes that dot the major cities of the country, and the ever expanding Defence Housing Societies that provide windfall profits to officers who can get plots of land allocated at heavily subsidized prices and then sell them at multiple times the market rate. The army also provided till recently regular 'batmen' or servants to all officers. Originally conceived in the British Indian Army as a valet for only the officer of the household, it became common practice for such soldiers (for they were indeed from the army and were trained as soldiers) to perform cooking, cleaning and other menial tasks around the officers' households. Some officers took advantage of their rank or affiliation with regiments or formations to get more than one batmen. A recent move by the army to provide such servants through an organized non-military provider is a small sign of progress but not as effective as giving an allowance that would allow officers to bear the administrative costs of hiring and using such help themselves.

The army also provides subsidized rations and consumer goods through the Central Stores Department or CSD, a form of PX (post exchange) in all cantonments, which allows military families to take advantage of bulk purchases and benefit from the relatively lower prices. This service is common to most military institutions worldwide. As a former army chief explained: 'Perks and privileges are given according to an institutionalised system approved by the government.' Army officers do not get many benefits in their 20 years of service. 'The service pyramid is very steep so successive benefits are given to a rapidly reducing number of people and only those who continue to progress in their career.' This benefits ladder has been defined by the army itself, over time, with officers now allowed access to subsidized housing plots at almost all their senior posting stations, where such valuable land is available for allocation at the discretion of the local army commanders and not the civilian government. Government has cut back on some perks. In 1997, it cancelled the right of service chiefs to import automobiles duty free and also stopped allocating them valuable housing plots in the capital, Islamabad.[11]

PENETRATION OF CIVIL SOCIETY

Other visible manifestations of military domination of the civil sector lie in the re-employment of retired or even serving officers in civil institutions and in the host of military-owned enterprises that provide longer term of employment for army officers. Today, military officers dominate education and training institutions in the civil sector. All the major civil service training establishments, for example, are now headed by army officers. They also head universities and state-owned corporations. While military rule or military-dominated rule has something to do with this, the role of the civilian rulers cannot be downplayed, for they have allowed the military free ingress into their domain over the years and indeed have elevated the military presence to the detriment of the civil sector.

The ISI is one of the world's better known and most effective counter-intelligence agencies, having secured Pakistan much valuable information on potentially hostile actions. It grew in stature and power in the aftermath of the Afghan war, when it became financially independent as a result of US cash flows. Since then, it has also tapped local business and banking sources, with the full knowledge and cooperation of at least one army chief, General Aslam Beg, who took money from the Mehran Bank for political purposes and passed it to the ISI. But the ISI's image has been gradually tarnished because of its domestic operations. It also has officers stationed in key embassies overseas, among other things, to keep tabs on the emigrant Pakistani community and visiting opposition politicians.[12]

A recent incident in Islamabad in which a retired, highly decorated brigadier and his family were reportedly abused and physically assaulted by staff of the ISI, acting on behalf of a senior ISI official whose children had gotten into an altercation with the brigadier's grandchildren, provides a good case study on how not to handle these matters. Newspaper reports such as the following by maverick commentator Ardeshir Cowasjee in *Dawn* led to much criticism of the army for allowing this kind of abuse of privilege and authority. Cowasjee quoted from the letter written by retired Brigadier Muhammad Taj, twice the winner of one of Pakistan's highest gallantry awards, the Sitara-e-Juraat, to President General Pervez Musharraf:

> Last night, an ISI major in plainclothes who called himself Tipu, with some 10 men also in plainclothes, armed with automatic weapons, entered my house and beat me, my daughter-in-law and my two grandsons.

A harrowing tale then followed of ISI high-handedness and the lack of respect for legal norms by its personnel. The brigadier's letter ends:

> I am 80 years old now and can only look to you, Sir, as the President of Pakistan and the Chief of the Pakistan Army that I also proudly served, to restore my dignity as an ex-army officer and protect my basic rights as a citizen of Pakistan, and to order immediate action against all officials involved in this criminal act.

The DG ISPR, Major General Shaukat Sultan expressed his regrets over the incident: calling it 'most unfortunate and extremely regrettable. This has been taken note of at the highest level. I assure you we are very concerned about the incident and action will be taken.'[13]

Much later, after a storm of criticism had emerged, the army's public relations spokesman released a statement that the president had called and apologized to the brigadier. There was no mention of any proceedings against the perpetrators or patrons of these illegal actions, nor any explanation of how and why military personnel were used to settle a private matter. The ISI officer involved in this incident, a major general, remained at the head of the ISI's political wing. Years of trying to build confidence in the army were nullified by this behaviour, relegating one more incident of army misconduct to the country's collective memory. The negative commentary on this incident from both civil and retired military officers was a sign that the army needs to change its approach to protecting its own, right or wrong. It is in the army's own interest and that of the country to eliminate such vigilantism by its uniformed staff and to shine the light on actions taken by the army to ensure that such actions would not be repeated.

Incidents such as the one quoted above as well as an autonomous handling of foreign relations have led to the growing sense that the ISI is a 'state within a state,' detracting from its mission of counter-intelligence. While bad behaviour such as the one exhibited in the incident mentioned here can occur in any institution at any level, the alleged autonomous nature of the ISI's operations have drawn much criticism at home and abroad. Former ISI head General Ehsanl ul Haq refused to acknowledge that the ISI was an independent actor. He maintained that the ISI does exactly what the government wants it to.[14] Indeed, given the regular posting and rotation of army officers from its ranks and the provision of a tight budget for its operations, it seems no longer likely to operate outside the government's direct control. This is a change from the days of the Afghan war when it had direct access to covert US and Saudi financing and therefore some financial independence from the army headquarters.

The ISI has also been accused of involvement in the case of numerous 'missing persons' who appear to have disappeared and the legal system has been unable to establish their whereabouts. In some cases, these persons may have been subject to summary rendition on behalf of the United States in its global war on terror. In other cases, domestic issues may be behind their disappearance. Even the secretary of the Ministry of Defence, a retired senior army officer, confirmed the 'lack of operational control over ISI, MI.' in response to the Sindh High Court's request for information about missing persons. In the case of a missing person, Munir Mengal, who headed a Dubai-based television channel called 'Voice of Baloch,' the 'Defence Secretary, retired Lt. Gen. Tariq Waseem Ghazi, confirmed in a sworn affidavit filed in the Sindh High Court on July 19 that his ministry had no operational control over the two rogue agencies and therefore was unable to enforce the court's order on either agency in matters relating to detentions. It could only pass on directions—that was all.'[15] Yet, when senior government officials were challenged to produce missing person or risk being jailed for contempt of court by the Supreme Court in late 2007, many such persons ended up being produced and then released.

It is an unequal contest between the ordinary citizen and organs of the state, especially the powerful Pakistan Army. This deteriorating relationship between the civil and the military is yet another challenge for the military leadership and its successor civilian government, if any.

DEFENDING THE HOMELAND

Pakistan's lack of national cohesion on the one hand and its location in a tough neighbourhood dictates that it should maintain a strong defence establishment. However, as assessments by the army itself have shown, there are different ways of achieving security without making the army so large and burdensome that it dwarfs and stifles economic development. There are sound military reasons for re-evaluating the nature, size, and organization of the army too. The army has conducted periodic reviews of its internal organization and structure. In 1962, it examined the rationale for maintaining a large standing force and decided on a slight reduction of about 10–15 per cent in its manning level by changing the service limits of the soldiers: with a service limit of four years and no pension and reserve liability of 7–15 years. In 1974, a new study brought about the concept of the 'cadrized unit' which maintained only a reduced but essential officer and soldier strength, while keeping arms and equipment for a full complement that could be activated from the reserves in times of need. This cut another 5–6 per cent of the combat strength but the reduction was short-lived and this new military system was dropped in due course. It was succeeded by another attempt to reduce manning levels to 75–90 per cent of combat strengths, but that too failed to gain any traction.

Today, Pakistan has a large conventional army, tasked by the nation's antiquated war directive with defending every inch of its borders: a hostile one on the east against India and a hot one in the west against Afghanistan, with a potential for unrest on the Iranian frontier, if the internal insurgency situation in that neighbour's Balochistan province becomes a cross border issue. Internally, the army needs to re-orient its training and force structure, not only for coping with external threats but also to combat internal insurgencies, starting with the current situation in FATA and the NWFP. It needs specialized units and training in low-intensity fourth generation warfare and indoctrination of both, officers and soldiers, in the principles of such warfare, where ideas not weapons alone matter. But underlying successful counter-insurgency warfare is the dictum:

> That the political power [not the army] is the undisputed boss…[as] a matter of principle and practicality. What is at stake is the country's political regime, and to defend it is a political affair. Even if this requires military action, the action is constantly directed toward a political goal. Essential though it is, the military action is secondary to the political one, its primary purpose being to afford political power enough freedom to work safely with the population.[16]

These words from David Galula, one of the pre-eminent experts on counter-insurgency warfare, are being heeded by other armies fighting similar battles. Galula, an expert commander from the Algerian war, also defines victory not as 'the destruction of the insurgent's forces in a given area' but 'that **plus** [emphasis added] the permanent isolation of the insurgent from the population, isolation not enforced upon the population but maintained by and with the population.' This is not the approach that Pakistan has taken to date in its border areas or even in Swat. But it can, and it does not need large conventional forces as much as a well-trained counter-insurgency force, working hand-in-hand with the political authorities. To make this work, the government will need to break out of its prevaricating behaviour vis-à-vis the Islamists and break all ties with their radical militia, even at the expense of finding another solution for the Kashmir issue.

CHANGING THE COMMAND SYSTEM

Despite the introduction of the Higher Defence Organization and the creation of the JCSC, composed of the chairman and the three service chiefs, command and control at the national level is unworkable and problematic since the army dominates all events and proceeds largely on its own. In almost all cases, the service chiefs pursue their own service's agenda rather than the common national agenda in the JCSC. The recent lack of consultation on the Kargil imbroglio with India is a case in point. Inter-service coordination is absent in most cases. The JCSC has become more of a redundant burden than the asset that it could be.

A suggestion made by US Centcom Commander, General Tony Zinni in the case of the US command structure might be worth pursuing in Pakistan. To make the JCSC truly 'joint' and to afford better coordination of national defence, it might be advisable to select the members of the JCSC from former chiefs or senior commanders, after they have retired from their regular appointments.[17] This would allow the JCs to better coordinate, set priorities, and manage the results of their plans and policies. By definition this would mean moving the overall budget controls and allocation of resources among the services to the new JCSC.

The internal structure of the army also needs to be re-examined. In 2007, the army announced a new command structure.

> As part of restructuring of the Army, three new commands are being established to improve the operational efficiency and working of the land forces. The Northern, Southern and Central Commands are being created that will be responsible for the administrative arrangements of the corps falling under the respective commands. The Northern and South Commands establishment has been finalized, while the Central Command will be raised subsequently.[18]

In some ways, this harkens back to partition when Pakistan had regional commands, including one for Waziristan. But with corps commanders and regional commander at the same rank (lieutenant general) there will be good cause for confusion about who has authority over whom.

A good idea, this regional command system needs to be expanded to three fully integrated regional commands, with air and naval components, as needed, and three strategic commands, including an integrated multi-service strike force, a central logistic command, and a reserve force for purely defensive purposes. The reserve force could then be the effective national guard that could be deployed in aid of civil power to tackle floods or other disasters. But to be truly effective, the army needs to be radically transformed into a leaner and highly mobile force, not the lumbering giant that it is today with a heavy tail-to-teeth ratio. This will require heavy and rapid investment in new equipment and training and shedding of a lot of fat. Further, to improve the operational readiness of the commands and their subordinate corps or divisions, the logistical work and responsibilities need to be separated from the military commanders. In other words, there needs to be a change away from the system that was introduced by Ziaul Haq, when Log area commanders began reporting to corps commanders. This unnecessarily involved corps commanders in administrative work and also introduced the prospects of corruption involving sale and handling of land and other assets or services in army cantonments.

A COUP-PROOF SYSTEM?

Finally, in a move that would allow the regional commanders greater freedom of action, they should all be full four-star generals and appointed by the same authority that currently appoints the COAS and the CJCS. The political spin-off benefit of such a move would be the elimination of the current all-powerful position of one person, the COAS, and the division of power among the regional commanders, while making the chairman of the JCSC the principal military advisor to the government of Pakistan. The COAS would then be much like the army chief in the current US system after Title X reforms of the US military structure, responsible for managing the support of the army as a whole and working with the regional commanders, as needed. It would also eliminate the possibility of a single person effecting a coup d'etat in the future, since the power of the army will be divided among 3–6 commanders, none of whom owes his job to the COAS or even the chairman of the JCSC.

The current system devolves an undue share of power in the country to the army chief, a factor in the clash between many army chiefs and prime ministers in recent years. In reply to a newspaper correspondent's question if he would be '[Prime Minister] Nawaz Sharif's man in the establishment,' the newly appointed army chief General Asif Nawaz responded with a broad smile: 'When half a million troops move with the direction of your finger, you are nobody's man but that of Pakistan Army and of your own conscience.'[19] While that may have been a statement of fact, it does not represent the ideal state of military–civil relations in Pakistan.

As the Indian experience shows, building up a viable political system helps stave off military coups.[20] It is only in the absence of political stability that a military can make a claim to act in the national interest. A broader-based recruitment policy also makes the army less dominated by any one province or language group. But its national nature and unified structure also can make it a useful deterrent to any centrifugal forces and allow it to act effectively in aid of civil power.

LOOKING AHEAD

It is important for the army to help create a stable national polity by subjecting itself in practice (not just in words) to civilian oversight and control by appearing before parliamentary bodies and committee, as needed, to explain its operations and policies. It needs to ensure that it does not become the instrument of civilian dictatorship by subjecting itself to wider parliamentary and controls and oversights of its operations rather than responding to a single individual in the civilian government. This should extend to senior appointments of the chiefs, the proposed regional commanders, and the chairman of the JCSC. And it must be prepared to expose more of its expenditures to scrutiny by government and parliament.

On its side, civilian government needs to ensure that it follows the constitution fully and does not involve the military in political disputes. As past experience shows, when politicians run to the army chief for help, it upsets the balance of the civilian system of government and eventually brings the army into power. Even Ayub Khan, an army man, learned this lesson to his discomfiture. As did Zulfikar Ali Bhutto, and Nawaz Sharif. If this cycle of a civilian interregnum followed by extended military rule is to end in Pakistan, then the politicians have to play their part faithfully and in the national interest. If they do, the army may play its part too and Pakistan may break out of this vicious circle that has kept it from developing into a true democracy and a progressive nation.

Underlying the army's actions in this regard is a wealth of experience from military regimes around the world, indicating the inability of such regimes to create stable political systems that can last. While the military has an advantage over the civil in employing force, it has a comparative disadvantage in building political loyalty from a civilian base. The reason is that 'a military government does not easily tolerate a normal level of dissension or debate needed to build or maintain coalitions with civilians.'[21] Few military regimes have attempted to 'build mass parties and where they have been created, they turned out to be ineffectual structures because genuine participation was not permitted.'[22] The military system of orders and obedience does not easily adjust to the noise of democracy and dissent. The Pakistani experience certainly supports these views, although successive military leaders, including Musharraf, felt that they could buck this trend.

Externally, Pakistan today faces on its eastern frontier, a newly emerging superpower: India. India's growing economy and armed forces, and especially its rapid development of a massive force projection capability, continues to be a concern to Pakistan and India's other neighbours. A large air force and navy with aircraft carriers, poised to fill the gap in the Indian Ocean created by the disappearance of the Soviet Union and the eventual retreat of the

United States, India may well become the region hegemon that Pakistan and its other smaller neighbours fear. How best can Pakistan respond to this possibility?

Matching India's military might along the lines of the past is a costly and untenable approach for the long run. In the face of hostility, Pakistan's defence lies in a smaller, highly mobile, and powerful military, relying on a nuclear and conventional weapons system, and the capability of delivering a damaging riposte. But an even better defence lies in creating a powerful, pluralistic polity residing in a strong economy, built on a society that values education and the welfare of its population. Such a system would be resistant to foreign interference or subversion and would allow Pakistan to restore balance to the current clash between power—the army—and authority (the civil administration). Normalization of ties with India is the first step in this direction. To be effective, such a policy needs the support of the military. General Musharraf's leanings toward rapprochement with India and the resolution of the Kashmir dispute offered a golden opportunity, but India appeared to be less than trusting, and progress has been slow and marked by fits and starts. A gradual thaw had occurred but needs to be enhanced by both sides so they can bury their historical enmities on the path to their economic and political development.

The composition of the Pakistan Army today better represents the society in which it operates than the army at independence. It is also more professional and better trained than ever before. As it expands its membership into other less represented areas and provinces, it can became a true national army and regain its position of trust and devotion. If it does not, and if the civilian politicians also fail to pay heed to the changes around them, then the rising tide of conservatism may be transformed into a radical Islamist wave that will sweep both civil society and the Pakistan Army into its embrace, with results that are entirely predictable and not what Pakistan nor its neighbours and friends desire. The longer the country remains under military domination, the greater the chance of failure of the state.

As the latest recruitment statistics indicate, Pakistan's army today is no longer the same homogenous force of the past with its limited recruitment base. It now reflects a broader range of the country's rapidly urbanizing population. The emergence of new and vibrant mass media and public discourse has also challenged the military's ability to control life in the country with an iron hand. Control, when it is applied, can only work temporarily. Today's emerging technologies provide ways for bypassing authoritarianism.

Military rule is inherently authoritarian and thus antithetical to democracy and pluralism, which are the bedrock of strong nation states. The army forces homogeneity, conformity, and obedience, whereas democracy thrives on debate, dissent, and argument. The army in Pakistan needs to recognize and understand these differences. Nations are made from willing participation of different and disparate communities and ethnicities that come together of their own volition and not as a result of centrally controlled political engineering or fiat.

'If Pakistan does not cohere as a modern more or less centrist state, if the Army loses its grip, and if regional separatist and radical Islamists grow in influence, Pakistan could become a grave threat to the United States and its neighbours, including Iran, China, Afghanistan, and India,' states Stephen Cohen, a Pakistan expert in the United States.[23] The reason is that Pakistan still provides ample opportunity for global terrorist networks to operate and recruit and train its soldiers in Pakistan, where they are provided protection by local militant groups with shadowy links, past or present, to the ISI Pakistan is also increasingly being used as a battleground by the Shia and Sunni regimes of Iran and Saudi Arabia respectively in their attempt to gain ascendancy in the Muslim World. A proxy war has been going on since the Zia period and has intensified after the recent Lebanese crisis and the invasion of Iraq. It is in Pakistan's interest to snuff out these relationships and eliminate these groups. But successive governments have not been able to do much in this regard, including the military government of Musharraf that talked in its early years about de-weaponization of civil society but failed to follow through.

While the army remains a conservative institution at heart, it is not yet a breeding ground for large numbers of radical Islamists that many fear. Islam, however, remains a visible force in Pakistani society and in the army today. Keeping the militant Islamists at bay remains a daunting task, but it need not be used only as a scary scenario to gain Western support. A progressive Pakistan needs to provide opportunities for its citizens to lead their lives without fear of the radical forces of Islam that are vying for power today. More important, given the dominant role of the army in Pakistan's polity, if Pakistan is to mature, thrive, and survive as a successful state and a nation, the army needs to take a back seat and allow the politicians and civil society to make their mistakes and allow the other critically important elements of society: mass media, educational institutions, businesses, professionals, lawyers, etc., to function unfettered. These are the challenges that both the army and civil society in Pakistan must surmount through a return to democratic norms so that they can fulfil their promises to the country and win the long war in this Age of Terror.

NOTES

1. Ustad Daman, 1959, quoted in 'The Colour Khaki' by Tariq Ali. *The New Left Review* 19, January–February 2003.
2. Paper presented at the NDC by a senior officer, who later on became a four-star general.
3. Chapter in a study done at the NDC, Rawalpindi.
4. Changing Recruitment Patterns and Composition of the Pakistan Army. Military Secretary's Branch, Pakistan Army GHQ paper given to author 1990.
5. Ibid.
6. Data supplied by Pakistan Army GHQ, 2006.
7. *The News*, Lahore, 5 January 2006. ISPR Directorate press release.
8. Study at the NDC in the late 1980s by a future four-star general of the Pakistan Army.
9. See for example Sherry Rehman, PPP member of the National Assembly, 'Enigma of the Defence Budget,' *Dawn*, 16 June 2005. She cites various expenses that need to be added to the official figure for defence spending raising it to Rs 277 billion.
10. IMF, Article IV Report 2005, Table 3a. Pakistan: Consolidated Government Budget, 2000/01–2005/06 and Table 17. Pakistan: Social- and Poverty-Related Expenditures, 2001/02–2005/06.
11. Jehangir Karamat (former COAS), 'Perceptions and Realities,' *The News*, 6 October 2000.
12. The ISI's reporting though sometimes leaves much to be desired. In 2006, the author interviewed Prime Minister Benazir Bhutto in mid-afternoon in the café of the Ritz Carlton in Washington DC for this book. The ISI report that was sent to the ambassador and Pakistan stated that I had a private lunch with her. My notebook and tape recorder were clearly visible during this meeting.
13. Ardeshir Cowasjee, 'Not on, General,' *Dawn*, 9 July 2006.
14. Interview with General Ehsan ul Haq, former CJCS and former DG ISI. October 2007. Washington DC.
15. Ardeshir Cowasjee, 'Insufficient Explanations,' *Dawn*, 23 July 2006.
16. David Galula, *Counterinsurgency Warfare: Theory and Practice* (Westport, Conn.: Prager Security International, 2006), pp. 62–63.
17. Tom Clancy and General Tony Zinni and Tony Kolz, *Battle Ready* (New York: G.P. Putnam's Sons, 2004), pp. 324–325.
18. Muhammad Saleh Zafar, 'Army to have three regional commands,' *The News*, 22 April 2007.
19. 'Pakistan—Change may not alter army position on NSC', *The News*, 8 October 1998.
20. See for example Lt. Gen. Dr M.L. Chibber, *Military Leadership to Prevent Military Coup* (New Delhi: Lancer International, 1986).
21. Alfred Stepan, *The Military in Politics: changing patterns in Brazil* (Princeton: Princeton University Press, 1971), p. 263
22. 'Soldiers in Mufti: The Impact of Military Rule upon Economic and Social Change in Non-Western States,' *American Political Science Review*, 64:1131–48. See also Richard Wintrobe, 'The Tinpot and the Totalitarian: an economic theory of dictatorships,' *American Political Science Review*, Volume 84, No. 3, September 1990 for an excellent survey of the literature and a model of the behaviour of dictatorships.
23. 'The Bad, the Ugly, and the Good: South Asian Security and the United States,' testimony by Dr Stephen Philip Cohen, Brookings Institution, before the House of Representatives, Committee on Armed Services. Defense Review Threat Panel, Washington DC, 25 September 2005.

Appendix 1

Timeline: Key events—Pakistan and its Army

ARMY	CIVIL
14 August 1947 General Sir Frank Walter Messervy appointed C-in-C of Pakistan Army.	**14 August 1947** Independence; Governor General Mohammad Ali Jinnah; Prime Minster Liaquat Ali Khan.
October 1947 First Kashmir War with India begins.	**11 September 1948** Jinnah dies; Khawaja Nazimuddin takes over as governor general.
15 February 1948 Messervy retires as army chief, replaced by General Sir Douglas Gracey.	**16 October 1952** Liaquat Ali Khan assassinated.
31 December 1948 Ceasefire declared in Kashmir.	**17 October 1952** Khawaja Nazimuddin takes over as prime minister; Ghulam Mohammad takes over as governor general.
17 January 1951 General Mohammad Ayub Khan appointed as first Pakistani army C-in-C, replacing Gracey.	**April 1953** Mohammad Ali Bogra takes over as prime minister.
9 March 1951 Prime Minister Liaquat Ali Khan reveals conspiracy by Major General Akbar Khan and others to overthrow government.	**July 1955** Ch. Muhammad Ali takes over as prime minister.
1954 Ayub Khan appointed defence minister.	**March 1956** 23rd March: Pakistan becomes a Republic under President Iskander Mirza.
May 1954 United States and Pakistan sign Mutual Defense Pact.	**October 1956** Huseyn Shaheed Suhrawardy becomes prime minister.
8 September 1954 Pakistan joins South East Asia Treaty Organization (SEATO).	**September 1957** I.I. Chundrigar becomes prime minister.
23 September 1955 Pakistan signs Baghdad Pact with Turkey, Iran, and Britain.	**December 1957** Malik Feroze Khan Noon becomes prime minister.
7 October 1958 Iskander Mirza declares martial law under Ayub Khan.	**October 1958** Iskander Mirza declares martial law with General Mohammad Ayub Khan as CMLA. Ayub then displaces Iskander Mirza and takes over as president.
24 October 1958 Ayub takes over as president, sending Mirza into exile. Appoints General Musa Khan as C-in-C.	

ARMY	CIVIL
17 February 1960 Ayub elected president.	**1967** Pakistan Peoples' Party formed by Zulfikar Ali Bhutto.
May 1961 Pakistan fights Afghan incursion in Bajaur area.	**March 1969** Ayub resigns and hands over to General A.M. Yahya Khan, C-in-C of Pakistan Army as CMLA and president. Elections held in both East and West Pakistan: National Awami Party in East and PPP in West win majorities.
April 1965 Pakistan and India fight battles in Rann of Kutch.	
August 1965 Pakistan sends infiltrators into Kashmir.	**21 March 1971** Sheikh Mujibur Rahman of National Awami Party declares independent Bangladesh.
6 September 1965 India retaliates across international border of West Pakistan. War declared. United States imposes sanctions.	**20 December 1971** Yahya hands over as CMLA and president to Zulfikar Ali Bhutto.
22 September 1965 Ceasefire between India and Pakistan.	**10 April 1973** New constitution of Pakistan approved by National Assembly.
3 January 1966 Ayub and Prime Minister Lal Bahadur Shastri of India sign Tashkent Agreement. General Agha Mohammad Yahya Khan appointed C-in-C replacing Musa.	**14 August 1973** Bhutto takes over as prime minister; Fazal Elahi Chaudhary becomes president under new parliamentary constitution.
July 1967 US withdraws military assistance advisory group. Pakistan turns to China, France and others for supplies.	**5 July 1977** General M. Ziaul Haq declares martial law and takes over from Bhutto.
26 March 1969 General Yahya Khan takes over from Ayub Khan as president.	**14 August 1978** Fazal Elahi Chaudhary resigns and hands over to Ziaul Haq as president.
25 March 1971 Army action launched against Awami League in East Pakistan. Civil war results in that province of the country.	**4 April 1979** Zulfikar Ali Bhutto hanged after trial and conviction on murder charges.
November 1971 India masses troops around East Pakistan; starts incursions.	**December 1979** Soviet Union sends troops into Afghanistan.
3 December 1971 Pakistan launches pre-emptive air strike against India from West Pakistan. War with India.	**1980** United States, Saudi Arabia finance Pakistani and Afghan 'jihad' against Soviets.

ARMY	CIVIL
16 December 1971 Dacca (now Dhaka) falls to Indian troops. Surrender ceremony at Dacca Race Course Ground. 90,000 Pakistanis, including troops, taken as prisoners of war. War ends.	**1983** Muhajir Qaumi Movement (MQM, later known as Muttahida Qaumi Movement) formed in Karachi by Altaf Hussain to represent Urdu-speaking refugees from India.
20 December 1971 Yahya hands over as president and CMLA to Zulfikar Ali Bhutto. Lt. Gen. Gul Hassan Khan appointed COAS (new designation). Martial Law imposed.	**March 1985** Mohammad Khan Junejo becomes prime minister under Ziaul Haq.
March 1972 Gul Hassan removed as army chief, replaced by General Tikka Khan.	**April 1986** Benazir Bhutto returns to Pakistan to start opposition campaign against Ziaul Haq.
April 1972 Martial Law lifted.	**April 1988** Soviet Union signs Geneva Accord with United States and Pakistan to withdraw from Afghanistan.
2 July 1972 Bhutto signs Simla (also 'Shimla') Accord with Indian Prime Minister Indira Gandhi.	**May 1988** Junejo dismissed
30 March 1973 Group of army officers arrested for planning coup d'etat against Bhutto. Attock Conspiracy Case tried under Major General Ziaul Haq. Bhutto launches army action against tribes in Balochistan (four-year conflict ensues).	**16 August 1988** Ziaul Haq dies in air crash. **17 August 1988** Chairman, Senate, Ghulam Ishaq Khan becomes president.
28 August 1973 India agrees to release Pakistani POWs.	**16 November** Elections held. PPP wins majority. Islami Jamhoori Itehaad (IJI) set up by ISI chief General Hamid Gul, including Nawaz Sharif, gains Punjab but sits in opposition.
1976 General Ziaul Haq appointed army chief.	**2 December 1988** Benazir Bhutto becomes prime minister.
4 July 1977 Ziaul Haq overthrows Bhutto and becomes CMLA under martial law.	**6 August 1990** Bhutto dismissed by President Ishaq, Ghulam Mustafa Jatoi becomes caretaker prime minister.
30 December 1985 Martial Law lifted.	**October 1990** President George H.W. Bush of United States imposes sanctions on Pakistan for its nuclear programme.
17 August 1988 Ziaul Haq dies in air crash near Bahawalpur. General Mirza Aslam Beg becomes COAS.	IJI led by Sharif wins huge majority in National Assembly and Senate.

ARMY	CIVIL
16 August 1991 General Asif Nawaz becomes COAS.	**1991** Kabul falls to Mujahideen. Sharif, Army Chief General Asif Nawaz visit city.
8 January 1993 General Asif Nawaz dies in office.	**April 1993** Sharif government dismissed by Ishaq Khan. Balkh Sher Mazari named caretaker prime minister.
12 January 1993 General Abdul Waheed (aka Abdul Waheed Kakar) appointed army chief by President Ishaq Khan.	**May 1993** Sharif restored by Supreme Court.
September 1994 Conspiracy uncovered to overthrow civil and military leadership. Major General Zaheer-ul-Islam Abbasi and others arrested, tried, and later convicted.	**July 1993** Both Sharif and Ishaq Khan resign under agreement crafted by Army Chief General Abdul Waheed; Moeen Qureshi named caretaker prime minister.
January 1996 General Jehangir Karamat succeeds General Waheed as army chief.	**6 November 1993** Bhutto becomes prime minister again. Farooq Ahmed Khan Leghari becomes president.
October 1998 After Karamat's speech at Naval Staff College suggesting a National Security Council, he resigns. Replaced by General Pervez Musharraf.	**4 November 1996** Leghari dismisses Bhutto government. Malik Mairaj Khalid becomes caretaker prime minister.
January 1999 Pakistan plan launched to take positions around Line of Control in Kashmir near Kargil.	**1996** Saudi Arabia, United Arab Emirates, and Pakistan recognize Taliban government in Afghanistan.
May 1999 India discovers incursions near Kargil, counter attacks in force.	**1997** Sharif wins large majority becomes prime minister for second time; Rafiq Tarar becomes president after Leghari resigns on 3 December.
4 July 1999 Prime Minister Sharif dashes to Washington, seeks President Clinton's help to end fighting. Agrees to withdraw Pakistani forces.	**4 May 1998** President Bill Clinton imposes sanctions against Pakistan and North Korea for secret missile deal.
12 October 1999 Musharraf's plane on return journey from Sri Lanka not allowed by Sharif to land in Pakistan. Sharif appoints Lt. Gen. Ziauddin as new COAS. Lt. Generals Mahmud Ahmed and Aziz Khan launch coup, remove Sharif from power. Musharraf suspends constitution, takes over as chief executive of	**28 May 1998** Pakistan tests five nuclear bombs in response to India's test of 12 May; tests sixth bomb on 30th.

ARMY	CIVIL

ARMY

Pakistan. Sharif sent into exile to Saudi Arabia.

9 September 2001
Al Qaeda Terrorists attack targets in US.

13 September 2001
US presents list of seven demands to Pakistan. Musharraf agrees to join US-led coalition in 'War on Terror' and attack against Taliban government of Afghanistan.

July 2007
US starts pushing Musharraf for more actions against Islamic extremists in NWFP and Al Qaeda. Insurgency widens and worsens in FATA and Swat.

8 October 2007
General Ashfaq Parvez Kayani appointed VCOAS and presumptive successor to Musharraf as army chief.

28 November 2007
General Kayani succeeds General Musharraf as army chief.

CIVIL

20 February 1999
Indian prime minister inaugurated bus service to Lahore and signed Lahore Declaration with Sharif two days later.

25 May 1999
India launches attacks on infiltrators in Kargil sector of Kashmir.

4 July 1999
Sharif rushes to Washington for meeting with Clinton to agree on Pakistani withdrawal from Kargil positions.

12 October 1999
General Pervez Musharraf takes over in coup d'etat from Sharif, becomes chief executive.

6 April 2000
Anti-Terrorism court sentences Sharif to jail for attempted hijacking of Musharraf's plane.

24 August 2000
Sharif sentenced to 14 years in prison for tax evasion and barred from politics for 21 years.

9 December 2000
Sharif and family exiled to Saudi Arabia.

20 June 2001
Musharraf dismisses Tarar, becomes president himself before visit to India.

July 2001
Agra summit fails on agreement between India and Pakistan.

11 September
Al Qaeda terrorists attack US sites in New York and Washington DC.

13 September 2001
Musharraf agrees to US terms; prepares to break ties to Taliban and assist US attack on Afghanistan.

ARMY	CIVIL

22 September 2001
US lifts sanctions against Pakistan.

13 February 2002
Musharraf welcomed by President George W. Bush at White House.

10 October 2002
In elections, PML (Q) party, favoured by Musharraf, wins majority in alliance with Muttahida Majlis-e-Amal (MMA), a coalition of Islamic parties. PPP becomes major opposition party.

21 November 2002
Mir Zafarullah Khan Jamali elected prime minister.

14 December 2003
Musharraf survives serious bomb blast. Air force personnel implicated.

2 February 2004
Dr A.Q. Khan acknowledges that he sold nuclear secrets to foreign customers. Musharraf pardons him next day. Proclaims him 'Hero'.

26 July 2004
Jamali resigns as prime minister, succeeded on 30th by Chaudhry Shujaat Hussain temporarily.

30 July 2004
Prime minister-designate Shaukat Aziz escapes assassination in bomb blast while campaigning for National Assembly seat.

27 August 2004
Aziz elected prime minister in place of Hussain.

15 September 2004
Musharraf backs out of his pledge to take off his uniform. Remains army chief and president.

14 October 2004
National Assembly allows Musharraf to retain both offices.

ARMY	CIVIL
	November 2004 Asif Zardari, husband of Bhutto, released from jail, re-arrested 21 December 2004 (later allowed to join his wife abroad).
	7 April 2005 Peace Bus crosses line of control in Kashmir, linking families.
	9 March 2007 Musharraf submits reference against Chief Justice of Supreme Court, Iftikhar Muhammad Chaudhry, for 'misconduct'; nationwide protests begin against this decision.
	July 2007 Armed militants operating out of Jamia Masjid (Lal Masjid or Red Mosque) in Islamabad and women's and men's seminaries attached to the mosque challenge government's writ. Siege of mosque ensues, ending in attack that left many dead and wounded. Extremists react throughout the country with attacks on army and civilians.
	20 July 2007 Thirteen-man Supreme Court bench under Justice Khalilur Rehman Ramday overturns Musharraf's decision to remove Chief Justice Iftikhar Muhammad Chaudhry.
	19 October 2007 Benazir Bhutto returns to Pakistan amid talk of a deal with Musharraf. Bomb disrupts her homecoming procession in Karachi.
	3 November 2007 General Musharraf declares a state of emergency, dismisses Supreme Court, puts constitution in abeyance, and muzzles broadcast media.
	25 November 2007 Nawaz Sharif returns to Pakistan with Saudi support.
	29 November 2007 Musharraf takes oath as civilian president of Pakistan.

ARMY	CIVIL
	27 December 2007 Benazir Bhutto assassinated outside Liaquat Bagh, Rawalpindi. **18 February 2008** PPP and PML (N) win elections.

APPENDIX 2

Primary Sources
Including interviews and direct communications

General Mahmud Ahmed, former DG ISI and former Commander X Corps, Rawalpindi, and earlier interview with then Brig. Ahmed. 20 August 1990, 17 April 2006.

Lt. Gen. Naseer Akhtar, Corps Commander V Corps, Karachi under General Asif Nawaz. Lahore, 18 April 2005.

Humayun Akhtar, Minister of Commerce (not taped, not for attribution).

Prince Turki al Faisal, Saudi Ambassador to United States, former head of the General Intelligence Department of Saudi Arabia 1977–2001. Washington DC. 3 October 2006.

Brig. F.B. Ali, Toronto. Telephone interview. 28 and 30 October 2006.

Richard L. Armitage, senior official Department of State under President George H.W. Bush and then Deputy Secretary of State in President George W. Bush. Arlington VA. 29 March 2007.

Sartaj Aziz, former Foreign Minister (during Kargil) and Minister of Finance in Nawaz Sharif government. Lahore, 17 April 2006.

Prime Minister Shaukat Aziz. Islamabad, 11 April 2006.

General Mirza Aslam Beg, COAS, 1988–91, interview, 8 January 1990.

Prime Minister Benazir Bhutto, Washington DC, 30 January 2006. Dubai, 18 and 19 March 2006.

Directorate of Monitoring, Radio Pakistan. Transcripts of broadcasts during 1971 crisis by world radio services (courtesy Kh. Shahid Hosain, former head Pakistan Broadcasting Corporation).

Lt. Gen. Asad Durrani, former DG MI, and DG ISI. Rawalpindi, 11 April 2006.

Major General Mahmud Ali Durrani, former Military Secretary to General Ziaul Haq, Commander 1st Armoured Division, Ambassador to US. Washington DC. 15 November 2006.

Robert Einhorn, Assistant Secretary of State for Non-proliferation. Washington DC, 13 June 2005.

Lt. Gen. Hamid Gul, former DG ISI and Corps Commander Multan. Rawalpindi, 14 April 2006.

Major General S. Shahid Hamid, former MGO under General M. Ayub Khan and Minister for Information, Broadcasting, and Tourism during Zia regime. Numerous conversations and written exchange.

Brigadier Khawar Hanif, Defence Attaché, Pakistan Embassy, Washington DC. Numerous conversations 2006–7.

General Ehsan ul Haq, former CJCSC, DG ISI. Washington DC, 31 October 2007.

Major General (later lieutenant general) Javed Hasan, former Commander FCNA. Lahore, 4 April 2006.

General Ahsan Saleem Hyat, VCOAS, Rawalpindi, 10 April 2006.

Karl Inderfurth, Assistant Secretary of State for South Asia. Washington DC, 29 June 2006.

Major General Afzal Janjua, former ISI Directorate. Lahore, 16 January 2007.

Major Farooq Nawaz Janjua, 4 Punjab Regiment 1971, numerous conversations 1965–90.

Lt. Col. Nasir Nawaz Janjua, former adjutant 16 Punjab Regiment in 1965 War. Numerous conversations 1965–85.

Ambassador Elizabeth 'Beth' Jones, former Deputy Chief of Mission, US embassy, Islamabad. Washington DC, 7 February 2006.

General Jehangir Karamat, COAS, 1996–1998, Washington DC, interview 9 March 2006, subsequent conversations and e-mail exchanges.

Lt. General Ashfaq Kayani, DG ISI. Islamabad, 14 March 2006.

President and C-in-C, Pakistan Army Agha Mohammad Yahya Khan, personal China file from Ali Yahya Khan, and conversations in Washington DC 1978.

Lt. Gen. Javed Hasan Khan, DG, Pakistan Administrative Staff College, former Force Commander Northern Area (FCNA) during Kargil conflict. Lahore, March 2006.

Air Chief Marshal Zulfiqar Ali Khan, Chief of Air Staff. Washington DC, 20 November 1989.

Lt. General Ziauddin Khwaja, former DG ISI, appointed COAS on 12 October 1999 by Prime Minister Nawaz Sharif in place of General Musharraf. Lahore, April 2006.

Major General M. Zaman Kiani, Indian National Army, unpublished memoir.

President Farooq Leghari. Lahore, 20 April 2006.

Lt. Gen. Abdul Ali Malik, Division Commander, 1971, unpublished memoir of 1965 War (courtesy of his nephew Major Saeed Akhtar Malik).

Lt. Col. (retd) J.D. Malik, former CO GHQ Signals Regiment 1955–58. Numerous conversations 1975–2004.

Captain Raheel Anjum Malik, 42 Punjab Regiment, 1971. Numerous conversations 1971 to present.

Major Saeed Akhtar Malik, telephone interview, California, 13 August 2006, subsequent conversations in Alexandria VA, and e-mail exchanges.

Ambassador John Monjo. Alexandria VA, May 2006.

President General Pervez Musharraf, Rawalpindi, 12 April 2006.

Lt. Gen. Javed Nasir, former DG ISI. Lahore, 1 April 2006.

General Asif Nawaz, COAS 1991–93. Numerous conversations 1971–1992.

Shahid Nawaz, younger brother, present in Pakistan at Army House, Rawalpindi, 1991–93. Alexandria VA. 15 April 2007.

Ambassador Robert Oakley, Washington DC 19 December 2005.

Pakistan Army GHQ Archives, Rawalpindi.

Thomas Pickering, Under Secretary of State, under President George W. Bush. Alexandria VA. 2 October 2006.

Paul R. Pillar, Chief Intelligence Officer, Near East and South Asia, CIA, 2000–2005. Washington DC, 1 May 2007.

Ambassador Nicholas Platt, New York, 5 July 2006.

Public Records Office, Surrey, UK.

Lt. General Javed Ashraf Qazi, former DG MI, MGO, and DG ISI, now Minister of Education. Rawalpindi, April 2005 and 11 and 23 April 2006.

Robin Raphel, Assistant Secretary of State for South Asia, Washington DC, 9 February 2005.

Bruce Riedel, Special Assistant to President Clinton, and Director South Asia, NSC. Washington DC. 31 January 2007.

General Brent Scowcroft, National Security Advisor to Presidents Gerald Ford and George H.W. Bush, Washington DC, 3 March 2006.

Major General Sikander Shami, currently DG National Institute of Public Administration, former PSC to COAS General Asif Nawaz and General Abdul Waheed. Lahore, 28 March 2006.

Prime Minister M. Nawaz Sharif. London, 25 May 2006.

I.A. Sherwani, Finance Adviser, Ministry of Defence, Washington DC, 18 July 1991.

Major General Irshadullah Tarar, former Commander FCNA. Lahore, 15 January 2007.

Lt. Gen. Mohammed Tariq, Corps Commander XXX Corps, Gujranwala, under General Abdul Waheed. Lahore, 16 April 2005.

US National Archives, Washington DC.

General Abdul Waheed, former COAS (not taped, not for attribution). Rawalpindi. 10 April 2006.

Major General Malik Abdul Waheed, former DG Martial Law and Deputy COS to General Ziaul Haq. Lahore, 20 April 2006.

Arnold Zeitlin, *The Sound of Thy Brother's Blood*, unpublished memoir of 1969–71 Pakistan.

General Anthony 'Tony' Zinni, C-in-C Centcom 1997–2000. Earlier Commanding General 1st Marine Expeditionary Force in Somalia and then Deputy C-in-C of Centcom. Herndon VA, 7 June 2007.

APPENDIX 3

Investigation into the Death of General Asif Nawaz

The sudden and suspicious death of the army chief, General Asif Nawaz, on 8 January 1993 produced a shock to the political system of Pakistan but it did not end in a clear resolution, as both the army and the political establishment found it hard to face the possibility that the army chief may have been murdered, and hindered the investigation at various stages. Neither approached the matter with alacrity or openness, even after his widow came out in public with her fears that he may have been the object of foul play. Both the government and the army closed ranks to protect themselves at a time when rapid and open disclosures about the general's health status and an open investigation would have allayed concerns.

What made the death especially suspicious was a series of ostensibly unrelated events in the months preceding and following his death that later took on greater import. Even during the days after his death, the author was approached by a nondescript individual in native garb who accosted me in the foyer of Army House where I would normally meet visitors who had come to condole my brother's death. After expressing his feelings of sorrow, he whispered in my ear that the general had been murdered and I should pursue the matter. Without much thought, I pushed the man away and asked the security officer, Major Janjua, to escort him out of Army House, whose gates had been opened to the general public during this period of mourning. Then I forgot about the incident, thinking it was just a crackpot idea from a hare brained individual. I returned to the United States.

However, after my return to the US, General Nawaz's wife, Begum Nuzhat Asif, began receiving anonymous letters (see Box 1) in Urdu allegedly written by individuals who said they worked in the prime minister's house and reported that they had been asked to 'polish' the general's plates with a special material that had been brought from overseas each time he came to dine at the prime minister's house.

The first letter alleged that because of differences between the prime minister and General Nawaz, the prime minister said he did not wish to see the general's face. The writer alleged that the prime minister had deputed a team of his close advisors to ensure that somehow General Nawaz be removed.[1] Begum Nuzhat Asif passed these on to General Waheed with a request that they be investigated. She did not hear back from him.[2] She also recalled that on 24 November 1992 General Nawaz had taken ill during a meeting at the joint chiefs of staff headquarters after taking some tea and snacks and had come home.

I too remembered that incident, since I had telephoned the family the next day and was surprised when the operator connected me to the living quarters of Army House and my brother answered the phone himself. I asked him why he was at home. He replied that he had had a 'case of food poisoning' and that the doctors had given him a shot to make him feel better.

A distraught Begum Nawaz wanted the army and the prime minister to investigate the matter after his death, because she suspected that the general had been subjected to foul play, given reports that the prime minister's inner circle had discussed removing him from the scene.

In the absence of any positive feedback from both the army and the prime minister, Begum Nawaz, took the matter to the president and then made public her wishes for an investigation of her husband's death. Given that her husband had been an active jogger and lifted weights regularly and had had a trip to the Siachen glacier at a height of above 20,000 without any ill-effects, she felt that there had to be another explanation for his sudden heart attack. In the politically charged atmosphere of those days and the growing rift between the president and the prime minister, her statement received a lot of publicity. The prime minister, of course, believed that the president had put up General Nawaz's widow to the job to discredit him and prepare the grounds for his dismissal. Within the military high command, the first reaction was denial and a feeling that an emotional widow was trying to lay the blame for her husband's death on external factors rather than the general's own health. The general's family history was raised in internal discussions at GHQ, since many members of his family had died of heart failure, including his

Box 1

Letter number 1:

Mess Waiter, Prime Minister House
Islamabad

Begum Sahiba, Assalamu Alaykum.

I was instructed by [Names of senior Nawaz Sharif government officials removed by author] to mix poison in the food and finish off General Asif Nawaz some way or the other, because he was a truth-loving general and was the biggest obstacle in the way of 'our government.' The bearer [waiter] had applied the poison, like a coating of polish, on General Asif Nawaz' plate. The poison was smuggled by [name of Sharif associate] in his pocket and was applied on the plates by the bearer/waiter of the Prime Minister House. They also wanted to kill some other army officers, but they could not lay their hands on them.

The Prime Minister House
Islamabad

Letter number 2:

Begum Sahiba, Assalamu 'Alaykum.

Mohtarema,

You are being informed that the operation launched by General Asif Nawaz in Sindh unmasked many well-known faces, implicating several important MQM leaders. Prime Minister Nawaz Sharif, Chaudhry Nisar, Ghous Ali Shah and Chaudhry Shujaat put pressure on General Asif Nawaz and asked him to go easy on this operation, because MQM was a part of the government. The 'Mujahid-e Millat' General Asif Nawaz did not heed their request at all. From that day on, after assembling all the mess waiters, cooks and all the staff involved in the preparation of food, only a select few mess waiters were given the duty of serving food [to General Asif Nawaz]. [They were told that] the one who would poison [the General] would be given land as well as a car and rupees five lakhs. Only a select few [waiters] were put on this duty. Their relatives were issued visas to go abroad. Mian Nawaz Sharif could not stand looking at late General Asif Nawaz.

When the operation [to poison General Asif Nawaz] was launched, Mian Nawaz Sharif cancelled his trip to Lahore, because he knew full well that 'today General Asif Nawaz is going to die.' And [names of Senior Sharif associates withheld by author] were given the task of announcing this news.
     For the night duty a mess waiter and a cook were appointed. They have been given a plot of land in CDA-Islamabad. Many big hands are involved in this case. Nawaz Sharif and Shahbaz Sharif --------- [part of sentence not clearly legible] were going to make ---- [not legible] ...the Chief of Army Staff, but President Ishaq Khan intervened. The plan/conspiracy to murder General Asif Nawaz was prepared by [Names withheld by author] quite a while ago. The mess waiters' duty was very strict. All the mess waiters of the Prime Minister's House know [about] this. [a couple of sentences could not be deciphered due to very poor and hazy copy]. Almost all the police officers at the Prime Minister's House and -----, who are with the Prime Minister, knew about the plot to murder General Asif Nawaz. On the day he died, the news was circulating that General Asif Nawaz was ill and that his condition was critical. This news had already gained wide circulation by the early morning. The person who spread this news was a mess waiter, and all the staff knew this.

father, uncles, and cousins, particularly Nasir Nawaz Janjua, whom the new army chief, General Abdul Waheed knew very well.

General Nawaz's own personal secretary, now serving in the same role with Waheed, Brigadier Sikander Shami, played a part in these discussions since he maintains that the general had had a medical check-up that indicated an aberrant ECG that the doctors wished to follow up,[3] but he maintains that General Nawaz reportedly had postponed it, fearing that news of his medical disability might leak, emboldening his political opponents. The military medical establishment also closed ranks. As their later testimony was to indicate, they had a different explanation for the general's illness of the previous November than the one he was given at the time of that incident. They attributed the general's nausea to an inner ear infection. Meanwhile, General Shamim Alam Khan, the chairman of the joint chiefs of staff, at whose headquarters the army chief had taken ill in November 1992, reportedly went to meet President Ishaq and pleaded with him not to push for an investigation since that would 'destroy the Joint Headquarters.' Ishaq conveyed this to Begum Nawaz.

The army did not wish to allow anything to happen that might impugn it. In choosing this approach, it was following a familiar path, protecting its corporate interest, even at the risk of allowing the death of a chief go uninvestigated, as it had done after the Zia crash. (No minutes of the discussions held at GHQ following Zia's death were in the GHQ archives that the author saw. But a review of the minutes of the first meeting of the joint chiefs of staff committee after Zia's death contains no mention of the crash. There was no talk about any investigation nor any discussion of its effect on the rank and file of the army.[4])

Rather than support a rapid investigation and exhumation, the army chose not to respond to the family's request to open a thorough investigation into General Nawaz's death, allowing the matter to fester for months. It did not share any of his medical files with the family either; their release could have resolved some issues. Amidst this uncertainty, media speculation arose that the general may have been murdered for political reasons. And it provided political capital to Prime Minister Sharif's opponents. Among them, the PPP stood to gain much traction, as did President Ishaq. Much was to happen in the meantime in Pakistani politics over the next nine months. Including the sacking of the Sharif government, its reinstatement, and then re-sacking by the army chief this time, who installed a caretaker government and arranged for new elections.

Prime Minister Sharif had been under some pressure to pursue the case of General Nawaz's death. Indeed, his government initially launched that effort on 12 April by setting up a judicial inquiry into the death of General Nawaz under Justice Shafiur Rahman of the Supreme Court of Pakistan in Rawalpindi.[5] But he did not anticipate being removed by the time the commission came into action and Begum Nawaz had to plead with the caretaker government of Prime Minister Moeen Qureshi to pursue this matter. Seeing an opportunity, the PPP had begun talking with the general's youngest brother, Shahid Nawaz, as a likely political candidate in the general's home district of Jhelum. It also may have provided legal help to Begum Nawaz through a pro-PPP lawyer, Barrister Shahzad Jehangir, who offered his services to the family *pro bono*, according to Salman Shah, Begum Nawaz's son-in-law. My niece, Aneela Shah, recalls that Major General Jehangir Nasrullah, the DG ISPR Directorate, was the one who introduced the family to Shahzad Jehangir. Benazir Bhutto's former ambassador in Switzerland, Mr M.U. Baqir, told me that he gave the name of a forensic expert, Michael Baden of the United States, to Mr Jehangir.

The judicial inquiry was a strange affair. It invited individuals to come forward and testify, although some were sent forward by the army and others came voluntarily. All statements were to be recorded without any questioning by lawyers or the family or any cross-examination. Also, the staff of Army House, who were asked to testify, reportedly had to meet with Brigadier Shami before they appeared before the commission. General Nawaz's ADC, a young Captain Qadeer of 5 Punjab Regiment, the only one of his staff who had been with him at the joint chiefs headquarters meeting when he took ill, did not appear before the commission.

During the hearings of the commission, military doctors, some of whom had treated the general and others who had not, all testified that he had suffered a heart attack and that the earlier episode at the joint chiefs headquarters was an ear infection. Major General Syed Tauqeer Ahmad Shah of the army medical service reportedly testified that the general had been under his care for cardiac disorder and had been under his treatment during the period 2–24 November 1992. Begum Nawaz challenged this by informing the commission that General Nawaz had been out of the country in Turkey on an official visit for two weeks during that period and then had gone to Makkah to perform *umra*. She also stated that Lt. Gen. Muhammad Yousaf, the personal physician of the late army chief, had informed her that 'tests carried out after 24th November 1992, showed that his blood pressure was normal, that no unusual enzyme levels were discovered. He had told me that General's ECG showed a slight aberration (sic), but that was normal for a man who had pursued a rigorous exercise regimen all his life.'[6] General Tauqeer (also spelt Tauqir by his own medical colleague Major General Yousaf) spoke with General Yousaf about the 24 November episode and had concluded that it was food poisoning. General Yousaf however thought it could also have been Vestibular Neuronitis (a viral disease that causes severe vertigo and nausea) due to infection of the ear. According to General Yousaf:

> Maj Gen Syed Tauqir Ahmed Shah and myself were unanimously of the view that the history, clinical findings and ECG findings were not suggestive of acute Ischaemic Heart Disease as the underlying cause of his symptoms. Both of us unanimously decided to do serial ECGs and cardiac enzyme profile to simultaneously monitor the cardiac status with a view to picking up any concomitant cardiac involvement at the earliest.[7]

Both doctors suggested hospitalization for rest purposes but the general said he would rest on his own. Later tests indicated 'absence of abnormality on the blood reports on (sic) 24 Nov 1992' and they then suggested among other things an exercise tolerance (stress) test and an ECG. They said they ruled out food poisoning, which was the diagnosis they had given General Nawaz himself at the time of his illness. The general's personal secretary, Brigadier Shami, testified that 'it was in the knowledge of army personnel that the late Asif Nawaz had a family history of heart ailment. He had been medically advised not to go for exercise till he was cleared after exercise tolerance test, he added. That test could not take place due to preoccupation of late general.'[8]

I was asked to get involved at this stage by the family in Pakistan, not having been involved in any of the earlier actions and having observed all earlier developments from my location in the United States. The commission had requested names of experts who might be involved in an exhumation and autopsy of the general's body. Following the advice of my lawyer friend, David Curtin of Alexandria VA, who gave me a list of solid contacts and suggested how a professional inquiry might proceed, I conducted interviews with more than half a dozen leading forensic pathologists in the United States and the United Kingdom, seeking those who might be available at short notice to go to Pakistan. This narrowed the choices considerably since I discovered that there were only a small number of internationally known forensic pathologists and they were all very busy. I sent a short list of names to be given to the commission. For whatever reason, only Dr Baden's name appeared in the final report, suggested by Mr Shahzad Jehangir. The police suggested four other names, two from the United States and two from the United Kingdom. The commission concluded that 'late General Asif Nawaz died a natural death on account of massive heart attack. The allegations of poisoning are not correct.'[9] It expressed an inability to order an exhumation and left that matter up to the administration. The report was forwarded to the law secretary on 12 May 1993 but no copy was made available to the family until mid-September, by which time a new caretaker government was in place.[10]

Prime Minister Qureshi inherited the unfinished investigation into the death of General Asif Nawaz, whose family was actively pursuing this issue afresh. During my search for forensic experts to proceed to Pakistan, should the Shafiur Rahman Commission demand them at short notice, I had discussed with Dr Cyril Wecht of Pittsburg, Pennsylvania, and Dr Fredric Rieders of the National Medical Services laboratory of Willow Grove, Pennsylvania, the case of my brother's death. They suggested that one way of ascertaining whether he had indeed been poisoned was to gather his hair samples and test them. Dr Rieders stated that the hair could be examined and through segmentation analysis it could be determined not only what had been ingested but also over what period. Among other things, I commissioned a search of the National Institutes of Medicine research files for cases of arsenic poisoning, an often preferred method for producing cardiotoxic shock. I received a computer generated set of studies that were almost two inches thick, establishing that relationship between arsenic and deaths due to heart attacks.

Then, I requested my niece, Aneela Shah, in Lahore to collect my brother's hair samples from his hairbrush and from his suits etc. She confirmed that she collected the samples herself and placed them in a plastic container. I collected these samples and the hairbrush on my way back from an official trip to Malaysia. During the same stopover in Pakistan, I called on General Waheed and spoke with him, in principle, on whether he might support an exhumation should we establish proof of poisoning. He agreed to do that. I did not inform him at the time of the hair samples, which I took back to Washington and dispatched as an anonymous sample on 9 July 1993 to Dr Wecht to be forwarded to Dr Rieders for testing. I did not wish my brother's name to be associated with this test. Dr Riders was to conduct 'analyses for 7 of the metals which have direct or indirect cardiotoxic effects which may lead to delayed cardiac death'.[11] A point made orally by Dr Wecht to me earlier was that having heart disease by itself did not mean that one died of heart failure. Many people with heart diseases die in car accidents, he said. So, he felt it is important to establish the real cause of death.

The summary results of the tests were faxed to me on 23 August 1993 and indicated that my brother's hair samples showed Arsenic '67 mcg/g' and Chromium '9mcg/g'. The report by Dr Dean F. Fritch (see facsimile of original report), the forensic toxicologist, also carried the following comments:

1. Normal concentrations of arsenic in unexposed healthy individuals are normally less than 4 mcg/g hair. The arsenic concentration in the hair of this individual is within the range which can be considered toxic and may be an amount which is fatal. Further analysis of other tissue specimens would be warranted to corroborate this finding.
2. Normal concentrations of chromium in unexposed healthy individuals are normally between 0.3 and 1.5 mcg hair.[12]

These results stunned me. My blood froze at what appeared to be incontrovertible evidence that General Asif Nawaz had indeed been poisoned. My first reaction was that that there might be a typographical error in the report. So I called Dr Fritch, who assured me that the report was correct. I immediately conveyed the results on the telephone to the family in Lahore and requested my niece's husband, Salman Shah, to help Begum Nawaz prepare a formal request for an exhumation and testing of my brother's body to confirm these findings. I also suggested that my younger brother, Shahid, not be included in any formal procedures on this matter, since he had decided that summer to contest the elections on a PPP ticket (against my advice) and his association would jeopardize the neutrality of this exercise.

I then called General Waheed at Army House at 1:51 p.m. (Eastern Standard Time) on 24 August 1993 and informed him of the results, following up with a call to General Qazi, who also happened to be my wife's cousin, and Prime Minister Qureshi, and followed up with faxes to each with letters suggesting prompt action on their part to resolve this issue. I suggested that foreign experts be brought in, including Dr Wecht, to conduct the exhumation and testing on tissue samples. General Waheed was very forthcoming on the telephone, after getting over the shock of the news, he said to me we should leave this to the army now 'We'll take care of it. We must follow up!' 'He [Asif] called me a brother' said Waheed. 'And even if he had not, he was our Chief.' I told him that my brother Shahid would not be involved in this case, because of his political connections. I told Waheed that I treated him and trusted him like a brother. This was to be our last direct conversation on this matter during that period. All subsequent communications on this issue were in writing and only from me to him, with no response.

Prime Minister Qureshi had been forewarned about the test results by Shahid Javed Burki, who happened to have arrived back in Washington the previous day. Qureshi was expecting my call at 1 p.m. (EST) on 25 August, late at night his time in Islamabad. I explained to him the background and that we were seeking prompt but discreet action so that the matter could be resolved speedily and not become entangled in election politics. He began by stating that the family had every right to seek further inquiry and tests, given the 'circumstantial evidence' that we had. He said that he had asked to see the report of the judicial commission and that he wished to proceed in a transparent manner so that no one could accuse his government of handling this secretly or conspiring against anyone. Irrespective of what government will say, it will look as if we helped engineer this situation at this particular time, he said, adding that the timing will be talked about. I repeated that we needed quick action. Qureshi promised that he would look at the medical test report that I would fax to him and that he might share this information with both Nawaz Sharif and Benazir Bhutto. He thought aloud about the possibility of getting the inquiry done in the period between the elections and the induction of the new government. I warned against that approach since he would become a lame duck the day the election results came out. Overall, I felt a sense of confidence in him and his response to our request for an exhumation and fresh autopsy. The next day I spoke again with General Qazi who told me that he had spoken with both the COAS and the prime minister and that they had some reservations about including Dr Wecht, who might be seen as 'our man.' I insisted that we needed to be sure of the validity of the findings and explained that I had kept Dr Wecht at arms length for professional reasons. Indeed, I had not even met him personally, having conducted all business with him by phone or in writing.[13]

Begum Nawaz then proceeded to file a First Information Report, a necessary first step to seek a formal police investigation into an alleged crime. This had the media abuzz and created a fair amount of noise in the political campaign, with both the PPP and the Sharif PML making charges and counter charges about General Nawaz's death. Almost a month went by and there had been no action, so I pressed both Waheed and Qureshi in writing to ensure that the inquiry was completed before the elections. To add to the pressure, I used my media contacts for the first time to provoke a prominent story in *Newsweek* about the issue. That appeared in September and garnered a lot of publicity. The government in the meantime had begun checking out both Dr Wecht and the laboratory in the United States through the ISI officer assigned to the Pakistan embassy in Washington, Lt. Col. Shuja Khanzada. He and the then CGS, Lt. Gen. Jehangir Karamat, also met me over lunch at the International Club on 19th street next to my office to probe further about what had happened and how I had handled the tests. I repeated all the details. But I was concerned that the government, through the ISI, might wish to 'fix' the results to avoid a major conflagration. Having done enough research on past Pakistan–US joint activities, I was fearful that the United States might go along with Pakistan's request to somehow find a way out of this potentially damaging situation for the army. I knew that General Qazi had been in touch with his counterparts in the US, UK, and France to get their help in setting up the team of forensic specialists. So, I approached and met senior officials at the Department of State to simply request the United States to stay out of this matter.[14]

FINDINGS OF THE FORENSIC EXPERTS

Eventually, a three-person team, including Dr Wecht, Dr John Clarke of Sheffield University, UK, and Dr Patrick Lambert from Seine Hospital, Romilly, France, were taken to Pakistan and took part on 30 September 1993 in the exhumation, examination, and taking of samples from my brother's body before it was re-interred in our family burial lot on a hill overlooking our village, Chakri Rajgan. Samples were taken back to Islamabad by the forensic team, now under the care of a deputy inspector general of police, Dr Shoaib Suddle, who had a doctorate in criminology. A special board was also constituted by the Health Department of the Punjab government consisting of Professor Dr Naseeb R. Awan (King Edward Medical College), Professor Dr A.H. Nagi (also of KEMC), Dr Muhammad Akram Sheikh (Chief Chemical Examiner, Punjab), and Lt. Col. Syed Mustafa Hussain Urakzai of the Army Medical College, Rawalpindi. A set of samples in glass jars filled with formaldehyde was also taken by the army but then brought back in a wooden box by a captain who accompanied Shahid Nawaz and Salman Shah back to the gravesite so that it could be re-interred close to the grave. (The army had said it intended to destroy the samples. The general's family thought it would be better to bury them.) Dr Wecht told me on his return that, on coming back from our village, he was taken by Dr Suddle to the hill station of Murree for a sightseeing trip. He assured me that the samples were safe during that period. Dr Wecht said that the three experts had agreed to talk before completing their reports and expected this to be done in about two weeks. A long silence followed. He was concerned about it and tried to raise his colleagues.

Eventually he sent me his report which stated that my brother had advanced heart disease and that none of the tissue, hair, or nail samples that he had tested showed any sign of arsenic. Separate reports by the other foreign experts carried similar results. I asked Dr Wecht if hair could be contaminated, say by proximity to animal hair in a brush. He said they would need to test the brush and asked the government about it and suggested testing the brush. They did not respond. But I had understood from Dr Rieders earlier that it is impossible to fake arsenic poisoning in hair since the poison has to be ingested naturally to grow into the hair over time and can be tested by doing 'segmentation analysis' by slicing and examining the hair from the bottom up. Soaking it in a solution cannot produce the same result and ingestion. In the absence of any other evidence, we had a serious disconnect between our initial tests and these final tests. And there was no firm evidence linking the poisoning with the prime minister or with anyone else.

The mystery remains. Nothing emerged to explain the apparent discrepancy between the results obtained from the samples that I received from the family and the 'final' test results that came out of the government-supervised tests later in the year. There was no direct evidence linking Prime Minister Sharif to the death. There was no evidence that linked any other party to Genral Nawaz's death. Politics took centre stage again and may have been behind this smoky ending of this episode.

Subsequent attempts to get information from the US government through the Freedom of Information Act for all communications about my brother have not yielded any results to date. The last communication from the Department of State only said that they are still gathering information from the field offices, almost two years after the request was filed. If there was some manipulation of the test samples, then only an insider with knowledge of that might break this impasse. Neither the Pakistan Army at that time or any government since then made any attempt to clarify the situation. A short governmental statement simply stated that no poison had been found in my brother's body. This was during the second Benazir Bhutto government. Surprisingly, she asked my niece through the governor of the Punjab to request her mother to seek a re-opening of the inquiry, an action that any government could initiate on its own. The family chose not to do so. In retrospect, an immediate inquiry and autopsy, followed by sharing with the family of General Nawaz's complete medical file may have avoided the politically charged drama that was allowed to be played out for months. But the army command apparently had closed ranks and was protecting itself, in a replay of the period after the death of General Ziaul Haq. Thus, yet another major suspicious death involving the Pakistan army and its politics remained unsolved.

NOTES

1. These letters written on plain paper and one carrying a handwritten home address of the prime minister's house, were given to me in May 1993 by Begum Nawaz.
2. She gave me copies of these letters.
3. Brigadier Shami spoke a number of times with the author about this issue and stressed that General Nawaz did not wish to undergo tests.
4. Pakistan Army, GHQ Archives.
5. The other two members of the commission were Justices Abdul Qadeer Chaudhry and Muhammad Rafiq Tarar (later president of Pakistan under Prime Minister Nawaz Sharif).
6. Begum Nuzhat Asif's statement before the judicial commission at Rawalpindi.
7. Note from Major General Yousaf to the Shafiur Rahman Commission.
8. 'Commission examines witnesses in Asif's case,' *The News*, 28 April 1993.
9. Shafiur Rahman Commission Report.
10. I was faxed a copy of the report on 16 September 1993.
11. Letter from Dr Frederic Rieders of NMS Inc., dated 30 July 1993.
12. Toxicology report of NAWAZ, NMS Control No. 983474, NMS Accession number 090944-93, dated 23 August 1993 sent to Dr Cyril Wecht. Signed Dean F. Fritsch Ph.D.
13. I kept detailed notes on most of these exchanges and other contacts during this period, typing up the gist of the conversations soon after they took place.
14. Meeting with John Holtzman and a junior colleague of his who looked after the Pakistan desk at the Department of State.

National Medical Services, Inc.
2300 Stratford Ave.
P.O. Box 433A
Willow Grove, Pennsylvania 19090
PHONE (215) 657-4900 • FAX (215) 657-2972

August 23, 1993

TO: Central Medical Center & Hospital
     ATTN: Dr. Cyril Wecht
     1200 Centre Avenue
     Pittsburgh, PA 15219

TOXICOLOGY REPORT OF: NAWAZ
     NMS Control No.   983474
     NMS Accession No.   090944-93

EXAMINATION: Check for Toxins with Delayed Cardiac Effect

SPECIMENS: 3.5 mg Hair was received on 07/14/93.

    n.b.:   The remainder of the submitted specimen is scheduled to be
               discarded six (6) weeks from the date of this report unless
               alternate arrangements are made by you prior thereto.

FINDINGS:

  Hair

    ARSENIC   67 mcg/g

    CHROMIUM   9 mcg/g

Other than the above findings, examination of the specimen submitted did not
reveal any positive findings of toxicological significance by procedures
outlined in the accompanying Analysis Summary Sheet.

COMMENTS:

1.   Normal concentrations of arsenic in unexposed healthy individuals are
     normally less than 4 mcg/g hair. The arsenic concentration in the hair of
     this individual is within the range which can be considered toxic and may be
     an amount which is fatal. Further analysis of other tissue specimens would
     be warranted to corroborate this finding.

2.   Normal concentrations of chromium in unexposed healthy individuals are
     normally between 0.3 and 1.5 mcg/g hair.

                                        Dean F. Fritch, Ph.D., DABFT
                                        Forensic Toxicologist

DFF:gfr

SELECTED BIBLIOGRAPHY

History of Pakistan and India

Ahmad, Syed Nur (Craig Baxter, ed.). *From Martial Law to Martial Law*. Lahore: Vanguard, 1985.

Ali, Chaudhri Muhammad. *The Emergence of Pakistan*. New York: Columbia University Press, 1967.

Arrian. Trans. by Aubrey de Selincourt. *The Campaigns of Alexander*. Middlesex: Penguin Books, 1971.

Ball, Charles. *The History of the Indian Mutiny*. Vols. I and II. London: London Printing and Publishing Company.

Bin Sayeed, Khalid. *Pakistan The Formative Phase, 1857-1948*. London: Oxford University Press, 1968.

Bowles, Chester. *Ambassador's Report*. New York: Harper & Row, 1954.

Bradley, John, ed. *Lady Curzon's India: Letters of a Vicereine*. London: Weidenfeld and Nicolson, 1985.

Burke, S.M. and Salim Al-Din Quraishi. *The British Raj in India*. Karachi: Oxford University Press, 1995.

Burki, Shahid Javed. *Historical Dictionary of Pakistan*. Lanham, Md.: The Scarecrow Press, 1999.

Burki, Shahid Javed. *Pakistan: A Nation in the Making*. Boulder, Colo.: Westview Press, 1986.

Campbell-Johnson, Alan. *Mission with Mountbatten*. New York: Atheneum, 1985.

Carter, Lionel, ed. *Mountbatten's Report on the Last Viceroyalty*. New Delhi: Manohar, 2003.

Ceram, C.W. *Gods, Graves, and Scholars*. New York: Alfred Knopf, 1962.

Collins, Larry and Dominique Lapierre. *Freedom at Midnight*. New York: Simon and Schuster, 1975.

Dasgupta, C. *War and Diplomacy in Kashmir, 1947-48*. New Delhi: Sage Publications, 2002.

De Schweinitz Jr., Karl. *The Rise & Fall of British India. Imperialism as Inequality*. London: Methuen, 1983.

Department of the Army. *U.S. Army Area Handbook for India*. U.S. Government Printing Office, 1964.

Dewey, Clive. *Anglo-Indian Attitudes*. London: Hambledon Press, 1993.

Galbraith, John Kenneth. *Ambassador's Journal*. Boston: Houghton Mifflin Company, 1969.

Gilbert Jr., William H. *Peoples of India*. Washington: Smithsonian Institution, 1944.

Habib, Irfan. *An Atlas of the Mughal Empire*. Delhi: Oxford University Press, 1986.

Hamilton, General Sir Ian. *Listening to the Drums*. London: Faber and Faber Ltd.

Hunter, Sir William Wilson. *A Brief History of the Indian Peoples*. Oxford: Clarendon Press, 1903.

Irvine, William. *The Army of the Indian Moghuls*. New Delhi: Eurasia Publishing House, 1962.

Jha, Prem Shankar. *Kashmir 1947*. Delhi: Oxford University Press, 1996.

Kashmir Study Group, 1947-1997. *The Kashmir Dispute at Fifty. Charting Paths to Peace*. 1997.

Keay, John. *When Men and Mountains Meet*. London: Century, 1987.

Keay, John. *India: A History*. London: HarperCollins, 2000.

Khan, Mazhar Ali. *Pakistan The First Twelve Years*. Karachi: Oxford University Press, 1996.

Korbel, Josef. *Danger in Kashmir*. Princeton, N.J.: Princeton University Press, 1966.

Lamb, Alastair. *Crisis in Kashmir, 1947 to 1966*. London: Routledge & Kegan Paul, 1966.

Lamb, Alastair. *Kashmir. A Disputed Legacy, 1846-1990*. Karachi: Oxford University Press, 1992.

Lamb, Alastair. *Incomplete Partition: The Genesis of the Kashmir Dispute 1947-1948*. London: Oxford University Press, 2002.

Lamb, Harold. *Alexander of Macedon*. Garden City, N.Y.: The Country Life Press.

Lelyveld, David. *Aligarh's First Generation*. Princeton: Princeton University Press, 1978.

Mehra, Parshotam. *A Dictionary of Modern Indian History, 1707-1947*. Delhi: Oxford University Press, 1987.

Raza, S. Hashim, ed. *Mountbatten and Pakistan*. Karachi: Quaid-i-Azam Academy, 1982.

Schofield, Victoria. *Kashmir in the Crossfire*. London: I.B. Tauris, 1996.

Scwartzberg, Joseph E. ed. *A Historical Atlas of South Asia*. Second impression. New York and Oxford: Oxford University Press, 1992.

Sen, Lt. Gen. L.P. *Slender was the Thread: Kashmir Confrontation 1947-48*. New Delhi: Orient Longman Limited.

Stephens, Ian. *Pakistan*. London: Frederick A. Praeger, 1967.

Streusand, Douglas E. *The Formation of the Mughal Empire*. Delhi: Oxford University Press, 1989.

Taylor, Edmond. *Richer by Asia*. New York: Time Incorporated, 1964.

Taylor, P.J.O., ed. *A Companion to the 'Indian Mutiny' of 1857*. Delhi: Oxford University Press, 1996.

Torrens-Spence, Johnny, *Historica Battlefield of Pakistan*. Karachi: Oxford University Press, 2006.

Wecht, Cyril, Mark Curriden and Benjamin Wecht. *Grave Secrets*. New York: Penguin Group, 1996.

Wikeley, J.M. *Punjabi Musalmans*. Lahore: The Book House.

Wirsing, Robert G. *India, Pakistan, and the Kashmir Dispute*. New York: St. Martin's Press, 1998.

British India and its Army

Allen, Charles. *Soldier Sahibs*. New York: Carroll & Graf Publishers, Inc., 2000.

Bayly, C.A. *Indian Society and the Making of the British Empire*. Cambridge: Cambridge University Press, 1990.

Beaumont, Roger. *Sword of the Raj*. Indianapolis: The Bobbs-Merrill Company, Inc., 1977.

Farwell, Byron. *Armies of the Raj*. New York: W.W. Norton & Company, 1989.

Fay, Peter Ward. *The Forgotten Army*. Ann Arbor: The University of Michigan Press, 1995.

Gardner, Brian. *The East India Company*. New York: Dorset Press, 1971.

Gaylor, John. *Sons of John Company: The Indian & Pakistan Armies, 1903-1991*. Tunbridge Wells, Kent: Spellmount Ltd., 1992.

Guy, Alan J. and Peter B. Boyden (Eds.). *Soldiers of the Raj: The Indian Army, 1600-1947*. Coventry: Clifford Press Ltd., 1997.

Hamid, Shahid. *Disastrous Twilight*. London: Leo Cooper, 1986.

James, Lawrence. *Raj: The Making and Unmaking of British India*. London: Abacus, 1997.

Leasor, James. *The Red Fort*. New York: Collier Books, 1957.

Lewin, Ronald. *The Chief*. New York: Farrar, Straus and Giroux, 1980.

Mason, Philip. *A Matter of Honour*. London: Jonathan Cape, 1975.

Mason, Philip. *The Men Who Ruled India*. New York: W.W. Norton & Company, 1985.

Moorhouse, Geoffrey. *India Britannica*. New York: Harper & Row, 1983.

Omissi, David *The Sepoy and the Raj*. London: The MacMillan Press Ltd., 1994.

Parkinson, Roger. *The Auk: Auchinleck, Victor at Alamein*. London: Granada Publishing, 1977.

Read, Anthony and David Fisher. *The Proudest Day*. London: Pimlico, 1998.

Roberts, Andrew. *Eminent Churchillians*. London: Weidenfeld & Nicholson, 1994.

Spear, Percival. *The Nabobs*. London: Oxford University Press, 1963.

Trench, Charles Chenevix. *The Indian Army*. New York: Thames and Hudson, Inc., 1988.

Warner, Philip. *Auchinleck: The Lonely Soldier*. London: Sphere Books, 1982.

Ziegler, Philip. *Mountbatten*. New York: Alfred A. Knopf, 1985.

India and its Army

Abraham, Itty. *The Making of the Indian Atomic Bomb*. London: Zed Books, 1998.

Akbar, M.J. *India: The Siege Within*. Middlesex, England: Penguin Books Ltd., 1985.

Ayook, Mohammed and K. Subrahmanyam. *The Liberation War*. New Delhi: S. Chand & Co., 1972.

Baranwal, J., ed. *Military Yearbook 1991-92*. New Delhi: Guide Publications, 1991.

Bhargava, G.S. *Their Finest Hour*. Delhi: Vikas Publishing 1972.

Chaudhuri, General J.N. *An Autobiography*, as narrated to B.K. Narayan. New Delhi: Vikas Publishing House, 1978.

Chibber, M.L. *Military Leadership to Prevent Military Coup*. New Delhi: Lancer International, 1986.

Chopra, Pran. *India's Second Liberation*. Delhi: Vikas Publishing House, 1973.

Dalvi, J.P. *Himalayan Blunder*. Bombay: Thacker & Company, 1969.

Ganguly, Sumit. *Conflict Unending: India-Pakistan Tensions Since 1947*. New York: Columbia University Press, 2001.

Jacob, J.F.R. *Surrender at Dacca: Birth of a Nation*. New Delhi: Manohar 1997.

Kargil Review Committee Report, The. *From Surprise to Reckoning*. New Delhi: Sage Publications, 2000.

Kaul, B.M. *Confrontation with Pakistan*. Delhi: Vikas Publications, 1971.

Khilnani, Sunil. *The Idea of India*. London: Hamish Hamilton, 1997.

Malik, V.P. *Kargil. From Surprise to Victory*. New Delhi: HarperCollins Publishers, 2006.

Maxwell, Neville. *India's China War*. Garden City, NY: Anchor Books, 1972.

Menezes, S.L. *Fidelity & Honour: The Indian Army*. New Delhi: Viking, 1993.

Palit, D.K. *The Lightning Campaign: Indo-Pakistan War 1971*. New Delhi: Thomson Press, 1972.

Palit, D.K. *War in High Himalaya: The Indian Army in Crisis, 1962*. New Delhi: Lancer International, 1991.

Perkovich, George. *India's Nuclear Bomb*. Berkeley: University of California Press, 1999.

Rao, K.V. Krishna. *Prepare or Perish: A Study of National Security*. New Delhi: Lancer Publishers, 1991.

Ray, Arjun. *Kashmir Diary: Psychology of Militancy*. New Delhi: Manas Publications, 1997.

Rikhye, Ravi. *The Fourth Round: Indo-Pak War 1984*. Jurong, Singapur: Mubarak and Sons, 1982.

Rikhye, Ravi. *The War That Never Was*. Delhi: Chanakya Publications, 1988.

Rikhye, Ravi. *The Militarization of Mother India*. Delhi: Prism India Paperbacks, 1990.

Singh, Harbaksh. *War Despatches: Indo-Pak Conflict 1965*. New Delhi: Lancer International, 1991.

Singh, Jogindar. *Behind the Scene: An Analysis of India's Military Operations, 1947-1971*. New Delhi: Lancer International.

Sinha, S.K. *Operation Rescue: Military Operations in Jammu & Kashmir 1947-49*. New Delhi: Vision Books, 1987.

Smith, Chris. *India's Ad Hoc Arsenal*. New York: Oxford University Press, 1994.

Srivastava, C.P. *Lal Bahadur Shastri, Prime Minister of India 1964-1966: A Life of Truth in Politics*. Delhi: Oxford University Press, 1995.

Sundarji, K. *Of Some Consequence: A Soldier Remembers*. New Delhi: HarperCollins Publishers, 2000.

Talbott, Strobe. *Engaging India. Diplomacy, Democracy, and the Bomb: A Memoir*. Washington, D.C.: The Brookings Institution, 2004.

Thomas, Raju G.C. *Indian Security Policy*. Princeton, NJ: Princeton University, 1986.

Thorat, S.P.P. *From Reveille to Retreat*. New Delhi: Allied Publishers, 1988.

Pakistan Politics

Ahmed, Khaled. *Pakistan. Behind the Ideological Mask*. Lahore: Vanguard Books, 2004.

Aijazuddin, F.S. *From a Head, Through a Head, To a Head: The Secret Channel Between the US and China Through Pakistan*. Karachi: Oxford University Press, 2000.

Akhund, Iqbal. *Trial & Error: The Advent and Eclipse of Benazir Bhutto*. Karachi: Oxford University Press, 2000.

Ali, Tariq. *Pakistan: Military Rule or People's Power*. New York: William Morrow & Co., 1970.

Ali, Tariq and Susan Watkins. *1968: Marching in the Streets*. New York: The Free Press, 1998.

Anwar, Raja. *The Terrorist Prince: The Life and Death of Murtaza Bhutto*. Lahore: Vanguard Books, 1998.

Awan, A.B. *Baluchistan. Historical and Political Processes*. London: New Century Publishers, 1985.

Banuazizi, Ali and Myron Weiner (Eds.). *The State, Religion, and Ethnic Politics: Pakistan, Iran and Afghanistan*. Lahore: Vanguard Books, 1987.

Baxter, Craig, ed. *Zia's Pakistan: Politics and Stability in a Frontline State*. Boulder, Colo.: Westview Press, 1985.

Bhutto, Zulfikar Ali. *The Myth of Independence*. Karachi: Oxford University Press, 1969.

Bhutto, Zulfikar Ali. *The Great Tragedy*. Karachi: Vision Publications, 1971.

Bin Sayeed, Khalid. *The Political System of Pakistan*. Karachi: Oxford University Press, 1967.

Blood, Peter R., ed. *Pakistan a Country Study*. Washington, D.C.: Library of Congress, 1994.

Burki, Shahid Javed. *Pakistan Under Bhutto, 1971-1977*. London: The MacMillan Press, 1980.

Burki, Shahid Javed. *Pakistan: The Continuing Search for Nationhood*. Boulder, Co.: Westview Press, 1991.

Choudhury, G.W. *The Last Days of United Pakistan*. London: C. Hurst & Co., 1974.

Cohen, Stephen Philip. *The Idea of Pakistan*. Washington, D.C.: Brookings Institution Press, 2004.

Constitution of Pakistan, 1973. Lahore: Mansoor Book House, 1973.

Constitution of Pakistan, 1973, With Amendments. Lahore: Mansoor Book House, 1989.

Corera, Gordon. *Shopping for Bombs. Nuclear Proliferation, Global Insecurity, and the Rise and Fall of the A.Q. Khan Network*. New York: Oxford University Press, 2006.

Feldman, Herbert. *From Crisis to Crisis: Pakistan 1962-1969*. Karachi: Oxford University Press, 1972.

Gankovsky, Yu. V. *The Peoples of Pakistan*. Lahore: People's Publishing House,

Gannon, Kathy. *I is for Infidel. From Holy War to Holy Terror: 18 Years Inside Afghanistan*. New York: Public Affairs, 2005.

Gardezi, Hassan and Jamil Rashid (Editors). *Pakistan: The Roots of Dictatorship*. London: Zed Press, 1983.

Government of Pakistan. *White Paper on Misuse of Media (December 20, 1971-July 4, 1977)*. 1978.

Government of Pakistan. *White Paper on the Conduct of the General Elections in March 1977*. Rawalpindi: 1978.

Government of Pakistan. *White Paper on The Performance of the Bhutto Regime, Vol. I*. Islamabad, 1979.

Government of Pakistan. *The Report of the Hamoodur Rehman Commission of Inquiry into the 1971 War: As Declassified by the Government of Pakistan*. Lahore: Vanguard.

Hamid, S. Shahid. *Early Years of Pakistan*. Lahore: Ferozsons, 1993.

Hasan, Mubashir. *The Mirage of Power: An Inquiry Into the Bhutto Years, 1971-1977*. Karachi: Oxford University Press, 2000.

Hasan, Parvez. *Pakistan's Economy at the Crossroads: Past Policies and Present Imperatives*. Karachi: Oxford University Press, 1998.

Hayes, Louis D. *The Struggle for Legitimacy in Pakistan*. Lahore: Vanguard Books, 1986.

Husain, Ishrat. *Pakistan. The Economy of an Elitist State*. Karachi: Oxford University Press, 1999.

Jaffrelot, Christophe, ed. *Pakistan: Nationalism Without a Nation?* New Delhi: Zed Books, 2002.

Jahan, Rounaq. *Pakistan. Failure in National Integration*. New York: Columbia University Press, 1972.

Jones, Owen Bennett. *Pakistan: Eye of the Storm*. New Haven: Yale University Press, 2002.

Jones, Philip E. *The Pakistan People's Party Rise to Power*. Karachi: Oxford University Press, 2003.

Kean, Thomas H. and Lee H. Hamilton. *The 9/11 Report: The National Commission on Terrorist Attacks Upon the United States*. New York: St. Martin's Press, 2004.

Khan, Roedad, Compiled and Selected by. *The American Papers: Secret and Confidential Indian, Pakistan, Bangladesh Documents 1965-1973*. Karachi: Oxford University Press, 2000.

Khan, Roedad, *The British Papers: Secret and Confidential India, Pakistan, Bangladesh Documents 1958-1969*. Karachi: Oxford University Press, 2002.

Lamb, Christina. *Waiting for Allah: Pakistan's Struggle for Democracy*. New Delhi: Viking, 1991.

Mehdi, Seyyed Ghaffar. *Politics of Surrender and the Conspiracy of Silence*. Markham, ON, Canada: Crescent International Newspapers, 2001.

Nasr, Seyyed Vali Reza. *The Vanguard of the Islamic Revolution*. Berkeley: University of California Press, 1994.

National Democratic Institute for International Affairs. *The October 1990 Elections in Pakistan*. 1991.

Newberg, Paula R. *Judging the State: Courts and Constitutional Politics in Pakistan*. New Delhi: Cambridge University Press, 1995.

Niazi, Kausar, *Aur Line Kut Gayee (And the line was severed)*, Lahore: Jang Publishers, 1987.

Noman, Omar. *The Political Economy of Pakistan, 1947-85*. London: KPI, 1988.

Rahman, Tariq. *Language and Politics in Pakistan*. Karachi: Oxford University Press, 2003.

Rafiuddin, Colonel, *Bhutto Key Akhri 323 Din (Bhutto's Final 323 days)* Lahore: Jang Publishers, 1991.

Rashid, Rao Abdul (interviewed by Munir Ahmed Munir) *Jo Mein Nain Dekha (What I Observed)*, Atish Fishaan,Publishers Lahore, 1985.

Sayeed, Khalid B. *Politics in Pakistan: The Nature and Direction of Change*. New York: Praeger Publishers, 1980.

Sharif, Nawaz (interviewed by Sohail Waraich), *Ghadaar Kaun? (Who's the Traitor?)*, Lahore: Ziaul Quran Publications, 2006

Siddiqi, Akhtar Husain. *Baluchistan (Pakistan) Its Society, Resources and Development*. Lanham, MD: University Press of America, 1991.

Sisson, Richard and Leo E. Rose. *War and Secession: Pakistan, India, and the Creation of Bangladesh*. Berkeley: University of California Press, 1990.

Syed, Anwar H. *The Discourse and Politics of Zulfikar Ali Bhutto*. London: MacMillan Press, 1992.

Tayeb, A. *Pakistan: A Political Geography*. London: Oxford University Press, 1966.

Truell, Peter and Larry Gurwin. *False Profits*. Boston: Houghton Mifflin Company, 1992.

Verghese, B.G. *An End to Confrontation (Bhutto's Pakistan)*. New Delhi: S. Chand & Co., 1972.

Verkaaik, Oskar. *Migrants and Militants: Fun and Urban Violence in Pakistan*. Princeton, NJ: Princeton University Press, 2004.

Von Vorys, Karl. *Political Development in Pakistan*. Princeton, NJ: Princeton University Press, 1965.

Weaver, Mary Anne. Pakistan. *In the Shadow of Jihad and Afghanistan*. New York: Farrar, Straus and Giroux, 2002.

Weissman, Steve and Herbert Krosney. *The Islamic Bomb*. New York: Times Books, 1981.

Wilcox, Wayne Ayres. *Pakistan: The Consolidation of a Nation*. New York: Columbia University Press, 1963.

Zaheer, Hasan. *The Separation of East Pakistan: The Rise and Realization of Bengali Muslim Nationalism*. Karachi: Oxford University Press, 1994.

Ziring, Lawrence. *The Ayub Khan Era: Politics in Pakistan, 1958-1969*. Syracuse, NY: Syracuse University Press, 1971.

Ziring, Lawrence. *Pakistan: The Enigma of Political Development*. Kent, England: Dawson & Sons, 1980.

Ziring, Lawrence. *Pakistan in the Twentieth Century: A Political History*. Karachi: Oxford University Press, 1997.

Ziring, Lawrence. *Pakistan: At the Crosscurrent of History*. Lahore: Vanguard, 2004.

Pakistan Army

Abbas, Hassan. *Pakistan's Drift Into Extremism*. Armonk, NY: M.E. Sharpe, Inc, 2005.

Ahmad, Brig Saeed. *The Indo-Pak Clash in the Rann of Kutch*. Rawalpindi: Army Education Press.

Ahmed, Gulzar. *Pakistan Meets Indian Challenge*. Rawalpindi: Al Mukhtar Publishers.

Ahmed, Lieutenant General Mahmud. *History of Indo-Pak War—1965*. Rawalpindi: Services Book Club, Army Education Directorate, GHQ, 2006.

Ali, Syed Ishfaq. *Fangs of Ice (Story of Siachen)*. Lahore: Pak American Commercial Ltd., 1991.

Ayub, Muhammad, *An Army, Its Role and Rule: A History of the Pakistan Army from Independence to Kargil, 1947-1999*, Pittsburg PA, Rose Dog Books, 2005.

Blinkenberg, Lars. *India-Pakistan. The History of Unsolved Conflicts*. Copenhagen, Denmark: Dansk Udenrigspolitisk Instituts, 1972.

Burki, Shahid Javed and Craig Baxter. *Pakistan Under the Military*. Boulder, Colo: Westview Press, 1991.

Chaudhry, A.A.K. *September '65*. Lahore: Ferozsons Ltd., 1977.

Cheema, Pervaiz Iqbal. *Pakistan's Defence Policy, 1947-58*. New York: St. Martin's Press, 1990.

Cheema, Pervaiz Iqbal. *The Armed Forces of Pakistan*. Karachi: Oxford University Press, 2002.

Cloughley, Brian. *A History of the Pakistan Army: Wars and Insurrections*. Karachi: Oxford University Press, 1999.

Cohen, Stephen P. *The Pakistan Army*. Berkeley: University of California Press, 1984.

Durrani, Mahmud Ali. *India & Pakistan: The Cost of Conflict and The Benefits of Peace*. Karachi: Oxford University Press, 2001.

Fitzpatrick, Mark (ed.). *Nuclear Black Markets: Pakistan, A.Q. Khan and the Rise of Proliferation Networks, a net assessment*. London: The International Institute for Strategic Studies, 2007.

Gill, John H. *An Atlas of the 1971 India-Pakistan War: The Creation of Bangladesh*. Washington, D.C.: Near East South Asia Center for Strategic Studies. Occasional Papers.

Haigh, R.H. and P.W. Turner. *Punjab Military History in the 19th Century*. Lahore: Vanguard Books, 1984.

Haqqani, Husain. *Pakistan. Between Mosque and Military*. Washington, D.C.: Carnegie Endowment for International Peace, 2005.

Husain, Major General Abrar. *Men of Steel: 6 Armoured Division in the 1965 War*. Rawalpindi: Army Education Publishing House, Army Education Directorate, GHQ, 2005.

Inter Services Public Relations. *Defence and Media: Role of Media in Promoting National Security*. Rawalpindi: The Army Press, 1990.

Jalal, Ayesha. *The State of Martial Rule*. Cambridge: Cambridge University Press, 1990.

Kamal, Dr K.L. *Pakistan: The Garrison State*. New Delhi: Inellectual Publishing House, 1982.

Kardar, A.H. *Pakistan's Soldiers of Fortune*. Lahore: Ferozsons Ltd., 1988.

Khan, Akbar. *Raiders in Kashmir: Story of the Kashmir War, 1947-48*. Pak Publishers, 1970.

Khan, Fazal Muqeem. *Pakistan's Crisis in Leadership*. Islamabad: National Book Foundation, 1973.

Khan, M. Asghar. *The First Round Indo-Pakistan War 1965*. London: Radnor House, 1979.

Khan, M. Asghar. *Generals in Politics: Pakistan 1958-1982*. New Delhi: Vikas Publishing House, 1983.

Khan, Major General Fazal Muqeem, *The Story of the Pakistan Army*, Lahore, Oxford University Press, 1963.

Kureja, Veena. *Military Internvention in Politics: A Case Study of Pakistan*. New Delhi: NBO Publishers, 1985.

Malik, Abdullah. *Fauj aur Pakistan (2) (Army and Pakistan)*. Lahore: Kausar Publishers, 1988.

Margolis, Eric S. *War at the Top of the World: The Clash for Mastery of Asia*. Toronto, Ontario: Key Porter Books, 2001.

Mazari, Shireen M. *The Kargil Conflict 1999*. Islamabad: Ferozsons, 2003.

Moore, Jr., Raymond A. *Nation Building and the Pakistan Army*. Lahore: Aziz Publishers, 1979.

Pakistan Army. *The Kashmir Campaign, 1947-48 (Restricted)*. Rawalpindi: Pakistan Army GHQ., 1971.

Pakistan Army. *Pakistan Army Green Book: Year of the Junior Leaders 1990*. Lahore: Ferozsons Ltd., 1990.

Qureshi, Hakeem Arshad. *The 1971 Indo-Pak War: A Soldier's Narrative*. Karachi: Oxford University Press, 2004.

Rahman, M. Attiqur. *Our Defence Cause*. London: White Lion Publishers, 1976.

Rahman, M. Attiqur. *The Wardens of the Marches: A History of the Piffers, 1947-1971*. Lahore: Wajidalis, 1980.

Riza, Shaukat. *The Pakistan Army War 1965*. Lahore: Wajidalis, 1984.

Riza, Shaukat. *The Pakistan Army, 1947-1949*. Lahore: Wajidalis, 1989.

Riza, Shaukat. *The Pakistan Army, 1966-71*. Lahore: Army Education Press, 1990.

Riza, Shaukat, Ihsan ul Haq Malik, Edgar O'Balance and A.R. Siddiqi, *The '65 War Analysed*. Karachi: *Defence Journal*, 1975.

Rizvi, S. Haider Abbas. *Veteran Campaigners. A History of the Punjab Regiment, 1759-1981*. Lahore: Wajidalis, 1984.

Rizvi, Hasan-Askari. *The Military & Politics in Pakistan 1947-86*. Lahore: Progressive Publishers Ltd., 1987.

Rizvi, Hasan-Askari. *The Military and Politics in Pakistan 1947-86*. Delhi: Konark Publishers Ltd., 1988.

Rizvi, Hasan-Askari. *Military, State and Society in Pakistan*. London: MacMillan Press, 2000.

Saeed, Ahmad. *Battle of Chhamb (1971)*. Rawalpindi: Army Education Press.

Siddiqa, Ayesha. *Military Inc. Inside Pakistan's Military Economy*. London: Pluto Press, 2007.

Siddiqa-Agha, Ayesha. *Pakistan's Arms Procurement and Military Buildup, 1979-99*. Lahore: Sang-e-Meel Publications, 2003.

Siddiqi, A.R. *The Military in Pakistan. Image and Reality*. Lahore: Vanguard Books 1996.

Tellis, Ashley J. C. Christine Fair and Jamison Jo Medby. *Limited Conflicts Under the Nuclear Umbrella*. Santa Monica, CA.: Rand, 2001.

Wirsing, Robert G. *Pakistan's Security Under Zia, 1977-1988*.New York: St. Martin's Press, 1991.

Yong, Tan Tai. *The Garrison State*. Lahore: Vanguard Books, 2005.

Zaheer, Hasan. *The Times and Trial of the Rawalpindi Conspiracy 1951*. Karachi: Oxford University Press, 1998.

Ziaullah, Syed and Samuel Baid. *Pakistan: An End without a Beginning*. New Delhi: Lancer International, 1985.

Afghanistan

Ahmed, Akbar S. *Pukhtun Economy and Society: Traditional Structure and Economic Development in a Tribal Society*. London: Routledge& Kegan Paul, 1980.

Anwar, Raja. (Translated by Khalid Hasan). *The Tragedy of Afghanistan: A First-hand Account*. London: Verso, 1989.

Borovik, Artyom. *The Hidden War*. New York: Grove Press, 1990.

Coll, Steve. *Ghost Wars*. New York: The Penguin Press, 2004.

Cordovez, Diego and Selig S. Harrison, *Out of Afghanistan: The Inside Story of the Soviet Withdrawal*. New York: Oxford University Press, 1995.

Durand, Algernon. *The Making of a Frontier*. Karachi: Oxford University Press, 2001.

Franks, General Tommy. *American Soldier*. New York: Reganbooks, 2005.

Grare, Frederic. *Pakistan and the Afghan Conflict, 1979-1985*. Karachi: Oxford University Press, 2003.

Harrison, Selig S. *In Afghanistan's Shadow: Baluch Nationalism and Soviet Temptations*. Washington, D.C.: Carnegie Endowment for International Peace, 1981.

Khan, Riaz M. *Untying the Afghan Knot. Negotiating Soviet Withdrawal*. Durham: Duke University Press, 1991.

Matinuddin, Kamal. *The Taliban Phenomenon, Afghanistan 1994-1997*. Karachi: Oxford University Press, 1999.

McCoy, Alfred W. *The Politics of Heroin*. Revised. Chicago: Lawrence Hill Books, 2003.

Meyer, Karl E., and Shareen Blair Brysac. *Tournament of Shadows: The Great Game and the Race for Empire in Central Asia*. Washington, D.C.: Counterpoint, 1999.

Rashid, Ahmed. *Taliban: Militant Islam, Oil and Fundamentalism in Central Asia*. New Haven: Yale Nota Bene, Yale University Press, 2001.

Rashid, Ahmed. *Jihad: The Rise of Militant Islam in Central Asia*. New Haven: Yale University Press, 2002.

Tamarov, Vladislav. *Afghanistan: A Russian Soldier's Story*. Berkeley: Ten Speed Press, 2001.

Waller, John H. *Beyond the Khyber Pass: The Road to British Disaster in the First Afghan War*. New York: Random House, 1990.

Weinbaum, Marvin G. *Pakistan & Afghanistan: Resistance and Reconstruction*. Boulder, CO: Westview Press, 1994.

Yousaf, Mohammad, and Mark Adkin. *The Bear Trap: Afghanistan's Untold Story*. Lahore: Jang Publishers, 1992.

Autobiography/Biography

Akhund, Iqbal. *Memoirs of a Bystander: A Life in Diplomacy*. Karachi: Oxford University Press, 1997.

Ali, Tariq. *Street Fighting Years: An Autobiography of the Sixties*. New York: Carol Publishing Group, 1991.

Arif, General K.M. *Working with Zia: Pakistan's Power Politics, 1977-1988*. Karachi: Oxford University Press, 1995.

Arif, General K.M. *Khaki Shadows. Pakistan 1947-1997*. Karachi: Oxford University Press, 2001.

Baxter, Craig, ed. *Diaries of Field Marshal Mohammad Ayub Khan, 1966-1972*. Karachi: Oxford University Press, 2007.

Burki, Lieutenant General (Rtd) W.A. *Autobiography of an Army Doctor in British India & Pakistan*. Rawalpindi: Burki House, 1988.

Bhutto, Benazir. *Pakistan: The Gathering Storm*. New Delhi: Vikas Publishing House, 1983.

Bhutto, Benazir. *Daughter of the East: An Autobiography*. London: Hamish Hamilton, 1988.

Bhutto, Benazir. *Daughter of Destiny: An Autobiography*. New York: Simon and Schuster, 1989

Bhutto, Benazir. *Daughter of the East: An Autobiography*. Reprint, London: Simon & Schuster, 2007.

Bhutto, Zulfikar Ali. *'If I am Assassinated...'* New Delhi: Vikas Publishing House, 1979.

Chishti, Lt. Gen. Faiz Ali (Retired). *Betrayals of Another Kind. Islam, Democracy and The Army In Pakistan*. Rawalpindi: PCL Publishing House, 1990.

Clancy, Tom, with General Tony Zinni and Tony Koltz. *Battle Ready*. New York: G.P. Putnam's Sons, 2004.

Clinton, Bill. *My Life*. New York: Alfred A. Knopf, 2004.

Collins, Larry, and Dominique Lapierre. *Mountbatten and the Partition of India, March 22-August 15, 1947*. Colombo, Sri Lanka: Peoples Publishing House, 1982.

Crile, George. *Charlie Wilson's War*. New York: Grove Press, 2003.

Fallaci, Oriana. Trans. by John Sepley. *Interview with History*. New York: Liveright, 1976.

Gauhar, Altaf. *Ayub Khan: Pakistan's First Military Ruler*. Lahore: Sang-e-Meel Publications, 1993.

Ispahani, M.A.H. *Qaid-e-Azam Jinnah As I Knew Him*. Karachi: Royal Book Company, 1976.

James, Sir Morrice. *Pakistan Chronicle*. London: Hurst & Company, 1993.

Khan, Gohar Ayub. *Glimpses into the Corridors of Power*. Karachi, Oxford University Press. 2007

Khan, Lt. Gen. Gul Hassan. *Memoirs of Lt. Gen. Gul Hassan Khan*. Karachi: Oxford University Press, 1993.

Khan, Mohammad Ayub. *Friends Not Masters: A Political Autobiography*. London: Oxford University Press, 1967.

Khan, Roedad. *Pakistan—A Dream Gone Sour*. Karachi: Oxford University Press, 1998.

Khan, Saadullah. *East Pakistan to Bangla Desh*. Lahore: Lahore Law Times Publications, 1975.

Khan, Sultan M. *Memories & Reflections of a Pakistani Diplomat*. London: The Centre for Pakistan Studies, 1997.

Latif, Maj. Gen. Rahat. *...Plus Bhutto's Episode. An Autobiography*. Lahore: Jang Publishers, 1994.

Mazari, Sherbaz Khan. *A Journey to Disillusionment*. Karachi: Oxford University Press, 1999.

Mirza, Humayun. *From Plassey to Pakistan: The Family History of Iskander Mirza, The First President of Pakistan*. Lanham, MD: University Press of America, 1999.

Mitha, Major General A.O. *Unlikely Beginnings. A Soldier's Life*. Karachi: Oxford University Press, 2003.

Mujahid, Sharif Al. *Quaid-i-Azam Jinnah. Studies in Interpretation*. Karachi: Quaid-i-Azam Academy, 1981.

Mukerjee, Dilip. *Zulfiqar Ali Bhutto: Quest for Power*. Delhi: Vikas Publishing House, 1972.

Musa, General (Retd.) Mohammad. *My Version: India-Pakistan War 1965*. Lahore: Wajidalis Limited, 1983.

Musharraf, Pervez. *In the Line of Fire: A Memoir*. New York: Free Press, 2006.

Niazi, Lt. Gen. A.A.K. *The Betrayal of East Pakistan*. Karachi: Oxford University Press, 1998.

Niazi, Kausar. *Last Days of Premier Bhutto*. Lahore: Jang Publishers, 1991.

Niazi, Kausar. *Zulfiqar Ali Bhutto of Pakistan: The Last Days*. New Delhi: Vikas Publishing House, 1992.

Pataudi, Sher Ali. *The Story of Soldiering and Politics in India and Pakistan*. Lahore: Bakhtyar Printers, 1983.

Qureshi, Saleem, ed. *Jinnah: The Founder of Pakistan*. Karachi: Oxford University Press, 1998.

Rabbani, Mian Ata. *I Was The Quaid's Aide-de-Camp*. Karachi: Oxford University Press, 1996.

Rahman, M. Attiqur. *Back to the Pavilion*. Karachi: Ardeshir Cowasjee, 1990.

Rashid, Haroon ul. *Fateh (Victor)*, Lahore, Jang Publishers, 199

Raza, Rafi. *Zulfikar Ali Bhutto and Pakistan, 1967-1977*. Karachi: Oxford University Press, 1997.

Salik, Siddiq. *Witness to Surrender*. Karachi: Oxford University Press, 1978.

Siddiqi, Brigadier A.R. *East Pakistan: The Endgame—An Onlooker's Journal 1969-1971*. Karachi: Oxford University Press, 2004.

Siddiqui, Irfan, *General Akhtar Abdur Rahman: Sheed-e-Jihad Afghanistan (General Akhtar Abdur Rahman: Martyr of the Afghan Jihad)*, Lahore: Jang Publishers, 1992.

Sirohey, Admiral Iftikhar A. *Truth Never Retires: An Autobiography*. Lahore: Jang Publishers, 2000.

Tenet, George, with Bill Harlow. *At the Center of the Storm: My Years at the CIA*. New York: HarperCollins, 2007.

Wolpert, Stanley. *Jinnah of Pakistan*. New York: Oxford University Press, 1984.

Wolpert, Stanley. *Zulfi Bhutto of Pakistan. His Life and Times*. New York: Oxford University Press, 1993.

Wolpert, Stanley. *Nehru: A Tryst with Destiny*. New York: Oxford University Press, 1996.

Yousaf, Brigadier (Retd.) Mohammad. *Silent Soldier: The Man Behind the Afghan Jehad*. Lahore: Jang Publishers, 1993.

The United States and Pakistan

Aandahl, Fredrick, ed. *Foreign Relations of the United States, 1951. Volume VI. Asia and the Pacific (in two parts) Part 2*. Washington, D.C.: United States Government Printing Office, 1977.

Aijazuddin, F.S., ed. *The White House & Pakistan. Secret Declassified Documents, 1969-1974*. Karachi: Oxford University Press, 2002.

Armstrong, David and Joseph Trento. *America and the Islamic Bomb: The Deadly Compromise*. Hanover, New Hamshire (USA): Steerforth Press, 2007.

Anderson, Jack with George Clifford. *The Anderson Papers: From the Files of America's Most Famous Investigative Reporter*. New York: Random House, 1973.

Barnds, William J. *India, Pakistan, and the Great Powers*. New York: Praeger Publishers, 1972.

Brown, W. Norman. *The United States and India & Pakistan*. Cambridge, Mass.: Harvard University Press, 1963.

Cohen, Craig. *A Perilous Course: US Strategy and Assistance to Pakistan*. Washington DC: Center for Strategic and International Studies, 2007.

Foreign Relations of the United States, 1948. Volume V. The Near East South Asia, and Africa (in two parts) Part 1. Washington, D.C.: United States Government Printing Office, 1975.

Glennon, John P., ed. *Foreign Relations of the United States, 1955-1957. Volume VIII. South Asia*. Washington, D.C.: United States Government Printing Office, 1987.

Kux, Dennis. *The United States and Pakistan, 1947-2000. Disenchanted Allies*. Washington, D.C.: Woodrow Wilson Center Press, 2001.

LaFantasie, Glenn W., ed. *Foreign Relations of the United States, 1958-1960. Volume XV. South and Southeast Asia*. Washington, D.C.: United States Government Printing Office, 1992.

Langewiesche, William. *The Atomic Bazaar: The Rise of the Nuclear Poor*. New York: Farrar, Straus and Giroux. 2007.

Levy, Adrian and Catherine Scott-Clark. *Deception: Pakistan, the United States and the secret trade in nuclear weapons*. New York. Walker and Company, 2007.

McMahon, Robert J. *The Cold War on the Periphery: The United States, India, and Pakistan*. New York: Columbia University Press, 1994.

Patterson, David S., ed. *Foreign Relations of the United States, 1964-1968. Volume XXV. South Asia*. Washington, D.C.: United States Government Printing Office, 2000.

Patterson, David S., ed. *Foreign Relations of the United States, 1969-1976. Volume I. Foundations of Foreign Policy, 1969-1972*. Washington, D.C.: United States Government Printing Office, 2003.

Qureshi, Saqib. *US Foreign Policy to Pakistan, 1947-1960: Re-Constructing Strategy.* Unpublished dissertation, London School of Economics, University of London, 2001.

Smith, Louis J., ed. *Foreign Relations of the United States, 1961-1963. Volume XIX. Asia.* Washington, D.C.: United States Government Printing Office, 1996.

Smith, Louis J., ed. *Foreign Relations of the United States, 1969-1976. Volume XI. South Asia Crisis, 1971.* Washington, D.C.: United States Government Printing Office, 2005.

Tahir-Kheli, Shirin. *The United States and Pakistan: The Evolution of an Influence Relationship.* New York: Praeger Publishers, 1982.

Tahir-Kheli, Shirin. *India, Pakistan, and the United States: Breaking with the Past.* New York: Council of Foreign Relations Press, 1997.

Wise, David and Thomas B. Ross. *The U-2 Affair.* New York: Bantam Books, 1962.

Wolpert, Stanley. *Roots of Confrontation in South Asia: Afghanistan, Pakistan, India & Superpowers.* New York: Oxford University Press, 1982.

Military Thought and Economy

Alexander, Bevin. *How Great Generals Win.* New York: W.W. Norton & Company, 2002.

Arnett, Eric, ed. *Military Capacity and the Risk of War. China, India, Pakistan and Iran.* New York: Oxford University Press, 1997.

Ball, Nicole. *Security and Economy in the Third World.* Princeton, NJ: Princeton University Press, 1988.

Birand, Mehmet Ali. Trans. Saliha Parker and Ruth Christie. *Shirts of Steel: An Anatomy of the Turkish Armed Forces.* London: I.B. Tauris & Co., 1991.

Blainey, Geoffrey. *The Causes of War.* New York: The Free Press, 1973.

Durschmied, Erik. *The Hinge Factor: How Chance and Stupidity Have Changed History.* London: Hodder & Stoughton, 1999.

Earle, Edward Mead, ed. *Makers of Modern Strategy: Military Thought from Machiavelli to Hitler.* Lahore: National Book Foundation, 1972.

Finer, S.E. *The Man on Horseback: The Role of the Military in Politics.* Middlesex, England: Peregrine Books, 1976.

Galula, David. *Counterinsurgency Warfare: Theory and Practice.* Westport, CT: Praeger Security International, 2006.

Huntington, Samuel P. *The Soldier and the State: The Theory and Politics of Civil-Military Relations.* New York: Vintage Books, 1957.

Janowitz, Morris. *Military Institutions and Coercion in the Developing Nations.* Chicago: The University of Chicago Press, 1977.

Johnson, John, J, ed. *The Role of the Military in Underdeveloped Countries.* Princeton: NJ: Princeton University Press, 1962.

Keegan, John. *The Mask of Command.* New York: Elizabeth Sifton Books Viking, 1987.

Kennedy, Gavin. *The Military in the Third World.* London: Gerald Duckworth & Co., 1974.

Kinzer, Stephen. *Crescent & Star: Turkey Between World Worlds.* New York: Farrar, Straus and Giroux, 2001.

Looney, Robert E. *Third-World Military Expenditure and Arms Production.* New York: St. Martin's Press, 1988.

Luttwak, Edward. *Coup d'Etat. A Practical Handbook.* Cambridge, MA: Harvard University Press, 1979.

McKinlar, Robert. *Third World Military Expenditure. Determinants and Implications.* London: Pinter Publishers, 1989.

McNeill, William H. *The Pursuit of Power.* Chicago: The University of Chicago Press, 1982.

Mullins, Jr., A.F. *Born Arming: Development and Military Power in New States.* Stanford, CA: Stanford University Press, 1987.

Nagl, John A. *Learning to Eat Soup with a Knife: Counterinsurgency Lessons from Malaya and Vietnam.* Chicago: The University of Chicago Press, 2002.

National Defense University Press. *Military Ethics.* Washington, D.C.: 1987.

Paukert, Liba, and Peter Richards, eds. *Defence Expenditure, Industrial Conversion and Local Employment.* Geneva: International Labour Office, 1991.

Perlmutter, Amos. *The Military and Politics in Modern Times.* New Haven: Yale University Press, 1978.

Poole, H. John. *Tactics of the Crescent Moon: Militant Muslim Combat Methods.* Emerald Isle, NC: Posterity Press, 2004.

Stepan, Alfred. *The Military in Politics: Changing Patterns in Brazil.* Princeton, NJ: Princeton University Press, 1974.

Stoessinger, John G. *Why Nations Go to War.* New York: St. Martin's Press, 1974.

Stoessinger, John G. *Nations in Darkness: China, Russia, and America.* Revised. New York: Random House, 1981.

Waltz, Kenneth N. *Man, the State and War: A Theoretical Analysis.* New York: Columbia University Press, 1959.

Weizman, Ezer. *On Eagles' Wings: The Personal Story of the Leading Commander of the Israeli Air Force.* New York: McMillan Publishing Co., 1976.

Whynes, David K. *The Economics of Third World Military Expenditure.* Austin: University of Texas Press, 1979.

INDEX